By the People

A History of the United States

Volume 2 – Since 1865

James W. Fraser
New York University

PEARSON

Boston   Columbus   Indianapolis   New York   San Francisco

Amsterdam   Cape Town   Dubai   London   Madrid   Milan   Munich   Paris   Montréal   Toronto

Delhi   Mexico City   São Paulo   Sydney   Hong Kong   Seoul   Singapore   Taipei   Tokyo

Dedication

To my children and grandchildren and all the students of their generations. May they find the American story in all its complexity as fascinating as I do.

Editor in Chief: Dickson Musslewhite
Publisher: Charlyce Jones Owen
Program Manager: Seanna Breen
Editorial Assistant: Maureen Diana
Project Manager: Emsal Hasan
Procurement Manager: Mary Fischer
Procurement Specialist: Mary Ann Gloriande
Associate Director of Design: Blair Brown
Cover Designer: Lumina Datamatics
Cover Art: Main photo: Civil rights march on Washington, D.C., photograph by Warren K. Leffler (Library of Congress Prints and Photographs Division/LC-DIG-ppmsca-03130); **Insert photos from left to right:** 1. Joseph Fayadaneega, called the Brant, the Great Captain of the Six Nations by George Romney (Library of Congress Prints and Photographs Division/LC-DIG-ppmsca-15712); 2. "His daughter! And he thought she was "just a little girl" by W.E. Hill. (Library of Congress Prints and Photographs Division/LC-USZC2-1205); 3. Two emigrants on the seashore, photograph by Underwood & Underwood (Library of Congress Prints and Photographs Division/LCUSZ62-35634); 4. "The first vote" by A.R. Waud. (Library of Congress Prints and Photographs Division/LC-USZ62-19234).
Digital Media Editor: Michael Halas
Media Project Manager: Elizabeth Roden Hall
Composition and Full-Service Project Management: GEX Publishing Services
Printer/Binder: RR Donnelly-Willard
Cover Printer: Phoenix Color-Hagerstown
Text Font: 10.5/13 Minion Pro-Regular

Acknowledgements of third party content appear on pages C1-C2, which constitute an extension of this copyright page.

Library of Congress Cataloging-in-Publication Data

Fraser, James W., 1944-
 By the people : a history of the United States / James W. Fraser, New York University.
 volumes cm
Includes index.
 ISBN 978-0-205-74309-4 (entire book) -- ISBN 978-0-205-74305-6 (volume 1) -- ISBN 978-0-205-74307-0 (volume 2) 1. United States--History--Textbooks. I. Title.
E178.1.F83 2014
973--dc23
                    2014026518

10 9 8 7 6 5 4 3 2 1

Brief Contents

Contents

Maps

Tables

Special Features

REVEL™

Educational technology designed for the way today's students read, think, and learn

When students are engaged deeply, they learn more effectively and perform better in their courses. This simple fact inspired the creation of REVEL: an immersive learning experience designed for the way today's students read, think, and learn. Built in collaboration with educators and students nationwide, REVEL is the newest, fully digital way to deliver respected Pearson content.

REVEL enlivens course content with media interactives and assessments — integrated directly within the authors' narrative — that provide opportunities for students to read about and practice course material in tandem. This immersive educational technology boosts student engagement, which leads to better understanding of concepts and improved performance throughout the course.

Learn more about REVEL
<http://www.pearsonhighered.com/revel/>

To the Student

I hope you enjoy reading *By the People* and that you learn the value of the study of American history and historical thinking skills as a result of reading it.

The title of this book—*By the People*—describes one of my key goals. This is a history of the many different peoples who have shaped the United States as it is today. Whenever possible, I have focused on the stories of average everyday women and men who have created this country. In a survey of U.S. History it is essential to tell the stories of the leaders—the people from George Washington to Barack Obama and also from Benjamin Franklin to Andrew Carnegie to Jane Addams—who have had been the best known leaders of their generation. At the same time I believe it is equally important to tell the story of some of those whose names have been forgotten—women and men who fought in the Revolutionary army, enslaved people who ran away or found other ways to resist and ultimately gain freedom, women who worked for decades to win the right to vote, immigrants who came to the United States in the hope of building a better life, American Indians of many different tribes who found ways to maintain their cultures in spite of formidable obstacles. These and many other people are essential to the story that is told in this book.

In focusing on the stories of the diverse peoples of this country I have also sought to foster a sense of agency—as well as historical knowledge. When history becomes one thing after another, it gets boring. When history becomes only a celebration of the good and greats among us, it is unbelievable. And when history is only a story of the bad things that some Americans have done to others, it is just plain depressing. On the other hand, if American history can be the story of those who fought back against injustice, who organized to win new rights, who found ways to build a better society, then our students can ask, "why not me?" And, I believe that such a history of people who made a difference in the past can lead today's students to join the list of those who have helped build a better and more hopeful country.

Please let me know what your experience is like. Email me at jim.fraser@nyu.edu. I am anxious to hear and to learn.

Jim Fraser
New York City, December, 2013

Features of *By the People*

The pedagogical approach of *By the People* is designed to provide numerous opportunities for students to engage in historical inquiry and to focus on historical analysis and interpretation. Each feature connects to the historical thinking skills that are an essential part of the study of history. They are intended to serve as points of discovery through which students learn and understand the past and its significance.

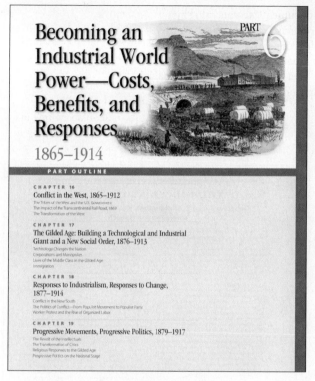

Part Opening Outlines

Each of the 4 parts opens with an outline of the text chapters covered in the Part.

Chapter Learning Objectives

Objectives for each main section of the chapter serve as a guide for the student learner to the chapter's main topics and themes.

Quick Review Questions

Questions that ask students to use historical thinking skills necessary for the practice and study of history conclude each main section of the chapter. These questions ask students to construct arguments, consider cause-and-effect, evaluate patterns of change, and evaluate comparisons and contrasts. Students are asked to use these skills as they relate to the content of the section.

American Voices

Primary source document excerpts bring history alive by introducing students to the words, thoughts, and ideas of people who lived and experienced the events of the time. Each document includes a brief head note and critical analysis questions to help students put the sources in their historical context.

Thinking Historically

This feature continues the emphasis of providing ample opportunity for the practice of historical thinking skills. The feature includes questions that connect to the skills.

In-text Explorer Activities

There is an Explorer activity feature in each part that focuses students on exploring and analyzing maps and topics related to key events in history.

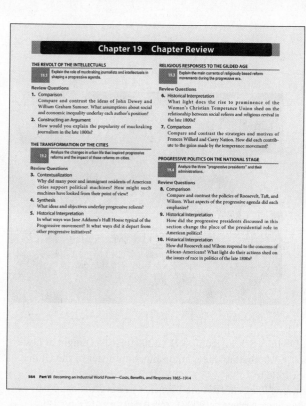

Chapter 19   Chapter Review

THE REVOLT OF THE INTELLECTUALS

19.1 Explain the role of muckraking journalists and intellectuals in shaping a progressive agenda.

Review Questions

1. Comparison
Compare and contrast the ideas of John Dewey and William Graham Sumner. What assumptions about social and economic inequality underlay each author's position?

2. Constructing an Argument
How would you explain the popularity of muckraking journalism in the late 1800s?

THE TRANSFORMATION OF THE CITIES

19.2 Analyze the changes in urban life that inspired progressive reforms and the impact of those reforms on cities.

Review Questions

3. Contextualization
Why did many poor and immigrant residents of American cities support political machines? How might such machines have looked from their point of view?

4. Synthesis
What ideas and objectives underlay progressive reform?

5. Historical Interpretation
In what ways was Jane Addams's Hull House typical of the Progressive movement? In what ways did it depart from other progressive initiatives?

RELIGIOUS RESPONSES TO THE GILDED AGE

19.3 Explain the main currents of religiously based reform movements during the progressive era.

Review Questions

6. Historical Interpretation
What light does the rise to prominence of the Woman's Christian Temperance Union shed on the relationship between social reform and religious revival in the late 1800s?

7. Comparison
Compare and contrast the strategies and motives of Frances Willard and Carry Nation. How did each contribute to the gains made by the temperance movement?

PROGRESSIVE POLITICS ON THE NATIONAL STAGE

19.4 Analyze the three "progressive presidents" and their administrations.

Review Questions

8. Comparison
Compare and contrast the policies of Roosevelt, Taft, and Wilson. What aspects of the progressive agenda did each emphasize?

9. Historical Interpretation
How did the progressive presidents discussed in this section change the place of the presidential role in American politics?

10. Historical Interpretation
How did Roosevelt and Wilson respond to the concerns of African-Americans? What light do their actions shed on the issues of race in politics of the late 1800s?

564   Part VI Becoming an Industrial World Power—Costs, Benefits, and Responses 1865–1914

Chapter Review

An extensive set of review questions based on the chapter learning objectives and key concepts.

MAP 20-5 Europe in 1919. The Treaty of Versailles created a number of new nations in eastern Europe out of what had once been the Austria-Hungary and Ottoman empires as well as new nations in the Middle East.

people like himself who had been excluded from the treaty-making process and his personal animosity to the president. Nevertheless, Lodge insisted that the issues were beyond party, that the United States "is the world's best hope but if you fetter her in the interests and quarrels of other nations, if you tangle her in the intrigues of Europe, you will destroy her power for good and endanger her very existence."

592   Part VII War, Prosperity, and Depression, 1890–1945

Exceptional Art and Illustration Program

A full complement of maps, photographs, and illustrations support the discussions within the text and provide geographic context as well as many iconic images of the past.

About the Author

James W. Fraser is Professor of History and Education at the Steinhardt School of Culture, Education, and Human Development at New York University. His teaching includes a survey course in U.S. History for future Social Studies teachers and courses in the History of American Education, Religion & Public Education, and Inquiries into Teaching and Learning. He holds a Ph.D. from Columbia University. Dr. Fraser is the President of the History of Education Society and a former member of the Editorial Board of the *History of Education Quarterly*. He served as Senior Vice President for Programs at the Woodrow Wilson National Fellowship Foundation in Princeton, New Jersey, from 2008 to 2012. He has also served as NYU liaison to the New Design High School, a public high school in New York's Lower East Side, and to Facing History and Ourselves.

Before coming to New York University Dr. Fraser taught in the Department of History and the program in education at Northeastern University in Boston, where he was the founding dean of Northeastern's School of Education. He was also a member and chair of the Commonwealth of Massachusetts Education Deans Council, the Boston School Committee Nominating Committee, and other boards. He was a lecturer in the Program in Religion and Secondary Education at the Harvard University Divinity School from 1997 to 2004. He has taught at Lesley University; University of Massachusetts, Boston; Boston University; and Public School 76 Manhattan. He is an ordained minister in the United Church of Christ and was pastor of Grace Church in East Boston, Massachusetts, from 1986 to 2006.

In addition to *By the People*, Dr. Fraser is the author or editor of twelve books including *The School in the United States: A Documentary History,* a third edition of which will be published in 2014, and *Preparing America's Teachers: A History* (2007), and *A History of Hope: When Americans Have Dared to Dream of a Better Future* (2002). He lives in New York City with his wife Katherine Hanson and their dog, Pebble.

Reconstruction

This popular picture, drawn by A. H. Ward for *Harper's Weekly* in November 1867, illustrated the prime meaning of Reconstruction for many African-Americans, whether former slaves or former soldiers in the Union army. The end of slavery brought—for the moment—the right to vote.

For those who had been enslaved it was a day of freedom. They celebrated as others had done. Houston H. Holloway, a slave sold three times before his 20th birthday recalled the day emancipation came to Georgia: "I felt like a bird out of a cage....The week passed off in a blaze of glory." Six weeks later, Holloway and his wife celebrated the birth of a new baby and "received my free born son into the world." For some former slaves, nothing mattered more than getting away from their old plantations. They moved short distances to be with friends and family or great distances to Louisiana, Indian Territory, or the North. For others, the news that they could now be wage-earning employees on the same plantations where they had previously worked without pay was the best option available. Whatever their situation and regardless of their previous status, emancipation changed every aspect of life for all people of the United States.

CHAPTER OBJECTIVE

Demonstrate an understanding of the development and decline of Reconstruction.

LEARNING OBJECTIVES

FEDERAL RECONSTRUCTION POLICY

Explain the political development of federal Reconstruction policy.

15.1

THE IMPACT OF RECONSTRUCTION

Explain the impact of Reconstruction on African-American life in the South.

15.2

TERROR, APATHY, AND THE CREATION OF THE SEGREGATED SOUTH

Analyze the reasons Reconstruction ended and the impact of Redemption.

15.3

Radical Republicans
A shifting group of Republican congressmen, who favored abolishing slavery and advocated full rights for former slaves in the South.

After January 1863, the Emancipation Proclamation made the Union Army an army of liberation for slaves during the war itself. Many slaves did not wait for the Union army to arrive. When Joseph Davis fled the plantation that he and his brother Jefferson Davis owned at Davis Bend on the Mississippi River in 1862, slaves took over the property and began running it themselves, much to the surprise of General Grant who arrived at Davis Bend with the Union army in 1863. Even for those still in slavery throughout the war, word passed quickly. In Mississippi, while the war was still far away, one slave responded to a planter's greeting "Howdy, Uncle" with an angry "Call me Mister." Other slaves refused to work unless they were paid or simply left, often in search of family members, sometimes just because, for the first time in their lives, they could.

In the aftermath of the Civil War, women and men who had been considered the property of others found that they could buy property. They could refuse to work for people who only recently had coerced their labor. They could travel without the hated passes from white masters. Sometimes they were reunited with family members from whom they had long been separated. People for whom literacy had been illegal now learned to read and write. They became teachers, started their own schools, and opened colleges and universities. Slaves and free blacks who had never dreamed of voting became voters and officeholders, members of state legislatures, and members of the United States Congress. They passed laws creating a system of public education and dreamed of better days ahead. The story of the era known as Reconstruction, its high hopes and its violent and tragic ending, is the focus of this chapter.

FEDERAL RECONSTRUCTION POLICY

15.1 Explain the political development of federal Reconstruction policy.

In December 1864, Senator Charles Sumner of Massachusetts thought Lincoln had agreed that former Confederate states must grant all citizens the same right to vote as whites (which meant the right of males to vote) to be readmitted to the Union. But while Lincoln had come to believe that blacks who fought in the Union army had won the right to vote, he also believed that the Constitution gave states the right to determine who voted and he did not yet seem ready, as far as anyone knew, to interfere.

When Lincoln died in April 1865, his own party was divided on the question of the vote for African-Americans and on how best to handle the readmission of the Confederate states within the nation. With the war just ending, the majority of Republicans, in and out of Congress, were still moderates. Many had begun the Civil War with the intention only to save the Union and had been won over in the course of the war to believing that the end of the war had to mean the end of slavery. Still, that revised intention was just a single goal; they were not committed to voting rights or the award of land for newly freed African-Americans. Other Republicans who were coming to be known as **Radical Republicans**—often called simply "the radicals"—in Congress were determined that the North's victory in the Civil War meant that the country should give formerly enslaved people not only their freedom but also the right to vote and to hold office. In addition, they believed the country should provide land to those who had previously worked other people's land as their slaves. In other words, formerly enslaved people should be given all the rights of white Americans.

American Voices

Jourdon Anderson, Letter to Colonel P. H. Anderson, 1865

After Jourdon Anderson and his wife Mandy were freed from slavery on a Tennessee plantation belonging to Colonel P. H. Anderson, they moved north and settled in Dayton, Ohio. A year later, with the war over and the Confederate army disbanded, Colonel Anderson wrote to his former slaves asking them to return as employees. Jourdan Anderson responded to his former master:

As to my freedom, which you say I can have, there is nothing to be gained on that score, as I got my free-papers in 1864 from the Provost-Marshall-General of the Department at Nashville. Mandy says she would be afraid to go back without some proof that you are sincerely disposed to treat us fairly and justly—and we have concluded to test your sincerity by asking you to send us our wages for the time we served you. This will make us forget and forgive old scores, and rely on your justice and friendship in the future. I served you faithfully for thirty-two years and Mandy twenty years. At $25 a month for me, and $2 a week for Mandy, our earnings would amount to $11,680. Add to this the interest for the time our wages has been kept and deduct what you paid for our clothing and three doctors visits to me and pulling a tooth for Mandy, and the balance will show what we are in justice entitled to....If you fail to pay us for faithful labors in the past we can have little faith in your promises in the future. We trust the good Maker has opened your eyes to the wrongs which you and your fathers have done to me and my fathers, in making us toil for generations without recompense. Here I draw my wages every Saturday night, but in Tennessee there was never any pay day for the negroes any more than for the horses and cows. Surely there will be a day of reckoning for those who defraud the laborer of his hire.

Jourdon Anderson

P.S. –Say howdy to George Carter, and thank him for taking the pistol from you when you were shooting at me.

Source: John David Smith, *Black Voices From Reconstruction, 1865–1877* (Gainesville: University Press of Florida, 1997), pp. 43–44.

Thinking Critically

1. **Documentary Analysis**

   What examples can you find in the document of Jourdon Anderson's sense of humor?

2. **Historical Interpretation**

   Why would Colonel Anderson invite Jourdon Anderson back to work on the plantation where he had been a slave? How do you think the former slave owner responded to this letter from Jourdon Anderson?

A similar kind of split existed over the proper ways to readmit states to the Union. Lincoln and many other Republicans had argued throughout the war that the Southern states had never left the United States; after all, preserving the Union had been the initial reason that the North went to war in 1861. If the Southern states had never left, there was little to do at war's end but for them to conduct elections for local and national office and resume their place in the nation. Others, however, especially the Radical Republicans, argued that after 4 years of fighting against the Union, the states of the former Confederacy were effectively out of the country and could be readmitted only after some period in which the federal government sought to reconstruct state governments to ensure that those who led the rebellion—traitors, as the radicals always called them—would not lead the new state governments and that the full civil rights of African-Americans would be ensured. The difference of opinion was significant, and compromise was not easy.

While Lincoln pondered the question of the vote and argued that the debate over the term *readmission* was a distraction from the work at hand, he did take another step that would have far-reaching significance in what was to come. Lincoln proposed establishing a federal Bureau of Freedmen, Refugees and Abandoned Lands.

Freedmen's Bureau
Agency established by Congress in March 1865 to provide social, educational, and economic services as well as advice and protection to former slaves.

Presidential Reconstruction
Name given to the immediate post–Civil War era, 1865–1866, when President Andrew Johnson took the lead to return full rights to the former Confederate states.

Congressional Reconstruction
Name given to the period 1867–1870 when the Republican-dominated Congress controlled Reconstruction era policy. Sometimes it is also known as Radical Reconstruction.

The **Freedmen's Bureau**, as it came to be known, would last longer and do more than Lincoln ever imagined when he signed the legislation authorizing it in March 1865.

Lincoln placed great faith in the new government established in Louisiana after the Union victories there. The new legislature pledged loyalty to the Union, created a public school system, and after it was proposed ratified the Thirteenth Amendment abolishing slavery. It had not, however, granted former slaves the right to vote. Lincoln pondered the question of whether Louisiana could be brought into proper practical relation with the Union sooner by sustaining, or by discarding, her new state government. His own answer was clear: he believed that the Louisiana government could *eventually* extend the vote and would provide a model of transition back into the Union for other Confederate states. The more radical members of Congress did not want to give Louisiana full rights as a state until it had guaranteed that blacks would be given the right to vote. They blocked counting Louisiana's electoral votes in the 1864 election and the seating of the state's new senators. They would soon do more.

The post–Civil War era is often described as including three distinct time periods. The first period is referred to as **Presidential Reconstruction** in 1865–66, when President Johnson sought to return states to their prewar status with only the institution of slavery being abolished. The next period is known as the more radical **Congressional Reconstruction** (sometimes Radical Reconstruction), which began when Congress began to challenge Johnson in 1867 and generally continued through

This illustration from *Harper's Weekly* shows agents of the Freedmen's Bureau trying to settle a dispute between white and black Southerners. The Freedmen's Bureau took an active role in the lives of citizens in a way that the federal government had never done before, managing disputes, organizing schools, and ensuring political rights for recently enfranchised African-Americans.

the end of Grant's two terms in 1877. The last period, known as **"Redemption"** (by its defenders but not by those who lost rights in the process), began with the election of Rutherford B. Hayes in November 1876 and involved the withdrawal of federal troops from the South as well as the return of white-only governments. That last period culminated in the 1890s with the virtual disenfranchisement of all blacks in the South.

Although this typical chronology is far too simplistic, it does provide an accurate framework for the reconstruction process. The reality of the process was much more complex. Many factions battled from 1865 well into the 1880s and 1890s. Johnson was challenged even during his first years in office. Congressional Reconstruction had many ups and downs. Grant generally agreed with the Congressional radicals, those Congressional leaders and their black and white allies in the South who sought to transform the former Confederacy into a racially integrated region with equal rights. Nevertheless, in every year between 1867 and 1877, those who sought a radical Reconstruction of the South met resistance, often very effective resistance in the South and a growing inclination of Northerners to look the other way as they grew tired of the effort. Perhaps most important, the end of Reconstruction did not come all at once. It was a long process involving defeats and successes throughout the country.

The Presidential Reconstruction of Andrew Johnson, 1865–1866

When Andrew Johnson became president on April 15, 1865, he had served as vice president for only 6 weeks. Even so, he came to the presidency with far more experience than Lincoln had in 1861. Like Lincoln, Johnson grew up in poverty, but he had risen in Tennessee politics from city alderman to member of the state legislature, to Congress, to two terms as governor to the U.S. Senate. When Tennessee seceded from the Union in 1861, Johnson—apart from any other Senator from a Confederate State—stayed loyal to the Union and stayed in the Senate. He had long seen himself as a spokesman for the "honest yeomen" of Tennessee, and he hated what he called the state's "papered, bloated…slaveocracy." During the Civil War, Johnson served with distinction as military governor of Tennessee in those parts of the state where the Union army had taken control. When the Republicans met in 1864 to nominate Lincoln for a second term, incumbent Vice President Hannibal Hamlin offered little to the ticket; his home state of Maine was sure to go Republican and he had played virtually no role in the war. The choice of Johnson as Lincoln's running mate—a border state senator and governor—might add essential votes. Although two previous vice presidents had succeeded to the presidency, no one expected it to happen again.

When Johnson became president after Lincoln died, many of those known as the Radical Republicans in Congress embraced him. These so-called radicals wanted to be sure that the end of the Civil War did not bring merely a return to a version of the prewar status quo minus slavery but, instead, wanted the whole South to be "reconstructed" to assure economic, educational, and political equality for the former slaves. The radicals were often a minority in the Congress and the country, where many were willing to accept second-class status for former slaves, but the radicals

Redemption
A term used by opponents of Reconstruction for the era in which the federal government ended its involvement in Southern affairs, and southern whites took control of state governments and ended black political rights.

had the clearest agenda for what they wanted to see happen, and every act of postwar Southern resistance tended to strengthen their hand. In 1864, Johnson had said, "Treason must be made odious, and traitors must be punished and impoverished." And he repeated similar views to members of Congress who met with him right after Lincoln's assassination. Ohio Senator Benjamin F. Wade said, "By the Gods, there will be no trouble now in running the government." Another was overheard saying, "I believe, that the Almighty continued Mr. Lincoln in office as long as he was useful, and then substituted a better man to finish the work."

When Johnson announced his plans for Reconstruction on May 29, 1865, there was widespread disappointment. Johnson supported the Thirteenth Amendment, already passed by Congress and ratified by several states, and insisted that support for the amendment be a condition for the readmission of any Confederate state to the union. But Johnson refused to go beyond that. He made it clear that he had little interest in political rights for former slaves. In contrast to his earlier claims, Johnson declared a full amnesty and pardon for most of those who had taken part in the rebellion as long as they were willing to pledge loyalty to the Union and support the end of slavery. The amnesty included restoration of all land taken by the Union army. There were exceptions to Johnson's amnesty, however. Major Confederate officials and individuals who owned more than $20,000 in taxable property had to seek individual presidential pardons.

At first glance, the policy seemed tough on the South or at least on the former slaveholders of the South—perhaps tougher than Lincoln would have been—and consistent with Johnson's pledge to keep slaveholders "out in the cold." But soon, many wondered how many individual presidential pardons would be granted as they realized that Johnson was granting many more than they had expected. Blacks, though now free, seemed destined to be excluded from most of the rights of citizenship in the Johnson plan. If former slaveholders were to be given back their land, what land would there be for former slaves? Illinois Congressman Elihu B. Washburne said, "I have grounds to fear President Johnson may hold almost unconquerable prejudices against the African race."

While the Radical Republicans in Congress were terribly disappointed, many Southern whites were delighted at the opportunity to create a "white man's government," if they accepted the end of slavery. Under Johnson's plan, former Confederate states were readmitted as soon as they ratified the Thirteenth Amendment, and the new state governments that were quickly organized in the South were recognized by Johnson as the legitimate government of these states. (Since most Republicans continued to insist that the rebellious states had never left the Union, there was no official way or time for them to be *readmitted*.) Once recognized, these state governments, dominated by many of the same people who had been in power before the Civil War, began passing laws strictly limiting black rights, most of all, the right to vote. In addition, hunting, fishing, free grazing of livestock, which whites all assumed were their rights and which some slaves had enjoyed, were now declared illegal for blacks in a series of what were known as **Black Codes**, passed by states across the South, beginning with Mississippi's code passed in November 1865. One part of the Mississippi code said:

Black Codes
Laws passed by states and municipalities denying many rights of citizenship to free blacks and to control black labor, mobility, and employment.

> All freedmen, free negroes and mulattoes in the State, over the age of eighteen, found on the second Monday in January, 1866, or thereafter, with no lawful employment or business, or found unlawful assembling themselves together, either in the day or nit time, and all white persons assembling with freedmen, Free negroes or mulattoes, or unusually associating…on terms of equality… shall be deemed vagrants.

In many states, Black Codes either made it illegal for an African-American to own a gun or taxed guns at high rates. In cities, new urban police forces, like the one in Mississippi in 1865, were designed to "keep good order and discipline amongst the negro population." Police patrols not only enforced the law but also often terrorized blacks, especially those who refused to sign long-term labor contracts with former slave masters. Any former slave who ran away from a labor contract could be either arrested and returned to the plantation holding that contract or sentenced to a chain gang to pay off the fine for running away. African-Americans in Louisiana noted how similar the contracts were to slavery and how similar the new police were to the old slave patrols. They also asked "why men who but a few months since were in armed rebellion against the government should now have arms put in their hands." Johnson's amnesty, especially his expectation that these states would reassume all the rights of any other state, made these oppressive developments almost inevitable.

Congressional Radical Reconstruction, 1867–1869

The new Congress that was elected with Lincoln in November 1864 did not assemble until December 1865—8 months after his death. This Congress had an overwhelming Republican majority, including many who had become disillusioned with Johnson by the time they met, especially as they saw what was happening in the states that had so recently been at war with the Union. The new president, they thought, was clearly siding with the former slaveholders rather than the former slaves.

Those in Congress most unhappy with Johnson, the Radical Republicans, were led by Charles Sumner in the Senate and Thaddeus Stevens in the House. Stevens told the House, "The whole fabric of southern society *must* be changed, and never can it be done if this opportunity is lost." For Stevens, the core values of the Republican Party remained, as the party's campaign slogan said, "free labor" by "free men" who earned their livelihoods by the sweat of their own brows. But with Johnson moving quickly to recognize the new state governments in the old Confederacy and those governments passing rigid Black Codes, the moment seemed to be quickly slipping away. Johnson focused on the Constitutional clause giving each state the right to set up its own government and arrangements for voting. Stevens and the radicals focused on a different part of the Constitution, the clause guaranteeing each state a republican form of government.

Most of the Republicans in Congress were not as radical as Stevens or Sumner. In 1865, a majority probably still had reservations about black voting rights. Even so, nearly all were disappointed at Johnson's easy amnesty of so many former Confederate leaders and the way Southern states were coming back into the Union with their old leaders in power. They discredited Johnson's version of Reconstruction because the results resembled the antebellum South in far too many ways. In particular, the fact that 58 members of the Confederate Congress, six Confederate cabinet officers, and the vice president of the Confederacy were all elected to Congress in 1865 and 1866 symbolized the failure of Johnson's policy to bring about meaningful change. However, the Constitution also gave Congress its own specific ways of asserting its authority.

Pennsylvania Congressman Thaddeus Stevens wanted Reconstruction to mean a thorough reordering of Southern society in which former slaves would receive land and guaranteed voting rights from the federal government.

Soon after convening in December 1865, Congress created a Joint Committee on Reconstruction. Moderate Senator William Pitt Fessenden of Maine was appointed chair, and most of the radicals, including Stevens, were excluded. Nevertheless, Congress undermined presidential Reconstruction by refusing to seat the Congressional delegates from the former Confederate states, even though Johnson considered those states to be fully restored to the Union. (Johnson's use of "restoration" rather than "reconstruction" irked many in Congress who wanted to see at least some change rather than restoring states to the place they had held in 1860.) Despite Johnson's insistence that the states had a right to be represented in Congress, the reality was that the Constitution made each house of Congress sole judge of the qualifications of its members, and neither house was ready to seat former Confederate leaders. Senator Ben Wade demanded that no Southern state be given a vote in Congress until African-Americans had the right to vote in that state. Others called for the creation of territorial governments in the former Confederate states, which would be under the control of Congress so that both voting rights and land redistribution could be assured. But Congress itself was divided, and action beyond rejecting the delegates from the South was hard to come by. Even legislation to give blacks in the District of Columbia the right to vote—something Congress clearly had authority to do—could not make it through both houses, especially after a December 1865 referendum of white voters in the District rejected black voting rights 6,951 to 35.

Early in 1866, Illinois Senator Lyman Trumbull proposed two new pieces of legislation. Unlike the more radical Republicans, Trumbull still maintained a good working relationship with Johnson and worried about the federal government exceeding its authority. But given developments in the South, Trumbull felt Congress had the authority—even the duty—to protect the rights of newly freed African-Americans under the Thirteenth Amendment, which included language giving Congress the power to pass laws to enforce the amendment.

First, Trumbull proposed extending the life of the Freedmen's Bureau. When Lincoln signed the legislation creating the Bureau, it was envisioned as a 1-year transitional body. However, through late 1865 and early 1866, the Freedmen's Bureau was the key federal agency distributing food to former slaves, supporting the establishment of schools, and in some cases, even helping former slaves gain their own land. After consulting with the head of the bureau, General O. O. Howard, Trumbull became convinced that its work would take many years and proposed extending it to 1870. He also proposed giving it new authority to ensure that blacks had all "civil rights belonging to white persons" and giving bureau agents the authority to press charges against state officials who denied those rights.

Trumbull then proposed the far-reaching Civil Rights Bill of 1866 that defined all persons born in the United States (except Indians) as citizens, permanently ending the Dred Scott distinctions between whites and blacks. Although the bill was silent on the issue of voting, given that many of the citizens it referred to—women and children, for example—could not vote, it explicitly guaranteed rights to make contracts, bring lawsuits, and have the equal benefit of the laws without regard to race. The law declared that such provisions were "fundamental rights belonging to every man as a free man." It also authorized federal authorities to prosecute violations in federal courts, a significant provision since Southern state courts were quickly reverting to their white-dominated ways.

Both of Trumbull's bills would have appeared radical a year or two earlier, but in 1866, they were seen as moderate proposals from a moderate Senator, and everyone expected smooth sailing for them. Then, after they passed Congress easily, President Johnson vetoed both bills. He called the Freedmen's Bureau an "immense patronage" system that exceeded the constitutional authority of the federal government, and he characterized the civil rights bill an as unwarranted "concentration of all legislative powers in the national Government." In his veto of the Civil Rights bill, Johnson also went out of his way to say that giving blacks citizenship rights was wrong and that "the distinction of race and color is by the bill made to operate in favor of the colored and against the white race."

The vetoes ended congressional efforts to work with the president on Reconstruction. Trumbull attacked the president. Senator William Pitt Fessenden, up to then considered a moderate, predicted that Johnson would "veto every other bill we pass." Johnson was prepared to do just that. He wanted to court Northern Democrats and Southern whites in his bid for a second term. Congress passed both pieces of legislation over Johnson's vetoes and began to use a veto-proof two-thirds majority to pass similar legislation in spite of presidential opposition. The era of presidential-led Reconstruction was fast coming to an end.

After passing Trumbull's two major bills over the president's veto in the spring of 1866, Congress proposed another amendment to the U.S. Constitution. Amendments to the Constitution proposed in Congress are not subject to a presidential veto, although three-fourths of the state legislatures need to agree to them. So in 1866, Congress set out to put the Civil Rights law into the Constitution itself. Agreement to do so came quickly; however, agreement on the other provisions of the amendment came much more slowly. Congress was not yet ready to give all black males the same voting rights that all white males had, but Sumner and some other radicals would never support an amendment that did not guarantee such rights. When their opposition was combined with the Democratic minority who did not want any new rights inscribed in the Constitution, crafting the amendment became a major hurdle. Many members of Congress wanted to punish any state that withheld the vote from black males, but they did not want to punish those states—currently all of them—that withheld the vote from women or those states—including several in the North—that made it hard for recent immigrants to vote. All of these issues led to months of wrangling, but the compromise that emerged as the Fourteenth Amendment guaranteeing rights of citizenship to former slaves and others born or naturalized in the United States was nevertheless significant.

The key provision of the Fourteenth Amendment said:

> All persons born or naturalized in the United States, and subject to the jurisdiction thereof, are citizens of the United States and of the State wherein they reside. No State shall make or enforce any law which shall abridge the privileges or immunities of citizens of the United States; nor shall any State deprive any person of life, liberty, or property, without due process of law; nor deny to any person within its jurisdiction the equal protection of the laws.

Other clauses of the Fourteenth Amendment stated changes drastically different from the Three-Fifth's clause and other previously accepted parts of the Constitution. They included language saying that any state that limited the voting rights of male inhabitants of a state would have its representation in Congress reduced, that any person who had held federal office and then participated in rebellion against the government could not again hold office, and that Confederate debts were null and void as far as the federal government was concerned.

Both houses of Congress finally passed the amendment in June 1866 and sent it to the states for ratification. Just as Johnson had refused to recognize a state as having returned to the Union until it ratified the Thirteenth Amendment, Congress now refused to seat the members of the House or Senate elected by a state until the state had ratified the Fourteenth Amendment. The amendment was popular in the North and many in the South were anxious to return to Congress, so approval from the required three-quarters of the states came quickly and the amendment was ratified in July 1868.

When Congress reconvened in December 1866, the majority of Republicans had no interest in working with Johnson. While the president called for immediate restoration of the "now unrepresented States" to Congress, Congress decided that, in fact, the states of the former Confederacy needed to be governed directly from Washington until "some indefinite future time." Some said that Congress was raising the bar after earlier requiring only assent to the Fourteenth Amendment, but the majority in Congress were no longer in any mood to compromise.

In January 1867, Congress quickly passed a law—over presidential veto—giving black males in the District of Columbia the right to vote. Since the district was directly controlled by Congress, they could pass such a law even though the Fifteenth Amendment, giving all black males the same voting rights as white males, was not yet contemplated. Congressional leaders then turned to more far-reaching legislation. They passed the Reconstruction Act of 1867, which declared all Southern state governments—already recognized by Johnson—to be inoperative and divided the former Confederate states into five military districts, ordering the military to oversee the writing of new constitutions that would guarantee universal male suffrage (see Map 15-1). Only after these new constitutions were in place, and after a state had ratified the Fourteenth Amendment, would Congress admit its representatives to Congress.

The president protested that the Reconstruction Act was, "the death-knell of civil liberty." African-Americans in the South, however, embraced the opportunity to participate in the political process. In addition to registering to vote and participating in constitution writing, blacks struck for higher pay in Charleston, Savannah, Mobile, Richmond, and New Orleans. Blacks in Richmond demanded integrated horse-drawn streetcars. Across the South, they created **Union Leagues** that became a base for political action and mutual support. The leagues offered opportunities to gain experience in the political process or, as one former slave said, "We just went there, and we talked a little, made speeches on one question and another." Former slaves became political leaders. By 1867, James H. Jones, the former "body servant" to Jefferson Davis, was a featured speaker at Republican meetings across the South.

Union Leagues
In the South, a Republican Party organization led by African-Americans, which became an important organizing device after 1865.

The Final Break—Johnson's Impeachment

By 1867, President Johnson had become virtually irrelevant to federal Reconstruction policy. Congress passed laws, the president vetoed them, and Congress passed them over the president's veto. But the Freedman's Bureau was under the control of the president even if he vetoed the bill that kept it going. The creation of military districts in the South also gave the president significant powers as commander-in-chief, even though he had opposed creating them.

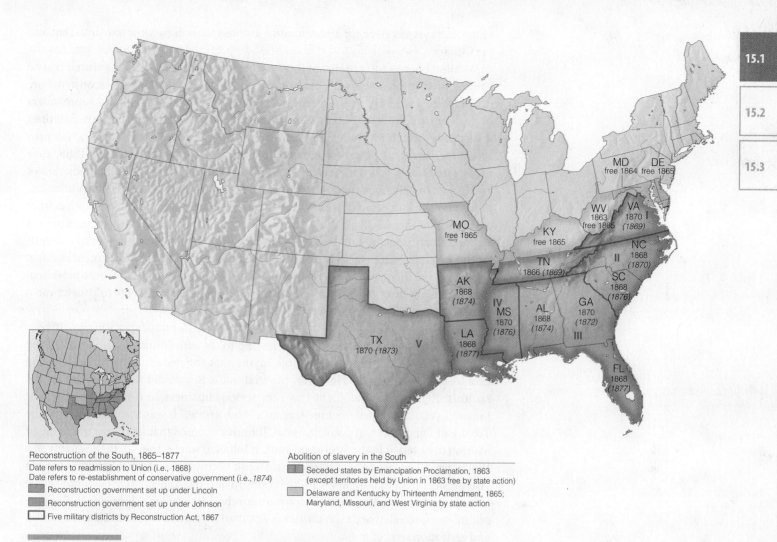

Reconstruction of the South, 1865–1877

Date refers to readmission to Union (i.e., 1868)
Date refers to re-establishment of conservative government (i.e., *1874*)

◼ Reconstruction government set up under Lincoln
◼ Reconstruction government set up under Johnson
▢ Five military districts by Reconstruction Act, 1867

Abolition of slavery in the South

◼ Seceded states by Emancipation Proclamation, 1863
(except territories held by Union in 1863 free by state action)
◼ Delaware and Kentucky by Thirteenth Amendment, 1865;
Maryland, Missouri, and West Virginia by state action

MAP 15-1 Southern Military Districts. Having lost all faith in President Johnson's leadership, the Congress in 1867 created five military districts to govern the states of the former Confederacy until new state constitutions that guaranteed the rights, including voting rights, of African-Americans were put in place.

Some in Congress began to consider removing Johnson in early 1867, but they were in a minority. Instead, Congress passed a number of laws that most hoped would keep Reconstruction moving in spite of the president. One law required all presidential orders to the military to pass through the army chief, General Grant, before going to commanders in the field. Grant was known to side with Congress, and this strategy seemed like an important safeguard and a significant limitation of Johnson's power. Congress also passed the Tenure of Office Act, which said that any person whose appointment required the Senate's consent, namely, members of the cabinet and ambassadors, could be replaced only when the Senate approved a successor. The goal of the act was to ensure that Secretary of War Stanton, who had been appointed by Lincoln and who took a tough stance on Reconstruction, stayed in office.

These Congressional actions might have worked had Johnson been willing to play a passive role, but Johnson could be stubborn, proud, and self-focused. His loyal Secretary of the Navy Gideon Welles said, "He has no confidantes and seeks none." As a result, unlike Lincoln, Johnson was often out of touch with congressional thinking.

These traits set the stage for an even more serious collision between the president and the Congress.

While Congress took charge of Reconstruction, Johnson became convinced that he had public opinion on his side and began to encourage opponents of Reconstruction, in the North and South. He also removed several of the tougher military commanders in the South and replaced them with officers who were willing to let events take their own course, which meant letting former Confederates take control of local governments and use their power to undermine black rights. Then in February 1868, after the Senate refused Johnson's request to remove Stanton, the president, in violation of the Tenure of Office act, fired him. It was a clear challenge to congressional authority.

Under the U.S. Constitution, a president can be removed only for "high crimes and misdemeanors," terms the Constitution does not define. But the procedure for impeachment is clear. The House of Representatives is required to act as a sort of Grand Jury, deciding whether or not to bring charges, called impeachment, against the president. Then the Senate, with the Chief Justice of the Supreme Court presiding, acts as a jury to hear and vote on the charges. Only with a Senate vote to convict can a president be removed from office.

Led by Thaddeus Stevens, the House, with every Republican voting positively, agreed on a long list of charges, most having to do with Johnson's violation of the Tenure of Office Act but also a charge saying that the president had tried to bring Congress "into disgrace." However, the trial in the Senate did not go as well for the radicals. Removing a president was very serious business, and it was unclear that Johnson's obstructionism met the level of a "high crime." It was also not clear that the Tenure of Office Act was constitutional. Johnson claimed that he meant the firing of Stanton to be tested in the Supreme Court. If Johnson were removed, then Senator Ben Wade, president pro tem of the Senate, would become president since there was no vice president, and many who disliked Johnson also disliked Wade. When the Senate finally voted in mid-May of 1868, Johnson survived by one vote. Johnson could serve out his term in relative peace, although his chances for the Democratic nomination and reelection were slim.

The Right to Vote—Grant's Election and the Fifteenth Amendment

After Johnson's impeachment was resolved, both parties turned to selecting nominees for the presidential election in the fall of 1868. For the Republicans, the choice was easy. Ulysses S. Grant as commander of the army had supported the Republicans in Congress on the issues of Reconstruction; his own attitudes on race had been significantly reshaped by the courage shown by black troops during the Civil War, and he was the nation's war hero. The Republicans easily nominated him along with the Speaker of the House Schuyler Colfax of Indiana as his running mate. Grant ran on a cautious platform that nevertheless embraced extending voting rights to former slaves. His slogan was, "Let Us Have Peace."

Democrats were divided on issues of personality, on their opposition to Congressional Reconstruction, and on fiscal policies—whether to continue to authorize the printing of money, or "greenbacks," based on the federal promise to pay. After 21 ballots in which a number of candidates, including Andrew Johnson, failed to win the nomination, they chose former New York Governor Horatio Seymour, who had flirted with supporting the Confederacy during the war and who had called protesters in the New York Draft Riot "my friends." For vice president, they nominated a former Union general from Missouri, Francis Blair, who called for an end to Reconstruction, which he called the rule of "a semi-barbarous race of blacks."

While neither party articulated a fully developed economic policy, the lines between the parties were drawn on the issues of race. August Belmont, one of the nation's leading bankers, said that, in the 1868 election, financial matters paled in comparison with black voting rights. In November, Grant carried most of the North and the parts of the South under federal control, including North and South Carolina and Alabama. Seymour's home state of New York, along with New Jersey, Georgia, and Louisiana favored Seymour. The state governments in Florida, Mississippi, and Texas had not yet been recognized, and those states did not vote. Grant won 53 percent of the popular vote but an overwhelming 73 percent of the electoral vote for an easy victory.

With Grant about to become president, Republicans in Congress moved quickly on the issue of voting rights. In February 1869, Congress passed the Fifteenth Amendment, which stated:

> The right of citizens of the United States to vote shall not be denied or abridged by the United States or by any State on account of race, color, or previous condition of servitude.

Harper's Weekly carried many illustrations of the changes happening in the South to Northern audiences. This issue of July 1868 showed the enthusiasm with which African-Americans, many of whom had been slaves only a few years before, were taking to electoral politics.

In a little less than a year, by February 1870, the required three-fourths of the states ratified the amendment and the right of former slaves, and other citizens, including the children of Chinese immigrants—who were citizens but had also been denied the right to vote—had been inscribed in the Constitution.

As powerful as the language of the Fifteenth Amendment is, it lacked some wording that many had wanted to include. The radicals had wanted the amendment to state that neither the right to vote nor the right to hold office could be abridged. But others feared that several Northern states, including California with its large Chinese population, might reject the amendment if the right of nonwhite people to hold office were included. Many also had wanted wording to prohibit the many tricks that some Southern governments were already using to limit the black vote, including literacy tests that could be manipulated to exclude whoever the test giver wanted excluded, or tests related to property or education. Supporters of the amendment, however, worried that they would lose too much Northern support if they included such clauses. Massachusetts and Connecticut used literacy tests to limit voting by foreign-born citizens, while Pennsylvania and Rhode Island had property or tax qualifications for voting, and no one wanted to risk losing the support of those states. As a result, important safeguards were not included.

Many women, especially the most prominent leaders of the women's rights movement, were deeply disappointed and angered by the Fifteenth Amendment. Women like Susan B. Anthony, Elizabeth Cady Stanton, and Sojourner Truth had labored long and hard in support of abolition and the Union cause, and now they saw women's right to vote ignored. Frederick Douglass was an advocate of women's rights in addition to African-American rights, but in 1869, he precipitated a long and painful, though temporary, break with Anthony and Stanton over the Fifteenth Amendment. Douglass argued for one step at a time, guaranteeing black men the same rights as white men, and then guaranteeing women of all races the right to vote. Douglass said, "I hold that women, as well as men, have the right to vote, and my heart and my voice go with the movement to extend suffrage to women." These were not just words. In the decade before and after battles around the Fifteenth Amendment, Douglass actively campaigned for women's right to vote. But between 1865 and 1870, Douglass was willing to compromise to achieve his immediate goal.

The compromise that Douglass proposed brought a sharp rebuke from the former slave and abolitionist Sojourner Truth. In 1867, at the height of the debate, Truth gave her own passionate response to Douglass. She said that she, too, had been born a slave and rejoiced that "They have got their liberty—so much good luck to have slavery partly destroyed; not entirely. I want it root and branch destroyed." For Truth, root and branch meant the vote for all. Partial justice would not do, "and if colored men get their rights, and not colored women theirs, you see the colored men will be masters over the women, and it will be just as bad as it was before."

In spite of compromises and disappointments, many hailed the Fifteenth Amendment as completing the work of abolition. As late as 1868, free blacks could vote in only eight Northern states. In 1870, by law, black men could vote everywhere in the United States. William Lloyd Garrison celebrated "this wonderful, quite sudden transformation…from the auction-block to the ballot-box." While there was already clear evidence of the many steps—by law and by violence—that would be taken to deny most blacks the right to vote for most of the next century, in 1870, there was also grounds for very real optimism.

15.1 **Quick Review** Compare Presidential Reconstruction and Congressional Reconstruction. What are the most significant differences between the two plans? Given these differences, was the tension between them inevitable?

THE IMPACT OF RECONSTRUCTION

15.2 Explain the impact of Reconstruction on African-American life in the South.

In the early years of Reconstruction, many of the South's former leaders returned to power. Only one Southern official was tried for treason and executed—Henry Wirz, commander of the infamous Andersonville prison where so many Union soldiers died. Jefferson Davis was imprisoned for 2 years but then was freed and retired to write his memoirs. Many other Confederate leaders quickly declared their loyalty to the Union after the war's end, received a pardon from Johnson, and resumed leadership in their states. Within a year of announcing his plan to exclude the wealthy and the political leaders of the Confederacy from the original amnesty conditions, Johnson had granted 7,000 individual pardons. The prewar status quo seemed to be returning in the Southern states. Then Congress took over Reconstruction, and everything changed. In state legislatures, local sheriff's offices, and school boards, former slaves, Northern abolitionists, and Southern Unionists took power under the banner of the Republican Party or local Union Leagues. A radical remaking of the South began in the late 1860s and continued into the 1870s.

Voting in the South

In January 1870, the Mississippi state legislature elected Hiram R. Revels to the United States Senate. Revels was the first African-American ever elected to the Senate. The legislature that elected Revels included 40 blacks and 100 whites—hardly a black-dominated body. He was elected, ironically, to fill Jefferson Davis's former seat, left vacant since Davis departed in 1861.

Hiram Revels, the first African-American senator (left) sits with six of the first blacks elected to the House of Representatives representing Alabama, Florida, South Carolina (three representatives), and Georgia.

Revels was born free in Fayetteville, North Carolina, in 1827. Like many of the African-American political leaders during Reconstruction, he was a minister in the African Methodist Episcopal Church, serving as a pastor in Baltimore, Maryland, when the Civil War began. Revels organized two all-black regiments and served as their chaplain. At the war's end, Revels went with his unit to Vicksburg, Mississippi, and then moved to Natchez. He was not initially a candidate for the Senate, but his lack of ambition for the post made him a perfect compromise candidate.

Senator Garrett Davis of Kentucky challenged the right of an African-American to be seated in the Senate. But Revels's key defender, James Nye of Nevada, told his colleagues, "In 1861 from this hall departed two senators who were representing here the state of Mississippi; one of them who went defiantly was Jefferson Davis." For Nye, and eventually for a majority in the Senate, nothing was a more fitting symbol of the outcome of the Civil War than the seating of an African-American in the place of the former president of the Confederacy.

Mississippi later sent Blanche K. Bruce to the Senate in 1874. Bruce was born a slave, but he attended Oberlin College and established himself as a planter in Mississippi in 1868. Unlike Revels, he worked his way up the political ladder, serving as the sergeant-at-arms of the Mississippi state senate, assessor and sheriff of Bolivar County, and a member of the Board of Levee Commissioners of the Mississippi River. Navigation on the Mississippi was a major concern of his during his U.S. Senate tenure, as was opposition to Chinese exclusion. Bruce was the last African-American to serve in the Senate until Edward Brooke was elected from Massachusetts in 1966.

More African-Americans were elected to the House. Twenty-two blacks served in Congress during Reconstruction, including 13 who had been born slaves. Between 1871 and 1873, South Carolina had three African-Americans in the House—Joseph H. Rainey, Robert B. Elliott, and Robert G. DeLarge. In the same sessions, Benjamin S. Turner represented Alabama; Josiah T. Walls, Florida; and Joseph Long, Georgia. Rainey served three terms in the House during which time he played an important role in arguing for the first major federal aid to education bill that was considered, although defeated, in Congress.

Reconstruction state governments, with black and white leadership, expanded the right to vote, abolishing restrictions that had existed for black and poor white voters. In addition, newly formulated state constitutions created public school systems and internal improvements designed to bring the South into the modern world. It was a heady time, yet not an easy one.

Schools for Freedom

Northern whites who came to the South with the Union army were amazed by the thirst for literacy demonstrated by former slaves. A member of an education society in North Carolina said, "he thought a school-house would be the first proof of their *independence*." Booker T. Washington, a well-known African-American educator remembered the immediate aftermath of emancipation: "Few people who were not right in the midst of the scenes can form any exact idea of the intense desire which the people of my race showed for education. It was a whole race trying to go to school."

Realizing that blacks saw the schoolhouse as "proof of their independence" surprised white observers. It did not surprise former slaves who had grown up in a world where literacy, for them, was a crime. As a slave child of seven or eight,

Frederick Douglass had been taught the alphabet by a white woman, but the lessons did not last long. He remembered:

> Mr. Auld found out what was going on, and at once forbade Mrs. Auld to instruct me further, telling her, among other things, that it was unlawful, as well as unsafe, to teach a slave to read....It would forever unfit him to be a slave."

Nothing appealed more to young Douglass than being made unfit for slavery. Douglass found secret ways to continue his studies, and by the time he made his escape to Massachusetts, Douglass had the literacy skills that would make him one of the great orators and writers of his day. Slave masters and slave-state legislatures who made it illegal to teach a slave to read or write, unwittingly also made literacy a powerful symbol of freedom.

While the majority of teachers who went South to teach were white women, an African-American, Charlotte Forten, began teaching in Port Royal, South Carolina, where she said, "The children are well-behaved and eager to learn. It will be a happiness

American Voices

John Roy Lynch, The Work of Reconstruction, 1869

John Roy Lynch was born a slave and elected as a Republican to the Mississippi legislature in 1869. In this essay, he described what Reconstruction meant to those who, like him, were trying to create a new political system, indeed a new culture, in the states that had been part of the Confederacy only a few years before.

The new administration had an important and difficult task before it. A state government had to be organized from top to bottom. A new judiciary had to be inaugurated, consisting of three justices of the state supreme court, fifteen judges of the circuit court, and twenty chancery court judges, all of whom had to be appointed by the governor, by and with the advice and consent of the [state] senate. In addition to this, a new public school system had to be organized and established. There was not a public school building anywhere in the state except in a few of the larger towns, and they, with possibly a few exceptions, were greatly in need of repair. To erect the necessary schoolhouses and to reconstruct and repair those already in existence so as to afford educational facilities for both races was by no means an easy task. It necessitated a very large outlay of cash in the beginning which resulted in a material increase in the rate of taxation for the time being, but the constitution called for the establishment of the system and, of course, the work had to be done. It was not only done, but it was done creditably and as economically as circumstances and conditions at that time made

possible. That system, though slightly changed, still stands as a creditable monument to the work of the first Republican state administration that was organized in the state of Mississippi under the Reconstruction Acts of the Congress.

It was also necessary to reorganize, reconstruct, and in many instances, rebuild some of the penal, charitable, and other public institutions of the state. A new code of laws also had to be adopted to take the place of the old one, and thus wipe out the black laws that had been passed by what was known as the Johnson legislature. Also it was necessary to change the statutes of the state to harmonize with the new order of things. This was no easy task, especially in view of the fact that a heavy increase in the rate of taxation was thus made necessary.

Source: John Hope Franklin, editor, *Reminiscences of an Active Life: The Autobiography of John Roy Lynch* (Chicago: The University of Chicago Press, 1970),

Thinking Critically

1. **Documentary Analysis**

   According to Lynch, what were the most important priorities of the new Republican governments?

2. **Historical Interpretation**

   What light does the document shed on the challenges faced by Republican governments during Reconstruction?

A school operated by the Freedman's Bureau in Richmond, Virginia, was shown in this September 1866 issue of *Frank Leslie's Illustrated Newspaper.*

to teach here." By 1870, several thousand teachers—whites and blacks, Northern immigrants, and veterans of the Confederate army—were teaching in schools for former slaves. Although a majority stayed for only a year or two, some found their life's work in these schools.

Many newly free African-Americans welcomed Northern white teachers for the long term, but they also wanted teachers from their own communities. The Freedmen's Bureau and Northern missionary groups helped in founding black colleges in the South, including Atlanta, Fisk, Hampton, and Tugaloo, which were specifically designed to train black teachers, often in a short course that lasted 1 or 2 years. The results of the new efforts at teacher preparation were impressive, and as early as 1869, the bureau reported that of the 3,000 teachers for the freedmen, the majority were now African-American.

The Reconstruction Act of 1867 also fostered the growth of Southern schooling. The 1867 act required states of the former Confederacy to call state conventions to rewrite their state constitutions, and the new constitutions were expected to include support for public education. Later, even as state after state returned to white rule, the public school system remained. In *Black Reconstruction in America*, W.E.B. Du Bois, a renowned African-American activist, wrote, "Public education for all at public expense was, in the South, a Negro idea."

The Reality of Sharecropping

For many newly freed slaves, another issue was as important as the vote or education—land. In Virginia, a freedman told a Union army officer that, if the army had a right to take away the master's slaves, then they "had the right to take master's land too."

In Alabama, a state convention delegate insisted, "the property which they hold was nearly all earned by the sweat of our brows." Those closest to the land, who had worked it for no pay, valued land and the promise of land ownership. Land provided independent economic opportunity on which freedom rested.

When Sherman's army arrived in Savannah, Georgia, in December 1864, the army of 60,000 troops was accompanied by some 20,000 former slaves. Sherman met with local blacks in Savannah. Garrison Frazier, a leader of that group, made it clear what they wanted: freedom and land, which meant "placing us where we could reap the fruit of our own labor." Four days later, Sherman's Special Field Order No. 15 provided for 40-acre parcels of land for black families, which was to be taken from the plantations of owners in active rebellion on the Sea Islands and coastal areas in Georgia and, later, in South Carolina (once his army got there). Sherman also offered army mules that were no longer needed. Thus, 40 acres and a mule became the symbol of freedom to many, and by June 1865, 40,000 newly freed people were settled on "Sherman land" in the former Confederacy. Sherman's order did not make it clear whether the land grant was temporary or permanent, but the link of freedom and land was permanent in the minds of many.

President Johnson wasted no time ending the redistribution of land after taking office. He ordered an end to the "40 acres and a mule" policy. As head of the Freedman's Bureau, General O. O. Howard had expanded Sherman's original South Carolina plan, instructing his agents to "set aside" 40-acre tracts for individual

THINKING HISTORICALLY

John W. Alvord's First Report to the Freedmen's Bureau, 1866

John W. Alvord was an unusually perceptive observer who was in charge of setting up schools for the Freedmen's Bureau. In his first report to the bureau in Washington, DC, in 1866, Alvord noted, somewhat to his surprise, that there were often black-initiated schools already in operation when he arrived to open schools. Thus, he wrote in his first report:

Throughout the entire South an effort is being made by the colored people to educate themselves....In the absence of other teaching they are determined to be self-taught; and everywhere some elementary text-book, or the fragment of one, may be seen in the hands of negroes....Native schools... are making their appearance through the *interior* of the entire country.

A more detailed reading of the report makes it clear that Alvord was surprised first by the commitment of the newly freed people to education, second by their sense of initiative in launching their own schools even before any federal or missionary teachers arrived, and third by the sense of self-respect and self-determination that those running the schools were maintaining.

Source: John W. Alvord, *Inspector's Report of Schools and Finances*. U.S. Bureau of Refugees, Freedmen and Abandoned Lands. Washington, D.C.: U.S. Government Printing Office, 1866, pp. 9–10, cited in James Anderson, *The Education of Blacks in the South, 1860–1935* (Chapel Hill: University of North Carolina Press, 1988), pp. 6–7.

Thinking Critically

1. **Documentary Analysis**
   What does Alvord's surprise at finding "Native schools" say about the way African-Americans were perceived?

2. **Historical Interpretation**
   How do you account for the determination to be self-taught and to develop their own schools by people who only a year before had been enslaved by others and who many portrayed as passive?

freedmen. Blacks across the South quickly began farming their own plots. Johnson overrode Howard's order, issued pardons to former plantation owners, and ordered Howard to restore the land to them, which meant taking it away from those who were currently using it. Once land had been returned to its former owners, there was very little chance that former slaves would regain their parcels.

In October 1865, General Howard made a painful journey to Edisto Island in South Carolina to announce the president's order. A committee of freedmen drafted their response:

> General, we want Homesteads…if the government having concluded to befriend its late enemies and to neglect to observe the principles of common faith between its self and us its allies in the war you said was over, now takes away from them all right to the soil they stand upon save such as they can get by again working for *your* late and their *all time* enemies.…You will see this is not the condition of really freemen.

Redistribution of land, it seemed, was not going to be part of Reconstruction.

In a few places, however, former slaves were able to purchase or win government land. Having spent their lives in unpaid labor, few slaves had any resources to buy land, even when it was being sold very cheaply in the aftermath of the war. In South Carolina, which had an exceptionally strong Reconstruction government, the legislature established a state land commission that provided grants of land to some 14,000 black families—perhaps one-seventh of the state's black population—in various parts of the state. They also created the town of Promised Land, which continues as a black-led community to the present.

The primary economic opportunity open to slaves was to return to the plantations where they had worked in the past, but do so as paid employees. Neither former slaves nor former slave owners found the prospect encouraging. One Georgia planter complained that, "Once we had reliable labor controlled at will. Now…it is both uncertain and unreliable." When railroads or new enterprises offered jobs, blacks left the plantations to take other work.

During the Johnson-dominated Reconstruction, Southern landowners not only reclaimed their lands but also ensured the passage of vagrancy laws made it a crime to be without a job, which meant former slaves had to take whatever was offered or be jailed. Some landowners agreed to hire only their own former slaves, making it extremely difficult for newly free people to bargain for wages or move to better opportunities.

Many in Washington were pleased to see blacks become wage earners, paid for raising the cotton, sugar, rice, and tobacco they had previously raised without pay as slaves. But former slaves did not like working for wages, especially the low wages that were offered for work in the same places where they had once labored as slaves. Wage-earning blacks resented their status as what some called "wage slaves." They wanted land of their own, and if they could not get land—and in most parts of the South they could not—they wanted a share in the profits of their work.

Given the dissatisfaction that both white landowners and black workers felt, a new economic arrangement was born: **sharecropping**. Sharecropping meant just what the name implied. Instead of working for wages, former slaves worked as independent entrepreneurs who were guaranteed a share of the crop in return for their labor. At the same time, landowners, who provided the land, the seeds, and the loans to get through the year, also received a share of the crop.

As this agricultural economy developed after the Civil War, the owner of a large tract of land (almost always a former plantation owner who had the land returned

Sharecropping
Labor system that evolved during and after Reconstruction whereby landowners furnished laborers with a house, farm animals, tools, and advanced credit in exchange for a share of the laborers' crop.

Edisto Island, off the coast of South Carolina, was one of the first places where the government provided land and mules—and mule carts. Former slaves quickly used the opportunity to become independent farmers.

by the Johnson administration) agreed to provide crude housing, a short-term loan for living expenses (known as the "furnish" and usually provided at the beginning of the growing season in March), seed, fertilizer, tools, and the right to grow cotton on a specified piece of land 15 to 40 acres in area. Landless tenants (almost always former slaves) agreed to work the land, plant, weed or "chop" the cotton through the growing season, and bring in a crop. Landowner and sharecropper would then split the profits after the harvest.

Once the harvest was done, just before Christmas at "the settle," the landowner would provide the sharecropper with a statement of accounts showing the value of the cotton harvest, the cost of the "furnish," and any other loans or purchases at the commissary on the plantation (usually the only place the sharecropper could buy goods and often a place where prices were very high), and the difference or profit due to the sharecropper. Everyone knew that many planters cheated their often illiterate tenants. Asking for a detailed accounting meant risking one's home and perhaps one's life. Few took the risk, though many sharecroppers were privately furious when the end-of-year payments were finally made and, somehow, the results for those who had worked all year were so modest.

Sharecropping began on the sugar plantations of Louisiana and quickly spread to the rest of the agricultural South. With sharecropping, black workers had a significant new incentive to work since they retained a portion of the profits they created. Women and children, who had resisted work in the field for wages, now returned to the fields as families sought to make a living.

At first, landowners were far from enthusiastic about sharecropping. While it meant that they no longer needed to supervise employees, they did not like the sense

Homes for sharecroppers were not much different from the cabins that had been built in the old slave quarters.

of independence that sharecropping brought to former slaves. They also disliked the shift from having farm work done by gangs of laborers, as had been the case in slavery and wage-earning times, to having the work done by family units on smaller plots. One South Carolina planter complained about the black-led Union Leagues that fostered sharecropping saying, "Their leaders counsel them not to work for wages at all, but to insist upon setting up for themselves." Nevertheless, by the early 1870s, sharecropping had become the primary means of agricultural organization in much of the South, especially the region's great cotton-growing heartland (see Map 15-2).

MAP 15-2 Sharecropping Reshapes a Plantation. These two maps show the changes in the living and work arrangements on the Barrow Plantation in Oglethorpe County, Georgia, between the last days of slavery in 1860 and the establishment of sharecropping in 1881. By the latter date, the old Slave Quarter had disappeared, replaced by dispersed cottages of the sharecropping families, each of whom worked a portion of the land.

Before long, plantation owners found ways to manipulate it for their own ends. Owners developed a credit system whereby a plantation-store sold everything from food to clothing on credit to the sharecroppers to be repaid when the crop was harvested. Many plantation owners made as much money with their stores as with their crops. With crops mortgaged before they were even planted, workers fell further and further into debt to the landowners. If sharecropping initially gave black families freedom that work for wages did not, it also tied them to the land in poverty for generations.

15.2 | **Quick Review** Consider the early impacts of Reconstruction up to 1877. Would you consider it a success or a failure? Give at least three reasons to support your position.

TERROR, APATHY, AND THE CREATION OF THE SEGREGATED SOUTH

15.3 | Analyze the reasons Reconstruction ended and the impact of Redemption.

During the first decade after the Civil War, Americans witnessed extraordinary changes. Slavery ended, and the Constitution was amended to give former slaves citizenship rights and the same right to vote as whites. Black males voted, held office, and served on juries, and black men, women, and children rode on integrated transit and attended school. Some even managed to own their own land. However, few of the advances of the first decade of Reconstruction lasted.

The rise and decline of black rights was an uneven process. Blacks were organizing and gaining new rights while the Civil War was still being fought. Many whites resisted black political and economic progress throughout Congressional Reconstruction. Although the withdrawal of federal troops in 1877 greatly hastened the process of undoing the gains of Reconstruction, what some white Southerners called "Redemption," that, too, was uneven. In some areas, white-only government had been reestablished well before 1877, while in other areas, blacks maintained political rights well into the 1880s and 1890s. Nevertheless, eventually, the high hopes of Reconstruction ended everywhere.

Opposition to Black Rights and the Roots of "Redemption"

Opponents of black rights were never completely excluded from power during Reconstruction. In September 1868, the white majority in the Georgia legislature voted to expel all 27 African-American representatives. Henry McNeal Turner, one of the 27, responded: "You may expel us, gentlemen, by your votes today; but while you do it, remember that there is a just God in Heaven." Two years later, in response to actions like the expulsion of the black legislators, President Grant reinstated military rule in Georgia. Black legislators returned to their seats along with white allies and opponents, and a majority in the legislature ratified the Fifteenth Amendment.

With Grant in the White House and Republican leaders in Congress who were willing to use federal troops if necessary to support the rights of former slaves and their allies, the Republican Party in the South was the party of black rights and racial equality. Blacks, often organized in Union Leagues, were at the heart of the party, but there were also large numbers of white Republicans in the South, including both Southern born and immigrants from the North. Southern whites who supported Republican and multiracial efforts were called **scalawags**, and they were a diverse lot. Some had

Scalawags
A disparaging term for southern whites who supported the Southern Republican Party during Reconstruction.

Carpetbaggers
Term used by white Southerners for Northern transplants who came to the South to help with Reconstruction.

opposed secession from 1861. Others, like Confederate General James Longstreet or army veteran Albert R. Parsons, embraced the Republican Party only after the war. Some, like Parsons, strongly supported equal rights for blacks. For others, support for black rights was secondary, but they saw the party as a place of personal opportunity.

Northern whites who came South were called **carpetbaggers** because, Southerners said, they could carry everything they owned in a single suitcase covered with carpet-like material. Resentful, Southerners claimed that carpetbaggers had come South to get rich. Carpetbaggers were on the whole younger and less prosperous than the scalawags. Some carpetbaggers were no doubt opportunists, coming to make their fortune, while others were abolitionists, coming South to implement policies they had long advocated. Many were veterans of the Union army, and some like Governor Adelbert Ames, the Republican Governor of Mississippi, had first been ordered South by the army and had stayed on.

In the 1860s and 1870s, there were virtually no black Democrats in the South. The post–Civil War Democratic Party was the party of "white only" government. Southern Democrats organized at every political level from small towns to state legislatures and governors' offices. Their twofold goal was to assure that, even if blacks were now free, they would have few rights and that whites committed to excluding blacks from power would dominate every aspect of society, politically, economically, and culturally. For these segregationist Democrats, African-Americans of the Union Leagues, scalawags, and carpetbaggers were all their enemies.

Lucius Quintus Cincinnatus Lamar of Mississippi, an example of the Southern Democratic Party leaders of his day, was from an old elite Southern family. He represented Mississippi in the U.S. Congress before the war and became a staunch secessionist. During the war, he was a general in the Confederate army. In the postwar period, he decided to enter politics again. Lamar wrote to a friend, "It does seem to me that if there ever was a time when the white people of this state…should rise & with one unanimous voice protest against the domination about to be piled upon them the present is that time." He proceeded to do everything he could to ensure white rule in Mississippi.

In November 1872, having long-since secured a presidential pardon, Lamar won a seat in the U.S. Congress. He also helped to organize the Democratic Party in Mississippi. In campaign speeches, Lamar attacked black voting rights. In Congress, he tried to ensure that the federal government did not enforce black rights. He helped defeat the Enforcement Act of 1875, which would have given President Grant more authority to implement the Fourteenth and Fifteenth Amendments in Mississippi. While he was engaged in partisan politics, Lamar also helped to develop another political organization outside of the Democratic Party—hidden from view but essential to his political victory—the Ku Klux Klan.

The Rise of Violence and the Ku Klux Klan

Ku Klux Klan
One of several vigilante groups that terrorized black people in the South during Reconstruction Era, founded by Confederate veterans in 1866.

The **Ku Klux Klan** was founded as a social club among Confederate veterans in Tennessee in 1866. It quickly turned into the largest of several secret and violent organizations bent on ensuring a reign of terror against not only Republican political leaders of either race but also teachers in black schools and blacks in general. The Klan was committed to ending Reconstruction and returning the South to white rule. The Klan assassinated Arkansas's Congressman James M. Hinds, members of the South Carolina legislature, and other members of state constitutional conventions. It had only just begun its work.

Similar organizations grew across the South. In Louisiana, the Knights of the White Camellia played a similar role, as did the White Line organizations in Mississippi. Although leaders like Lamar maintained a public distance, they secretly kept close ties to these violent extralegal organizations. By political organizing and sheer violence and intimidation, they were confident that they could return the South to its prewar ways.

Even before the emergence of the KKK, African-Americans and their white Republican allies faced violence. Just after the war's end in May 1866, a bloody riot in Memphis, Tennessee, which began when two carriages, one driven by a black and one by a white, collided. The riot resulted in the burning of black schools, churches, and over 90 black homes as well as the killing of at least 48 people; all but two of whom were black. A Memphis teacher was murdered, and others were told they would be killed if they did not leave the city immediately. The following fall, only 13 of the 40 teachers in the black schools of Memphis returned. A few weeks later, a similar riot in New Orleans, Louisiana, resulted in at least 100 injuries as well as the killing of 34 blacks and three of their white supporters.

By the spring of 1873, what could only be described as a civil war was going on in Louisiana. Tension mounted after the November 1872 elections in which one group of voters elected a Republican governor and another group, a Democratic one. When a federal judge ruled in favor of the Republican slate, President Grant sent troops to New Orleans to oust the Democratic governor and install the Republican administration. But in the small town of Colfax, Louisiana, two sheriffs had also been elected, and federal troops were a long way off. On Easter Sunday, April 13, 1873, tensions reached a boiling point. Several dozen black families along with William Ward, who was the Republican sheriff as well as a former slave and Union army veteran, barricaded themselves inside the town and sent urgent telegrams to the governor in New Orleans, asking for the army to rescue them. Help was too late in coming. Two to three hundred whites marched on the town, led by the Democratic sheriff, Confederate veteran Christopher Columbus Nash. Nash and his army attacked the town and killed everyone they could find. At least 60 blacks, perhaps many more, were killed. The next day, witnesses saw only piles of bodies everywhere. Colfax was far from an isolated incident.

Some of the greatest violence was in Mississippi. On July 4, 1874, as the Republican Party held a meeting in Vicksburg, Mississippi, armed whites arrived and shot and killed many of those, white and black, in attendance. Peter Crosby, the sheriff in Vicksburg, demanded federal intervention, but did not get help. On September 1, 1875, at a Republican meeting in Yazoo City, Henry Dixon began shooting at the mixed-race gathering. One person was killed instantly. Before long, those who were at the meeting scattered and a company of organized Mississippi White Liners—the Mississippi version of the Klan—took over the town and forced its elected government to flee.

On Election Day, the Democrats won statewide in Mississippi. In Port Gibson, black voters arriving at the polls were met by some 80 whites armed with Remington rifles, who started firing at them. One old man, John Morris, was killed, six others wounded, and none voted. At Peytona, not a single Republican vote was cast.

Klan members quickly adopted hoods and masks both to hide their identity and to frighten those who opposed them.

The Memphis riot was but one of many in which whites, enraged by new black rights, attacked homes, schools, and churches belonging to newly free blacks and any whites who supported them.

Democratic sentries on the Tombigbee River ensured that black voters could not cross the river to get to polling places. Governor Ames fled for his life before his term ended, while Democratic Party teams warned politically active Republicans, black and white, to leave the state before they were killed. Reconstruction ended in Mississippi with the 1875 elections.

Efforts to Defend Reconstruction

The antiblack, anti-Republican violence with which the South was slowly "redeemed" from Reconstruction met resistance at every step, sometimes very significant resistance. In March of 1870, just as the Fifteenth Amendment was ratified, Congress also passed the first Enforcement Act, making the denial of the right to vote because of race through force, fraud, bribery, or intimidation a federal crime. Up to that time, protecting voting rights had been completely a state issue, but in 1870, Congress had significant reasons not to trust that all the states would protect voting rights, especially for newly enfranchised African-Americans. Two further Enforcement Acts gave the federal government the right to intervene when elections were unfair. In addition, the Ku Klux Klan Act of April 1871 made conspiracies to deprive citizens of the right to vote a punishable federal offense. In June 1870, Congress also created the U.S. Department of Justice with a specific mandate to enforce Reconstruction. (Up until then, the U.S. Attorney General had been a kind of in-house lawyer and legal advisor to the president and cabinet but with no agency to lead.) All of these acts represented a major expansion of federal power. Because of the new legislation, crimes against individuals could, for the first time, be prosecuted by the federal government, especially if state governments did not step in and do their duty.

President Grant used this legislation forcefully. In October 1871, the president proclaimed nine counties of South Carolina to be in a "condition of lawlessness" and sent federal troops to restore order and arrest several hundred Klan leaders, some of whom ended up serving terms in federal prison. In addition, perhaps 2,000 Klan members left the state. Seven hundred leaders of the Klan were also arrested in Mississippi and several hundred more in North Carolina. By the end of 1872, the Klan, as an organization, had been destroyed.

The Klan would rise again, but not for many decades later. Nevertheless, despite its absence, violence against blacks and their white Republican allies continued in the 1870s. In the North, people were growing more and more willing to let the South settle its own affairs. When the Democrats nominated newspaper editor Horace Greeley for president in 1872, they adopted a platform attacking Republican corruption and calling for civil service reform while also promising a general amnesty for former Confederates and an end to federal intervention in the South. Grant was easily renominated by the Republicans and won the election handily, but Democrats gained power in Congress. As it turned out, Greeley died before the electoral votes were counted, which caused some confusion, but no one doubted that Grant had won the election. In his inaugural address at the beginning of his second term in March 1873, Grant told the nation, "The effects of the late civil strife have been to free the slave and make him a citizen. Yet he is not possessed of the civil rights which citizenship should carry with it. This is wrong, and should be corrected. To this correction I stand committed, so far as Executive influence can avail." Grant did his best, but it was not enough.

In 1875, Grant sent fellow Civil War General Philip Sheridan to Louisiana to investigate the political violence. Sheridan documented the killing of 2,141 blacks and the wounding of 2,115 more since the war had ended. All of these crimes remained unpunished. Another Civil War veteran, former slave Henry Adams, organized a committee of 500 blacks to "look into affairs and see the true condition of our race." In northern Louisiana around the Red River area alone, the committee documented 683 murders, including the following notations:

> Sam Maybury, whipped to death, December 1865
> Henry West, badly whipped, November 1874
> George, a colored man, killed by white men 1873
> Nancy Brooks, badly whipped by a white man, 1873

In most cases, the list included the name of the victim and the unpunished killer. The reality that Sheridan and Adams documented would not change for a very long time.

A Changing National Mood and the End of Reconstruction

A number of factors led to the growing national weariness with federal intervention in the South. Southern Reconstruction governments were regularly accused of corruption, and some office holders, black and white, certainly enriched themselves. P.B.S. Pinchback of Louisiana, the only black governor in the Reconstruction-era, admitted that he made considerable profit for himself in his political career. South Carolina's white Republican Governor Robert K. Scott speculated in state bonds, and North Carolina's Governor William Holden was aware of "damnable rascality." In truth, the Reconstruction governments were probably no more corrupt than those that came before or after, but the charges tarnished Reconstruction.

The Grant administration also faced one corruption scandal after another. During Grant's first year in office, Jay Gould and James Fisk, the nation's leading bankers, tried to corner the nation's gold supply and thus control the economy, with possible support from administration insiders including Julia Grant, the president's wife. One after another, cabinet officers resigned and were replaced after they were charged with taking bribes or other forms of corruption. In 1870, former Ohio Governor Jacob Cox resigned as secretary of the interior to protest the administration's failure to implement civil service reform. In perhaps the biggest scandal, a congressional investigation uncovered the workings of the so-called Whiskey Ring, a group including elected officials, government employees, and whiskey makers who defrauded the U.S. Treasury of excise taxes on whiskey. Over 200 distillers and revenue agents were indicted, and Grant's personal secretary, Orville E. Babcock, resigned. Grant directed the investigations to continue saying, "Let no guilty man escape if it can be avoided," and he ordered the Attorney General not to grant immunity to any suspects, but he was seriously tarnished by the widespread corruption.

The sheer size of the federal interventions in the South also undermined public support. In late 1874, White League militants ousted the Republican governor, William P. Kellogg, in Louisiana and took over the legislative hall. Since Louisiana was still under military supervision, Grant ordered General Sheridan to restore order. With 5,000 U.S. Army troops, Sheridan restored Kellogg to the governor's office and forcibly removed Democrats from the legislative hall. The spectacle of U.S. Army soldiers marching into a legislative chamber and removing people who claimed to have been elected created a huge backlash. Newspapers that had supported the Union cause now compared the White League to the founding fathers defending their freedom from the tyranny of the British.

Debates in Congress reflected the change in Northern public opinion and the increasing swagger of Southern leaders. Joseph R. Hawley, a Connecticut Republican who called himself a "radical abolitionist," nevertheless argued that the "social, and educational, and moral reconstruction," of the South could "never come from any legislative halls." The Democrats in Congress praised "local self-government," while insisting that black and white Republicans in the South should stop depending "upon external aid." In that context, it was difficult for the federal administration or the U.S. Army officers in the South to get support.

The U.S. Supreme Court was not sympathetic to Reconstruction. In the *Slaughterhouse Cases* of 1873, the court severely restricted the reach of the Fourteenth Amendment. A group of butchers in New Orleans had challenged the right of the Louisiana legislature to grant a monopoly to one meatpacking company because, they said, it violated their Fourteenth Amendment rights to due process of law and citizenship rights. But the court ruled that the Fourteenth Amendment did not include such rights, making it much harder to bring other suits about state infringement of citizen's rights.

In March 1876, the court's decision in *United States v. Cruikshank* struck a further blow to Reconstruction. William J. "Bill" Cruikshank was a white participant in the attack on Colfax, Louisiana, in 1873. He was indicted on federal charges for violating the civil rights of blacks who were killed in the attack. But 3 years later, the Supreme Court ruled that the charges were unconstitutional. Chief Justice Morrison R. Waite wrote that protecting the rights of individual citizens was a state, not a federal duty. *Cruikshank* took away one of the federal government's most important enforcement powers—the right to bring federal charges against those who attacked the basic rights of African-Americans.

Finally, in 1883, the court ruled that the Civil Rights Act of 1875 was unconstitutional because the Fourteenth Amendment gave Congress only the right to outlaw state government actions, not discrimination by individuals, which the court left to the states to deal with. The legal foundation of Reconstruction seemed to be crumbling or, perhaps, the court was simply following public opinion. Associate Justice Samuel Miller, a Grant appointee, wrote to a friend, describing what many Americans were also feeling, "I am losing interest in these matters."

As the country prepared for the 1876 presidential elections, the loss of interest in Reconstruction was evident. The Republicans nominated Ohio Governor Rutherford B. Hayes, who was on good terms with all factions in the party and especially popular with some because of his crackdown on nascent labor unions in Ohio. The platform said surprisingly little about Reconstruction. The Democrats nominated New York Governor Samuel Tilden, who had made a fortune as legal counsel for some of the country's richest bankers and railroads and gained fame for fighting corruption in government. Promising to continue the fight against corruption and foster prosperity, and never mentioning Reconstruction, Tilden was the strongest candidate the Democrats had nominated in some time.

The campaign was intense, especially in the South where violence and confusion reigned. In November, Tilden outpolled Hayes, winning the popular vote 4,286,808 to 4,034,142, but it was the electoral votes that counted. In three states, Florida, Louisiana, and South Carolina, Republican election boards discarded enough votes to declare Hayes the winner, which meant that he would also win the electoral count. Not surprisingly, the Democrats challenged these decisions.

The months between the election and the inauguration were as tense as any since the Jefferson–Adams contest of 1800. Some Democrats vowed "Tilden or War." Congress created an Electoral Commission of 10 congressional representatives, five from each party plus five Supreme Court justices, to determine the outcome since the Constitution gave no guidance beyond saying that the votes "shall be counted" in the Senate. After intense negotiations, the Electoral Commission ruled 8 to 7 for Hayes. But the Constitution specified that a president could not be declared elected until the Senate actually counted the votes cast by the presidential electors from the various states. Democrats refused to convene the Senate to count that vote, thus making it impossible to resolve the crisis. Finally on February 26, a group of Southern Democrats met with Ohio Republicans and negotiated a compromise. Hayes, who promised to treat the South with "kind consideration," agreed that, if he were made President, he would use his power to end Reconstruction, most of all by withdrawing the federal troops that were in the South protecting Republican governments. The Southern Democrats liked the offer and agreed to let the Senate meet and count the votes including—following the Electoral Commission's recommendation—the votes of the Republican electors from Florida. On Inauguration Day, March 4, 1877, Hayes became president and moved quickly to fulfill his promises.

Southern Republicans who had supported Hayes were outraged. A former slave from South Carolina commented angrily, "To think that Hayes could go back on us when we had to wade through blood to help place him where he is now." Little could now be done, however. Hayes did not immediately remove federal troops from the South, but he made it clear that the troops who remained would not intervene in the South's internal matters as Grant had ordered. The changes in federal policy had been coming for some time, but after March 1877, there was little reason to expect any federal support for Reconstruction anywhere.

After 1877, the direction was clear. John C. Calhoun, an Arkansas planter and grandson of the South Carolina senator of the same name, told Congress that "left to ourselves," the white South could settle "all questions" about the region's political arrangements. And they did. Blacks, carpetbaggers, and scalawags were slowly excluded from offices, though some stayed on into the 1890s. Many were forced to leave the South altogether if they wanted long lives. In addition, blacks were excluded from voting altogether, education budgets were slashed, and the regulation of sharecropping shifted further in favor of plantation owners. After 1877, white rule in the South was assured.

The Birth of the Segregated South

Disenfranchisement and segregation did not happen overnight. African-Americans were still being elected to office in the 1880s and 1890s. George H. White of North Carolina, who was described as "the last of the Negro congressmen," bade a final farewell to the House of Representatives in 1901 saying: "This, Mr. Chairman, this is perhaps the Negroes' temporary farewell to the American Congress. But let me say, phoenix-like, he will rise up someday and come again." The absence of blacks from Congress lasted for 28 years until Oscar De Priest was elected from Chicago. Only after another civil rights movement many decades later did African-Americans reach the number of representatives in Congress that they had in the 1870s.

Various forms of what came to be called **Jim Crow segregation** developed at a rapid pace. (Jim Crow was a derogatory character in a minstrel show designed to denigrate blacks, but his name has been applied to the whole era of rigid racial segregation that was the rule in many parts of the United States from the 1870s to the 1960s.) Schools, public facilities, transportation, and most every other aspect of life were segregated. In addition to losing the vote, blacks were marginalized economically so that sharecropping became virtually the only option for most. A vicious campaign of lynching controlled blacks through fear and intimidation. Perhaps the capstone of this segregation was the U.S. Supreme Court's 1896 *Plessy v. Ferguson* decision that "separate by equal" facilities were quite acceptable under the United States Constitution. By the time that decision was issued, the high hopes of Reconstruction were a dim memory and most Americans—white and black—were living in a very different world.

Jim Crow segregation
Segregation laws that became widespread in the South during the 1890s, named for a minstrel show character portrayed satirically by white actors in blackface.

15.3 **Quick Review** Considering the events and trends of the later years of Reconstruction, or Redemption as it was called, who were the winners and who were the losers? Who was most responsible for what happened?

CONCLUSION

During the 12 years after the Civil War, Americans grappled with what the future held for newly freed slaves and how best to return to the Union those states that had been in rebellion during the Civil War. The so-called Radical Republicans in Congress sought ways to protect the educational, political, and economic rights of the freedmen—as former slaves, male and female, were called. Andrew Johnson, who became president upon Lincoln's death in April 1865, seemed indifferent to African-American rights and soon alienated congressional radicals by restoring power to former rebels intent on limiting the freedoms of former slaves.

Congressional Republicans had their own plans for consolidating the Union victory, however, and eventually, the House of Representatives impeached Johnson for obstructing its plans to reconstruct the South. Although he was acquitted of "high crimes and misdemeanors" by the Senate, which allowed him to stay in office, Johnson's political career was over. But Congress passed a number of laws, including the 1866 Civil Rights Act and the Fourteenth and Fifteenth Amendments to the Constitution, designed to protect black rights as citizens and voters. Across the South, African-Americans and whites committed to Reconstruction were elected to local and national office in larger numbers and began to reshape their states. In 1868, Ulysses S. Grant, the Republican nominee, was elected president. Grant was committed to the Reconstruction of the South in ways that would protect black rights, especially black voting rights.

After the war, African-Americans pursued full citizenship rights, education, and economic independence. Terrorized by white supremacists and lacking money and credit, most African-Americans never achieved either true equality or independence. At the same time, white veterans of the Confederate army were organizing to deny those rights, not only legally through the Democratic Party but also illegally through the Ku Klux Klan and other similar organizations. As time passed, and as public support for federal intervention in the affairs of the South eroded, the promise of Reconstruction's early days evaporated. By 1877, a new president, Rutherford B. Hayes, began to bring Reconstruction to an end, assuring white rule in the South and the disenfranchisement and "Jim Crow segregation" of African-Americans for generations to come.

CHAPTER REVIEW Why might the historian Eric Foner call Reconstruction "America's Unfinished Revolution"?

Chapter 15   Chapter Review

FEDERAL RECONSTRUCTION POLICY

15.1 Explain the political development of federal Reconstruction policy.

Review Questions

1. **Historical Interpretation**
   What do Johnson's policies before his impeachment tell us about his vision of the post-Reconstruction South?

2. **Constructing Arguments**
   How would you explain the increasingly radical nature of Congressional Reconstruction? What factors pushed Congress toward more aggressive intervention in Southern society and politics?

3. **Comparison**
   Compare and contrast Presidential Reconstruction and Congressional Reconstruction. What were some of the ways that Congress forced the states of the former Confederacy to accept Reconstruction that Johnson opposed?

THE IMPACT OF RECONSTRUCTION

15.2 Explain the impact of Reconstruction on African-American life in the South.

Review Questions

4. **Historical Interpretation**
   What aspects of the history of the 1860s and 1870s would a historian report to emphasize the success of Congressional Reconstruction? What aspects of those years would a historian report to emphasize Congressional Reconstruction as a failure?

5. **Contextualization**
   Why did newly freed slaves place such a high priority on education?

6. **Constructing Arguments**
   Defend or refute the following statement. "By the end of the 1870s, from an economic perspective, most Southern blacks were almost as closely tied to the land and dependent on white landowners as they had been under slavery." What evidence can you produce to support your position?

TERROR, APATHY, AND THE CREATION OF THE SEGREGATED SOUTH

15.3 Analyze the reasons Reconstruction ended and the impact of Redemption.

Review Questions

7. **Contextualization**
   What groups made up the Republican coalition during Reconstruction? What did each group hope to gain from its support of the party?

8. **Historical Interpretation**
   Is it fair to describe the Democratic Party during Reconstruction as the party of white supremacy? Why or why not?

9. **Constructing Arguments**
   Defend or refute the following statement. "The Ku Klux Klan of the Reconstruction era was, at its essence, a terrorist organization."

Becoming an Industrial World Power—Costs, Benefits, and Responses

1865–1914

PART OUTLINE

16 Conflict in the West

BUFFALO BILL'S WILD WEST
CONGRESS OF ROUGH RIDERS OF THE WORLD.

Buffalo Bill's Wild West Show created the image of the American West for many people, which was more fantasy than reality.

CHAPTER OBJECTIVE

Demonstrate an understanding of the post–Civil War changes in the American West

LEARNING OBJECTIVES

THE TRIBES OF THE WEST AND THE U.S. GOVERNMENT

16.1 Explain western development from an Indian perspective and the way Indian and white cultures shaped each other.

THE IMPACT OF THE TRANSCONTINENTAL RAILROAD, 1869

16.2 Analyze the building of transcontinental railroads and its impact on the nation, especially the West.

THE TRANSFORMATION OF THE WEST

16.3 Analyze how indigenous people, ranchers, farmers, miners, outlaws, politicians, and mythmakers shaped the West and our understanding of its history.

I n the midst of the Civil War, Abraham Lincoln worried about the potential for alliances between the Confederate States and some western Indian tribes. He met with 14 western chiefs at the White House in March 1863. He did not offer much but urged them to adopt the "peaceful ways of the white people." Chief Lean Bear of the Cheyenne reminded the president that whites were responsible for most of the violence in the West. He did not mention the irony of Lincoln's statement coming in the midst of the bloodiest war in American history.

Subsequent presidents had similar, usually unproductive, meetings. President Grant tried hard to implement what came to be known as the Grant Peace Policy, but, though well intentioned, that policy ultimately depended on the U.S. Army to settle matters in the West, and the army in the field was often anything but peaceful. While the most intense interaction between white settlers and Indian tribes east of the Mississippi River lasted for over 200 years, the major battles between the western tribes and the U.S. Army lasted for less than 30 years. What began as a series of bloody skirmishes during the Civil War erupted into the Great Plains Wars in the 1870s and 1880s. By the 1890s, the armed conflict was all over as tribes were defeated and moved into ever shrinking reservations.

At the same time, white ranchers, farmers, and miners built new settlements across the West. What began as great cattle ranches were replaced within 30 years by smaller-scale farms producing beef and wheat for national and world markets. These agricultural developments of the post–Civil War era depended on new technologies—most of all the development of railroads that brought supplies to isolated farmers and shipped their products—and on new economic and political arrangements. This chapter examines the growth and changing nature of the American West between 1865 and 1890.

THE TRIBES OF THE WEST AND THE U.S. GOVERNMENT

16.1 Explain western development from an Indian perspective and the way Indian and white cultures shaped each other.

Native Americans fought on both sides in the Civil War and sometimes used the country's division to expand their territory, forcing both North and South to divert troops from other battles. The Civil War also changed the lives of American Indians. For most whites, however, Indian matters existed only on the margin of their attention during the war. Once the Civil War ended, white relationships with Indian tribes, especially on the Great Plains, took on greater significance. As many Americans, whites and some blacks, began to look for more land in the aftermath of the war, they ran directly into newly empowered Indian tribes.

The Comanche Empire

For the Comanches, arguably the most powerful tribe on the western frontier in 1860, the Civil War was a great gift. The U.S. Army, the Texas Rangers, and other whites who had been harassing them for decades were called to fight against each other on distant battlefields. The Comanches welcomed their absence.

In 1700, the Comanches were a small tribe who had recently moved into what is now the Southwest of the United States. They developed expertise using two European imports, rifles and horses, becoming the much-feared "Lords of the South Plains." The Comanches built a way of life based on hunting the buffalo, and like the buffalo, they traveled widely over the Great Plains. They also made alliances (especially with the Utes), traded (with everyone), and fought bloody battles (especially with the Apaches and the Europeans) while they stole horses and supplies as well as kidnapped settlers and people from other tribes. By the early 1800s, although they were without a permanent capital, borders, or bureaucracy, the Comanches ruled an empire that was equal in size and power to the United States or the Republic of Mexico.

Nevertheless, by the late 1850s, the Comanches seemed to be in decline. Working with Texas Rangers and with smaller tribes who had been Comanche victims, the U.S. Army began to gain the upper hand in Texas. The Comanches needed ample space for hunting, trading, and fighting; they had no interest in being settled in any permanent locations. In battles during 1858, over 100 Comanche warriors, including chiefs, were killed and a large number of women and children taken prisoner. Some Comanches were ready to seek peace. The Penateka Comanches, who had split from the larger tribe, gave up warfare and settled on a Texas reservation just before the Civil War.

The Civil War and, later, Reconstruction, opened up new opportunities for the Comanches. The war diverted troops from Texas to distant battlefields, and as early as 1863, Comanche raiding parties began to move back into parts of Texas they had left in the 1850s, stealing horses and cattle. When Texas joined the Confederacy, Comanches developed a brisk trade selling stolen Texas cattle to Union Army agents in New Mexico. With the coming of peace in 1865, the U.S. Army demilitarized any forces in Texas that had fought for the Confederacy in the Civil War, including the feared Texas Rangers. While U.S. Army troops were stationed in Houston, San Antonio, and along the border with Mexico, west Texas, with several million cattle wandering on huge range lands, was only lightly protected. The Comanche saw their opportunity. They developed a rich trade with prosperous New Mexicans who came to be known as the *comancheros* because of the trade.

Significant Dates	
1858	John Butterfield opens overland stage route
1862	Congress passes the Homestead Act
1864	Navajo Long Walk to Bosque Redondo
1865	Civil War ends, units of U.S. Army return to patrol the West
	Chicago Union Stock Yards opens
1867	Chisholm Trail to Abilene, Kansas
	Medicine Lodge Creek Treaty between U.S. government and Comanche
1868	Treaty of Fort Laramie with Lakota Sioux
	Treaty of Bosque Redondo with Navajos
1869	Transcontinental Railroad completed at Promontory Point, Utah
	President Grant announces new Grant Peace Policy for American Indians
1872	Modoc uprising in California
1873	Panic and Depression
1874	U.S. Army defeat of the Comanche
	Black Hills Gold Rush into Sioux territory in the Dakotas
1876	Battle of the Little Bighorn
1877	Nez Perce under Chief Joseph surrender to U.S. Army
1878	Billy the Kid and Lincoln County War in New Mexico
	El Fronterizo, Spanish-language newspaper begins publication in Arizona Territory
1879	Beginnings of Carlisle Indian School
1881	Gunfight at the OK Corral
	Beginning of Great Dakota Land Boom
1882	Gustavus Swift creates new refrigerated rail car allowing shipment of meat
	Opening of Anaconda Copper Mine in Montana
1883	Buffalo Bill's Wild West Show
	Four standard time zones created for the United States
1887	Dawes Act begins dividing Reservations into private allotments
1889	Oklahoma Land rush; North Dakota, South Dakota, Montana, Washington become states
1890	Lakota Sioux Ghost Dance and massacre at Wounded Knee
	White Cap resistance to land development in New Mexico
	Idaho and Wyoming become states
1892	Johnson County War—Wyoming Stock Growers Association drive out smaller ranches
1896	Utah admitted as a state
1907	Oklahoma admitted as a state
1912	New Mexico and Arizona admitted as states

16.1

16.2

16.3

From the mid-1860s into the early 1870s, great annual trading gatherings took place where *comancheros*, often backed by investors from the eastern United States, traded salt, hard bread, flour, sugar, tobacco, blankets, and knives as well as the ever-in-demand latest issue revolvers and rifles in exchange for cattle that the Comanches had recently acquired in Texas. The Comanches also continued to trade in people—Mexican and Indian captives, especially women, who were in great demand as brides in New Mexico. While these trading gatherings integrated the Comanches into U.S. markets, the stolen cattle and the continued trade in humans were sources of serious tensions between the Comanches and the governments of the United States and the state of Texas.

To restore order to the Southwest and open up new land for white settlement, U.S. peace commissioners met with more than 5,000 Comanches as well as Kiowas, Naishans, Cheyennes, and Arapahoes at Medicine Lodge Creek in Texas in October 1867. The U.S. delegation was led by William Tecumseh Sherman, head of the army of the West, a post he had also held during the Civil War. As a show of strength, the army team included 500 well-armed soldiers in dress uniform. A newspaper reporter also at the meeting wrote that the Comanches arrived "with all their war paraphernalia, their horses striped with war paint, the riders bedecked with war bonnets and their faces painted red." They also knew a thing or two about a show of strength.

After elaborate opening ceremonies and the exchanges of gifts—including 6,000 pounds of coffee, 10,000 pounds of bread, and 3,000 pounds of tobacco from the government—the U.S. representatives made it clear they had come to Medicine Lodge Creek to end the Comanche status as a sovereign people. The government would help them become farmers on a reservation, but would not tolerate a continuation of the old hunting, trading, and stealing ways. Sherman concluded, "You can no more stop this [change] than you can stop the sun or the moon. You must submit and do the best you can."

The Comanche chiefs were outraged by the government's demands. Several, including Paruasemena, the leader of the Penateka Comanches, expressed their anger in eloquent responses, but in the end, the chiefs signed a treaty, although it was one that left much open to interpretation. The **Medicine Lodge Creek Treaty** provided for a Comanche reservation but also gave them the right to hunt on open plains below the Arkansas River in Indian Territory (Oklahoma). The government representatives assumed that the Comanches would become farmers on the reservation while venturing out on occasional hunting trips to track the buffalo. The Comanches thought that the reservation would make a perfectly good winter campground, and they were more than happy to receive government rations, but they had no intention of becoming settled farmers. Along with hunting buffalo, the Comanches expected to continue hunting for Texas cattle and trading them to New Mexico buyers.

The radically different interpretations of the Medicine Lodge Creek Treaty between the Comanches and the U.S. government became clear the next spring when several thousand Comanches, having spent the winter on the reservation, collected their government payments and began raiding cattle and horses in Texas, New Mexico, and Indian Territory. According to one report, 6,255 horses and 11,395 cattle were lost to Indian raids in Texas between 1866 and 1873.

After several unsuccessful peace efforts, the United States gave up on negotiations and ordered the army to attack and force the Comanches onto a permanent reservation. From 1871 to 1873, the army and the Comanches fought. While the army attacked, American buffalo hunters decimated the buffalo herds as industries found new uses for their hides. The buffalo had been at the heart of Comanche life, not only as food but also as a way to understand the universe, and their destruction undermined the Comanche way of life.

During the fighting from 1871 to 1873 a new Comanche leader emerged. Quanah Parker was the son of a Comanche chief and Ann Cynthia Parker, a white Texan who had been captured by the Comanches. He became the fiercest opponent of compromise with whites. Then in 1874, Isa-tai, a young Comanche spiritual leader or shaman, became prominent, sharing a message heard many times among different Indian tribes—that if they would get rid of white ways and end their dealings with white

Medicine Lodge Creek Treaty

An 1867 treaty between the Comanches and the U.S. Army in which the Comanches agreed to settle on a reservation.

American Voices

Paruasemena (Ten Bears), Speech at Medicine Lodge Creek Treaty Meeting, 1867

Paruasemena was one of the Indian leaders to visit Lincoln at the White House in 1863. Four years later, the 75-year-old leader spoke to the U.S. peace commission at Medicine Lodge Creek. The passion and pathos of the speech touched many.

My people have never first drawn a bow or fired a gun against the whites. There has been trouble between us…my young men have danced the war dance. But it was not begun by us. It was you who sent out the first soldier.…

Two years ago I came upon this road, following the buffalo, that my wives and children might have their cheeks plump and their bodies warm. But the soldiers fired on us…The blue-dressed soldiers and the Utes came out from the night…and for campfires they lit our lodges. Instead of hunting game they killed my braves, and the warriors of the tribe cut short their hair for the dead.

So it was in Texas. They made sorrow in our camps, and we went out like the buffalo bulls when the cows are attacked. When we found them we killed them, and their scalps hang in our lodges. The Comanches are not weak and blind, like the pups of a dog when seven sleeps old. They are strong and farsighted, like grown horses. We took their road and we went on it. The white women cried, and our women laughed.

But there are things which you have said to me which I do not like. They were not sweet like sugar, but bitter like gourds. You have said that you want to put us on a reservation, to build us houses and make us medicine lodges. I do not want them. I was born under the prairie, where the wind blew free and there was nothing to break the light of the sun. I was born where there were no enclosures and everything drew a free breath. I want to die there and not within walls. I know every stream and wood between the Rio Grande and the Arkansas. I have hunted and lived over that country. I live like my fathers before me and like them I lived happily.

When I was in Washington the Great Father told me that all the Comanche land was ours and that no one should hinder us in living upon it. So, why do you ask us to leave the rivers and the sun and the wind and live in houses? Do not ask us to give up the buffalo for the sheep. The young men have heard talk of this, and it has made them sad and angry. Do not speak of it more. I love to carry out the talk I get from the Great Father. When I get goods and presents I and my people feel glad, since it shows that he holds us in his eye.

If the Texans had kept out of my country, there might have been peace. But that which you now say we must live in, is too small. The Texans have taken away the places where the grass grew the thickest and the timber was best. Had we kept that, we might have done the things you ask. But it is too late. The whites have the country which we loved, and we wish only to wander on the prairie til we die.

Source: Taylor, Nathaniel G., et al., (1910) Papers Relating to Talks and Councils Held with the Indians in Dakota and Montana in the years 1866-1869. Washington: Government Printing Office. (Original in the National Archives, Records of the Indian Division, Office of the Secretary of the Interior, Record Group 48.)

Thinking Critically

1. **Documentary Analysis**

   How did Paruasemena characterize the conflict between his people and the United States government?

2. **Contextualization**

   What light does this document shed on the differences between white and Indian cultural values in the 1800s?

---

people, the buffalo would return and life would be good again. In a great camp meeting in June 1874, several hundred Comanche warriors led by Isa-tai and Parker joined with Kiowas, Cheyennes, and Arapahoes to eliminate the white presence from the Great Plains. The Comanche attacked the buffalo hunters.

The army counterattacked. On September 28, 1874, U.S. forces attacked Parker's main encampment, and though nearly all of the Indians fled, the army destroyed the camp, taking the horses and burning tents, blankets, and food. Faced with starvation, the Comanches began to surrender in small groups, coming to the army post at Fort Sill in Indian Territory over the course of the winter where they gave up their horses and rifles and moved to the reservations assigned to them. Isa-tai was discredited among the Comanches from then on.

The winter of 1874–75 was the low point of Comanche life, but it was not the end. Quannah Parker was only 27 when he surrendered to federal authorities. Over the next 4 decades, he became principal chief of the Comanches and led them from warfare to farming and ranching. Parker was a tough negotiator with the federal Bureau of Indian Affairs for expanded land allotments. He had eight wives, built a fine 10-room house, and before he died he had his own telephone, owned a car, traveled by train, and went hunting with President Theodore Roosevelt. The life Parker and his people lived as he grew older was radically different from the life he had lived as a youth, but he helped create the foundation for tribal survival in a new era.

The Navajos and the Apaches

The Navajos, or Diné as they prefer to be called, were as warlike as the Comanches and dominated large swaths of New Mexico, Colorado, and Kansas. The Union army ended their rule and that of the Mescalero Apaches, too. In August 1862, Union Brigadier General James H. Carleton arrived in New Mexico in command of California volunteers, but when he learned that Confederates in the region had already been defeated, he ordered his troops to attack the Apaches and Navajos instead. In early 1863, the army invaded Apache lands and soon confined some 400 Apaches at a new reservation at **Bosque Redondo** in central New Mexico. Carleton then appointed Kit Carson to lead the attack on the much larger Navajo tribe of some 10,000 people. Carson told the Navajos, "Go to Bosque Redondo, or we will pursue and destroy you. We will not make peace with you on any other terms." Carson kept his word, marching into Canyon de Chelly, the sacred Navajo heartland, attacking Navajo encampments as well as destroying orchards, crops, and livestock. By the spring of 1864, some 6,000 Navajos had surrendered rather than die of starvation. U.S. troops pursued other resisters, and eventually 8,000 Navajos were forced on the "Long Walk," 300 miles south to a strange way of life at Bosque Redondo.

The Bosque Redondo reservation was a complete failure. The Mescalero Apaches considered the Navajos to be their "inveterate enemies," and the two tribes had no interest in cooperating. The arid land of mid New Mexico could not support thousands of families, even if they did turn to farming as the government asked them to do. In addition, the Comanches saw the confined reservation as an opportunity to attack old enemies.

After the Civil War, a congressional peace commission visited Bosque Redondo and realized that the government had created a disaster. On June 1, 1868, they signed a new treaty with the Navajos that allowed them to return to a reservation in their own homelands. A new Mescalero Apaches reservation in central New Mexico was established by executive order in 1873 and expanded in 1883. Navajo leaders negotiated several expansions of their reservation between 1868 and 1886 so it covered a large part of New Mexico and Arizona up to the four corners area with Colorado and Utah. They also managed to avoid the division of the reservation into individual allotments that destroyed tribal ways for other tribes. With the shared experience of suffering at Bosque Redondo and the substantial new lands, the Navajo tribe had become the Navajo Nation. They kept their promise to stop raiding and recreated much of their old ways, living on lands they considered sacred and making a living by herding sheep, goats, and horses. The tribe grew from 10,000 in 1864 to 30,000 in 1900, an unusual experience for American Indians.

Bosque Redondo
A reservation in central New Mexico where the majority of the Navajos and Mescalero Apaches were confined during the Civil War.

Navajos under guard at Bosque Redondo, ca. 1864.

The Modocs, the Nez Perce, and the Pacific Coast Tribes

Well before the Civil War, the rapid influx of white settlers who came to California with the gold rush was a catastrophe for the many small tribes that dotted the state. The California tribes had already been weakened by decades of Spanish and Mexican efforts to turn them into workers on the missions and the large rancheros of the state. The new American presence only made things worse. Federal commissioners negotiated treaties with 139 tribes to create small reservations, mostly in northern California, but Congress did not ratify the treaties and white settlers ignored them. In spite of the efforts of federal Indian agents to create reasonable safeguards for the Indians of California, settlers and miners ignored restrictions on Indian land if they thought they could find gold or plant a settlement. California Indians were starved and all too often simply murdered. In 1845, before the United States took control of California, there were some 150,000 Indians in California—down from probably 300,000 when the Spanish missionaries first arrived; just a decade after California became a state, only 25,000 remained.

In the fall of 1872, Kintpuash, a leader of the Modoc tribe in southern Oregon and northern California, led his people out of a reservation the Modocs had shared with the Klamaths and Snakes since signing a treaty in 1864. Kintpuash did not like reservation life, and the Modocs returned to their homelands on Lost River in California. The U.S. Army followed and attacked them, but the Modocs knew the territory, especially the great black lava fields that provided hiding to those who had grown up among them. The Modocs resisted, killing soldiers, settlers, and government negotiators. Orders came from Washington "that the name of Modoc should cease," because they had violated their treaty and killed federal negotiators. Eventually, the army won. Surviving Modocs were relocated in Indian Territory far from their homeland.

The Nez Perce, the tribe without whom Lewis and Clark would have perished, had long lived in Oregon and Idaho, but they were a deeply divided tribe. One group, known as the "progressives," signed a treaty in 1855 agreeing to live on a large reservation in Idaho. Another group, the so-called "nonprogressives," refused. They lived independently in an area encompassing the Salmon River in Idaho and the Snake River in Oregon.

For some time, the nonprogressive Nez Perce were allowed to live in peace, but as white settlement grew in the Snake River's fertile Wallowa Valley, pressure came to force them and their leader Chief Joseph, or Hin-mah-too-yah-lat-kekt, onto the Idaho Reservation. They resisted, but by 1877, the Nez Perce knew they could no longer live unmolested in the Wallowa Valley. They began a long retreat to preserve their independence, a retreat that turned into a well-chronicled but tragic journey. Initially, the Nez Perce moved east across the Bitterroot Mountains into Montana hoping to find sanctuary with the Crow or Sioux. Then they turned north, hoping to cross into Canada. All along the way, the U.S. Army pursued them. Finally, when they were less than 40 miles from Canada, the army caught up. A few escaped across the border, but the majority, led by Chief Joseph, surrendered. The chief said, "I am tired of fighting. Our chiefs are killed.…It is cold and we have no blankets. The little children are freezing to death.…My heart is sick and sad. From where the sun now stands, I will fight no more forever." Most of those who had made the long journey with Chief Joseph ended up on a reservation in Indian Territory, although some, eventually including Chief Joseph, were allowed to return to the Pacific Northwest but never to their ancestral lands (see Map 16-1).

The Lakota Sioux—From Fort Laramie to the Little Big Horn and Wounded Knee

The Sioux, by far the largest group of tribes in the northern Great Plains, also fought fierce battles with the U.S. Army. Teton and Santee Sioux had been embroiled with U.S. settlers and army troops through the 1860s, but the largest battles of the 1870s were with the powerful Lakota Sioux.

In December 1866, the Lakota attacked and killed U.S. troops. Rather than risk further fighting, the government sought peace with the Lakota as well as their

Chief Joseph of the Nez Perce who led the epic journey of his people.

MAP 16-1 The Plains Indian Wars. As trails and then railroads brought more settlers, the great battles between the U.S. Army and the Plains Indians erupted all across the Great Plains.

Cheyenne and Arapaho allies. In the 1868 Treaty of Fort Laramie, the Lakota Sioux, led by Red Cloud, promised to avoid war, and the army agreed to abandon three provocatively placed forts. (An earlier Fort Laramie Treaty of 1851 was negotiated simply to keep peace between the tribes and give the U.S. Army and settlers rights-of-way across the plains to California and Oregon.) Although the 1868 Fort Laramie Treaty could be seen as a victory for the Sioux, one faction, led by Sitting Bull, derided the treaty, reservation life, and the government annuities that were promised, saying to those who signed, "You are fools to make yourselves slaves to a piece of fat bacon, some hard-tack, and a little sugar and coffee." Indeed, the treaty that Sitting Bull criticized did not protect the Lakota or the other tribes involved.

Less than a decade after the treaty was signed, when gold was discovered in the Black Hills and miners and settlers descended on the region, the government ordered the Lakota to leave winter camps and settle near the agency headquarters. The Lakota resisted. The Great Sioux War of 1876–77 had begun.

General George Armstrong Custer led a battalion of troops in an attack on the Sioux who were refusing to move. At the Little Bighorn River on June 25, 1876, Custer and his troops were surrounded by a much larger force of Sioux and Cheyennes. None of the army troops survived. It was perhaps the most famous Indian victory, but that success was soon followed by defeat. Less than a month after the Little Bighorn battle, General Philip Sheridan led a huge force that attacked and defeated the Sioux. The government then broke up the Great Sioux Reserve in the Black Hills of Dakota Territory, creating six much smaller reservations: Standing Rock, Cheyenne River, Lower Brule, Crow Creek, Pine Ridge, and Rosebud, while giving some of the best land, now declared "surplus," to white settlers and miners.

General William Tecumseh Sherman led the U.S. delegation in negotiations with tribal leaders, which led to the Fort Laramie Treaty of 1868.

The defeats of 1876–77, along with the destruction of the great buffalo herds, led to an era of depression, disease, and poverty for the Sioux. A little more than a decade later, in 1890, the religious phenomenon that had been seen among other tribes appeared among the Sioux. A spiritual leader, Wovoka, initiated the **Ghost Dance** movement, promising a return of the buffalo and the disappearance of white people if only the Sioux would take up the dance and return to their ancient ways, freeing themselves of dependence on white culture. The rise of the Ghost Dance frightened the white community, and the army was sent to Pine Ridge to investigate. A former Indian agent, Valentine McGillycuddy, appealed for calm saying, "I should let the dance continue….If the Seventh-Day Adventists prepare their ascension robes for the second coming of the Savior, the United States Army is not put in motion to prevent them. Why should not the Indians have the same privilege?"

McGillycuddy also warned that "If the troops remain, trouble is sure to come." He was right. One band of Sioux under the leadership of Big Foot left the reservation while the Ghost Dance continued, and U.S. troops went after them. When Big Foot and his band were caught, they returned to Pine Ridge without a fight but maintained their freedom. The next day, however, those who had followed Big Foot were asked to surrender themselves as prisoners. Ghost Dance leaders convinced them to make a stand. It was a fatal move. Gunfire erupted on the reservation and between 100 and 200 (some estimate as high as 300) Indians were killed. Armed Indian resistance in the West ended at Wounded Knee. The Sioux faced a bleak future after 1890, and it was decades before they made some of the same adjustments as the Navajos and Comanches.

Ghost Dance
Part of a religious awakening among the Lakota Sioux in 1890 in which they believed that if they returned to their traditional ways and ceremonies, the whites would be driven from their land.

Government Policy—The Grant Peace Plan and the Dawes Act

The rapid expansion of the nation after the Civil War added complex new issues to the government's Indian policy. The U.S. Army represented the U.S. government to Indians west of the Mississippi. Before the Civil War, the army's goal was to limit warfare with and among the tribes while allowing white settlers transit across the Great Plains to California and Oregon. Few whites settled on the Great Plains before the 1860s, and the government was content to leave the Plains Indian tribes to themselves unless, like the Comanches, they fought directly with the army. The first Treaty of Fort Laramie in 1851 did not limit Indian land use except to try to keep the peace by keeping tribes

Artist Frederick Remington depicted the 1890 Ghost Dance, which represented a hope for a new age.

apart from one another. No reservations were established. Rather, in exchange for gifts, the army asked the tribes to avoid conflict with one another, with military forts, and with the transit routes for the mail and for settlers. Asking for anything more was beyond the limits of what the 270 soldiers at Fort Laramie could reasonably ask in a meeting attended by perhaps 10,000 American Indians, including the Sioux, Arapaho, Cheyenne, Assinboins, Shoshones, Arikaras, Hidatsas, Mandans, and Crows.

After the Civil War, the pressure for space for white settlement greatly intensified. At the same time, U.S. Army units that had been fighting the Civil War were now available for service in the West. Among these units were segregated African-American units that were sent to the West and came to be known as Buffalo Soldiers because their white commanders thought their hair was like that of the buffalo. Even though most military units were demobilized after the war, there were more than sufficient numbers of soldiers—white and black—remaining in the army to provide a formidable fighting force in the West.

In 1862, a Republican Congress had passed, and President Lincoln had signed, the **Homestead Act**, fulfilling a major Republican campaign promise to make more federal land available for white settlement. The act provided 160 acres of federal land to a family that would settle and maintain the land for 5 years. The act, however, did not specify where the land would come from. Much of the initial homestead settlements were in Minnesota, Iowa, Nebraska, and Kansas, all on lands that had been prime buffalo hunting locations for various tribes. Unlike before the Civil War when most whites had moved across the Great Plains and kept going under the protection of U.S. Army, after the Civil War, whites were coming to the plains to stay and larger army forces were coming with them. In addition to farming, the discovery of mineral wealth in places like the Black Hills of the Dakotas brought more whites and further racial conflict.

Immediately after the war, the same Congress that was taking control of Reconstruction also created its own Indian peace policy and assigned the army to implement it. The battles with the Lakota Sioux led those in Congress to seek a peaceful way of proceeding, so they created the Indian Peace Commission to negotiate treaties with the Plains tribes. The congressional commission developed the idea of tribal reserves or reservations, large tracts of land that would, they hoped, be set aside for the Indians, protecting the tribes from encroaching white civilization while ensuring their eventual assimilation into white culture. It was same policy that had been used in negotiating with tribes that originally lived east of the Mississippi but with one big difference. The majority of eastern tribes had been forced onto reservations in the West, specifically, in Oklahoma or Indian Territory. There was no place further west to push the western

Homestead Act
Law passed by Congress in 1862 providing 160 acres of land free to anyone who would live on the plot and farm it for 5 years.

American Voices

Charles W. Allen, Report from Wounded Knee, 1890

Charles W. Allen, a white newspaper editor who had spent most of his life among the Sioux and was friendly with them, reported the event he saw while visiting his wife's family at the Pine Ridge Reservation on December 29, 1890. The first part of this report is taken from Allen's autobiography published in 1938. The second part is from a newspaper article he wrote for the Chadron Democrat *three days after the events took place.*

Presently all the Indian men began coming in bunches of from two to a dozen or more, stringing leisurely along then taking their seats in a circle on the grass before the commander and his staff....Then General Forsyth addressed in a firm but conciliatory manner....[H]e told them that for the time being they were prisoners, and as such they were to give up their arms peaceably....He then told them to go back to their lodges, bring all their firearms, and turn them over to him. The Indians departed for their camp in a reluctant, obviously sulky mood....

After what seemed an unreasonable length of time the Indians came strolling back pretty much as they had come to the first meeting, except that they seemed purposely to adopt a more independent swagger in approaching the council field. Many of them were painted hideously and conspicuously grim of visage.... Quite a number of their wives had accompanied the braves to this meeting, robed in long blankets reaching almost to the ground, and each took a position immediately behind her husband....The women who stood close behind their men concealed, under each blanket, a repeating rifle and well filled cartridge belt....

Chief Big Foot had been escorted from his tent, and urged his followers to maintain peace and comply with the general's orders....I also observed a Hotchkiss gun that had been placed in commanding position on a small knoll at the north edge of the camp, not far from the site on which the Catholic church now commemorates the tragedy....

Gen. Forsyth ordered a detail of dismounted troops under Capt. Wallace to close in and surround them at a distance of about twenty paces....During this procedure, which was very interesting, an Indian ghost dance master, arrayed in full paraphernalia, began to make medicine, holding his hands up to the sun and calling upon the Messiah to visit his wrath upon the soldiers. He would take up hands full of dirt and scatter it, then hold up his hands as if momentarily expecting the earth to open and swallow up the troops. It was evident that he was getting the Indians worked up and he finally told them to be brave and that bullets would not hit them if the soldiers did shoot at them. The commander was told of what he was saying, and he ordered him to sit down, which order he finally complied with after he had walked clear around the circle as though he owned the earth....They had proceeded to disarm but some eight or ten of these, when the brave who had been inciting them jumped up and said something and fired at the soldier who was standing guard over the arms that had been secured. The first gun had no sooner been fired than it was followed by hundreds of others and the battle was on. The fighting continued for about a half hour, and then was continued in skirmish for another hour.

Source: Charles W. Allen, *From Fort Laramie to Wounded Knee: In the West That Was,* edited with an introduction by Richard E. Jensen (originally published 1938, republished Lincoln: University of Nebraska Press, 1997), pp. 192–202.

Thinking Critically

1. **Documentary Analysis**

   As Allen told the story, who was responsible for the fighting at Wounded Knee?

2. **Historical Interpretation**

   In what ways did Wounded Knee mark the end of an era in American history?

---

tribes, so the government tried to move them onto as limited an amount of land as possible. At the same time, of course, confining the tribes on reservations would ensure that most of the land of the West could be opened for white development. The plan was not a great success. Tribes like the Sioux, Nez Perce, and Comanches resented the confinement of reservation life and often wandered far beyond their assigned bounds.

When Ulysses S. Grant became president in 1869, he initiated a new Indian Peace Policy that became known as **Grant's Peace Policy**. Grant's thinking was shaped by the terrible bloodshed he had seen in the Civil War and by his identification with the emancipation of slaves. He wanted to end the corruption that he saw in the Indian Bureau, and he wanted to treat the Indians with dignity. His goal was peace. At the same time, Grant wanted room for white settlement and was certainly not planning to keep whites out of the vast tracts of western land that the Indians used for hunting. In his first annual message to Congress in December 1869, Grant said there was no turning back the clock, that the past "cannot be undone, and the question must be met as we now find it." Meeting the question, he believed, meant assimilating Indians

Grant's Peace Policy

A new effort by President Grant to end the Plains Indian wars by creating a series of reservations on which tribes could maintain their traditional ways.

into white society, or as the president asked, "cannot the Indian be made a useful and productive member of society by proper teaching and treatment." Since most of the Indians did not want to become "useful and productive members" of white society, Grant's policy may have been doomed from the beginning, but he tried to find a humane solution to the clash of quite different cultures in the American West.

When Grant announced his Peace Policy he said,

> The building of rail-roads and the access thereby given to all the agricultural and mineral regions of the country is rapidly bringing civilized settlements into contact with all the tribes of Indians....I see no remedy for this except in placing all the Indians on large reservations...and giving them absolute protection there.

Grant then appointed a member of the Seneca tribe, Ely S. Parker, as the first Native American Commissioner of Indian Affairs, the first nonwhite to hold a high government position. Grant also turned to Christian missionaries, not the army or the Indian Office, to take the lead in managing reservation affairs. He declared the reservations off limits to the army, even troops who were chasing Indians with whom they had been in battle.

The missionaries, people like the Quaker Lawrie Tatum who was appointed to lead the Comanche and Kiowa reservation, tried to make the peace policy work. But government supplies were slow in coming and often of shoddy workmanship. Many Indians resisted the confinement of reservation life. The army was frustrated by the rule that they could not follow Indians into the reservation asylum even as they were expected to police the non-Indian territories. General Sheridan condemned the Peace Policy saying, "If a white man commits murder or robs, we hang him or send him to the penitentiary; if an Indian does the same, we have been in the habit of giving him more blankets." The Indians, seeing through the references to peace, considered the whites as thieves who were stealing their land.

Although the Indian Peace Policy remained in force, the army simply ignored it. Sherman's defeat of the Comanches in 1874–75 was in violation of the policy that army units could not enter reservations, but the general was praised, not reprimanded. Within a year after Custer's 1876 defeat, the army had subdued nearly all of the Sioux. Crazy Horse, one of the Sioux who was at the Little Big Horn the day Custer died, became an army scout and was killed at an army post in September 1877. Sitting Bull was arrested in 1881 after returning from exile in Canada. He toured briefly with Buffalo Bill Cody's Wild West Show in the 1880s and then retired to the Standing Rock reservation where, as the Ghost Dance movement grew, he was killed in a standoff with other Sioux sent by the army to arrest him. But the Grant Peace Policy had unofficially died long before the old chief met his end.

Within a decade of the last major Indian wars in the 1870s and the settlement of most western Indians on reservations, the U.S. government again began to change policy. By the 1880s, reformers in and out of government were concluding that the assimilation of Indians into white society—a goal many shared—would not happen as long as they maintained their ancient ways on reservations. If the key to Indian survival was for them to become independent farmers who attended churches and schools just as whites did, then why, reformers asked, should they live on reservations? Why not give them all the benefits of the Homestead Act and allow Indians, like whites, to gain free title to their own 160-acre farm and American citizenship?

In response to these arguments, Congress passed the General Allotment Act, known as the **Dawes Act** for its prime sponsor Massachusetts Senator Henry L. Dawes, in 1887. The Dawes Act divided the reservations into 160-acre tracts to be assigned to each family. After a 25-year waiting period, Indian families could sell the land like their white neighbors. Indians who took possession of a homestead also became U.S. citizens. At first glance, the Dawes Act might seem like an enlightened piece of legislation and at least some of its sponsors certainly believed that it was.

The Dawes Act had other provisions, however, that led to negative results. Indian culture was tribal and communal, and hunting was a major activity; however, the Dawes Act pushed Indians to be farmers and to join an individualistic culture that many found to be quite alien. Beyond that, the most immediate impact of the act

Dawes Act

An 1887 law terminating tribal ownership of most reservation land and allocating some parcels to individual Indians while the remainder was opened for white settlement.

was that, after each family on a reservation was allotted its 160 acres, all "surplus" land could then be sold by the government to white families. Later, after the 25-year waiting period, Indian families sometimes sold their land, giving them a profit but alienating them from their tribe. A few tribes, the Navajos and the Senecas, were able to avoid implementation of the Dawes Act and retain communal ownership of their reservations. But for many, the act was an economic and cultural disaster.

In 1881, 155 million acres were set aside as reservations belonging to Indian tribes. As a result of the Dawes Act, Indians controlled only 78 million acres by 1900. While the Dawes Act broke up tribal lands, other federal perspectives undercut Indian culture. Few white authorities believed that the First Amendment protections of religious freedom applied to Indian religion, especially because Indian religion and Indian warfare were often linked. It was not until 1978 that Congress declared traditional Indian religions to have First Amendment rights.

Sending Indian young people to special schools was also seen by officials as one of the surest ways of implementing Grant's promise to "favor any course towards them which tends to their civilization and ultimate citizenship." In 1875, the army ordered 72 Indian prisoners—among them, Cheyenne, Arapahos, Kiowas, Comanches, and Caddos—moved from Fort Sill in Indian Territory to a new federal prison in St. Augustine, Florida. Lieutenant Richard Henry Pratt, a Civil War veteran who was put in charge of the prisoners, decided to create a model Indian school. He hired Sarah Mather from Mt. Holyoke College, and the two began what they believed was an essential mission to teach the prisoners American-style dress, the English language, and Protestant Christianity. The isolation of the prisoner-students made the process easier. Soaring Eagle, a Cheyenne warrior, said, "It is good to go to church....When I go home, I hope to sit down and sing God's hymns." Of course, Soaring Eagle and the other prisoners knew that about the only chance they had to actually go home was to comply with the school's policies.

Pratt and Mather's experiment drew widespread praise. They were authorized to expand their efforts and open the **Carlisle Indian School** in old army barracks in Carlisle, Pennsylvania. Twenty-five Indian boarding schools, eventually both Catholic and Protestant, were built on the Carlisle model between 1879 and 1902. Using federal tax dollars, these schools taught religion, western customs, and values to their Indian students.

Indian students resisted the goal of the boarding schools to transform them, though such resistance was harshly punished. Francis La Flesche, an Omaha who attended a Presbyterian mission school in the 1860s, reported that he and his friends spoke English during the day, but at night when the missionaries were gone, they continued to tell each other the Omaha stories and speak the Omaha language.

Carlisle Indian School
A boarding school for Native American children opened in Carlisle, Pennsylvania to teach white ways and separate Indian children from tribal culture.

16.1 **Quick Review** How did actions after the Civil War—in particular, reassigning U.S. Army units to the West and offering land for white settlement through the Homestead Act—irrevocably change life for Indians in the West?

THE IMPACT OF THE TRANSCONTINENTAL RAILROAD, 1869

16.2 Analyze the building of transcontinental railroads and its impact on the nation, especially the West.

When he proposed his Indian Peace Policy in December 1869, Grant said that it was needed because "[t]he building of rail-roads…is rapidly bringing civilized settlements into contact with all the tribes of Indians." Only 7 months earlier at Promontory Point, Utah, Leland Stanford, governor of California and president of the Central Pacific Railroad, and T. C. Durant, vice president of the Union Pacific Railroad, had driven the last spike—made of California gold—to connect the first rail line that spanned the North American continent.

The dream of a **transcontinental railroad** gained widespread support in the 1850s. An army survey in 1853 offered four possible routes across the country variously ending in

Transcontinental railroad
The Union Pacific rail line from California and the Central Pacific line connected with Chicago and other eastern cities, it was the first rail line to allow train travel all across the United States.

When crews building the Union Pacific Railroad and the Central Pacific Railroad met at Promontory Summit, Utah, in May 1869, the nation celebrated the completion of the first transcontinental railroad.

Portland, San Francisco, Los Angeles, or San Diego, each of which was considered. Even more serious debate focused on where the routes should begin. Illinois Senator Stephen A. Douglas wanted them to start in Chicago, while Mississippi Senator Jefferson Davis wanted them to begin in Memphis or New Orleans. It had been Douglas's dream of a route starting in Chicago that originally led him to propose the Kansas-Nebraska Act. But before the issue of the best transcontinental rail route could be settled, the Civil War had intervened. Once the war began in 1861, the departure of Southerners from Congress meant that a more northerly route became the obvious choice of the remaining members. The Pacific Railroad Act passed easily in 1862. The California-based Central Pacific started building east from San Francisco and Sacramento while the Union Pacific started building west across the Great Plains from various terminals in Kansas, Nebraska, and Missouri, all of which were already connected to the east coast by existing rail lines. The federal government provided a 400-foot right of way, federal loans, and major land grants to the two railroads. Construction moved very slowly during the war, but the coming of peace in 1865 brought a rush to complete the work.

The hard physical labor of actually laying track was done mostly by Irish workers on the Union Pacific and by Chinese laborers on the California-based Central Pacific. Those starting in the east were sometimes able to lay track at the rate of four rails per minute, covering 500 miles and reaching Cheyenne, Wyoming, by November 1867. Those starting in California had the far more difficult task of crossing the Sierra Nevada Mountains. They had to build snow sheds and blast through solid rock to make their way. Finally in the spring of 1869, the lines connected, and the nation was knit together as never before.

The first rail connection across the continent was only the beginning. By the early 1890s four major lines reached across the country, connecting to a large network of midwestern and eastern rail lines. The major cities within California, Oregon, and Washington were connected by their own lines. All of the country's large cities, and most of the medium-sized ones, were connected by rail. A city without a rail link was doomed to wither.

Technological changes helped extend the railroads. George Westinghouse's invention of an air brake system in 1873 made trains safer and the rides smoother as it became possible to stop all of the cars of a train at once rather than needing to coordinate the work of a brakeman on each car. Eli Janney invented a safer system for coupling and decoupling railway cars, saving the lives of innumerable railway workers. Safer construction of tracks and bridges, the replacement of iron rails with steel, and new improved locomotive production all improved speed and safety. Although travel to the California Gold Rush in 1849 took 6 to 8 weeks or more, by the 1870s, a person could travel across the United States in 10 days and, if one could afford it, do so in the comfort of a Pullman sleeping car.

The railroads linked communities with a speed that created a new sense of time. When a traveler moved by horse or wagon, the exact time of day did not matter that much. Trains, however, needed to follow a schedule if passengers and freight were to depart and arrive on time and collisions were to be avoided. Schedules, particularly coordinating trains over great distances, required something no one had considered before—standardized time. Although some objected, like the Cincinnati editor who asked why his city should shift its clocks "so as to harmonize with an imaginary line through Pittsburgh," the clear majority of the country readily agreed to the plan. On Sunday, November 18, 1883, known as the "Day of Two Noons," all but the most isolated American communities adjusted their clocks to place them in one of the four time zones into which the nation was being divided—time zones that still regulate daily life today.

What had once been isolated regional economies quickly became part of a national commercial network because of railroads. The cost of moving food and other goods dropped dramatically. People followed the same time schedule. The railroads that crossed the continent

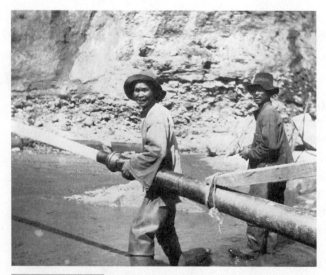

Chinese crews, working in the isolated mountains of California, had to blast tunnels and build bridges to complete the rail line.

ended at docks where ocean-going steamships carried food, lumber, and other materials from the United States to Asia and South America. Within three decades of acquiring the West Coast, the United States was connected to a Pacific market of international trade and commerce that would create work for many—from lumberjacks in Oregon and Washington to miners in Idaho or the Dakotas to wheat farmers across the Midwest—creating wealth for a few and linking the nation's economy to the rise and fall of world markets. After 1890, a glut of wheat in Argentina could impact the life of a farmer in Nebraska, and a drop in the value of silver in Japan could hurt a miner in Idaho. Even though the United States was not quite yet a major world power, it was connected to the world as never before (see Map 16-2).

16.2 **Quick Review** How did railroads improve transportation and communication in ways that other innovations such as canals and steamboats could not?

THE TRANSFORMATION OF THE WEST

16.3 Analyze how indigenous people, ranchers, farmers, miners, outlaws, politicians, and mythmakers shaped the West and our understanding of its history.

The defeat of the Indian tribes and the Homestead Act, along with extraordinary changes in time, speed, and transportation brought on by the railroads, transformed the American West. Land that had been part of Mexico in the 1840s and that people from the East Coast only wanted to get across in the 1850s became the site of vast new ranches, settled farms, and rapidly expanding towns. By the 1880s and 1890s, a new region was becoming part of the nation's cultural, economic, and political networks.

Of course, not all of the new settlers in the American West got along with each other. Cattle ranchers depended on vast wide-open spaces to feed and move their herds. Farmers seeking to establish 160-acre homesteads depended on barbed wire to fence off their land, and keep cattle out. Older residents of what had been the northern parts of Mexico had relied on sometimes vague property lines and depended on communal grazing lands while the newly arriving Americans wanted precise lines and built fences across the land that had once been held in common. Settlers seeking to establish farms or build towns depended on law and order while others—outlaws and gunfighters—thought that the best way to make one's fortune was to take it from others. As these groups battled for control, they soon came to create political organization if not always social order.

Cowboys, Cattle, the Open Range, and Barbed Wire

White families seeking to make their fortune, or at least a living, raising cattle moved into southwest Texas in the 1850s, expanding throughout the West by the 1860s and 1870s. Allowing the cattle to graze the vast open areas enabled herders to manage larger numbers than if they had to confine them to pens with feed. Texas Longhorn cattle, the result of interbreeding cattle of Spanish origin and Anglo-American stock, seemed especially perfect for the region. They could survive on easy-to-find grass on the wide plains, did not need additional feed, and were resistant to Texas fever, the tick-born disease that killed other cattle. Further north in Kansas, Nebraska, and the Dakotas, other cattle ranchers also discovered that cattle thrived on the bunchgrasses of the northern prairies, which dried out by mid-summer but retained its protein and fed cattle well, even when they had to find it through the snow.

By the time the Civil War called most of the cattlemen off to distant battlefields and left the cattle to fend for themselves, there were probably 5 million cattle in west Texas. Although the Comanches took their share of the abandoned cattle, many remained by the end of the war, and some herds grew substantially, having been allowed to breed without being slaughtered for food for several years.

In the summer of 1865, returning veterans reconnected with families and sought to reestablish the herds on which their families depended. Lee Moore remembered helping his veteran father reassemble a herd in southwest Texas, "We didn't call it roundup

MAP 16-2 Connecting the Nation. Rail lines and cattle trails connected far flung parts of the West. Gold and silver mines, cattle ranches, and wheat farmers were suddenly part of a worldwide market.

in those days. We called it cow-hunts and every man on this cow-hunt was a cattle owner just home from the war and went out to see what they had left and to brand up."

Most of those trying to reassemble herds in 1865 could not be called ranchers. They did not own or maintain ranches, as such. Rather they allowed their cattle to graze freely on the open Texas land officially owned by the federal government, though contested by various Indian tribes. They identified their cattle by branding them when they were young. Unbranded cattle—known as mavericks—were free for the taking. The few who did own ranches managed vast operations, like the huge King Ranch where Richard King owned 84,000 acres at the end of the Civil War, eventually expanding to 1,270,000 acres. The King Ranch was one of several huge ranches in Texas and New Mexico, but much of the cattle raising in the 1860s and 1870s was a much more informal affair that depended on respect for cattle brands rather than fenced private lands.

Several developments account for the huge increase in cattle ranching in the decades after the Civil War. Americans started to eat a lot of beef, and in prosperous times, they could afford to do so. Cookbooks reported new ways to prepare beef while telling readers that pork, which had fed much of the nation in earlier times, was unwholesome and hard to digest. Hiram Latham, a publicist for the Union Pacific Railroad wrote a pamphlet, *Trans-Missouri Stock Raising*, in 1871 that declared the only way to support the nation's manufacturing workers was to ensure they had a large supply of clothing and cheap food, food that needed to include a healthy amount of beef (see Map 16-3).

In spite of the ease of raising cattle, particularly in Texas, Colorado, Wyoming, or Montana, it was a long distance from those areas to the mouths of most Americans, whether on the Pacific Coast or in the Midwest or on the Atlantic Coast. In 1867, Joseph G. McCoy founded Abilene, Kansas, one of the nation's first cattle towns, to facilitate the loading of cattle onto transcontinental trains that would speed the beef to consumers. Jesse Chisholm began herding cattle along what came to be known as the Chisholm Trail from Texas, across Indian Territory, to Abilene to connect with those railroad lines. In 1867, some 30,000 cattle made their way along the Chisholm Trail, and over the next 20 years, 2 million more followed.

Not surprisingly, Abilene and other towns at the end of the drive became wild places when the cattle drive reached town. Cowboys, young single men who had spent many months following the herds, were ready for a party when they got to town. The infamous Longbranch Saloon and the Dodge House Hotel, both in Dodge City, Kansas, hosted many celebrating cowboys. These environments offered some of the only economic opportunities for women in the cattle industry, and those opportunities were less than reputable. Prostitution was often the only way to survive and sometimes was a route to independence. A Wichita newspaper reported on the "ten bawdy houses" in Newton, Kansas, in 1871: "Here you may see young girls not over sixteen drinking whisky, smoking cigars, cursing and swearing." Most prostitutes in the cattle towns were very young, between 14 and 23, and from the eastern United States, Europe, and even Indian Territory. Few stayed in the business for very long.

As the demands for beef increased and cowboys brought more cattle into the railroad towns, developments in rail transport made the cattle industry more profitable. In 1882, Gustavus Swift created a new fleet of refrigerated railroad cars. Beef spoiled or took on an odd and unappetizing look in earlier refrigerator cars when it was packed in ice. Swift kept the ice separate and above the beef so the beef stayed cold without touching ice. A few Chicago packinghouses—Swift, Armour, Morris, and Hammond—along with smaller ones in Kansas City, Omaha, and Forth Worth, came to dominate the nation's meatpacking industry. By 1900, 82 percent of the nation's cattle were killed and packed in such places. The Chicago's Union Stock Yards, first opened in 1865 to distribute cattle to these facilities, became the hub for feeding the world.

As the beef industry became more centralized in the 1870s and 1880s, it continued to depend on the muscle of cowboys who cared for cattle, kept track of them when they drifted away, and handled the roundups and cattle drives. The greatest era of the cowboys of the American West was between the Civil War and 1900. The cowboys who did the work of the cattle industry were mostly poor, mostly young, and of many different backgrounds.

In spite of the lonely days and only rare occasions to celebrate, cowboys themselves often did all they could to contribute to the romantic legend that surrounded them. Nat Love, for one, was born a slave in Tennessee in 1854. After the Civil War, he moved west and worked as a cowboy. He was good at the work and in 1876 won roping and shooting contests in Deadwood, South Dakota, that gave him a prize of $200. From then on, he was known as Deadwood Dick and his own autobiography as well as the popular dime novels that told Deadwood Dick stories made him a legend, even if some of those who repeated his story left out the crucial fact that Deadwood Dick was an African-American cowboy.

In the 1860s, many of the cowboys in Texas were white Confederate veterans, and those in Kansas or Montana were Union veterans. Still, there were a relatively large number of African-Americans and American Indians among them. Cattle companies, especially in Texas, soon began replacing the Anglo cowboys with those of Mexican descent whom they could pay substantially less. In 1883, white cowboys in Texas

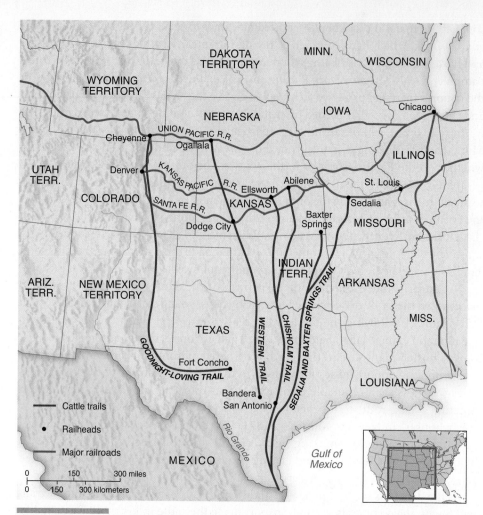

MAP 16-3 Cattle Trails and Rail Lines. Cattle were driven north from Texas and parts of Kansas and Nebraska to rail lines where they could be moved to world markets.

struck for higher wages, but the Panhandle Cattleman's Association quickly broke the strike and found new sources of labor among poor single men of all races who wanted any job or who thought the work might be glamorous.

As the cattle business came to be controlled by larger ranches and corporations in the 1880s and 1890s, cowboys became less independent and more like hired workers in other industries, liable to be assigned to fence building one day and cattle branding the next. Nevertheless, herding cattle over great distances required skill, especially using a rope to lasso and understanding the behavior of herds. The most successful cattle producers knew that they had to provide for their staff. Cowboys had originally carried their own food, but cattle owners began to supply the food from specially constructed wagons, accompanied by a cook, who provided the meals on the range. The first rancher to carry food and bedding for the roundups and trail drives was Charles Goodnight, and in his honor, the wagons came to be known as "Chuck Wagons."

Although the cattle industry prospered, it also experienced significant changes and downturns. Branding cattle—using a hot iron to create a scar on the left flank of a calf that was easy to identify—was key to identifying cattle who roamed over very large areas of range, perhaps a hundred miles or more. While branding continued, by the 1880s, cattle owners began using barbed wire fences to set off their ranges. Barbed wire fences kept herds in more contained areas and protected the best grass. Of course, protecting the grass meant identifying who had the rights to certain areas, which brought cattle ranchers into conflict with each other and with the federal government since most of the western ranges were federal lands. The conflict often turned violent, perhaps most

Most of a cowboy's life was hard, lonely work.

dramatically in the Johnson County War of 1892 when the Wyoming Stock Growers Association hired gunfighters to force smaller ranchers out of the state.

Success also depended on the price of beef staying high and a ready supply of cattle, both of which were problematic. The winters of 1880–81, 1884–85, and 1886–87 were all unusually harsh. Cattle died for lack of food, or they drifted in front of a storm until they piled up against a barbed wire fence and died. In addition, economic recessions in the 1870s and again in the late 1880s led Americans to eat less beef. By the mid-1880s, the market for the 20 million cattle in the American West was declining. After a recovery, another depression in the 1890s made it hard to predict what the value of cattle would be in any given year.

By the end of the 1890s, the era of open ranges, roundups, and huge cattle drives was coming to an end. Growing demand for high-quality beef and new knowledge about the best feed enabled the cattle industry to shift to smaller scale ranches where a rancher could maintain a few hundred cattle, ensure that they were well fed and cared for, and bring them to market at the best moment.

The male world of the cowboys was replaced by ranch families. Men still did most of the work with the cattle while wives and daughters tended houses and gardens doing the "inside work." But in isolated communities, rigid gender lines were hard to maintain. A woman who lived on a Wyoming ranch in 1899 wrote, "The heavy work of the ranch naturally falls to men, but I think most ranch women will bear me out in saying that unless the women… be always ready to do anything that comes along…the ranch is not a success." Cowboys still worked on these ranches and urban Americans still ate beef, but the world of beef production and life on the plains was quite different than it had been only a short time before.

Latino Resistance in the Southwest

Mary A. Fulgenzi, a long-time resident of San Miguel County in New Mexico Territory, recalled the time in the late 1880s when tensions in her county exploded:

> In the early days of Las Vegas the wealthier people wanted to take possession of most of the lands. They fenced in any land they fancied, whether it belonged to them or not. The poor people also needed land to graze their stock and felt that they should have their share, for, according to the land grant, lands not allocated to individuals were to be used by the community in general.

Throughout much of the West, the battle between those who wanted to fence and control the land and those who wanted free grazing land for their herds was one of the great divides. The emergence of cheap barbed wire changed the face of the West. The specific details about contained and open grazing were different in different places and for

Explore the New Economy of the West, 1850–1893 on MyHistoryLab

WHAT NEW ECONOMIC PATTERNS EMERGED IN THE WEST?

The second half of the 1800s brought quick expansion of the United States into the West. Railroads quickly spread across the region, spurring town development and creating a giant national marketplace that stretched from coast to coast. The federal government established post offices through the West to help further connect the nation. Settlers streamed from the East in search of cheap land on which to raise their crops and livestock. The West became an important agricultural region as farm products then moved along the railroad network linking western towns with eastern and international markets.

This patriotic lithograph, titled "Across the Continent—Westward the Course of Empire Takes Its Way," represents the expansion into the American West made possible by the nation's first transcontinental railway, which was completed in 1869.

GROWING POPULATION IN THE WEST

	1860	1890
Montana	N/A	142,924
Idaho	N/A	88,548
Wyoming	N/A	62,555
Colorado	34,277	413,249
New Mexico	93,516	160,282
Arizona	N/A	88,243
Utah	40,273	210,779
Nevada	6,857	47,355
Washington	11,594	357,232
Oregon	52,465	317,704
California	379,994	1,213,398

Source: "United States Resident Population by State", http://lwd.dol.state.nj.us/labor/lpa/census/1990/poptrd1.htm

KEY QUESTIONS   Use MyHistoryLab *Explorer* to answer these questions:

Cause ▶▶▶ *How did railroad expansion shape population growth in the West?*

Map the growth of the railroad network and the development of western towns and cities.

Analysis ▶▶▶ *How did western agriculture develop during the late 1800s?*

Map the importance of agricultural commodities produced in the West.

Response ▶▶▶ *How did the federal government's presence manifest itself as settlers moved west?*

Trace the spread of post offices.

different groups of people, but across the West there were clashes between those who wanted to fence off private property and those who wanted open prairies.

At the heart of the battle in San Miguel County were two different views of the nature of land ownership. The majority of Mexicanos—as people of Mexican descent in New Mexico preferred to be called at the time—saw themselves as *las masas de los hombres pobres* (the masses of the poor). Their assumption was that any land that was not specifically part of the home or the irrigated farmland of one family was held in common—open grazing land that all could use. By the 1880s, however, Anglo-Americans with very different views of land ownership were arriving after the Atchison, Topeka, and Santa Fe Railroad opened a line in 1879. Representatives of investors from the East Coast of the United States and from Britain, who could not imagine any alternative to private ownership of land, began buying up land and fencing off their property to create their own cattle ranches.

For some longtime residents, if the fences were threatening their way of life, the remedy was simple: get rid of the fences. When the ranchers did not comply with requests to take down their fences, a secret organization called the White Caps cut the fences, destroyed the posts, and opened the range again. In response to widespread fence cutting, the territorial governor requested federal troops. In spite of federal troops, most citizens of San Miguel County were sympathetic with the fence cutters. By the summer of 1890, San Miguel County's dissidents were running for political office and soon controlled the balance of power between Republicans and Democrats in the territorial legislature. What had started as an outlaw movement had become part of the political process.

Latino resistance took different forms across the Southwest. In New Mexico, which retained a Mexicano majority well into the 1900s, it was possible for resistance to move into the political process and prevail. In Texas, where racial tensions were especially sharp and where the white majority grew rapidly, older Latino communities had fewer options. Police power rested with the Texas Rangers, who were seen by the Latino community as simply the force of the Anglo community. While the Rangers saw their opponents as outlaws, many in the Mexican-American community saw them as heroes. Perhaps most famous was the case of Gregorio Cortez (1875–1916) who came to Texas from the Mexican city of Matamoros. Cortez shot the sheriff of Manor, Texas, in 1901 when he tried to arrest Cortez for a crime he did not commit. After a long manhunt by the Texas Rangers, Cortez was arrested and sentenced to life in prison, but eventually pardoned by the governor of Texas. For generations, Latino songs and ballads—known as *corridos*—celebrated Cortez's story within the Mexican-American community.

Mexican-American resistance also took other forms. Carlos Velasco immigrated from Sonora to Tucson, Arizona, and in 1878 launched *El Fronterizo*, one of many Spanish-language newspapers in the southwest. The paper continued to be published until 1914, successfully supporting the election of Mexican-Americans to local office and promoting Mexican customs, pride, and links across the international border.

Farmers and Farm Towns

As the cattle industry was transitioning to a more settled ranching industry, farmers were also arriving on the Great Plains in numbers never before thought possible on the arid grasslands. Large numbers of them were responding to massive advertising by the railroads, who also owned much of the western lands. New techniques of farming enabled these farmers to cultivate areas where only buffalo herds had roamed only a short time before.

Those who began creating new homesteads and businesses as well as new lives in these lands of the West came from widely varying backgrounds. They included people of different faiths, Americans from eastern regions of the United States, immigrants from Europe and Mexico, former slaves, and Indians, among others.

Joseph Fish, a Mormon, lived a little upstream from Salt Lake City in the village of Parowan, Utah, where he worked as a miller and a tanner as well as farmed, exchanged work with neighbors, pulled sagebrush, built fences, and harvested wheat and oats to make his living.

Gro and Ole Svendsen moved from Norway to Emmet County, Iowa, in 1863. Ole cut and sawed timber, broke ground, and harvested wheat. Gro made and sold butter and taught her children in Norwegian and English. Drops in agricultural prices and grasshoppers undermined their profits, but they carried on. For others, the challenges were too great. In the 1880s, a group of Ukrainian Jews created a utopian community in South Dakota, but the transition to the plains of South Dakota was too difficult and the community failed. Many other settlers and homesteaders also failed, and wagons traveling west to Kansas emblazoned with "Kansas or bust" met other returning wagons that said "Busted by gosh." But people kept coming.

Thomas Johnson, a former slave from Kentucky, joined over 300 former slaves, known as Exodusters, in settling Nicodemus, Kansas, a town that was attracting people across the post-Reconstruction South with advertisements that said, "All Colored People that want to GO TO KANSAS, on September 5, 1877, Can do so for $5.00." Initially, there was not much to this town. The wife of the first pastor said that she "began to cry" when she first saw it, but people stayed on, eventually building it up.

Rosie and Henry Ise arrived at a new homestead in Osborne County, Kansas, in 1873 with their team of horses and their small herd of cattle. The Ises were lucky. They were moving to an already established homestead that had a small cabin with a bed, a stove, and boxes for chairs. It also had a sod chicken house and a patch of corn, wheat, and oats already planted.

Mariano G. Samaniego moved north from the Mexican state of Sonora in the 1850s to Tucson, Arizona. He did not establish a homestead but opened a clothing store. Later, he earned a college degree from Saint Louis University and then expanded his business, supplying the Union army during the Civil War. By the 1880s, Samaniego shifted his focus to cattle ranching and was known as a respected leader of the Mexican community in Arizona.

Steven Arrow and Big Eagle took advantage of the Homestead Act and acquired their own homesteads in South Dakota, separate from the reservation land. They were an exception to

THINKING HISTORICALLY

Cutting Fences in New Mexico

As Los Gorras Blancas, or the White Caps, formed a secret militia and cut fences in an effort to retain the traditional communal grazing lands in the face of new development in San Miguel County, New Mexico, they also announced the reasons for their illegal activity. In March 1890, members of the organization rode through the town of Las Vegas, New Mexico, posting Nuestra Platforma, a platform announcing their goals that said:

Not wishing to be misunderstood, we hereby make this our declaration.

Our purpose is to protect the rights and interests of the people in general; especially those of the helpless classes.

We want the Las Vegas Grant settled to the benefit of all concerned, and this we hold is the entire community within the grant.

We want no "land grabbers" or obstructionists of any sort to interfere.

We will watch them.

There is a wide difference between New Mexico's "law" and "justice." And justice is God's law and that we must have at all hazards....Be fair and just and we are with you, do otherwise and take the consequences.

The White Caps, 1,500 Strong and Growing Daily

Source: Robert J. Rosenbaum, Mexicano Resistance in the Southwest (Dallas: Southern Methodist University Press, 1998), p. 166.

Thinking Critically

1. Compare and Contrast

How do the "rights and interests" described in this platform fit with the "rights and interests" of private property that many new arrivals brought with them to New Mexico?

2. Historical Interpretation

How does a Mexican-American perspective change or complicate the traditional story of the history of the West in the post–Civil War era?

Many different people filed homestead claims, including Lizzie Chrisman and her three sisters, who established a claim and a sod hut in Nebraska in 1887.

the American Indian experience, but a Sioux Falls merchant said of the Sioux Homesteaders that they "gave more indication of civilization and industry and a show of living like white people than the same number of Norwegian families located a few miles below."

Fifteen percent of homestead claims were filed by single women. Married women could not file their own claim, being already part of a household. Elinore Pruitt Stewart wrote,

> any woman who can stand her own company, can see the beauty of the sunset, love growing things, and is willing to put in as much time at careful labor as she does over washtubs…will have independence, plenty to eat all the time and a home of her own in the end.

The move by farm families into the West was relatively steady. The Homestead Act of 1862 made 160-acre tracts available to those who settled, and Congress later allowed larger homesteads in the more barren lands. The railroads advertised for farmers to settle on their lands. James J. Hill arranged for the settlement of over 200,000 farmers on lands the Great Northern Railroad owned in Montana alone. People who had moved west wrote to friends and families and invited them to join them. Some farm families moved often in search of better prospects. Other families put down deep multigenerational roots, providing stability to their communities.

Farms and homesteads dotted Minnesota, Nebraska, Kansas, and northwestern Iowa in the 1860s as well as California, Oregon, and Washington territory. Stage coach and wagon transport companies maintained links between rail centers and the isolated farms and towns. Throughout the 1870s and 1880s, settlements continued to increase. Between 1881 and 1885, 67,000 new settlers claimed homesteads in North and South Dakota in the "Great Dakota Land Boom." In 1889, homesteaders rushed in to Oklahoma when the federal government declared a large swath of the former Indian Territory to be separate from any tribal reservation and opened it to white settlement.

As farmers and small town businesses filled the land, Indians felt the pressure on their reservations. Some sold land under the provisions of the Dawes Act, while the government sold off other previously tribal lands. In addition, cattle ranchers were forced to confine herds that had previously roamed freely. Long-standing Mexican communities in west Texas, New Mexico, Arizona, and California lost economic and political power to newcomers who had little respect for the older inhabitants of the region. Even so, the number of new farmers kept growing. In 1850, there were 1.5 million farms in the United States, just 119,000 of them west of the Mississippi River. By 1910, there were 6.4 million farms in the nation, and a very large number of them west of the Mississippi.

Successfully growing crops in these new areas required discovering which ones thrived best. While corn grew well in the eastern United States, the hot temperatures and the lack of water made it hard to grow in much of the West. Mennonite settlers brought Russian hard winter wheat with them, and in Kansas and the surrounding "Golden Belt," this wheat became the staple crop by the 1880s. In other areas, spring wheat did better while, in the high plains, sorghum crops resisted drought well. Experimentation, luck, and watching what worked for the neighbors all were essential to the success of farming in areas never before farmed.

Farming was not for the poorest people. It cost money to start a farm, even the most modest homestead. An 1862 farm publication estimated that the cost of starting a farm was $968. Homesteaders had to cover expenses in getting a family to a new place as well as in breaking the sod, clearing forest, building fences, buying farm implements, purchasing livestock and seed, and building a house. Nevertheless, there were thousands, eventually hundreds of thousands, of American families who saved or borrowed funds and began the farms that fed much of the world and settled much of the North American continent.

Mining and Miners

The Gold Rush to California was the first rush of people to seek wealth in the minerals of the West, but it was far from the only mineral rush. As early as 1859, Henry Comstock found silver along the Carson River in Nevada, and thousands of California miners rushed east into Nevada to seek new opportunities for wealth. Comstock himself sold his claim, but corporate interests made fortunes in Nevada. In 1874, thousands of miners, many fresh from the now played-out California goldfields and the Nevada silver mines, made their way to the Black Hills of South Dakota. The land was part of the Sioux reservation, but neither the U.S. Army nor the Sioux were able to stop many of the more than 15,000 prospectors who had come for gold. Some of them got rich, many of them died in the effort, and all of them helped launch some of the most intense of the Plains Indian Wars.

Mining and the quest for mineral wealth continued to lead to fortunes and to death in the West. In 1882, a poor Irish immigrant, Marcus Daly, persuaded California investors to back his claim to a silver mine near Butte, Montana. Very little silver was ever found at the Anaconda mine, but it turned out to be one of the richest deposits of copper in the world, making millions for Daley, his backers, and the Anaconda Copper Company. Others found mining wealth in gold, silver, copper, and lead mines in Idaho, Montana, Colorado, and as far away as Arizona and Alaska. The mineral wealth of the West seemed endless, and many from around the world sought to find it, though only a very few gained any real wealth.

Seemingly overnight, new towns emerged wherever there was mining for copper, silver, and gold, including Carson City, Nevada; Deadwood, South Dakota; and Anaconda, Montana. Like the cattle towns, these overwhelmingly male mining towns made up of transients could be violent places where the smallest disagreement could erupt into violence. In addition, ethnic rivalries often divided the miners. As in California's gold fields, Chinese miners were soon driven out of most mining operations, in spite of the fact that Chinese immigrants were 10 percent of Montana's population and 25 percent of Idaho's in the 1870s. When not driven out, the Chinese were forced to take low-level jobs working water cannons or doing laundry for other miners. Miners of European origin also drove Mexican-American miners out of the fields.

Mining was male work and typically did not lead to a settled life. In 1860, the mining camps of Virginia City and Gold Hill, Nevada, reported a population of 2,300 men and 30 women. The towns also reflected the transient nature of the population. In 1879 Leadville, Colorado, had four banks, four churches, and 120 saloons, plus a fair share of brothels. While some mining towns later became important commercial centers, many soon became empty ghost towns once the mining played out.

Most prospectors sought wealth from their individual discoveries, but most of the money in mining was made by large corporations like the Anaconda Copper Company that could afford expensive mining equipment to extract deeply buried ore. Work in the mines dangerous. Jobs were often divided by ethnicity, with Chinese and

Latino miners given the least-skilled and lowest paying jobs and miners from Europe getting the better paying positions. Nevertheless, with little attention to safety, all of the miners faced explosions, floods, cave-ins, and asphyxiation from poisonous gasses. Only the emergence of new unions among the miners began to address the dangers, if not the ethnic divides, in the 1890s (see Chapter 18).

Outlaws, Gunfighters, and Mythmakers—Legends of the Old West

The West of the late 1800s could be a very violent place. Contrary to Hollywood images, cowboys and Indians tended to keep their distance from each other. It was the army that fought the Indian wars, not the cowboys. But there was plenty of violence among whites. Ranch owners and land developers hired professional gunfighters to eliminate people they saw as troublemakers. Angry people on the margins, or those pushed to the margins of society, struck back violently, cutting fences in New Mexico or becoming outlaws and counting on the vast distances and easy anonymity of the West to protect them. Cowboys in town at the end of a long and dull cattle ride shot each other. Much of the violence was local and personal, some was between people wanting very different development in the region, especially between cattle ranchers and farmers, and some was also a carryover from the Civil War.

In Tombstone, Arizona, the local elite hired Wyatt Earp and his brothers, Virgil, Morgan, and Warren, along with Doc Holliday to make the town safe enough to encourage investors from California and the East Coast. The local elite and the Earp brothers all had strong Union Army and Republican Party connections. They were bothered by an outlaw group, ex-Confederate cattle rustlers led by the Clanton brothers and McLaury families. On October 26, 1881, at the O.K. Corral, the two sides met. Both Clanton brothers and one of the McLaurys were killed, and Tombstone became a more respectable place.

Another crime wave took place in Missouri, Kansas, Oklahoma, and Arkansas. During the Civil War, Confederate raiders led by William Quantrill and including Jesse and Frank James terrorized Union supporters in Missouri and Kansas (see Chapter 15). Quantrill was killed before the war ended, but the James brothers continued a long reign as postwar outlaws, starting with a bank robbery at Liberty, Missouri, on February 13, 1866, and continuing in the new and lucrative arena of train robberies well into the 1880s. Many robbers like the James brothers found widespread, though quiet, support by farm families who would never attempt illegal behavior but who hated the railroads and the large commercial ranchers. These families privately cheered when those more powerful forces suffered losses at the hands of these outlaws, however violent and self-serving the particular rebels might be.

In New Mexico, the so-called Lincoln County War of 1878 pitted two groups of ranchers seeking to dominate the county. Both hired outlaws, one of whom was a young teenager named Henry McCarty who changed his name to William Bonney (a famous pirate) and who came to be known as "the Kid." After the Lincoln County War ended, the hired outlaws drifted away. After trying unsuccessfully to find honest work, and after being promised a pardon but then having it revoked by New Mexico's governor, "the Kid" turned to cattle rustling and robbery until he was shot by Lincoln County Sheriff Pat Garrett. But Billy the Kid, who was 21 when he died, had killed 10 people in his short and violent life. His legend grew far beyond his life as a whole publishing industry came to thrive on the retelling and expansion of his legend.

Stories of gunfighters like Billy the Kid and Wyatt Earp became legends of the American West, but the person who did the most to create the legend of the Wild West was a former army scout named William Cody who created his highly successful Buffalo Bill's Wild West Show in the 1880s. According to his autobiography, Cody was born in Iowa in 1846, but his family soon moved to Kansas where his father was killed by the "border ruffians" from Missouri in the battles of "Bleeding Kansas." Cody took a job herding cattle to support his family when he was 11 years old. During the Civil War, he was part of a local militia that protected the territory from attacks by Quantrill and the James brothers. Later, he hunted buffalo and served as a scout. On one occasion, Cody scouted for a party that included James Gorden Bennett of the *New York Herald,* one of

Creede, Colorado, was a typical western mining town with quickly built buildings and a transient, virtually all-male population.

the nation's great publicists. Bennett fictionalized Cody as the hero of one of the popular dime novels of the time, *Buffalo Bill: the King of the Border Men,* which gave Cody the chance to launch his "Wild West, Rocky Mountain, and Prairie Exhibition."

Buffalo Bill's Wild West Show was everything eastern crowds wanted it to be. It included scenes from Indian battles, Indian dancing, stagecoach robberies, and always the shooting prowess of Annie Oakley, who epitomized the "good" frontier woman of wholesome character who could outshoot any man. In the 1880s, Sitting Bull himself traveled with the show, giving it an "authentic" aura for many who were anxious to see the leader who had defeated Custer in 1876.

The Wild West show was a long way from any true representation of the West. Although the Indians performed amazing feats of horseback riding, they nearly always ended up fulfilling stereotypical images in the minds of their white audiences. Similarly, while the true cowboys were an ethnically diverse lot—white, Mexican, Indian, and African-American—all of Cody's cowboys were white. The U.S. Army units in the show were also white, in spite of the active role of African-American Buffalo soldiers in the West. Annie Oakley, who was an amazing shot with a rifle, lived in Ohio and never traveled further west except on tour with the show. Indians almost never had the battles with the cowboys that Cody portrayed; Indians fought with the army, and cowboys avoided those battles. However, Indians facing desperate poverty on the reservations found work in the shows that brought needed income, and they were allowed to dance traditional dances in the shows that were banned by federal authorities on the reservations.

Cody's shows were performed all across the United States and in Europe, twice before Queen Victoria, and one of his riders performed in Outer Mongolia. Prince Albert I of Monaco came to Cody, Wyoming, to hunt with Buffalo Bill. When the show declined in popularity, Cody reinvented himself once again as an advisor to the new Hollywood studios—as did Wyatt Earp—on "realistic" ways to portray the old West in the new medium that was sweeping the nation. In the process, an image of the Wild West was formed that still persists.

Becoming States

Annie Oakley (1860–1926) won fame for her shooting ability and often traveled with Buffalo Bill's Wild West show.

For much of the 1880s, much of the western United States was organized into territories that were directly controlled by the federal government rather than as states that sent senators and representatives to Congress and voted in presidential elections.

California was admitted in 1850, just after the war with Mexico and the discovery of gold. Minnesota was admitted in 1858 and Oregon in 1859. Kansas became a state in 1861, Nevada in 1864, Nebraska in 1867, and Colorado in 1876. More than a decade later, in 1889 and 1890, six new western states were all admitted almost at once—the former territories of North Dakota, South Dakota, Montana, Washington, Idaho, and Wyoming. Utah was admitted in 1896, Oklahoma in 1907, and New Mexico and Arizona in 1912. Several unique issues account for the time lags.

In some cases, local elites found that they could prosper by controlling the federal appointments and federal funds in their territory while bypassing the democratic processes that statehood brought. Many in Congress also liked, and profited from, these arrangements. The federal government owned much of the land in western states, and until the Indian wars came to an end, the U.S. Army was the chief protector of western citizens. The U.S. Geological Survey and the U.S. Army Corps of Engineers mapped and shaped the land of the West. Through the territorial stages and beyond, the federal government was a more important part of life in the West than in the East.

Some of the states posed unique issues. Long before it was admitted as a state, the territorial legislature in Wyoming granted the 1,200 women living in the territory the right to vote. When Wyoming became a state in 1890, it also became the first state to grant women the right to vote, allowing women in Wyoming to vote for president while their sisters elsewhere could not. Three years later, the State of Colorado granted women the right to vote. After that, campaigns for women's votes stalled. A commitment to women's rights was not universal in the West, but it was more popular there than elsewhere (see Map 16-4).

A more complicated issue arose in Utah and delayed statehood for years. The area around the Great Salt Lake had been settled by Mormon families in 1846 and 1847 when it was still part of Mexico (see Chapter 10). After the region became part of the United States in 1848, the federal government initially left the Mormons on their own, and Brigham Young served as territorial governor as well as spiritual leader. However, in the late 1850s, President Buchanan forced Young out of office and appointed a non-Mormon governor.

The issue for Buchanan was the Mormon commitment to plural marriage. Mormon men—but not Mormon women—were encouraged to take more than one spouse. The majority of Mormon men had only one wife, but a significant number had two, and Brigham Young himself had 27 wives and 56 children. As with more traditional families, some extended Mormon families succeeded quite well while others were torn. When questioned, the majority of Mormon women, including women whose husbands had other wives, defended their arrangement.

Plural marriage horrified most people in the rest of the United States, however. While Presidents Lincoln and Johnson had been too preoccupied with war and Reconstruction to worry much about the Mormons, Presidents Grant, Hayes, Garfield, and Arthur all promised to deal with the "Mormon Question." As early as 1862, Congress passed the Morrill Anti-Bigamy Act, making it a federal crime to take multiple wives, but Utah was far away and Mormon juries were not about to convict anyone accused of that crime.

In spite of all of the controversy and hostility generated by the issue of plural marriage, the Mormon community prospered. By the 1860s, there were enough people living in Utah Territory to qualify for statehood. By 1870, the population stood at 87,000. Unlike other parts of the West, where white men far outnumbered white women, Utah had a balanced gender ratio. Women and men prospered in a community of strict morality and hard work, including work for women outside of the household. Women ran their own industries, cooperative stores, as well as relief societies and charities.

The rest of the United States remained dissatisfied with Utah's practices, however, and eventually, the Mormon leadership decided that statehood was more important than maintaining plural marriage. In 1890, the Mormon Church announced the end of plural marriage, and although there were those who continued to practice it, the majority of members went along with the decision. With that key issue resolved, Utah was admitted as a state in 1896. One of the first moves by the new state legislature was to, again, give women the right to vote and hold office, making Utah the third state, after Wyoming and Colorado, to do so.

Issues of race delayed the admission of the last three western states. Oklahoma had been established as Indian Territory when Andrew Jackson's Indian removal policies forced some northern tribes and the five southeastern tribes to move there. By the late 1800s, the tribes had put down roots, developed new communities, and were thriving. Other western tribes had also been forced to settle in Indian Territory. Nevertheless, the Dawes Act and other federal policies opened much of the western part of the territory to white settlement. In 1905, representatives of the tribes proposed establishing two separate states—Sequoyah in the eastern portion would be made up of the Indian Reservations. Oklahoma in the west would be made up of the white areas. Indiana Senator Albert J. Beveridge, Chair of the Senate Committee on Territories wanted to have just one territory dominated by "Americans," by which he did not mean Indians, and President Theodore Roosevelt agreed. Oklahoma was admitted in 1907 as a single state.

The Territory of New Mexico initially included all of Arizona and New Mexico. The population quickly reached the level required for statehood but, unlike the other areas acquired from Mexico, especially Texas and California, the majority of the people living

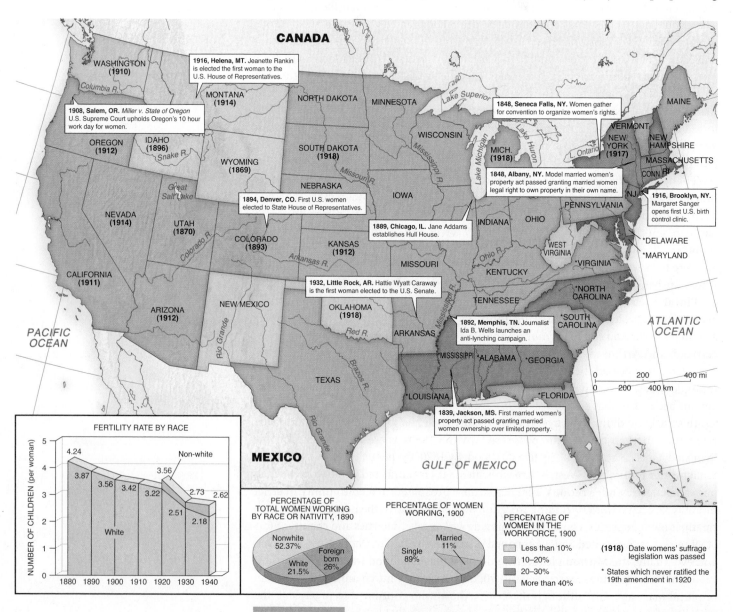

MAP 16-4 Early States Granting Women Suffrage. Before 1920, a number of states, especially in the West, granted women the right to vote as indicated on this map.

in New Mexico Territory were of Mexican descent. In spite of the fact that they were now U.S. citizens, Congress was not prepared to admit a self-governing state with a Mexican-American majority. In 1902, Senator Beveridge proposed uniting them again and admitting them as a single state since that would ensure a larger "American" (or non-Mexican) population, but that proposal failed. President William Howard Taft signed legislation in 1912 admitting New Mexico and Arizona as the 47th and 48th states of the Union.

Well before New Mexico and Arizona became states, the political, economic, and cultural shape of the vast region known as the West was settled. The original inhabitants who had fought with each other and with whites and had hunted buffalo across the plains or lived comfortably on the rich resources of the Pacific Coast were moved to distant reservations where they were alternatively ignored and challenged by federal authorities while building new cultures for themselves and the surrounding communities. By 1900, much of the West was divided into settled communities of farms, large and small, and growing towns connected by railroads. There was still plenty of desolate empty country to be found, but the West of the 1800s was a receding memory.

16.3 **Quick Review** What were the major concerns involved in admitting new states in the West? How were these issues similar to or different from those involved in admitting states in the East?

CONCLUSION

The American West changed dramatically between 1865 and 1890. In the midst of the Civil War, Abraham Lincoln had urged tribal leaders to adopt the "peaceful ways of the white people," without noticing the irony of such a plea in the midst of the Civil War. The end of the Civil War brought two of the most violent decades in the West as units of the U.S. Army fought with various tribes trying to force the Native Americans to give up their traditional hunting and nomadic ways to settle on reservations. By the 1890s, conflict between whites and Indian tribes was over as tribes were defeated and moved into ever-shrinking reservations. While the impacts of white settlement and the Civil War on American Indians varied from tribe to tribe, in the long run, they were a disaster.

After the Civil War, white ranchers, farmers, and miners built new settlements across the West. What began as great cattle ranches were replaced by smaller farms producing beef and wheat for national and world markets. The agricultural developments of the post–Civil War era depended on new technologies—most importantly, railroads that brought supplies to isolated farmers and shipped their products to world markets. What had once been isolated regional economies quickly became part of a national and international commercial network because of railroads, and the United States was connected to the world as never before. As more and more people settled the West, access to vast regions for grazing cattle became limited and tensions began to mount. Still, the West was largely rural, and disputes were often settled by hiring outlaws rather than by more traditional means. Farmers came to the West for many reasons, including the desire for land, the search for better economic opportunities than were available in the East, and a longing for adventure. Although most farmers established homesteads in hopes of establishing permanent roots, mining towns sprang up around impermanent mines, and they were often violent places.

Once a distant frontier, by 1890, the American West was becoming part of the nation's cultural, economic, and political networks and by 1912 the last of the western territories had become a state. The large areas that had been governed as territories were not settled and populated enough to be considered as states, but some of these areas posed unique issues. However, despite debates over economic issues, voting rights of women, concern about the plural marriage of Mormon communities, and the racial diversity of parts of the Southwest, all of the once isolated territory of the American West had been divided into new states that were admitted to the Union by 1912.

CHAPTER REVIEW How do the typical depictions of the American West in the late 1800s differ from the realities of life in the region?

[Handwritten margin notes: Indian relocation (to small reservation); Beginning of Industrial Revolution; Farmers moving to west looking for new opportunities]

THE TRIBES OF THE WEST AND THE U.S. GOVERNMENT

 16.1 Explain western development from an Indian perspective and the way Indian and white cultures shaped each other.

Review Questions

1. **Cause and Effect**

   What new opportunities did the Civil War create for the Comanche people?

2. **Contextualization**

   What does the Ghost Dance phenomenon tell us about how the Sioux of the 1890s saw their recent history?

3. **Historical Interpretation**

   Why did the U.S. government come to believe that it needed new approaches to Indian policy in the 1870s and 1880s? Whose interests did the new policies serve?

THE IMPACT OF THE TRANSCONTINENTAL RAILROAD, 1869

16.2 Analyze the building of transcontinental railroads and its impact on the nation, especially the West.

Review Questions

4. **Historical Interpretation**

   How did railroads contribute to the growth of a national economy?

5. **Craft an Argument**

   What factors might explain the widespread support for a transcontinental railroad in the 1850s and 1860s?

THE TRANSFORMATION OF THE WEST

16.3 Analyze how indigenous people, ranchers, farmers, miners, outlaws, politicians, and mythmakers shaped the West and our understanding of its history.

Review Questions

6. **Cause and Effect**

   What factors contributed to the boom in cattle ranching in the second half of the 1800s?

7. **Contextualization**

   What motives brought white farmers to the West in the decades following the Civil War?

8. **Historical Interpretation**

   How did issues of race and gender impact the admission of western states into the Union?

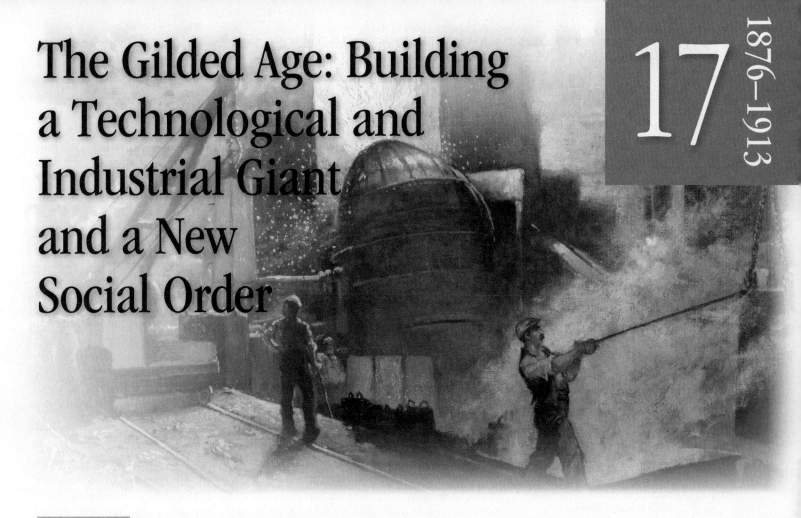

The Gilded Age: Building a Technological and Industrial Giant and a New Social Order

If anything symbolized the new industrial might that began to characterize the United States in the Gilded Age, it was the production of steel at one of Andrew Carnegie's plants.

O n May 10, 1876, Ulysses S. Grant, then in his 8th year as president, traveled to Philadelphia to open the Centennial International Exhibition of Industry. The event celebrated the 100th anniversary of the signing of the Declaration of Independence with a massive show of the nation's progress in science, technology, and industry. The exhibition covered 285 acres on the banks of Philadelphia's Schuylkill River and included pavilions from each state and from many foreign countries. Among them, Colorado and Kansas displayed corn 20 feet high, and Germany displayed a giant artillery piece from the Krupp works. Between the pavilions were refreshment stands selling popcorn, waffles, soda water, root beer, and German *lager bier* as well as a fountain built by the Sons of Temperance, which was serving ice water. The focus was on the great mechanical achievements of the United States, symbolized by the giant Corliss steam engine that provided power for all the exhibits in Machinery Hall and that seemed to be without vibration or noise (because its boiler was outside the building) as well as by the many mowers, reapers, sewing machines, typewriters, fans for ventilating mines, and the Pullman sleeping cars. Most of all, the fair told the world that the United States had arrived as a manufacturing and technological giant.

The event represented a cross-section of the nation in 1876, both as it was and as it wanted to be, filled with new inventions, including Alexander Graham Bell's new telephone, which Bell demonstrated to

CHAPTER OBJECTIVE

Understand how the United States became an industrial giant, at what cost, and with what impact on its diverse peoples and cultures.

LEARNING OBJECTIVES

TECHNOLOGY CHANGES THE NATION

Explain the inventions of the late 1800s and their impact. **17.1**

CORPORATIONS AND MONOPOLIES

Analyze the role of the new giant corporations in American life. **17.2**

LIVES OF THE MIDDLE CLASS IN THE GILDED AGE

Analyze daily life, popular ideas, and political direction for the middle class during the Gilded Age. **17.3**

IMMIGRATION

Explain the reasons immigrants came to the United States in such large numbers during the Gilded Age and what their experience was. **17.4**

17.1

17.2

17.3

17.4

Significant Dates

1859	Edwin Drake discovers oil in Titusville, Pennsylvania
1870	Standard Oil Company launched by John D. Rockefeller and Henry M. Flagler
1871	Thomas Edison demonstrates Universal Stock Printer
	Treaty of Washington settles U.S.–Canadian border and claims between United States and Britain
1873	Panic of 1873—Economic panic and depression
	Senate rejects United States acquisition of Dominican Republic
1875	Dwight L. Moody launches religious revivals
1876	Alexander Graham Bell patents the telephone
	Thomas Edison establishes research laboratory in Menlo Park, New Jersey
	President Grant opens Philadelphia Centennial Exhibition
1877	Cornelius Vanderbilt, richest man in America, dies in New York City
1878	Edison demonstrates new phonograph
1879	Edison's first successful incandescent lamp burns for 16 hours on November 17
1882	Edison Illuminating Company lights southern Manhattan
	Chinese Exclusion Act
1886/1888	George Westinghouse and Nikola Tesla discover alternating current to transmit electricity
1887	First Electronic Trolley cars built
1890	Greatly increased immigration from Eastern Europe and Asia begins
1892	Ellis Island immigration station opens in New York Harbor
1893	Panic of 1893—Major U.S. depression
1896	Edison demonstrates first moving pictures
1901	U.S. Steel becomes the largest corporation in history
1902	Victor Talking Machine Company begins mass producing recording disks
1903	Wright Brothers make first flight at Kitty Hawk, North Carolina
1913	Henry Ford's moving assembly line begins operation at Highland Park, Michigan

an appreciative audience that included the Emperor of Brazil. It was a fitting opening to an era in which business, manufacturing, and technology would dominate the nation's political, economic, and cultural life, bringing prosperity and power that was previously unimagined. It would also bring clashes between those who benefited and those who did not, which frightened many and nearly tore the nation apart. This chapter explores how the nation came to be that giant, at what cost to its people and the world, and with what results in the culture—or, rather, the many different cultures—of the country.

TECHNOLOGY CHANGES THE NATION

17.1 Explain the inventions of the late 1800s and their impact.

Alexander Graham Bell saw himself as a teacher more than an inventor. While teaching deaf students at Boston University, Bell sought new ways to help deaf people hear. In July 1874, he discovered that if a person were to speak into a vibrating set of reeds, it created a fluctuating current that could, at the other end of an electronic wire, be turned back into the same sound through another set of tuned reeds. He patented his new invention in March 1876 and demonstrated it first by calling his assistant Thomas Watson from the next room. Later, he showed it at the Massachusetts Institute of Technology and then at the World's Fair. While Bell returned to teaching, others organized the Bell Telephone Company. By 1880, there were 30,000 telephone subscribers. By 1900, the number had grown to 1.3 million, and by 1920, to 13 million. In four decades, Bell's experiment had become a necessity of modern life. For most Americans, the telephone replaced the telegraph, developed by Samuel F. B. Morse from earlier inventions in 1835. By the 1840s, telegraphs were relaying messages and news in Morse code, consisting of dot and dash signals, over miles of telegraph wires—215,000 miles of wires by 1900. But the telephone quickly made the telegraph outdated.

Before Bell gained fame for his telephone, Thomas Edison was already on his way to being known as the greatest inventor of the era. Edison was born in Milan, Ohio, in 1847, the same year as Bell. At 16, with little formal schooling, he became a telegraph transmitter. Several people in the telegraph industry were trying to design what they called a "diplex," a way to send two messages—one in each direction—on the same telegraph wire at the same time. In 1873, Edison produced both a diplex and a quadruplex that could send two messages simultaneously each way on a single wire, greatly increasing the value of every telegraph line in the nation and securing Edison's fame and fortune. While he was toying with that invention, Edison had also invented the Edison Universal Stock Printer in 1871, a greatly improved version of the stock ticker tape machine.

In 1876, Edison established an independent research laboratory at Menlo Park, New Jersey. The many employees there were made to understand that they worked only at Edison's direction and he got all of the credit. Eventually, he had 1,000 patents to his name, thus becoming the most productive American inventor of all time. He tinkered with ways to record a human voice and music. On April 18, 1878, he demonstrated his new phonograph at the National Academy of Sciences in Washington, DC, and, later that night, at a midnight show at the White House.

Edison's most important invention was the electric light bulb. In the 1870s, large meeting halls were lit by arc lamps, and gas lights were popular in many places. The rest of the nation—city as well as country—depended on kerosene lamps or candles when the sun went down. The electric light bulb changed things across the country. Given Edison's fame, he was able to assemble a consortium of financiers, led by J. Pierpont Morgan, to support his research. After toying with different options, the Edison labs created a bulb that lit a room for 16 hours on November 17, 1879. Almost immediately, everyone wanted electric lights, and Edison wanted everyone to have them. He made London, Paris, and New York the priority cities because he knew that what happened in those places would quickly be reported elsewhere. Within 2 years, all three cities had buildings lit by electric lights. On September 4, 1882, Edison pulled the switch that lit a number of buildings in southern Manhattan, including the House of Morgan, the New York Stock Exchange, and the headquarters of the *New York Times* and *New York Herald*.

Thomas Edison with his phonograph.

The inventions just kept coming. George Westinghouse and Nikola Tesla found that alternating current was a much more efficient way to transmit electricity than the direct current that Edison used. Edison was initially skeptical, but by the 1890s, alternating current produced at generating plants from New York to California was powering much of the nation. Frank J. Sprague introduced the first electric streetcars in Richmond, Virginia, in 1888, and these cars, which were cheaper and cleaner and safer than horse-drawn or steam cars, caught on quickly.

In 1892, the General Edison Electric Company merged with a rival to create General Electric, the company that not only produced light bulbs but also all things electric. By 1896, using film developed by George Eastman of Rochester, New York, Edison moved from small-scale to large-screen moving pictures, and in 1902, the Victor Talking Machine Company began mass-producing recording disks and players. The country was radically different because of Edison's work and that of other prolific inventors who gave the country elevators invented by Elisha G. Otis, machine tools from Pratt and Whitney, steam boilers from Babcock and Wilcox, newspaper linotype compositors, and typewriters. A total of 440,000 patents issued between 1860 and 1890 transformed modern life.

In the 1890s, a number of independent manufacturers began experimenting with gasoline-powered vehicles, putting a gasoline engine on bicycles or carriages, which led to automobiles. Although by 1899 only 2,500 automobiles were produced per year, many were predicting that the new vehicles would replace horse-drawn carriages. They were right. By 1916, 1 million automobiles were produced in the United States, which created massive change as work with horses declined and a new set of jobs in the automobile industry began as more and more Americans experienced the freedom that an automobile gave them.

The key to the vastly expanded production of automobiles was the vehicle itself, which was relatively simple, given other inventions that existed. Rather, expanded production was possible only after inventing a way to produce large numbers of cars at low cost. The genius who revolutionized the *production* of automobiles was Henry Ford. Ford, a former machinist, built his first automobile in 1896 after many others had done so, but it was his invention of the assembly line that made possible the mass-production of cars at reasonable costs. Ford took the idea of interchangeable parts, first developed for guns by Eli Whitney, and applied it to cars. Then he created a process whereby those parts could be assembled in a routinized fashion that greatly speeded production, thus lowering cost, even if it made the role of most workers extremely boring.

Ford opened a plant for the production of the Model T Ford in Highland Park, Michigan, in 1910 and added a moving assembly line in 1913. Each worker was assigned one small task to be repeated over and over. As Ford described it, "Every piece of work in the shop moves. There is no lifting or trucking of anything other than materials." Worker after worker did his assigned task over and over again. At the end of the process, a fully assembled Model T emerged from the assembly line. Ford paid his workers well. He had to. They found the work mind numbing, but valued the pay—high enough that they, too, could afford their own Model T. He transformed an industry, bringing the cost of an automobile to within the reach of many Americans and spawning a whole set of new industries from highway construction to automobile repairs. The success of the automobile dramatically expanded the nation's need for oil, now refined into gasoline to power the rapidly growing numbers of vehicles (see Table 17-1).

TABLE 17-1 Factory Sales of Passenger Cars per Year

Year	Numbers of Vehicles Sold
1900	4,100
1905	24,200
1910	181,100
1915	895,000
1920	1,905,500

While Ford, Walter Chrysler, and the founders of General Motors were creating the automobile industry in Detroit, Michigan, other inventors were tinkering with additional ways to advance transportation. Wilbur and Orville Wright, two bicycle makers from Dayton, Ohio, were determined to develop a flying machine. On December 17, 1903, on a deserted beach at Kitty Hawk, North Carolina, their machine took off. By 1908, Orville Wright had a contract with the Army Signal Corps to conduct test flights at Fort Myer, Virginia. The Wright brothers conducted test flights around the country, including Los Angeles and Chicago. Air travel did not transform the lives of most Americans as quickly as the automobile because it remained inefficient and dangerous for some time. Nevertheless, watching people actually leave the ground on machines confirmed for many that, in the realm of technology, anything was possible.

17.1 **Quick Review** How did the inventions of the late 1800s and early 1900s better connect the nation?

CORPORATIONS AND MONOPOLIES

17.2 Analyze the role of the new giant corporations in American life.

The kinds of inventions that were appearing in the 1880s and 1890s, like the earlier railroads and telegraph systems, could not be produced by a family business. Railroads crossed the continent. Electric generation required huge investments. Telephones were useful primarily if they connected large numbers of people. Most of the country's earliest corporations had been for public benefit—building universities and hospitals—or for temporary partnerships for specific ventures. New corporate structures emerged during the Jacksonian era in response to larger, more expensive ventures to process cotton and manufacture other materials. After the Civil War, those corporate structures achieved a level of size and power undreamed of by earlier generations of manufacturers. Managing the investments involved in the great new industries also required a new kind of financing. In the absence of a federal bank—nothing had replaced the Bank of the United States that Jackson had abolished in the 1830s (see Chapter 10)—private bankers played an increasingly important role. Post–Civil War corporations and banks were of a size and a level of power the nation had not seen before. They made a few Americans extremely wealthy—richer than any American ever had been before—and they made other Americans very nervous about the new concentrations of wealth and the accompanying power. The outsized wealth of the era, sometimes lavishly spent, inspired the humorist Mark Twain to name this post–Civil War era the "**Gilded Age**," a reference to coating items with gold. For some, the Gilded Age produced an excess of money, taste, and power; for others, it created poverty.

Gilded Age

Term applied to America in the late 1800s that refers to the shallow display and worship of wealth characteristic of the period.

Financing and Controlling the Railroads—Jay Cooke, Cornelius Vanderbilt, and Others

At the end of the Civil War, the most powerful banker in the United States was Jay Cooke, who saved the Union's finances during the war (see Chapter 14). In the early 1870s, however, he almost wrecked the nation's economy.

Cooke financed the Northern Pacific Railroad (see Chapter 16), telling European investors that a rail line from Duluth, Minnesota, to the Pacific coast would connect the world's breadbasket to shipping across the Pacific and across the Atlantic. He insisted, "There is nothing on the American continent equal to it.…There is no end to the possibilities of wealth here." The promise of wealth was enticing, and investment poured in. However, there were too many railroads, and few were making profits. At the same time, the end of the seemingly faraway Franco-Prussian War (1870–1871) caused world grain prices to drop precipitously as European countries produced more of their own wheat. The result was further reduced profit on the rail lines that hauled American wheat. A government investigation into the Union Pacific Railroad's shaky finances during this period undermined public confidence in rail investments. As a result, Cooke could neither sell new railroad bonds nor meet obligations on the old ones. On September 18, 1873, Jay Cooke and Company declared bankruptcy and closed its doors.

The news that the nation's most prestigious banker could not meet his obligations undermined financial confidence, launching what was known as the **Panic of 1873**. *The Nation* magazine described Wall Street: "Great crowds of men rushed to and fro trying to get rid of their property, almost begging people to take it from them at any price." The Stock Exchange closed for 10 days. Banks collapsed. Railroad construction stopped. By 1874, 500,000 people had lost their jobs, and breadlines were seen not only in New York but also wherever railroad construction and the demand for steel rails, wooden ties, or products that moved by rail had been boosting the economy. The depression of 1873 demonstrated the boom-and-bust cycle of the new economy and the degree to which railroads and banking connected all parts of the nation's financial structure.

As the economy recovered after 1873, the man who profited more than any other was already very rich Cornelius Vanderbilt. After Robert Fulton invented the steamboat in 1807, Vanderbilt created a steamboat empire, first in New York Harbor, and then around the world. After 1815, Vanderbilt's steamers began to travel to Boston, New Orleans, and—during the California gold rush—to Nicaragua to meet other steamers that took gold seekers up the coast to California. Controlling the transit to California was far more profitable than seeking gold there. His style of doing business was illustrated on one occasion when, in an argument with competitors he said, "Gentlemen: You have undertaken to cheat me. I won't sue you, for the law takes too long. I will ruin you." During the Civil War, Vanderbilt kept his ships moving between New York and Union-held New Orleans and beyond to South America in spite of Confederate efforts to stop them.

After the Civil War, Vanderbilt shifted from steamships to railroads. Vanderbilt did not build railroads; he bought them. In addition, he created new and much more profitable ways to manage them. Vanderbilt created corporations of a size not previously known in the United States and launched a managerial revolution. The corporations that Vanderbilt led involved levels of managers reporting to powerful central offices. The new bureaucracies could ensure safety: trains that ran on schedule were less likely to collide, and trains that ran on well-laid tracks were less likely to derail. They also created great new wealth even as they reduced the role of any one individual manager or boss. Vanderbilt was hardly alone in fostering either of these developments, but he was certainly an innovative leader.

In 1863, Vanderbilt bought a major interest in the New York & Harlem Railroad, a small line that ran to the heart of Manhattan. Vanderbilt improved its tracks, cars, and service and purchased the connecting Hudson River Railroad. Then in 1867, he forced

Panic of 1873
A major economic downturn, launched when the country's leading financier, Jay Cooke, went bankrupt during which thousands lost their jobs and from which the country took years to recover.

the directors of the state's largest railroad, the New York Central, to sell to him or be shut out of New York City. His New York Central Railroad empire made Cornelius Vanderbilt the richest man in America when he died in 1877.

Others also became major speculators in the United States in the 1860s and 1870s. Daniel Drew, along with Jay Gould and Jim Fisk, came to be known as corporate pirates. They simply extracted wealth from a company. As a young man, Drew herded cattle from farms to slaughterhouses. He once claimed to have perfected a technique of feeding salt to his cattle and then, just before reaching the slaughterhouses, giving them all the water they wanted so they would arrive looking plump and, thus, fetch a good price. In later life, he certainly did the same thing with stocks: buying companies, issuing stock far beyond the company's value—called watering the stock in honor of his experience with cattle—and then leaving the company almost bankrupt while he walked away with the profit from the stock sales.

Later, in 1869 Drew, Gould, and Fisk teamed up to corner the nation's gold supply (see Chapter 15). First, they convinced President Grant to appoint Daniel Butterfield to the key treasury post overseeing the nation's gold supply. They then bribed Butterfield to join in their conspiracy. As they kept buying and hoarding gold, the price kept going up and up because of the demand they were creating. Grant discovered, or at least guessed, what Butterfield and the trio were up to, and he ordered the government to sell up to $4 million in gold, bringing the price back down. The trio sold their gold just before Grant issued his order. Although they no longer controlled the gold supply, they emerged very well-off. Many others who had invested in gold were ruined, and what became known as "Black Friday" created a significant drag on the nation's economy. Henry Adams, grandson and great-grandson of presidents, who was just beginning his own career as one of the nation's major intellectuals, wrote:

> For the first time since the creation of these enormous corporate bodies, one of them has shown its power for mischief, and has proved itself able to override and trample on law, custom, decency, and every restraint known to society, without scruple, and as yet without check.

It would be another 30 years before there were effective checks on the corporate gamblers.

The fortunes that the Vanderbilts, Drews, and others like them made in the 1870s and 1880s allowed them to spend lavishly, creating the public image of gilding a lily— a flower that when cut would be thrown away in a few days—with gold, a lot of gold. In grand parties in New York and at summer "cottages" or mansions in Newport, Rhode Island, or elsewhere, they showed off their wealth to the delight of some and the disgust of others.

New Industries: Rockefeller's Oil, Carnegie's Steel, and Morgan's Banking

Before the 1800s were over, however, a new generation of corporate leaders exceeded the most optimistic hopes of the Vanderbilts and their generation. Among them was John D. Rockefeller, who, though he did not discover any oil nor invent new ways to refine oil into kerosene or gasoline, did discover new ways to make money from oil, amassing more money from the fuel than anyone had previously imagined possible. Mark Hanna, a childhood friend who later became President McKinley's closest advisor, remembered saying of John D. that he was "sane in every respect save one—he was money mad!"

When Rockefeller was 20 years old, he heard news that got as much national attention as John Brown's raid on Harper's Ferry that same year. On August 28, 1859, Edwin Drake struck oil while drilling a well near Titusville, Pennsylvania. "Rock oil" as the oil that came from the ground was called (as opposed to whale oil and oil refined from coal), was in great demand. Before the invention of electric lights in 1879, kerosene lights were the brightest and most popular form of illumination. They were significantly

John D. Rockefeller (1839–1937) created the Standard Oil Company which came to have monopoly control of the sales of oil in the United States making Rockefeller an extraordinarily rich man as he drove competitors out of business.

brighter than candles and safer than gas lights. With kerosene lights, families could read in the evening, and the mills could start earlier and operate later. In addition, the machinery that the country was using, from railway engines to factory presses and looms, needed to be lubricated with oil to avoid seizing up. However, the oil had been scarce and expensive. Drake's oil well significantly changed the potential supply of oil.

A rush ensued to sink oil wells in western Pennsylvania. Rockefeller, however, did not like the dirt or the risk of drilling in which some struck it rich while others with a dry well or two went bankrupt. (He also did not like the risk of fighting as a soldier and quickly paid the $300 for a substitute to fight for him in the Union army.) He focused instead on refining the oil that others produced. With two partners, Rockefeller built a refinery in Cleveland where he could take advantage of nearby supplies of crude oil and get his products to market by using Great Lakes shipping and the rail lines between the East Coast and Chicago that ran through Cleveland.

Rockefeller was determined to dominate the Cleveland refining market. He kept his products better and his prices lower than any of the competition. He quickly bought out his partners, one of whom later commented, "John had abiding faith in two things: the Baptist creed and oil." He might have added that Rockefeller also had great faith in his own ability to strike a good bargain and manage his business, which meant cutting costs in every possible way. He brought in a new partner, Henry M. Flagler, who was as religious and as cost-conscious as himself. Rockefeller's Cleveland refinery was soon shipping more oil than any other in the region, which gave him great influence with the railroads. Jay Gould offered a rebate to Rockefeller if he would ship on the Erie system, and Rockefeller accepted but then convinced the Erie's primary competition, the Lake Shore Railroad, to give an even better one. When word of the secret rebates leaked out, other oil producers complained, but Rockefeller and Flagler had already made enough money to buy several of the competitors.

Horizontal integration
The merger of competitors in the same industry.

In 1870, the Rockefeller–Flagler partnership became the Standard Oil Company, and the two set out to gain control of the nation's oil business. They bargained with oil producers to keep costs low. They bought up every rival refining company they could, leaving producers with little option but to sell their oil to Standard Oil at whatever price Standard Oil was willing to pay. When a company would not sell to them, they went into direct competition, cutting prices, until the competitor either sold to Standard Oil or went out of business. They created the Standard Oil Trust, a separate corporation, to buy up virtually every other refinery in the nation. While competition kept prices low, Rockefeller thought competition was a terrible waste of effort and a drain on his profits, and he meant to end it. By the 1880s, companies under the control of Standard Oil refined nine out of 10 barrels of oil produced in the United States. This control over oil production came to be known as **horizontal integration** or, in cases like Standard Oil where nearly all of the industry was integrated, a horizontal monopoly. Standard Oil kept growing. Rockefeller produced his own tank cars and leased them to the railroads, making it difficult for competitors to transport oil. When pipelines started replacing oil tank cars, Standard Oil bought the pipelines. In the 1890s, tired of haggling with oil producers, Standard Oil simply started buying oil wells and became the largest producer and refiner of oil in the nation. In the 1890s, the United States had no meaningful antimonopoly laws in force, and Rockefeller's tireless work had made him the master of oil from its production to its refining to its sales.

Just as Edison's light bulb was starting to reduce demand for kerosene, Henry Ford's automobiles created a demand for gasoline, refined from the same crude oil as kerosene. Automobiles would dwarf all previous markets for Standard Oil's products. In addition, the world's navies were also turning from sail to oil-powered steamships. After 1900, everyone knew that with the development of these gas- and oil-powered vehicles, Standard Oil's greatest days were still ahead (see Map 17-1).

Andrew Carnegie was only a little older than Rockefeller. In 1848, when he was 12 years old, his family came to the United States from his native Scotland after his father, a successful linen weaver, was thrown out of work by the mechanization of the industry. Andrew Carnegie's first job was in a textile mill in Allegheny, Pennsylvania, where he earned $1.20 per week. He soon moved to higher paying jobs and eventually became the personal assistant to the division superintendent of the Pennsylvania Railroad, a position in which he quickly learned the inner workings of American industry.

Like Rockefeller, Carnegie paid someone to serve as his substitute in the Union army—a practice that was entirely legal, though ethically questionable, during the Civil War. In 1863, he decided to leave salaried work because he was confident he could make more money by investing, and he valued his independence. He advised others that the key to success was "Put all your eggs in one basket and then watch that basket." Carnegie's basket was steel, which he quickly realized was coming to dominate American commerce.

In the early 1870s, Carnegie persuaded several investors to join him in opening a new state-of-the-art steel mill just outside Pittsburgh. Pittsburgh was near the coal fields, and steel mills used a lot of coal. The location was also near rivers and competing railroad lines, so no one rail line could squeeze Carnegie's profits. Having established himself as the head of a giant corporation, Carnegie, like Rockefeller, set out to dominate the field. He found ways to track and cut costs. Seeing him around the plant looking at inventories, one foreman said, "There goes that damned bookkeeper." He replaced wood buildings, which could burn, with iron ones; he developed an assembly line approach to steel production; and he constantly updated and replaced equipment.

Carnegie built or bought everything needed for the steel business, from the coal mines to the coke ovens that prepared fuel to the iron mines that produced iron ore. He purchased railroads and steamships to transport the coal and ore to Pittsburgh. In addition, he did whatever was needed to keep workers' salaries as low as possible. He once said, "Show me your cost sheets. It is more interesting to know how well and how cheaply you have done this thing than how much money you have made." Other steel mill owners who worried only about profits were defeated by Carnegie's constant focus on costs.

Type of Plants:

△ Blast furnace

○ Rolling mill, steel work

□ Bridge building plant

Companies:

▨ The Carnegie Co.

▨ Federal Steel Co.

▨ National Steel Co.

▨ National Tube Co.

▨ American Steel and Wire Co. of New Jersey

▨ American Tin Plate Co.

■ American Steel Hoop Co.

▨ American Sheet Steel Co.

▨ American Bridge Co.

▨ Lake Superior Iron Mines

Independent Firms:

◇ Blast furnace

◇ Rolling mill

Companies:

▨ Republic Iron and Steel Co.

▨ Bethlehem Steel Co.

▨ Lackawana Iron and Steel Co.

▨ Pennsylvania Steel Co. of New Jersey

▨ Cambria Steel Co.

▨ Crucible Steel Co. of America

▨ Tennessee Coal, Iron, and Railroad Company

▨ Jones and Laughlins Ltd

Pittsburgh

Cleveland

MAP 17-1 The Nations's Industrial Heartland. The giant corporations of the Gilded Age tended to concentrate in the northwest of the United States. The factories of the region attracted immigrants from around the world and within the United States while also concentrating wealth and increasing the country's transportation networks.

By the late 1890s, Carnegie Steel was the largest single company in the steel business. In contrast to the Standard Oil Trust, which was the model of horizontal monopoly, controlling all of the nation's oil refining, Carnegie Steel was the model of **vertical integration**, controlling all means of steel production from raw materials through sales. For Carnegie, those means included the materials of coal and iron in the ground, the mining and transport of the materials, and the production and sales of the steel that came from these materials. Like Rockefeller, Carnegie became a very rich man.

Vertical integration

The consolidation of numerous production functions, from the extraction of the raw materials to the distribution and marketing of the finished products, under the direction of one firm.

Chapter 17 The Gilded Age: Building a Technological and Industrial Giant and a New Social Order **487**

More important than enjoying a lavish lifestyle and sometimes supporting various charities, emerging corporate leaders used their money to ensure their political influence and power. While Rockefeller and Carnegie were the best known, and probably the most successful, builders of monopoly trusts, other leaders built monopolies and grew almost as rich. In 1892, the *New York World* listed 3,045 millionaires in the United States. Gustavus Swift dominated meat, Charles Pillsbury grain, Henry Havemeyer sugar, Frederick Weyerhaeuser lumber, and James B. Duke tobacco. In addition, companies in other fields established trusts as they replaced competition with easier and more profitable coordination—the cottonseed oil trust, the linseed oil trust, the lead mining trust, the whiskey distilling trust, and the cord (rope) manufacturing trust. Free enterprise, as previous generations had known it, was quickly being replaced by a single corporation or trust that had many employees who simply took orders while the trust dominated the market for its product, ending competition and setting prices that consumers large and small had no choice but to pay or do without the product. The owners of these trusts had enough political power to make sure that no government intervened.

While Rockefeller and Carnegie were amassing their fortunes, another American was amassing the greatest economic power that the country had ever seen. Although never as personally wealthy as Rockefeller or Carnegie, John Pierpont Morgan was the banker that everyone else, including the richest industrialists and often the U.S. government, looked to. Like Rockefeller and Carnegie, Morgan was born in the 1830s, and like them, he paid for a substitute rather than let the Civil War divert him from banking. In the financial chaos of the Civil War, Morgan launched J.P. Morgan & Company. During the war, Morgan made great profits. He once sold reconditioned army rifles back to the federal government at a considerable profit. Working with European banks, Morgan helped finance the transcontinental railroad in the United States and the Suez Canal in the Middle East (both of which were completed in 1869). Using his skill and formidable resources, Morgan helped pick up the pieces of the American economy after the collapse of Jay Cooke & Company had launched the Panic of 1873.

In 1877, after Cornelius Vanderbilt died, Morgan helped Vanderbilt's son, William, sell off some shares of the New York Central Railroad. In return Morgan got a $3 million fee but, more valuable to him, a seat on the board of directors of the New York Central. He helped others with similar sales and gained seats for himself on other equally powerful boards. As a result, Morgan knew more about American industries than any other banker. In particular, he knew that the railroads were overbuilt and he was determined to reduce the competition among them.

In the late 1880s, two of the largest railroads, the New York Central and the Pennsylvania Railroad, ran competing lines from Philadelphia to Pittsburgh and from New York to Chicago. Morgan decided to be a very forceful peacemaker. He invited—or summoned—the principal directors of each railroad to his yacht, the *Corsair*, and then ordered the captain to sail up and down the Hudson until finally, in exhaustion, they agreed to a settlement. The result of the agreement—some called it collusion—was better organization and higher profits for both lines, especially for stockholders and directors like Morgan himself, who also always collected a hefty fee for his services, but at considerable cost to shippers who had benefitted from the cutthroat competition.

The Panic of 1893 showed Morgan's power as much as prosperity did. In May 1893, the National Cordage Company, known as the rope trust, which was producing far more rope than the market demanded and issuing far too many promissory notes, went bankrupt, launching a major drop in stock prices among related businesses. In an economy as deeply interconnected as the U.S. economy had become, a drop in one area meant a drop in many others. In the course of the ensuing depression, the Philadelphia and Reading, Northern Pacific, Union Pacific, and Santa Fe Railroads as well as a host of other businesses all followed into bankruptcy.

People much lower on the economic scale also felt the depression, sometimes more so. In the fall of 1893, a Methodist minister from Lincoln, Nebraska, told the

American Voices

Andrew Carnegie, Wealth, 1889

In this article, known as "The Gospel of Wealth," Carnegie justified his vast fortune (he would be the richest person in America by 1901) and laid the foundation for his late-in-life generosity that built Carnegie libraries and created the Carnegie Corporation of New York in 1911.

The price which society pays for the law of competition, like the price it pays for cheap comforts and luxuries, is also great; but the advantage of this law are also greater still, for it is to this law that we owe our wonderful material development, which brings improved conditions in its train....We accept and welcome therefore, as conditions to which we must accommodate ourselves, great inequality of environment, the concentration of business, industrial and commercial, in the hands of a few, and the law of competition between these, as being not only beneficial, but essential for the future progress of the race....The question then arises...What is the proper mode of administering wealth after the laws upon which civilization is founded have thrown it into the hands of the few?...

There are but three modes in which surplus wealth can be disposed of. It can be left to the families of the decedents; or it can be bequeathed for public purposes; or, finally, it can be administered during their lives by its possessors....Why should men leave great fortunes to their children? If this is done from affection, is it not misguided affection? Observation teaches that, generally speaking, it is not well for the children that they should be so burdened. Neither is it well for the state....

As to the second mode, that of leaving wealth at death for public uses, it may be said that this is only a means for the disposal of wealth, provided a man is content to wait until he is dead before it becomes of much good in the world....Besides this, it may fairly be said that no man is to be extolled for doing what he cannot help doing...

There remains, then, only one mode of using great fortunes... Under its sway we shall have an ideal state, in which the surplus wealth of the few will become, in the best sense the property of the many, because administered for the common good, and this wealth, passing through the hands of the few, can be made a much more potent force for the elevation of our race than if it had been distributed in small sums to the people themselves....

This, then, is held to be the duty of the man of Wealth: First, to set an example of modest, unostentatious living, shunning display or extravagance; to provide moderately for the legitimate wants of those dependent upon him; and after doing so to consider all surplus revenues which come to him simply as trust funds, which he is called upon to administer, and strictly bound as a matter of duty to administer in the manner which, in his judgment, is best calculated to produce the most beneficial results for the community—the man of wealth thus becoming the mere agent and trustee for his poorer brethren, bringing to their service his superior wisdom, experience and ability to administer, doing for them better than they would or could do for themselves....

Such, in my opinion, is the true Gospel concerning Wealth, obedience to which is destined some day to solve the problem of the Rich and the Poor, and to bring "Peace on earth, among men of Good-Will"

Source: Andrew Carnegie, "Wealth," *North American Review*, Vol. 148, No. 391 (June, 1889).

Thinking Critically

1. Documentary Analysis

In Carnegie's view, what importance should be attached to economic inequality? How did he believe the wealthy should use their fortunes?

2. Crafting an Argument

Defend or refute the following statement. "Andrew Carnegie's views on wealth were nothing more than a thinly veiled effort to justify exploitation and social injustice."

---

story of "an honest Methodist farmer" who sold his year's harvest for $31 and "with this he paid his taxes and half his grocery bill, and went home without dinner because there was not a nickel left in his pocket." A lot of honest Methodist, Baptist, and Presbyterian farmers were in the same boat, as well as factory workers and members of the rising middle class who lost their jobs and their hopes in the 1893 depression.

As European investors watched the collapse of the U.S. economy, they started withdrawing gold held in U.S. banks. The European run on the U.S. gold supply almost bankrupted the U.S. government. At the beginning of 1895, the federal government's gold supply, kept in vaults in New York City, was $100 million. By the end of January, it was down to $50 million and falling quickly as investors withdrew their gold. In early February, Morgan traveled from New York to Washington, DC, in his private rail car to offer help. President Grover Cleveland, a Democrat, did not want the political embarrassment of being rescued by—or being seen under the control of—J. P. Morgan. However, by the time the two met, Morgan informed Cleveland (since Morgan always had the most up-to-date financial information) that there was but $9 million in gold still available and that a $10 million draft was on its way. The banker told the president, "You can't meet it. It will be over before three o'clock."

Morgan also had a solution to offer. He reminded the president and the treasury secretary of a long-forgotten piece of Civil War legislation that said, "The Secretary of the Treasury may purchase coin with any of the bonds or notes of the United States, authorized by law, at such rates and upon such terms as he may deem most advantageous to the public interest." He then offered $65 million in gold in return for 30-year government bonds. The president asked Morgan whether he could promise that the deal—which not only provided gold but put the full faith and credit of the House of Morgan behind the credit of the United States—would end the rush on the treasury and Morgan said, "Yes sir, I will guarantee it."

The deal worked. European bankers who had lost faith in the United States had faith in Morgan. They bought the bonds and stopped demanding payments in gold. The government had been protected from going the way of National Cordage and the Reading Railroad. The publisher Joseph Pulitzer called the deal an "excellent arrangement for the bankers," but "[f]or the nation it means a scandalous surrender of credit and a shameful waste of substance." Morgan made a fortune on the deal but also saved the U.S. economy. In the absence of any federal bank, the House of Morgan essentially served that role until the Federal Reserve Bank was created in 1916.

No project of J.P. Morgan's was as great, however, as the one he launched in 1900. It began with the kind of competition that Morgan always hated. Illinois Steel, which Morgan had helped finance, was making a direct run at Carnegie Steel for control of the market. Charles Schwab, one of Carnegie's partners, organized a holiday dinner with Morgan to see whether they could work out a deal to end the competition. Carnegie had talked of retiring, and his wife was anxious for him to enjoy life and devote himself full time to his charities. Carnegie was asked his price and, after a night's sleep, offered to sell Carnegie Steel for $480 million. Morgan agreed and later shook Carnegie's hand saying, "Mr. Carnegie, I want to congratulate you on being the richest man in the world." Morgan, Schwab, and Elbert Gary, the head of Illinois Steel, then negotiated with Rockefeller, whom Morgan disliked personally, to buy out Rockefeller's ownership of iron deposits in the Mesabi Range and the ore boats that went with them. In March 1901, Morgan announced the creation of the U.S. Steel Corporation, bringing together Carnegie's formidable assets, Illinois Steel, the Rockefeller iron mines, and other assets worth a total of $1.4 billion, the largest corporation ever seen at the time. The giant monopoly corporation was now the dominating fixture of the U.S. economy.

17.2 **Quick Review** How did the businessmen of the Gilded Age and their tactics revolutionize American industry? Whom do you think had the greatest impact?

LIVES OF THE MIDDLE CLASS IN THE GILDED AGE

17.3 Analyze daily life, popular ideas, and political direction for the middle class during the Gilded Age.

During the Gilded Age, what came to be known as middle-class values emerged in the United States. More Americans than ever before achieved a level of comfort and social respectability that, while it was a long way from the wealth of the Rockefellers, Carnegies, and Morgans, was also a long way from the poverty of most of rural America or those who worked on the railroads or in the refineries. As Americans moved from farms to towns, some of the urban residents became comfortable professionals and managers and, in the process, created a set of norms for "middle-class respectability" that had not been known before.

Middle-Class Life and Expectations

John Lewis came to the United States from Great Britain before the Civil War and got a job in the wholesale grocery business in New York City. By the 1870s, Lewis was the proprietor of his own store and a solid member of America's emerging urban middle class. While achieving a middle-class life for himself and his family, Lewis wrote letters to his brother in England describing his life. For the Christmas of 1875, Lewis took the train to visit relatives in Philadelphia. In addition to the feasting, which greatly impressed Lewis, he also noted the Christmas tree decorations:

> As *large* and fine a tree as can be accommodated being procured and set up, it is covered with every conceivable shape into which coloured and gilt paper and card can be cut and…little pictures, glass balls, chains, garlands &c, anything to make a gay and imposing display.

Lewis also noted that the enjoyment of the trees seemed to be a prime adult occupation while the children wanted candy. He noted, "The candy stores are among the gayest and most prosperous, and the consumption of their wares by women and children all the year round is enormous and is often spoken of by writers as a great national failing."

In maintaining his own store, traveling easily from city to city, celebrating holidays with feasts, decorations, and parties, Lewis was participating in the emerging middle-class culture of the late 1800s. Before the Civil War, Christmas celebrations among American Protestants were limited affairs, but after the war, the fondness for that holiday, and the economic resources to celebrate more grandly than ever before, grew rapidly. A larger group of people had the resources to own homes, decorate them, and travel to visit relatives than in any previous generation in the United States.

Those in the rising urban middle class were redesigning not only their private homes but also their expectations, particularly for city buildings and services that supported their emerging tastes and desires. Huge new department stores offered the opportunity to shop for the things that middle-class people, like John Lewis, wanted in their lives. The architect Daniel Burnham, the leading voice of what came to be known as the City Beautiful movement, designed public buildings in a classical style that showed a permanence and beauty that this emerging class expected. City Beautiful planned major revitalization efforts in Washington, DC, Cleveland, San Francisco, and Chicago, designing buildings such as the grand new Boston Public Library, based on the model of a Renaissance palazzo; the new building for the Library of Congress, which was completed in 1897; and the new New York Stock Exchange that opened in 1903.

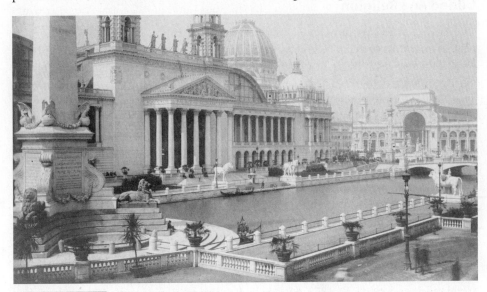

Architect David Burnham's City Beautiful movement made its debut in 1893 at the World's Columbian Exposition, Chicago, Illinois. In this photograph, the Palace of Mechanic Arts and lagoon showcase the classical style that characterized the movement.

The architect Louis Sullivan, Burnham's professional rival, sought a much simpler and, he said, more American style of architecture that reflected the energy of a culture that constructed buildings soaring to heights previously unimagined. Sullivan hated classical Renaissance style and preferred more simple lines. Frederick Law Olmsted designed major new park systems, including Central Park in New York, Boston's chain of connected parks around the city known as the Emerald Necklace, and the Mall in Washington, DC, all of which spoke to the commitment to beauty and permanence for a new and growing class of people who had the time and inclination to use such public spaces for leisure and uplifting pastimes.

While architects designed new buildings and park systems designed to show permanence and prosperity, other urban planners found ways to make cities more livable for the growing middle class or to help the middle class to escape what they found difficult to live with. These planners found new ways to bring pure water into city neighborhoods, perhaps most important to the life—and health—of city dwellers. Cholera and other waterborne diseases had long been a fact of city life. Once a cholera epidemic began to spread, wealth and class did little to protect people from it. Cities, like small towns, tended to depend on well water and on small, individual cisterns that collected rain water for their water supply. However, in growing urban areas, stagnant cisterns were a breeding ground for disease, and wells easily became contaminated. Beginning in 1842, New York started building a reservoir for water to be piped into the city from rural areas to provide a healthier water supply. As New York grew, a large new plan—the New Croton Aqueduct—was built from 1885 to 1893 to bring water to all of the city's neighborhoods. Other cities followed the same pattern. Water, which had been a source of disease, became one of the healthiest aspects of urban life.

Even as city life improved, many in the middle class wanted to put some distance between themselves and the cities. Railroads, which had initially connected cities over long distances, began to build shorter lines that would allow people who worked in cities to live in suburbs—a new development in American life during the Gilded Age. They commuted between their homes in semirural settings and their work in the commercial centers of urban America. Cities also quickly took to adding electric lights that kept cities alive at night, electric elevators that allowed much taller buildings to be built, and electric trolleys that made it easier to get from one part of a city to another. The cities of the Gilded Age were cleaner, brighter, and faster paced than anything known in the United States before that time.

Gilded Age Religion

The Gilded Age saw new levels of religious activity among white middle-class Protestants. Most of the middle class were, indeed, both white and Protestant, and they viewed themselves as living in a "Christian America," by which they meant a Protestant Christian culture. Between 1860 and 1900, the major Protestant denominations—the Methodists, Baptists, Presbyterians, Congregationalists, and Episcopalians—tripled their membership from 5 million to 16 million. Americans not only joined Protestant churches but also participated in nondenominational religious organizations, including the YMCA as well as Bible, mission, and social reform societies. The theology that was being preached changed with the times, becoming more individualistic and more optimistic. And no one represented the changes in white American Protestantism as much as the great revivalist of the era, Dwight L. Moody.

Like many Americans of his generation—the same generation as Rockefeller, Carnegie, and Morgan—Moody grew up on a farm but moved to a city. When the Civil War began, Moody gave up his shoe business to work full time for the YMCA. He led a Sunday school for poor immigrant children and supported the YMCA's social service missions. By 1875, Moody had an international reputation. He launched the Northfield and Mount Hermon schools as well as a new Bible training school in Chicago in 1886 that eventually became the Moody Bible Institute.

Electric lights, electronic trolleys, and fast-moving trains not only speeded transportation but also created a new kind of energized night life in cities like New York.
W. Louis Sonntag, Jr., *The Bowery at Night,* watercolor, 1895. Copyright Museum of the City of New York. 32.275.2.

Another prominent minister, Lyman Abbott, described Moody's preaching in 1899 saying, "As he stood on the platform, he looked like a business man; he dressed like a business man; he took the meeting in hand as a business man would." If other business men were dominating the culture and the economy, a preacher who acted like a business man could be a success. Moody did not shout. He gave a simple message focused on the need for conversion and the love of God. The preacher was deeply critical of both sides in the growing debates that pitted liberal biblical scholarship against those who insisted the Bible was the literal truth. He did not see any fresh views on either side of the argument and wondered whether both could not just "let us get on with the practical work of the kingdom."

The sins Moody denounced were attending the theater, disregarding the Sabbath, and believing atheistic teachings. Coming home to Jesus was the key for Moody, and home and Jesus often represented the same thing. He preached a gospel perfectly fitted to the growing sense of individualism in the United States. In describing his mission, he said, "I look upon this world as a wrecked vessel. God has given me a lifeboat and said to me, 'Moody, save all you can.'"

Ira D. Sankey's music was as important as the preaching at Moody's revivals. Some of the most popular hymns that Sankey led people in singing were written by Fanny J. Crosby, who wrote over 8,000 of them. The hymns, like the popular *Pass Me Not, O Gentle Saviour,* reflect an individualistic faith in which the focus is on divine comfort and love far more than on sin, divine judgment, or great social change. Protestant Americans sang these hymns during Sunday morning services and at home around a piano—which those of the emerging middle class could now afford.

Electoral Politics

Between 1876 and 1896, electoral politics reflected the dominant middle-class interests of the era. While groups within the major parties and new political parties like the Populists (see Chapter 18) protested against the poverty and corruption that was part

Stalwarts
A faction of the Republican Party in the 1870s and 1880s who wanted the party to stay true to its earlier support for Reconstruction in the South and who were less connected to the emerging big-business interests than others.

of the backdrop of the Gilded Age, the major parties, Republicans and Democrats alike, reflected the ideas and aspirations of the middle and upper classes. In a nation where a few were growing exorbitantly wealthy and a larger number were moving into new comforts, the leaders of the political parties had no interest in challenging the status quo.

In the 1870s and 1880s, the Republican Party was the political voice of most corporate leaders and most Protestants outside of the South. But the party was split between the heirs of the antislavery wing of the party—**Stalwarts** they called themselves—and others who believed that it was time to forget about slavery and the goals of Reconstruction and simply embrace the nation's growing prosperity. The party was also split along lines of personal animosity, none deeper than the hatred between Roscoe Conkling, Stalwart leader of the New York delegation in the Congress, and James G. Blaine, a Congressman from Maine since 1862 who had quickly risen over many more senior members to be Speaker of House. Blaine was among those ready to focus on the future; embrace the economy that Rockefeller, Carnegie, and Morgan were creating for the nation; and forget about reform efforts, whether in the form of the now-fading Reconstruction goals or the needs of the urban poor. Blaine was a man of great charm and eloquence but often seen as being too smooth and probably a participant in some of the worse corruption of the Grant administration.

After the tensions of the 1876 Hayes-Tilden election (see Chapter 15), the Republicans did not want to renominate President Hayes and turned instead to another Civil War veteran and compromise candidate from Ohio, James A. Garfield, who defeated the Democrats' Union war hero Winfield Scott Hancock in the November 1880 election. Unlike many in either political party, Garfield was committed to civil service reform—ending the use of government jobs to reward political favorites—and to uniting Stalwarts and their opponents. His running mate was the New York customs collector Chester A. Arthur, better known for his ability to find government jobs for friends than for any reform agenda. Three months after the inauguration, Garfield was shot by a disgruntled office seeker, and although he seemed to be healing from his wounds, he died on September 19, 1881. Arthur became the president and, as some said, served a less undistinguished term than expected.

In 1884, Blaine was determined to stop Arthur's renomination. He tried hard to convince yet another war hero, William T. Sherman, to run for president, but Sherman's unequivocal response was, "If nominated I will not run, if elected I will not serve." Eventually, the Republicans gave Blaine his turn as their candidate.

Governor Grover Cleveland was the Democratic nominee. Cleveland had fought corruption when he was mayor of Buffalo, New York, a reputation that propelled him to the governor's office in 1882 and only 2 years later to the White House. Given Cleveland's reputation for honesty and Blaine's for corruption, a number of long-time Republicans campaigned for the Democrats. These party crossovers became known as **Mugwumps**, a word they claimed came from an Indian word for "big chief" but that their opponents said meant someone whose mug was on one side of a fence while their "wump" was on the other.

Mugwumps
A reform faction of the Republican party who supported Cleveland, the Democratic nominee over the Republican Blaine in the 1884 election.

In the midst of the 1884 campaign, a preacher from Buffalo revealed that Cleveland had fathered a child with a young widow, Maria Halpin, and then paid child support. Cleveland supporters said that Halpin had many boyfriends and that Cleveland was only protecting the others, some of whom were married. The nominee ordered his campaign to "Tell the truth." While the nation faced serious economic choices, the campaigns fell to chanting "Blaine, Blaine, James G. Blaine, continental liar from the state of Maine," against "Ma, ma, where's my pa?" Just before the election, another preacher who supported Blaine castigated the Democrats as the "party of rum, Romanism, and rebellion," a phrase that may have cost the Republicans key Catholic votes in New York state where Cleveland won by only 1,100 votes, which gave him a majority in the Electoral College.

Cleveland was not significantly different than the Republicans who served before him, though he did take a strong stand against the annexation of Hawaii and other expansionist efforts that Republicans had been pursuing. But as African-Americans in the South suffered from ever-increasing segregation and inequality, white and black farmers faced poverty, and workers began efforts to organize unions to end starvation wages, Cleveland, like the Republicans, tended to ignore their needs or, when pushed, sided with the corporations and their owners (see Chapter 18).

In a close race, Cleveland was defeated for reelection in 1888 by the Republican nominee, Civil War general and presidential grandson Benjamin Harrison, whose main campaign issues were Cleveland's veto of a pension bill for all Civil War veterans and Cleveland's return of Civil War banners to Southern states. A tactic called "waving the bloody shirt"—reminding everyone in the North that Republicans had won the Civil War while Democrats represented the states of the Confederacy—seemed to win elections for Republicans. Yet 4 years later, Cleveland, in a return match, defeated Harrison and served a second term from 1893 to 1897—the only president in history to serve nonconsecutive terms. It was Cleveland's bad luck to begin his second term just as the Panic of 1893 began, and while his negotiations with J. P. Morgan may have avoided even worse disaster, the economic crisis of 1893 hurt many Americans. The political stability of the 1870s and 1880s seemed to be coming to an end in the 1890s.

Global Connections

American influence around the world grew dramatically during the Gilded Age. Americans had been sending missionaries to foreign countries since the early 1800s, but far greater numbers went abroad in the 1880s and 1890s. Dwight L. Moody called on young converts to consider careers as foreign missionaries, and some of them launched the China Inland Mission to convert China. Another Moody convert, John R. Mott, organized the Student Volunteer Movement that eventually sent over 5,000 missionaries to India, Africa, China, Japan, and the Middle East (the Movement later became the World Student Christian Federation). Individual churches and religious bodies sent their own preachers, teachers, and medical missionaries to all parts of the globe. Missionaries brought western values, a respect for human rights—especially women's rights. However, they also brought American commercialism interests,

While political leaders like Hayes, Garfield, and Cleveland vied for the presidency, many reformers were coming to the conclusion that the business trusts led by people like Rockefeller, Carnegie, and Morgan really controlled the country. This political cartoon from 1889 showed who many thought actually ran the Senate and the country.

perhaps unwittingly, to cultures that may or may not have wanted them. The missionaries were quickly followed by merchants and industrialists, though missionaries sometimes led the protests against the commercialization of international relations. Returning missionaries became the voice of the world in many American communities, describing people and cultures unfamiliar to American audiences.

Missionaries were far from the only Americans to visit other parts of the globe during the Gilded Age. As the United States grew in population and industrial production, it became a player of growing importance in world markets, second only to Great Britain. After the Panic of 1873, many worried that the rapid growth in U.S. industrial productivity could become a problem rather than a boon. If the country produced more and more and depended only on domestic markets, then prices and income were doomed to keep falling. The only solution, some argued, was to find foreign markets, lots of foreign markets, to be sure that American products were sold all over the world, bringing new income to American producers. Exporting goods was nothing new to the United States, but after 1870, many U.S. business leaders intensified exporting efforts to sustain the nation's economy. The total value of U.S. exports jumped from $234 million in 1865 to $1.5 billion in 1900, and the country was transformed from a debtor to a creditor nation.

In terms of commercial efforts, the United States had long been interested in Cuba. Southern Senators regularly suggested making the island a slave state before the Civil War, and in 1854, the American ambassadors to Europe's leading powers issued the so-called Ostend Manifesto, demanding that Spain sell Cuba to the United States. After the Civil War, Cuba was no longer of value as a slave state, but interest in the island never disappeared from American politics. When a rebellion against Spanish rule broke out in Cuba in1868, perhaps 100,000 Cubans died as a result while the island's economy was devastated. U.S. merchants took advantage of the situation and bought sugar plantations, mines, and ranches in Cuba while U.S. diplomats forged an agreement with Spain for free and open trade between the island and the United States. By 1890, the United States was the dominant economic force on the island, and trade with Cuba was important for the U.S. economy.

The United States also had longstanding interests in Mexico. During the Civil War, Napoleon III had sent French troops to Mexico, installing Austrian Archduke Maximilian and his wife Carlotta as rulers of the country. Secretary of State Seward warned the French that their meddling was an "act of hostility," and U.S. General Philip Sheridan informed Mexican revolutionaries that he had placed a substantial supply of weapons at the border and would look the other way if they disappeared. The supply vanished, and Maximilian was overthrown by a new government led by reform-minded Benito Juárez. Maximilian was executed by a revolutionary firing squad in June 1867. Later, Porfirio Díaz, who did not share Juárez's reform agenda, claimed dictatorial power in Mexico. Diaz was anxious to expand U.S. investment in Mexico, and Americans bought railroads, mines, and oil exploration companies. By 1900, Americans had some $500 million invested in Mexico, enough to make the country a major trading partner and, indeed, to give American businesses significant influence in the Mexican economy and political life. Some feared Mexico was becoming almost an economic satellite of the United States.

U.S. commercial interests extended far beyond the Americas. In the 1870s, Belgium's King Leopold II created a private colony around the Congo River in Africa. It was a brutal affair. Residents of the Congo were pressed into slave labor on the vast rubber plantations that were meeting growing demands for rubber, and they were making Leopold very rich. Anxious to gain a new market, some businessmen persuaded President Arthur to recognize King Leopold's rule as the legitimate government of the Congo in 1884; however, Arthur's successor, Grover Cleveland reduced U.S. involvement in light of the violent conditions.

In Europe, the growth of U.S. exports almost provoked a trade war between the United States and Europe's leading economic powers, including Britain, Germany, and France. Bad harvests in Europe starting in 1879 led to significant demand for American food, lifting the U.S. economy out of the last vestiges of the Panic of 1873. But European governments became nervous about their growing dependence on U.S. food and claimed that U.S. pork and beef was not safe, leading to a huge fall off in exports. The *New York Herald* urged "avenging the American hog" with a boycott of French wine and German sugar, but an eventual compromise led meat exports to be doubled.

In Asia, a U.S. Navy squadron sailed to Korea in 1867 but was sent away. But the U.S. Navy kept trying, as it had with Japan and China, and in 1882, Korea agreed to open itself to U.S. markets. The two governments signed the Treaty of Chemulpo after which Korean officers studied at the U.S. Military Academy at West Point and the Brooklyn Navy Yard. While Korea remained a relatively small trading partner, the determination to open a country known as the "Hermit Kingdom" was typical of the era. From Korea to Latin America, the Congo, and Europe, the United States emerged from the Gilded Age as a trading partner of some importance not only in familiar countries but also in parts of the world previous generations had barely heard about.

17.3 **Quick Review** How did the expansion of industry contribute to changes in noneconomic arenas during the Gilded Age?

IMMIGRATION

17.4 Explain the reasons immigrants came to the United States in such large numbers during the Gilded Age and what their experience was.

In the 75 years between 1815 and 1890, 15 million people immigrated to the United States, the great majority from northern Europe—Britain, Ireland, Germany, Scandinavia, Switzerland, and Holland. In the next 25 years, from 1890 until the start of World War I in 1914, 15 million additional immigrants came to the United States, and those immigrants came from new places—80 percent of them from Italy, Greece, Russia, the Empire of Austria-Hungary, Romania, and Turkey, and others from Japan, China, and Korea, as well as Mexico and other parts of Latin America. With their arrival, they changed the complexion of the nation. What all these immigrants had in common was a "push-pull" experience in which various factors pushed them to leave their home countries and, at the same time, other factors pulled them to try a new life in the United States.

The Push from Around the World

When Sadie Frowne described the desperate poverty of Poland or when the Lithuanian, Antanas Kaztauskis, expressed his family's fear that he was about to be drafted into the Russian army, they were relating reasons that pushed hundreds of thousands of people to move not only from southern and eastern Europe—Italy, Greece, Poland, Russia, and so on—but also from China, Japan, and Korea to start new lives in the United States. Most of those who emigrated to the United States between 1890 and World War I did so in large part because something, often grinding poverty and fear of persecution, pushed them to get out of the places where they and their families had lived for many generations, and the pull of hoped-for new lives and new prosperity attracted them to the United States (see Map 17-2).

Nowhere was the push to leave greater than in Russia and Russian-dominated parts of eastern Europe including the Ukraine, Lithuania, and Poland. Abraham Cahan, who came to the United States from Russia as a young man, explained what

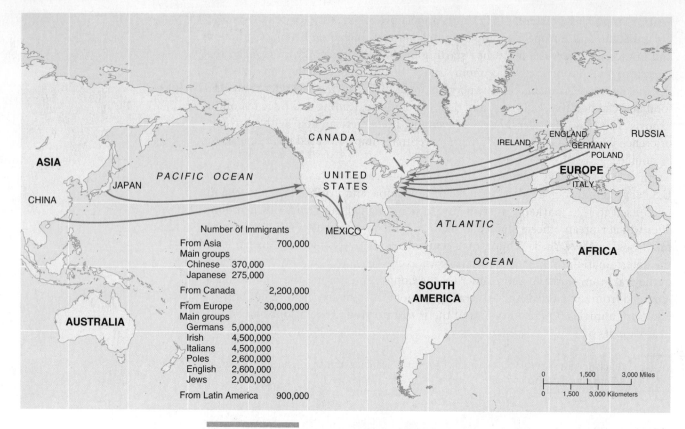

MAP 17-2 Immigration to the United States. Between 1820 and 1914, but especially between 1880 and 1914, immigrants transformed the United States. This map shows where they came from and how many arrived.

drove him: "The government itself had set off the pogroms in order to save the throne from a revolutionary upheaval. By making the Jews the scapegoats, it had confused the common people so that in the end the peasants were certain that the Jews and not the Czar were the cause of their troubles." Golda Meir, who became a school teacher in Milwaukee and one day would be Prime Minister of Israel, remembered,

> I can still recall distinctly hearing about a pogrom that was to descend on us... with the rabble that used to surge through town, brandishing knives and huge sticks, screaming 'Christ killers' as they looked for the Jews.

Pogroms

Government-directed attacks against Jewish citizens, property, and villages in tsarist Russia beginning in the 1880s; a primary reason for Russian Jewish migration to the United States.

Pogroms—anti-Jewish attacks—became increasingly common in Russia at the end of the 1800s. They were not only tolerated but also often actively encouraged by the Russian government and the Russian Orthodox Church.

After the assassination of Czar Alexander II in 1881, the government ordered that all Jews in Russia must move to the Pale of Settlement, a region that stretched from the Baltic in the north to the Black Sea in the south. Jews were not allowed to travel into the rest of Russia. Within the Pale, though there was a thriving Jewish community and culture, there was desperate poverty. Jews were not allowed to own land. Another immigrant remembered, "There were ten times as many stores as there should have been, ten times as many tailors, cobblers, barbers, tinsmiths." Leaving Russia seemed the only solution to such conditions.

For Italian peasants there were no pogroms, but there was plenty of violence and poverty. When Italy was united as a nation in 1871—following a movement known as the *Risorgimento*—wealth and industry were concentrated in the north and the *Mezzogiorno*, as southern Italy was known, was a land of poverty where massive soil erosion made farming almost impossible. In 1906, Mount Vesuvius erupted, destroying towns and some of the rich grape-growing farmland that remained. Facing

American Voices

Sadie Frowne, A Polish Sweatshop Girl, 1906

Sadie Frowne's account of her move from a small village in Russia to become a garment worker New York City's Lower East Side is representative of the life experience of thousands of immigrants.

My mother…kept a little grocer's shop in the little village where we lived at first. That was in Poland, somewhere on the frontier…She had a wagon in which she used to drive about the country, selling her groceries, and sometimes she worked in the fields with my father.

When I was a little more than 10 years of age my father died. He was a good man and a steady worker, and we never knew what it was to be hungry while he lived. After he died troubles began, for the rent of our shop was about $6 a month, and then there were food and clothes to provide. We needed little, it is true, but even soup, black bread, and onions we could not always get.…

Mother wrote to Aunt Fanny, who lived in New York, and told her how hard it was to live in Poland, and Aunt Fanny advised her to come and bring me.…She said we should both come at once, and she went around among our relatives in New York and took up a subscription for our passage.

We came by steerage on a steamship in a very dark place that smelt dreadfully. There were hundreds of other people packed in with us, men, women and children, and almost all of them were sick. It took us 12 days to cross the sea, and we thought we should die, but at last the voyage was over and we came up and saw the beautiful bay and the big woman with the spikes on her head and the lamp that is lighted at night in her hand (Goddess of Liberty).…

So I went to work in Allen Street (Manhattan) in what they call a sweatshop, making skirts by machine. I was new at the work and the foreman scolded me a great deal.…

In Poland I and my father and mother used to go to the synagogue on the Sabbath, but here the women don't go to the synagogue much, though the men do. They are shut up working hard all week long, and when the Sabbath comes they like to sleep long in bed and afterward they must go out where they can breathe the air.…

Some of the women blame me very much because I spend so much money on clothes. They say that instead of a dollar a week I ought not to spend more than 25c a week on clothes, and that I should save the rest. But a girl must have clothes if she is to go into good society at Ulmer Park or Coney Island or the theater. Those who blame me are the old country people who have old-fashioned notions, but the people who have been here a long time know better. A girl who does not dress well is stuck in a corner, even if she is pretty, and Aunt Fanny says that I do just right to put on plenty of style.

Source: Sadie Frowne, "A Polish Sweatshop Girl," in Hamilton Holt, editor *The Life Stories of Undistinguished Americans as Told by Themselves* (originally 1906, republished New York: Routledge, 2000), pp. 21–28.

Thinking Critically

1. Documentary Analysis

According to the author, what led to her mother's decision to move to America?

2. Synthesis

What elements of the author's story make it typical of immigrant stories of the period?

---

poverty, criminal gangs, and chaos, some 4 million Italians, almost all from the south, left Italy between 1880 and 1914. Unlike the Jews coming from Russia, many of the Italian immigrants hoped one day to return home after making some money, and perhaps one in four did return. Those who came, whether temporarily or permanently, settled in major American cities and took on some of the hardest work at the bottom ranks of the American economy.

Russian Jews and southern Italian Catholics were far from alone. All across Europe, the population was growing faster than the land could support. Immigration provided a way out. Political upheaval in many places led to violence. Turkish violence against the Christian minority, especially the massacres of 1894, 1895, and 1896, led many Armenians to leave for America. Roman Catholics in Orthodox areas like Lithuania and Orthodox believers facing persecution in Catholic or Muslim countries wanted to move.

Chinese immigrants had been coming to the West Coast since the Gold Rush of 1849, but poverty and continued political turmoil kept them coming, though the numbers were slowed significantly after 1882 when Congress passed the **Chinese Exclusion Act**. Until 1882, immigration had been a relatively easy matter for the Chinese. If one could afford the passage, one simply booked it and then walked off the ship in San Francisco.

Chinese Exclusion Act
Federal legislation that suspended Chinese immigration, limited the civil rights of resident Chinese, and forbade their naturalization.

This Italian woman with her children at Ellis Island, the main Atlantic coast port of entry for immigrants, represented the way many families came to the United States. A father would come first and, later, after making some money, send for his wife and children, who followed on their own.

However, many in California and other parts of the West were threatened by the Chinese who by their sheer numbers increased the competition for jobs or mining claims. After a string of anti-immigrant petitions led Congress to change the law—the first time an entire nationality was barred from the country—only Chinese who could prove to the satisfaction of new immigration agents that they were either returning citizens or that they brought with them educational, economic, or diplomatic skills were allowed into the United States. Japanese immigrants, however, began to arrive, especially after 1885 when the emperor ended a ban on emigration and increased taxes to build up the government, causing many farmers to lose their fields.

In addition, about 300,000 French-Canadians moved from Quebec into the United States between 1860 and 1900, especially into New England and New York. Remote villages in Mexico experienced almost constant revolutionary violence in the late 1800s and early 1900s as regime followed regime. As a result, many Mexicans moved across the Rio Grande into the United States to find jobs on farms, mines, or fields in Texas and California, greatly expanding an earlier Mexican-American community that had been in the United States since the changing border made them Americans in the 1840s. Eventually some 4 million Italians, 2 million Russian Jews (one-third of all of the Jews in Russia), and 9 million other immigrants from almost every other part of the planet came to the United States in the 30-year period before 1920.

The Pull from an Industrializing United States

While there was good reason to leave Russia or Italy or Japan or Mexico, among other places, in the late 1800s, there were also reasons to want to come to the United States. The pull of opportunity was as important as the push of poverty and oppression. Although stories of the wealth to be found in the United States often led to terrible disappointment, the conditions in the United States were often still significantly better than what immigrants had left behind.

Prospective immigrants learned about jobs and opportunities from many sources. In a small village in Lithuania, Antanas Kaztauskis heard a man who lived in his village talk about the success of his son who was working in the stockyards in Chicago and who had sent his father a Lithuanian language newspaper from Chicago where the old man read of the rights of "life, liberty, and the getting of happiness."

American employers, often short of workers during economic boom times, advertised for help, even publishing a guidebook, *Where to Emigrate and Why,* in 1869. Steamship companies advertised for passengers, who could now, they claimed, take advantage of quicker travel times—14 days in 1867 and perhaps 6 days by 1900—all in safer and healthier conditions.

In Japan, farmers heard that a plantation laborer in the Kingdom of Hawaii could earn six times more than in Japan. It might be possible in a few years of working in Hawaii or the United States to save enough to return home, buy new land and make a fresh start in Japan. Many Japanese women saw the opportunity to start a new life as a "picture bride" for a Japanese immigrant who was already in Hawaii or the United States. In a culture in which arranged marriages were the norm and in which women were encouraged to become educated and make their own way in the world, the idea of women, traveling to a new land, starting a new life with a new husband, did not seem so strange. Riyo Orite, said of her experience, "I was engaged at the age of 16 and didn't meet Orite until I was almost 18. I had seen him only in a picture at first.... Being young, I was unromantic. I just believed that girls should get married....[P] eople around me praised the match."

Mexicans who returned after spending time in the United States came back to families and friends with "shoes and good suits of clothes." Others who moved north wrote to family and friends, "Come! Come! Come over, it is good here!" Jesus Garza remembered, "As I had heard a lot about the United States it was my dream to come here." And many did come.

The Reality—Jobs, Cities, and Americanization

When immigrants arrived in the United States, they did not always find what they had been expecting or hoping for. Italian immigrants often summed up their experience:

> Back in the old country, the young and naïve immigrants had been told that the streets of America were paved with gold. But when they got here, they discovered three important things: First, the streets weren't paved in gold; second, they weren't paved at all; and third, they were expected to pave them.

Few immigrants were quite as naïve as the story implies, but the popularity of the story in Italian immigrant communities says a lot about the reality of the immigration experience.

When arriving immigrants from Europe first landed, the authorities were not always welcoming. New York was the prime point of entry. In 1892, the federal government built a new immigration center on Ellis Island in the harbor, which replaced the old one at Castle Garden at the tip of Manhattan. Ellis Island combined quarantine, customs, and reception. Twelve million people came through Ellis Island before it closed in 1954. It could be an intimidating experience as clerks asked a battery of questions, trying to be sure that no physically or mentally ill people or troublemakers were allowed into the country. They did not make life easy for anyone. Nevertheless, only about two percent of those who arrived at Ellis Island were actually turned away. Those who were not permitted to enter typically either carried disease or came across in some way as unlikely to be able to support themselves.

During this process at Ellis Island, the clerks often gave immigrants a new anglicized name. A Russian named Cooperstein became Cooper, a Finn named Huttama became Hanson, or a Greek named Kiriacopoulis became Campbell. In one case, a German Jew became so confused with all the questions he was being asked that he forgot his own name. When he responded to the clerk's question about his name with "Ich vergesse" ("I forget"), the clerk registered him as Ferguson.

Steamships from Europe also docked in Boston or Philadelphia where the government established similar centers. Immigrants from Canada and Mexico were sometimes processed at border crossing points, while at other times, they simply walked or rode across the long borders between the countries. In the Southwest, people had long traveled back and forth across the Rio Grande, and they did not stop doing so.

On the Pacific coast, most immigrants came through the Port of San Francisco. In 1910, the federal government created a processing center on Angel Island in San Francisco Bay that was designed to be a kind of West Coast Ellis Island. Over the next 30 years 175,000 immigrants entered the United States through Angel Island, the vast majority of them Chinese. Similar but smaller stations were created in other ports, especially Seattle. Although Angel Island might have been designed as a counterpart to Ellis Island, it was a very different place. At both islands, immigrants faced frightening medical inspections and batteries of questions from federal immigration agents. But while most of those coming through Ellis Island left within a day, many on Angel Island were kept for weeks or months, occasionally for years. From the time of the passage of the Chinese Exclusion Act in 1882 until changes in U.S. policy in 1943, only Chinese immigrants who could prove that they were returning U.S. citizens or the children of U.S. citizens were allowed into the country. The Chinese immigrant population was essentially frozen at its 1882 levels. However, the destruction of all federal records in the earthquake and fire in San Francisco in April 1906 meant that if someone claimed to be a U.S. citizen, it was hard to disprove the claim. So-called "paper sons," came to the United States with high hopes that they could answer the required questions and gain admission to a country where they could make some money and avoid the wars and famine in China. Some succeeded. Others were deported back to China. As a result, Angel Island became a place of constant tension. Paul Chow, whose parents had come through Angel Island, remembered the fear the place evoked in his family. "Whenever my mother would mention it, she'd say, 'Angel Island, shhh,'" he said. "I thought it was all one word 'Angelislandshh.'"

Arrival at Angel Island in San Francisco might mean long waits in confining conditions for Asian immigrants like these Japanese women.

Melting pot
An often popular idea that somehow immigrants from other countries should quickly lose their culture and language and "melt" into being just like other Americans.

Although the phrase "**melting pot**" became a popular way to describe the influx of immigrants during the height of the immigration boom, the reality in United States was not quite what the popular phrase indicated. The term *melting pot* came from a play by Israel Zangwill, produced in New York in 1908, in which the hero wants to forget the pain of his life as a Jew in czarist Russia and announces that he is happy to be in America "God's Crucible," where he can be part of "the great Melting-Pot where all the races of Europe are melting and reforming." In fact, many of those who arrived had no interest in "melting" into a common American culture but were, instead, creating a richly diverse nation of far more ethnic and cultural variety than had ever been seen before.

For Jews arriving in New York, the next step after leaving Castle Garden or Ellis Island was often to make their way to the Lower East Side of Manhattan, the heart of the Jewish community. To be in the Lower East Side in the 1880s and 1890s was, as Rose Cohen said, as though "we were still in our village in Russia." There was little actual cultural melting going on, though people slowly took on more and more American ways. While one found friends there, living conditions were hard in some of those most crowded blocks in the country. The *American Magazine* described Lower East Side tenement housing in 1888:

> They are great prison-like structures of brick, with narrow doors and windows, cramped passages and steep rickety stairs....The narrow court-yard... in the middle is a damp foul-smelling place, supposed to do duty as an airshaft....In the hot summer months...these fire-escape balconies are used as sleeping-rooms by the poor wretches who are fortunate enough to have windows opening upon them.

Bathrooms were at the end of the hall and were shared by multiple apartments.

Most apartments were packed with people as families crowded into tiny rooms and took in borders who would help pay the rent. One 1908 survey found that 50 percent of families slept three or four persons to a room and another 25 percent had five or more persons per room.

Jewish immigrants found work where they could. Jewish peddlers sold nearly everything—fruit, vegetables, fish, clothing, kitchen utensils—filling streets like

Hester Street in New York's Lower East Side was the heart of the city's immigrant community.

Delancey Street with pushcart after pushcart, all selling something different and trying to convince passers-by to purchase. Even more Jewish immigrants found work in the garment industry. Many Russian Jews had survived as tailors (the Singer sewing machine was a major export from the United States to Russia). In America, skill with a needle meant a job. The demand for uniforms for the Union army led to the establishment of standard sizes for clothing, first for men and later for women, and this change allowed the development of mass-produced rather than individualized clothing. Because of the development of standard sizes, the garment trade was able to shift from made-to-order work for the elite to mass production of clothing for everyone. Men's suits and pants, women's dresses and shirtwaists, as blouses were called, were produced in the thousands, making the clothing business a major industry.

At first, garment work was done at home as families or small groups took in piece work and returned the finished products. Later, larger factories, known as **sweatshops**, brought together sometimes hundreds of workers who were expected to sew at a fast pace for long hours to ensure that they kept their jobs and the owners made a decent profit. One could walk for blocks in southern Manhattan and see nothing but such

Sweatshops
Small, poorly ventilated shops or apartments crammed with workers, often family members, who pieced together garments.

Garment workers sewing by hand in a small New York City sweatshop in 1908. Photograph by Lewis Hine.

work going on from early morning to late evening. In spite—or perhaps because—of the harsh living and working conditions, New York's Jewish community grew strong. Russian Jews had no intention of returning to Russia where pogroms and poverty reigned. They established synagogues, foreign language newspapers provided news, and some 300 Hebrew schools maintained their language and culture.

Italian immigrants also created their own neighborhoods. In Chicago, Taylor Street became the heart of Little Italy. In Milwaukee, the Third Ward on the east side was the heart of the Italian community where some 20 Italian grocery stores existed on Brady Street alone. In Boston, the North End and East Boston housed Italian communities. And in New York, many Italian immigrants, like Russian Jewish immigrants, moved to the Lower East Side of Manhattan.

THINKING HISTORICALLY
The Pull of Nostalgia, the Push to Continue

In 1906, the *Jewish Daily Forward*, a Yiddish-language newspaper serving Jewish immigrants, began carrying an advice column in which the editor, Abraham Cahan responded to letters. One writer, a recent immigrant from Russia, said:

Oh, my poor dear parents, how saddened they were at my leaving. The leave-taking, their seeing me on my way, was like a silent funeral....I came to America and became a painter. My great love for Hebrew, for Russian, all my other knowledge was smeared with paint. During the year that I have been here I have had some good periods, but I am not happy because I have no interest in anything. My homesickness and loneliness darken my life....I want to run back...and I beg you to be my counsel as to how to act.

The editor was blunt noting that "almost all immigrants yearn deeply for dear ones and home at first," but that the young man "must not consider going home, but try to take root here. He should try to overcome all these emotions and strive to make something of himself so that in time he will be able to bring his parents here."

That same year, Hamilton Holt, editor of the New York *Independent*, published *The Life Stories of Undistinguished Americans As Told by Themselves,* 27 accounts of the immigrant experience including several by those who considered a return to their homeland but who had decided against it. An Italian immigrant who shined shoes in New York City who wrote:

We had said that when we saved $1,000 each we would go back to Italy and buy a farm, but now that the time is coming we are so busy and making so much money that we think we will stay.

A Swedish immigrant who prospered as a farmer in Minnesota wrote:

Father and mother kept writing to the children in America that now they had made their fortunes they should come home and live, but they put it off....I am going over to

Sweden soon to keep Christmas there....but will come back again, and maybe bring other people with us. Some Swedes go to the old country every Christmas.

A modern researcher, Erika Lee, found that her great-great-great-grandfather, Moy Dong Kee, had come to California in 1854, before the Chinese Exclusion Act limited Chinese mobility. Though he stayed in the United States for 52 years, he was able to make at least three trips to visit his family who remained in China. He finally retired to China in 1906 at the age of 72.

Some immigrants indeed traveled back and forth often. Others made their fortunes in America and then returned to their homelands. Perhaps a quarter or more of all Italian immigrants eventually returned to Italy, an unusually high percentage among immigrant communities, but a little money earned in America could translate into land ownership in Italy. In other immigrant communities—especially among Russian Jews facing pogroms and conscription into the czarist army—very few ever returned. The pull of nostalgia and the usually stronger push to continue to make a life in their new adopted home was part of the life of almost every immigrant.

Source: Isaac Metzker, *A Bintel Brief: Sixty Years of Letters from the Lower East Side to the Jewish Daily Forward* (New York: Doubleday, 1971), pp. 117–118. cited in Robert D. Marcus, et al, *America Firsthand: Volume Two, Readings from Reconstruction to the Present* (Boston: Bedford/St. Martins, 2004), pp. 121–122.

Thinking Critically

1. Crafting an Argument
What do the reasons immigrants gave for wanting to leave or wanting to stay tell you about their reasons for immigrating in the first place?

2. Contextualization
Why might some immigrants have found it easier than others to return to their home country? Why was such a trip almost impossible for others?

Since most Italian immigrants came from the rural poverty of southern Italy, they had few marketable skills when they got to the United States. Like Russian Jews, some became pushcart owners, selling fruits and vegetables. Others opened restaurants. More than a few became the laborers who built the cities where they lived: New York, Chicago, Milwaukee, and Boston all have water and sewer lines dug by Italian laborers. Gender roles were, perhaps, more rigidly defined in the Italian immigrant communities than elsewhere. Italian families tried every way they could to encourage married women to stay at home and to depend on the men to earn a living for the family.

For the 900,000 French Canadians who emigrated to the United States between 1840 and 1930, the move south meant escape from rural poverty and a chance for a new start, especially in the mills of New England. More than most immigrant groups, those coming from Quebec tended to bring their priests (nearly all French Canadians were Catholic), doctors, lawyers, and grocers with them, all of whom were sure that life might be better—or at least marginally more prosperous—in rapidly industrializing New York and New England than in the isolated farms of Quebec.

Like the Italians and the French Canadians, Mexican immigrants often moved back and forth between the United States and home communities, but in their case, that move meant crossing only a river rather than an ocean. Nevertheless, more and more immigrants from Mexico eventually made permanent homes in the United States, creating the *barrios,* which were often extensions of Mexican communities that had long stretched along the border from Texas to California.

Mexican-American communities, like those of European immigrants, often reflected quite different home regions. One immigrant remembered, "We came to know families from Chihuahua, Sonora, Jalisco, and Durango. Some had come to the United States even before the revolution, living in Texas before migrating to California." The barrio was also home in other ways. Immigrants from Mexico could find familiar food, including tamales, frijoles, tortillas, and menudo. They could see traditional clothing, enjoy traditional holidays and festivals, and feel much less like strangers in someone else's land.

For all Catholic immigrants, the Catholic Church was an essential link with their faith and their past. At the end of the U.S. Civil War, there were 42 dioceses and 3,000 Catholic churches in the United States. By 1900, there were 70 dioceses and 10,000 churches, many serving specific ethnic communities. The Italian parish, the Polish parish, the Mexican parish, and the German parish might be in very close proximity, but they served their own group, often offering parochial schools and classes in a home language that was important to parents coping with children growing up in an English-speaking society.

Those who entered the United States from Asia found different kinds of work in their own ethnic communities. Chinese immigrants such as Lee Chew found work when they could:

> When I got to San Francisco…[a] man got me work as a house servant in an
> American family, and my start was the same as that of almost all the Chinese
> in this country. The Chinese laundryman does not learn his trade in China;
> there are no laundries in China….All Chinese laundrymen here were taught in
> the first place by American women just as I was taught.

For the Japanese in Hawaii (an independent country until 1898), housing and work were found on the sugar plantations, which were new to them. Hawaiian companies encouraged whole families to immigrate, believing that "dependable married men" made better workers, though both women and men were given jobs in the fields. Japanese communities were able to establish themselves with their own traditions, religious practices including Buddhist temples, Japanese-language schools for children, and festivals including the Emperor's Birthday when work ceased in spite of the frustration of the plantation owners. In time, Japanese, Portuguese, Chinese, and native Hawaiian workers got to know one another other, exchanged food, and developed real if tenuous friendships.

17.4 **Quick Review** Which were more important in bringing immigrants to the United States in the late 1800s and early 1900s—the push factors or the pull factors? Give at least three reasons to justify your answer.

[handwritten margin notes: Gilded Age / wealthy / middle class / poverty / creation of / new cultures]

CONCLUSION

The well-named Gilded Age was a time of great extremes. In the decades after the Civil War, Americans built bigger corporations, cities, and buildings than ever before. Some made huge fortunes and lived a life of lavish spending. Other Americans created a new middle class. Still others, especially immigrants living in tightly packed urban communities, lived on the edge of poverty while also creating new cultures with their own values and norms. All of them created a vastly different nation than any previous generation had known.

During the Gilded Age, America emerged as an industrial giant. Technological innovation and vast reserves of coal, oil, steel, and timber, along with well-established but expanding railroad networks, fueled a growing economy. New forms of corporate ownership developed to direct and manage large-scale industrial operations, and private investment banks grew immensely rich and influential along with the industrialists whose ventures they helped to finance. The few who managed to generate great wealth often spent lavishly on homes and possessions as a reflection of their power and position, sealing the reputation of the period as one of shameless excess gotten by ruthless economic exploitation.

While a few grew enormously wealthy, a new middle class also emerged in the Gilded Age. Made up mostly of the families of men who worked at the middle levels and managed the large new corporations, the middle class created its own new lifestyle. City services—from a healthy supply of water to new high-rise buildings with elevators to giant department stores catered to the needs of this growing middle class. Many in the middle class also sought some distance from the cities, and the rail and trolley lines facilitated the growth of suburbs in which large private homes replaced apartments and people enjoyed a mix of urban and rural amenities. From religion to sports to politics, the United States catered to the new middle class.

The rapidly expanding new industries needed workers, and the call for workers exerted a pull on people living in far distant places, including Russia, Italy, China, and Japan. At the same time, developments in these and other countries were creating a push that led many to want to leave. Whether it was the anti-Jewish pogroms in Russia or the grinding poverty of Italy or the civil wars that wracked China, the chance to leave for a better life was so appealing that the United States experienced a massive era of immigration between 1880 and 1914. Once in the United States, immigrants were not always welcomed. Many native-born Americans distrusted what they saw as foreign cultures. Many immigrants resisted giving up old ways. But the jobs—though low level and low pay—were there and immigrants began working in agriculture and in the booming urban sweatshops that were clothing the country and the world.

As a result of all of these changes, by 1900, the United States was a very different place than it had been only a few short decades earlier.

CHAPTER REVIEW What were the three biggest differences in the United States in 1900 as a result of the events, trends, and innovations of the Gilded Age?

Chapter 17   Chapter Review

TECHNOLOGY CHANGES THE NATION

17.1 Explain the inventions of the late 1800s and their impact.

Review Questions

1. **Crafting an Argument**
   In your opinion, what was the most important technological innovation of the late 1800s? Why?

2. **Historical Interpretation**
   How does the rise of the automobile industry illustrate the connection between technological innovation and industrial growth and consolidation in the late 1800s and early 1900s?

CORPORATIONS AND MONOPOLIES

17.2 Analyze the role of the new giant corporations in American life.

Review Questions

3. **Historical Interpretation**
   What does the Panic of 1873 tell us about the role of speculation in the American economy of the late 1800s?

4. **Comparison**
   Compare and contrast American manufacturing in the early 1900s and the late 1900s. What had changed? Why?

5. **Historical Interpretation**
   What does J. P. Morgan's involvement in the Panic of 1893 and in its resolution tell us about the nature of American industry at the turn of the century?

LIVES OF THE MIDDLE CLASS IN THE GILDED AGE

17.3 Analyze daily life, popular ideas, and political direction for the middle class during the Gilded Age.

Review Questions

6. **Contextualization**
   How did architecture and urban design of the late 1800s reflect middle-class values and aspirations?

7. **Synthesis**
   What connections can you make between the growth of American business and changes in American religious life in the late 1800s?

IMMIGRATION

17.4 Explain the reasons immigrants came to the United States in such large numbers during the Gilded Age and what their experience was.

Review Questions

8. **Cause and Effect**
   What factors explain the migration of large numbers of eastern European Jews to the United States at the turn of the century?

9. **Comparison**
   What did immigrants hope to find in America? How did their expectations compare with reality?

10. **Historical Interpretation**
    What might explain the formation of ethnic neighborhoods in the late 1800s? What advantages did such neighborhoods provide to new immigrants?

18 Responses to Industrialism, Responses to Change

Drivers and mules with young laborers in a West Virginia coal mine in a 1908 photo by Lewis Hine.

CHAPTER OBJECTIVE

Demonstrate an understanding of how the rapid industrialization after the Civil War impacted the lives of diverse people and the rise of distinct resistance movements.

LEARNING OBJECTIVES

CONFLICT IN THE NEW SOUTH

18.1 Analyze how the combined impact of industrialism and the end of Reconstruction created the unique character of the New South.

THE POLITICS OF CONFLICT—FROM POPULIST MOVEMENT TO POPULIST PARTY

18.2 Analyze how agrarian unrest and protest came to have a significant impact on American politics.

WORKER PROTEST AND THE RISE OF ORGANIZED LABOR

18.3 Explain the tensions in industrial America that led to major labor strife between the 1870s and 1914.

When he accepted the nomination of the newly growing Socialist Party for president in the 1912 presidential elections, Eugene V. Debs said:

> The world's workers have always been and still are the world's slaves. They have…produced all the world's wealth and supported all the world's governments. They have conquered all things but their own freedom.

It was the goal of the Socialist Party, Debs said, to win that freedom. Debs had an expansive goal for his political organization—a party for women and men, blacks and whites, struggling farmers as well as factory and railroad workers. When the presidential election was held in November, Debs won some 900,000 votes, or 6 percent of the total. Although that percentage was small, it reflected nonetheless unusual support for a nontraditional candidate.

In a nation in the midst of rapid social change, Debs sought to speak for those being hurt by the changes. Although he failed to rally as many as he hoped to his political banner, his campaign reflected the deep tensions in the United States in the late 1800s and early 1900s. In the face of extraordinary technological and industrial change, many were angry. This chapter traces the reasons so many Americans were angry in the years between 1877 and 1914 and the results of that anger in reshaping the political and cultural life of the nation. Chapter 19 traces the ways that yet other Americans began to tackle the problems of this era.

CONFLICT IN THE NEW SOUTH

18.1 Analyze how the combined impact of industrialism and the end of Reconstruction created the unique character of the New South.

In 1886, the young editor of the *Atlanta Constitution*, Henry Grady, was invited to New York City to speak at the prestigious New England Society of New York, one of the city's most elite groups. Coming 20 years after the end of the Civil War, the invitation was quite an honor for a Southern newspaper editor. The society, like Grady, was ready for a fresh start regarding the nation's regional differences. Grady was in New York to tell his audience that a **New South** had been born. The New South was not like the old version. It had been born, Grady said, out of the defeat of the South's "brave armies" in the late war and the ending of slavery. A new day had begun. But it had begun under leaders who, though moving in new ways, were proud of their past and wanted to be clear, "The South has nothing for which to apologize.…The South has nothing to take back."

The New South meant several things to Grady. First, Grady was saying that that the South was done apologizing for the Civil War, for slavery, and for the increasingly rigid social, political, and economic segregation that was developing in place of slavery. On race relations, the South, Grady said, wanted to be left alone. Grady was also announcing that the South had come of age economically. It was building railroads and industrializing at an impressive pace, and Southerners wanted to be fully integrated into the economic prosperity of the rest of the nation. On the economic front, the New South that Grady was discussing was indeed different from the Old South.

Economic Development and Economic Optimism

The pre–Civil War South had been dominated by agriculture. In the New South, sawmills, factories, mines, and railroads were being built, and old wooden buildings were being replaced with new brick ones in many towns. Optimism was growing, though not everyone was celebrating. The decline in the price of cotton was devastating farmers, and for most African-Americans, segregation and exclusion made life almost unbearable. Nevertheless, for a fortunate subset of white Southerners, the years between 1875 and 1900 were a time for optimism.

Before the Civil War, the South had far fewer miles of railroad track than the North. Catching up on railroad construction was a key element in defining the **New South**. The new railroads brought all sorts of change. The investment in building railroads—much of it Northern or European money—brought work to many Southerners, not only those who did the actual work of laying track but also those supporting them. As one Mississippi resident noted, "The women and children were busy producing vegetable crops, chickens, eggs, milk and butter, and the men were butchering and delivering fresh meat and other supplies to the men working on the railroad." Once the new lines were in place, there were also jobs working on the railroads. The work was dangerous and injuries were common, but the pay was better than anything many Southerners had seen.

The rail lines provided Southerners with important new connections to the outside world (see Maps 18-1A and 18-1B). A generation earlier, rail lines had connected many parts of the North, but when the rail lines finally reached an isolated town like Harrison, Arkansas, in February 1900, the local newspaper announced, "Harrison is a Rail-road Town At Last." Henry Hammond, an astute observer of Southern life, pointed out that country people "who formerly were satisfied with their weekly paper, who went to town annually or semiannually, in some instances not more than two

Significant Dates

1877	Great Railroad Strike
1882	Agricultural Wheel farmers' organization launched
1886	Haymarket bombing
	Henry Grady announces the "New South"
	Charles W. Macune elected president of the Farmers' Alliance beginning its rapid growth
1890	New Mississippi state constitution effectively excludes blacks from voting
	Farmers' Alliance establishes headquarters in Washington, DC
	United Mine Workers of America founded in Columbus, Ohio
1891	The People's Party (Populists) launched
1892	Homestead strike
1893	American Railway Union organized
1894	Coxey's Army marches on Washington, DC
	Pullman strike
1896	U.S. Supreme Court's *Plessy v. Ferguson* decision
	William Jennings Bryan runs for president on Democratic and Populist Party tickets
1905	Industrial Workers of the World organized
	Niagara Movement organized
1909	National Association for the Advancement of Colored People launched
1911	Triangle Shirtwaist Fire
1912	Bread and Roses strike in Lawrence, Massachusetts
1914	Colorado miner's strike

18.1

18.2

18.3

New South
An ideology developed by some elite Southerners that declared an end to the nostalgia for slavery and plantation life and a beginning for the economic development of the South while protecting the growing racial segregation of the region from any Northern interference.

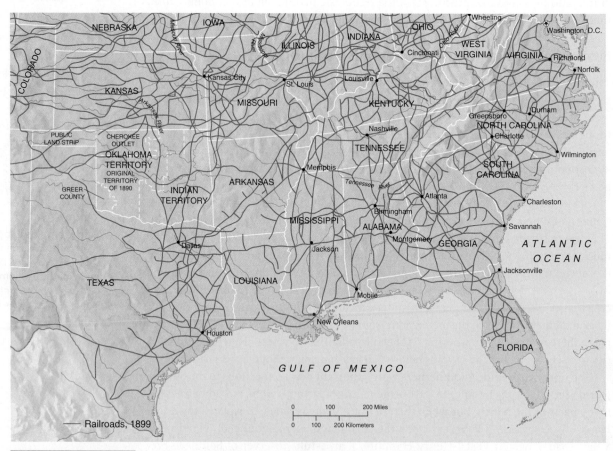

MAP 18-1A and MAP 18-1B Expanding Southern Railroads, 1859–1899. Map 1A at top illustrates the extent of railroad lines in 1859 on the eve of the Civil War. Map 1B illustrates the expansion of rail lines by 1899.

or three times during a long life, can now go quickly, safely, pleasantly and cheaply several times a day." Farms were connected to towns, and towns to cities beyond the imaginings of people's parents and grandparents.

The railroads that brought people to town also brought goods from around the world while shipping goods that the South produced to world markets. Country stores sold manufactured goods that made life easier and fertilizer that made the land more productive.

In many small towns, stores also sold goods on credit, making them virtually banks. In this capacity, stores also accepted fields planted in cotton as collateral for loans, as cotton remained the prime cash crop of the South.

In addition to cotton, new industries were growing in the South in the 1880s. Sawmills and turpentine camps produced lumber and turpentine that was shipped around the world. Phosphate mining expanded but was then eclipsed by coal mining as new markets demanded coal. Tobacco, which the South had shipped to the world since the 1600s, became a growth industry. Using effective advertising and marketing skills, Julian Carr shipped his Bull Durham tobacco bags worldwide, and Washington Duke and his son James shipped prerolled cigarettes that quickly became the most popular way to enjoy "clean, quick, and potent" tobacco. Iron and steel were produced at the South's fastest growing city of Birmingham. The South's textile production, which had involved 10,000 people in 1870 (as it had in 1850), employed almost 100,000 by 1900. Finally, a new product, Coca-Cola, developed by Asa G. Candler in 1889, became highly popular and, eventually, a drink of choice for many on every continent.

Nostalgia and Celebration of the "Lost Cause"

The rapid changes in the South made some uneasy. The movement of Southerners—white and black—in search of jobs and economic opportunities created a sense of dislocation. C. L. Pettigrew of North Carolina, like many others, remembered a slower pace and complained about "that striving, rough and eager crowd." Others mourned to see "the white-columned porticos of the favorite colonial architecture now maundering in decay," as ambitious young people moved to opportunities elsewhere.

Simmering in the South were deep generational tensions between Confederate veterans and those who had been born too late to remember the war. A Texas veteran wrote to the legislature, asking them to be sure that "the sons of Confederates and the public generally" remember the Lost Cause. Another ex-Confederate, Wade Hampton, insisted, "I believe now, as always, that the South was right." For veterans like Hampton and others and for Southern widows of those who had died in the war, the memory of the "Lost Cause" as a glorious time and a righteous fight made the pain of a sometimes lonely and often economically challenging present more bearable.

Southern writers produced romantic stories of the "Lost Cause" of the Civil War and the days of slavery that preceded it. Thomas Nelson Page, of a prominent Virginia family, created the "plantation school" of writing, recounting tales of a chivalrous past. Page also started the tradition of the wise and loyal slave, who, Page told his white readers, longed for the days before the war when everyone had a secure place in a well-ordered society. The most famous author of the plantation school, Joel Chandler Harris, created the fictional elderly black man, Uncle Remus, and his animal alter-ego, Brer Rabbit. The Uncle Remus stories first published in the *Atlanta Constitution* in 1879 and then as a popular book, portrayed the Old South as a romantic and happy place.

This ad from the 1890s introduces the new drink, Coca Cola, which was one of the many new industries that emerged in the South.

Religion in the New South

Religion also played a crucial role in the post-Reconstruction South. Southerners did not actually attend church in greater numbers than their Northern counterparts, but religious imagery and biblical language were a strong part of the South's culture. With the coming of freedom, Southern blacks quickly joined or established their own churches. By 1890, there were 1.3 million black Baptists in the South. Northern black churches, especially the African Methodist Episcopal and African Methodist Episcopal Zion denominations, also built churches for Southern blacks. The black church became the place in the segregated South where former slaves could meet with a measure of safety, share and build and new communal identity, and control the intellectual and cultural life of their own institution.

White Southerners also gravitated to churches in the 1880s and 1890s. Baptist bodies were the largest group of white churches in the South, but the Methodists claimed almost as many members. Also strong were the Disciples of Christ, the Presbyterians, and in certain areas of the South, Episcopalians and Roman Catholics. In white and black churches, nearly all of the clergy were male, but women could play a large role in the churches, particularly through women's associations and mission groups, which provided necessary support to these churches and through which women could exercise a level of autonomy.

Creating the Segregated South

The railroads that knit the New South together quickly became the focus of the South's great unresolved issue—race. Even though the political rights of African-Americans had been declining in the South since the defeat of Reconstruction in the 1870s, the South of the 1880s and early 1890s was not the rigidly segregated place it would become by 1900. Churches were segregated by custom and choice. Schools, hospitals, and hotels were generally segregated by law. Blacks were confined to the balcony in most theaters, and the races did not mix in restaurants. However, in many places of work, at many political gatherings, and in travel, blacks and whites could be found together in the South of the late 1800s. The railroads were certainly not going to build separate lines or even run separate trains, and most railroads saw all talk of racial segregation as potentially troublesome and expensive. Nevertheless, trouble was brewing.

As passenger railroads developed in the South between 1865 and 1880, they generally offered two classes of service—a first-class car for women and men who did not smoke or chew tobacco, and a second-class car—often a section of the baggage car—for men who used tobacco or people too poor to buy a first-class ticket. In some cases, blacks were assumed to belong in the second-class car with the tobacco-using white men; however, in many cases, blacks rode first class without incident. In any case, a trip that might start without incident could quickly turn ugly. In the early 1880s, a black man was asked by the conductor to leave the first-class car after the train crossed the state line from Tennessee to Georgia. When he refused, he was badly beaten by other passengers. In 1889, a delegation from the first African Baptist Church of Savannah, Georgia, started their journey to a church convention in Indianapolis, Indiana, on the East Tennessee, Virginia and Georgia Railroad. The well-dressed delegates started out comfortably in first class, but they were met at a subsequent train stop by a mob of 50 white men with pistols and clubs who attacked them and threatened to "blow your G-d-d brains out."

While the railroads did not want to take action, state legislatures did. In railroad cars, people of different races—and equally important,

A conductor evicts a well-dressed black man from a first-class coach. Enforcing segregation on the railroad coach was seen by many white southerners as somehow essential to protecting white women.

genders—might mix in especially close contact given the close seating. During the late 1800s, whites were developing an especially great fear of any contact between black men and white women. As one person wrote, a man "would be horrified at the idea of his wife or daughter seated by the side of a burly negro." Tennessee was the first state to respond, enacting a law saying, "All railroad companies shall furnish separate cars, or portions of cars cut off by partition wall, which all colored passengers who pay first-class rates of fare may have the privilege to enter and occupy." The law seemed to imply that it was up to blacks whether they wanted to be segregated or not, but clearly that idea was not the way the arrangement worked. Across the South, trains were rigidly segregated a decade before the 1896 U.S. Supreme Court's 7-to-1 decision in *Plessy* v. *Ferguson* declared that "separate but equal" transportation—and, by implication, other matters—did not violate the equal protection clause of the Fourteenth Amendment to the U.S. Constitution.

The Politics of Exclusion

The end of the racially integrated governments of the Reconstruction era and the almost complete exclusion of African-Americans from the political life of the South took place in two distinct stages between the 1870s and 1900. These stages are often merged in the popular mind as if they happened all at once, though they did not.

The first step in ending Reconstruction took place in the 1860s and 1870s (see Chapter 14). Black legislators and white legislators who supported them (all of whom were Republicans) were defeated by white Democratic segregationists at different times in different states, nearly always in elections marked by violence and voter intimidation. Virginia was the first to shift from a Republican to a Democratic legislature in 1869. Conservative Democrats soon also won large majorities in other states—North Carolina in 1870, Georgia in 1871, Texas in 1873, Alabama and Arkansas in 1874, and South Carolina and Mississippi in 1876. Finally, contested elections in Louisiana and Florida were awarded to the Democrats in 1877 as part of the same compromise that put Hayes in the White House. The withdrawal of most federal troops that the newly inaugurated Hayes ordered in 1877 was thus the culmination, not the cause of the end of Reconstruction.

However, the defeat of Reconstruction was not the end of the story. While every Southern state had a conservative Democratic legislature and governor after 1877, quite a few blacks still voted and some were still elected and appointed to public offices in the South for another decade. Black voters could provide the margin of victory in close contests. Most state legislatures had at least a few African-American representatives, and many federally appointed officials from postmasters to census officials were black. In 1891, as the Arkansas legislature was debating railroad segregation, it was a black legislator, John Gray Lucas, who objected. It was also a black delegate to Mississippi's 1895 state constitutional convention, Thomas E. Miller, who told the majority that they needed to remember, "It was your love of power and your arrogance which brought Reconstruction on you."

In most cases, the few black office holders remaining were too few in number to have an impact. Nevertheless, some whites objected to the close interactions that challenged racial and gender conventions in certain offices such as when a white woman visited the post office to be helped by a black male postmaster. When the Republicans won the White House and Congress in 1888, some white Southerners feared a repeat of Reconstruction, perhaps even the appointment of federal election officials who would monitor Southern election procedures. At the same time, a new generation of Southern whites were tired of the Klan-style violence that accompanied elections. An1889 article in the Jackson, Mississippi, *Clarion-Ledger* said, "The old men of the present generation can't afford to die and leave the election to their children and grandchildren, with shot guns in their hands, a lie in their mouths and perjury on their lips in order to defeat the negroes." The solution to the election violence that the newspaper wanted was not to hold fair and race-neutral elections but, rather, to establish legal means to exclude all blacks from all political participation.

Fears of black political involvement grew in the 1890s when the Populist movement disrupted Southern politics. It was one thing for a handful of blacks in the state legislature to raise questions about a bill before the white majority voted for whatever it wanted. It was a different matter if the white Democratic majority was split between Populist and traditional factions and the black representatives had the tie-breaking votes or if, as happened in North Carolina, a Populist-Republican ticket, with black support, could actually win the majority of seats in a state legislature. In 1896, South Carolina's arch-segregationist Governor Ben Tillman warned of an "unholy alliance between the independents and the negroes."

For many Southern whites, the solution was a new set of laws that would ensure "white supremacy" forever. Political leaders called new state constitutional conventions to ensure that they secured absolute power. Blacks and their white allies had been marginalized by the violence and the voting that ended Reconstruction, but the new state constitutions of the 1890s moved from marginalization to complete exclusion. When the work of these new constitutional conventions was done, extremely few black voters and no black office holders remained anywhere in what came to be known as the "solid South," which meant solidly white and Democratic.

Mississippi rewrote its state constitution in 1890, creating what looked like color-blind obstacles that would, in practice, stop all blacks from voting. The most obvious restrictions—a literacy test or a poll tax or a property qualification for voters—would also exclude many poor whites who were themselves illiterate and who could not meet a property qualification or pay a poll tax. So Mississippi's delegates created a complex set of limitations on voting and office. To be able to vote, the new constitution said, a person had to have lived in the state for at least 2 years and in the election district for at least 1; a sharecropper who moved for a better chance at life thus lost the right to participate in elections at least for a time. Other states instituted "grandfather clauses" that said anyone whose grandfather had been a voter was exempt from other restrictions, a privilege no descendent of slaves could claim. Those intending to vote in Mississippi and elsewhere could not do so if they had been convicted of petty crimes such as arson, bigamy, or petty theft, crimes that blacks were routinely charged with. Ironically, conviction for murder, rape, or grand larceny did not exclude one from voting. The Mississippi convention did require a modest poll tax. Finally, the convention adopted a requirement that every voter be able to understand and interpret the state constitution. White state-appointed registrars would decide whose interpretation was "reasonable." An editorial in the Jackson, Mississippi, *Clarion-Ledger* described the new system: "[I]f every negro in Mississippi was a graduate of Harvard…he would not be as well fitted to exercise the right of suffrage as the Anglo-Saxon farm laborer." Once the new Mississippi Constitution took effect, it had its intended impact. Once other Southern states observed what was happening in Mississippi, they too adopted the approach.

After the U.S. Supreme Court declared poll taxes and literacy tests to be constitutional in their 1898 ruling in *Williams* v. *Mississippi,* there was little chance that any Southern state would fail to enact such Mississippi-style voting tests. In 1908, Texas became the last state of the former Confederacy to add a poll tax, and across the region, that tax was usually one of several mechanisms that ended black voting.

Then, as though all of the new laws were not enough, a new form of violence toward African-Americans emerged in the late 1800s. Where the Klan and other groups had terrorized black communities during Reconstruction, the spectacle of public lynching became widespread in the following years. Individual African-Americans, often young men, were singled out, often accused with little or no evidence of raping a white woman, and hung in a public spectacle. The issue was rarely an actual rape but, more often, a young black man's failure to observe the customs of stepping out of the way for a white person to pass or a black man's challenging the payment of a landowner at the sharecroppers settle, or a black man asserting his political rights. Most of all, lynching was a way to strike terror into the black community while asserting and celebrating white dominance. In 1900, the New South was fast becoming a region governed exclusively by white voters and white elected officials and would remain so until the black Civil Rights movement of the 1950s, 1960s, and 1970s transformed the region and the nation.

African-American Responses

As the rigid segregation of "separate but equal," which everyone knew meant separate and very unequal, settled on the South and, indeed, much of the country, especially after 1896, African-Americans debated how to respond to a legal system that excluded them from voting. In addition, they considered their response to being barred from access to quality schooling and to any but the most menial jobs as well as to being restricted from entering rail cars, hotels, or theaters that served whites. They also argued responses to cultural expectations that they "give way," allowing whites to pass in front of them in stores and on sidewalks, that they call all whites by their last names while they were called by their first names by whites, and that they live with the oppressive knowledge that even the slightest challenge to segregation could be met with not only ostracism but also unimaginable violence.

Ida B. Wells (1862–1931) was one of the African-Americans who challenged the lynchings that were a key part of the violence used to maintain segregation. Between 1889 and 1918, 386 lynchings took place in Georgia, 373 in Mississippi, and similar numbers in several other states. Wells argued that the rape charge, which was often the excuse for lynching a black man, was a "thread-bare lie" and a cover for punishing any black man who challenged the rules of segregation. In response to her writing, a white mob destroyed her printing press at her *Memphis Free Press,* but throughout her life, she continued to write, publish, and organize legal challenges to segregation and especially its maintenance through the violence of lynchings.

In the face of the harsh reality of segregation and exclusion, Booker T. Washington (1856–1915), perhaps the nation's best-known African-American leader, argued that it was time to adjust to segregation rather than challenge the laws and customs excluding blacks. Washington urged blacks to create an economic foundation for themselves. In the midst of the harsh realities of the 1890s, Washington's course of action seemed the only realistic option.

Not all African-Americans agreed with Washington, and a young African-American scholar, W.E.B. Du Bois (1868–1963), became his harshest critic. Du Bois criticized compromises and wrote that "the problem of the twentieth century is the problem of the color line." He described the kind of "double consciousness" or "twon-ess" that African-Americans were forced to develop in a country that proclaimed liberty but excluded them by law and custom.

In 1905, Du Bois joined other African-American leaders meeting at Niagara Falls—in a hotel on the Canadian side because no hotel on the American side would give them rooms—to begin a campaign for "every single right that belongs to a free-born American, political, civil, and social" without compromise. The **Niagara Movement** that emerged from the conference fought for an end to segregation and for full equality for African-Americans. Four years later, in February 1909, Du Bois, others from

Ida B. Wells-Barnett became the most effective national spokesperson for the antilynching crusade.

Niagara Movement
African-American group organized in 1905 to promote racial integration, civil and political rights, and equal access to economic opportunity; the movement later helped organize the NAACP.

THINKING HISTORICALLY

Debating Booker T. Washington's "Cast Down Your Buckets Where You Are" Speech

On September 18, 1895, Booker T. Washington gave a speech to a mostly white audience at the Cotton States and International Exposition in Atlanta, Georgia. Washington came to the exposition at the height of his career to offer what came to be known as the **Atlanta Compromise**—that African-Americans would accept segregation in return for being able to develop economically. So Washington said:

> To those of my race...I would say: "Cast down your bucket where you are"—cast it down in making friends in every manly way with the people of all races with whom we are surrounded. Cast it down in agriculture, mechanics, in commerce, in domestic service, and in the professions. . . . In all things that are purely social we can be as separate as the fingers, yet one as the hand in all things essential to mutual progress. . . .The wisest among my race understand that the agitation of questions of social equality is the extremist folly, and that progress in the enjoyment of all the privileges that will come to us must be the result of severe and constant struggle rather than of artificial forcing. No race that has anything to contribute to the markets of the world is long in any degree ostracized. It is important and right that all privileges of the law be ours, but it is vastly more important that we be prepared for the exercise of these privileges. The opportunity to earn a dollar in a factory just now is worth infinitely more than the opportunity to spend a dollar in an opera-house.

At the time, the speech was greeted with great applause, most of all, on the part of Northern white philanthropists who poured money into Tuskegee and other ventures supported by Washington.

Eight years later in 1903, W. E. B. Du Bois published *The Souls of Black Folk*. Du Bois was unsparing in his judgment, writing:

> Mr. Washington represents in Negro thought the old attitude of adjustment and submission . . . . . .In answer to this, it has been claimed that the Negro can survive only through submission. Mr. Washington distinctly asks that black people give up, at least for the present, three things—
>
> First, political power,
>
> Second, insistence on civil rights,
>
> Third, higher education of Negro youth—

And concentrate all their energies on industrial education, the accumulation of wealth, and the conciliation of the South. This policy has been courageously and insistently advocated for over fifteen years, and has been triumphant for perhaps ten years. As a result of this tender of the palm-branch, what has been the return? In these years there have occurred:

1. The disfranchisement of the Negro.
2. The legal creation of a distinct status of civil inferiority for the Negro.
3. The steady withdrawal of aid from institutions for the higher training of the Negro.

These movements are not, to be sure, direct results of Mr. Washington's teachings; but his propaganda has, without a shadow of doubt, helped their speedier accomplishment. The question then comes: Is it possible, and probable, that nine millions of men can make effective progress in economic lines if they are deprived of political rights, made a servile caste, and allowed only the most meager chance for developing their exceptional men?

Considering these quotes, the lines between Du Bois and Washington could not have been starker. In reality, they were not as stark as the two documents imply. Privately, Washington provided funds for court challenges of segregation and challenged lynchings, but unlike Du Bois, he had been born in slavery and lived and worked in Alabama in the heart of a segregated world. Du Bois, a generation younger, was raised in the North, and had much less patience with any form of accommodation. Nevertheless, between them, the two leaders outlined differences that remained in the African-American community for decades.

Source: Booker T. Washington, *Up From Slavery: An Autobiography* (New York: Doubleday-Page, 1901); W.E.B. Du Bois, *The Souls of Black Folk* (Chicago: A.C. McClurg, 1903).

Thinking Critically

1. **Comparison**

   What do you see as the starkest differences between Washington and Du Bois?

2. **Contextualization**

   Why did Du Bois believe that economic and political progress for African-Americans were inextricably linked? Why did Washington think they could be separated?

the Niagara Movement, and additional African-American leaders, including Ida B. Wells, Mary McLeod Bethune, and Mary Church Terrell, joined with white reformers, including Jane Addams, John Dewey, Clarence Darrow, and Lincoln Steffens. They created the **National Association for the Advancement of Colored People** (the NAACP) to fight for full enforcement of the Fourteenth and Fifteenth Amendments; bring public exposure and legal challenges to the mostly unpunished wave of lynchings that were happening in all parts of the country; and begin what would be a long, slow legal process of court challenges to the "separate but equal" laws that provided the legal foundation for black exclusion.

Atlanta Compromise
An 1895 proposal from Booker T. Washington that African-Americans remain separate from whites while focusing on economic self-help.

National Association for the Advancement of Colored People (NAACP)
An interracial organization founded in 1910 dedicated to restoring African-American political and social rights.

| 18.1 | **Quick Review** Is "New South" an appropriate name for the society that emerged after Reconstruction? Consider the economics, politics, and social aspects of the region in formulating your answer. |

THE POLITICS OF CONFLICT—FROM POPULIST MOVEMENT TO POPULIST PARTY

| 18.2 | Analyze how agrarian unrest and protest came to have a significant impact on American politics. |

In the 1870s and 1880s, American farmers were living very difficult lives. The work was backbreaking. They had no time for much of an education and far too little time for family or community life. The economic cycles seemed structured against them. Whenever farmers started to get ahead financially, they faced a downturn because of a glut of wheat in Russia or overproduction of cotton in Egypt or some other issue, leaving them in a pattern of debt. Even in good times, it seemed that the railroads and middlemen in New York or New Orleans or London or Paris took the profits that they produced. Perhaps most galling to many farmers was the sense that the rapid changes happening in the rest of the country seemed to be leaving them behind. It is not accidental that the derogatory word "hayseed," entered the nation's vocabulary at this time. Urban America saw itself as up to date and modern but saw farmers, living in isolated rural areas, as backward and out of date. Moreover, the new technologies that enabled rapid communication let these farmers know just what others in the country thought of them. Jefferson's agrarian ideal seemed like part of a very dim past.

The Farmers' Alliance and Other Farm Groups

By the beginning of the 1880s, many farmers were deeply in debt to the banks on which they depended for their mortgages and for loans to obtain equipment and supplies for the planting year. Railroads, that might give a break to John D. Rockefeller's Standard Oil, kept raising the rates to haul farm products to market. By the time farmers paid off their loans and paid to get the wheat, corn, and other farm products to market, they had little, if any, money left. Eventually, farmers started to do something to change their circumstances. Nelson Dunning of the Farmers' Alliance, wrote, "Nothing could withstand their power, if the farmers of America would organize," particularly, as he believed, in ways the Standard Oil Company had done. In the Farmers' Alliance and eventually in their own political party, farmers, who had indeed been observing what the Rockefellers and Carnegies of the nation were doing, tried to create their own power base.

The earliest nationwide farmer organization was the Patrons of Husbandry, also known as "**the Grange**." Farmers gathered in Grange Halls to celebrate their work and foster a sense of community, but they also organized to deal with the chronic debt and the sense that the nation's financial arrangements were stacked against them. Especially in the South, local Grange chapters organized cooperative buying and selling through their own cotton gins and warehouses, knowing that they would get better prices for their crops

The Grange
The National Grange, or the Patrons of Husbandry, a national organization of farmers formed after the Civil War to promote the rights and dignity of farmers.

The Grange, the first national farmers' organization, painted an idealized picture of farming. Later, farmers' organizations were less idealistic and more militant.

Agricultural Wheel

An organization of farmers, begun in Arkansas in 1882. More militant than the Grange, it sought to advance farmer's economic status.

Farmers' Alliance

A broad mass movement in the rural South and West during the late 1800s, encompassing several organizations and demanding economic and political reforms; it helped create the Populist Party.

and better rates from the railroads if they banded together. The national leadership of the Grange focused on lobbying for agricultural colleges, attracting more people to farming, encouraging crop diversity, and promoting a richer home life for farm families.

Farmers also started additional organizations. In 1882, Arkansas farmers launched the **Agricultural Wheel**. By 1885, the Agricultural Wheel had 1,105 local chapters in four states. The Wheel became a tough organization that excluded any but working farmers. The organization used its size to negotiate price reductions with manufacturers of farm implements and got up to 50 percent reductions on the prices of wagons, buggies, reapers, and mowers, while organizing its own warehouses to hold crops until prices met expectations.

A number of similar organizations coordinated similar efforts, but the largest by far was the **Farmers' Alliance**, which began as the Texas Alliance in Lampasas County, Texas, in the 1870s by ranchers who were dealing with issues of communal and private grazing lands. After Charles W. Macune was elected president of the Texas organization in 1886, the Alliance grew rapidly. Macune had trained as a pharmacist and a physician before he settled in Milam County Texas in 1879 where he practiced medicine while farming on the side. But his rural medical practice gave him a sense of the problems the ranchers and the farmers faced, particularly, the isolation and the lack of economic clout.

Under Macune's leadership the Farmers' Alliance became a business organization—organizing the farmers (including ranchers) of Texas, and eventually the nation, to use the best of corporate practices to fight with the organizations they saw oppressing them. The Alliance sought to get a better financial deal for farmers through the negotiating power of a large organization demanding lower prices for the things they bought and higher prices for the products they sold.

The Texas Farmers' Alliance grew from 38,000 members in 1886 to 225,000 members in 1889—almost half of all of the eligible farmers in Texas. In 1887, the Alliance merged with the Arkansas-based Agricultural Wheel and continued to grow with local units stretching from North Carolina to California and from Texas to the Dakotas. In 1890, Macune moved to a national headquarters in Washington, DC, and the Alliance had over 1 million members.

Under Macune's leadership, the Farmers' Alliance steered clear of direct political involvement. The goal of the Alliance was simple: farmers would combine their power to equal the power of other businesses. They were not opposed to monopolies; they wanted to be one. The Washington office published the *National Economist*, mailed to farmers across the country, while sponsoring lecturers, organizers, and corresponding secretaries to spread Alliance ideas. The organization sought to overcome rural isolation and lack of educational opportunities through lending libraries, schools, conferences, and social occasions for farm families. Most of all, the Alliance sought to open a "new era" of prosperity for farmers through tough negotiations on their behalf.

Macune believed that whites and blacks had different economic interests and insisted that the Farmers' Alliance should include only white farmers. When the Agricultural Wheel joined the Alliance, it dropped its black members. In response to Macune's segregationist policy, African-American farmers created their own **Colored Farmers' National Alliance and Cooperative Union** that had 1.2 million members by 1890. Given the political and social disenfranchisement that black farmers faced, they organized primarily through black churches. In many communities, the black Baptist Church and the Colored Farmers' Alliance had virtually the same membership. Lacking the resources to publish their own materials or hire lecturers or organizers, the black organization never had the clout of the white alliance, even though it had more members.

Colored Farmers' National Alliance and Cooperative Union
An organization of Southern black farmers formed in Texas in 1886 in response to the Southern Farmers' Alliance, which did not accept black people as members. It helped launch the Populist Party.

While the Farmers' Alliance was racially segregated, it welcomed women as members and leaders, as did the Colored Farmers' Alliance. Fully a quarter of the members of the Colored Farmers' Alliance were women. In contrast to the Grange, which had special positions for women, the Farmers' Alliance opened all positions to both women and men. Annie L. Diggs of Kansas was one of the senior editors of the National Reform Press Association, the white Alliance's publishing house. Mary E. Lease of Kansas was the most famous of the Alliance's many speakers, while Marion Todd of Illinois was considered to be the most effective theoretician for the movement. Bettie Munn Gay, who had turned a highly mortgaged Texas farm into a successful cotton growing operation, became one of the leaders in the Texas Alliance. Women and men within the Alliance debated women's suffrage and occasionally argued over the prohibition of alcohol. But they were united in a commitment to improve the life of farm families, economically as well as intellectually and culturally, ending the terrible isolation that farm families experienced.

Defining a National Agenda

While Macune focused the Farmers' Alliance on cooperative economic efforts and stayed out of electoral politics, other leaders wanted more direct political involvement. In California, the president of the state Farmers' Alliance, Marion Cannon, became convinced after long battles with the Southern Pacific Railroad that only public ownership of the railroads would allow farmers to get a fair deal. Alliance lecturer Marion Todd published *Railways of Europe and America* in 1893 in which she argued for

American Voices

Mary E. Lease, Women in the Farmers' Alliance, 1891

Mary E. Lease, a well-known speaker for the Farmers' Alliance, rose to national fame telling Kansas farmers to "raise less corn and more hell" and then traveling the nation to recruit members and build support for the organization. In 1891, she gave a speech to the National Council of Women of the United States, part of which is presented here.

Madam President, Friends, and Fellow-Citizens,—I use that term with somewhat pardonable pride when I remember that the Alliance League of Kansas has given to the women of my sunflower, humanity-loving, temperance-loving State of Kansas the right of political suffrage.

The subject assigned to me to-day, Women in the Farmers' Alliance, cannot be intelligently discussed nor fully understood until the necessity for the formation of the Farmers' Alliance is first shown, and its aims and purposes briefly stated. It must be evident to every intelligent man and woman to-day that there is something radically wrong in the affairs of this Nation....

My friends, the lash of the slave-driver's whip is no longer heard in this country, but the lash of necessity is driving thousands to unrequited toil. Conscienceless capital is robbing manhood of its prime, mothers of their motherhood, and sorrowful children of sunshine and of joy. Look around you! What do you behold to-day? A land which less than four hundred years ago we received fresh from the hands of God, a continent of unparalleled fertility... and yet, in this land of plenty and unlimited resources, the cry of humanity is going up from every corner of this Nation. The plaint of motherhood, the moans of starving children! Capital buys and sells to-day the very heart-beats of humanity....

Oh, yes; we can point to the rivers bridged, to the transcontinental railway connecting ocean with ocean, to wonderful churches and cathedrals; he can point to the most wonderful system of agriculture that ever brought joy to a hungry world; he can jostle his rags against the silken garments his toil has secured; he can walk shelterless and sad by the side of the home he has helped to build; he can wipe the sweat from his weary face, and reflect that the twenty thousand of American millionaires who own one billion five hundred million dollars, gathered from the toils and tears of sixty-four millions of American people, have it in their power to name their Governors and our legislators and representatives and Congressmen,— and they *do* name them, and they *have* named them for the last quarter of a century, and they have it in their power to fix the price of labor, to fix the price for every ton of coal.

Source: Mary E. Lease, *Speech to the National Council of Women of the United States, Assembled in Washington, DC, Feb 24, 1891*

Thinking Critically

1. Documentary Analysis

According to Mary Lease, why was there a "necessity for the formation of the Farmers' Alliance," and what should be its political agenda?

2. Historical Interpretation

What importance should we attach to the fact that a number of women, Mary Lease among them, played prominent roles in farmers' movements and the People's Party?

---

subtreasury system
A proposal for a unit of the U.S. Treasury Department (or "subtreasury") to own warehouses that would store farmer's crops until prices rose.

managing railways in ways similar to how the government managed post offices. Some in the Alliance wanted a federal commission to limit the power of the railroads, but Cannon and Todd were convinced that the railroads were too big to be tamed and that a government takeover was the only answer.

Even Macune came to advocate for what he called the **subtreasury system**, a unit he wanted to have created within the U.S. Department of the Treasury that would provide low-interest loans to farmers. These loans would be secured by cotton, wheat, and other staple crops. The subtreasury would protect its investment and support farmers through a federal system of warehouses and grain elevators in 1,000 counties across the country where the government would ensure minimum prices for crops and hold them until they sold at that price. If speculators could use the telegraph to make money buying and selling crop futures, why couldn't farmers, with the right government support, use the same technical arrangements to ensure their own profits?

Although Alliance leaders took up the subtreasury idea and some politicians, like Tom Watson of Georgia, became advocates, the leadership of the Democratic Party resisted, as did virtually all Republicans. In the end, the subtreasury was never created. As a result, many within the Alliance began to question the value of staying out of politics.

More than public ownership of railroads or the subtreasury idea, the political issue that engaged U.S. farmers was federal fiscal policy. When the government limited the supply of currency, farmers had a very difficult time paying their debts, getting loans, or getting the price they wanted for their crops. When the government made more funds available, the resulting inflation made it easier to pay debts (because the debt amounted to less in current dollars) and made it easier to sell the products of the farms. Although easing the supply of money improved the situation of farmers, one policy made it difficult to do: the nation's adherence to the gold standard, requiring that every dollar in circulation be backed by a dollar's worth of gold in a bank vault.

During the Civil War, the federal government had temporarily dropped the gold standard. Instead, it created federal bank notes, known as "greenbacks" because of their color, essentially printing dollars based not on gold but on the "full faith and credit" of the government's promise to pay. The government also allowed the additional use of silver as backing for currency during the war. Both of these policies eased the supply of money significantly, but they also fueled inflation since, with more dollars available, any dollar was worth less. Farmers liked inflation, but investors and bankers hated it. After the Civil War, the nation's bankers demanded a return to the gold standard by gradually withdrawing greenbacks from circulation as the government paid down its Civil War debt and then in 1873 "demonetizing" silver so only gold, and not silver, could be used for coins or backing for dollars in circulation. These policies were effective in curbing inflation, but they led to an extremely tight money supply, tight credit, and challenging times for farmers. The tight money of the 1880s was thus a direct result of federal policy, and the Farmers' Alliance as well as the other farmer organizations were determined to change the policy. Some advocated expanding the number of greenbacks, others supported the coinage of more silver and some called for both, but all agreed that something needed to be done.

Populism Becomes a Political Party

The rapid growth of the Farmers' Alliance in the 1880s brought into the organization many state leaders who advocated direct political involvement. Leonidas L. Polk of North Carolina was the strongest of all these leaders. A Confederate hero, Polk made his fortune in real estate development when the Carolina Central Railroad crossed his old family plantation in 1873. He was active in the Methodist Church and in the Grange. He also helped ensure the end of Reconstruction in his state while helping recreate the Democratic Party there. Polk lobbied for the creation of a state Department of Agriculture, became its first commissioner in 1877, and in 1886, published his own newspaper, *Progressive Farmer*. In 1888, he brought the state organization he led into the Farmers' Alliance, and within the year, 42,000 North Carolina farmers were members of the national organization.

Other states had similar leaders. South Carolina's Benjamin R. Tillman had served in a militia that kept blacks and Republicans out of politics. He became active in the state Grange in the 1880s and became convinced that "the yoke of the credit system" was keeping farmers down. He convened a large meeting of white farmers in 1886, lobbied for a state agricultural college, and created a 20,000 member South Carolina Alliance that remained independent of the national organization. Georgia's Tom Watson was a lawyer and "friend and follower" of the Farmers' Alliance, though as a nonfarmer he could not join. Nevertheless, he was elected to Congress as a Farmers' Alliance candidate in 1890, expanding the movement of the Alliance into politics.

As the price of cotton fell to the lowest level in 30 years in 1891—and the farm economy continued to worsen throughout the 1890s—Watson, Tillman, Polk, and others rallied for a change. The nation's largest labor unions, the Knights of Labor and the Women's Christian Temperance Union, had recently launched a new political organization, the **People's Party**, also known as the **Populist Party**, at a convention in Cincinnati in 1891 that was advocating for many of the reforms to currency

People's Party
Usually known as the **Populist Party**, a major third party of the 1890s formed to fight for the rights of working people.

and regulation of railroads that the Alliance wanted. If the Farmers' Alliance were to merge with the People's Party, they could win elections and have their voices heard in state capitals, in Congress, perhaps even the White House.

Macune continued to oppose such political involvement, preferring farmer-controlled cooperative economic development. Polk became the leader of those who said yes to political involvement and specifically to joining the People's Party. Everyone knew that the 1892 convention of the Farmers' Alliance would decide the issue. Polk won. Macune retired from the Alliance and spent the next 30 years practicing medicine and law while preaching in Methodist churches in rural Texas.

The People's (or Populist) Party grew dramatically. The Colored Farmers' Alliance and smaller groups like the Farmers' Mutual Benefit Association also joined. The widespread assumption was that when the People's Party, now a multiracial coalition of farmers, labor, and women's groups, held their national convention in Omaha, Nebraska, in July 1892, they would nominate Leonidas Polk for president. A month before the convention, however, Polk suddenly died. The People's Party nominated James B. Weaver of Iowa, a former Union general, and James G. Field, a former Confederate from Virginia, as his running mate. Polk's charisma did not adhere to the new nominees. Nevertheless, Weaver won over a million votes in the 1892 presidential election that ultimately returned Cleveland to the White House. Not since the late 1850s, when the Republican Party had come out of nowhere, had the nation witnessed anything like the phenomenal growth of the Populists, as the members of the People's Party quickly came to be known. Populist candidates won the governor's office in Colorado and Kansas in the 1892 elections. Populists elected Marion Cannon to Congress from southern California as well as Congressmen from Colorado, Kansas, Nebraska, and North Carolina. They elected eight representatives to the California state legislature, a group that held the balance between the Democrats and Republicans and almost succeeded in electing California's U.S. Senator.

Two years later, Populist candidates won over 1.5 million votes, electing seven to the U.S. House, six to the U.S. Senate, and many to state legislatures. In a partnership with Republicans, Populists won control of the North Carolina legislature—the only time since Reconstruction when the Democrats had lost control of a state—and sent Marion Butler to the U.S. Senate. In 1894, Populist candidates won 41 percent of the vote for statewide offices in Colorado, 39 percent in Washington State, 39 percent in Kansas and 36 percent in Texas. Populists were elected to Congress from Alabama, Kansas, Nebraska, and North Carolina. The Populists, it seemed, were gaining power.

As the Populists approached the 1896 presidential elections, the Republican and Democratic Parties were keeping a worried eye on them and, at the same time, borrowing parts of their message. No one borrowed more from the Populists than the young former congressman from Nebraska, William Jennings Bryan. Bryan was a Democrat, not a Populist, but his views on many issues, most of all his advocacy for the unlimited coinage of silver, were the same as those of the Populists and anathema to leaders of the Democratic Party, including President Cleveland, who was not seeking reelection but who wanted a successor more like himself. Nevertheless, Bryan worked tirelessly for the Democratic nomination, courting as many "silver" delegates to the party's 1896 convention in Chicago as possible.

When the Democrats finally met in early July, the debate on the platform was intense, pitting those who wanted to hold to the gold standard against the "free silver" Democrats who agreed with the Populists. Bryan spoke to the convention, electrifying the gathering as he concluded:

> If they dare to come out in the open field and defend the gold standard as a good thing, we shall fight them to the uttermost, having behind us the producing masses of the nation and the world. Having behind us the commercial interests and the laboring interests and all the toiling masses, we shall answer their demands for a gold standard by saying to them, you shall not press down upon the brow of labor this crown of thorns. You shall not crucify mankind upon a cross of gold.

After the cheering stopped, the Democrats not only adopted a silver platform but also nominated Bryan for president. The Populists were torn about what to do since Bryan's views seemed so close to their own, and with him, they might actually win the White House. Although divided between those who wanted to maintain their independence and those who were willing to compromise, the Populist Convention that met in July nominated Bryan as their candidate for president. By joining forces with the Democrats, they were confident of victory.

The Republicans nominated William McKinley, a genial Congressman from Ohio, and the last Civil War veteran to run for president. In the fall campaign, managed by Marcus Alonzo Hanna, a wealthy supporter who was emerging as something close to a modern professional political advisor, the Republicans equated a vote for Bryan with a rebellion against the nation. They linked the Republican ticket with the flag, patriotism, and economic caution. They called McKinley the "advance agent of prosperity" and some, like a young Theodore Roosevelt, described the Democrats and Populists as "plotting a social revolution and the subversion of the American Republic." In the contest, the notions of patriotism, economic caution, and northeast regional distrust of the South and West won. A comfortable majority elected McKinley, though the results show how deeply divided the country had become (see Map 18-2).

The Populists never recovered from their loss in 1896. Those who had supported Bryan and the alliance with the Democratic Party blamed those who did not. Populists who had not wanted to compromise blamed those who had "sold out" and supported a Democrat. African-Americans whose votes had been essential to Populist victories in many close contests, were deeply disillusioned at how quickly Populist leaders like Tom Watson turned into arch segregationists after 1897.

The Populist Party continued for a short time, but the enthusiasm and confidence were destroyed by the divisions over the 1896 election. In 1900 and 1904, the party nominated Tom Watson who, having courted black voters in the 1890s, now campaigned on a platform of white supremacy even while he maintained the Populist economic program. The Democrats renominated Bryan in 1900, but he did poorly without Populist support and in the face of prosperity and McKinley's considerable popularity. The new Socialist Party, emerging from Northern labor unions, began to contest presidential elections, taking many of the Populists labor union supporters. A moment and a movement had passed, although its efforts did, in the end, lead to the adoption of the silver standard. In the early 1900s, national interest turned elsewhere, although many elements of the Populist platform were adopted and became the basis for a later progressive movement championed by both Republicans and Democrats after 1900. The farmers of the South and West, who had organizing themselves so successfully and had bridged heretofore uncrossed gender barriers, were never able to resolve their racial divisions. Never again would they have the same level of political power.

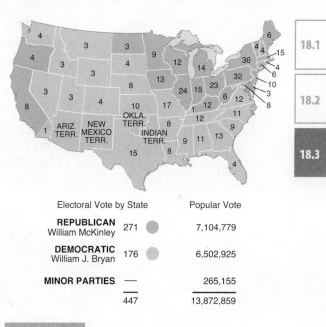

Electoral Vote by State | Popular Vote

REPUBLICAN William McKinley   271   7,104,779

DEMOCRATIC William J. Bryan   176   6,502,925

MINOR PARTIES —   265,155

447   13,872,859

MAP 18-2 The Election of 1896. This map of the electoral votes in the 1896 presidential election shows how deeply divided the country was. States where farming was dominant voted overwhelmingly for Bryan.

18.2   **Quick Review**   Was politics the best way for the farmers to address their grievances? Why or why not? What might have been a more effective strategy?

WORKER PROTEST AND THE RISE OF ORGANIZED LABOR

18.3   Explain the tensions in industrial America that led to major labor strife between the 1870s and 1914.

The Great Railroad Strike of 1877 began spontaneously in Baltimore, Maryland, and Martinsburg, West Virginia, on July 16 and 17, 1877, after the management of several railroads announced a wage cut. At Camden Junction, 2 miles from Baltimore, a fireman simply refused to keep the train moving. Soon others joined, and before long, all traffic on the Baltimore & Ohio Railroad had come to a halt. The management then fired the strikers. In response, others joined the strike, and by July 19, rail workers prevented all freight from leaving Pittsburgh. Now mostly forgotten, the strike inspired some Americans, frightened others, and for decades shaped people's responses to the country's rapid growth and industrialization.

The strike was marked by widespread violence. A large crowd of strikers and their supporters in Baltimore attacked state militia troops who then fired on the crowd, killing 11 people. In Pittsburgh, a huge crowd hurled insults and rocks at a militia unit who then started shooting, killing 20. The crowd vented its fury on the Pennsylvania Railroad, burning everything in sight. By July 22, some 39 Pennsylvania Railroad buildings, 104 engines, and more than 1,200 freight cars had been destroyed. As news of the violence spread, strikes took place all along the major rail lines from New York and New Jersey to Indiana and Illinois. Black and white workers went out on strike together. In St. Louis, Missouri, a week-long general strike led workers to take control of the city. Workers went on strike as far away as Kansas City and San Francisco.

Women played a crucial role, and the *Baltimore Sun* reported about the "very active part taken by the women, who are the wives and mothers of the firemen. They look famished and wild, and declare for starvation rather than have their people work for the reduced wages."

In response to a plea from the railroad management, President Hayes declared that a state of insurrection existed and called out federal troops who, armed with rapid-fire Gatling guns, put an end to the strike. Former President Grant criticized his successor, noting the irony that he himself had been criticized for sending the army to protect black voting rights but, "Now, however, there is no hesitation about exhausting the whole power of the government to suppress a strike on the slightest intimation that danger threatens." But in the eyes of the new president, attacks on black voters and attacks on the property of the railroad companies were two different things.

Others drew their own lessons from the 1877 uprising. E. L. Godkin, editor of *The Nation,* called for doubling the size of the U.S. Army, but instead something new was created, the National Guard, made up of part-time soldiers who could be called out when needed. After 1877, states created National Guard units and built massive National Guard armories, stern stone buildings where arms might be stored in case of a new insurrection. These National Guard armories can still be seen in many cities—a monument to the 1877 rail strike.

Twisted track and the wheels of burned out rail cars show some of the $10 million damage caused by the 1877 railroad strike.

The strikes also inspired the rise of labor unions that sought to help workers organize to demand new rights rather than just vent their fury. These unions sometimes led to additional uprisings, but in addition, they brought about changes in how corporations did business.

The Knights of Labor

Founded by tailors in Philadelphia in 1869, the **Knights of Labor**, quickly emerged to become the country's largest and most powerful labor union after the 1877 strike. The Knights welcomed white and black workers, immigrants as well as the native-born, and skilled and unskilled workers. Terence V. Powderly was the head, or Grand Master Workman, of the Knights of Labor in the 1870s and 1880s. Powderly believed that isolated workers and small local unions were doomed to defeat when facing railroads and other large corporations, and he wanted his union to have the same organizational power as the largest corporations.

Under Powderly's leadership, the Knights tried to avoid violence. The Knights believed that workers and owners had more in common than their differences and hoped that eventually many workers could become independent owners rather than a permanent labor force. The union campaigned for government support of agricultural cooperatives, an 8-hour work day, equal pay for women, and government ownership of railroads and banks. Powderly took the commitment to racial integration seriously. At their October 1886 convention in Richmond, Virginia, Powderly caused quite a stir in the local community by inviting an African-American delegate, Francis Ferrell, to introduce him to the meeting. In 1883, they organized a successful strike against the Western Union Telegraph Company and, in 1885, were strong enough to win a strike against several railroads that agreed to restore lost wages and hire back all striking workers. For Powderly, the success of the 1885 strike showed what a strong union could do. By 1886, the Knights had 700,000 members. In an even larger railroad strike that began in Marshall, Texas, in 1886, some 9,000 workers stopped freight on lines in Texas, Missouri, Arkansas, and Kansas. Strikes, it seemed, were becoming a national phenomenon, and the Knights were in the forefront. However, while national leaders of the Knights urged peaceful negotiations, in the 1886 strike, strikers pushed rail cars off tracks and set fires to railroad buildings. To avoid further violence, the Knights called off the strike while claiming a victory that was not really theirs.

The railroad strike of 1886 showed the power of a union to bring the trains, and thus the country, to a halt. It also demonstrated the split between many members of the Knights who harbored deep hatred for industrial owners and union leadership that still sought conciliation. While the Knights remained strong and were an essential element in the Populist political campaigns of the 1890s, the split was never fully healed. In time, other unions, some more moderate, some more radical, would replace the Knights.

The Knights of Labor
Labor union that included skilled and unskilled workers irrespective of race or gender; founded in 1869.

The American Federation of Labor

While the Knights of Labor attempted to organize all workers, those in some of the more skilled trades created their own separate unions. In 1886, many of these small elite unions came together to create the **American Federation of Labor** with 50,000 members. Samuel Gompers of the Cigar Makers Union was elected as its president and, except for 1 year, served as president of the A. F. of L. until his death in 1924, by which time it had grown to 3 million members, by far the strongest labor union in the United States.

Under Gompers's leadership, the A.F. of L. continued to organize workers in separate craft unions with membership in each union restricted to workers in a specific trade such as cigar makers or plumbers or iron molders. Gompers carefully avoided larger issues, preferring to negotiate specifically for immediate ends—increased wages, job security, an 8-hour day, benefits, and the right of the union to bargain collectively for workers. "We fight only for immediate objects. . .that can be realized in a few years," Gompers said. He was happy to leave political ideology and more far-reaching social change to others. If the growth in the A. F. of L.'s membership is a measure, it was a successful strategy.

American Federation of Labor (A.F. of L.)
Labor organization formed in 1886 as a federation of smaller elite craft unions.

Haymarket, 1886

On May 4, 1886, many of the tensions in the United States exploded at Chicago's Haymarket Square. Between 40,000 and 60,000 of Chicago's workers went on strike on Saturday, May 1, chanting their demands for an 8-hour work day, "eight hours for work, eight hours for rest, eight hours for what we will." The A. F. of L. supported the strike. So did socialists and anarchists in Chicago's diverse immigrant communities.

Socialism and anarchism, though quite different political philosophies, were both very strong in Chicago. Socialists believed that the workers should own the means of production and that private ownership of factories, businesses, and lands should be abolished in favor of ownership by all, which often meant government ownership. Anarchists deeply distrusted any government—including a Socialist government—and disdained elections as fraudulent exercises in futility. In place of government, anarchists wanted small, local, voluntary organizations. They believed that by abolishing higher authorities, a new era of peace and freedom would come. Nevertheless, for two anarchist leaders, Albert Parsons and August Spies, the 8-hour movement was an opportunity to bring skilled and unskilled workers together as a step toward their larger goal.

As the strike continued on Monday, May 3, Spies issued a call for a mass meeting to be held the following night at Haymarket Square and asked Albert Parsons to join him. Perhaps 3,000 people showed up at the Haymarket rally. But just as the rally was ending and Parsons himself was enjoying a beer at a nearby tavern, a police contingent marched into the rally to end it. Someone—no one ever found out who—threw a bomb into the middle of the police ranks, killing one police officer. Six more officers soon died of their wounds.

As news of the Haymarket bomb spread, newspapers blamed anarchists and socialists for the violence. Eventually, Albert Parsons, August Spies, and six others were tried and convicted for being part of "a general conspiracy to annihilate the police force and destroy property," even though none of them could possibly have thrown the actual bomb. Appeals and a nationwide campaign for clemency ensued. Samuel Gompers, who certainly disagreed with anarchists, nevertheless said that Parsons, Spies, and the others had been "fighting for labor from different sides of the house." In spite of all the appeals, four, including Parsons and Spies, were hung on November 11, 1887.

Haymarket
The name given to the strike, rally, and bombing that took place around Haymarket Square in Chicago in May 1886 as well as to the subsequent executions of four leaders of the incident.

Haymarket—as the strike, rally, bombing, and executions all came to be called—was a pivotal moment in American labor history. For some, the trial and executions were a validation of the rule of law. For others, the trial and execution of men who never threw the bomb and did not have any known links to whoever did, provided proof that justice was not possible for those who protested in Gilded Age America. Lucy Parsons, Albert's widow, spent the rest of her long life speaking and writing about their cause. Emma Goldman, a young girl at the time, traced her own career as a life-long radical organizer to the stories of the Haymarket martyrs.

Homestead Strike, 1892

While the 1886 strike for an 8 hour-day was a national event, other strikes followed, none more important than the 1892 Homestead Strike at Andrew Carnegie's plant at Homestead, Pennsylvania. By the 1890s, Carnegie owned a dozen plants in western Pennsylvania and northern West Virginia. Workers at these huge mills turned out a quarter of the nation's steel supply and earned $40 million per year in profits for Carnegie. Carnegie wanted to be seen as a friend to working people, but profits still came first. In 1892, when workers at Carnegie's Homestead Steel Mill went on strike, Carnegie left his top lieutenant, Henry Clay Frick, in charge while he remained at his castle in Scotland. Frick decided that the time had come to break the 24,000-member Amalgamated Association of Iron, Steel, and Tin Workers.

In June 1892, when it came time to negotiate a new contract, Frick offered only a cut in salary. When the union rejected the offer, Frick closed the plant, fired all of the workers, and built an 8-foot fence around it. He then hired new nonunion workers and 300 Pinkerton agents to protect them. The Pinkerton Agency had been created to support the North during the Civil War but turned into a quasi-police force for industrial owners who were caught in conflict with unions in the late 1800s. The Homestead workers fought back.

On July 6 when two barges of Pinkerton detectives came down the river to the plant, strikers who had been patrolling the area rushed the pier. No one knows who shot first, but both sides kept shooting. Eventually, between five and nine steelworkers and between three and ten Pinkerton agents were killed. Pennsylvania's governor sent 8,000 militia troops to Homestead to keep the peace, and Frick brought in new workers who began operating the mill. Union leaders were arrested, but were acquitted (it was hard to find an antiunion jury in the region). Public opinion generally blamed Carnegie and Frick for the bloodshed. Nevertheless, Frick had won his battle. He had defeated the union and reopened the mills with nonunion workers. Unlike Andrew Carnegie, he did not care about public opinion. Carnegie also blamed Frick for the troubles, and the two never spoke again, but Carnegie also did not reinstate the union.

Coxey's Army, 1893–94

In 1893, a grand world's fair, the Columbian Exposition, opened in Chicago. Like earlier fairs, this one displayed the nation's technological marvels and industrial success, including 400 buildings lit with 10,000 electric lights. While the fair was a booming success, the nation's economy was collapsing in the Panic of 1893. J. P. Morgan rescued the country's gold reserves (see Chapter 17) but did not end the terrible unemployment. By the end of the year, one-fifth of those who had been working before the panic were out of a job. Many were desperate, and the contrast between the desperation and the fair's glitter was obvious.

An Ohio businessman, Jacob Coxey, was dazzled when he attended the Chicago fair, but deeply touched by the poverty and desperation he saw among unemployed in the city. Back in his hometown of Massillon, Ohio, near Akron, Coxey announced a plan to put the unemployed to work building roads. Coxey argued that America needed to improve its mostly dirt roads and also end unemployment. The solution was clear to him. Congress should appropriate $500 million in government bonds and offer every man who wanted to work $1.50 per day for an 8-hour day fixing the country's highways. (Coxey assumed that the key was putting men, not necessarily women, to work.) And, Coxey insisted, if Congress did not act, the unemployed should march to Washington and demand action.

Although only about 100 marchers assembled at the beginning of the march, by the time the march got to Homestead, Pennsylvania, site of the Carnegie strike, it had grown to 600. All along the way, people gave them food and shelter. Coxey marched into Washington, DC, on schedule on May 1, 1894. The *New York Times* called the march a "Battle between Law and Anarchy." Federal troops were put on alert. By mid-May, some 800 Coxeyites were in the District of Columbia, a number that grew to 1,200 in August. But Congress, dominated as it was by the corporate interests, did not pass Coxey's legislation or do anything else to aid the unemployed. In August, police scattered **Coxey's Army**, as they were called by the press. Coxey returned to Ohio where he lived to the age of 97 and died in 1951, still advocating federally financed highway improvement and pleased to see his goals partially fulfilled by the New Deal's employment programs in the 1930s.

The American Railway Union, the Pullman Strike of 1894, and the Socialist Party

The American Railway Union was created in 1893 and led by Eugene V. Debs, who would go on to play an important role in American labor and political life for the next several decades. Debs was born in 1855 in Terre Haute, Indiana, and left school at 15 to take a job on the railroads. In 1875, he joined the Brotherhood of Locomotive Firemen but soon came to believe that having different unions for engineers, firemen, brakemen, and for the workers who maintained the tracks, was a recipe for defeat. His response was to help organize one union for everyone who worked on the railroads.

Coxey's Army

A protest march of unemployed workers, led by businessman Jacob Coxey, demanding a public works highway program and guaranteed jobs during the depression of the 1890s.

Coxey's Army with their supporters marched though towns from Ohio to Washington, DC, on their way to make their demands of Congress.

Almost immediately after its founding, the American Railway Union won a strike against the Great Northern Railroad in 1894. It looked like a new force was emerging. But then Debs found himself pulled into a strike he did not want, and the early successes of the American Railway Union turned to failure when the new union was involved in another strike at the Pullman Palace Car Company.

George Pullman did not operate a railway; he made railway cars—the very best railway cars anywhere in the United States. Pullman cars were elegant sleeping cars that cost four times as much as other railway cars and that allowed travelers who could afford the accommodations to cross the country in comfort. Having designed and manufactured the cars, Pullman leased the cars and their staff to various rail lines that attached them to regular trains. Both Pullman and the lines profited handsomely from the exchange.

To keep his employees out of industrial strife, Pullman built his own town, Pullman, Illinois, 12 miles outside of Chicago. In Pullman, 8,000 workers and their families lived in 1,400 houses that they rented from the company. They were provided with schools, an athletic club, free lectures, a local theater, and health care. The housing at Pullman was substantially better than housing available to most other industrial workers, but the rents were high and the rules strict. Pullman did not allow alcohol, and he had "spotters" who kept an eye on the behavior and home life of his employees.

Facing the Panic of 1893, Pullman thought that the only prudent thing was to lay off some workers and cut wages for the rest. He did not, however, reduce rents in Pullman since he also expected the town to pay its own way. Nevertheless, in spite of the depressed economy, the Pullman Company paid its standard dividends to its shareholders. In response, the workers went on strike. Ninety percent of the residents of Pullman did not show up for work. They called on Debs and the American Railway Union for support.

Debs told the Pullman workers that the midst of a depression was a terrible time to call a strike and urged them to postpone. They refused and Debs felt bound to support them. The American Railway Union refused to handle any train that had a Pullman car attached. By June, rail traffic through Chicago had stopped. The union took special care to keep the mail trains running so there would be no reason for federal intervention, but the federal government intervened anyway.

The Cleveland administration obtained an injunction ordering the strikers back to work, and when they refused, Cleveland ordered 14,000 federal troops to Chicago to end the strike. When the army arrived in Chicago, there was a riot and 34 people were killed. Federal authorities not only ended the strike but also arrested Debs and disbanded the union.

The strike and the jail term transformed Debs. He went to jail a charismatic labor leader. He came out convinced that the American economic system was permanently stacked against workers and their unions and that the only way to bring about change was political. He supported the Populist movement in the 1896 election but then founded the **Socialist Party** in the United States. The Socialists advocated government ownership of the nation's major industries and a mandate for higher salaries for workers. In the national elections of 1904 through 1920—except 1916—Debs ran for president as the party's candidate, winning hundreds of thousands of votes and giving himself a platform to advocate for a completely different economic system.

Miners and Their Unions

The steel that was transforming America required two key ingredients, iron ore and coal to fuel the smelting process that turned iron into steel. Coal also heated most of the nation's cities, and coal-fired generators produced much of the nation's electricity. These two ingredients had to be mined from deep in the earth, as did several other resources of great importance to the United States. Gold and silver were still the most valued forms of exchange. Lead pipes provided water to most houses. Bringing these resources to the industrial process required the backbreaking and dangerous work of miners. As the United States industrialized, the need for mines and miners grew exponentially. However, since every dollar paid to a miner increased the cost of finished products, or reduced the profits of those who owned the manufacturing process, mine owners were determined to keep the pay of miners as low as possible; recruiting new immigrants who found themselves with few options.

Federal troops, on orders from President Cleveland, escorted trains and destroyed the union in the aftermath of the Pullman Strike.

Even before the Great Railway Strike of 1877, the country's coal miners had been an angry lot. Coal had been mined in Pennsylvania's Schuylkill Valley for generations, but in the 1860s and 1870s, miners had to dig deeper than ever, using pumps to lower the water table and machinery to ventilate the mines. Those deep mines were dangerous. The pumps could fail or a new stream could break through and drown miners. Tunnels could collapse. Methane or other dangerous gasses could collect and kill miners before they knew what was happening. And of course, the very properties that made coal valuable made fire an ever-present danger.

In the aftermath of the Panic of 1873, the mine owners cut pay, and in response, the miner's union called a strike. By January 1875, Pennsylvania coal production stopped. Since cities were heated with coal, midwinter seemed like a good time to win a strike, but the mine owners had stockpiled coal and the cities stayed warm while miners starved. By July 1875, the strike was defeated and the miners went back to work, at the reduced wages.

The failure of the 1875 strike produced a secret organization among the Irish immigrant coal miners in Pennsylvania, the Molly Maguires, who attacked and sometimes murdered foremen, superintendents, and even a mine owner. The mine owners hired the Pinkerton Detective agency, which had played an important role in the Homestead Strike. A Pinkerton agent infiltrated the Mollys, and eventually 10 men were convicted of murder based on their involvement in the Molly Maguires and were executed in June 1877.

In the 1880s and 1890s, new efforts were made to create a new and stronger union among the coal miners of Pennsylvania, Ohio, Virginia, and West Virginia that was focused not on violence against owners but on victories for the workers. The **United Mine Workers of America** was founded in Columbus, Ohio, in 1890. The new union's charter called for ensuring that the miners received a fair share of the wealth they created, "fully compatible with the dangers of our calling." The United Mine Workers of America was open to all races and religions to avoid the divisions that had undermined earlier unions. During an 1894 coal strike in Alabama, the *Chicago Tribune* reported, "For the first time in this district, no distinction as to color was made. Negroes marched in companies sandwiched between the white men. A negro and a white miner carried a banner." It was an all too rare moment in American labor history.

Under the leadership of a former Knights of Labor member, John Mitchell, who knew how to call a strike and when to call for arbitration, the United Mine Workers won a 10 percent raise in 1900 and then in 1903 won another raise along with recognition for the union and guarantees of fair weighing of the coal (since miners were paid by the weight of the coal they dug and often felt that they were cheated). By the early 1900s, the mine workers of the Eastern part of the country were better paid and living in better conditions than had been thought possible even a few years earlier, although it had been a hard road for them to get there.

Mining developed later in the West than in the East (see Chapter 16) but expanded rapidly. In 1883, gold was discovered in the Coeur d'Alene region of Idaho, the narrow northern part of the state. Before long, the gold was played out but deposits of silver, lead, and coal were found. The lead and coal, however, were buried much deeper than silver and gold, and Western miners found themselves working deep underground in dangerous conditions as employees of large corporations that were financed by Eastern stockholders. Several unions merged in 1891 to create the Miners' Union of the Coeur d'Alenes. When the price for silver and lead fell on national markets in 1892, the Miners' Union went on strike to protest a cut in wages from $3.50 a week to $3.00 a week, for a 7-day week of 10-hour days.

As in Pennsylvania, the mine owners hired the Pinkerton agency to infiltrate the union, and pitched battle broke out between unionized miners and nonunion workers. The governor of Idaho called for federal troops to end "a state of insurrection and rebellion." In April 1899, striking miners used dynamite to blow up the Bunker Hill Mine in the Coeur d'Alene region after the mine superintendent fired all union workers. The governor of Idaho, Frank Steunenberg, who had been elected with union support in

United Mine Workers of America
A new union organized in 1890 to bring together mine workers in the Eastern half of the United States in one organization that eventually became a national union.

1896, called for federal troops to restore order. When Steunenberg was assassinated in 1905, the Western Federation of Miners was blamed, but none of its leaders were convicted. The struggles in the West continued, and some of the union leaders, especially the charismatic William D. (Big Bill) Haywood, became national labor leaders.

The Industrial Workers of the World

On June 27, 1905, over 200 delegates gathered in Chicago to found a new union, the **Industrial Workers of the World**, known as the **Wobblies**. The IWW's founders wanted to create "one big union" of all workers no matter what their trade or skill. Western Federation of Miners leader Big Bill Haywood opened the convention saying, they were there to build, "a working class movement that shall have for its purpose the emancipation of the working class." Eugene V. Debs expressed the hope that the time had come to "begin the work of forming a great economic or revolutionary organization of the working class." Mother Jones, Lucy Parsons, and other labor leaders joined in launching the IWW.

Industrial Workers of the World (IWW) Popularly known as **Wobblies,** organized in 1905 to bring together the nation's workers in "one big union" to fight for a radically different economic system that favored workers over owners.

American Voices

Mother Jones, "Victory at Arnot" 1897

Mother Jones became a union organizer and traveled the country supporting mine workers, other unions, and later the Socialist Party and the Industrial Workers of the World. She was arrested often but continued leading strikes with approaches such as described below from her autobiography, most likely an incident that took place during the United Mine Workers strike of 1897.

In Arnot, Pennsylvania, a strike had been going on 4 or 5 months. The men were becoming discouraged....Sunday afternoon I held a meeting...."You've got to take the pledge," I said. "Rise and pledge to stick to your brothers and the union till the strike's won!"

The men shuffled their feet but the women rose, their babies in their arms, and pledged themselves to see that no one went to work in the morning....

Then the company tried to bring in scabs [nonunion workers]. I told the men to stay home with the children for a change and let the women attend to the scabs. I organized an army of women housekeepers. On a given day they were to bring their mops and brooms and "the army" would charge the scabs up at the mines....I selected as leader an Irish woman who had a most picturesque appearance. She had slept late and her husband had told her to hurry up and get into the army. She had grabbed a red petticoat and slipped it over a thick cotton night gown. She wore a black stocking and a white one. She had tied a little fringed shawl over her wild red hair. Her face was red and her eyes were mad. I looked at her and felt that she could raise a rumpus.

I said, "You lead the army up to the Drip Mouth. Take that tin dishpan you have with you and your hammer, and when the scabs and the mules come up, begin to hammer and howl. Then all of you hammer and howl and be ready to chase the scabs with your mops and brooms. Don't be afraid of anyone."

Up the mountain side, yelling and hollering, she led the women, and when the mules came up with the scabs and the coal, she began beating on the dishpan and hollering and all the army joined in with her. The sheriff tapped her on the shoulder.

"My dear lady," said he, "remember the mules. Don't frighten them."

She took the old tin pan, and she hit him with it and she hollered, "To hell with you and the mules!"

From that day on the women kept continual watch of the mines to see that the company did not bring in scabs. Every day women with brooms or mops in one hand and babies in the other arm wrapped in little blankets, went to the mines and watched that no one went in. And all night long they kept watch. They were heroic women. In the long years to come the nation will pay them high tribute for they were fighting for the advancement of a great country....

The last of February the company put up a notice that all demands were conceded...before I left, the union held a victory meeting.... The women came for miles in a raging snow storm for that meeting, little children trailing on their skirts, and babies under their shawls. Many of the miners had walked miles. It was one night of real joy and a great celebration.

Source: Mary Harris Jones, *The Autobiography of Mother Jones* (Chicago: Charles H. Kerr, 1990), pp. 30–39.

Thinking Critically

1. **Documentary Analysis**

   What unique strategy did Mother Jones employ during the 1897 miners' strike?

2. **Comparison**

   Compare the strategy used by Mother Jones with that used by workers during the Homestead Strike. Do you think the different strategies help explain the differences in outcome that you note?

The convention adopted a constitution that began, "By organizing industrially we are forming the structure of the new society within the shell of the old." This mission was very different from the incremental goals of the American Federation of Labor. For the IWW, contract negotiations and strikes were only a step "within the shell of the old" to help launch the new world.

In the early 1900s, workers were not embarrassed to sing about their dreams and the IWW *Song Book* described them in songs, including one that mocked the idea that the poor should hope that, "You'll get pie in the sky when you die" instead of taking action now. Another IWW song promised that, "If the workers took a notion," they could bring the current economy to a halt.

The IWW was attacked by the press, the corporate world, and the government. It was also torn by ideological splits, personality tensions, and factional divisions. But for 15 years, the IWW was a major force in labor organizing around the country and included some of the country's most charismatic labor leaders among its members.

The Garment Industry and the Triangle Shirtwaist Fire of 1911

The garment industry, one of the nation's largest, employed mostly women. Between 1900 and 1910, New York City became the nation's center in the manufacture of ready-to-wear clothing. Led by innovative owners, much of the work moved from the small sweatshops of the Lower East Side to larger factories in the new high-rise buildings of 10 and 12 stories in southern Manhattan. Max Blanck and Isaac Harris operated their factory, the Triangle Shirtwaist Company, in Greenwich Village. There, over 500 workers, most of them young Jewish and Italian women, assembled the popular shirtwaists (as women's blouses were called) that were sold in department stores across the country.

In New York City alone, over 40,000 people worked in the garment trades in the early 1900s. Although divided by language—Yiddish, Italian, English and a host of other languages—the garment workers joined together to protest low salaries. The International Ladies' Garment Workers Union (ILGWU) had a tough organizer, Clara Lemlich, who had emigrated from Russia in 1903 and who led women in a number of strikes. During some of the strikes, factories hired replacement nonunion workers while police arrested strikers or thugs beat them up. Women from New York's social elite, including Anne Morgan, daughter of J. P. Morgan, sometimes joined the picket lines and they, too, were sometimes arrested or beaten.

In the late fall of 1909, as the ILGWU considered a general strike in the garment industry, many, including A. F. of L. president Samuel Gompers, urged caution. But Clara Lemlich said, "I have no further patience for talk. . . .I move that we go on a general strike." Workers cheered and the strike began. Factories all over Manhattan were picketed that fall. The garment industry owners organized their own association and refused to give in to the striker's demands.

Striking garment workers got help from the national leadership of the A.F. of L., and from the Western Federation of Miners whose leader, Big Bill Haywood, sent word that "the Western miners are hearty admirers of your courage and fighting qualities." They also got support from society women like Morgan and from African-American women who were being recruited as strikebreakers but who refused, though in a meeting they asked the union to "exercise a proper consideration of the claims and demands of the men and women of color who desire to enter the various trades." The long strike ended in exhaustion for both sides in early 1911 when the union and the owners agreed to a compromise.

On Saturday March 25, 1911, only a month after the strike ended, a fire started under one of the cutting room tables

The IWW supported strikes all over the country, like this one by women from the Ladies Tailors union on the picket line during the "Uprising of the 20,000" garment workers strike.

at the Triangle Shirtwaist Factory. Perhaps a cigarette butt had been tossed in the bin of cotton scrap and dust, which exploded in a massive fire. Workers tried to put the fire out with buckets of water they kept on each floor, but it spread too rapidly. The fire started on the eighth floor and quickly filled the cutting room with smoke. Flames spread up airshafts to the ninth and tenth floors. Workers ran for exits, some of which had been blocked by the owners who, fearful of theft, insisted that all workers use only one exit. New York's firefighters arrived, but none had ladders that could reach to the eighth or higher floors. Some workers were quickly consumed by flames. More than 50 jumped from the windows, and 20 were killed when a flimsy fire escape on the outside of the building collapsed. In the end, 146 workers, most of them young women, were killed in the **Triangle Shirtwaist Factory Fire**, the deadliest industrial catastrophe in Manhattan for decades. Eventually, the Triangle Shirtwaist Fire led to new industrial regulations and important labor reforms. At the time, however, when devastated husbands, parents, friends, and relatives lined up at the makeshift morgue on Twenty-Sixth Street to try to identify the bodies, only the terrible loss seemed real.

Victims of the Triangle Shirtwaist Fire fell from the eighth and ninth stories to their death on the sidewalk below.

Triangle Shirtwaist Factory Fire
A fire in the Triangle Shirtwaist Factory in New York City in 1911 that killed 146 workers and that later led to new factory inspection and safety laws.

Bread and Roses: The Lawrence Strike of 1912

A few months after the Triangle Fire, on New Year's Day 1912, a new Massachusetts law limited the work week to 54 hours, a cut from the 56-hour norm in the mills of Lawrence. The management of the mill companies complied with the law and cut wages accordingly. They saw little reason to worry about any protest. The workers of Lawrence spoke 45 different languages and were divided into different crafts; less than one in ten was a union member. Cutting their pay seemed both prudent and low risk. But when the pay cuts appeared in the pay envelopes, workers immediately started to walk off the job. An estimated 14,000 workers were on strike by the end of the first day. In response to the strikers' spontaneous action, the IWW, then at the height of its influence, sent some of its top organizers to Lawrence. They planned smaller meetings by language groups and large rallies on the Lawrence Common. To get around a city ordinance that banned gatherings in front of any of the mills, the strikers devised a new tactic—a moving picket line in which strikers did not stop but kept walking in a continuous line around the mill.

When IWW leaders were accused of putting women in the front lines, the IWW's Elizabeth Gurley Flynn responded, "The IWW has been accused of putting the women in the front. The truth is, the IWW does not keep them in the back, and they go to the front." At some point in the strike, when women, with their babies in their arms, marched through the streets of Lawrence with signs reading, "We Want Bread and Roses, Too" the strike was given a new name. The public generally supported the strikers, and the mill owners eventually agreed to an increase in salary and no discrimination against strikers. The **Bread and Roses strike** was a success; probably the greatest success in the IWW's short history.

Bread and Roses Strike
A spontaneous strike of workers in the mills of Lawrence, Massachusetts in 1912.

Ludlow, Colorado, 1914

In the mountains of southern Colorado, brutal working conditions persisted in the coal mines that were owned by John D. Rockefeller. On September 15, 1913, delegates from the mining camps gathered at Trinidad, Colorado, and voted for a strike demanding recognition for their union, a 10 percent increase in wages, an 8-hour day, the right to elect those who would weigh the coal, free choice of stores and doctors (rather than only company stores and doctors), and enforcement of Colorado mining laws. Mother Jones told the miners, "Don't be afraid boys. . .Fear is the greatest curse we have." Within a week, 80 to 90 percent of the miners were on strike.

The strike lasted 14 months. It was long and bloody. The coal companies evicted the striking miners from their company-owned housing and the union arranged tent camps. Violence erupted between the coal company's guards and strikers, and by the end of the first month, more than 20 people had been killed. Worse violence followed.

On April 20, 1914, militia troops recruited by the coal company took up positions around the miners' camp at Ludlow, Colorado, and the nervous inhabitants then took up their own positions. No one knew who fired the first shot, but one shot quickly led to several hours of murderous fighting. Tents burst into flame, possibly from a bullet striking something explosive. Over 30 people were killed, including several women and 11 children found under one of the tents where they had huddled for safety. The **Ludlow Massacre** became a rallying cry for labor, and the loss of life, especially of children, permanently tarnished and troubled the Rockefeller family. President Woodrow Wilson sent U.S. army troops to restore order and the United Mine Workers Union declared that ending the strike was "doing the best thing possible for the men on strike who have suffered so long in order that justice might be done." Further justice would take much longer.

Ludlow Massacre
Violence during a coal strike in Ludlow, Colorado, in 1914 in which at least 30 people, including 11 children, were killed.

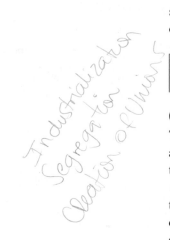

Industrialization
Segregation
Creation of Unions

18.3	**Quick Review** Was the violence that accompanied many strikes inevitable? Why or why not?

CONCLUSION

The rapid industrialization of the United States after the Civil War generated wealth and progress for some Americans and serious new problems for others. Very quickly, the disparities that emerged created new and violent tensions in the United States.

In the South, the end of Reconstruction set the region on a path that would continue to deny civil rights and economic opportunities to African-Americans for many decades to come. Combined with the country's growing indifference to the original goals of Reconstruction, the New South successfully limited the advancement of African-Americans through legal exclusions. Even as the South was opening up to the world with the introduction of new railroad lines and the diversification of its economy, power and prosperity came only to some. Those who were excluded fought back, particularly African-Americans, who challenged segregation, violence, and their economic exclusion.

Farmers, white and black, also challenged their economic exclusion from the prosperity that Gilded Age America was generating. Through a number of organizations, especially the Farmers' Alliance and later the Populist Party, farmers sought economic might equal to the giant corporations and political access at the highest levels.

Industrial workers also organized to fight for their rights. New Unions—the Knights of Labor, the American Federation of Labor, the United Mine Workers of America, and the Industrial Worker of the World—sought to protect worker's rights. The nation was wracked by strikes, from the Railroad Strike of 1877 to the Miners Strike in Pueblo, Colorado, in 1914 as well as tragedies including the Triangle Shirtwaist Fire of 1912. Between the railway strike of 1877 and the Colorado strike of 1914, American workers fought to better their lives and working conditions. While some owners were sympathetic, the nation was divided by a great gulf between those who owned the industries and those who worked in them. Grand visions of a different kind of society were born but not achieved. More basic demands—for higher pay, safer conditions, shorter work days—were only partially met, and it would be another 2 decades, during the Great Depression and New Deal era, that industrial workers could get much of what they were asking for from 1877 onward.

CHAPTER REVIEW	How did some of the disenfranchised (workers, blacks, farmers, etc.) attempt to make their voices heard in the late 1800s and early 1900s? Why were their tactics different? How successful were they?

Chapter 18   Chapter Review

CONFLICT IN THE NEW SOUTH

18.1 Analyze how the combined impact of industrialism and the end of Reconstruction created the unique character of the New South.

Review Questions

1. **Historical Interpretation**
   What was new about the New South?

2. **Constructing an Argument**
   What factors contributed to the increased rigidity of racial segregation and renewed white efforts to exclude blacks from political life in the late 1800s?

3. **Comparison**
   Compare and contrast the response of Booker T. Washington and W.E.B. De Bois to racial segregation and discrimination. To what groups within the white community might each appeal? Why?

THE POLITICS OF CONFLICT—FROM POPULIST MOVEMENT TO POPULIST PARTY

18.2 Analyze how agrarian unrest and protest came to have a significant impact on American politics.

Review Questions

4. **Historical Interpretation**
   What factors contributed to the rise of farmers' organizations in the late 1800s?

5. **Crafting an Argument**
   How would you explain the emphasis that farmers' political representatives placed on federal fiscal policy?

6. **Contextualization**
   What factors contributed to the nomination of William Jennings Bryan by both the People's Party and the Democrats?

WORKER PROTEST AND THE RISE OF ORGANIZED LABOR

18.3 Explain the tensions in industrial America that led to major labor strife between the 1870s and 1914.

Review Questions

7. **Comparison**
   Compare and contrast the Knights of Labor and the American Federation of Labor. How would you characterize the approach of each to the challenges facing American workers in the late 1800s and early 1900s?

8. **Historical Interpretation**
   What role did government play in the labor disputes of the late 1800s?

9. **Crafting an Argument**
   What group or groups bears greatest responsibility for the violence that often accompanied labor disputes in the late 1800s and early 1900s?

19 Progressive Movements, Progressive Politics

CHAPTER OBJECTIVE

Demonstrate an understanding of the many ideas that were labeled progressive and the impact of those ideas on life in the United States.

LEARNING OBJECTIVES

THE REVOLT OF THE INTELLECTUALS

19.1 Explain the role of muckraking journalists and intellectuals in shaping a progressive agenda.

THE TRANSFORMATION OF THE CITIES

19.2 Analyze the changes in urban life that inspired progressive reforms and the impact of those reforms on cities.

RELIGIOUS RESPONSES TO THE GILDED AGE

19.3 Explain the main currents of religiously based reform movements during the progressive era.

PROGRESSIVE POLITICS ON THE NATIONAL STAGE

19.4 Analyze the three "progressive presidents" and their administrations.

No one individual symbolized the Progressive movement as much as Theodore Roosevelt. As an advocate of the outdoor life, a "trustbuster," and a conservationist, he captured the hearts of many Americans in the early 1900s.

Theodore Roosevelt had been president for less than 4 months in December 1901 when he sent his first annual message to Congress. The new president said that, in light of the "tremendous and highly complex industrial development" in the country, the "old laws, and the old customs which…were once quite sufficient to regulate the accumulation and distribution of wealth…are no longer sufficient." He asked Congress for new laws and new presidential authority to meet the new situation. Roosevelt was ready to act.

Roosevelt rejected the radicalism of Democrats like William Jennings Bryan or Socialists like Eugene V. Debs. He insisted, "it cannot too often be pointed out that to strike with ignorant violence at the interest of one set of men almost inevitably endangers the interests of all." He was full of praise for the corporate leaders who had created great wealth. Nevertheless, he asserted, "There is a wide-spread conviction in the minds of the American people that the great corporations known as trusts are in certain of their features and tendencies hurtful to the general welfare." And since the "conditions are now wholly different," therefore "wholly different action is called for." As Roosevelt defined those "wholly different" actions in the weeks and months that followed, it became clear that he was charting a new course in American politics. He was no radical, but he was not a McKinley Republican either. He was determined to address the anger that fueled strikes—though certainly not to adopt the economic changes advocated by many strikers. In addition, he was committed to changing urban and industrial conditions and conserving the country's natural resources.

As a result of his efforts, Roosevelt and the two presidents who followed him, William Howard Taft and Woodrow Wilson, came to be known as the progressive presidents. Presidential politics, however, were far from the only aspect of the larger Progressive movement that dominated American life between 1890 and 1917 and, indeed, led to the electoral success of Roosevelt and his successors. This chapter seeks to understand the many ideas that were labeled progressive and the impact of those ideas on life in the United States.

THE REVOLT OF THE INTELLECTUALS

19.1 Explain the role of muckraking journalists and intellectuals in shaping a progressive agenda.

Long before Theodore Roosevelt became president, numerous people in the United States were thinking about how best to respond to the extraordinary changes brought about by immigration, urbanization, and the rapid industrialization of the country. Upper-class reformers, newspaper reporters, ministers, writers, and college professors proposed new ways of ordering economic and political life. At the end of the 1800s, rapid industrialization and urbanization across the United States produced a radically different intellectual climate. New ideas, and those who envisioned them, began to shape the future of industrialized America.

Utopian Idealists

Henry George, a young journalist in California, was deeply troubled by the railway strike of 1877. Two years later, he published *Progress and Poverty*. The book quickly became a bestseller. George understood that there were benefits from industrialization, but the result, he said, was that "[f]rom all parts of the civilized world come complaints…of want and suffering and anxiety among the working classes."

As a solution, George proposed a 100 percent tax on any increase in the value of land or any rents on land. He argued, "We already take some rent in taxation. We have only to make some change in our modes of taxation to take it all." George said that his proposal would reduce the value and cost of land, thus allowing workers to turn to farming if they wished, which would create a labor shortage that would inevitably raise wages and improve conditions in factories. While many economists argued with George's logic, the **single tax movement** became a political force, and single tax clubs sprang up everywhere. In 1886, New York's Central Labor Union persuaded George to run for mayor of the city. Although George lost, his campaign led to a permanent reform coalition in New York.

Ten years after George's book, Edward Bellamy, a journalist from Massachusetts, published *Looking Backward* in 1888. The book described a new perfect society in which class and class warfare had disappeared in a country of prosperous citizens who enjoyed their lives free of poverty or wealth and also free of lawyers and politics.

In contrast to Bellamy's hopeful work, Ignatius Donnelly wrote *Caesar's Column* in 1891, a book that described a country rigidly divided between a large working class living brutal lives and a small, comfortable elite. In Donnelly's fictional story, a few Americans are able to escape from their world and start a happy new community organized around the platforms of the Greenback Party, the Knights of Labor, and the Farmers' Alliance.

George, Bellamy, and Donnelly and other authors like them were often unrealistic. Their images of a new perfect society seem romantic and their economic proposals unworkable. Nevertheless, in a county groping its way to a different economic order, all of them gave ideas, energy, and optimism to other reformers.

Significant Dates

1879	*Progress and Poverty* by Henry George published
	Frances E. Willard elected president of Woman's Christian Temperance Union
1881	Henry Demarest Lloyd publishes exposé of Standard Oil Company
1889	Ellen Starr and Jane Addams open Hull House in Chicago
	Hazen S. Pingree elected as reform mayor of Detroit, Michigan
1893	*McClure's Magazine* publishes first issue
1897	Samuel M. "Golden Rule" Jones elected reform mayor of Toledo, Ohio
1899	John Dewey's *School and Society* published
1901	Theodore Roosevelt becomes president at William McKinley's assassination
1904	Ida Tarbell's *History of the Standard Oil Company* published
1906	Upton Sinclair's *The Jungle* published
1912	Woodrow Wilson defeats Theodore Roosevelt, William Howard Taft, and Eugene V. Debs for the presidency and launches New Freedom
1913	Federal Reserve System launched
1914	Clayton Anti-Trust Act
1917	Walter Rauschenbusch's *A Theology for the Social Gospel* published

single tax movement
Proposed by Henry George in 1879, the single tax—a 100% tax on any increase in the value of real estate—was designed to keep property values low and therefore limit the accumulation of wealth while spreading opportunity more broadly in the society.

The Professors

John Dewey is best remembered for his educational ideas, but his goal was a wider philosophical response to industrialism. Dewey was born in 1859 in a small town in Vermont, studied philosophy at Johns Hopkins University, and taught at the University of Michigan. In 1894, Dewey was invited to the new University of Chicago. Dewey accepted the offer with enthusiasm. Chicago in the 1890s was the center of social reform in which Dewey and his wife Alice Chapman Dewey were deeply interested. When it came time to make the move, however, Dewey had a hard time getting to Chicago.

When Dewey set out for Chicago in July 1894, most of the nation's rail lines were shut down because of the Pullman strike. He found transit on a Michigan Central train that did not use Pullman cars. Traveling in the midst of a nationwide strike was informative to the young philosophy professor. He spoke with one of the American Railway Union organizers and wrote to his wife that "my nerves were more thrilled than they had been for years." He wondered "if I had better resign my job teaching & follow him round till I got into life." Dewey was considerably less impressed by another passenger who was "voluble on the outrage" of the strike because it was preventing him from getting home for dinner. For Dewey, the focus was on higher considerations.

Young intellectuals like Dewey were then challenging the dominant economic theory of the time, "**Social Darwinism**." The foremost American exponent of Social Darwinism, the economist William Graham Sumner, opposed what he called "the absurd effort to make the world over." For Sumner, Charles Darwin's description of biological evolution showed that the fittest of each species survive and thus shape the future. So, Sumner argued, in the social order, the fittest were rightfully the owners and the dominant class of society. Those less fit are condemned by their natural "un-fitness" to be laborers and employees. Any interference with the system, Sumner argued, would destabilize the economy and weaken the nation. Herbert Spencer, a British writer, proposed similar ideas, coining the phrase "survival of the fittest." He, too, had a large following in the United States, especially among the wealthy.

Dewey saw the ideas of Spencer and Sumner as easy but unethical justifications for privilege. Instead, Dewey believed that wise people could and should intervene in the economy to make it more just. His thinking was shared by a generation of philosophers, including William James, Charles S. Peirce, and future Supreme Court Justice Oliver Wendell Holmes, who in the 1880s and 1890s doubted all ideological certainties and certainly did not want to see Social Darwinism become the dominant mindset in society.

Another young scholar, Richard Ely at Johns Hopkins University, also attacked the Social Darwinists. Ely had visited the town of Pullman before the strike and noticed that workers would not talk to him, fearing that he was a spy. He called the town's culture "benevolent, well-wishing feudalism." As a counter to Social Darwinism, Ely was developing a very different economic theory that allowed for—indeed called for—government to intervene directly in the economic affairs of the country.

While Dewey focused on philosophy and Ely on economics, Albion Small was helping to build the new academic discipline of sociology. For Small, sociologists did not simply study society; they meant to reform it. In 1896, Small sought to help define his field when he wrote in the new *American Journal of Sociology* that "action, not speculation, is the supreme teacher." Dewey, Ely, and Small were all part of a generation of academics who shared the goal of changing society.

The Muckraking Journalists

Although newspapers had been important in the United States since well before the American Revolution, newspapers changed significantly in the late 1800s. When Joseph Pulitzer bought the *New York Evening World* in 1887, he made it the largest circulation paper in the country with several innovations—banner headlines, comic strips, and investigative journalism. The *World* did an exposé of the speculative adventures of the managers of the Equitable Life Assurance Society, which the paper said were

Social Darwinism
The application of Charles Darwin's theory of biological evolution to society, holding that the fittest and the wealthiest should thrive and lead, the weak and the poor "deserve" their fate, and government action is unable to alter this "natural" process.

"gambling with the people's money." Public anger over this news of the insurance industry's excesses led to the election of a reforming Republican, Charles Evans Hughes, as governor of New York in 1906 and to new regulations on the insurance industry. In addition, the huge response to the exposé made the *World* a very successful paper.

Almost a decade later, William Randolph Hearst, who had used the Pulitzer formula for his *San Francisco Examiner* exposés of the Southern Pacific Railroad, purchased the *New York Morning Journal* to compete directly with Pulitzer. Hearst hired some of the country's best reporters, Edward Markham, Ambrose Bierce, and Winifred Black, and published his own exposés of New York City corruption. Many other newspapers began to imitate Pulitzer and Hearst.

The trend toward investigative reporting to expose misconduct of important people or organizations was emerging even before Pulitzer and Hearst took advantage of it. Henry Demarest Lloyd, who wrote for Chicago newspapers, became one of the first of the so-called **muckraking journalists**. The term *muckraking* referred to the job of raking through filth. Muckraking journalists saw it as their duty to expose the filth of corruption. Not everyone liked the new investigative journalism, and those who objected included more than just those being investigated. President Theodore Roosevelt thought the journalists described problems but failed to offer solutions. It was Roosevelt who coined the term *muckrakers*. He said the journalists were simply raking up the muck from the bottom of society's pond, and the name muckraker stuck. For many, however, it became a term of respect.

Early in his career, Lloyd covered the 1877 railroad strike. He wrote that if something did not happen to improve the lot of the country's workers, "the country will drift into a convulsion as much greater than the convulsion that wrecked the Roman Empire." Lloyd's 1881 exposé of Standard Oil Company and his 1894 book, *Wealth Against Commonwealth*, denounced the monopolies as a threat to the welfare of everyday people.

Hearst also launched *Cosmopolitan* magazine as a vehicle for investigative journalism. In 1893, S. S. McClure launched *McClure's Magazine*, which until 1926 was the

muckraking journalists
Journalism exposing economic, social, and political evils, so named by Theodore Roosevelt for its "raking the muck" from the bottom of American society.

The Jungle, by muckraking journalist Upton Sinclair, exposed the inhumane and unhealthy conditions of meat processing in Chicago. One result was typical of progressive legislation designed to improve people's lives, the Pure Food and Drug Act, which regulated the meatpacking industry.

leader in the investigative field. Investigative journalists—writing with the conviction that if people knew more of what was wrong in society they would act to change it—played a key role in the Progressive movement.

The January 1903 issue of *McClure's* included articles by Ida M. Tarbell as part of her continuing analysis of John D. Rockefeller and the Standard Oil Company, later published as *The History of the Standard Oil Company* in 1904; Ray Stannard Baker's report of visiting striking coal miners and their families; and the report by Lincoln Steffens on "The Shame of Minneapolis" about the trial of the infamous four-term mayor of Minneapolis who got rich from payments from opium joints, unlicensed saloons known as "blind pigs," and "disorderly houses" of prostitution. Issue after issue of *McClure's*, *Cosmopolitan*, and daily newspapers were forcing cities to clean up corruption, compelling sometimes reluctant legislators to enact new restrictions on monopolies, and helping political reformers gain office.

In 1906, a young reporter named Upton Sinclair took a job in Chicago's slaughterhouses to report, from the inside, on the meatpacking industry. He found a world where workers suffered terrible injury, animals suffered inhumane treatment, and unsanitary conditions poisoned the meat consumed by Americans. When Sinclair's exposé, *The Jungle*, was published in 1906, the public response was immediate. Consumption of meat fell precipitously, and within months, Congress passed the Federal Meat Inspection Act and the Pure Food and Drug Act regulating the meat industry as well as the food and drug industries. While Sinclair's main goal had been to draw attention to inhumane working conditions, the primary result of his efforts was sanitary regulation of meatpacking plants. As Sinclair reflected years later, "I aimed at the public's heart and by accident I hit it in the stomach." Nevertheless, the passage of reform legislation within months of a Sinclair's book showed the power of such reporting and, at the same time, raised journalism to new heights as a respectable profession.

> **19.1** **Quick Review** Which was more important to launching the Progressive movement: the theory behind it or the identification of specific problems? Why?

THE TRANSFORMATION OF THE CITIES

> **19.2** Analyze the changes in urban life that inspired progressive reforms and the impact of those reforms on cities.

The United States grew from a little under 40 million people in 1870 to just over 75 million people in 1900 (for comparison, the 2010 census showed the United States at over 300 million people). Perhaps one-third of the growth between 1870 and 1910 was due to immigration and two-thirds to a high-birth rate. While the population almost doubled, it also became concentrated in cities. Many of the nation's cities were much larger and more densely populated in 1900 than they had been in 1870, when the majority of people still lived on farms and in rural communities. In 1870, the United States had only seven cities with over 250,000 people and none yet held a million people. Thirty years later, three cities had passed the 1 million mark—New York with 3.4 million, Chicago with 1.7 million, and Philadelphia with 1.3 million. There were also dozens of large cities scattered among most of the states and territories of the union. Americans were adjusting to urban life, and the adjustment was not always easy.

The Rise of Machine Politics and the Progressive Response

As cities grew, a new kind of urban politics took root in the United States, shaped by the fact that cities were the major points of entry for new immigrants to the nation. Many immigrants desperately needed services, especially help with a job. Some took quickly to city political life, finding in politics a way to gain social respectability.

Nowhere was the mix of urban growth, immigration, and the need for new services greater than in New York City. Within that mix in New York, a new kind of political organization, the political machine, was created. In political machines, constituents supported a candidate in return for anticipated favors, which would be repaid when that candidate was elected. New York's Democratic political machine was known as **Tammany Hall**, named for the building where it first met. Tammany effectively ruled New York for most of the years from the 1850s to the 1930s. Many other urban political machines were often associated with Irish political leaders, but Tammany predated the Irish influence. In fact, gaining access to Tammany was part of the Irish rise to power in New York City.

The most famous, or infamous, of early Tammany bosses was William M. (Boss) Tweed, who led Tammany in the 1860s and 1870s. Tweed was a Protestant of English background. After holding the office of alderman (city council member) and then being elected to Congress, Tweed turned to where he saw the real power, in Tammany.

In 1863 at the age of 40, Tweed became the chief of Tammany. He made sure one of his close allies, Abraham Oakley, was elected mayor while he stayed in the background and kept control of the political process. Tweed became immensely wealthy as he and his Tammany associates benefited from—some said stole from—development projects like the Tweed Courthouse in lower Manhattan (now the home of the city's school department) and Riverside Park, built over the New York Central Railroad tracks—beautiful municipal improvements that provided jobs but cost many times what they should have, with large kickbacks going to the chosen developers and to Tweed himself.

Tweed and the New York political bosses who came after him robbed the city shamelessly, by one estimate taking 45 million dollars (1 billion in current dollars). At the same time, the political machine made sure that the city's poor—or more specifically, those among the city's poor who supported them on election day—got jobs when they needed them. When necessary, Tammany created more jobs than the city needed

19.1

19.2

19.3

19.4

Tammany Hall
New York City's Democratic Party organization, dating from well before the Civil War, that evolved into a powerful political machine after 1860, using patronage and bribes to maintain control of the city administration.

Political cartoons like this one showing a corrupt political boss handing out special privileges and demanding votes in return, did much to turn public opinion against machine rule in politics.

to be sure that every loyal voter got one, even if that meant that the city had 20 inspectors for its four water pumps and Central and Riverside parks were kept immaculate by an impressively large number of park workers. Tammany and other political machines could also be counted on for more direct aid when it was needed—a handout to tide a family over a rough spot, a basket of food for the holidays, someone to show up at court and indicate to the judge or district attorney when charges should be dropped.

Tweed's corruption was attacked by the cartoonist Thomas Nast and eventually provoked a public backlash. Tweed was arrested, convicted of theft, and died in jail in 1878. Some of his collaborators fled the country. But Tammany survived, and the new leader, John (Honest John) Kelly was the first of a long line of Irish politicians to direct Tammany. Kelly avoided the kind of theft that led to Tweed's downfall. But he did ensure that a tightly organized political machine maintained close links to immigrant communities and Catholic parishes, as well as local and district bosses. Kelly controlled the city's 40,000 jobs and made sure that loyal Tammany supporters—those who remembered to vote the Tammany ticket on election day—got those jobs.

One of Tammany's district leaders, George Washington Plunkitt, was also a state senator. In 1905, Plunkitt described how New York politics worked. He said that reformers failed to draw "the distinction between honest graft and dishonest graft. There's all the difference in the world between the two." Plunkitt would have nothing to do with "dishonest graft—blackmailin' gamblers, saloon-keepers, disorderly people, etc." But there was another way, he said, "There's honest graft, and I'm an example of how it works. I might sum up the whole thing by sayin': 'I seen my opportunities and I took 'em.'" He explained, "Well, I'm tipped off, say, that they're going to lay out a new park at a certain place.…I go to that place, and I buy up all the land I can in the neighborhood.…ain't it perfectly honest to charge a good price and make a profit on my investment and foresight?" It was an arrangement that Plunkitt saw no reason to hide. Reformers might not have liked it, but that was how cities worked in Plunkitt's day.

New York was far from alone in the rise of machine politics that was often Irish dominated. Most large cities had something similar. Politics in Boston was played at the neighborhood level, where a number of legendary figures—Patrick J. Kennedy in East Boston, John F. (Honey Fitz) Fitzgerald in the North End, P.J. Maguire and later James Michael Curley in Roxbury, and most powerful of all Martin Lomasney in the West End—each ruled their neighborhood. In 1905, Fitzgerald won election as mayor. He served two terms and was succeeded by his arch-rival James M. Curley, who dominated Boston politics for the next half century. Fitzgerald's favorite daughter, Rose, married Patrick Kennedy's son Joseph, and their son, John Fitzgerald Kennedy, became the first Irish Catholic elected president.

While the political machines met real needs for their poor and working-class constituents (and along the way made a few of their leaders very wealthy), the closed-door deals, the graft—"honest" or "dishonest"—and the political favoritism dismayed many. The political machines greatly increased the cost of municipal government. They also shut many out of office, especially the children and grandchildren of the native-born elite who thought it was their duty and destiny to rule. A new generation of political reformers began challenging the political machines, making municipal reform an important element in the progressive agenda.

The Progressive Challenge to City and State Government

Progressive reformers believed that the country's political and economic systems could be fixed if honest people of good will put their minds to it. They had little interest in radical reforms like socialism and little sympathy for the old-line politicians like Boston's Martin Lomasney. They were what they said they were, reformers, trying to reform current structures of government.

In their campaigns for efficient urban management, progressive reformers sometimes came across as cold and heartless to residents who preferred the

American Voices

Lincoln Steffens, "Boston—1915," 1908

Lincoln Steffens, one of the leading "muckraking" journalists, was invited to support a reform effort in Boston—called Boston 1915—by local businessmen in 1908. Boston taught Steffens some important lessons about not only the role of political machines but also the place of reformers like himself in the life of the urban poor.

My sponsor, E. A. Filene, called together a group of earnest, representative men, some of them reformers, not all…I [asked them], Who was the worst, the most impossible, man in Boston?

"Martin Lomasney," they said, all in quick agreement. A politician he was.…and the next morning early I took my little dog, Mickey Sweeney, and went over in the bad wards where Martin Lomasney was the boss.…

"Who do you want?" he demanded.

"Martin Lomasney."

"That's me," he said. "Who are you?"

I told him. "Sure," he said. "I've read your stuff. What do you want?"…

"The reformers sent me to you,"…"I asked them who was the worst man in town, and they named you. So I've come to get the low-down on things, and—will you give it to me?"…

"You must want something," Martin grumbled at me.…

"Yes," I said. "Police graft. What do you do about the petty crooks?"

He was cross, or he pretended to be. "What do you mean by petty crooks?"

"Oh, you know, the dips, the burglars and thieves, the regular professional crooks that we honest grafters call criminals."

"And what do you mean by what I do about them?"

"Well, you go to the front for them, don't you? See the district attorney or a judge or the cops—you get them off, don't you?"

"Yes, I do," he said, dropping his feet and facing me with three fingers thrust under my nose. "Three times."

I laughed. "Ah, now, don't you sometimes do it four times?"

He was defying me. "Seven times? Martin, don't you even get 'em off seventy times seven times?"

"Yes, I do," he burst. "I never quit some of 'em, not the way you do."

"Of course," I said. "You stick, but tell me, how do you justify it to yourself, saving these hopeless crooks over and over and over again when you know they'll come back and do it over and over and over again!"

I did not expect him to answer this question. It was more of an exclamation on my part, but he did answer it; inarticulate people can sometimes express themselves.

"I think," said Martin Lomasney, "that there's got to be in every ward somebody that any bloke can come to—no matter what he's done—and get help. Help, you understand; none of your law and your justice, but help."

That hit me hard, and we got no further that day.… They provided help and counsel and a hiding-place in emergencies for friendless men, women, and children who were in dire need, who were in guilty need, with the mob of justice after them. And, as I sat there and thought I saw that if we were to build up in Boston an organization to replace the political machine and so win the town the loyalty that now went to the boss and his party, we must provide for that service.

Source: Lincoln Steffens, *The Autobiography of Lincoln Steffens* (New York: The Literary Guild, 1931), pp. 612–618.

Thinking Critically

1. Documentary Analysis

What did Lincoln Steffens, and the men who invited him to Boston, think about the way that Martin Lomasney ran his ward in Boston? What did Lomasney think of the reformers?

2. Historical Interpretation

How did Lomasney justify his politics? What do his justifications suggest about the challenges faced by the reformers who hoped to supplant him?

face-to-face dealings of old-style political bosses. Moreover, in their desire to cut costs, some reformers attacked services that others thought essential. Progressive reform was also seen—sometimes accurately—as an effort by an older Protestant and native-born elite to reclaim power from more recent immigrant groups, especially the Irish, who had built up their own political organizations.

Nevertheless, candidates committed to cleaning up urban corruption and providing more efficient urban services came to power in a number of cities. Progressive reform cut across the political parties. Republicans and Democrats alike included both reformers and those who resisted reform.

Grover Cleveland was elected mayor of Buffalo, New York, as a Democrat in 1881 with a promise to clean up the municipal corruption. Cleveland established a reputation for honesty, especially after he rejected a street-cleaning contract approved by the city council as a "bare-faced, impudent, and shameless scheme." Cleveland's honesty led to his election as a reform governor of New York and, only 2 years later, to the presidency and the White House.

Hazen S. Pingree was elected mayor of Detroit, Michigan, as a Republican reformer. Born in Maine in1840, Pingree served in the Union army, then moved to Detroit where he went to work in a shoe factory, and by the 1880s, owned one of the largest shoe manufacturers in the Midwest. In 1889, Republican business leaders, determined to oust Detroit's Democratic machine, sought out Pingree who quickly took to politics, was a tough campaigner, and became a popular mayor. Pingree challenged the awarding of city contracts for the schools, ferries, toll roads, and street and sewer services. When the private City Railway Company wanted a long-term contract, Pingree forced them to cut fares from 5 cents to 3 cents, a significant benefit to Detroit's citizens.

When the depression of 1893 put 25,000 of Detroit's 250,000 people out of work, Pingree, who did not want to increase municipal spending, convinced owners of vacant lots to allow the city to use them, provided seeds and farm implements to the unemployed, and urged people all over the city to start their own potato patches and vegetable plots. In time, he became known as "Potato Patch Pingree" for his efforts.

Samuel M. Jones, known as "Golden Rule Jones," served as mayor of Toledo, Ohio, from 1897 until 1904. Jones started work as a day laborer, but eventually started his own oil company. When Jones sold the company to Standard Oil, he emerged a rich man. Reform-minded business leaders nominated Jones for mayor in Toledo in an effort to dislodge a corrupt machine. Jones spent municipal funds freely, opening kindergartens, building parks, and instituting an 8-hour day for city workers. He also called on voters to renounce political parties, believing that a nonpartisan approach to politics would work best. The Republican Party, unhappy with Jones's free-spending ways, refused to renominate him, but he was elected as an independent and continued to serve as a popular mayor until his death. His successor in office, Brand Whitlock, continued his policies through four terms until President Woodrow Wilson appointed Whitlock as U.S. ambassador to Belgium on the eve of World War I. Between them, Jones and Whitlock gave Toledo a national reputation for good government and effective public services when many cities were still mired in corruption and inefficiency. Other cities were also known for their progressive mayors, including San Francisco's James D. Phelan, 1897–1902, and Cleveland's Tom Lofton Johnson, 1899–1909.

Grover Cleveland and Hazen S. Pingree both moved from the mayor's office to become governor of their states. The move was not merely upward political mobility. Many progressive reformers became convinced that legislation at the state level was essential to limit the power of corporations or corrupt urban machines. Other state reforms became core progressive issues, especially proposals for **initiative**, **referendum**, and **recall**, measures aimed at limiting the power of political elites by giving voters the chance to change government policy. South Dakota in the 1890s, Oregon in 1902, and then other states, especially in the West, began adopting these measures. Initiative laws allowed voters to put new laws on the ballot through a petition process while a referendum allowed a similar process to review legislation already in force in a state. Finally, recall petitions and votes allowed voters to remove public officials—legislators, mayors, governors—from office before their terms ended. Never as popular east of the Mississippi as in the West, initiative, referendum, and recall were typical progressive measures, based on the same assumption that drove muckraking journalists: an educated and informed public would do the right thing once the right information was in hand.

Governors and legislatures also adopted other reforms in the progressive era. Workers who were injured on the job had been left on their own or blamed for accidents, but progressives passed worker's compensation laws. Some passed limits on

initiative
Procedure by which citizens can introduce a subject for legislation, usually through a petition signed by a specific number of voters.

referendum
Submission of a law, proposed or already in effect, to a direct popular vote for approval or rejection.

recall
The process of removing an official from office by popular vote, usually after using petitions to call for such a vote.

This young Pittsburgh miner lost his leg in a mine accident. Referring to people like this worker helped progressives pass worker's compensation laws.

the length of the work day, especially for women, and tried to regulate the safety of working conditions.

Reform came to New York City by a different route. Seth Low, the president of Columbia University, was elected mayor of New York as an anti-Tammany candidate in 1901. He fought graft and instituted civil service reform, but Low was not popular, especially in communities that depended on Tammany, and he was defeated for reelection 2 years later. At that point, New York was back in Tammany hands, and Tammany's boss, Charles Murphy, was also the most powerful politician in the state although he held no office. After state elections in 1910, however, Murphy launched his own reform efforts. He selected two Tammany loyalists who were among the youngest and newest in the legislature, 33-year-old Robert F. Wagner in the Senate and 38-year-old Alfred E. Smith in the House, to be the party leaders. Wagner and Smith were known as the "Tammany Twins." In their long political careers, they were also among the most important reformers in American history.

After the Triangle Factory Fire in 1911 (see Chapter 18), Murphy knew they had to do something or lose the support of families who had lost so many daughters and sons in the fire. Murphy directed Wagner and Smith to sponsor the creation of the New York Factory Investigating Commission, which the legislature approved within 3 months. Where Tammany-controlled police officers had harassed striking garment workers only months before, the Tammany-created Factory Investigating Commission hired some of the same strikers to investigate conditions in the city's garment industries, where they found unsafe and unworkable fire escapes and locked exits. A social worker, Frances Perkins, who had witnessed the Triangle Fire, was one of many to volunteer her services to the Factory Investigating Commission. Perkins also wrote much of the legislation that came from the commission's work. In the 2 years, Wagner and Smith, working closely with Perkins, pushed 36 measures through the New York legislature, including those requiring sprinklers in high-rise buildings, fire drills in large shops, unlocked exits, and a reorganization of the state Department of Labor to enforce the new regulations.

Later, these New Yorkers would bring progressive legislation to a national stage. Frances Perkins served as the head of the state's Department of Labor and then from 1933 to 1945 as the U.S. Secretary of Labor, the first woman to serve in a presidential cabinet. Robert Wagner went to Washington as a U.S. Senator where he sponsored legislation creating the Social Security system and legislation guaranteeing unemployment insurance and workers' compensation. In addition, he sponsored the Wagner Act, which gave labor unions the right to bargain effectively—the most important piece of labor legislation enacted in the United States in the 1900s. Al Smith served as a progressive governor of New York in the 1920s and as the Democratic nominee for U.S. president in 1928, the first Catholic nominated by a major party. Progressive reform had influenced one of the most powerful political machines, Tammany, and in turn, Tammany had cultivated powerfully effective legislators who generated historic reforms.

Progressive Education

In 1899, John Dewey wrote *The School and Society,* describing what he thought a progressive approach to education should be, one that he had tried to create with his wife, Alice Chapman Dewey, and Ella Flagg Young, a Chicago teacher leader (who would later be superintendent of schools in Chicago, the first woman to lead a big city system). Together, they opened the Laboratory School at the University of Chicago in 1896, a child-centered approach. For Dewey and others, the focus was not on structure at all, but on the child. These child-centered progressives wanted to shift the emphasis in schools from the curriculum to the needs of the child. Progressive education meant many different things to different people, and Dewey represented only one aspect of it. Other educators who also called themselves progressives argued bitterly with him. For some, progressive education meant reorganizing schools to be more business-like, with centralized administrations and bureaucratic top-down modes of decision making. Progressive teachers wanted to restructure schools to give themselves more voice and more influence while also earning better pay and teaching smaller classes. For yet others, the goal was to make education scientific and to use standardized testing to improve schools. Certainly in the field of education there were many movements that called themselves progressive, and no one definition fit all of them.

Jane Addams and the Settlement House Movement

In 1913, when Jane Addams had been living at Hull House on Halsted Street in Chicago for more than 20 years, she summed up her belief about the role of the settlement house and all efforts to improve society. "We have learned to say," she wrote "that the good must be extended to all of society before it can be held secure by any one person or any one class; but we have not yet learned to add to that statement, that unless all men and all classes contribute to a good, we cannot even be sure it is worth having." While many progressives might have agreed that society must find a way to extend the good things of life to all citizens, far fewer would have agreed with Addams that all citizens needed to play a role in defining what "good" looked like. Nevertheless, she held firm on both points. At Hull House, social reformers met those they were trying to help in face-to-face encounters, and all involved learned from each other.

Addams was born to a comfortable life in 1860 (her father was a friend of Abraham Lincoln's) and moved to Chicago in 1889 when she and her friend Ellen Starr opened Hull House. Chicago's Hull House, though not the first American settlement house, became the model for most others. Addams said she was at Hull House to be a part of the community, not to offer help from above. She knew that she was living there as much to learn as to help her economically poorer neighbors.

Hull House and similar settlement houses in other cities organized badly needed social services in poor urban neighborhoods. Lillian Wald and Mary Brewster founded the Henry Street Settlement and the Henry Street Visiting Nurse Services in New York City's Lower East Side. Others settlement houses, including Hull House, did the same. Visiting nurses based in settlement houses visited the tenement apartments of the poor and brought medical help.

Jane Addams (1860–1935) spent all of her adult life at Hull House in Chicago, living among the city's poor. She not only provided social services but also learned much from her neighbors.

American Voices

Jane Addams, *Twenty Years at Hull House*, 1910

Jane Addams was a younger contemporary of Mother Jones but from a very different background. She and her good friend Ellen Starr opened Hull House in one of Chicago's poorest neighborhoods in September 1889, and Addams lived there for the next 45 years serving successive generations of Chicago's poor. In the process, she became a nationally and internationally known advocate for settlement houses and, later, for political reform and an end to war. Nevertheless, for all of her national and international travel and fame, her home and her roots remained on Halsted Street where she lived until she died in 1935.

The next January [1889] found Miss Starr and myself in Chicago, searching for a neighborhood in which we might put our plans into execution. In our eagerness to win friends for the new undertaking, we utilized every opportunity to set forth the meaning of the Settlement as it had been embodied in Toynbee Hall, although in those days we made no appeal for money, meaning to start with our own slender resources....

In those early days we were often asked why we had come to live on Halsted Street when we could afford to live somewhere else. I remember one man who used to shake his head and say it was "the strangest thing he had met in his experience," but who was finally convinced that it was "not strange but natural." In time it came to seem natural to all of us that the Settlement should be there. If it is natural to feed the hungry and care for the sick, it is certainly natural to give pleasure to the young, comfort to the aged, and to minister to the deep-seated craving for social intercourse that all men feel. Whoever does it is rewarded by something, which, if not gratitude, is at least spontaneous and vital and lacks that irksome sense of obligation with which a substantial benefit is too often acknowledged....

From the first it seemed understood that we were ready to perform the humblest neighborhood services. We were asked to wash the newborn babies, and to prepare the dead for burial, to nurse the sick, and to "mind the children."...

But in spite of some untoward experiences, we were constantly impressed with the uniform kindness and courtesy we received. Perhaps these first days laid the simple human foundations which are certainly essential for continuous living among the poor: first, genuine preference for residence in an industrial quarter to any other part of the city, because it is interesting, and makes the human appeal; and second, the conviction in the words of Canon Barnett, that the things which make men alike are finer and better than the things that keep them apart, and that these basic likenesses, if they are properly accentuated, easily transcend the less essential differences of race, language, creed, and tradition.

Perhaps even in those first days we made a beginning toward that object which was afterward stated in our charter: "To provide a center for a higher civic and social life; to institute and maintain educational and philanthropic enterprises, and to investigate and improve the conditions in the industrial districts of Chicago."

Source: Jane Addams, *Twenty Years at Hull House* (originally published 1910).

Thinking Critically

1. **Documentary Analysis**
   Why did Jane Addams believe that living among the poor was a central part of her mission?

2. **Contextualization**
   How did Addams see her relationship with the people she served? What aspects of the Progressive movement were reflected in her views?

Under Addams leadership, Hull House did more than provide services to the poor. It also took the side of the poor in labor and legal disputes. When Addams realized that young women strikers were in danger of losing their company housing, Hull House launched a cooperative women's boarding house. Such direct support for strikers did not endear Addams to some of Chicago's most powerful leaders who were willing to tolerate, even support, social services but were hostile to her involvement in a strike. Nevertheless, such efforts solidified her base within the communities that mattered the most to her.

19.2 **Quick Review** Why were political reforms, school reforms, and assistance for the working class deemed necessary to improve life in American cities? Which were the most beneficial? Were some harmful?

RELIGIOUS RESPONSES TO THE GILDED AGE

19.3 Explain the main currents of religiously based reform movements during the progressive era.

In the late 1800s, reform movements seeking to improve the lives of working people, bring an end to municipal corruption, and build a just economic order often took on the language and style of evangelical religion. Both reform movements and religious revivals emphasized personal and social transformation. Both wanted changes in people's hearts and were unafraid to use government to bring about changes in behavior. Many reformers were themselves Protestants, and reform efforts were often rooted in the ideas and individualistic ethos of Protestant Christianity.

Temperance and the Woman's Christian Temperance Union

Certainly no political renewal movement was more rooted in Protestant Christianity than the women's campaign against alcohol that began in the 1870s (see Map 19-1). Early in the 1800s, many Protestant ministers began to oppose excessive drinking, and some Protestants took a strong stand against liquor. Still, most Americans continued to drink alcohol. The Panic of 1873, however, led a group of Midwestern women to start a new temperance movement. Many women seemed to reach the same conclusion at about the same time: liquor was consuming their husbands' wages while leading the men to arrive home drunk and ready to abuse wives and children. The answer to this problem, and the key to defending their homes and families, they said, was a campaign against "Demon Rum."

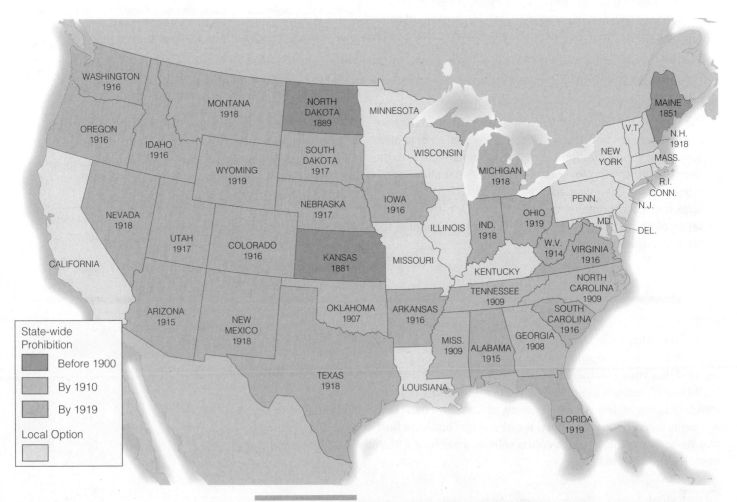

MAP 19-1 Prohibition in the States. The power of the Woman's Christian Temperance Union is shown in the number of states that, starting with Kansas in 1881, prohibited the sale of alcohol outright and those many more that passed local option laws giving cities and towns the right to ban alcohol.

In Hillsboro, Ohio, women began to meet to pray and then to take their prayers into the local saloons or, if banned, to stand outside and pray. Through the depression winter of 1873–1874, Ohio women claimed credit for closing some 3,000 saloons. The following fall, in November 1874, 200 women from 17 states met in Cleveland and formed the **Woman's Christian Temperance Union** (WCTU). They were determined to make temperance—abstinence from liquor—the key moral and political issue of the decade. In the process, the WCTU empowered a generation of women who had been taught that ladylike behavior meant quietly taking care of home and family and leaving politics to men.

When the WCTU began, Frances E. Willard, dean of women and professor at Northwestern University in Chicago, was too busy with her academic duties to pay much attention. Soon thereafter, however, she left Northwestern to become a full-time organizer for the WCTU. Five years later in 1879, Willard became its second president, and she led the WCTU for the next 24 years until her death in 1898, becoming probably the most prominent woman in the United States at the time.

Under Willard's leadership, the WCTU broadened its goals while never losing sight of ending the use of alcohol. Willard was convinced that "much of the evil by which the country is cursed," especially the evil of drink, is the fault of "the men in power whose duty is to make and administer the laws." She took the organization into the political arena, demanding for women the right to vote so they could vote on matters affecting drink and the home. She coined the phrase "home protection" to describe the WCTU's agenda. If drink was destroying families, she argued, then women needed the right to defend their families. If the WCTU was going to pursue its mission of saving homes and reconstructing the nation, then Willard insisted, "We must show power."

By the time Willard died, the WCTU had almost 200,000 members, a 12-story national headquarters in Chicago, and a powerful national presence.

Others took the temperance cause in very different directions. Carry Nation, from Kiowa, Kansas, was married to a man who turned out to be a hopeless drunk. After he died, Nation moved and married a nondrinker. In response to what she believed was a call from God, Nation went back to Kiowa and smashed up the local saloon, breaking bottles, mirrors, and pictures. She followed up with "hatchetations" of other saloons and became a national symbol of one version of the temperance movement.

Whether in the direct action of Carry Nation or the more organized approach of Frances Willard, the temperance movement changed the United States. It laid a solid foundation not only for the Eighteenth Amendment that in 1919 banned the manufacture and sale of liquor but also for the Nineteenth Amendment that a few months later in 1920 gave women the right to vote. The temperance crusade also demonstrated the power of organized religion, both in churches led by clergy and in extradenominational organizations often led by women. The United States in the late 1800s was still an overwhelmingly Protestant country, and a movement that could tap the Protestant religious fervor of the nation's majority could go far.

The Social Gospel

In 1897, Charles M. Sheldon, a young Congregationalist pastor in Topeka, Kansas, published a novel, *In His Steps,* which eventually sold 15 million copies. *In His Steps* told of a fictionalized minister who asks his congregation, "What would be the result, if in this city every church member should begin to do as Jesus would do?…What would Jesus do in the matter of wealth?" In the novel, the question "What would Jesus do?" transformed the town. Similarly, *In His Steps* also struck a chord in the country. Sheldon's question, "What would Jesus do?" led many Protestants to embrace reform movements.

Other religious leaders began to talk of what they called the **Social Gospel**, which was based on the idea that improving society was both the right thing for religious

Frances Willard (1839–1898) led the Woman's Christian Temperance Union from 1879 to 1898, making it a powerful force in the United States.

Woman's Christian Temperance Union
National organization formed after the Civil War dedicated to prohibiting the sale and distribution of alcohol.

Social Gospel
Application of religious ethics to industrial conditions and thereby alleviating poverty, slums, and labor exploitation.

THINKING HISTORICALLY
How the Other Half Lives

Jacob A. Riis, an immigrant from Denmark working as a newspaper police reporter, published *How the Other Half Lives* in 1890. In that book, Riis sought to describe to the city's well-off residents the housing conditions of New York's poor, especially through his photographs. He described parts of lower Manhattan:

> The death of a child in a tenement was registered at the Bureau of Vital Statistics as "plainly due to suffocation in the foul air of an unventilated apartment."…Another was the case of a hard-working family of man and wife, young people from the old country, who took poison together in a Crosby Street tenement because they were "tired." There was no other explanation, and none was needed when I stood in the room in which they had lived. It was an attic with sloping ceiling and a single window so far out on the roof that it seemed not to belong to the place at all. With scarcely room enough to turn around in they had been compelled to pay five dollars and a half a month in advance. There were four such rooms in the attic, and together they brought in as much as many a handsome little cottage in a pleasant part of Brooklyn.

Riis said, "the proprietors frequently urged the filthy habits of the tenants as an excuse for the condition of their property, utterly losing sight of the fact that it was the tolerance of those habits which was the real evil, and that for this they themselves were alone responsible." In pinning responsibility for poverty and misery directly on those who profited from it, Riis created considerable hostility toward himself but also great publicity for the book.

Later, Riis described the difficulty he had in getting the *How the Other Half Lives* published:

> For more than a year I had knocked at the doors of the various magazine editors with my pictures, proposing to tell them how the other half lived, but no one wanted to know.… [I]n the church one might, at all events, tell the truth unhindered. So I thought; but there were cautious souls there too.

Eventually, Riis met Dr. Schauffler, the manager of the City Mission Society, and Dr. Josiah Strong, the author of *Our Country*.

They were impressed with the photos and arranged for Riis to tell the stories within *How the Other Half Lives* to a group at the Broadway Tabernacle, a Congregational church associated with Schauffler and Strong. Riis continues the account:

> One of the editors of *Scribner's Magazine* saw my pictures and heard their story in his church, and came to talk the matter over with me. As a result of that talk I wrote an article that appeared in the Christmas *Scribner's*, 1889, under the title "How the Other Half Lives," and made an instant impression.… It could not have been long after I wrote "How the Other Half Lives" that he [Theodore Roosevelt, then Police Commissioner of New York City] came to the *Evening Sun* office one day looking for me. I was out, and he left his card, merely writing on the back of it that he had read my book and had "come to help."…There is very little ease where Theodore Roosevelt leads, as we all found out.…Mr. Roosevelt was a member of the Health Board, and sometimes it was the tenements we went inspecting when the tenants slept. He was after the facts, and learned speedily to get them as he could. When as Governor, he wanted to know just how the Factory Law was being executed, he came down from Albany and spent a whole day with me personally investigating tenements in which sweating [sweatshop manufacturing done at home] was carried on.

Source: Jacob A. Riis, *The Making of an American* (New York: Macmillan, 1901), pp. 191–225.

Thinking Critically

1. Contextualization
What might have been some of the reasons Riis had trouble getting his pictures published? How do you think real estate owners responded to his pictures and his explanations of conditions?

2. Comparison
Compare and contrast the contributions of Riis, Roosevelt, and Addams to the Progressive movement. What common beliefs, approaches, and goals did they share?

people to do and, indeed, God's will. There were many social gospel preachers, but the most prominent was Walter Rauschenbusch whose 1917 book *A Theology for the Social Gospel* broadened the definition of sin from a focus on individual flaws to include social institutions that oppressed others. Rauschenbusch was far from alone in advocating a social gospel. George D. Herron was a pastor whose most famous sermon, "The Message of Jesus to Men of Wealth" claimed simply that "a rich Christian is a contradiction of terms." Josiah Strong edited a social gospel magazine, *The Gospel of the Kingdom*, and published a book, *Our Country*, pleading for missionary work within American cities and around the world. In every city, local city mission societies carried out their own social gospel mission.

Even more than his writing, the photographs that Jacob Riis made, like this one titled "Sleeping Quarters Areaway, Mulberry St.," showed middle-class America the poverty in which "the other half" lived.

While the social gospel was a Protestant movement, social issues also swept Catholic America. Cardinal James Gibbons, the long-time archbishop of Baltimore and nominal leader of American Catholics, defended the American labor movement and the role of Catholics in it to a wary Vatican. Gibbons argued that the rise of monopolies with their "heartless avarice" demanded action.

Not all religious communities shared in the social gospel movement, however. Many first-generation Jewish immigrants put all of their religious energy into secular political reform and labor movements. Some rabbis, in turn, worried that the focus on secular politics would undermine the spiritual world of the immigrants. Parish priests in Italian, German, and Czech parishes in Chicago tangled with the anarchists and union radicals whom they saw as taking people away from the faith. Some Catholics focused on private devotional activities or large street festivals often devoted to the Virgin Mary, seeing their faith as a refuge from the larger society rather than a way to change society. They valued the ministry of individuals like Frances Xavier Cabrini—Mother Cabrini—sent to the United States by an Italian bishop in 1889 to serve the needs of the Italian immigrants but who, unlike Cardinal Gibbons, avoided labor organizing and politics. Religious people, like others, had widely differing ideas about how to live well in the new urban and industrial society of the United States.

19.3 **Quick Review** How were religiously inspired progressives similar to or different from other progressive reformers?

PROGRESSIVE POLITICS ON THE NATIONAL STAGE

19.4 Analyze the three "progressive presidents" and their administrations.

A significant turning point in American politics came early in the morning of September 14, 1901, when President William McKinley died in Buffalo, New York. He had been visiting the Pan American Exposition when he was shot by a lone anarchist, Leon Czolgosz, on September 6. The president survived the bullet but died of the infection that followed. McKinley was the third American president to be assassinated after Abraham Lincoln in 1865 and James A. Garfield in 1881. The fact that Czolgosz described himself as an anarchist led to a strong backlash against the anarchist movement, just regaining its political standing after the widespread hostility to anarchism engendered by the Haymarket violence of 1886 (see Chapter 18).

Vice President Theodore Roosevelt, who had been on a camping trip with his family in New York's Adirondack Mountains when McKinley was shot, arrived in Buffalo to take the oath of office. Sitting on the train bringing McKinley's body from Buffalo to Washington, DC, was Ohio Senator Mark Hanna, who had helped McKinley select Roosevelt as Vice President. Hanna understood what the transition meant for many like him who constituted the old guard of the Republican Party. "Now look!" Hanna muttered, "That damned cowboy is President of the United States!"

There was a reason that some referred to the new president as a cowboy. Theodore Roosevelt had already had an extraordinary career in and out of politics when he ascended to the presidency. Born to a wealthy New York family whose roots went back to Dutch New York, he grew up as a sometimes awkward and sickly child. He compensated by lifting weights and learning to box. He attended Harvard College, was elected to the New York state assembly at 23, a year after his marriage to Alice Hathaway Lee. When his wife died, Roosevelt abandoned politics for a cowboy life in the Dakotas. He soon returned to New York, married Edith Kermit Carow, and started on his rapid political ascent. He was appointed U.S. civil service commissioner at age 31, police commissioner of New York at 37, and assistant secretary of the Navy at 39. During the Spanish-American War, Roosevelt took command of a unit in Cuba known as the Rough Riders, making himself a war hero. He was elected governor of New York when he had just turned 40 and was already plotting his own campaign for the presidency.

Roosevelt's hopes for the presidency were almost derailed by his differences with the old guard in the New York Republican Party. As governor, Roosevelt wanted to end corruption, tax the street railways, and provide for industrial safety as well as workmen's compensation for those injured on the job. He had advocated for the inspection of tenement housing since being shown their conditions by Jacob Riis. But not everyone in New York, Democrats or Republicans, liked those new ideas.

The boss of the Republican Party in New York, state Senator Tom Platt, supported Roosevelt for governor in November 1898 because his war hero popularity and anticorruption image seemed the only way to win the election and maintain Republican power. But once Platt discovered that Roosevelt actually meant what he said, the boss decided he needed to get rid of the governor before he wrecked the Republican machine. Platt planned to sideline Roosevelt by getting him the nomination as McKinley's running mate for 1900. Roosevelt did not want the nomination. In 1900, no sitting vice president had been elected president since Martin Van Buren succeeded Andrew Jackson more than half a century earlier. Even so, the nomination was hard to reject without seeming disloyal to the party. McKinley and Roosevelt won the election, and state politics in New York returned to normal. Then, only months into McKinley's second term, the president was dead and the reforming politician from New York was the president of the United States. At the age of 42, he was also the youngest president ever.

Teddy Roosevelt—Progressive President

Taking the oath of office, the new president promised "to carry out absolutely unbroken" the former president's policies. One observer responded, "yes, the same way one carries out the trash." That comment represented an accurate view of the new president. After a brief period of mourning, very brief for him personally, the White House and the country started to experience Roosevelt's considerable reforming energy, which New Yorkers had known for some time.

Theodore Roosevelt

THE TRUSTBUSTER AND THE SQUARE DEAL   Roosevelt soon outlined his departure from McKinley and his determination to limit the power of industrial corporations. TR (as he came to be known to everyone) told Congress that "there are real and grave evils" that come from the power of the great corporations, and the federal government needed to assume the authority to supervise and limit that power.

Only a month before Roosevelt spoke to Congress, James J. Hill, owner of the Great Northern Railroad, and E. H. Harriman, who controlled the Union Pacific Railroad, met with representatives of J. Pierpont Morgan, who controlled the Northern Pacific Railroad. These three lines were competitors across the northern plains. The competition among them kept prices low and helped farmers and industries who wanted to ship their products. As had been the case with steel less than a year before, such competition struck Morgan as terribly inefficient and a drain on profits. Hill, Harriman, and Morgan solved their problem by creating a new entity, The Northern Securities Company Limited, to which they then sold all of their railroads. In place of competition, the transcontinental railroad routes would now be one happy family.

Roosevelt did not mention Northern Securities in his December speech, and some industrialists hoped that his speech was mere rhetoric. Then in February 1902, the attorney general announced that, at the president's request, he was filing suit under the 1890 **Sherman Antitrust Act** to break up Northern Securities. To the new president, the Northern Securities Company was too big and too powerful, and the lack of competition on the rails meant that the new trust could charge virtually any rates it wanted to haul freight and passengers.

Roosevelt's actions were not the first time that the Progressive movement led the federal government to take action. In response to the assassination of President Garfield by a disappointed office seeker in 1881, Congress passed the **Pendleton Civil Service Reform Act** of 1883, which sought to replace political patronage with merit in the selection of government employees. Chester A. Arthur, the vice president who became president when Garfield died, strongly supported the act and lost the backing of the bosses in his own party for doing so. The act created the Civil Service Commission whose job it was to give federal employees a measure of protection from losing their jobs over their political ideas while keeping federal civil servants—not elected officials—from actively fundraising or campaigning. In addition, in response to public pressure about the power of monopolies, Congress had passed the Sherman Antitrust Act in 1890, which its sponsor Senator John Sherman of Ohio said was to outlaw any business practices that would unfairly raise costs for the consumer.

The Pendleton Act, however, covered only about 10% of federal employees when it was passed and none at the state or local level. The Sherman Act had been a virtual dead letter after a series of court cases reduced its scope soon after it was passed. Suddenly, with the Northern Securities suit, a new administration was bringing the Sherman Act back to life and warning of further progressive initiatives to follow.

Soon after the suit was announced, J. P. Morgan visited the White House for a private meeting with the president and the attorney general. Morgan told the president, "If we have done anything wrong, send your man to my man and they can fix it up." Roosevelt, who saw things quite differently said, "That can't be done," and Attorney General Philander Chase Knox added, "We don't want to fix it up, we want to stop it." Morgan then asked if the government was now going to attack his other interests, especially U.S. Steel, and Roosevelt responded, "Certainly not—unless we find out that in any case they have done something that we regard as wrong." After Morgan left, Roosevelt told Knox he found it quite revealing that Morgan could deal with him only as "a big rival operator," with whom to make a deal. But there would be no deal.

The Northern Securities case took 2 years to move through the federal courts, but in March 1904, the U.S. Supreme Court affirmed Roosevelt's interpretation of the Sherman Act. The majority opinion said that "No scheme or device could…more

Sherman Antitrust Act
The first federal antitrust measure, passed in 1890; sought to promote economic competition by prohibiting business combinations in restraint of trade or commerce.

Pendleton Civil Service Reform Act
A law of 1883 that reformed the spoils system by prohibiting government workers from making political contributions and by creating the Civil Service Commission to oversee their appointment on the basis of merit rather than politics.

effectively and certainly suppress free competition" and ordered the Northern Security trust broken up into competing lines. From then on, Roosevelt would be known as the "trustbuster," and he liked the title.

Roosevelt kept up the pressure for change. In a series of speeches in the summer of 1902, he told audiences, "The great corporations which we have grown to speak of rather loosely as trusts are the creatures of the State, and the State not only has the right to control them, but it is in duty bound to control them wherever need of such control is shown." His natural inclination to expand the government's power to supervise corporations was supported by many in Congress and by muckraking publications like *McClure's*, which Roosevelt may have disliked, but which nonetheless provided him with new ammunition with every issue. Roosevelt wanted a new cabinet-level Department of Commerce with investigative authority, a ban on secret deals between railroads and specific companies (of the sort that launched Rockefeller's oil empire), and additional funds for the Department of Justice to expedite antitrust cases. Ironically, once Roosevelt had won his Northern Securities victory and gained the tools that Congress gave him, he did not pursue many other antitrust cases. The Taft and Wilson administrations would use the new tools more than Roosevelt himself. The president had made his point. As was often the case during his 7 years in office, having done so, he moved on to other issues.

CONSERVATION IN NATURE As a child, Theodore Roosevelt was a birdwatcher and developed an intense love of nature. Years later, he walked into a cabinet meeting and asked, "Gentlemen, do you know what has happened this morning?" The members of the cabinet waited for important news. Roosevelt told them, "Just now I saw a chestnut-sided warbler—and this is only February!" The birds did not usually appear in Washington on their return from Central America until much later in the spring.

While Roosevelt loved nature, watched birds, and as president saved thousands of acres of land from development, he was also an avid hunter who loved to shoot bear, cougar, or just about anything in the wilderness. However on one bear hunt in 1902, Roosevelt refused to shoot a bear that had been captured and tied to a tree so the president could have the honor of the shot. He was happy to kill many other bears on real hunts, but attacking a tied-up bear was unsportsmanlike. His refusal made national news and sparked a new craze, fostered by the Steiff and Ideal toy companies—a new toy known as a Teddy Bear in honor of the president who would not shoot one.

Just before he became vice president, Roosevelt published *The Strenuous Life* in which he argued that Americans were getting far too little time to replenish their bodies and souls in the great outdoors. But the strenuous life in nature that he advocated was only possible if the wilderness and the wildlife were preserved for future generations to enjoy. Once he became president, Roosevelt combined all of this considerable enthusiasm for nature with his political skill to become perhaps the most conservation-minded of any president.

Although a keenly passionate advocate, Roosevelt was not, however, the first president to care about conservation. Harrison, Cleveland, and McKinley all set aside federal lands for permanent parks, and both Yellowstone and the Grand Canyon were federal reserves before Roosevelt took office. But from Roosevelt's perspective, too few animals were protected, too little land had been put aside, and too little was being done to protect the environment.

Even though his attack on the trusts got most of the headlines, a short line in TR's December 1901 message to Congress said, "The preservation of our forests is an imperative business necessity." People like his friend Gifford Pinchot and members of the Audubon and Sierra clubs cheered. Western senators were furious at an attack on the prime source of wealth in their states. Again, some hoped that it was a mere rhetorical flourish. They soon learned differently. When Roosevelt came to the presidency in 1901, 43 million acres of land were included in U.S. forest reserves. When he left office in 1909, that number had increased more than fourfold to 194 million acres.

Roosevelt also professionalized the protection of nature. He wrote that the "Nation as a whole should earnestly desire and strive to leave to the next generation the National honor unstained and the National resources unexhausted," and only new conservation efforts would preserve either honor or resources. He appointed a former Rough Rider, David E. Warford, as a federal forest ranger with authority to protect the 4.15 million acres of federal land in Arizona and Colorado. He nominated Gifford Pinchot, who shared the president's commitment, to be head of the Division of Forestry and, later, head of the U.S. Forest Service in the Department of the Interior and gave him "an absolutely free hand."

Between 1906 and 1908, Roosevelt used—or misused, as his critics said—authority given to him by the Antiquities Act of 1906 to declare a 295-acre stand of giant redwood trees just north of San Francisco as Muir Woods National Monument; 800,000 acres in Arizona as the Grand Canyon National Monument; and 2,500 acres, later expanded to 26,000 acres, as the Pinnacles National Monument in California. He also set aside the Natural Bridges National Monument in Utah and a dozen other similar monuments, ensuring that the land would never pass into private hands (see Map 19-2).

The president's continued expansion of the amount of land protected by the federal government provoked resistance in Congress. In early 1907, Senator Charles W. Fulton, a Republican from Oregon, attached an amendment to the Department of Agriculture's appropriations bill that said that no further forest reserves or expansions of reserves could be created within six western states without an act of Congress. When the bill reached the president, he had 10 days to sign it or risk having no funds to operate the Department of Agriculture. Roosevelt quickly approved a total of 21 new forest reserves in the six states—Medicine Bow Forest in Colorado, Priest River Forest in Idaho and Washington, Toiyabe Forest in Nevada, Blue Mountain in Oregon, and

MAP 19-2 Major National Parks. While the federal government claimed ownership of much of the land in the West, no president matched Theodore Roosevelt in setting aside large tracts of that land as national parks and forests so it would be preserved for future generations rather than be sold or developed.

Olympic and Rainier forests in Washington. When the paperwork creating these new forests was done, Roosevelt then signed the agriculture bill with Fulton's amendment, saying that no *additional* forests would be created.

Roosevelt and African-Americans

One of Roosevelt's first moves as president was to invite Booker T. Washington, the country's best known African-American, to the White House for a meeting and then, in October 1901, for dinner with the president and his family. No African-American had ever before eaten a meal as a guest at the White House. Roosevelt was making a very public statement about race relations in the United States. He was also taking a first step toward securing a full term as elected president for himself. Booker T. Washington controlled a block of delegates to the Republican nominating conventions since even though blacks could not vote in the segregated South of Roosevelt's day, they could and did win election as delegates to national Republican nominating conventions.

Although neither Roosevelt nor Washington discussed the dinner in public, the press made a great deal of the evening. While some reports were positive, papers like the *Memphis Scimitar* called the dinner "The most damnable outrage which has ever been perpetrated by any citizen of the United States."

For the rest of his 7 years in the White House, Roosevelt had a decidedly mixed record on African-American concerns. He did not mention black disenfranchisement or lynching in his first presidential message to Congress. However, in his 1906 annual message to Congress, he said, "The members of the white race…should understand that every lynching represents by just so much a loosening of the bands of civilization." They were important words, though with too little follow-up. In symbolic ways—the White House dinner and speeches on lynching—Roosevelt did more to support African-Americans than several of his predecessors or successors. In comparison to the energy he gave to other issues he considered important, however, his track record was certainly lackluster.

Roosevelt's Continuing Popularity

Roosevelt's obvious joy at life and enjoyment of the presidency was infectious. People loved having a young and enthusiastic chief executive. A friend once said of Roosevelt that he "wanted to be the bride at every wedding and the corpse at every funeral."

Roosevelt's large family brought life and vitality to the previously staid White House. Alice, daughter of his first marriage, was a young adult who flirted with and charmed everyone she met, including Ohio Congressman Nicholas Longworth whom she married in a White House wedding. She would continue to charm Washington society for the next three-quarters of a century. The president and Edith's younger children, Ted, Kermit, Ethel, Archie, and Quentin played at the White House, chasing rabbits on the White House grounds, marching with the White House police, and riding bicycles on the lawn and occasionally down the stairs.

In 1904, the Republicans easily nominated Roosevelt for a full term. Having lost with Bryan in 1896 and 1900, Democrats were looking for a fresh face and nominated Alton B. Parker, chief justice of the New York Court of Appeals. It was not a close contest. Parker was a colorless candidate, but it is unlikely that any Democrat could have won. Republicans were the country's major party and Roosevelt's energy carried the day. He won by a landslide.

After his reelection, Roosevelt's popularity only grew, and he and everyone knew that he could easily win a third term or, as his daughter Alice kept saying, "a second elected term" if he were a candidate in 1908. Nevertheless, he had promised himself and the country in 1904 that he would not seek a third term, saying as he claimed victory in November 1904, "The wise custom which limits the President to two terms regards the substance and not the form." As 1908 approached, the president was tempted to break the pledge but did not. Roosevelt's goal in 1908 was to find a candidate who would carry on the policies that he had championed. He thought he had found just the right candidate in Secretary of War, William Howard Taft.

Taft Wins, Taft Loses—The Elections of 1908 and 1912

William Howard Taft, who had served as a federal district court judge in Ohio before becoming governor general of the Philippines and then secretary of war, would have loved an appointment to the Supreme Court, one he finally won in 1921 when Warren Harding appointed him. But in 1908, Roosevelt had picked Taft as the successor most likely to continue his programs, and once Roosevelt had made up his mind, there was little that Taft or anyone else could do to stop him.

Having failed miserably with the conservative Alton Parker in the 1904 election, the Democrats returned to William Jennings Bryan for a third try for the White House. The Socialist Party was also growing in strength and their candidate, Eugene V. Debs, made a respectable showing. But the election was never really in doubt, and Taft won easily on the promise to continue Roosevelt's progressivism.

TAFT'S ADMINISTRATION, TAFT'S POLICIES Not surprisingly, given their very different personalities, tensions between the outgoing and the incoming president began even before Taft's inauguration. Roosevelt expected Taft to keep most of the existing cabinet; Taft wanted some of his own people. Most disappointing to the conservationist Roosevelt, Taft replaced Secretary of the Interior James R. Garfield, an ardent conservationist, with Richard A. Ballinger, a Seattle lawyer and former reform mayor, who was more interested in exploiting public lands than conserving them. Nevertheless, Taft kept Gifford Pinchot on at the U.S. Forest Service, and Roosevelt sailed for Africa soon after the inauguration, confident that the country was in good hands.

Taft kept a key Roosevelt-Taft pledge and called Congress into special session in early 1909 to lower the nation's tariff rates. Ida Tarbell, one of the best known muckraking journalists, insisted that the poor could not afford warm clothing because of the high tariff charged on imported wool, and many economists felt that overly high tariffs were protecting industries that no longer needed protection. Income and inheritance taxes seemed more equitable ways to pay for the government. But not everyone in Congress agreed, especially Rhode Island Senator Nelson Aldrich and House Speaker Joe Cannon.

New York Representative Sereno Payne proposed reducing the tariff rates and substituting an income tax. But when the bill reached the Senate, Aldrich dropped the income tax and revised the tariffs up—significantly. Aldrich acknowledged that the Republican platform had promised to revise the tariff, but he asked, "Where did we ever make the statement that we would revise the tariff downward?" Everyone knew that the downward revision had been the promise, but it was not the outcome. Even most moderate Republicans criticized the Payne-Aldrich tariff, but Taft signed the bill. When Congress later passed bills to lower the tariff on cotton, wool, steel, and iron, Taft vetoed them. In the process, he built an alliance with the conservative Aldrich wing of the party, losing the support of many Roosevelt progressives.

While Roosevelt was in Africa, word came to him in January 1910 that Taft had fired Pinchot. Pinchot wrote to the former president, "We have fallen back down the hill you led us up." The tariff might be abstract to Roosevelt, but conservation was the issue nearest and dearest to him, and Pinchot was the agent TR had counted on to keep the movement alive in the new administration.

On many fronts, Taft kept his pledge to carry out Roosevelt's policies, in some cases with more vigor than TR had ever shown. It was Taft, not Roosevelt, who decreed an 8-hour workday for government employees and who advocated the Sixteenth Amendment to the Constitution, passed in 1913, to ensure that federal income taxes could be collected. In addition, Taft was a far tougher trustbuster than Roosevelt, breaking up John D. Rockefeller's Standard Oil Company and bringing more antitrust suits in his 4 years than Roosevelt did in 7.

A widely distributed cartoon showed former president Roosevelt's disappointment with his hand-picked, but ensnarled, successor president Taft.

THE UNIQUE ELECTION OF 1912   Roosevelt was not alone in his estrangement from the Taft administration. Critics abounded, and Senator Robert La Follette of Wisconsin was hinting broadly that he might challenge Taft for the Republican presidential nomination in 1912. La Follette was a different kind of progressive from Roosevelt. He advocated a more open nominating process for candidates and an income tax to limit the power of the very rich. He wanted to destroy the monopolies that Roosevelt wanted only to regulate. La Follette was also appalled by concessions to the white South, believing that if African-Americans "had been fairly treated," then they would have been able to take the places now denied them as farmers and businessmen.

As Roosevelt waited, La Follette campaigned for the nomination. Then in February 1912, La Follette gave a speech in Philadelphia in which, either exhausted or drunk, he went on for over 2 hours, repeating himself again and again. He lost not only his audience but also the nomination with that speech. A week later, seven Republican governors asked Roosevelt to run. TR announced, "My hat is in the ring" and wrote, "I will accept the nomination for President if it is tendered to me." He also set out to be sure that the 1912 nomination was, in fact, so tendered.

Through the spring, Taft and Roosevelt fought it out—Taft always reluctantly, Roosevelt with his usual exuberance. In the South, Taft used the party machinery to control the delegates. Roosevelt defended his challenge saying, "If that be revolution, make the most of it." Taft responded, "This wrenches my soul....I do not want to fight Theodore Roosevelt, but sometimes a man in a corner fights. I am going to fight."

Taft won in the states where delegates were controlled by caucuses while Roosevelt won nearly all of the states that held primary elections, including Pennsylvania, California, Minnesota, Nebraska, Maryland, South Dakota, and even Taft's home state of Ohio. After seeing the primary returns, Idaho Senator William E. Borah declared, "There can be but one result, and that is the nomination of Mr. Roosevelt," and Nebraska's Senator George Norris happily said, "Taft is out of the race."

Taft, however, was not out of the race. He still controlled the party machinery. When delegates were contested—and 254 convention seats were contested—the Republican National Committee decided who should vote at the convention. The committee awarded 235 of the contested delegates to Taft and only 19 to Roosevelt, sealing the nomination for Taft.

Two months after the Republican convention, in early August 1912, a new Progressive Party held its convention in the same hall. The 14,000 delegates were mostly middle-class reformers—social workers, teachers, and owners of small businesses.

It was the first major political convention to include female delegates, and there were many. Also attending were a few African-American delegates from border states and New England, none from the Deep South where Taft controlled the party. Few of the farmers and laborers representing past Populist Party conventions were there. The platform included support for the rights of labor unions, conservation, women's suffrage, the 8-hour workday, workplace safety, as well as unemployment and old age insurance. In a doomed effort to court white Southern votes, the platform was silent on the rights of African-Americans. By acclamation, the convention nominated Theodore Roosevelt for president and California Governor Hiram Johnson for vice president. In the first convention speech by a woman, Jane Addams seconded Roosevelt's nomination. Roosevelt, saying that he felt "as fit as a Bull Moose," happily accepted the nomination. A convention like no other launched a presidential election like no other.

Many Democrats saw the Republican split as the chance for a Democratic presidency. Champ Clark of Missouri, the speaker of the house, was the frontrunner. He was popular within the party, but was a dull speaker. Oscar Underwood of Alabama was more conservative, but perhaps a better speaker than Clark. Others hoped to be kingmakers. Charles Murphy, the boss of Tammany, controlled the New York delegation while William Jennings Bryan controlled many other delegates. Finally, the governor of New Jersey, Woodrow Wilson, campaigned for the nomination.

Wilson had only held elected office for 2 years. He was an expert on constitutional law with a Ph.D. from Johns Hopkins, who had served as the president of Princeton University from 1902 to 1910. He had sought to transform Princeton from a country club for rich boys to a serious academic institution. He battled with faculty, alumni, and trustees and showed little aptitude for compromise.

In 1910, just as Wilson saw some of his most cherished goals defeated at Princeton, the political bosses who ran the Democratic Party in New Jersey were looking for an appealing candidate for governor. They offered Wilson the nomination, and he surprised even his supporters by being a magnetic candidate, winning easily. Then, to the surprise of the bosses, Wilson kept his word that he would be independent, broke with those who had put him in the governor's office, and refused to follow their lead in patronage. He governed as a progressive, getting the state to adopt workmen's compensation, a commission to regulate public utilities, and more open election laws, winning great popularity as well as the undying hatred of political bosses. Wilson entered the Democratic nominating convention as a strong candidate, but not the leader. While Clark led on the first ballots, Wilson kept gaining; on the 46 ballot, exhausted delegates gave Wilson their party's nomination.

With the nominations of Roosevelt, Taft, and Wilson—a former, the current, and a future president—the 1912 election was unique. In addition, a fourth candidate, Eugene V. Debs, was once again the candidate of the Socialist Party, and by 1912, the Socialists were a force to be reckoned with. In local elections the year before, Socialist candidates had been elected as mayor in 56 cities and towns, and one of the party's candidates, Victor Berger, was elected to Congress from Wisconsin. The Socialist Party, always highly factionalized, enthusiastically nominated Debs as their standard bearer for a fourth time. Some Socialists worried that Roosevelt's Progressive Party would steal their platform, but while the Progressive Party called for governmental oversight of the monopolies, the Socialists called for government ownership of all large-scale industries—especially the railroads. Like the Progressives, the Socialist platform also called for shorter working hours, workers' compensation, electoral reform, and giving women the right to vote. However, unlike the Progressives, it also called for ensuring blacks the right to vote.

Wilson wrote to a friend that "Roosevelt's strength is altogether incalculable. The contest is between him and me, not between Taft and me." He was right. It was difficult for Wilson, who was running as a progressive Democrat, to differentiate himself from Roosevelt's Progressive Party. If the contest was to be one of personal popularity, no one was more popular than Teddy Roosevelt. Boston attorney Louis D. Brandeis

New Freedom
Woodrow Wilson's 1912 program for government intervention in the economy to restore competition by curtailing the business monopolies, thereby providing opportunities for individual achievement.

suggested a way forward to Wilson. While Roosevelt spoke of the New Nationalism and governmental controls over the monopoly trusts, Brandeis suggested Wilson should speak of a **New Freedom** that would give people the greatest freedom by simply breaking up the great trusts and fostering competition at every level. Four years later, Brandeis would receive his reward when Wilson appointed him as the first Jew to serve on the U.S. Supreme Court.

In the fall campaign, Wilson called Roosevelt a "self-appointed divinity" who wanted to control the trusts and people's lives. Wilson, in contrast, wanted freedom from trusts and from government regulation. "Ours is a program of liberty," he said, "theirs is a program of regulation." Roosevelt struck back, saying that Wilson's approach was "simply the laissez-faire doctrine of…three-quarters of a century ago." Taft morosely stayed on the sidelines. Debs went after them all.

While Roosevelt was speaking in Milwaukee, Wisconsin, in October, a would-be assassin shot him at close range. The bullet lodged in Roosevelt's chest but a heavy coat and the text of a long speech that was in the coat pocket prevented a serious injury. Roosevelt, with typical pluck, went ahead with an hour-long speech before allowing himself to be taken to a hospital. His chances of victory improved as stories of his courage spread. In the end, however, the deep division within the Republican ranks, their failure to crack the Democrats' hold on the "solid South," and Wilson's use of Brandeis's antitrust rhetoric all ensured the outcome. Wilson won the popular vote with over a million votes more than Roosevelt, who defeated Taft by another half-million. Debs came in fourth with just over 900,000 votes (see Map 19-3).

Woodrow Wilson's New Freedom

Woodrow Wilson planned four major initiatives for his administration—conservation, access to raw materials, banking and finance, and the tariff and taxes. He announced that he would call the new Democratic-majority Congress into a special session in April 1913, a month after his inauguration and months ahead of when it would normally meet.

While Wilson spoke to the importance of conservation in his inaugural address, and while he did push the creation of the National Park Service, his commitment to conservation did not come close to Roosevelt's. Wilsonian progressivism focused elsewhere.

Only a month after the inauguration, Wilson broke a custom followed by every president since Jefferson and gave a speech in person to a joint session of Congress. Widely televised presidential addresses to Congress are now such a normal feature of American life that is it easy to forget that no president from Jefferson to Taft ever spoke directly to Congress. Nevertheless, Wilson did, and he continued to do so throughout his two terms in office.

Wilson's first congressional victory was the passage of the Underwood-Simmons tariff, which the new president signed in October 1913. Cleveland, McKinley, Roosevelt, and Taft all failed to get tariff reductions through Congress, mostly because of the power that lobbyists had with the Senate. But Wilson managed to embarrass several senators with a very public investigation of the role of lobbyists. He also met privately with several Democratic senators to hear their concerns and shore up their support. In the end, Wilson got a new tariff that reduced the tax on goods imported into the United States by at least 10 percent across the board, more on some things. The new law also used the power given in the new Sixteenth Amendment to introduce the first federal income tax since the Civil War, starting at 1 percent on incomes above $4,000 (considerably more than most Americans made in 1913).

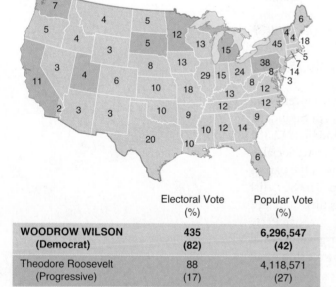

	Electoral Vote (%)	Popular Vote (%)
WOODROW WILSON (Democrat)	435 (82)	6,296,547 (42)
Theodore Roosevelt (Progressive)	88 (17)	4,118,571 (27)
William Taft (Republican)	8 (1)	3,486,720 (23)
Eugene Debs (Socialist)	–	900,672 (6)

MAP 19-3 The Election of 1912. This map shows the breadth of Woodrow Wilson's electoral victory after Roosevelt and Taft split the Republican vote and Debs failed to gain traction as the Socialist Party candidate.

Woodrow Wilson broke a precedent going back to Thomas Jefferson and began the modern practice of presidential speeches to a joint session of Congress.

Wilson then turned to reform of the nation's banking system. Since Andrew Jackson closed the Bank of the United States in the 1830s, the federal government's role in the nation's banking system had been very limited. In the financial panics of 1893 and 1907, J. P. Morgan had acted as the nation's banker, ensuring that the nation's credit system stayed intact. While Morgan's interventions were essential to protect the government and the nation's largest banks, they did little to help farmers or proprietors of small businesses or to allow the government to control the supply of money, a role that Bryan and his followers had been demanding for a long time.

Working closely with Virginia Senator Carter Glass, Wilson was able to create the Federal Reserve system in a matter of months. Following the advice of Brandeis that "concessions to big business interests must in the end prove futile," the president spent no time with representatives of business but, instead, built a coalition of the many factions within the Democratic Party and of progressive Republicans. The final bill passed the House 287 to 85, and the Senate, after a desperate last-minute attempt to derail the bill by Frank A. Vanderlip of the National City Bank of New York, passed the bill 54 to 34. Before the end of his first year in office, Wilson and the Congress had created the Federal Reserve that remains the core of the nation's banking system.

During the presidential campaign, Wilson had differentiated himself from Roosevelt with his claim that he was the real "trustbuster." In office, he supported his Attorney General James McReynolds in attacking the American Telephone and Telegraph Company, United States Steel, and the New Haven Railroad, all companies in which J. P. Morgan had an interest. Then he went to Congress and asked for more authority. The Clayton Anti-Trust Act, signed in October 1914, outlawed interlocking directorates (under which the same individuals might serve on the boards of directors of supposedly competing companies), and defined unfair trade practices, including the kind of collusion over prices that had allowed John D. Rockefeller to create the

Federal Trade Commission
Government agency established in 1914 to provide regulatory oversight of business activity.

Standard Oil monopoly. Perhaps most important, the Clayton Act exempted labor unions and farmer cooperatives from the definition of a "combination in restraint of trade," a charge that had been used in federal court cases against unions since Eugene Debs was sent to jail the 1890s. Although the bill did not give unions everything they wanted, Samuel Gompers declared it to be the "Magna Carta," of labor union organizing. Separate legislation also strengthened the investigative powers of the Interstate Commerce Commission and created a new **Federal Trade Commission** with a specific, if somewhat vague, mandate to limit the growth and power of monopolies.

While Wilson delivered quickly on some of his reformist campaign pledges, he deeply disappointed other followers. When the House passed legislation outlawing child labor in February 1915, Wilson did nothing and the bill died in the Senate. Only much later in his presidency did he support effective child labor legislation. He also disappointed farmers, a key Democratic constituency, when he quietly allowed a plan for rural credits to help farmers with mortgages to die in congressional conference committee.

African-Americans were greatly disappointed with Wilson. Booker T. Washington had a long-standing link to the Republican Party, but during the 1912 campaign, younger blacks, including African Episcopal Zion Bishop Alexander Walters and W.E.B. Du Bois, endorsed Wilson. It was a significant departure from the African-American–Republican Party alliance that had existed since Reconstruction. Perhaps, these leaders argued, this Virginia-born and Georgia-reared intellectual could finally break the hold of segregationists on the Democratic Party. During the campaign, Wilson was happy to receive their support, but once in office, Wilson spoke only vaguely of a federal commission to investigate race relations in the United States and allowed his cabinet to set policy that did not support the African-American cause.

Citing what they said was white anger at "racial mingling," especially in Southern post offices, Post Master General Albert S. Burleson and Secretary of the Treasury William Gibbs McAdoo ordered the segregation of offices, rest rooms, and eating facilities at the Post Office, Treasury Department, and Bureau of Printing and Engraving. Federal employees who had long worked in racially integrated settings were now segregated by race. The Democratic majority in Congress allowed segregationist senators like James K. Vardaman of Mississippi to block black appointments to federal jobs that previous Republican presidents had provided.

The black press attacked Wilson for the segregation policy and the lack of federal appointments. Wilson's most pointed confrontation about his racial policies was with the African-American editor William Monroe Trotter of Boston. In November of 1913, Trotter met with the president to lay out a long list of specific concerns about segregation in the federal service and the lack of African-Americans being hired in the government. Wilson responded blandly, saying, "Now, mistakes have probably been made, but those mistakes can be corrected." A year later, Trotter led another delegation to the White House and received another round of bland vagueness. Trotter lost his temper saying, "We are here as full-fledged American citizens" and reminded Wilson of the support he had received from African-Americans. Wilson in turn lost his temper, telling Trotter, "You are an American citizen…but you are the only American citizen that has ever come into this office who has talked to me with [such] a tone." The president insisted that Trotter be excluded from any future meeting, but there would be few future meetings with African-Americans with or without Trotter.

Wilson's reputation in the African-American community was further tarnished when in early 1915 he allowed one of the first full-length motion pictures, D. W. Griffith's *Birth of a Nation,* to be shown at the White House. The National Association for the Advancement of Colored People was actively protesting the film, which, though a masterpiece of cinematography, was also a glorification of the Ku Klux Klan. Wilson did not endorse the film, but the president also refused to announce his nonendorsement. Later, Wilson signed a letter prepared by his personal secretary saying that "the President was entirely unaware of the character of the play before it was presented and has at no time expressed his approbation of it." Nevertheless, the film incident, along with the segregation of the federal work force, seriously undermined Wilson's reputation among African-Americans.

When Wilson became president, his agenda focused exclusively on domestic policy. In his first year in office, with the Underwood Tariff, the Clayton Anti-Trust Act, as well as the creation of the Federal Reserve System and the Federal Trade Commission, he had extraordinary success. A little more than a year after the inauguration, however, a political assassination in the far off town of Sarajevo, Bosnia, began a chain of events that would change the president's and the nation's focus in succeeding years. After 1914, international matters, far more than his domestic agenda, dominated his administration. Indeed, the assassination in the Austrian Empire in June 1914 can be seen as the ending of the progressive era. In the new era, discussed in the next chapter, international matters are central.

19.4 **Quick Review** Which progressive president had the greatest effect on living and working conditions for the American people? Give three reasons to support your answer.

CONCLUSION

population increased

Between 1870 and 1900, America's population almost doubled, from 40 million in 1870 to 75 million in 1900, with immigration responsible, perhaps, for one-third of this growth. As more and more Americans crowded into the nation's cities, drawn there by jobs in America's rapidly expanding industrial economy, a new urgency to focus on the challenges of immigration, urbanization, and industrialization took hold. By 1900, a rising cohort of Americans—including intellectuals, social reformers, and political leaders—seemed to recognize that new ideas and new levels of activism would be needed to create a solid foundation for the country's future.

Muckraking journalists such as Ida Tarbell, Upton Sinclair, and Lincoln Steffens sought to convince other Americans to heed the call to solve a wide range of problems related to the health and well-being of American society. Some reformers attempted to rein in the excesses of industrialists and the financial markets; others focused their attentions on the urban poor, the nation's education system, preservation of the natural world, electoral reforms, decent wages for the laboring classes, industrial safety and sanitation, or—in one of the strongest movements—ending the use of alcohol by Americans.

Beginning at the city and state level, progressive reformers sought elected office and sought to use their offices to implement many progressive reforms in the conduct of elections and in the protection of individuals through such things as pure food and drug laws. Theodore Roosevelt, who gained the presidency after the assassination of William McKinley in 1901, successfully brought progressivism to the White House. He expanded the powers of the presidency to control the power of giant corporations, protect the nation's natural resources, and bring a new vitality to electoral politics. The two presidents who followed him, William Howard Taft and Woodrow Wilson, shared some of Roosevelt's reformist tendencies and furthered the goals of progressivism, changing, in particular, the relationship between business and government in the decades leading up to World War I.

CHAPTER REVIEW How progressive was the "Progressive Era"? Include the work of individuals, government policy, and philosophy in your answer.

Chapter 19   Chapter Review

THE REVOLT OF THE INTELLECTUALS

19.1 Explain the role of muckraking journalists and intellectuals in shaping a progressive agenda.

Review Questions

1. **Comparison**
   Compare and contrast the ideas of John Dewey and William Graham Sumner. What assumptions about social and economic inequality underlay each author's position?

2. **Constructing an Argument**
   How would you explain the popularity of muckraking journalism in the late 1800s?

THE TRANSFORMATION OF THE CITIES

19.2 Analyze the changes in urban life that inspired progressive reforms and the impact of those reforms on cities.

Review Questions

3. **Contextualization**
   Why did many poor and immigrant residents of American cities support political machines? How might such machines have looked from their point of view?

4. **Synthesis**
   What ideas and objectives underlay progressive reform?

5. **Historical Interpretation**
   In what ways was Jane Addams's Hull House typical of the Progressive movement? It what ways did it depart from other progressive initiatives?

RELIGIOUS RESPONSES TO THE GILDED AGE

19.3 Explain the main currents of religiously based reform movements during the progressive era.

Review Questions

6. **Historical Interpretation**
   What light does the rise to prominence of the Woman's Christian Temperance Union shed on the relationship between social reform and religious revival in the late 1800s?

7. **Comparison**
   Compare and contrast the strategies and motives of Frances Willard and Carry Nation. How did each contribute to the gains made by the temperance movement?

PROGRESSIVE POLITICS ON THE NATIONAL STAGE

19.4 Analyze the three "progressive presidents" and their administrations.

Review Questions

8. **Comparison**
   Compare and contrast the policies of Roosevelt, Taft, and Wilson. What aspects of the progressive agenda did each emphasize?

9. **Historical Interpretation**
   How did the progressive presidents discussed in this section change the place of the presidential role in American politics?

10. **Historical Interpretation**
    How did Roosevelt and Wilson respond to the concerns of African-Americans? What light do their actions shed on the issues of race in politics of the late 1800s?

War, Prosperity, and Depression

1890–1945

PART 7

20 Foreign Policy and War in a Progressive Era

CHAPTER OBJECTIVE

Demonstrate an understanding of the ways in which the United States engaged with the world and the impact of that engagement on the people of the United States.

LEARNING OBJECTIVES

CONTINUING EXPANSION

20.1 Explain continued U.S. expansion, particularly U.S. acquisition of what would much later be the 49th and 50th states.

THE SPLENDID LITTLE WAR…WITH SPAIN—CUBA, PUERTO RICO, AND THE PHILIPPINES, 1898

20.2 Analyze the causes and consequences of the U.S. War with Spain in 1898.

FOREIGN POLICY, FOREIGN ADVENTURES, 1900–1914

20.3 Explain developments in U.S. policy in Panama, Asia, and Mexico between the War with Spain and World War I.

THE UNITED STATES AND THE GREAT WAR

20.4 Analyze the causes and consequences of U.S. involvement in World War I.

I n 1914, all of Europe went to war. President Woodrow Wilson was determined to stay out of the conflict and campaigned for reelection in 1916 with the slogan "He kept us out of war." Although Wilson would not continue to keep the nation out of the European war, the man he defeated in the 1912 presidential election, former President Theodore Roosevelt, was ready to go to war much sooner than Wilson. As president, Roosevelt liked to summarize his foreign policy with the proverb, "Speak softly and carry a big stick." When Europe began what was then called the Great War, the former president was speaking less and less softly and arguing that the United States should prepare for war and that Wilson's neutrality was a sign of personal and national weakness.

Roosevelt's enthusiasm for a more activist approach to foreign policy was not out of character with his own presidency. When he became president in 1901, the United States had already acquired Alaska, Hawaii, and other islands in the Pacific. Many Americans wanted more land, or at least greater influence around the world. Other than his very active involvement in the acquisition of the Panama Canal Zone, Roosevelt had been surprisingly cautious in international relations. He reduced U.S. involvement in the Philippines, negotiated an end to war between Russia and Japan, brokered an agreement to soften Japan's sense of insult at California's anti-Japanese measures, and sought successfully to keep peace with the world. Many of Roosevelt's strongest political supporters, progressive senators like Robert La Follette and reformers like Jane Addams, adamantly opposed U.S. endeavors abroad and U.S. involvement in World War I.

Nevertheless, although foreign policy is always shaped by many people and many forces, presidents Roosevelt and Wilson were certainly the dominant figures in U.S. international relations between 1898 and 1920. Their story, and the world they and so many others shaped, is the subject of this chapter.

CONTINUING EXPANSION

20.1 Explain continued U.S. expansion, particularly U.S. acquisition of what would much later be the 49th and 50th states.

The geographical expansion of the United States that had continued from the time it declared independence persisted throughout the Progressive Era. Admiral Alfred Thayer Mahan of the U.S. Navy persuasively laid the foundation for continued expansion in his book, *The Influence of Sea Power upon History*, published in 1890. Few books were ever as influential in the development of U.S. foreign policy. Mahan argued that all great nations in history had great navies that could control the world's oceans and, specifically, that the U.S. Navy needed to be large enough to be a significant player in the Pacific. He worried that the U.S. Navy was too small and that the lack of U.S. control of Pacific islands limited the nation's reach. The popularity of his book accelerated developments already underway, and within a decade, the U.S. Navy had been expanded to the third largest in the world while the United States had annexed Hawaii and Puerto Rico in 1898 and had assumed control of Samoa, the Philippine Islands, and Cuba.

Not surprisingly, some have called the late 1800s the age of **U.S. imperialism**. Whether that term correctly describes U.S. expansion in this era continues to be debated. Certainly, thinking in the United States was influenced by the ways Britain, France, and Germany were seeking new colonies in Africa and the Middle East. Many Americans did not want their country to be left behind. Some people in the United States agreed with those Europeans who insisted that the white race was destined to rule the world's people. Immigrants or the children of immigrants sometimes wanted the United States to intervene in their old homelands to protect the rights of compatriots. Even so, a surprisingly diverse array of Americans did not want their country involved in anything beyond its borders. Expansion beyond North America was never without controversy, even as the United States became involved around the globe.

Alaska

Long before Mahan argued for greater U.S. control of the oceans, the United States assumed ownership of the huge Russian territory known as Russian America, or Alaska. In the 1740s, Vitus Bering, a Danish captain serving the Russian Navy explored the Arctic Oceans between Asia and North America. Soon thereafter, Russia had joined Britain, France, and Spain in claiming large parts of North America. A Russian governor moved to Sitka, Alaska, in 1799 to administer Russian communities that dotted the coast of what is today Alaska, Canada, Washington, Oregon, and northern California. Control and management of the vast Russian territory was vested in the private Russian American Company. Russians fished and traded in sea otter skins, providing support for the colony and modest returns to Russia itself.

The value of Alaska to the Russian company or government was never great. Tensions with native residents ran deep. Russians exploited Native Alaskans while Western diseases took a heavy toll of the native population. In response, Native Alaskans massacred Russian communities at Sitka and Nulato. By 1860, the government was unhappy with the Russian American Company and worried about defending the long Alaskan coast from the British Navy.

American settlers in Washington Territory were learning about the rich fishing, whaling, and fur trapping that was possible in Alaska. Secretary of State Seward envisioned its value and coordinated negotiations to purchase it from Russia. The negotiators agreed on a price of $7.2 million, and on October 18, 1867, the Russian flag was

20.1

20.2

20.3

20.4

Significant Dates

1890	U.S. Navy Admiral Alfred Thayer Mahan publishes *The Influence of Sea Power upon History*
1893	United States supports overthrow of Hawaiian government, but new Cleveland administration blocks U.S. annexation of the islands
1898	Hawaii annexed by United States
	U.S. War with Spain leads to American control of Cuba, Puerto Rico, and Philippine Islands
1904	U.S. support for revolution in Panama followed by Panama Canal Treaty
1907–08	Gentlemen's Agreement with Japan limiting Japanese immigration to United States
1912	Alaska granted territorial status
1914–1917	U.S. intervention in Mexico
1914	World War I begins in Europe
1915	British liner *Lusitania* is sunk with loss of American lives
1917	United States enters World War I on side of Britain and France
1918	World War I ends
1919	Treaty of Versailles negotiated including League of Nations, then rejected by U.S. Senate

U.S. imperialism
A term used to describe the U.S acquisition of Hawaii, Puerto Rico, and the Philippine Islands in 1898.

hauled down at Sitka and the Stars and Stripes rose in its place. Congress balked at appropriating the funds for the purchase, and critics called the whole transfer "Seward's folly," but the nation had gained valuable new territory. Fishing, mining, the fur trade, and indeed the sale of ice to Californians made Alaska a good investment. However, Aleuts, Sitkas, Kolosh, and other Alaskan tribes found that they had only substituted one overlord for another. U.S. troops, miners, and settlers fought with Alaskan tribes as they had with native peoples further south.

Having purchased Alaska, the U.S. government was slow to do much with it. Only in 1884 did Congress create any official form of government for what they called the District of Alaska. Soon thereafter, gold was discovered in the district, and the Klondike gold rush of the late 1880s expanded the American population of Alaska as did 1898 legislation that extended the provisions of the 1862 Homestead Act to Alaska. Finally in 1912, President Taft signed legislation giving Alaska full territorial status, and the elected legislature first met at Juneau the following year.

Hawaii

Although the United States was a major influence in Hawaii long before Mahan argued for a wider Pacific influence for the nation, it was in Mahan's time that the United States annexed Hawaii. While the American Revolution was being fought, a British explorer, James Cook, landed on a chain of islands that he named the Sandwich Islands, which came to be known as Hawaii. Before Cook's arrival in 1778, there had been no contact between the native Hawaiians and Europeans. The Polynesian people whom Cook encountered were governed by a stable if loosely held feudal monarchy. Unfortunately, like other native peoples, they had no immunity to Western diseases, and the contact initiated by Cook took a terrible toll.

Hawaii's strategic location halfway between California and Japan and its harbors that were perfect for American whaling vessels greatly interested American and European merchants and U.S. Navy officers. By the early 1800s, Hawaiian harbors were filled with U.S. Navy ships and private whaling vessels, and Americans mixed with Hawaiians on a regular basis. In 1820, a group of New England missionaries and three American-educated Hawaiians arrived to convert Hawaiians to Christianity and interest them in American culture.

U.S. control of California with its large Pacific harbors in 1848 and the completion of the Transcontinental Railroad in 1869 expanded U.S. commercial and military interest in the kingdom of Hawaii. Trans-Pacific steamship lines that began at the Pacific docks where the railroad ended sought fueling stations on their way to Asia, and Hawaii's Pearl Harbor was the perfect stopping place. At the same time, American-owned sugar plantations had become a major economic force in Hawaii. Native Hawaiians, who were now a minority within their own country and controlled perhaps 15 percent of the land and 2 percent of the capital, did not want to further U.S. influence in their country, but the Hawaiian government agreed that it would not grant special trading rights or naval bases to any other country in return for a promise that Hawaii could ship a steady supply of sugar duty-free to the United States. Hawaii's King Kalakaua visited the United States in 1874 to formalize the agreement.

By the 1880s, American economic power in Hawaii was overwhelming, but the islands remained independent. When King Kalakaua died, his sister Queen Liliuokalani succeeded him. She sought to regain "Hawaii for the Hawaiians" and reduce the economic and political power of the United States. Most of the American planters on the island did not like the queen's moves and formed the Annexation Club. In 1893, the annexation group overthrew her and seized power. The U.S. minister in Hawaii, John L. Stevens, cabled Washington, "The Hawaiian pear is now fully ripe and this is the golden hour for the United States to pluck it." The U.S. Navy landed sailors "to preserve order," thus securing the queen's overthrow. Hawaii would have been annexed to the United States if the recently inaugurated Democratic President Grover Cleveland had not sensed that there was something unseemly about the whole affair and ended negotiations with the rebels. Cleveland announced his firm opposition to annexation.

Hawaii's Queen Liliuokalani was overthrown in an uprising led by American planters. A century later, the U.S. government apologized to native Hawaiians for this illegal act.

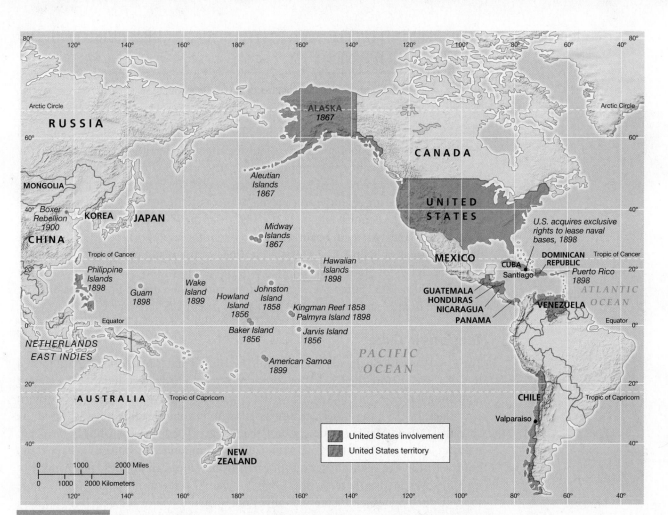

MAP 20-1 The U.S. in the World, 1900. By 1900, the United States had claimed many islands in the South Pacific and had strong involvement with other Pacific islands as well as Latin American countries.

Under Cleveland, the United States might have supported Liliuokalani's restoration had she not insisted that she would execute all of the rebels. That action was too much for Cleveland, and his administration ignored Hawaii, which continued as an independent nation under the control of the American planters who had overthrown the queen's government.

When William McKinley was elected president in 1896, he demonstrated none of Cleveland's resistance to U.S. acquisition of Hawaii as the next step in the nation's "Manifest Destiny." McKinley said, "We need Hawaii as much…as in its day we needed California." In June 1897, McKinley proposed a treaty of annexation, to which the planter government agreed. McKinley realized that anti-imperialists in the Senate could block the two-thirds vote required to approve the treaty, so the president used the same strategy that John Tyler had used half a century earlier for Texas. He asked both houses of Congress to annex the territory by joint-resolution, which required only a majority vote. By June 1898, to the protests of native Hawaiians and the cheers of the planters, Hawaii became a permanent territory of the United States. In that same year, the United States annexed tiny Midway and Wake islands and, a year later, agreed to divide Samoa with Germany. Across the Pacific, Mahan's dream of stations for the growing navy was a reality (see Map 20-1).

20.1 | **Quick Review** How did worry about other nations, as well as domestic events and developments in the United States, contribute to the nation's interest in acquiring Alaska and Hawaii as new territories?

THE SPLENDID LITTLE WAR…WITH SPAIN—CUBA, PUERTO RICO, AND THE PHILIPPINES, 1898

20.2 Analyze the causes and consequences of the U.S. War with Spain in 1898.

The U.S. War with Spain in 1898 (often called the Spanish-American War) followed decades of U.S. expansionism—much of it expansion into territory that had previously been part of Spain's once-vast empire in the Americas. Spain had at one time exercised political control of all of Latin America, except for Brazil, and it had ruled the Philippine Islands for centuries. As a result of successful independence movements, all that was left of the Spanish empire in the 1890s was the Philippines and a collection of Caribbean islands. Many in Spain wanted to retain those outposts for their own value and as symbols of Spain's past glory. Nevertheless, as a result of a short war—which future Secretary of State John Hay called "a splendid little war"—Spain lost the last of its holdings. The United States gained long-term influence in both Cuba and the Philippine Islands, and made Puerto Rico a permanent U.S. territory.

Tensions in Cuba

The U.S. War with Spain started in Cuba. The United States had long been interested in Cuba. Well before the Civil War, southern Senators had suggested that the United States ought to acquire Cuba as a slave state to offset the growing number of Northern free states. In 1854, the American ambassadors to Europe's leading powers issued the so-called Ostend Manifesto, demanding that Spain sell Cuba to the United States, but it did not happen. After the Civil War, Cuba was no longer of value as a slave state, but interest in the island never disappeared from American politics, and American investors were active there. By the 1890s, almost 90 percent of Cuban exports came to the United States, and American investors owned much of the best farm land on the island.

Cubans wanted to throw off Spanish rule and win independence. An 1890 agreement with Spain had reduced the tariff on sugar, launching a boom in the Cuban economy, but a new U.S. tariff in 1894, strongly influenced by lobbying from the Sugar Trust in the United States, significantly raised the tariff on imported sugar. The increased cost of Cuban sugar in the United States, significantly reduced the sales of Cuban sugar and devastated the Cuban economy. Cuban revolutionaries led by José Martí, who had been living in exile in New York City, saw the resulting Cuban depression as the ideal moment to gain independence. Martí returned to Cuba in 1895, and his revolutionary forces began burning cane fields, killing Spanish soldiers, and making Spanish rule more costly. Spanish authorities responded by creating concentration camps where they held Cubans in controlled enclaves that separated them from the rebels. Many in these camps suffered from malnutrition and disease.

When William McKinley was inaugurated as U.S. president in 1897, he made it clear that he wanted Spain out of Cuba. American public opinion was on the side of the rebels. New York newspaper editors William Randolph Hearst and Joseph Pulitzer engaged in what was called "yellow journalism" (named for a popular cartoon character of the day known as the "Yellow Kid"), publishing sensationalized accounts of Spanish atrocities in Cuba. They sent well-known artists like Frederic Remington, and writers like Richard Harding Davis, to Cuba to report on Spanish actions to increase circulation for their publications.

While many Americans saw the Cuban revolution of the 1890s as a simple question of good Cubans against bad Spaniards, American business leaders with investments in Cuba also worried that a revolutionary victory would threaten their investments. Martí, while grateful for American support, worried about long-term American influence, insisting that, "To change masters is not to be free."

The Spanish government in Madrid did not want a war with the United States, and they worried—correctly, it would turn out—that the government, and indeed the Spanish monarchy, could not survive the overthrow of the last bastion of Spain's empire in the Americas. As U.S. public opinion became more belligerent, so did public opinion in Spain. Spanish people rallied to their flag, and in one town a mob attacked the U.S. consulate.

War in Cuba, Puerto Rico, and the Philippine Islands

In February 1898, over 200 American sailors were killed when the battleship USS *Maine* blew up in Havana Harbor. The explosion may well have been the result of a bad boiler; however, Americans blamed Spain, and "Remember the *Maine*" became a rallying cry. McKinley managed to get Congress to declare war without ever asking for it.

The U.S. invasion of Cuba was not well managed. American troops arrived wearing wool uniforms—hardly the right material for a hot Caribbean summer. Even though Theodore Roosevelt gained fame for leading mostly African-American troops (shown as white in subsequent pictures) in a rapid assault on San Juan Hill, the battles in Cuba were generally slow and difficult. In 4 months of fighting, 345 Americans were killed in action while 5,000 died from disease.

Since the United States was at war with Spain, McKinley also approved the orders that had been issued by Assistant Secretary of the Navy Roosevelt (issued just before he resigned that position to fight in Cuba) to Admiral George Dewey to sail the U.S. fleet to the Spanish-owned Philippine Islands. The six warships under Dewey's command quickly sank the Spanish fleet at the Battle of Manila Bay on May 1, 1898, giving the United States control of a Pacific territory much larger than Cuba. The American Pacific fleet also captured the Spanish garrison on Guam Island and took control of the uninhabited atoll of Wake Island.

Finally, the United States decided to take the last Spanish outpost in the Caribbean, Puerto Rico. Once control of Cuba seemed assured in July 1898, McKinley ordered General Nelson A. Miles to Puerto Rico. He wanted to be sure the troops arrived before peace talks began with Spain. In 1898, some Puerto Ricans welcomed the U.S. overthrow of Spanish authority, and the indigenous independence movement in Puerto Rico was not as strong as that in Cuba.

By August 1898, Spain was ready to ask for peace. Much to McKinley's displeasure, the congressional resolution authorizing the war had included the Teller Amendment, named for Senator Henry Teller of Colorado, which said the United States could not permanently annex Cuba. If the United States could not annex Cuba, Puerto Rico seemed like the next best permanent U.S. territory in the Caribbean. In the case of the Philippines, which had not been an initial focus of the war, McKinley felt that he could "see but one plain path of duty—the acceptance of the archipelago." In the Treaty of Paris of December 1898, Spain ceded control of Cuba, Puerto Rico, and the Philippines to the United States for a payment of $20 million. Afterward, the United States promised eventual independence for Cuba. Suddenly, the United States was a world power, joining the nations of Europe with its own far-flung empire. What to do with that empire would be a subject of considerable debate in the future.

A large number of the troops who fought in Cuba, including those commanded by Theodore Roosevelt in his assault on San Juan Hill, were African-American soldiers like these from the 9th Cavalry.

The Anti-Imperialists

When the U.S. War with Spain ended, the United States had to decide what to do with its new territory. In spite of the Teller Amendment, President McKinley did everything possible to maximize U.S. involvement in Cuba, including ensuring that the U.S. Navy would have a perpetual base at Guantanamo Bay. The United States was going to keep Puerto Rico, but what about the distant Philippines? The war had begun and ended in the Caribbean over issues of Spanish control of Cuba; however, as part of the war, the United

After liberating the Philippine Islands from Spain, the United States quickly found itself at war with the Filipino people who wanted independence and, as this picture shows, took many of the people of the island prisoner.

States also found itself in control of a chain of seven thousand islands with 7 million people living thousands of miles from the United States.

President McKinley told a group of visiting Episcopal clergy that he had lost sleep and had prayed long and hard about what to do with the islands and that the answer had come to him: "[T]here was nothing left for us to do but to take them all, and to educate the Filipinos, and uplift and civilize and Christianize them." The United States could not give them back to Spain or another country and, he insisted, "they were unfit for self-government."

Nearly all Filipinos were already Christian since Catholic Spain had ruled the islands for nearly 400 years, but McKinley meant Protestant Christianity. The Constitution might prohibit the government's direct involvement with the religious beliefs of the Filipinos, but allowing missionaries was easy.

A greater difficulty with the president's plan was the fact that many Filipinos did not want to be annexed by the United States. A revolt against Spain had been underway long before Commodore Dewey sank the Spanish fleet in Manila Bay. In addition, Dewey had encouraged Emilio Aguinaldo, leader of the Filipino insurrection, to establish an interim government for the islands. Aguinaldo expected U.S. recognition of Philippine independence, and even after it became clear that this was not President McKinley's plan, Aguinaldo hoped for either the defeat of McKinley's treaty in the Senate or a victory in the 1900 presidential elections by William Jennings Bryan, who strongly opposed annexation of the Philippines. When the Senate ratified the treaty with Spain and Bryan lost the election, Aguinaldo led a revolt against the United States. What the U.S. government called the "Philippine Insurrection," Aguinaldo called a war for independence.

Between 1898 and 1902, and beyond, the U.S. Army engaged in a brutal battle with Filipino insurgents. Many more American soldiers were killed in the postwar insurgency in the Philippine Islands than were killed in the war with Spain. Thousands of Filipinos were killed—perhaps 20,000 in combat and 200,000 from war-related causes—and many more left homeless.

Within the United States, broad-based opposition to the war in the Philippines was organized as the Anti-Imperialist League, founded at Boston in June 1898. The league included unlikely allies. Andrew Carnegie offered to buy the islands from the United States to secure their independence and wrote to one member of McKinley's cabinet, "You seem to have finished your work of civilizing the Filipinos; it is thought that about 8,000 of them have been completely civilized and sent to Heaven; I hope you like it." Charles Francis Adams (descendent of two presidents), former abolitionist Thomas Wentworth Higginson, reformers including Jane Addams and Henry Demarest Lloyd, labor leaders including Samuel Gompers, rival Democrats William Jennings Bryan and Grover Cleveland, and university presidents like Harvard's Charles W. Eliot and Stanford's David Starr Jordan all opposed the annexation.

The nation's best-known authors, Mark Twain and William Dean Howells, turned biting humor on McKinley's efforts. Twain said that the U.S. efforts in the Philippines meant that the United States had become "yet another Civilized Power, with its banner of the Prince of Peace in one hand and its loot-basket and its butcher-knife in the other." Booker T. Washington said, "Until our nation has settled the Indian and the Negro problems, I do not think we have a right to assume more social problems."

Most anti-imperialists insisted that the Constitution did not allow for the United States to acquire any territories that it did not plan to eventually admit as states and that **"the Constitution follows the flag"**—meaning all of the civil and political rights guaranteed in the Constitution also applied to other people under U.S. control. The advocates of territorial expansion did not agree, and in May 1901, the U.S. Supreme Court in a series of 5-4 decisions in the Insular Cases declared that the Philippines and Puerto Rico were territories, not future states, and that therefore those residing there were "subjects" not "citizens." It was a bitter moment for the anti-imperialists.

"the Constitution follows the flag"
An argument that the rights of U.S. citizens should be extended to any people living in a territory conquered by the United States.

While Roosevelt had been one of the staunchest advocates of going to war in 1898 and of keeping control of the Philippine Islands after the war, by the time he became president in 1901, the U.S. effort was increasingly unpopular and he had other priorities. In 1901, the Army captured Aguinaldo. William Howard Taft, who had been governor general of the Philippines, was welcomed home, and a truce settled on the islands, though U.S. troops remained until the Japanese invasion at the start of World War II. United States' attention turned elsewhere.

20.2 | **Quick Review** Was the U.S. War with Spain a triumph for the United States?

FOREIGN POLICY, FOREIGN ADVENTURES, 1900–1914

20.3 Explain developments in U.S. policy in Panama, Asia, and Mexico between the U.S. War with Spain and World War I.

When Theodore Roosevelt became president in September 1901, he inherited two major foreign policy issues from McKinley—the ongoing war in the Philippines, which he quickly put behind him, and the question of a Central American canal connecting the Atlantic and Pacific oceans, which he embraced with Rooseveltian enthusiasm. Roosevelt considered the Central American canal one of his proudest achievements.

A Canal in Panama

Ever since the California Gold Rush of 1848, there had been talk of building a canal across Central America that would allow shorter travel by ship from the Atlantic to the Pacific oceans, but the hurdles were significant. The narrow point of land between North and South America was hot and damp, and mosquito-born diseases made working there a death sentence. The land was also mountainous, and for any canal to be built, engineers had to design a series of locks to raise and lower ships. Nevertheless,

Mostly West Indian workers, using steam shovels and hand tools in backbreaking labor, built the Panama Canal once the United States gained control of the territory.

Roosevelt Corollary

President Theodore Roosevelt's policy asserting U.S. authority to intervene in the affairs of Latin American nations; an expansion of the Monroe Doctrine.

in 1850, the United States and Britain negotiated the Clayton-Bulwer Treaty, stating that any canal would be a joint venture though neither controlled the territory. Fifty years later, few in the United States still wanted a joint venture with Britain, and in November 1901, Secretary of State John Hay and the British Ambassador to the United States, Lord Pauncefote, concluded a treaty that gave the United States the exclusive right to build an interocean waterway in Central America. McKinley had created an Isthmian Canal Commission that recommended building a canal in Nicaragua, but Roosevelt preferred a shorter route through Panama.

The canal was not the first time Roosevelt involved the United States in Latin America. In 1902, shortly after he came to office, the government of Venezuela held back on debt payments to European banks. Britain, Italy, and Germany sent ships to Venezuela, but Roosevelt, citing the Monroe Doctrine, pressured them to withdraw. A year later when the Dominican Republic seemed set to follow the same route as Venezuela, Roosevelt sent U.S. forces to the island and took control of its customs operation, dividing the revenue between the country and the European creditors, an involvement in the finances of the Dominican Republic that lasted until 1941. Then, in 1904, he formalized U.S. action in the Dominican Republic, announcing the "**Roosevelt Corollary**" to the Monroe Doctrine, stating that the United States had a right to intervene in any nation in the Americas that could not manage its own affairs.

Roosevelt's greatest interest in Latin America, however, remained constant. He wanted a canal, and he wanted it built in the territory of Panama that then belonged to Colombia. Even though the government of Colombia did not agree, many in Panama saw the situation differently. Panama was a frontier province of Colombia, distant enough that it could take 15 days for messages from Panama City to reach the national government in Bogotá. Many in Panama were ready to declare independence. There is no evidence that Roosevelt actively urged a revolution, but he certainly did nothing to discourage one either. In November 1903, when Panama revolted against Colombian rule, Roosevelt sent orders to U.S. Navy ships standing by on both the Pacific and Atlantic coasts of Panama to "prevent landing of any armed force with hostile intent, either government or insurgent." Since the insurgents were already in Panama and the only forces that wanted to land were from the Colombian government, the impact of the order was clear. Describing the independence movement in Panama, Roosevelt told the U.S. Congress that the people of Panama had risen up against Colombia, "literally as one man." Senator Edward Carmack retorted, "Yes, and the one man was Roosevelt."

Once Panama declared independence, the United States quickly—with "indecent haste," one critic said—recognized the independent Panamanian government and then proposed the canal to them. Three months later, in February 1904, both nations ratified a treaty giving the United States the right to a canal zone 10 miles wide, which "the United States would possess…[as] if it were the sovereign of the territory", while the new government in Panama City got the $10 million that had originally been offered to Colombia. Roosevelt got the route he wanted, if not the good will of Latin America.

Late in his term, Roosevelt visited Panama. Ever the energetic enthusiast, he climbed up to the driver's seat of the biggest steam shovel digging the canal, spoke with some of the 19,000 West Indian laborers who were doing the backbreaking work (and who died at an astounding rate—85 just in the month of the president's visit), met with authorities of the new government, and envisioned ships passing through the canal and towns rising on the banks of what was still, at that point, a muck-filled ditch. The canal did not open until 1914, long after Roosevelt had left office. With or without Roosevelt, the United States would most likely have built a canal between the oceans at some point. Nevertheless, the route and the speed were a result of Roosevelt's efforts.

The United States, Russia, Japan, and China

Across the world, Russia had long been expanding its territory. Russian Cossacks had asserted control of Asian Siberia for Russia in the 1600s and then looked west to North America and south in Asia. All Russian expansion came to an abrupt halt in early 1904, however. Japan, which had emerged as a modern military and diplomatic power, was determined to stop Russia from acquiring influence in Manchuria and Korea. The Japanese fleet under Admiral Heihachiro Togo attacked and destroyed a Russian fleet anchored at Port Arthur. To America, the war seemed far away, and the United States quickly declared neutrality. A year later, in May 1905, another Russian fleet was destroyed. The Japanese Navy sank twenty-two Russian ships, killed some 4,000 Russian sailors, and captured several more ships along with the Russian commander Admiral Rozhdestvenski. Nevertheless, no peace treaty emerged, and Japanese resources were spent.

The Japanese government sent a secret message to Roosevelt, asking if he would "directly and entirely of his own motion and initiative…invite the two belligerents to come together." Roosevelt loved the idea of playing mediator and proposed arbitration to the tsar. Russia agreed, and the announcement of the peace conference won Roosevelt worldwide praise.

Once Roosevelt got representatives of both countries to Portsmouth, New Hampshire, in August 1905, they argued about borders, money, and a postwar plan. But eventually, Roosevelt's arm-twisting led to a peace agreement. The war ended, and Roosevelt was praised by the Russian tsar and the Japanese emperor. A year later, Roosevelt was rewarded with the Nobel Peace Prize.

While the czarist government was grateful for Roosevelt's role in ending the war, Russian immigrants to the United States had their own grievances against the tsar's rule. When hundreds of Russian Jews were killed in pogroms between 1903 and 1906, Jewish immigrants in the United States pressured the U.S. government to do something about the situation, and President Roosevelt and Secretary of State John Hay issued a formal protest. The Russian ambassador responded to the protest saying that it was "unbecoming for Americans to criticize" Russia in light of American lynching of African-Americans and the bad treatment of Chinese immigrants.

Japan, too, though appreciative of Roosevelt's efforts to mediate with Russia, was not pleased by San Francisco's segregation of Japanese students. California was the port of entry for immigrants from Japan and China. It was also the place where anti-Asian feelings ran strongest. In October 1906, in the aftermath of the city's great earthquake, as they reorganized and reopened the city's schools, the San Francisco School Board adopted a policy of racial segregation for Chinese, Korean, and Japanese children. The government of China protested but was too weak to do more. In Japan, however, anger at the insult led to calls for war. Roosevelt tried to convince Californians to rescind the segregation order while encouraging the government of Japan to ignore the insult, but failed at doing both.

Gentlemen's Agreement
A diplomatic agreement in 1907 between Japan and the United States curtailing, but not abolishing, Japanese immigration.

Great White Fleet
A U.S. Navy fleet sent around the world from December 1907 to February 1909 by President Theodore Roosevelt to show American strength and to promote good will.

dollar diplomacy
The U.S. policy urged by President Taft of using private investment in other nations to promote American diplomatic goals and business interests.

However, in 1907 and 1908, he successfully negotiated the **Gentlemen's Agreement** by which the United States agreed not to pass any formal limit on Japanese immigration and the Japanese government agreed to limit the emigration of laborers to the United States. For Japan, it was important not to face anything as insulting as the Chinese Exclusion Act of 1882 had been. For Californians, Roosevelt had accomplished the goal of establishing a limit on Japanese immigration. At the same time, Roosevelt used Japan's threat of war to ask Congress to appropriate funds to expand the U.S. Navy and then sent the **Great White Fleet**—16 battleships painted gleaming white rather than navy grey—around the world with a dramatic stop at Tokyo Bay. The 1908 tensions with Japan had receded, though they were hardly ended.

In China, tensions were also rising against the United States. The Society of Righteous and Harmonious Fists, (called Boxers by foreigners) a secret society consisting of local farmers, peasants, and others who were victims of disastrous floods and opium addiction, led the Boxer Rebellion in 1901, attacking all foreigners, including American businessmen and missionaries, whom they blamed for their plight. Although the Boxer Rebellion was quickly quashed by an international force, Chinese citizens, carrying anti-American posters and singing anti-American songs, organized a massive boycott of U.S. goods in 1905.

Woodrow Wilson's Asian Policy

While he was president, Theodore Roosevelt had insisted that the long-standing Open Door Policy allowing the United States and Britain free trade with China be continued in spite of Japan's desire to dominate all Asian markets. President Taft had less lofty goals for America's role in the world, and though he was wary of political ties, he strongly encouraged American investment wherever there was an opportunity, leading critics to call his policy **dollar diplomacy**. Late in Taft's term, J.P. Morgan negotiated a large international loan to China to support the building of new rail lines there. Upon becoming president, Woodrow Wilson found himself immediately involved with Asian matters and specifically the Morgan loan. Wilson's new secretary of state, William Jennings Bryan, had deep reservations about the loan. Within 2 weeks of the inauguration, Wilson announced that the government of the United States opposed the loan because its terms undermined "the administrative independence of China." China did not get the loan. Unfortunately, it also did not get the railroads that the loan was supposed to finance, something that weakened the country in its future dealings with Japan.

Tensions with Japan that had been brewing since Roosevelt's time continued. Just as Wilson assumed office, the California legislature adopted a law that no one "ineligible for citizenship" could buy land in California. Since Japanese immigrants could not become citizens, everyone knew at whom the law was directed. Secretary Bryan made two trips to California to try and get the law rescinded, but failed. Japan's government reacted angrily, as it had with school segregation in 1906, and again a war seemed possible. Wilson and Bryan did everything they could to diffuse the situation. The leaders in Tokyo also did not want a war, but in Japan, feelings of deep anti-American animosity were furthered by California's continuing determination to marginalize Japanese immigrants.

Wilson and Bryan also tried to end U.S. control of the Philippines. They convinced Congress to pass legislation granting eventual independence to the islands, but Republican opponents succeeded in deleting any specific deadline. Only after World War II did the United States recognize the independence of the Philippines, though it had been promised in 1916.

Mexico and Latin America

The most difficult foreign policy issue for Wilson in his first term involved Mexico. In February 1913, just before Wilson's inauguration, Mexican army general Victoriano Huerta led a military coup against the elected moderate, President Francisco Madero, who was killed in the bloody overthrow. Many American investors wanted the U.S. government to support the new Huerta administration, but Wilson announced, "We can have no sympathy with those who seek the power of government to advance their own personal interests or ambitions." Wilson and Bryan believed that the coup was part of a battle between British and American oil companies, and they wanted none of it.

Wilson desperately wanted to let Mexico work out its own future. As he told the journalist Ray Stannard Baker, he "felt shame as an American over the first Mexican war" of 1848. He continued that it was "his resolution that while he was president there should be no such predatory war." He also believed that a people had the right "to do as they damned pleased with their own affairs." Baker added that the president did, indeed, use the word *damned*.

In spite of the president's intentions, Americans had major investments in Mexico, and thousands of American citizens worked in Mexico as teachers, nurses, and construction workers. Wilson could not ignore the country, and he sent envoys to try to persuade Huerta to resign, but failed. He spoke passionately about "the self-restraint of a really great nation." When a revolution against Huerta led by Venustiano Carranza and Francisco "Pancho" Villa broke out, Wilson recognized it. In April of 1914, when Wilson got word that a large shipment of European arms for Huerta's government was on its way to the Mexican port of Veracruz, Wilson ordered the Navy to land at the port and stop the arms. The arms were stopped, but to Wilson's surprise, Mexico did not welcome the intervention, Mexican forces fought the U.S. Marines, and 17 Americans were killed. Not only Huerta but also Carranza condemned what they called a U.S. invasion. The end result was good for Carranza. Without the new arms, Huerta resigned and went into exile, and Carranza rode into Mexico City as the victor. Argentina, Brazil, and Chile agreed to negotiate a solution, and the Americans withdrew from Veracruz.

Unfortunately, a new civil war began in Mexico when Villa split with Carranza. In March 1916, Villa, who was now leading a full-scale revolt, led several hundred troops in an attack on the U.S. border town of Columbus, New Mexico. They wanted arms that were stored at nearby U.S. Army Fort Furlong, but more important, the wily Villa wanted to create an international incident. He did not get the arms, but he did get the incident.

Wilson notified Carranza of his intention to respect Mexican sovereignty, but also ordered the U.S. Army, under General John J. Pershing, to enter Mexico and find Villa.

Mexican revolutionary Pancho Villa clashed with others in Mexico but also conducted a long-running battle with U.S. forces.

Chapter 20 Foreign Policy and War in a Progressive Era   **577**

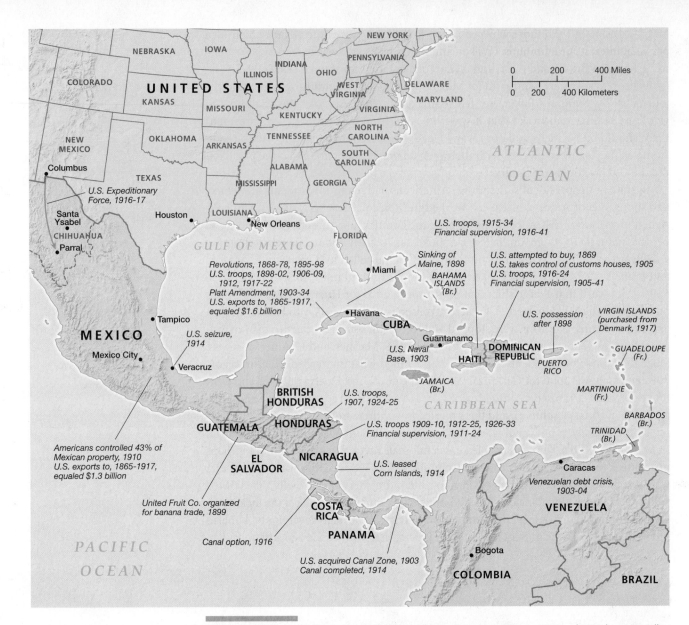

MAP 20-2 U.S. Intervention in the Caribbean and Latin America. Between 1865 and 1933, but especially under the administrations of McKinley and the "progressive presidents"—Roosevelt, Taft, and Wilson—the United States intervened regularly in the nations of the Caribbean and Latin America.

Carranza had much to benefit from eliminating Villa and stayed out of the battle. Some 10,000 U.S. troops under Pershing's command were well-equipped with motor vehicles and airplanes, but they never found Villa though they engaged in some bloody battles as they chased him through northern Mexico for months. Eventually in early 1917, as Wilson became more and more concerned with the war in Europe, the U.S. forces withdrew without success, and Villa survived until he was assassinated in 1923.

The United States intervened in several other Latin American matters during Wilson's administration (see Map 20-2). Bryan offered an apology to Colombia for the U.S. role in the revolution that had separated Panama and negotiated a $25 million payment to Colombia. Roosevelt was furious at an obvious slap at his administration, and his friend Henry Cabot Lodge blocked authorization of the funds in the Senate. The United States sent Marines to end unrest in Nicaragua, the Dominican Republic, and Haiti; they stayed in Haiti until 1934. For all of their talk of nonintervention, Wilson and Bryan seemed quite willing to intervene in the Americas.

20.3 **Quick Review** How would you summarize the similarities and differences in Roosevelt's, Taft's and Wilson's foreign policy? Give specific examples of ways they differed.

THE UNITED STATES AND THE GREAT WAR

20.4 Analyze the causes and consequences of U.S. involvement in World War I.

20.1

20.2

20.3

20.4

Just after the November 1912 election, while he was still living in Princeton, President-elect Wilson told one of his former faculty colleagues, "It would be an irony of fate if my administration had to deal chiefly with foreign problems, for all my preparation has been in domestic matters." It was an irony that would come to pass with a vengeance.

War in Europe

On June 28, 1914, the Austrian Archduke Franz Ferdinand, heir apparent to the throne of the Austria-Hungarian Empire, and his wife, Sophie, were assassinated in the town of Sarajevo by a Serbian nationalist who wanted independence for Serbia. Nothing could have seemed as far removed from the United States than the murder of members of a central European royal family. However, within a very short time, the impact of the assassination was felt everywhere in the world.

In the summer of 1914, Europe was at peace. Even so, independence movements within the Austria-Hungarian and Ottoman Empires, particularly in Balkan states (including Serbia), were challenging the empires' central governments (see Map 20-3). In addition, a newly united Germany was angry at being shut out of the colonies in Africa and Asia by the speed with which the British and French had moved. An arms race had developed among the continent's greatest powers, and in their quest for security, European nations had developed a complex series of defensive alliances. Germany, Austria-Hungary, and the Turkish Ottoman Empire were known as the Central Powers. Russia, France, and Great Britain were known simply as the Allies. All of these factors quickly led Europe to tumble into all-out war when Austria set out to punish Serbia and Russia came to the aid of the Serbians. By August, all of Europe was engulfed in what was called the Great War. (The term World War I was coined only after the outbreak of another great war in 1939, one which quickly came to be known as World War II.)

At the beginning of the war, many Europeans were caught up in patriotic fervor. Young men signed up promptly and marched off proudly. Both sides expected an easy victory. The German army attacked France by moving through neutral Belgium. It was a move that cost Germany dearly in public support, but it allowed the German army to get within 30 miles of Paris early in the war. Then an allied counteroffensive drove the Germans back, and by November 1914, both sides were dug in for the long trench warfare that would not move very much—though every small move cost thousands of soldiers their lives—until March of 1918. The long years of trench warfare were ghastly. In 1916 at the Battle of the Somme, 60,000 British soldiers were killed in a single day. In a year-long battle for the town of Verdun, a million soldiers were killed. New forms of artillery, tanks, and flamethrowers, along with the introduction of poisonous mustard gas, caused what seemed like never-ending waves of death while life in the trenches involved living for months with mud, rats, and rotten food. Despite these costs, the battle lines did not change significantly. Wilson called it "this vast gruesome contest of systematized destruction."

The United States saw all of these developments as a distant tragedy. A young American mining engineer, Herbert Hoover, organized the Commission for Belgian Relief, which along with the American Red Cross, sent aid to people caught in the path of war. Hoover gained international fame as the "Napoleon of mercy," for his efforts. However, most Americans preferred not to get involved and agreed with U.S. ambassador to London Walter Hines Page, who said, "I thank Heaven for many things—first the Atlantic Ocean." President Wilson declared neutrality. He wanted to stay out of the war, and he understood that any European war would stir up deep tensions in a nation made up of immigrants from every one of the nations at war. Neutrality, however, would not be easy to maintain.

MAP 20-3 Europe and the Middle East Before and During World War I. This map shows the areas dominated by the Austria-Hungarian and Ottoman Empires, both of which would disappear at the end of World War I. Also shown is the area in northern France where the greatest fighting of the war took place.

The warfare on land and on the oceans around Europe cut into U.S. trade, hurting wheat farmers and cotton growers who could not get their goods to European markets. Britain began to place large orders for farm products and for munitions while using its powerful navy to maintain a blockade of the Central Powers. War-torn Britain needed money to buy these things, but when J.P. Morgan began to float large loans, Secretary of State Bryan imposed a ban on loans to belligerents, seeking the "true spirit" of strict neutrality. Bryan's ban hurt U.S. commerce, and Britain and France claimed it was prejudicial toward them, so Bryan and Wilson announced that "commercial credit" could be extended to the allies. No one understood the difference between "commercial credit" and loans, but the distinction allowed the European allied powers to get the goods they wanted, U.S. farmers and manufacturers to profit, and everyone to pretend that neutrality was still maintained.

The Wilson administration had to steer a difficult course while facing considerable internal pressures. Former president Roosevelt urged massive buildup of the army and navy as well as a military draft, all in the name of preparedness for an eventual war on the side of the British and French. From Roosevelt's perspective, Wilson was dangerously passive.

In contrast, Progressive Senator Robert La Follette of Wisconsin and other politicians, especially those from states with large German populations led a peace movement, fearing that Wilson was edging toward war. Jane Addams led a large woman's movement for peace. Many union leaders saw the war as a battle between European capitalists in which the working class should not be involved. Anarchists and socialists condemned the war. Between 1914 and 1916, in spite of Roosevelt's best efforts to build support for preparedness and war, most Americans in and out of office favored keeping as far distant from Europe's problems as possible.

Of the many diplomatic tensions that the war in Europe created, by far the greatest had to do with the German use of a new kind of sea power—the submarine, or U-boat. Britain's navy ruled the waves, but German U-boats could glide under the waves and strike at ships bringing supplies to Britain and France. On February 4, 1915, the German Admiralty announced that the waters around Britain were a "war zone" and its submarines would freely attack any ship bringing supplies to Britain. Wilson and Bryan sent a formal diplomatic note that sinking ships without warning was "an act so unprecedented in naval warfare" that the United States would hold them to "a strict accountability for such acts." No one defined what "strict accountability" meant. Somehow, submarine warfare—having a ship struck by a torpedo seemingly out of nowhere—terrified people in a way that direct ship-to-ship combat did not. Submarine warfare also threatened the profitable U.S. trade with Britain. For Wilson, it also raised the issue of basic rights of U.S. citizens, as neutrals, to travel freely. On the last point, the president and his secretary of state differed strongly. Bryan asked "whether an American citizen can, by putting his business above his regard for his country, assume for his own advantage unnecessary risk and thus involve his country in international complications." For Wilson, the freedom of neutrals to travel was "in the interests of mankind," and protecting the rights of neutrals under international law was a national duty.

In March 1915, a submarine sank a small British passenger ship, the *Falaba,* and an American citizen was killed. Then on May 7, 1915, a submarine sank the British liner *Lusitania,* the grandest and fastest ocean liner then in service. The *Lusitania* sank in 18 minutes and 1,198 people were killed, including 127 American citizens. The United States demanded an apology from Germany. When Bryan suggested also issuing a formal warning to American citizens not to travel on ships belonging to countries that were at war, Wilson refused.

In response to the American note, the German government sent secret orders to its submarine captains to avoid large passenger liners, but their official word to the United States was evasive. Wilson promised that if Germany would give up submarine warfare, he would also press Britain to end the blockade of goods flowing to Germany and Austria, but he also prepared a second note to Germany saying that the sinking of the *Lusitania* involved "principles of humanity."

Bryan argued for protesting the British blockade and for linking the second note to a policy that would bar passenger ships from carrying munitions (the *Lusitania* may well have been carrying munitions in addition to passengers). Wilson thought that Bryan's plan would undermine the needed message of protest. Bryan resigned rather than sign the second *Lusitania* note. He told the president that he was risking war by creating a situation where a foolish move by the German government could drag the United States into a war and that he could do more for peace building public opinion outside the administration than within. Bryan's departure was a sad parting between two people who had come to like and admire each other but who deeply believed in different courses of action. Robert Lansing became acting secretary and signed the note. Congress debated but did not pass a law barring Americans from travel on belligerent ships. Sinkings and diplomatic notes continued, as did American domestic politics and new developments in Woodrow Wilson's personal life.

Especially before the United States entered World War I, songs like "I Didn't Raise My Boy to Be a Soldier" were popular among many who did not want to see young American men caught up in the fighting.

In the summer of 1914, as Europe began to move toward war, Ellen Wilson, the president's wife of 30 years whose warmth offset Wilson's sometimes dour personality, became desperately ill. Her kidneys were failing, and through the summer, the president read diplomatic cables while sitting by his wife's bedside. She died at the White House at the beginning of August. The president wrote, "I never understood before what a broken heart meant." Less than a year later, Wilson met a vivacious 42-year-old widow named Edith Bolling Galt and quickly fell in love. Although some in the cabinet worried about how the public would respond to a new marriage so quickly after the loss of his first wife, the two were married in December 1915. The nation had a new First Lady who would support Wilson and have a significant role in policy as war and illness later sapped his energy.

While Wilson was seeking to maintain neutrality and dealing with his personal life, 1916 was also an election year. After Ellen's death, he had seriously considered not running, but his new personal life and his desire to see the diplomatic crisis through led him to declare his candidacy for a second term. The Republican Party was reunited and nominated Supreme Court Justice Charles Evans Hughes. Hughes had served two terms as governor of New York, but he had also been on the Supreme Court since 1910 and thus sat out the Roosevelt-Taft split. Roosevelt called him "the bearded iceberg," but campaigned strongly for the ticket as did Taft. It was a very close contest, but in the end, Wilson carried California by 4,000 votes and, with it, the Electoral College.

A month after the election Wilson tried to broker a peace between Europe's warring powers. He asked both sides for their demands. Germany indicated that it was willing to discuss peace, but a new British government led by Prime Minister Lloyd George said it had no interest in American mediation. Then in December, Lloyd George indicated willingness to talk while the Germans backed off. In the midst of this diplomacy, the German government made two fateful mistakes. On January 31, 1917, it announced to the United States that it was resuming "the full employment of all the weapons…at its disposal." At the same time, German Foreign Minister Arthur Zimmermann sent a secret cable to the German embassy in Mexico with an offer to the Carranza government—long estranged from Wilson and the United States—that if it would attack the United States, Germany would see to the restoration of the territory from Texas to California that had been taken from Mexico in 1848.

The British government managed to intercept and decode the Zimmermann telegram and release it to the public, turning much of American public opinion against Germany. Wilson was more concerned with unrestricted submarine warfare than any interference from Carranza. He broke diplomatic relations with Germany. He then asked Congress for authority to arm merchant ships, but La Follette and other Republican Progressives blocked the bill in the Senate. Wilson called them "a little group of willful men" and claimed the authority to arm the ships on executive authority. At the same time, other Americans, including former President Roosevelt were pressing Wilson to do more for Britain. As early as January 1915, Roosevelt, although out of office, wrote to British Foreign Minister Sir Edward Grey, calling Wilson's lack of greater support for the British "very obstinate." Roosevelt thought Wilson was stumbling in 1915 and was ready to march. In the end, when war came, it brought Roosevelt political and personal tragedy. Wilson would accept neither his advice to help Britain nor his offer of service, and in July 1918, Roosevelt's beloved son Quentin was killed in combat in France.

From the German perspective, an immediate attack on supplies going to Britain and France was the only way to win the war. If they could block food and munitions from getting to the allies, then the Germans believed they could win the war before the United States could organize itself to do much harm. In March, U-boats sank three U.S. merchant ships with the loss of 15 American lives. As Bryan had warned, Wilson's hard line meant that Germany had the initiative. The president felt he had run out of options. On April 2, 1917, Wilson appeared before a joint session of Congress and asked for a declaration of war against Germany.

American Voices

Woodrow Wilson, War Message 1917

Wilson had spoken directly to Congress many times before. Nevertheless, when he decided that the United States needed to go to war on the side of Britain and France the words took on a new level of importance. Everyone knew what he would ask, but they waited to hear his reasons.

Gentlemen of the Congress:

On the 3d of February last I officially laid before you the extraordinary announcement of the Imperial German Government that on and after the 1st day of February it was its purpose to put aside all restraints of law or of humanity and use its submarines to sink every vessel that sought to approach either the ports of Great Britain and Ireland or the western coasts of Europe.... Vessels of every kind, whatever their flag, their character, their cargo, their destination, their errand, have been ruthlessly sent to the bottom without warning and without thought of help or mercy for those on board, the vessels of friendly neutrals along with those of belligerents....

With a profound sense of the solemn and even tragical character of the step I am taking and of the grave responsibilities which it involves, but in unhesitating obedience to what I deem my constitutional duty, I advise that the Congress declare the recent course of the Imperial German Government to be in fact nothing less than war against the Government and people of the United States; that it formally accept the status of belligerent which has thus been thrust upon it....

What this will involve is clear. It will involve the utmost practicable cooperation in counsel and action with the governments now at war with Germany....It will involve the organization and mobilization of all the material resources of the country to supply the materials of war....It will involve the immediate full equipment of the Navy in all respects but particularly in supplying it with the best means of dealing with the enemy's submarines. It will involve the immediate addition to the armed forces of the United States already provided for by law in case of war at least 500,000 men, who should, in my opinion, be chosen upon the principle of universal liability to service....It will involve also, of course, the granting of adequate credits to the Government, sustained, I hope, so far as they can equitably be sustained by the present generation, by well conceived taxation....

One of the things that has served to convince us that the Prussian autocracy was not and could never be our friend is that from the very outset of the present war it has filled our unsuspecting communities and even our offices of government with spies and set criminal intrigues everywhere afoot against our national unity....That it means to stir up enemies against us at our very doors the intercepted note to the German Minister at Mexico City is eloquent evidence....

The world must be made safe for democracy. Its peace must be planted upon the tested foundations of political liberty. We have no selfish ends to serve. We desire no conquest, no dominion. We seek no indemnities for ourselves, no material compensation for the sacrifices we shall freely make. We are but one of the champions of the rights of mankind.

Source: Woodrow Wilson, *War Messages*, 65th Cong., 1st Sess. Senate Doc. No. 5, Serial No. 7264, Washington, D.C., 1917; 2 April 1917

Thinking Critically

1. **Documentary Analysis**

   As Wilson described it, what led to his decision to ask Congress to declare war on Germany?

2. **Contextualization**

   How did Wilson justify American military intervention on moral ethical grounds? What does the speech tell you about Wilson's vision of America's place in the world?

The War at Home—Support and Opposition

Not everyone was convinced by Wilson's eloquence. In the Senate, Wisconsin's La Follette and George Norris of Nebraska led the opposition to a declaration of war. Norris, a Republican long part of the Progressive movement, said, "We have loaned many hundreds of millions of dollars to the allies in this controversy." And he saw the war as simply a way to defend those loans, insisting, "We are going into war upon the command of gold." He would have none of it. When the vote came, six Senators, three Republican and three Democrats, opposed the war. In the House, 50 Representatives voted no on the war resolution. The most dramatic vote came from Jeannette Rankin of Montana. Rankin was the only woman in the House, elected at a time when women in most states still did not have the vote. She was under intense pressure from some suffragists, who planned to demand votes for patriotic women as a war measure, to vote for the war, but in the roll call Rankin answered, "I want to stand by my country, but I cannot vote for war. I vote no." (In 1941, after a long absence, Rankin would

20.1

20.2

20.3

20.4

Committee on Public Information
Government agency during World War I that sought to shape public opinion in support of the war effort through newspapers, pamphlets, speeches, films, and other media.

be on the floor of Congress again and would be the single no vote against U.S. entry into World War II.) Once the United States was formally at war, the previous antiwar constituency split between those including Bryan, who believed that once the United States had made the decision to go to war everyone should support the war effort, and others—from Jane Addams to Eugene V. Debs to Emma Goldman—who continued to oppose the war no matter what the president asked or how the Congress voted. Despite the opposition, once the United States was formally at war in the spring of 1917, the Wilson administration set out to do everything possible to assure the support of every citizen. In his war speech Wilson had said, "If there should be disloyalty, it will be dealt with with a firm hand of stern repression." He meant it.

To build support for the war, Wilson created the **Committee on Public Information** (CPI) and appointed the respected progressive journalist George Creel as its head. No one could challenge Creel's progressive credentials as a muckraker, supporter of women's rights, and political reformer. Creel rejected crude propaganda, insisting that "[a] free people cannot be told what to think. They must be given the facts and permitted to do their own thinking." Creel also insisted that he and the Wilson administration would be the ones to decide what "facts" to give people and, more seriously, what alternative "facts" should be blocked.

Creel announced, "It was a fight for the minds of men, for the 'conquest of their convictions,' and the battle-line ran through every home in the country." Under his leadership, the CPI hired other muckraking journalists, including Ray Stannard Baker and Ida Tarbell, and published 75 million pamphlets supporting the U.S. war effort. They recruited 75,000 "Four Minute Men," volunteers who were ready to speak at a moment's notice in favor of the war effort and against Germany at any theater or neighborhood meeting. He worked with the still-new movie studios to create films like *The Kaiser: Beast of Berlin.* Creel's CPI launched a special "War Americanization Plan" to encourage foreign-born immigrants, especially those from the Central Powers, to buy Liberty Bonds and otherwise assert their American patriotism. He also hired Charles Dana Gibson, famous for creating the nation's model of feminine beauty in the "Gibson Girl," to produce prowar posters that would glorify the American war effort and call on all Americans to purchase war bonds and tend home vegetable gardens—or victory gardens—as well as for young men to serve in the army. The government also launched "war study courses" to encourage patriotism and loyalty among public school students. Creel was confident enough of his efforts that he opposed more blatant limitations on civil liberties. After the war, he wrote, "Better far to have the desired compulsions proceed from within than to apply them from without."

Herbert Hoover, who had gained fame organizing support for people in war ravaged Belgium, became the head of the U.S. Food Administration and urged Americans to support the war by eating less and conserving more so that food could be sent to the troops or the Allies. Like Creel, Hoover believed that voluntary compliance was most effective, so he rejected rationing in favor of what he described as mobilizing "the spirit of self-denial and self-sacrifice in this country." People got the widely touted message, "FOOD WILL WIN THE WAR—DON'T WASTE IT." The federal government also created the Fuel Administration and the War Industries Board and took direct control of the nation's railroads. Most of the new agencies were led by business executives, and the criticism of business leaders that had characterized Wilson's first term virtually disappeared as the nation's corporate elite became essential supporters of the war effort.

While Creel led the government's "fight for the minds" of the American people and Hoover tried to change their eating habits, other self-styled patriots had their own agendas. The nongovernmental American Protective League (APL), which eventually grew to 250,000 members, included some who had opposed German immigrants or domestic political radicals and who saw the war as a time to further their agenda. APL members, without government authority, opened mail and listened in on telephone calls, looking for spies and traitors. Fearing such animosity, many German-Americans

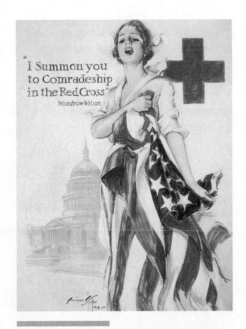

The U.S. government and private organizations like the Red Cross used advertising that had been effective in other sectors of American life to recruit Americans to support the war effort, as in this poster of a young woman summoning Americans to service.

were careful to demonstrate their loyalty. The Deutsches Haus of Indianapolis became the Athenaeum of Indiana; sauerkraut became liberty cabbage; and German language classes, schools, and newspapers were closed. On occasion, the split between those who supported and those who opposed U.S. involvement in the war turned violent. A few months after the United States entered the war, during the hot summer of 1917, some 2,000 members of the APL along with the sheriff of Bisbee, Arizona, raided a mass meeting of the Industrial Workers of the World—the large and radical union that strongly opposed the war—and rounded up over a thousand IWW members and supporters, a third of whom were Mexican-American, leaving them out on the desert without food or water for 2 days before letting them escape to New Mexico. A German-American, Robert Prager, was lynched by a mob in Collinsville, Illinois. An IWW organizer, Frank Little, was lynched in Butte, Montana, after he told striking copper miners that they were battling an "imperialist, capitalist war." An editorial in the *Washington Post* said of the violence, "In spite of excesses such as lynching, it is a healthful and wholesome awakening in the interior of the country."

In 1917 and 1918, Congress passed several acts to control the country's responses to the war, including the Sedition Act of 1918 and the Espionage Act of 1917, giving the government vast new powers to limit free speech and the press that had not been seen in the United States since the Alien and Sedition Acts of the John Adams administration. The **Sedition Act** of 1918 made illegal "uttering, printing, writing, or publishing any disloyal, profane, scurrilous, or abusive language about the government of the United States…or the military or naval forces of the United States." Postmaster General Albert Burleson banned from the U.S. mail anything that he thought violated the act. Attorney General Thomas W. Gregory and his successor A. Mitchell Palmer prosecuted violators or left it to local U.S. attorneys to do so.

Sedition Act
Broad law restricting criticism of America's involvement in World War I or its government, flag, military, taxes, or officials.

In spite of government policies and the efforts of many in organizations like the APL to force all Americans to support the war, dissenters continued to speak out. Jane Addams, leader of the Women's Peace Party as well as Chicago's Hull House, spoke to the City Club of Chicago just after war had been declared, saying, "That the United States has entered the war has not changed my views of the invalidity of war as a method of settlement of social problems a particle, and I can see no reason why one should not say what one believes in time of war as in time of peace.…" Her words were greeted only by silence from the club women. The National Federation of Settlements, which Addams had helped to found, said, "It has been very painful to many of us who hold Miss Addams in deep affection and wholly respect her, to find that we cannot think or act in unison with her."

Jane Addams continued to oppose the war and seek international mediation to end it. She not only wanted the United States out of the war but also wanted to end the war wherever it was fought. At the same time, Addams, ever the practical settlement house leader, sought to ensure that there was "bread in time of war," no matter who needed to eat. She happily cooperated with the U.S. government's Food Administration though she objected to its slogan, "Food Will Win the War." Nevertheless, Addams urged residents of Chicago to plant vegetable gardens and consume less so that more could be sent to those in greatest need.

While Addams was snubbed for her antiwar stance, others paid a much higher price. Radical leaders were watched carefully for "unpatriotic" words and actions. Over a hundred IWW and Socialist Party leaders were arrested and jailed on charges of violating the Sedition Act. In June 1918, Eugene V. Debs told a huge rally in Canton, Ohio, "I realize that, in speaking to you this afternoon, there are certain limitations placed upon the right of free speech." But Debs also made it clear that he was equally as opposed to the leadership of Germany as to that of the Allies for, he said, all sides were using working people to fight their battles. So he continued, "The master class has always declared the wars; the subject class has always fought the battles." In particular, he added, "[T]he working class who make the supreme sacrifices, the working class who freely shed their blood and furnish the corpses, have never yet had a

Espionage Act

Law whose vague prohibition against obstructing the nation's war effort was used to stop dissent and criticism during World War I.

voice in either declaring war or making peace. It is the ruling class that invariably does both." Debs was arrested for the speech and sentenced to 10 years in prison under the **Espionage Act** of 1917.

War and Victory

Many of those who supported U.S. entry into the war assumed that the country would limit its role to patrolling the oceans and providing material to the Allies. But once Wilson led the nation to war, he wanted full-scale involvement just as he had told the Congress. He was determined to defeat Germany and to win a place for himself at the table of the peace negotiations that he knew must come at the war's end.

General John J. Pershing, fresh from the failed effort to find Villa in Mexico, became the commander of the American Expeditionary Forces (AEF) in large part because he had kept silent when others were criticizing Wilson's lack of early preparation for war. Wilson refused an offer by former President Roosevelt to raise his own all-volunteer unit. Pershing's orders were to work closely with the British and French while protecting the separate identity of the American forces.

Deciding to send troops to fight in Europe was one thing. Actually getting an army raised and across the ocean was quite another. Over significant opposition, Congress passed a military draft, and draft boards across the country began processing the not-always-willing recruits. Training camps were set up. Regardless, it took time to raise and train an army. It also took both time and ships to get them across the Atlantic, and the United States was short on both. Since the Civil War, the U.S. merchant marine, needed to transport troops and supplies, had shrunk even as the navy had grown, and German attacks had reduced Britain's shipping capacity significantly.

On July 4, 1917, a token force of "doughboys" as the American troops were called, paraded in France to enthusiastic acclaim. But it would be many months before large numbers of U.S. troops arrived in France and an even longer time before Pershing thought they were ready to fight.

While the United States was raising, training, and transporting its army, the Allies came close to losing the war. The German government knew that it needed to win quickly before Americans arrived in force. In the long run, the United States had more people, and thus more potential soldiers, than any of the combatants except Russia.

This picture of men—and horses—bogged down in mud is a more accurate portrait of the experience of those who fought in World War I than the romanticized posters.

THINKING HISTORICALLY

Limiting Free Speech

Once the United States voted to go to war, most Americans supported the war effort, but a sizeable minority did not, and their claim to opposition under the free speech clause of the U.S. Constitution caused great tension. Many years later, Miriam E. Tefft, whose family supported the war, still remembered the fear when she was 15 years old and "the tragic hysteria which was World War I broke out in the copper mining camp of Bisbee, Arizona, where I lived and the citizens took over the law." In Bisbee the IWW was leading a miner's strike but since the union was also opposed to U.S. involvement in the war, the two issues—the right of the miners to strike and loyalty or opposition to the war effort, merged. "You could almost smell fear," Tefft remembers. "Men didn't look at each other in the face. Everyone was under suspicion. Loyalties were divided. One could sense an undercurrent of outrage seething." Then on July 12, 1917, Tefft recalled seeing

> that the deputies and armed citizens were keeping the strikers in line as they were herded into the ball park behind the high board fence. The men had evidently been taken completely by surprise; some were still in their nightshirts, many in long underwear; some apparently hadn't been given time to put on their shoes. "Where are they taking them?" people asked. A few days later the answer came. "The loads of strikers had been shipped to New Mexico, where they were turned out into the desert near Columbus."

Many other Americans were arrested and sent to jail under the Espionage Act. Charles Schenck mailed pamphlets urging people to resist the military draft and was convicted and sent to prison. Speaking to farmers in North Dakota, Kate Richards O'Hare said, "Any person who enlists in the army of the United States of America will be used for fertilizer," and a federal judge sentenced her to 5 years in prison. Perhaps the most famous American to oppose the war, Eugene V. Debs, was sentenced to 10 years in prison for his speech in Canton, Ohio.

Schenck, O'Hare, Debs, and others appealed that their basic rights under the Constitution were being undermined. Some were eloquent in their testimony. O'Hare told the judge who sentenced her,

> I am dangerous to the war profiteers of this country who rob the people on the one hand and rob and debase the Government on the other...You can convince the people that I am dangerous to these men; but no jury and no judge can convince them that I am a dangerous woman to the best interests of the United States.

Deb, in perhaps his best known statement, told the judge who was sentencing him:

> Your Honor, years ago I recognized my kinship with all living beings, and I made up my mind that I was not one but better than the meanest on earth. I said then, and I say now, that while there is a lower class, I am in it, while there is a criminal element I am of it, and while there is a soul in prison I am not free.

Despite the eloquence, no courts overturned the Espionage Act convictions. The U.S. Supreme Court upheld enforcement of the Espionage Act. In the case of Charles Schenck, *Schenck v. United States,* Justice Oliver Wendell Holmes wrote that Congress could limit free speech if the words "are used in such circumstances as are of such a nature as to create a clear and present danger." In *Debs v. United States,* the court upheld Debs's conviction even though he had not urged violation of the draft laws. And later, when foreign-born opponents of the war were deported, the court upheld those rulings also.

Finally, in the case of the IWW miners in Bisbee, Arizona, Tefft concluded,

> It was anticlimax when President Wilson, breathing fire and brimstone, sent a commission to investigate. The commission was headed by Felix Frankfurter [later appointed to the U.S. Supreme Court]. They found the government was helpless to punish anyone. No law could be found against kidnapping people en masse and dumping them in another state.

Many Americans who did not agree with Debs or Addams were still appalled by the Wilson administration's attacks on free speech and the court's decisions. Samuel Gompers, president of the American Federation of Labor, supported the war but also condemned the attacks on other unionists, including on members of the IWW. Even Theodore Roosevelt criticized the president for the excessive force of the Espionage and Sedition Acts, which he called "sheer treason to the United States," and dared Wilson to send him to jail because it "would make my voice carry farther." After Wilson had left office, his successor, Warren Harding, pardoned Debs who had served some 2 years in federal prison. The country moved on, but the laws remained on the books.

Source: Miriam E. Tefft, interview dated February 2, 1982 from arizona.edu/bisbee/docs2/rec_teff.php; The Trial of Kate Richards O'Hare for Disloyalty, Bismark, North Dakota, 1917, reprinted in Robert Marcus and Anthony Marcus, editors, On Trial: American History Through Court Proceedings and Hearings, Vol. 2 (St. James, NY: Brandywine Press, 1998), pp. 96-104); William A. Pelz, editor, The Eugene V. Debs Reader (Chicago: Institute of Working Class History, 2000).

Thinking Critically

1. **Synthesis**

   What larger fears and tensions within American society were revealed by the multifaceted efforts to suppress dissent during World War I?

2. **Comparison**

   To what degree does Tefft's description of the era as one of "wartime hysteria" account for the decisions? Do such limits on speech always happen in time of war? Can or should they be avoided?

Schenck v. United States
The first of several decisions by the U.S. Supreme Court upholding the Sedition and Espionage Acts.

20.1

20.2

20.3

20.4

Knowing that the Americans were coming, the British and French launched a major offensive in the summer of 1917. As with previous efforts, the offensive was turned back, and the terrible losses led to mutinies throughout the French army. The Allied armies seemed to be losing the will to fight.

On Germany's eastern front, the Bolshevik Revolution in Russia in November 1917 led to a new government that wanted nothing to do with the war. The Bolsheviks signed the Treaty of Brest-Litovsk which ended the war between Germany and Russia on German terms, the most important term of all being that Germany could now focus exclusively on the western front and attack France in the spring of 1918.

The treaty did not come in time to save Germany, however. By 1918, 850,000 fresh U.S. troops had arrived, and they quickly went into combat, while the German troops were exhausted by 4 years of war. For the German soldiers, the fact that they were facing so many well-armed fresh troops undermined morale as much as any specific American victories, though those victories were not without importance. At Château-Thierry in June of 1918, U.S. forces helped stop a German offensive toward Paris. By that fall, the Americans were part of an Allied effort that had driven the German army out of France and back inside Germany. The end was becoming clear. An armistice was signed, and on November 11, 1918, at 11:00 a.m., the guns of Europe fell silent.

Peace Talks, and the Failure of the Treaty of Versailles

No one knows exactly how many were killed and wounded in World War I or how many more died of disease and exposure. By some estimates, as many as 65 million men fought, of whom 8 million were killed. In Europe, hardly a family escaped losing

American Voices

Mathew Chopin, "Advancing Over the Top and Carrying Wounded Comrade Under Shell-Fire," 1918

U.S. soldiers began arriving in France in the summer of 1918 and were quickly moved to the front lines. While presidents and generals planned, those doing the actual fighting—recent arrivals to war from farms and crowded city neighborhoods—told their own stories of fighting, fear, bravery, and sorrow, including this one recorded by Mathew Chopin while still in France, waiting for a ship home in early 1919.

At early dawn we continued advancing "over the top" through clouds of gas and smoke—under rain of machine gun bullets, shrapnel and steel. The Huns [as most Americans called the Germans during the war] were shelling heavily the edge of the roadside. It was freezing cold; we were out of water and had just a small ration of salmon and hard-tack. Completely exhausted and thirsting for a drink, I remember grabbing a canteen from a passing artillery caisson to soothe my parched lips, when the explosion of a shell sent over deadly gas, getting four of our men. We got down in a valley for awhile during a machine gun barrage and then up again, firing away at the enemy as fast as our automatics could work....

So many of our men were getting wounded and as the litter-bearer was killed while going out under fire for wounded, my sergeant sent me with another man to replace him. It was a dangerous situation going over rounds of Hell, as we had to go up and get them under machine gun and rifle fire....We began picking up the wounded as fast as they came and bandaging those in need of first aid. It was a heartrending sight that weakened the strongest, for everywhere were wounded and lifeless forms—some all torn to pieces, their limbs and heads entirely severed from their bodies! I remember making a trip about a mile under heavy gun fire to get a wounded stretcher-bearer whose partner had been killed. He was a game little Yank, yet a pitiful sight, with his side all ripped open by shrapnel. As I laid him gently on the stretcher, I still remember his last uttered words, "Oh God, if I could only live to die at home!"

Source: Mathew Chopin, *Through the Valley of Death*, 1919 From www.geocities.com/louisiana_doughboy/index.htm and cited in P. Scott Corbett and Ronald C. Naugle, Life, Liberty, and the Pursuit of Happiness: Documents in American History, Volume II, 1861 to Present (Boston: McGraw Hill, 2004), pp. 109–109.

Thinking Critically

1. **Analysis**
   What impression of the fighting do you get from Chopin's description?

2. **Historical Interpretation**
   What light does Chopin's account shed on the impact of new military technology on the fighting during World War I?

someone, and for a generation, young women outnumbered young men by significant numbers. Ships were sunk, villages and towns destroyed, national economies wrecked. While some including Wilson wanted to use the end of the war to secure "a just and lasting peace," others wanted vengeance, and still others wanted to forget all about war and simply have a good time in a life that they knew could be cut all too short. Amid all these conflicting political and emotional cross-currents, leaders of the victorious nations met in Paris at the beginning of 1919 to write a peace treaty.

Woodrow Wilson, who had broken precedent early in his term by speaking directly to Congress, broke precedent again when the war ended. He sailed for Paris to personally lead the American delegation at the Paris peace talks. No American president had ever left the United States while in office, and some even wondered whether it was constitutional to do so. Wilson waived the concerns aside. Modern communications would allow him to remain in close touch with Washington while he was across the Atlantic. The British, French, and Italian Prime Ministers were all going to be present, and Wilson had no intention of handing the American role off to anyone else.

When the president and Mrs. Wilson arrived in Brest, France, on December 13, 1918, they were greeted as heroes, and they continued to be honored as they toured France, Britain, and Italy. A banner on the Champs-Élysées in Paris announced, "Honor to Wilson the Just," and an American newspaper reporter wrote, "No one ever had such cheers." It must have been a satisfying moment for the war-weary president. For Wilson, one ominous cloud over the negotiations

The peace talks at Versailles brought together a wide range of world leaders but were dominated by the leaders of Great Britain, France, and the United States.

was the fact that Republicans had made substantial gains in the congressional elections of November 1918 in spite of his impassioned appeal to the voters to keep the Democrats in charge while he negotiated a treaty. Then, while he was in France in January 1919, Wilson received a telegram that his arch-rival Theodore Roosevelt had died. A reporter said he thought he saw a look of pity and then a smile of triumph on the president's face, though Wilson was far too diplomatic to say anything.

When the Paris peace talks convened at the old royal palace of Versailles, Wilson thought he was in a very strong bargaining position given the role of U.S. resources and troops in bringing the war to a successful conclusion for the allies. His counterparts thought differently. Georges Clémenceau, the tough 77-year-old French premier, wanted vengeance for France's terrible losses, and British Prime Minister David Lloyd George, though more moderate than Clemenceau, harbored nothing like Wilson's generous spirit. France and Britain had lost 10 to 20 times as many soldiers as the United States, most of the battles had been fought in France, and neither leader nor their followers were in any mood to be generous. The losers—Germany, Austria, and the Ottoman Empire—were excluded from the conference. The new communist government of Russia, which had signed its own separate treaty with Germany in early 1918, was also excluded from the peace conference, and Wilson sent troops to try and support the overthrow of the communist government, which would lead to long-term tension between Russia and the United States.

Since 1916, Wilson had been telling his fellow Americans what he wanted from a peace conference. He insisted the traditional U.S. isolationism could not continue and the nation must be willing to "become a partner in any feasible association of nations to maintain the peace." In October, just before the presidential election, he told an audience in Omaha, Nebraska, "we are part of the world." And in January 1917, he told the Senate that the United States wanted "peace without victory." His goal was to avoid future wars based on the "covenant" of a new international organization that would ensure that "no such catastrophe shall ever overwhelm us again."

Fourteen Points

The proposed points outlining peace offered by President Woodrow Wilson in 1918 after World War I; the treaty agreed to at the Versailles peace conference did not, however, include all 14.

In January 1918, as the United States went to war, Wilson outlined what came to be known as his **Fourteen Points**. The president said that America insisted on "open covenants of peace, openly arrived at." The commitment to openness was a mix of Wilsonian idealism and a reaction to the release by the new Russian leader, V. I. Lenin, of secret agreements that had been negotiated by the czarist government, Britain, and France. Although he did not use the word "self-determination," Wilson condemned old-style European imperialism and, indeed, any wars fought for territory. He insisted that the many diverse nationalities living within the Austria-Hungarian and Ottoman Turkish empires should have "an absolutely unmolested opportunity of autonomous development (see Map 20-4)." Most of all, he called for a "general association of nations" to preserve peace.

Wilson stayed at the peace conference for 6 months except for one 2-week return trip to the United States. He did not have as much success as he expected. He was not well-staffed. He found himself in painful meetings with the three European premiers who had different goals from his and who, especially Clemenceau, obviously did not respect him.

The treaty that emerged from the peace conference was, perhaps inevitably, a disappointment to everyone. Wilson got his League of Nations, which would include not just the allies—as Clemenceau initially wanted—but would be open to every nation of the world. The league's covenant included Article X in which member nations agreed to "respect and preserve as against external aggression the political integrity and existing political independence of all Members of the League." However, though the League now existed, Wilson had also paid a high price to get it.

Clemenceau compromised on his initial goal of dividing Germany into several smaller nation-states, but he won on achieving strict limits to German military power, temporary occupation of the Rhineland, and a "war guilt" clause, which meant that Germany should pay most of the war's cost. Most of the world's non-European

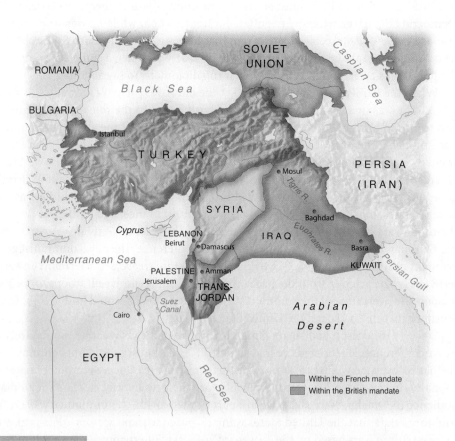

MAP 20-4 A Changing Middle East. While the major impact of the Treaty of Versailles was within Europe, the peace conference also created several new Middle Eastern nations, including Syria, Iraq, and Trans-Jordan—later Jordan and Israel—out of the former Ottoman Empire.

peoples were bitterly disappointed with the treaty. Middle Eastern and African colonies that had belonged to the defeated Central Powers expected to be granted their independence by the peace conference. Instead, they became "mandates" assigned to various victorious powers that were supposed to grant them independence at some unspecified future date. Japan, which had played only a modest role in the war, won the right to continue its control over Shandong province in China, leading a young Mao Zedong to call the treaty "really shameless." In addition, protests erupted in India, Egypt, Korea, and China over other provisions in the treaty.

African-American leaders also protested the failure of the Treaty of Versailles to respect the right of citizens of former German colonies in Africa or mention racial discrimination in the final treaty. W.E.B. Du Bois tried to organize a Pan-African conference in Paris to protest the treaty's failings, but the British government would not give passports to Africans from British colonies who wanted to attend, and the U.S. State Department refused permission to American delegates, including Madame C. J. Walker, the first African-American woman millionaire, and journalists Ida Wells-Barnett and William Monroe Trotter. Du Bois made it to the meeting only by signing up as a cook on a freighter bound for France.

During the peace negotiations, several new nations were created within Europe—Poland, Yugoslavia, Romania, and Czechoslovakia—that were supposed to recognize the hopes for independence by ethnic groups who had been dominated by the old tottering Austria-Hungary and Ottoman empires, but the mapping of those boundaries set off its own ethnic tensions, especially for people who suddenly became an ethnic minority in a new country (see Map 20-5).

Wilson convinced himself that he had gotten as good a treaty as he could—which was perhaps true given the other actors at the peace conference—and he invested his greatest hopes in the idea that the League of Nations could resolve any remaining issues. He signed the treaty at Versailles in June 1919 and sailed for home. On July 10, Wilson personally spoke to the U.S. Senate, asking them to ratify the treaty. He reminded his audience of the nation's high ideals in going to war and the fact that "in the settlements of the peace we have sought no special reparation for ourselves." The key to the whole treaty and, indeed, to future peace, Wilson continued, was that the League of Nations was "the only hope of mankind." So he begged the Senate to ratify the treaty immediately without any amendments, asking, "Shall we or any other free peoples hesitate to accept this great duty? Dare we reject it and break the heart of the world?" The Senate, which had final authority to approve any treaty, would take 8 months to give Wilson his answer.

Wilson was greeted as a hero when he arrived home in the United States, and public opinion seemed to be on his side, but there were problems lurking for the Versailles Treaty. The battle over the treaty has often been portrayed, as it was by Wilson, as one between his internationalism and an older isolationist view of America; however, the issues were more complex. Wilson had made the treaty needlessly partisan by campaigning vigorously, but unsuccessfully, for a Democratic victory in the 1918 elections and then failing to take any Republican leaders with him to Paris. He had also lost many of his strongest supporters who were disillusioned by the attack on civil liberties that he had allowed during the war and the compromises he had made at Paris. Some senators such as California's Hiram Johnson and Idaho's William Borah opposed any binding promise to intervene in other nation's affairs. Borah said that he wanted "not isolation but freedom to do as our own people think wise and just."

The greatest threat to the treaty came from Massachusetts Republican Senator Henry Cabot Lodge, chair of the Senate Foreign Relations Committee, who hated the treaty and hated Wilson even more. Lodge objected to the treaty for many reasons. He feared the treaty, he said, because it gave an international organization "the power to send American soldiers and sailors everywhere"—a power, Lodge insisted, "which ought never to be taken from the American people or impaired in the slightest degree." Some thought Lodge was less concerned about the league than about the insult to

20.1

20.2

20.3

20.4

**Changes in European
boundaries after World War I**

▨ Areas lost by Russian Empire

▨ Areas lost by Austro-Hungarian Empire

▨ Areas lost by German Empire

▨ Areas lost by Bulgaria

Names of the newly independent nations created
at the Versailles Conference of 1919 are in bold

MAP 20-5 Europe in 1919. The Treaty of Versailles created a number of new nations in eastern Europe out
of what had once been the Austria-Hungary and Ottoman empires as well as new nations in the Middle East.

people like himself who had been excluded from the treaty-making process and his
personal animosity to the president. Nevertheless, Lodge insisted that the issues were
beyond party, that the United States "is the world's best hope but if you fetter her in
the interests and quarrels of other nations, if you tangle her in the intrigues of Europe,
you will destroy her power for good and endanger her very existence."

As he had done at Princeton and in New Jersey state politics when he faced opposition, Wilson appealed over the heads of his immediate opponents to a wider audience, in this case, the whole nation. In the fall of 1919, Wilson began a 10,000-mile tour of the country, giving 40 speeches in 21 days to enthusiastic audiences, asking them to tell their senators to support the treaty. The public response was gratifying but did not move votes in the Senate. The trip also broke the president's already fragile health. On September 25 at Pueblo, Colorado, after a speech in which he said that with the treaty he had negotiated, "international law is revolutionized by putting morals into it," and promising that his beloved league would "lead us, and through us the world, out into pastures of quietness and peace such as the world never dreamed of before," he collapsed and admitted that he could not go on. After he returned to the White House, Wilson suffered a life-threatening infection and a massive stroke that left him partially paralyzed. The medical conditions may also have clouded his judgment and made him more stubborn.

The Senate Foreign Relations Committee recommended approval of the treaty but with 14 reservations, including one insisting that the U.S. military could not be sent to defend Article X without specific congressional approval. Wilson adamantly refused to consider the reservations. In a final vote on November 18 and 19, 1919, the Senate first came to a tie vote for the treaty with reservations—far short of the two-thirds majority needed to approve a treaty. Then on a second vote in which they considered the treaty without reservations, the Senate defeated the entire treaty by a vote of 55 to 39. The League of Nations would be launched in Geneva, Switzerland, but without the participation of the United States. Wilson's grand vision for a world at peace with the United States as a leader was dead. Many argued that the president's refusal to compromise had been among the forces that killed it. Colonel House, who had once been Wilson's closest confidant, wrote that he had once thought that Senator Lodge was the worst enemy of the treaty, but before the debates and votes were over, he had decided that the worst enemy had actually been Wilson himself.

With the end of World War I, Europe had a dramatically different map and the United States had a dramatically different political situation. People who had fervently gone to war in 1917 were tired and cynical by 1919. The cost of the war in lives, money, and liberties led many to question the governmental and business leaders who had been most enthusiastic about it. By 1920, many in the nation were ready to forget high-sounding idealism, progressive or otherwise. It was, perhaps, time for more joy or, at least, the election of a more genial and less idealistic president.

20.4 **Quick Review** How did U.S. participation in World War I shape Wilson's presidency?

CONCLUSION

During the Progressive Era, the United States began to look outward more than in the past and to extend its power and influence further across the globe. The three American leaders known as the "progressive presidents"—Theodore Roosevelt, Taft, and Wilson—all spent much of their administrations dealing with foreign policy. In what some have called "the age of U.S. imperialism," the United States took control of vast new territories, including Hawaii, a number of Pacific islands, the Canal Zone in Panama, as well as Cuba, Puerto Rico, and the Philippine Islands. Alaska, which had previously been purchased from Russia now became an official U.S. territory, Hawaii was annexed after an American-led revolt on the island, and the Canal Zone was acquired by treaty after complex negotiations with Panama and Colombia. Most of the other territories came under U.S. control as a result of the 1898 War with Spain. While Cuba and the Philippine Islands eventually attained independence, U.S. influence continued there for a long time.

The increased involvement of the United States in international affairs in the late 1800s and early 1900s, and its expanded territorial reach, made the United States a major world power. Consequently, diplomatic tensions began to mount, especially between the United States and Latin America, where construction of the American-controlled Panama Canal and military interventions in Mexico, Nicaragua, the Dominican Republic, and Haiti created resentment. Although the United States had successfully brokered a peace agreement between Russia and Japan in 1905, further U.S. involvement in Asia coupled with anti-Asian legislation in California, embittered the Japanese. Many within the United States also opposed American involvement in the affairs of the rest of the world, especially after the 1898 War with Spain and the continued U.S. occupation of the Philippine Islands.

After the assassination of Archduke Franz Ferdinand in 1914, the Central Powers (Germany, Austria-Hungary, and the Ottoman Empire) went to war against the Allies (Russia, France, and Great Britain). Americans were divided about the conflict and looked to President Wilson to maintain U.S. neutrality. However, for some Americans, feelings changed when German U-boats sank three U.S. merchant ships and a British ocean liner, which killed 127 American citizens. The publication of a secret German cable to Mexico—known as the Zimmermann telegram—in which Germany promised the return of Texas to Mexico if Mexico would attack the United States, turned more of American public opinion against Germany. In 1917, when Germany expanded its submarine attacks, the United States entered the war.

Support for U.S. involvement in the war was not universal, and a large and vocal peace movement emerged. But the Wilson administration pressed for a series of laws to silence dissent. In particular, the Sedition Act and the Espionage Act gave the government unprecedented power to restrict free speech. The Supreme Court upheld these laws, and many antiwar protesters were prosecuted and jailed.

By 1918, the Allies, with support from American troops, had defeated the Central Powers and an armistice was signed. At the Paris peace talks, President Wilson hoped to secure a lasting peace and favored treaty provisions that called for a League of Nations. Republican opposition to the league blocked U.S. adoption of the treaty, and the League of Nations was launched without American involvement.

| CHAPTER REVIEW | How was U.S. foreign policy between 1898 and 1918 different from that of the pre–Civil War period? |

Chapter 20 Chapter Review

CONTINUING EXPANSION

20.1 Explain continued U.S. expansion, particularly U.S. acquisition of what would much later be the 49th and 50th states.

Review Questions

1. **Cause and Effect**
   How did Alfred Thayer Mahan's *The Influence of Sea Power Upon History* shape American foreign policy in the late 1800s and early 1900s?

2. **Contextualization**
   Why did Hawaii become a major focus of American activity in the Pacific in the 1800s?

THE SPLENDID LITTLE WAR…WITH SPAIN—CUBA, PUERTO RICO, AND THE PHILIPPINES, 1898

20.2 Analyze the causes and consequences of the U.S. War with Spain in 1898.

Review Questions

3. **Historical Interpretation**
   What role did economic considerations play in propelling America into war with Spain in 1898?

4. **Cause and Effect**
   How did the U.S. War with Spain and the fighting in the Philippines that followed help spark anti-imperialist sentiment in the United States?

5. **Constructing an Argument**
   Defend or refute the following statement. "The United States went to war with Spain to seize control of parts of the Spanish Empire, not to defend the rights of the Cuban people."

FOREIGN POLICY, FOREIGN ADVENTURES, 1900–1914

20.3 Explain developments in U.S. policy in Panama, Asia, and Mexico between the War with Spain and World War I.

Review Questions

6. **Historical Interpretation**
   What does the Roosevelt Corollary tell us about the way American policy makers viewed Latin America during the early 1900s?

7. **Cause and Effect**
   How did American actions in the early 1900s contribute to long-term tensions between Japan and the United States?

8. **Comparison**
   Compare and contrast Wilson's foreign policy in Asia with his actions in Mexico and Latin America. How would you explain the differences you note?

THE UNITED STATES AND THE GREAT WAR

20.4 Analyze the causes and consequences of U.S. involvement in World War I.

Review Questions

9. **Historical Interpretation**
   What factors contributed to the outbreak of World War I in 1914?

10. **Contextualization**
    Why did Wilson find it so difficult to maintain American neutrality?

11. **Comparison**
    What connections can you make between efforts to suppress dissent during World War I and earlier periods in American history when limits were placed on individual liberties?

21 A Unique, Prosperous, and Discontented Time

1919–1929

CHAPTER OBJECTIVE

Demonstrate an understanding of the unique aspects of a decade in U.S. history that lasted from 1919 to 1929.

LEARNING OBJECTIVES

THE PRELUDE—THE RED SUMMER OF 1919

21.1 Explain how events at the end of World War I shaped the decade that followed.

THE 1920s—THE EXUBERANCE OF PROSPERITY

21.2 Analyze how Prohibition and other developments of the 1920s reshaped American culture.

THE 1920s—THE CONFLICTS ABOUT AMERICAN IDEALS

21.3 Explain the elements of discrimination, hardship, and fundamentalism that also shaped American life in the 1920s.

HARDING, COOLIDGE, AND HOOVER—NATIONAL POLITICS AND POLICIES IN THE 1920s

21.4 Analyze the political and policy developments of the decade.

The 1920s was known as the Jazz Age not only because of its most popular music but also because jazz music provided the background to an era in which many Americans wanted to forget the past and have fun dancing, drinking, and riding in increasingly popular automobiles.

Almost as soon as the era ended, journalists and historians began talking about the "Jazz Age" or simply, "the 1920s," as a way to describe a distinct era in American history. The 11 years that was framed by the end of World War I in November 1918 and the stock market crash of October 1929 was unique in many ways. As troops returned to the Unites States from their service in Europe during World War I and as national leaders debated the Treaty of Versailles at the start of this era, many Americans wanted to forget about the rest of the world and its troubles. They expected the resulting peace to usher in a time of pleasure and plenty.

For many white middle-class Americans, the twenties were, indeed, a time of great prosperity and a time to enjoy the freedom of the Jazz Age. However for others, including many white farmers in the Midwest and South, southern black sharecroppers, and American Indians living on isolated reservations, the twenties were not prosperous at all. For many recent immigrants and for residents of small towns and rural areas the 1920s were a decade when they felt especially marginalized; when it was clear that sophisticated urban dwellers looked down on them and their cultural and religious values and their resentment took many forms. Understanding the differing experiences of those who lived through this decade is the focus of this chapter.

THE PRELUDE—THE RED SUMMER OF 1919

21.1 Explain how events at the end of World War I shaped the decade that followed.

When the guns of World War I fell silent on November 11, 1918, the world celebrated. While the United States had been spared much of the war's cost, many Americans were not sure what to make of the postwar world. Some Americans had talked of socialism, even communism, since the strikes of the 1870s, but most did not follow their lead. As a result of World War I, communists had seized control of Russia. Some Americans celebrated the new Russian government, but many more feared it and wondered whether there might be links between America's homegrown radicals and Russia. For African-Americans who had fought in the war, had risked their lives for democracy, and had seen different cultures, the idea of returning to a United States with rigid segregation generated new tensions and determination. Other African-Americans had moved North to take war-time jobs, and they had no intention of returning to the segregated South. To the surprise of some, within months of the armistice, the country quickly became a very tense place.

With the coming of peace, American workers wanted a part of the new postwar prosperity and tried to gain back the money they had lost from stagnant wages in an era of wartime inflation. In January 1919, 35,000 shipyard workers went on strike in Seattle, Washington, and a month later, 60,000 workers in other industries joined them. The week-long Seattle General Strike, when virtually no one in the city went to work, stands as the largest citywide strike in U.S. history, and it frightened many.

The Seattle strike was the largest but hardly the only strike in 1919. Textile workers in Lawrence, Massachusetts, the scene of the 1912 Bread and Roses strike (see Chapter 18), engaged in a short and successful strike to demand a 48-hour work week in January 1919. In September, the police force of Boston, Massachusetts, who had not received a raise since 1913, went on strike. Without a police force in Boston, mobs looted stores and bars, the police commissioner created a temporary voluntary force, and Massachusetts Governor Calvin Coolidge gained national fame when he fired all of the striking police officers, saying, "There is no right to strike against the public safety by anybody, anywhere, any time."

While people debated the right of public employees to strike, steel workers went out on strike in September 1919 after the chairman of U.S. Steel, Judge Elbert Gary, refused to meet with union representatives. A month later, coal miners walked off the job, just as the nation's demand for coal for winter heat was beginning.

Strikes were not the only signs of political chaos in 1919. In April, bombs arrived in the mail of Postmaster General Albert Burleson, Attorney General A. Mitchell Palmer, several members of the U.S. Senate, Seattle's antistrike Mayor Hanson, and federal immigration authorities and judges. Not one of them was injured, but no one ever discovered who sent the bombs. On May Day, an international Socialist holiday in honor of the Haymarket events (see Chapter 18), riots erupted in several cities, including Cleveland, Ohio, where one socialist was killed and 40 injured in a parade. A few days later, a protester in Washington, DC, was shot and killed when he refused to stand for the national anthem. The crowd applauded. The American Legion, a new organization of returning soldiers, promised to uphold Americanism and attack radicals. In Centralia, Washington, an IWW group killed four parading Legion members, and the Legion lynched an IWW organizer.

At the same time, the worldwide influenza pandemic that began in 1918 came to the United States. During 1919, half a million Americans died of the flu, many more than had died in the war. The influenza did not discriminate between young and old or rich and poor. Although its source was microbes, not radicals, the influenza epidemic contributed to the sense that something was terribly wrong in the postwar world.

Significant Dates

1919	Palmer raids and Red Summer Major strikes in many industries Chicago race riot
1920	Eighteenth Amendment creating Prohibition takes effect.
	Nineteenth Amendment giving women the right to vote takes effect
	Congress again defeats Treaty of Versailles
	Charles Ponzi's scheme collapses
	Warren Harding elected U.S. President
	First radio broadcast as Station KDKA reports election returns
1921	Margaret Sanger founds American Birth Control League
	Washington Conference agrees to limit growth of world's navies
1923	Warren Harding dies Calvin Coolidge becomes president
1924	Calvin Coolidge defeats John W. Davis for president
1925	*The Great Gatsby* published Scopes trial in Dayton, Tennessee
1927	Babe Ruth hits 60 home runs Sacco and Vanzetti executed Kellogg-Briand Pact outlawing war negotiated
1928	Herbert Hoover defeats Al Smith for president
	Mickey Mouse born

The influenza epidemic of 1918 killed far more Americans than World War I—more than 500,000. Police and public officials, like these members of the St. Louis Red Cross Motor Corps, wore masks to protect themselves. Images such as this one, like the disease, helped spread fear around the country.

Palmer Raids

A series of raids by U.S. government agents in 1919 and 1920 to find, arrest, and sometimes deport people considered to be dangerous radicals.

For many Americans, the chaos of 1919 proved that there was a link between U.S. labor unions, socialists, and the Bolshevik communist regime in Russia. Communism seemed to be spreading with a revolt in Hungary and uprisings in the old capitals of Vienna and Berlin. Maybe, some said, it was coming to the United States. Seattle Mayor Ole Hanson toured the country proclaiming that he had put down a Bolshevik uprising in his city. The *Los Angeles Times* told people that they needed to wake up to the Bolshevik menace, while former president William Howard Taft said that the Bolsheviks were "crusaders, pushing their propaganda in every country, seeking to rouse the lawless, the discontented, the poor, the lazy, and the shiftless to a millennium of plunder and class hatred." The Senate ordered an investigation of Russian Bolshevik influence in the United States. Attorney General Palmer presented what he said was evidence of communist influence in the country. Palmer's proof was a witness who had heard one striker say, "The IWW was not as bad as it was supposed to be." It was hardly overwhelming proof of an international conspiracy. Inflation and stagnant wages seemed to have more to do with the strikes and protests than international intrigue.

Nevertheless, people were frightened and the federal government responded. The Wilson administration not only asked Congress to extend the war-time Lever Fuel Act that had prohibited the obstruction of coal distribution during the war but also asked for a peace-time sedition law to continue some of the wartime restrictions on civil liberties. Using the Lever Act, Attorney General Palmer persuaded a federal judge to issue an injunction against the coal strike. Palmer also ordered an all-out effort to find dangerous radicals and appointed a young Justice Department staffer, J. Edgar Hoover, later the first director of the Federal Bureau of Investigation, to lead it. By the end of November, the so-called "**Palmer Raids**" had led to many arrests, and 249 of those arrested who had not been born in the United States were ordered deported, among them, the well-known radical Emma Goldman, who told federal authorities:

> Ever since I have been in this country—and I have lived here practically all my life—it has been dinned into my ears that under the institutions of this alleged Democracy one is entitled to think and feel as he pleases. What becomes of this sacred guarantee of freedom of thought and conscience when persons are being persecuted and driven out for the very motives and purposes for which the pioneers who built up this country laid down their lives?

Goldman and the other deportees, along with an impressive number of guards, left New York on the liner *Buford*, bound for exile in Russia. At the same time, Congress expelled its one Socialist member, the strongly anticommunist representative Victor Berger from Milwaukee, who had opposed the war and remarked that all the American people had gotten out of it was flu and inflation. Milwaukee was not represented in Congress until 1921. The November arrests and deportations were not the end of the hysteria. On January 2 and 3, 1920, Justice Department agents led by J. Edgar Hoover arrested 5,000, perhaps even 10,000, suspected radicals in 33 cities. This second round of Palmer Raids destroyed the tiny U.S. Communist Party and caught many others. The size and scope of the raids and the lack of evidence of a widespread conspiracy undercut public support for Palmer. By the spring of 1920, more Americans were starting to question the raids. Maybe there were not as many Bolsheviks in the country as Palmer thought.

Fears about communists and labor unions were not the only concerns to rock the country in 1919. The city of Chicago had been on edge for weeks in the hot summer of 1919. While nearly 5,000 public employees—from garbage collectors and street sweepers to city hall clerks—were on strike, someone put up signs in Chicago's black community that said, "We will get you July 4." Somehow, the fear of communists and the fear of expanded rights for African-Americans merged as it often did. Black residents, fearing an assault, armed themselves. Then on July 27, a black boy swimming in Lake Michigan drifted across the line that supposedly separated the races on Chicago's lakefront beaches. A white mob beat the boy to death while a policeman ignored them. Blacks attacked the policeman and the white mob.

In the days that followed, armed whites attacked Chicago's black community, and blacks fought back. An injured black military veteran confronted a white crowd yelling, "This is a fine reception to give a man just home from the war." The crowd beat him to death. When a group of whites drove a truck armed with a machine gun into a black neighborhood, blacks killed them. When the riot ended 5 days later, 23 blacks and 15 whites had been killed and over 500 people had been injured. Unlike previous race riots in other cities, which had been almost exclusively white attacks on blacks, the black community in Chicago had fought back. The black-owned *Chicago Defender* noted that "the youngest generation of black men are not content to move along the line of least resistance as did their sires."

While the Chicago race riot was by far the worst, it was not the only one that summer. In Charleston, South Carolina, a brawl between white sailors and local blacks left two blacks dead and several white sailors injured. In Longview, Texas, a white mob beat up a black school teacher for distributing the *Chicago Defender*. As in Chicago, blacks retaliated. After the *Washington Post* published a series of stories about black crime, especially rape, a riot between white soldiers and black residents left six dead and hundreds injured.

Thirty-six blacks were lynched in 1917. In 1919, 76 lynchings were recorded, including some of veterans recently home from World War I. In one Mississippi lynching, the Jackson newspapers announced plans in advance. In September, in Omaha, Nebraska, a mob attacked the jail where a black prisoner was being held, beat up the mayor who tried to stop them, and then lynched the prisoner, William Brown. Only U.S. Army troops under General Leonard Wood brought order to Omaha. As the African-American writer James Weldon Johnson looked at the racial violence and the fear of communists that were roiling the country, often being mixed, he called the season the "Red Summer" of 1919. That Red Summer was a strange and violent start to a decade of prosperity and discontent that followed.

21.1 **Quick Review** To what extent did America's growing involvement in the world contribute to domestic events in 1919?

THE 1920s—THE EXUBERANCE OF PROSPERITY

21.2 Analyze how Prohibition and other developments of the 1920s reshaped American culture.

On May 11, 1921, when Prohibition had been in effect for a little over a year, the *New York Times* reported that an attractive 24 year-old legal stenographer from West 156th Street in Manhattan, Claire Fiance, had been arrested when a detective stopped her to ask about a suspicious looking package she was carrying and, "with a bright smile and a shake of her bobbed hair," Fiance replied that she was carrying a bottle of whiskey (a violation of the law that prohibited the transportation of alcohol). Fiance's arrest, and those of many more women like her, was a symbol of two of the most important shifts in American law and culture that took place in the 1920s—shifts in many American's attitudes toward the consumption of alcohol and toward the appropriate role of women in American society.

During the course of the 1920 presidential campaign, the Republican nominee Warren G. Harding coined a new word that described the nation's mood. He said, "America's present need is not heroics but healing; not nostrums but normalcy."

21.1

21.2

21.3

21.4

Harding's normalcy
A word coined by Warren G. Harding while he was the 1920 Republican presidential candidate to convey what he thought the country wanted—a new kind of "normal" free from war, international entanglements, and reform efforts.

Harding's normalcy was less a return to some previously "normal" era than a plea to give the reforming spirit of the previous decades a rest. People were as tired of Roosevelt-era reforms as they were of Wilson's internationalism. Many wanted to enjoy themselves, take part in the growing national prosperity, and keep the reformers and the government out of their lives. There was nothing very normal about the era—especially in terms of a national law that banned alcohol, or in terms of the changing roles of women or the new technologies that changed the culture—but it seemed to summarize what many Americans wanted for themselves and their country.

Prohibition—The Campaign for Moral Conformity

Just at the time when many sought "normalcy," the greatest reform experiment in the nation's history—the prohibition of alcohol—took effect. Even though prohibition seemed like a reform more typical of the Progressive Era, the way prohibition was implemented was typical of the 1920s. Indeed, prohibition—and resistance to it—defined the 1920s for many.

Americans had long been fond of alcohol. But some Americans had also long worried about the nation's drinking habits. In the 1830s, the army ended the traditional whiskey ration for the troops. By the 1850s, school children learned to read from *McGuffey's Readers* that included stories about the "scene of desolation" that liquor created. Some religious groups concluded that drinking and Protestant Christianity were incompatible. The Women's Christian Temperance Union (WCTU) became the primary voice of temperance reform in Protestant America in the 1880s (see Chapter 19).

While the WCTU sought to persuade people to give up drink, a new organization, the Anti-Saloon League, sought to banish alcohol by law in the 1910s. The male-dominated league had a solid financial base, greatly helped by John D. Rockefeller, and relied on professional experts to organize campaigns, lobby legislators, and attack opponents. In political campaigns, the Anti-Saloon League supported "dry" (supporting prohibition) candidates of any party and attacked any politician it considered either "wet" (opposing prohibition) or insufficiently dry. As elected officials saw colleagues elected or defeated because of the league's political acumen, they started to support prohibition whatever their personal feelings or drinking habits.

The campaign to prohibit alcohol can be understood as no small part of a larger effort by native-born white Protestants, especially those living on farms and small towns, to retake control of a national culture that they saw increasingly under the sway of recent immigrants. As native-born Protestant America became more and more hostile to drink, many immigrants did not appreciate the campaign for moral conformity that they saw in the prohibition movement.

The Protestant evangelist, Charles Stelzle, though a prohibition leader, was more understanding of the role of the neighborhood saloon than many of his compatriots. While many prohibitionists described saloons as dens of iniquity, Stelzle remembered growing up on New York's Lower East Side where "the working men…held their christening parties, their weddings, their dances, their rehearsals for their singing societies, and all other social functions" in the neighborhood tavern. Saloons were often where ethnic groups could maintain language and tradition. In the evening, Germans could have their beer, Italians their wine, and Irish their whiskey, while enjoying the company of others like themselves. For people who gathered over a drink, prohibition was an attack on the freedom and acceptance they had come to America to find.

Anti-Saloon League leader, William Anderson, condemned immigrant resistance to prohibition. The Board of Temperance, Prohibition, and Public Morals of the Methodist Church said, "If it is true that foreign-born laborers are rebellious against the country because of Prohibition, it may be said that the country is not being run for their benefit. If they do not like the way things are being done let them go back to Europe." As a result of statements like that, many recent immigrants experienced prohibition as an attack on their cultures and some of prohibition's strongest advocates did little to discourage such an assumption.

With the coming of World War I, the Anti-Saloon League had made support for prohibition a test of patriotism. The league had successfully inserted a clause into the Lever Food and Fuel Control Act banning the use of grain for hard liquor, while giving the president authority to regulate wine and beer production. Wilson was no fan of prohibition, but it was hard for him to reject a call for national sacrifice in support of the war. In December 1917, Congress—with intensive lobbying by the Anti-Saloon League—passed the Eighteenth Amendment to the U.S. Constitution prohibiting the manufacture, transport, and sale of liquor. The league worked quickly to ensure that the required three-quarters of the state legislatures acted and, in January 1919, Nebraska became the 36 state to ratify, putting the amendment over the line. In October 1919, Congress passed the Volstead Act, sponsored by Minnesota Representative Andrew J. Volstead, banning not only hard liquor (which many even among the amendment's supporters thought was its purpose) but also wine and beer—anything with more than ½ of 1 percent alcohol. Violating the law carried as much as a $1,000 fine. The U.S. Treasury was given authority for enforcement. Like the Eighteenth Amendment, the Volstead Act did not ban the possession of alcohol, only its manufacture, transportation, and sale—a loophole that made enforcement extremely difficult. The act also allowed doctors to prescribe whiskey for medical needs and drugstores to dispense it, and it allowed sacramental wine for religious purposes and industrial use of alcohol— all loopholes that would be exploited in the 1920s.

When Prohibition took effect on January 16, 1920, Americans observed the day in widely different ways. Liquor stores sold out. People who could afford to do so filled their basements with bottles (since possession remained legal), and that night, saloons, hotels, and private clubs gave one last grand party. Assistant Secretary of the Navy Franklin D. Roosevelt drank champagne with former Harvard classmates at the Metropolitan Club in Washington.

Other Americans held very different celebrations. The best known evangelist of the day, Billy Sunday, told worshipers in Norfolk, Virginia, "The reign of tears is over.... The slums will soon be only a memory. We will turn our prisons into factories and our jails into storehouses and corncribs. Men will walk upright now, women will smile, and children will laugh. Hell will be forever for rent." In fact, Prohibition unleashed a crime wave not only because illegal liquor produced great profits, emboldening criminals to new levels of creativity and violence, but also because so many average Americans were willing to disobey the law.

A Scandalous Age—Bootleg, Ponzi, and Teapot Dome

As Prohibition began in 1920, a Chicago gangster known as "Big Jim" Colosimo owned saloons and brothels across the city. Colosimo's nephew and business manager, Johnny Torrio, had moved from Brooklyn to Chicago to work for him in 1909, and both men had become millionaires. Prohibition meant they had to change some of their ways, but they certainly planned to continue, expecting increased profits. One day, Torrio asked Colosimo to meet a load of whiskey that Torrio was having delivered to one of their cafés. Colosimo showed up on schedule and, as he walked through the dining room, someone emerged

With the coming of Prohibition, federal agents and local police regularly raided establishments that served alcohol and poured it into sewers. In spite of many such raids, alcohol consumption was hardly slowed by the Eighteenth Amendment or the Volstead Act as illegal production and sales filled the gap.

from the cloakroom and shot him. Colosimo died instantly. While no evidence was ever found that Torrio or his new bodyguard from Brooklyn, Al Capone, was involved in the murder, Torrio—aided by Capone—quickly took control of the liquor business in Chicago. The Colosimo murder was only the start of the violence to come with Prohibition—all across the country. Organized crime had existed long before Prohibition, but once Prohibition took effect, criminals from Los Angeles to Boston, in powerful gangs or as individual operators, took control of the now-illegal liquor business in their cities, expanding their operations and criminal networks beyond anything seen before, often violently.

The single most violent incident in Prohibition came near its end. By 1929, Capone had consolidated his control of illegal liquor in Chicago. He also controlled much of the police force, the elected political leadership, and the courts of Chicago and had his own squad of gunmen and rumrunners to bring illegal alcohol to the city, especially from Canada. When an upstart gangster known as "Bugs" Moran tried to take part of his business away, Capone hired professional killers. On February 14, 1929, five men, two dressed as police officers, arrived at Moran's headquarters. They lined up the seven men there against a wall, shot and killed them, and calmly drove off. That bloody St. Valentine's Day massacre provided a fitting capstone to a bloody decade wherein gangsters killed each other and innocent bystanders. Many other people were killed in drunken brawls in the illegal saloons, or speakeasies, that proliferated or by drinking improperly made bootleg liquor that poisoned them.

By 1929, after all the killing and dying, Americans were wondering whether Prohibition was such a good thing after all. Capone's influence with politicians and police made him safe from arrest in Chicago, but after 1929, the newly elected Herbert Hoover demanded that the U.S. Treasury Department do something to uphold the law, even in Chicago, and Capone was eventually arrested and imprisoned for income tax evasion in 1931. The liquor trade continued unabated.

While Prohibition-related crimes made the headlines in the 1920s, they were not the only criminal enterprise to flourish in a decade that many experienced as particularly lawless. In 1919, Charles Ponzi opened a new investment firm in Boston, announcing an extraordinarily high rate of return because of the skill he claimed in international trade. In fact, he simply paid old investors with money provided by new investors. Other than using the profits to live a very high life, Ponzi did not invest at all. The scheme made Ponzi rich and famous, but newspapers and bank investigators started asking questions and Ponzi's world collapsed in August 1920. He was arrested and eventually deported from the United States. Investors lost all their money. The Ponzi scheme was neither the first nor the last time that someone tried to get rich by catering to the greed of others, but it became the term used to describe that kind of fraud.

Perhaps the largest criminal enterprise of the 1920s was conducted within the federal government itself. In 1909, the government set aside three large oil reserves, two in California at Elk Hills and Buena Vista and one in Wyoming at Teapot Dome. They were managed by the Navy Department until the Harding administration came into office in 1921.

Harding, a most genial president, hated to say no to anyone, especially old friends whom he met for poker games and illegal drinking throughout his administration. When Harding's Secretary of the Interior Albert B. Fall asked to have the oil reserves transferred from the Navy Department to the Department of the Interior, Harding agreed. Fall's long-standing ties to the oil industry might have helped him manage the national assets.

In 1922, officials in the U.S. Navy were growing nervous about the growth of Japan's Navy and wanted some of the reserve oil pumped and transferred to Pearl Harbor. To meet the Navy's needs, Fall secretly leased the reserves to oil companies owned by his friends Harry F. Sinclair and Edward Doheny for very low rates. The two pumped oil from the reserves, paying a royalty, in oil, to the Navy. The Navy got the oil it needed in Hawaii. Sinclair and Doheny made a considerable profit. After a congressional investigation led by Montana Senators Burton K. Wheeler and Thomas Walsh began in 1924, it was discovered that Sinclair had made a gift of $260,000 to Fall while Doheny had lent the secretary $100,000 with no interest or deadline for payment. A great deal of additional money seems to have changed hands behind the scenes as Sinclair and Doheny not only stole from the government but from their own companies. Once Congress began to unearth the trail of oil and money, what became known as the **Teapot Dome** scandal kept spreading. Eventually, the U.S. Supreme Court declared both leases "illegal and fraudulent," Fall was found guilty of accepting a bribe and spent a year in prison, and the Harding administration was tagged as one of the most corrupt in history.

While the Teapot Dome scandal was the largest of the Harding scandals, there were plenty of others. Harding's appointee as head of the Veterans' Bureau, Charles R. Forbes, managed to lose some $200 million in 2 years, buying new goods at a high price from friends and selling goods on hand as cheap surplus. The arrangement made money for his friends but cost the government a fortune. Similar scandals involved the Alien Property Custodian office, which was supposed to manage German assets in the United States, and the Prohibition Enforcement Division of the Treasury Department which, it was said, would ignore violations as long as the right amount of money was left in a fishbowl in a New York City hotel room. With senior-level officials of the U.S. government behaving in such a manner, it was no surprise that regular citizens viewed obedience to the law as optional.

The Vote for Women

In August 1920, just months after the Prohibition amendment had been ratified, the U.S. Constitution was amended again to say "The right of citizens of the United States to vote shall not be denied or abridged by the United States or by any State on account of sex." The Nineteenth Amendment took effect in time for women in every part of the United States to vote in the presidential election of November 1920. Women's suffrage and the new roles for women that evolved in the 1920s helped shape that decade as much or more than Prohibition or any other development.

The women most associated with the two amendments—Susan B. Anthony and Elizabeth Cady Stanton, leaders in the long-lasting women's suffrage movement, and Frances Willard of the Women's Christian Temperance Union—all died before the campaigns they led achieved their goals. It was Carrie Chapman Catt's privilege to preside over the victory. Catt was an active member of both the Women's Christian Temperance Union and the National American Woman Suffrage Association. The organizations provided a network for her to meet other women, and those connections would determine the rest of her career. Catt served two terms as president of the NAWSA from 1900 to 1904 and again during the crucial years from 1915 to 1920.

As World War I began in Europe, Catt was active in the Women's Peace Party but left it after the United States entered the war. Other women such as Jane Addams and Jeanette Rankin, the first woman in Congress, continued to oppose the war when such views were seen as dangerously unpatriotic. Catt, in contrast, demanded a suffrage amendment as a "war measure." If the United States was going to fight for democracy, Catt argued, then expanding democracy in the United States to include women was essential. In 1919, the Northeastern Federation of Colored Women's Clubs extracted a promise from a sometimes reluctant Catt not to agree to any compromise language in the constitutional amendment that could leave enforcement to the states. They knew all too well what Southern state legislatures would do with the votes of African-American women. Sadly, after the war, Catt did all too little to support voting rights for African-American women, South or North.

In spite of differences about the war itself, women found ways to work together. Jeannette Rankin introduced the "Anthony Amendment," the woman's suffrage amendment, to the House of Representatives on January 10, 1918. The amendment passed

Teapot Dome
The name given to a major scandal of the Harding presidency in which U.S. Navy oil reserves, including those at Teapot Dome, Wyoming, were used to enrich the secretary of the interior and his friends.

THINKING HISTORICALLY

Understanding Different Perspectives on Women's Rights

Very soon after women gained the vote, Carrie Chapman Catt helped the National American Woman Suffrage Association turn itself into the League of Women Voters and served as its honorary president until her death in 1947. Some NAWSA veterans debated whether women should affiliate with the Democratic and Republican parties or remain independent. Different women followed different courses of action. The newly organized league—initially an all-white organization—committed itself to nonpartisan education and helping women join parties and vote wisely.

While the league encouraged women to engage in politics, other women who viewed the right to vote as merely a first step toward gaining other rights, pushed for a much more militant approach to women's rights. Alice Paul led the National Woman's Party that adopted a Declaration of Principles in 1923, which in part, insisted:

> In short—that woman shall no longer be in any form of subjection to man in law or in custom, but shall in every way be on an equal plane in rights, as she has always been and will continue to be in responsibilities and obligations.

In their quest for these rights, the Woman's Party began a long fight for an Equal Rights Amendment to the U.S. Constitution.

Other women took a very different view of the place of women in society. Opposition to women's suffrage did not disappear in 1920, and one antisuffrage group changed the name of its journal from *Protest* to *The Woman Patriot: Dedicated to the Defense of Womanhood, Motherhood, the Family and the State AGAINST Suffragism, Feminism and Socialism*. It was a long title but it spelled out their agenda as did a 1921 article in *The Woman Patriot* that said that they "fought the grant of the ballot because they foresaw that it was the logical boundary line between the old institution-of-marriage ideal of the Family as the unit of society and the Feminist revolt against nature." Battle lines of a contest that would continue for the next hundred years were being drawn.

African-American women had their own concerns. During the 1920s, rigid segregation made voting almost impossible for African-American women or men. They also faced other pressing issues as Charlotte Hawkins Brown (1883–1961) of the National Colored Woman's Club told a conference of mostly white women that was meeting in Memphis, Tennessee, in 1920:

> I came to Memphis crushed and humiliated....[O]n my way to this conference...I had a premonition of trouble [as she was in a sleeping car, but found] twelve young white men sitting around. A young man leaned forward and said, "We have wired ahead to have you taken off this train. Now, we give you your choice, to get off this car right away and go into the day coach, or be taken off."...The leader of the crowd said, "Let's march," and these young men got in front of us and two or three behind and we were ushered into the colored day coach....Friends, what do you say about the cold-heartedness that we have felt?...We have begun to feel that you are not, after all, interested in us...We feel that so far as lynching is concerned that, if the white woman would take hold of the situation that lynching would be stopped, mob violence stamped out and yet the guilty would have justice meted out by due course of law and would be punished accordingly....I want to say to you when you read in the paper where a colored man has insulted a white woman, just multiply that by one thousand and you have some idea of the number of colored women insulted by white men.

Source: Ellen Skinner, editor, *Women and the National Experience: Sources in Women's History* (Boston: Prentice Hall, 2011); Mari Jo Buhl, Teresa Murphy, Jane Gerhard, editor, *Women and the Making of America* (Upper Saddle River, NJ: Pearson/Prentice Hall, 2008).

Thinking Critically

1. **Cause and Effect**

   How did the passage of the Nineteenth Amendment change the place of women in American political life? What aspects of women's participation in politics were not changed by the amendment?

2. **Comparison**

   Compare and contrast the responses of to the passage of the Nineteenth Amendment included here. How would you explain the differences you note?

the House 274 to 136. The Senate moved more slowly, but under Catt's leadership, the NAWSA helped defeat four antisuffrage senators in November 1918, and the amendment was approved and sent on to the states in June 1919. A little more than a year later, the Tennessee legislature gave the amendment the required 36 state. On August 26, 1920, the secretary of state announced that the amendment had been ratified.

That fall, more than 26 million women across the country voted in the presidential election. One of them, Charlotte Woodward, at 91, was the only surviving signer of the Seneca Falls Declaration of 1848. It had been 72 years since Elizabeth Cady Stanton and her allies proclaimed their right to vote.

Many women in the 1920s asserted new freedoms not only in dress and style but also in claiming the right to hold a job, though too often the jobs that were available were at the bottom of the economic ladder in places like the typing pool.

A Revolution in Culture—Manners, Morals, and Automobiles

Both gaining the right to vote and Prohibition played a part in fostering a new life-style for a generation of young women who came to be known as "flappers." Flappers cut their hair short and dressed in ways that exposed more skin—on their necks, arms, and legs—than any previous generation. Some flappers embraced their own sexual freedom, objecting to the older rules about sexuality, and many chose to drink or smoke. Certainly the flappers of the 1920s were not the first women to rebel against the sexual double standard that made women guardians of morality. Women had broken out of assigned spheres to fight for the right to vote and for social reform. But in the 1920s, having won the right to vote, the activism of many women changed drastically.

Flappers were determined to have equal freedom as men to do as they pleased in work and in their social lives. The emergence of the flappers was one—but only one—aspect of that new activism. Preprohibition saloons and bars had been male preserves. No respectable woman would enter one. However, the illegal speakeasies that replaced the old bars in the 1920s—often in the same location—catered not only to men but also to women, and not just flappers. As Elmer Davis, a thoughtful observer of his times, said of Prohibition, "The old days when father spent his evenings at Cassidy's bar with the rest of the boys are gone, and probably gone forever; Cassidy may still be in business at the old stand and father may still go down there of evenings, but since Prohibition mother goes down with him."

It was not only young middle-class women—flappers—who challenged their status in the United States in the 1920s. The voices of those advocating for women had become stronger, and elected officials began to listen to the newly expanded electorate. In 1921, Congress passed the Sheppard-Towner Act providing federal funds for prenatal and infant care. In 1922, Congress passed the Cable Act, protecting the citizenship rights of American women who married noncitizens. By 1923, three women, all Republicans, were serving in the House of Representatives. Women became active in both political parties and ran for office in all parts of the country. In New Mexico, a descendent of one of the old Spanish land-holding families, Adelina Otero Warren, who had been honored for her leadership when New Mexico ratified the Nineteenth

American Voices

Ellen Wells Page, A Flapper's Appeal 1922

Middle- and upper-class young women known as flappers were the symbols of the revolution in morals that took place after World War I. In previous generations, young women from "good families," were expected to be the guardians of morality, but in the 1920s, these women became the leaders of a revolt against the social norms. Flappers wore make up and exposed parts of their bodies—necks and arms—that no decent woman of earlier generations would have shown. They stopped wearing corsets, danced closely with men, and rode in automobiles that gave them privacy. Some smoked, drank, and engaged in premarital sex. Far from hiding their revolt, they gloried in it. One self-described flapper appealed for understanding of her generation.

If one judges by appearances, I suppose I am a flapper. I am within the age limit. I wear bobbed hair, the badge of flapperhood. (And, oh, what a comfort it is!) I powder my nose. I wear fringed skirts and bright-colored sweaters, and scarfs, and waists[blouses] with Peter Pan collars, and low-heeled "finale hopper" shoes. I *adore* to dance. I spend a large amount of time in automobiles. I attend hops, and proms, and ball-games, and crew races, and other affairs at men's colleges. But none the less some of the most thoroughbred superflappers might blush to claim sistership or even remote relationship with such as I. I don't use rouge, or lipstick, or pluck my eyebrows. I don't smoke (I've tried it, and don't like it), or drink....

I want to beg all you parents, and grandparents, and friends, and teachers, and preachers—you who constitute the "older generation"—to overlook our shortcomings, at least for the present,

and to appreciate our virtues. I wonder if it ever occurred to any of you that it required *brains* to become and remain a successful flapper? Indeed it does! It requires an enormous amount of cleverness and energy to keep going at the proper pace. It requires self-knowledge and self-analysis. We must know our capabilities and limitations. We must be constantly on the alert. Attainment of flapperhood is a big and serious undertaking!

"Brains?" you repeat, skeptically. "Then why aren't they used to better advantage?" That is exactly it!..."The war!" you cry. "It is the effect of the war!" And then you blame Prohibition....But this is my point: Instead of helping us work out our problems with constructive, sympathetic thinking and acting, you have muddled them for us more hopelessly with destructive public condemnation and denunciation....

We are the Younger Generation. The war tore away our spiritual foundations and challenged our faith. We are struggling to regain our equilibrium. The times have made us older and more experienced than you were at our age.

Source: Ellen Welles Page, "A Flapper's Appeal to Parents," *Outlook*, December 6, 1922.

Thinking Critically

1. Documentary Analysis

How did Page define "flapperhood"?

2. Contextualization

What does the document tell us about typical 1920s explanations of the flapper phenomenon? What was Page's attitude towards such explanations?

Amendment, ran for Congress in 1922, winning the Republican nomination but losing the final election. Had Warren won her close race, she would have been the first Latina among the first women in Congress.

In 1921, Margaret Sanger, who became a birth control advocate while working as a visiting nurse in New York City, organized a birth control conference for physicians and researchers in New York City and later the same year founded the American Birth Control League. In 1923, she opened a physician-run birth control clinic since, by law, only physicians, not nurses like Sanger, were allowed to dispense birth control information in the 1920s. She organized several international conferences on birth control in the 1920s. In the 1930s, she tested federal laws against the importation of foreign-made contraceptives and won. In 1942, the American Birth Control League became Planned Parenthood with Sanger as honorary chair. Planned Parenthood also supported the research that led to the first birth control pill, approved by the U.S. Food and Drug Administration in 1960.

While responses to Prohibition and women's issues were changing the culture, technological changes of the 1920s also reshaped the ways Americans thought about culture and morality. For many Americans, urban and rural, the radio and motion pictures brought news of national and international events and shaped a more unified and fast-changing national culture. The relatively low-cost automobile made it possible for more Americans to travel while giving younger Americans a degree of privacy unheard of by previous generations—especially once enclosed sedans replaced open cars in the mid-1920s. Washing machines, refrigerators, vacuum cleaners, and toasters, reshaped traditional housework for women. In addition, new forms of financing allowed people to buy all of these goods on installment plans, dramatically increasing consumer debt while making the new inventions available to more people.

When the nation's first radio station KDKA in Pittsburgh began operating, broadcasting the election returns in the Harding-Cox presidential contest in November 1920, it ushered in a new era in news and entertainment. Within a very short period of time, hundreds of stations were reporting news; playing records; covering religious services, sports events, and political campaigns; and broadcasting live concerts (once they had figured out how to manage acoustical control). In 1927, Congress passed the Radio Act, which created a plan to license radio stations and regulate the wavelengths at which they broadcast. A decade after KDKA started its first broadcast, half of all American households owned a radio.

Although automobiles had already been introduced, they became increasingly common during the 1920s. Fords, Chryslers, Chevrolets, Cadillacs, Lexingtons, Maxwells, and Hudsons showed up in front of American homes. During that decade, the number of cars registered in the United States tripled from 9 million to 26.5 million.

Margaret Sanger

Auto-related industries such as steel, paint, textile, and tire production along with highway construction boomed in the 1920s. Auto dealerships, gas stations, repair shops, roadside restaurants, and hotels grew. Congress provided funds for the federal Bureau of Public Roads in 1921, and metropolitan areas expanded as distances became easier to traverse. New York City built the Bronx River Parkway, connecting large parts of the city, and Los Angeles opened new highways into the heretofore farming country of the San Fernando Valley.

The 1920s was the first decade in which more Americans lived in cities and towns than on farms. It was also a decade in which suburbs expanded dramatically as the automobile and growing roadways allowed people to spread further than the train and streetcar tracks had during the first wave of suburbanization in the 1880s. The pace of suburbanization was quickened when General Motors purchased a number of streetcar companies and tore up the tracks, replacing the service with General Motors buses. From New York to Los Angeles, the nation's trolley system slowly withered, replaced with buses that could move more freely but that later added to growing traffic congestion.

Like the automobile, silent motion pictures had been invented well before World War I, and they, too, became an important part of the culture of the 1920s. By the end of the decade, an average of 100 million Americans, out of a total population of 123 million, attended a movie every week. Movies offered fun, escape, and entertainment. For people in small towns and rural areas, movies brought the larger world into their community. After 1927, motion picture technology enabled the addition of sound and voice, and "talkies" became popular. Whether people watched the comedies of Charlie Chaplin, the cartoons of Walt Disney's Mickey Mouse (created in 1928), the religious enthusiasm of *The Ten Commandments* and *The King of Kings,* or the sexually suggestive acting of Clara Bow and Rudolph Valentino, movies gave them new ways of looking at the world. Not insignificantly, movie theaters were air-conditioned well before most other buildings, making a summer evening at the movies especially appealing.

Movies, newspapers, and magazines such as *Time* (started in 1923) created an age of new heroes. Heroes seemed to be emerging all the time, including "Babe" Ruth of the New York Yankees, who hit 60 home runs in 1927 in the increasingly popular game of baseball, or boxers like Jack Dempsey and Gene Tunney, whose matches generated over a million dollars in revenue, or Gertrude Ederle, the first

Listening to the radio became possible for many in the 1920s, uniting the culture in shared information and shared tastes as never before.

woman to swim the English Channel in 1926, or the decade's most celebrated hero, Charles A. Lindbergh, who flew solo across the Atlantic in his airplane the *Spirit of St. Louis* in 1927 and was welcomed home with what was becoming a New York institution, a ticker-tape parade down Fifth Avenue.

In addition, a new form of self-defined, sophisticated culture took hold. When *The New Yorker* appeared in 1925, its editor Harold Ross said that it was "not edited for the old lady in Dubuque," but, rather, was "a reflection in word and picture of metropolitan life." Part of *The New Yorker*'s success was the guidance it gave to members—or aspiring members—of New York's "smart set" on how to navigate the city's nightlife— which nightclubs, speakeasies, cafes, and hotel lounges provided the best entertainment, the grandest design, and (though it didn't overtly say so) the best drinks.

The U.S. writers of the 1920s spoke to a generation and class disillusioned with the idealism of past decades as well as the business and money making that characterized so much of 1920s bourgeoisie culture. Many lived abroad and were dubbed the "Lost Generation" by Gertrude Stein, who herself lived most of her life in Paris. Among them were Ernest Hemingway and other writers as different as T. S. Eliot and John Dos Passos. Sinclair Lewis published *Main Street* in 1920 and *Babbitt* in 1922, which both looked at the stifling conformity and hypocrisy of small town America. F. Scott Fitzgerald dropped out of Princeton, where he had spent most of his college career at parties, and then described that culture he knew so well in *This Side of Paradise* in 1920 and *The Great Gatsby* in 1925. In their literature and their assumptions, the social and artistic elite who lived between the end of the First World War in 1918 and the coming of the Great Depression in 1929 lived at a unique, prosperous, and discontented moment in American history and literature.

The Harlem Renaissance and Marcus Garvey

In 1920 as in 1820, 90 percent of African-Americans lived in the South. However, by 1920, some blacks had begun to move away from rural poverty and segregation in the rural South to new opportunities in Southern cities and in the larger industrial cities of the North. Although the height of the **Great Migration**—the great movement of African-Americans from rural South to urban North—took place in the 1940s and 1950s (see Chapter 24), it had its beginnings during and immediately after World War I. The result was both a population shift and a cultural flowering (see Map 21-1).

World War I created new opportunities for African-Americans. As work expanded, factories in the North needed more workers. The Illinois Central Railroad, which ran straight from the heart of the cotton-growing Mississippi Delta to job-rich Chicago, enabled those who were moving. The nation's most widely read black newspaper, the *Chicago Defender,* announced "The Great Northern Drive" in May 1917. The newspaper called on Southern blacks to make "The Flight Out of Egypt," commissioned songs like "Bound for the Promised Land," and negotiated special group rates with the Illinois Central. The paper told sharecroppers about jobs available in the stockyards and meat-packing houses in Chicago.

Black music reflected the emotions of those who moved North. The blues, music born out of gospel, ragtime, and jazz, began on back porches, small town bars and dance halls, and prison cells in the Mississippi Delta early in the 1900s. At first, blues musicians sang of hard lives in the South. John Hurt sang, "Avalon [Mississippi] my home town, always on my mind," and Bill Broonzy sang, "Anywhere in Mississippi is my native home." But in the 1920s, the blues moved north. Those who had sung about life in Mississippi began to sing, "I'm going to Detroit, get myself a good job. Tired of stayin' round here with the starvation mob."

Some 50,000 African-Americans moved from the South to Chicago during World War I and another 100,000 in the 10 years that followed. Chicago's black population grew from 44,000 in 1910 to 109,000 in 1920 to 234,000 in 1930. During and after World War II, many more blacks would follow. In addition to Chicago,

Great Migration

The mass movement of African-Americans from the rural South to the urban North, spurred especially by new job opportunities that began during World War I and the 1920s.

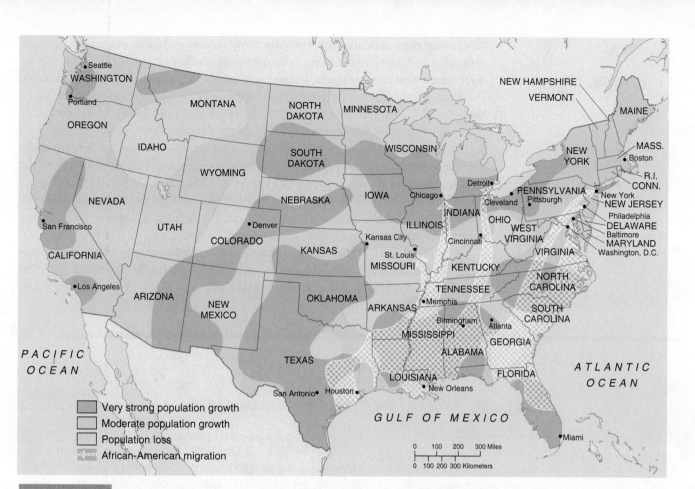

MAP 21-1 People Moving in the 1920s. Many Americans chose to, or were forced to, move during the 1920s. Cities and suburbs grew rapidly. Throughout the era, African-Americans moved from the South to Northern cities such as Chicago, Detroit, and New York. In some areas, the farmers' depression meant giving up on cultivated land and starting over to farm another region or become a city worker.

African-Americans moved to New York; Detroit; Los Angeles; Philadelphia; Syracuse, New York; Oakland, California; Milwaukee; Newark; Gary, Indiana; and other cities that offered jobs and a modicum of freedom.

Cotton planters did everything possible to stop the northern migration. The *Chicago Defender* was branded as dangerously subversive. Plantation owners opposed anything more than rudimentary education for blacks so they would have few skills to take north. In Greenville, Mississippi, the town's leading white citizen, LeRoy Percy, opposed the Klan because he feared that their brand of terror would lead to "an exodus within a year," of the black people who were essential to the economy. African-Americans kept moving.

The novelist Richard Wright described the experience of many of the early migrants in his novel *Native Son* and his autobiography *Black Boy*. Wright was born to a sharecropper family in Natchez, Mississippi. He left the rural South for Memphis and then in 1927 for Chicago to experience, he said, "the warmth of other suns." It was not an easy move. Wright remembered, "I had fled a known terror, and perhaps I could cope with this unknown terror."

The North to which the Southern immigrants came was not always a welcoming place. After World War I, some whites sought to reclaim the industrial jobs they had held before the war at the same time that wartime demand for workers ebbed. Salaries were much higher in the North, but so were rents. Living conditions in increasingly segregated and rapidly growing urban neighborhoods made for tightly packed homes. Race riots in Chicago and St. Louis in 1919 made it very clear just how unwelcoming the North could be.

African-Americans had long lived in cities like New York, Providence, and Philadelphia. Free black communities emerged before the Civil War in places like Pittsburgh, Cleveland, and Cincinnati. In 1910, only a tiny percentage of Northern

Harlem Renaissance
A new African-American cultural awareness that flourished in literature, art, and music in the 1920s.

blacks were professionals, mostly preachers or teachers in African-American churches and schools. Most Northern black men were janitors, porters, servants, or waiters while black women were cooks, laundresses, maids, or servants. Still, there was often conflict between these long-time urban blacks and the newcomers from the South who started arriving in large numbers after 1917. Each found the social and economic position of the other threatening.

Nevertheless, in spite of fear, pain, and segregation, something very important started happening in the expanding black communities of the urban North in the 1920s, most of all in New York City's Harlem (see Map 21-2). When the philosopher Alain Locke published *The New Negro* in 1925, the book he hoped would define the **Harlem Renaissance**, he wrote that in that era, the African-American was, "moving forward under the control largely of his own objectives."

While the intellectual and cultural leaders of Harlem celebrated their Renaissance, other African-Americans, especially those on the lowest rungs of the economy, looked to the charismatic Marcus Garvey (1887–1940) to foster racial

American Voices

Alain Locke, *Voices of the Harlem Renaissance* 1925

When Howard University professor Alain Locke edited The New Negro, Voices of the Harlem Renaissance *in 1925, a collection of the work of many of the artists, poets, and novelists, whose work was part of the movement, the word "Negro" was the preferred term of respect for most Americans of African descent—just as the term "African American" would be in future decades. Locke became known as the "dean" of the New Negro movement, an artistic and intellectual flowering of an assertive new cultural identity. The acknowledged capital of this new movement was New York City's Harlem, and during the 1920s, the "Harlem Renaissance" defined elite black culture.*

From Alain Locke's "Foreword"—

This volume aims to document the New Negro culturally and socially,—to register the transformations of the inner and outer life of the Negro in America that have so significantly taken place....Negro life is not only establishing new contacts and founding new centers, it is finding a new soul. There is a fresh spiritual and cultural focusing. We have, as the heralding sign, an unusual outburst of creative expression. There is a renewed race-spirit that consciously and proudly sets itself apart. Justifiably then, we speak of the offerings of this book embodying these ripening forces as culled from the first fruits of the Negro Renaissance.

From James Weldon Johnson's essay in *The New Negro*, "Harlem: The Culture Capital"—

In the history of New York, the significance of the name Harlem has changed from Dutch to Irish to Jewish to Negro. Of these changes, the last has come most swiftly. Throughout colored America, from Massachusetts to Mississippi, and across the continent to Los Angeles and Seattle, its name, which as late as fifteen years ago had scarcely been heard, now stands for the

Negro metropolis. Harlem is indeed the great Mecca for the sight-seer, the pleasure-seeker, the curious, the adventurous, the enterprising, the ambitious and the talented of the whole Negro world; for the lure of it has reached down to every island of the Carib Sea and has penetrated even into Africa.

In the make-up of New York, Harlem is not merely a Negro colony or community, it is a city within a city, the greatest Negro city in the world. It is not a slum or a fringe, it is located in the heart of Manhattan and occupies one of the most beautiful and healthful sections of the city. It is not a "quarter" of dilapidated tenements, but is made up of new-law apartments and handsome dwellings, with well-paved and well-lighted streets. It has its own churches, social and civic centers, shops, theaters and other places of amusement. And it contains more Negroes to the square mile than any other spot on earth....

I believe that the Negro's advantages and opportunities are greater in Harlem than in any other place in the country, and that Harlem will become the intellectual, the cultural and the financial center for Negroes of the United States, and will exert a vital influence upon all Negro peoples.

Source: Alain Locke, editor, *The New Negro: Voices of the Harlem Renaissance*, new Introduction by Arnold Rampersad (originally 1925, new edition New York: Simon & Schuster, 1992)

Thinking Critically

1. **Documentary Analysis**

   According to the authors, what made Harlem different from other African-American communities?

2. **Contextualization**

   What did Locke and Johnson see as the hallmarks of the "Negro" or "Harlem" Renaissance?

MAP 21-2 Harlem in the 1920s. Before World War I, only a few blocks of New York City's Harlem neighborhood had an African-American majority. By the end of the 1920s, nearly all of Harlem, from Central Park to the Harlem River, was an African-American community, and for many—including the voices of the Harlem Renaissance but also the followers of Marcus Garvey—it was the capital of black America.

pride and self-determination. Garvey established the Universal Negro Improvement and Conservation Association and African Communities League (UNIA) in Jamaica in August 1914.

For poor blacks, especially those seeking to adjust to life in Northern cities, Garvey's message rejecting integration with white America and focusing on self-help, self-determination, and African nationalism struck a powerful chord. At the beginning of 1918, the New York branch of the UNIA had about 1,500 members. By 1920, Garvey claimed a membership of 2–4 million in 30 branches across the country.

In the early 1920s, Garvey outlined an independent path for blacks, "not to hate other people," but to take responsibility for their own fate. "We are organized," he said, "for the absolute purpose of bettering our condition, industrially, commercially, socially, religiously and politically."

Garvey was at the height of his popularity in the early 1920s. In 1919, the UNIA purchased a large auditorium in Harlem, and in August 1920, 25,000 delegates from Africa, the Caribbean, and the United States adopted the Negro Declaration of Rights. A UNIA parade in Harlem included UNIA men of the African

Marcus Garvey, pictured with some of his followers, used lavish uniforms and parades to foster pride and self-confidence in his mostly poor, African-American supporters.

Chapter 21 A Unique, Prosperous, and Discontented Time **611**

Legion in uniform and a delegation of 200 women of the Black Cross Nurses marching in a show of strength and pride.

Garvey created a shipping company, the Black Star Line, to carry passengers and freight between the United States, the islands of the Caribbean, and Africa. This crown jewel of Garvey's economic development plan was launched in 1920 and eventually owned a number of ships. It was also Garvey's downfall. Selling stock at $5 per share, Garvey eventually collected over $750,000, perhaps much more. But whether through mismanagement or corruption, or both, the line floundered.

The Black Star Line was attacked by blacks as well as whites. In December 1920, W.E.B. Du Bois published an indictment of the Black Star Line. The finances of the Black Star Line collapsed and with it the rest of Garvey's U.S.-based efforts. He was arrested for fraud, convicted, and sentenced to 5 years in federal prison in 1923 and began serving his term in the Atlanta Federal Penitentiary in February 1925. In November 1927, President Calvin Coolidge commuted Garvey's sentence but had him deported to Jamaica. Garvey continued to build the UNIA in Jamaica and traveled through much of the world, but his influence, though significant, declined in the United States.

> **21.2** **Quick Review** How did changes in American culture reflect the postwar desire for fun and leisure? When was that not the cause of change?

THE 1920s—THE CONFLICTS ABOUT AMERICAN IDEALS

> **21.3** Explain the elements of discrimination, hardship, and fundamentalism that also shaped American life in the 1920s.

While the 1920s are often remembered as the Jazz Age—the decade of Prohibition, speakeasies, new automobiles, flappers, and parties—large numbers of Americans lived quite different lives. For many, the crime and the drinking were an evil to be shunned. Some who refused to violate the Prohibition laws lived quiet and law-abiding lives; others joined organizations that were determined to enforce Prohibition, not always by lawful means. Growing confidence and hope among African-Americans particularly threatened white Southerners, and long-simmering tensions heated dangerously. Despite the relative prosperity, many people on farms and in the poor neighborhoods of big cities still lived lives of desperate poverty. In addition, many native-born Americans came to distrust and fear immigrants or those who were different, and the teaching of evolution threatened the very fabric of faith for others. These conflicts challenged core American ideals on many levels, and reactions ranged from quiet frustration to vocal defiance.

The Rise of the Ku Klux Klan in the 1920s

As Prohibition came into force, the Ku Klux Klan was also revived as a defender of Prohibition as well as an opponent of immigration, rights for African-Americans, and anything that undermined the dominance of white native-born Protestants in the nation's life. The original Klan had been one of several white terrorist organizations that opposed Reconstruction after the Civil War, killing blacks and their white supporters and burning black schools and churches. Because of prosecution by the Grant administration, the Reconstruction-era Klan virtually disappeared in the 1870s. In 1915, a Georgian, William Joseph Simmons, inspired by nostalgia for a bygone era, recreated the Klan. During its first few years, Simmons's Klan was an insignificant organization of a few hundred members. Then in the early 1920s, a Texas dentist, Hiram Wesley Evans, pushed Simmons aside and turned the Klan into a hugely successful hate organization aimed at African-Americans, immigrants, Catholics, Jews, and anyone who challenged the Prohibition laws. Under Evans's leadership, the Klan increased from a few hundred to as many as 5 million members, including a female auxiliary that became the separate Women of the Ku Klux Klan (WKKK). As the Klan struck fear into many, it enriched a few leaders who controlled access to everything from membership dues to Klan robes and paraphernalia, which had to be ordered directly from the national headquarters.

The Klan slogan was, "One flag, one school, one Bible." It advocated for strict enforcement of Prohibition and—ironically, some thought—a cabinet-level Department of Education that would ensure that all American children were taught Klan-defined patriotism, or "100% Americanism." It gave flags and Bibles to public schools while demanding the firing of Catholic and Jewish teachers. The Klan sought to require every student to attend public schools and, in Oregon, got the state to outlaw private and parochial schools, though the law was overturned by the U.S. Supreme Court before it took effect.

The Ku Klux Klan staged massive rallies and demonstrations such as this one in Washington, DC, in 1925.

Most people understood that the Klan also had another agenda: maintaining rigid racial segregation and, by using terror if need be, keeping African-Americans from asserting the right to vote or getting ahead economically. If a black man was accused of flirting with a white woman, he might expect a whipping or worse from robed Klan visitors. If the Klan discovered an interracial couple, they attacked them. If a black did not want to sell land at a price offered by a Klan member, he or she might expect a lashing until agreeing to sell. In 1920, Nathan Taylor, an African-American attorney in Mississippi who previously had been protected by white attorneys was abducted by the Klan and taken out to the middle of the Mississippi River and warned that, one way or another, he was to leave the state. Preferring to leave alive, Taylor moved to Chicago.

The Klan, often with the Women of the Klan in the lead, launched boycotts of stores owned by blacks, Catholics, or Jewish people. Klan publications condemned the "foreign influence" of the Catholic Church and reprinted articles from Henry Ford's fiercely anti-Semitic *Dearborn Independent* about what they called the "money grasping Jews." The Klan's Constitution defined a goal

> to unite white male persons, native-born Gentile citizens of the United States of America, who owe no allegiance of any nature to any foreign government, nation, institution, sect, ruler, person, or people…to shield the sanctity of the home and the chastity of womanhood; to maintain forever white supremacy.

The Klan provided entertainment in isolated small towns where there was not much to do. A hundred thousand people attended a Klan rally on July 4, 1923, in Kokomo, Indiana, which featured music and food. Almost as many attended a speech by Imperial Wizard Evans at Ku Klux Klan Day at the Texas State Fair in Dallas that fall. The Klan was especially strong in the Midwest and the South, but there was Klan activity from Maine to California.

A number of groups, from the Catholic Knights of Columbus to the African-American press to the new, and specifically the anti-Klan American Unity League (AUL), began to challenge the Klan. Where the Klan spoke of "pure Americanism," the AUL spoke of "true Americanism." In some places, pitched battles erupted between

21.1

21.2

21.3

21.4

eugenics

A movement that claimed scientific basis to apply Darwinian theory to the "natural selection" of the "fittest" human beings to reproduce and improve the human race.

Klan members and their opponents, but one of the most effective anti-Klan tactics was simply to find and publicize lists of members in the secret organization, asking, "Is Your Neighbor a Kluxer?" Opposition to the Klan, battles among its leaders, and exposure of internal corruption all weakened the organization, and by 1930, the Klan, which had once had more than 5 million members, had dropped to 50,000. Although it did not disappear, the Klan as a power in American life was a phenomenon of the 1920s.

Eugenics and I.Q. Tests—The Science of Discrimination

It was not only the Klan that sought to marginalize African-Americans, Asians, Catholics, and Jews in the United States in the 1920s. The eugenics movement used ideas from evolutionary biology, derived loosely (inaccurately and simplistically, many said) from Charles Darwin, to "prove" that some ethnic groups were more highly evolved than others. The **eugenics** movement was begun in England in the 1880s by Francis Galton, who concluded that the social elite—people like himself—were significantly higher on the evolutionary scale than England's working class, who in turn were more evolved than society's poor and criminal element. Eugenics quickly became popular in the United States. Eugenics gave a scientific patina to efforts to limit the immigration of ethnic groups from southern and eastern Europe and from Asia. Southern segregationists quickly latched on to eugenics as a "scientific" justification for racial segregation.

Margaret Sanger, the advocate for family planning and birth control, was a lifelong advocate of eugenics, particularly its focus on preventing inherited traits and weaknesses, which had been a long-used approach to agricultural breeding. The eugenics movement applied this knowledge to human concerns, including various efforts to limit possibilities for those with disabilities such as deafness or limited intelligence—the "unfit"—to procreate.

Henry Goddard, a prominent American psychologist and eugenicist established an intelligence testing program on Ellis Island in 1913, which was used to "sort" the thousands of immigrants entering the country, helping to create some of the notions about higher or lower intelligence in various ethnic groups. Efforts to predict intelligence and ability grew as a result of the development of scientific intelligence testing that began with the Army during World War I. By the 1920s, educators led by Stanford University's Lewis M. Terman and Columbia University's Edward L. Thorndike believed that "Whatever exists at all exists in some amount," and that by measuring the amount of intelligence in a given child—through the newly popular IQ (or Intelligence Quotient) test—educators could assign him or her a "mental age" and sort the more advanced for college and the rest for menial jobs. These tests actually measured the kind of culturally specific knowledge that children of native-born Protestant and northern European families learned at home, so test-takers from those backgrounds tended to score considerably higher than the children of southern Europeans, who still scored higher than eastern European Jews. Those of African and Asian descent tended to score the lowest on the IQ tests. Such "science" reinforced immigration restriction and racial segregation in the 1920s.

Interest in eugenics faded in the 1930s, especially as Adolph Hitler embraced the idea in *Mein Kampf* and used it as the basis of his anti-Semitic and anti-Slavic efforts to achieve a "pure" race and eliminate any they considered "unfit." IQ tests remained popular much longer, being used well after World War II to sort and track students in school. In the 1920s, however eugenics and IQ testing enforced popular opinion in the United States.

Immigration Restriction, 1924

While groups like the Anti-Saloon League and the Klan were often hostile to African-Americans, Catholics, and Jews, they found allies in Congress who were also trying to end further immigration into the country. In 1924, the opponents of immigration succeeded spectacularly when Congress cut off virtually all immigration from southern and eastern Europe, Africa, and Asia. In addition to anti-immigrant groups like the Klan, labor unions and some African-American organizations feared that a never-ending stream of new immigrants could depress wages or take jobs. Cultural elitists, supported by the eugenics movement, worried that the traditional Anglo-American culture was being diluted. Hostility to new immigrants was not new. In the 1840s, the Know-Nothing Party attempted to limit Irish immigration. In 1882, Congress excluded Chinese immigrants. The largest movement to limit immigration to the United States, however, was led by the Immigration Restriction League (IRL), founded in 1894.

In 1917 on the eve of U.S. entry into World War I, Congress passed a literacy test for new immigrants over President Wilson's veto. Similar legislation had also been vetoed by presidents Cleveland and Taft, but by 1917, the anti-immigrant vote in Congress was strong. More immigrants than expected were, in fact, literate and the literacy test did not significantly reduce the number of immigrants coming to the United States. People like Wilbur Carr of the U.S. Consular Service warned that Poland's Jewish ghettos were about to empty into the United States after World War I, fueling new fears of a new "horde" of immigrants from war-torn Europe. In response, Congress passed an emergency Immigration Restriction Act in 1921, for the first time setting quotas for the numbers of immigrants who could enter the United States.

One of the architects of even tougher anti-immigrant legislation was Congressman Albert Johnson of Washington State. Johnson hated radical organizations like the IWW and was convinced (incorrectly) that most of its members were immigrants. He was also strongly anti-Japanese and a member of the Asiatic Exclusion League. In addition, he was influenced by the "scientists" who argued that eugenics and IQ tests proved that Asians as well as southern and eastern Europeans were inferior people to "Nordic" stock. Johnson became chair of the House Committee on Immigration in 1919 and set out to write new legislation.

In setting the quota for the number of immigrants, Johnson decided not to refer to the 1910 census, which had been the basis of the 1921 restriction but which was taken well after large numbers of Russian, Italian, and other southern European immigrants had arrived in the United States. Instead, he referred to the 1890 census, taken just before that wave of immigration, to set new quotas. Using the 1890 census, and limiting the percentage of immigrants allowed into the country to 2 percent of that number, Johnson cut the total number of immigrants allowed into the United States per year from 357,803 to 161,184. The proposed law also tilted the ethnic makeup of the new arrivals against ethnic groups that had arrived in large numbers between 1890 and 1910. Italy was cut from 42,057 immigrants per year to 3,912, Poland from 21,076 to 5,156, and Russia from 5,638 to 474. Yugoslavia, created out of the pre-World War I Austria-Hungarian Empire, was cut from 6,426 to 851 immigrants. Russian Jews, Italians, and Slavic immigrants were reduced to a trickle. In contrast, German immigration was only cut from 67,607 to 51,299 and Britain's from 77,342 to 62,458. Northern Europeans did not generally fill their quotas, but the rest of the world was reduced drastically. Under the Johnson formula, Japan should have been allowed 240 immigrants, but Johnson insisted that the bill ban all Japanese immigration to the United States.

Urban representatives led by New York's Fiorello LaGuardia protested. The American Jewish Committee criticized the bill. It did no good. The new 1924 immigration restriction passed the House and Senate by wide margins, and President Coolidge, who had already told Congress that "America must be kept American," signed the bill. Although some modifications were made, from 1924 until 1965, immigration to the United States from most of Europe and all of Asia and Africa was severely limited.

The 1924 legislation, however, did not impact all immigration. It did not stop Irish immigration since large numbers of Irish immigrants had come to the United States before 1890, which under Johnson's formula kept the quota high. It also had no impact on immigration from North and South America, since the bill allowed unlimited immigration from Canada and Mexico. Approximately 500,000 Mexican workers came to the United States during the 1920s. They filled agricultural jobs in the West previously held by Japanese immigrants as well as railroad jobs and industrial jobs in Chicago; Gary, Indiana; and Detroit, Michigan. The Mexican community in Los Angeles, a city founded by Mexican immigrants, grew rapidly.

The 1924 immigration restrictions created deep tensions between the United States and some other countries, most of all China and Japan. The government of Japan, which had sought to work with several American administrations to construct "Gentlemen's Agreements" limiting immigration, was incensed at the disrespect in the ban of even the 200 immigrants per year that the quota would have allowed. Coming on the heels of previous insults like the 1906 segregation of Japanese students in the San Francisco public schools, the 1924 legislation contributed to deep-seated, anti-American feelings in Japan. Other governments, including those of Italy and Rumania, objected to the legislation. Nevertheless, the United States was in an isolationist mood after the end of World War I, and the protests did not stop the closing of America's previously very open gates. Members of Congress responded to foreign protests by saying that, "the nation's immigration laws should be made for Americans and not to please foreigners," and "No foreign government has the right to tell the United States who we shall or shall not admit."

Just as the United States was closing its doors, the trial of two recent immigrants polarized the nation. Nicola Sacco and Bartolomeo Vanzetti were arrested on May 5, 1920, for robbery and the murder of a paymaster and guard of a shoe factory in South Braintree, Massachusetts. They were tried in the midst of the antiradical, anti-immigrant hysteria sweeping the country and were convicted in July 1921. After a long series of appeals, reviews, and massive public protests, during which Sacco and Vanzetti maintained their innocence, their conviction was upheld and they were executed at Charlestown Prison on August 23, 1927.

The case of Sacco and Vanzetti took on enormous symbolic importance during the 1920s. Opponents of immigration and of political radicalism generally assumed that they were guilty simply because they were immigrants and self-confessed anarchists. For others, winning freedom for Sacco and Vanzetti could be, depending on one's view, a blow struck for the cause of anarchism, or for the rights of immigrants, or simply the right to a fair trial. For observers during the 1920s, the Sacco and Vanzetti case symbolized how much a nation made up of immigrants had turned against those immigrants who arrived most recently.

The Farmers' Depression

For many farmers, World War I had brought prosperity as the prices for wheat, cotton, and other agricultural products went up significantly. With new money to be found in every bushel or bale, farmers extended production between 1914 and 1918. Farmers enjoyed amenities as never before. In the early 1920s, one farm wife wrote about the "running water in the house! What a constant cause of thankfulness! What a joy to use all I need and want!" No more would she have a long, hot walk to the spring for a pail of water to sooth a thirsty child or to wash a dipper because "the water from that same spring is in our pressure-tank…."

Farmers kept expanding the areas they cultivated. The rich lands of the Delta in northwest Mississippi were still more than 60 percent wilderness in 1914. Bears were seen in cornfields and wolves attacked livestock. But in the war years, the world needed more cotton than ever, and planters cleared land as fast as they could. By the war's end, much of the Mississippi Delta was in cotton production and land sold for up to

Nicola Sacco and Bartolomeo Vanzetti's trial symbolized the fears of immigrants to some and the hopes for justice for others. Vanzetti defined the way he wanted to be remembered. In May 1927, he told a journalist who visited him in the Dedham jail, "If it had not been for these things, I might have lived out my life talking at street corners to scorning men....Never in our full life could we hope to do such work for tolerance, for justice, for man's understanding of man as now we do by accident."

$1,000 an acre. Agricultural centers like Greenville, Mississippi, "The Queen City of the Delta," had 15,000 people with paved streets and factories in 1920. Some 20 railroad trains stopped every day, and agents in Greenville sold cotton directly to buyers in New York, Chicago, and New Orleans as well as the European cotton markets at Liverpool, England. Prosperity, it seemed, had finally arrived in the Delta.

Similarly, in the arid cattle country of southern Kansas and the panhandle region of Oklahoma, land that had never been plowed was being turned into farmland as fast as developers and settlers could break the sod with a plow and set up windmills to bring water from deep below. Driven by the insatiable wartime need for wheat and encouraged by the Union Pacific Railroad, which brought settlers, plows, and windmills, settlers filed 53,000 new homestead claims in the Great Plains in 1914 alone. The former grassland was now producing wheat, and many families who started out living in a mud-walled dugout imagined that there was a fortune in store if only they could turn over enough sod. "Plant more wheat to win the war," the government said, and farmers in the Midwest and the Plains, happy to mix patriotism and profit, did just as the nation asked.

Then, the war ended. Europe began planting its own wheat again. Disbanded armies did not need uniforms. By 1920 and 1921, most of the world was caught up in an economic downturn that drastically reduced the demand for everything, especially wheat and cotton. The general economy started to recover in 1922 and 1923, but the farm economy did not. Even with its new prosperity, the United States could not consume all of the wheat and cotton and meat produced on the nation's farms. For many farmers, the Great Depression of the 1930s began in 1920 or 1921.

Not all farmers were impacted in the same way. Due to the new popularity of ice cream and increased use of milk in American diets, dairy farmers prospered. Vegetable farmers sold celery, spinach, and carrots to city people who had discovered vitamins. But those producing the staple crops—wheat, cotton, and corn—did not prosper. In 1921, cotton, which had brought a dollar a pound only a year before, sold for only 20 cents a pound—if a buyer could be found. Wheat prices also fell drastically However, the price of the fertilizer farmers needed for their crops and the coal they needed to heat their homes kept rising.

Desperate to maintain their incomes, farmers did what seemed logical: they worked harder. If the price for a bushel or bale dropped, the only thing to do was to produce more. What was logical on an individual basis was disastrous on a national one. The more the farmers produced, the more the oversupply led prices to fall. There seemed to be no way to break the pattern.

Senators and representatives from the farm states were desperate for help, and Congress passed the McNary-Haugen bills under which the federal government would set a minimum price for farm products and buy them when the price fell to that level. The government would then store the goods until prices rose. But President Coolidge vetoed the bills as unsound government intervention in free markets. Midwestern progressives complained, but they did not have the votes to override the veto.

In 1927, nature seemed to turn against rural America. It rained a lot that spring. Farmers generally like spring rains, but in 1927, there was too much rain. One of the most intense storms in history came on Good Friday, April 15, 1927. In New Orleans alone, 14.96 inches of rain fell in less than a day. The Mississippi River flooded from Illinois to Louisiana (see Map 21-3). Engineers had been building levies to contain the Mississippi and its tributaries for decades, and by the 1920s, levies were everywhere. Behind the levies, farmers had cleared and planted thousands of acres of land. Cities and towns had grown up. However, prosperity, even survival, depended on the levies holding. That April in 1927, they did not hold. The flood of 1927 covered an area 150 miles long and 50 miles wide along the Mississippi River with water, some of it 20 feet deep, and made 200,000 people homeless, perhaps even three times that number. Secretary of Commerce Herbert Hoover directed the rescue efforts, and the Red Cross provided aid across a stricken country. Many criticized rehabilitation efforts that spent an average of $20 per flood victim as too little too late.

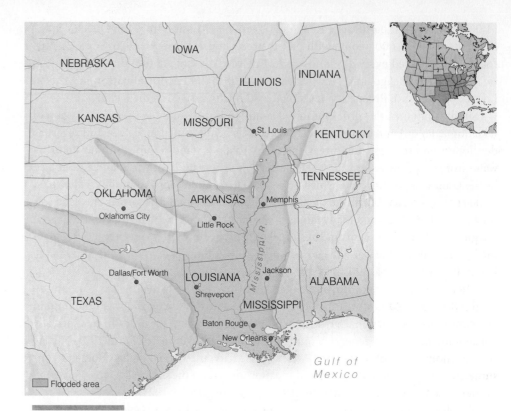

MAP 21-3 The Mississippi River Flood. This map gives some sense of the huge territory that was impacted when the Mississippi River flooded in 1927.

In the aftermath of the flood, many never recovered. Crops planted later that year were beset by disease and an early frost. Pellagra, the result of poor diet, afflicted 50,000 people in the Mississippi Delta. Farmers gave up on the land. Sharecroppers simply moved away. More blacks moved north, and more farmers—black, white, and Latino—moved to town. Soon, the generally prosperous nation quickly forgot the flood and the devastation.

The Scopes Trial

The general prosperity of the 1920s drove many social changes. High schools began to spring up in small towns and scattered rural communities, offering educational opportunities that had been limited to big cities before 1920. In 1890, a total of 200,000 American youth were enrolled in high school. Thirty years later, that number was 2 million and growing—a 10-fold increase.

With the growth of high schools, some Americans started to worry about just what was being taught in them—in particular, biology. The new high school biology classes were greatly influenced by the 1859 publication of Charles Darwin's *Origin of Species,* which described all changes in plant and animal life, including the emergence of human beings, as natural selection—a process by which random biological changes in individuals within a species that are beneficial for survival become passed on to subsequent generations.

The book was at once controversial, particularly in terms of its theological implications. Most scientists embraced Darwin's work and saw no conflict between the new biology and traditional religious teachings. Even those scientists who questioned it acknowledged the important contribution. Harvard's Asa Gray wrote a popular high school botany textbook in the late 1800s that presented evolution as showing that all life was "part of one system," showing "One Mind." After 1900, however, a new generation of scientists stopped talking about One Mind. George William Hunter's textbook, *A Civic Biology,* simply said "Species have been modified during a long course of descent, chiefly through natural selection."

Popular religion was also evolving. Before 1900, most Protestants, liberal or conservative, assumed that the Bible was a fairly accurate historical record, but that assumption was challenged by German-inspired "higher criticism" of the Bible that sought to understand the Bible in terms of the social context in which it was written. In reaction, a new movement known as Fundamentalism began within American Protestantism in the early 1900s. Fundamentalist ministers called for a literal reading of the Bible and rejected any other interpretation of the "unchanged word of God." Fundamentalism represented a new militant form of Protestantism and a much more pessimistic view of modern society. Protestants have traditionally been optimistic about the future. Fundamentalists were pessimistic about a sinful world. They saw the United States of the 1920s, with its open flouting of Prohibition laws, the questionable moral standards of the flappers, the growth of Catholic and Jewish immigrant communities, and the teaching of evolution in the schools, as full of evil.

For growing numbers of American parents and political leaders worrying about the high school curriculum, the changes in scientific thinking and the increasing influence of fundamentalism came into a dramatic collision in the trial of a local high school biology teacher, John Thomas Scopes, in the small town of Dayton, Tennessee, in 1925. Scopes, as required by Tennessee regulations, used Hunter's *A Civic Biology* textbook in his classes. In following the mandated state curriculum, he also violated a Tennessee law against the teaching of evolution.

Between 1922 and 1925, a number of states under pressure from fundamentalists, including Tennessee, outlawed the teaching of evolution. The American Civil Liberties Union (ACLU), however, saw these new laws as an assault on free speech and placed ads in newspapers, including the *Chattanooga Times,* asking for volunteers to test the law and promising legal counsel. Business leaders in Dayton, Tennessee, thought the town could use some publicity and asked Scopes if he would volunteer for the test case. He agreed, and one of the most famous trials in U.S. history resulted.

Although they had long been on the same side of political battles, the nation's leading attorney, Clarence Darrow, and three-time presidential candidate William Jennings Bryan, represented opposite sides in the trial of Tennessee biology teacher John T. Scopes that captured national attention.

Dayton and the nation got quite a show. Clarence Darrow, the best known lawyer in the country, volunteered to join the ACLU team. Former presidential candidate William Jennings Bryan volunteered for the prosecution. Every major newspaper in the country covered the trial. Most people thought Darrow got the better of Bryan in the arguments, but on the facts, Scopes was clearly guilty. Scopes admitted he had violated the law, and he was found guilty and fined $100, though the Tennessee Supreme Court threw the case out on a technicality to avoid appeal to the U.S. Supreme Court, which the ACLU wanted.

Cautious textbook publishers changed their books. In future editions, *A Civic Biology* stopped calling Darwin "the grand old man of biology" and instead simply said that he was a "leading biologist." Evolution, which in the earlier editions had been a "wonderful discovery" now became merely Darwin's "interpretation of the way in which all life changes." Only in the late 1950s would a full discussion of evolution return to high school textbooks.

> **21.3** **Quick Review** To what extent were the racism, anti-immigration efforts, and fundamentalism of the 1920s the result of changes throughout the United States?

HARDING, COOLIDGE, AND HOOVER—NATIONAL POLITICS AND POLICIES IN THE 1920s

21.4 Analyze the political and policy developments of the decade.

Three Republican presidents led the United States during the 1920s. The election of Warren Harding in November of 1920 was almost a foregone conclusion given the general disenchantment with Woodrow Wilson's policies, the war, and the League of Nations. A politician who promised to return the nation to "normalcy" was just what people wanted. Harding and his running mate Massachusetts Governor Calvin Coolidge defeated the Democratic nominee, Ohio Governor James Cox, and his running mate, the young Franklin Roosevelt, by 16 million to 9 million popular votes. In what was his last race, the Socialist Party candidate, Eugene V. Debs polled close to a million votes while still in prison for violating the World War I sedition laws. Late in 1921, Harding commuted his sentence, and Debs was freed.

Although Harding was remembered mostly for the scandals of his administration, he also made some very strong appointments. Three months after coming to office, he appointed former President William Howard Taft to the job Taft had always wanted, Chief Justice of the Supreme Court, where Taft served until 1930. Charles Evans Hughes, the 1916 Republican presidential candidate, became secretary of state. Knowing that there was no chance of U.S. participation in the League of Nations but wanting to foster peace in the postwar world, Hughes called the **Washington Conference** in 1921 to try to end the competition among the United States, Britain, and Japan to build up their navies. To the surprise of many, the result of the conference, the **Five Powers Treaty** of February 1922, slowed the worldwide navy build up and established limits on battleships, battle cruisers, and aircraft carriers in a ratio of 5 each for the United States and Britain, 3 each for Japan, and 1.75 each for France and Italy. No limits were set for other types of ships. In 1922 Hughes also ended the long-standing U.S. occupation of the Dominican Republic.

Harding also appointed Andrew Mellon, one of the wealthiest people in the United States, to serve as secretary of the treasury. Mellon, who served through the Harding, Coolidge, and Hoover administrations, ensured that there was a close and comfortable relationship between government and business. He cut government spending, cut taxes, and retired half of the World War I debt while in office. He was often hailed as "the greatest secretary of the treasury ever" until the coming of the Great Depression raised serious questions about his policies. Herbert Hoover, perhaps the most liberal

Washington Conference
A conference called by the United States in 1921 that led to the adoption of the **Five Powers Treaty** in 1922 in an ultimately ineffective effort to limit the growth of the world's navies and thus preserve peace.

member of the cabinet, served as secretary of commerce for Harding and Coolidge, encouraging cooperation between businesses to stabilize industrial production and the economy.

Harding died suddenly in August 1923, probably the result of a heart attack. His wife's refusal to allow an autopsy led to rumors that he was poisoned or committed suicide, though there was never any evidence for either. His death came just as the Tea Pot Dome scandal was about to come to light. He was reported to have asked Herbert Hoover "what a President should do whose friends had betrayed him?" Harding was deeply mourned, but as the scandals of the Harding administration surfaced, his reputation was tarnished before the year was out.

Fortunately for the Republican Party, Harding's vice president, the stern and distant Calvin Coolidge, had no connection to the scandals and quickly took steps to investigate them. News of Harding's death reached the vice president while he was vacationing with his father in a rustic Vermont farmhouse. Since the house had no electricity, Colonel John Coolidge administered the presidential oath of office to his son by the light of a kerosene lamp—a reassuring image that perfectly fit the tone of austerity and adherence to old-time values that the new president wanted to set. More important to Coolidge's success, the economic downturn of 1921 had eased, and by 1923, many Americans were experiencing an economic boom, known as the "Coolidge prosperity." To no one's surprise, Coolidge, a man of so few words he came to be known as "silent Cal," was nominated for a full term by the Republican Party in the summer of 1924.

As this cartoon shows, the Tea Pot Dome scandal that came to light in 1923 soon after President Harding's death threatened to steamroll over many leaders of the Republican Party. However, the fact that the new Republican president, Calvin Coolidge, had nothing to do with it allowed party leaders to distance themselves from the scandal and, in the end, have an easy road to the White House in the November 1924 elections.

The Democratic Party was deeply divided between a southern and western wing that was primarily white, Protestant, rural, and supportive of Prohibition and a northern wing that, though also very white, included many Catholics and Jews, and was highly urban as well as strongly anti-Prohibition. The Klan was a force at the summer nominating convention where their opposition to a Catholic candidate who wanted to repeal Prohibition made itself felt. The two leading contenders for the nomination included former Treasury Secretary William G. McAdoo, a "dry" who favored Prohibition and was supported by the southern and western wing of the party, and New York Governor Al Smith, a Catholic and a "wet" staunch opponent of Prohibition. They battled for 103 ballots before the delegates turned to the West Virginia lawyer and former congressman John Davis in an exhausted compromise. Others, disgusted with both parties, rebuilt the old Progressive Party of 1912 and nominated Wisconsin's popular progressive Senator Robert La Follette for president.

Coolidge's victory in the 1924 elections was as decisive as Harding's had been in 1920. He won 54 percent of the total with only 28.8 percent for the Democrats and 16.6 percent for the La Follette Progressives. Except for Wisconsin, which went for La Follette, Coolidge carried every state outside of the then solidly Democratic South.

The Coolidge administration took some important steps in foreign policy. Just before he took office as Coolidge's vice president, Charles G. Dawes negotiated the so-called Dawes Plan to help ameliorate the German financial crisis brought on by the huge reparations payments to Britain and France. In 1925, Coolidge appointed Frank Kellogg as secretary of state. Two years later in 1927, French foreign minister Aristide Briand proposed a joint U.S.-French alliance, but Kellogg turned the conversation to a multilateral treaty. **The Kellogg-Briand Pact** outlawing war was signed in Paris in

The Kellogg-Briand Pact
1928 international treaty that denounced aggression and war but lacked provisions for enforcement.

August 1928, and eventually, 62 nations were signatories to the much acclaimed agreement. Unfortunately, unlike the plan for the League of Nations, there was no enforcement mechanism to the Kellogg-Briand Pact. While passive at home, U.S. government under Coolidge also enthusiastically encouraged engagement with Latin America, maintaining military force in some countries and doubling investment in others. After coming to office in 1929, Hoover tried to improve relations with Latin America, removing American troops from Nicaragua and Haiti. In addition, while not officially recognizing the government of the new Soviet Union, the Coolidge and Hoover administrations encouraged business investment and the Soviet government welcomed it, especially the mass-production of automobiles that they called "Fordism."

The 1928 presidential election that brought Hoover to office was very different and much closer than the previous two. The tone of the contest was angrier. When Calvin Coolidge announced that he would not seek another term as president, the Republicans nominated Hoover. The Democrats, tired of their losses in 1920 and 1924, decided that Al Smith's charisma and enthusiastic support in the North would make him a winner. After all, many asked, didn't the South vote for the Democratic nominee no matter who he was?

On many issues, Hoover and Smith were not far apart. Hoover was more liberal than Coolidge and privately worried that the Coolidge prosperity was a balloon that would surely pop. He said that he looked forward to the day when "poverty will be banished from this nation," though he saw business success, not government intervention, as the key to accomplishing that goal. Coolidge once called him "that damn Bolshevik." Smith was also a friend to big business. Once nominated, Smith chose John J. Raskob of General Motors to run his campaign and included several leading industrialists in his inner circle.

Nevertheless, there were two huge differences between the candidates. Hoover was a "dry" who favored continuing Prohibition, and Smith was a "wet" committed to ending it. Hoover called Prohibition "a great social and economic experiment, noble in motive and far-reaching in purpose." Smith told the convention that nominated him that "there should be fundamental changes in the present provisions for national prohibition." With many people becoming disillusioned with Prohibition, on that issue alone Smith might have had the edge.

However, another issue influenced the race. Hoover, a Quaker, was a Protestant. Smith was a Catholic. Many Catholic voters in places like Boston, New York, Chicago, and San Francisco rallied to Smith with an enthusiasm they had never shown for any previous presidential candidate. Meanwhile, in much of the nation's Protestant heartland, Smith's Catholicism was the heated issue of the campaign. The candidate himself thought he had addressed the issue, but as he campaigned in the Midwest and South, Smith could see burning crosses on the hillsides and his rallies were met by Klan members. At one rally in Oklahoma, Smith eyed the crowd and commented to a reporter, "I don't know those people out there. I don't speak their language." On election day in November 1928, Hoover won, carrying states in the South that had not voted Republican since the end of Reconstruction and even Smith's home state of New York. Smith won 40 percent of the vote and carried Massachusetts, Rhode Island, and parts of the South, but Hoover's 58 percent of the vote and 444 electoral votes guaranteed that he could enter the White House with a solid mandate. The stock market responded to Hoover's election by reaching greater heights than ever before. The new president kept his reservations about the stock market bubble to himself. The nation seemed confident in their new president, the economy, and the way society had been moving for the last 10 years. It would be Hoover's bad luck that none of this confidence would last through his first year in office.

21.4 **Quick Review** How were the elections of 1924 and 1928 similar? How were they different?

CONCLUSION

The 1920s marked a period of significant social and political change in the United States. This period, known by many as the "Jazz Age," began at the conclusion of World War I and ended with the stock market crash in 1929. For many Americans, especially those in the middle and upper classes, the 1920s were a time of prosperity. For other Americans, however, the 1920s were harsh.

In the so-called Red Summer of 1919, many working people in the United States were deeply dissatisfied with the terms and conditions of their employment. They wanted their salaries adjusted to reflect the inflation generated by the war, and they also wanted a share of the postwar boom. Strikes were common as were violent confrontations between wage earners and business elites, whose fear of bolshevism intensified their opposition to organized labor. Racial tensions also boiled over in that summer, and race riots took place in cities around the country.

In January 1920 when the Eighteenth Amendment to the Constitution outlawed the "manufacture, sale, or transportation" of any alcoholic beverage, the resulting era of Prohibition set off a wave of opposition. Bootleggers found ways to manufacture and sell alcohol in defiance of the Eighteenth Amendment, and average citizens found ways to drink alcohol as they flouted the law. The widespread prosperity and contempt for Prohibition also set the stage for other law breaking during the decade, including investment fraud and corruption in the federal government.

In this turbulent period, women gained the right to vote when the Nineteenth Amendment was passed. With their newly gained power, some younger women declared themselves to be "flappers," flouting social conventions, and many women began reforms around prenatal care and birth control as well as other issues relevant to them. The presidential election of November 1920 was the first election in which women in every state in the United States took part.

Technological innovations combined with favorable government policies toward business resulted in high corporate profits throughout the decade. The economic growth of 1920s sustained a new mass culture focused on materialism and consumerism and was characterized by the automobile, the radio, and the movies. Social and cultural change affected all Americans. African-Americans began the Great Migration, a movement of large numbers of Southern blacks from the rural South to the urban North, which continued from the 1920s to the 1960s. Newly arriving African-Americans in the North launched the Harlem Renaissance, a flowering of black culture in music, novels, and poetry, centered in New York City's Harlem while others became followers of Marcus Garvey.

For many other Americans, the 1920s were a difficult time. While sweeping changes of the 1920s were welcomed by many, a large portion of American society objected to what they saw as the erosion of traditional American values, leading to a resurgent Ku Klux Klan among other things. The black community faced brutal racism in both the North and the South. Race riots swept across the country from Chicago, Illinois, to Charleston, South Carolina, wherever blacks began to push for greater equality and economic opportunity. A nation built on immigration turned against immigrants, and 1924 legislation drastically reduced immigration to the United States. White farmers in the Midwest and South also suffered greatly as crop prices plummeted. The government largely ignored the plight of these Americans. Other Americans turned to a new kind of religious fundamentalism challenging such things as the teaching of evolution in the public schools.

Three Republican presidents—Warren G. Harding, Calvin Coolidge, and Herbert C. Hoover—presided over the nation during the 1920s and while they differed among themselves, all three supported the growth of a business-oriented culture and saw business success as the key to prosperity for all.

CHAPTER REVIEW Why is the 1920s a unique era in American history?

Chapter 21   Chapter Review

THE PRELUDE—THE RED SUMMER OF 1919

21.1 Explain how events at the end of World War I shaped the decade that followed.

Review Questions

1. **Cause and Effect**
   What factors contributed to the Red Summer of 1919?

2. **Contextualization**
   How did issues and tensions emerging from World War I create the anger and violence of 1919?

THE 1920s—THE EXUBERANCE OF PROSPERITY

21.2 Analyze how Prohibition and other developments of the 1920s reshaped American culture.

Review Questions

3. **Construct an Argument**
   Defend or refute the following statement: "If it were not for American participation in World War I, Prohibition would never have been enacted."

4. **Historical Interpretation**
   What light does the Teapot Dome scandal shed on the nature of Republican government in the 1920s?

5. **Comparison**
   Compare and contrast the domestic ideal of womanhood of the late 1800s with the "new woman" epitomized by the flappers of the 1920s. What was new about the "new woman"?

THE 1920s—THE CONFLICTS ABOUT AMERICAN IDEALS

21.3 Explain the elements of discrimination, hardship, and fundamentalism that also shaped American life in the 1920s.

Review Questions

6. **Comparison**
   Compare and contrast the Ku Klux Klan of the 1860s and 1870s with the Klan of the 1920s. How did the new Klan differ from the original Klan?

7. **Synthesis**
   How did anti-immigrant sentiment shape the culture of the 1920s?

HARDING, COOLIDGE, AND HOOVER—NATIONAL POLITICS AND POLICIES IN THE 1920s

21.4 Analyze the political and policy developments of the decade.

Review Questions

8. **Constructing an Argument**
   What accounts for the Republican dominance of national politics in the 1920s?

9. **Synthesis**
   What connections can you make between the election of 1928 and the general social and cultural trends of the 1920s?

Living in Hard Times

During the Great Depression, lines of unemployed impoverished workers seeking food and shelter could be seen in cities and towns across the United States.

I n late October 1929, the value of shares sold on the New York Stock Exchange, known as Wall Street, collapsed. Prices kept dropping for the next 3 years in a dizzying decline in which paper wealth simply evaporated. For most Americans, the stock market crash seemed irrelevant at first. For industrial workers, who rarely owned stock, the value of shares in the enterprises where they worked was not important, but the subsequent drop in industrial jobs as production of automobiles, radios, appliances, and clothing dried up was all too real. For many farmers in the Deep South and those trying to get by farming small mountainous farms in Appalachia, the Depression had come much earlier, beginning with the drop in agricultural prices in 1920 (see Chapter 21). For other farmers, especially those who had plowed the plains and created the wheat farms of Oklahoma and Kansas in the 1910s and 1920s, the full impact of the Depression came later. Wheat farmers struggled with the fact that a glut in the world supply of wheat kept prices low all through the 1920s, but it was with the terrible dust storms of the 1930s, storms in which the child of one farmer remembered, "you couldn't see your hand in front a' your face," that the full impact of the Depression was felt in this region. This chapter traces the story of the many causes that led to the long years of the Great Depression, and the impact of the Depression on the political climate in the United States and the world.

CHAPTER OBJECTIVE

Demonstrate an understanding of the causes and consequences of the Great Depression.

LEARNING OBJECTIVES

THE COMING OF THE GREAT DEPRESSION

Explain the coming of the Great Depression and the initial response to it.

22.1

THE NEW DEAL

Explain the goals and results of the New Deal and the responses to change on the part of diverse Americans.

22.2

THE DEEP ROOTS OF WAR—THE UNITED STATES, EUROPE, AND ASIA

Analyze the international impact of the Depression, German and Japanese military expansion, and the initial U.S. response.

22.3

THE COMING OF THE GREAT DEPRESSION

22.1 Explain the coming of the Great Depression and the initial response to it.

The Great Depression was a worldwide crisis. The crash of the American stock market was but one of many causes of the economic catastrophe. People lost their jobs in Japan. In Chile, mineral exports, the mainstay of its economy, collapsed, leading to joblessness, and the government, which lost tax income, could do little. In Germany, already suffering from a precarious economy, industries went bankrupt and millions of workers were laid off. Industrial production collapsed in Great Britain leading to hunger marches by the unemployed. Jobs disappeared in Canada. And in the United States, the combined impact of the stock market crash (which had an impact worldwide), the continuing farm depression, and the rapid decline in industrial production led to national paralysis.

The Great Crash: October 1929 and the Coming of the Great Depression

Speculative booms and busts had occurred regularly in economies (and continue even in modern times) as people allowed prices to rise far beyond value and then the inevitable crash in prices came. In the 1600s, Dutch investors were caught up in speculation in tulip bulbs, and in the 1720s, English investors lost fortunes in what came to be known as the Great South Sea Bubble. In the mid-1920s, many Americans began to buy Florida real estate that later became worthless.

The Great Crash of 1929 was a prime example of this phenomenon. The U.S. economy did well in the 1920s, and it would have been strange if the value of stocks had not gone up. Stocks, after all, are merely partial ownership in a company, so a share of stock purchased on the New York Stock Exchange for a company (U.S. Steel or General Electric, for example) is a share in the ownership of that company. If the company makes a sufficient profit, dividends are paid to shareholders. If a company increases in value, the value of each share increases. However, if a company does poorly, or a lot of people start to worry that a company *will* do poorly, shares will probably decrease in value. The stock market is—in theory—a place where people who want to sell a share of stock meet people who want to buy one and agree on a price; the price of the most recent sale of stock is then listed as the current value of the stock.

During the 1920s, stock prices generally rose, with some modest downturns between 1924 and 1928. Toward the end of 1928, especially after Herbert Hoover's election victory in November, the stock market started going up much faster. Many people—including president-elect Hoover, as he later wrote in his memoirs—were worried that the prices were showing all the hallmarks of a speculative boom. Still, people continued to buy stocks. The Radio Corporation of America, known on the stock market simply as "Radio," was a relatively new company that had never paid a dividend. Radio sold for $85 a share at the beginning of the year, and the price rose to $420 a share by the end of the year. (Stock prices are reported simply as whole numbers, so Radio sold for 85 and 420.) Other companies followed the same course: DuPont began the year at 310, ending at 525; department store giant Montgomery Ward began at 117, ending at 440. At the height of the market in September 1929, still without distributing a single dividend, Radio was selling for 505.

As people saw the chance to make money, they also borrowed money to buy stocks, a process called buying on margin. If a person could invest $85 in Radio and a year later have a stock worth $420, why not borrow enough to buy ten shares for $850 and fairly quickly reap $4,200? And brokers were more than happy to lend the money. Buyers were expected to use their own money for 25 percent to 50 percent of the value of a stock but could easily borrow the rest. Early in the 1920s, perhaps a billion dollars of loans were provided to cover stock purchases; by the end of 1928, those loans reached six billion dollars.

In the spring of 1929, the outgoing President Calvin Coolidge reported that the economy was "absolutely sound," and stocks were "cheap at current prices." The more cautious Hoover, who understood economics better than his predecessor, believed instead that the "growing tide of speculation" was not merely a problem but was, indeed, a "crime," yet worried that his saying so might cause a devastating loss in confidence. By September 1929, a respected economist Roger Babson warned, "Sooner or later a crash is coming and it may be terrific." Factories will shut down, he predicted, and "men will be thrown out of work." The speech precipitated a drop in stock prices, but the so-called "Babson Break" lasted only for 1 day. Most economists thought Babson was wrong.

Stock prices kept going up through the spring of 1929, and then in the summer they skyrocketed. From the beginning of June to the end of August, Westinghouse stock went from 151 to 286, General Electric from 268 to 391, and U.S. Steel from 165 to 258. At the sight of those kinds of profits, most investors simply forgot about the warnings.

The market reached its high point on the day after Labor Day in 1929. There was a small downturn in September and by October, everyone started to worry. Then in late October, speculation turned to panic as stock prices just kept falling. Tuesday, October 29, known as Black Tuesday, was the worst single day in the history of the stock exchange. Crowds formed all up and down Wall Street. Contrary to contemporary rumors and latter-day myths, there were no suicidal leaps from windows, though a few speculators did die by their own hand on that and the following days. Most quietly watched their life savings disappear as prices continued to fall.

In the months and years that followed, stock prices continued to fall. On November 11, the *New York Times Industrial Average* closed at 224; a drop by half from 452 from September. The worst possible news was followed by even worse news as prices kept falling through 1930, 1931, and 1932. By July 1932, the *New York Times* reported the Dow Jones Industrial Average as 58—a little more than a tenth of what it had been only 3 years earlier. Value, it seemed, had simply disappeared from American businesses.

The loans that had enabled many to buy stock "on margins" made things worse. When the value of a stock fell to the actual percentage the buyer had invested, 50 percent or 25 percent, the stock broker who had arranged the loan would notify the owner that he or she had to produce more money to pay off the loan or else the stock would be taken over by the broker and sold to recoup the loan. Since many investors had put all their savings into the stock market, they had no funds to cover such "calls" and were wiped out. Even if the market later rallied, they had no investment left. In addition, the brokers often were not able to sell the stock in time to protect the loan either, so brokers lost money, too.

The stock market crash was far from the only problem with the nation's economy in 1929. At the same time, basic underpinnings of the American economy, including banking, manufacturing, farming, and international trade, were also surprisingly fragile. When the economy came apart, it came apart thoroughly. A sizable number of Americans, perhaps as many as half—farmers, farm workers, and sharecroppers; American Indians living on reservations; factory workers; widows; and the elderly—had been living on the edge of poverty throughout the boom.

This picture reflects some of the chaos on New York's Wall Street on October 29, 1929, as stock values crashed and people saw their life's savings disappear.

In 1930, before even the initial impact of the Depression, 60 percent of American families had a total income of less than $2,000 per year, which was then considered the poverty line.

Between 1929 and 1932, farms across the country were foreclosed on—and more would have been had not armed groups of farmers banded together to prevent the sales. Factories, which had been overproducing, now closed and workers lost their jobs. One out of four people in the United States was out of work by 1932. Many were living in shanties, and others rode the rails as stowaways or waited in bread lines. In the winter of 1932–33, the nation's banking system started to collapse as banks that had also invested in stocks or offered mortgage loans on property that was now worthless failed, and state governors announced "bank holidays" in their states to stop further failures.

The Hoover Years, 1929–1933

Herbert Hoover had been president for only 7 months when the stock market crashed. Given his background, Hoover seemed the ideal president for a moment of crisis. As a trained engineer who had helped feed a starving Europe during World War I and served as Secretary of Commerce, he understood economics; moreover, he was far more flexible than Coolidge. As the economy worsened, Hoover called on people to engage in voluntary collective action—asking business leaders to keep wages and prices up, asking bankers to pool resources to help weaker banks, encouraging farmers to form cooperatives and keep excess crops off the market. He cut taxes and supported federal public works such as construction of dams, bridges, and hospitals to stimulate the economy. After 1932, he reluctantly agreed with a Democratic Congress to create the Reconstruction Finance Corporation to provide funds to keep banks and railroads from bankruptcy as well as the Emergency Relief and Construction Act to lend money to states for relief and public projects.

As the economy worsened, however, Hoover's call for voluntary solutions seemed weak. Farmers were reluctant to cut back on their crops if their neighbors would simply fill the gap. Bankers were too worried about staying solvent to bail out other banks. The Reconstruction Finance Corporation never invested enough to save all the banks that needed saving. Hoover tried but failed to negotiate a reduction in the reparations that were wrecking the German economy and thus undermining U.S. trade with Europe. Then in 1930, Congress passed the Smoot-Hawley Tariff, a disastrous move that was designed to protect American industries by raising the cost of imported goods, but resulted in a trade war as other nations also raised their tariffs in return, leading to a huge decrease in international trade with devastating results. Despite the dire circumstances, Hoover, though no orthodox conservative, could not bring himself to support further government intervention and debt.

Perhaps it was simply Hoover's bad luck to preside over the beginning of the Depression. People would have blamed him no matter what he did. When he tried to restore confidence by announcing that, "The fundamental business of the country, that is production and distribution of commodities, is on a sound and prosperous basis," things just kept getting worse and people lost confidence in him. When homeless families built communities of shacks, they called them **Hoovervilles**. When out-of-work veterans marched to Washington as the "**Bonus Army**" to demand a pension, he ordered the army to disperse them and people called him heartless. When he had lost his bid for reelection and tried to get the incoming administration to cooperate on a plan for the banking crisis in early 1933, Roosevelt ignored him. Hoover's was an unhappy presidency in an unhappy time.

In early 1932, U.S. Army troops and local police attacked the Bonus Marchers camp within sight of the U.S. Capitol Building. The attack on former soldiers who had come to Washington from all parts of the United States seeking pensions from Congress infuriated many and further undermined Hoover's reputation.

Hoovervilles
Shantytowns, sarcastically named after President Hoover, in which unemployed and homeless people lived in makeshift shacks, tents, and boxes. Hoovervilles cropped up in many cities in 1930 and 1931.

Bonus Army
A protest movement of World War I veterans in 1932 demanding early payment of service bonuses not due until 1945 to help them through the Great Depression and to provide a stimulus for the economy.

Quick Review How did the fragile economy of the 1920s combined with the stock market crash create a dire situation for the American people? What actions did the Hoover administration take to address the situation? What other actions could Hoover have taken?

THE NEW DEAL

22.2 Explain the goals and results of the New Deal and the responses to change on the part of diverse Americans.

In the desperate situation that the United States faced in 1932, probably the most desperate economic moment in American history, most thought that whoever won the 1932 Democratic nomination would win the election. After all, the crisis had occurred under the leadership of previous Republican presidents. Among the Democrats, Al Smith entered the race again along with Speaker of the House of Representatives John Nance Garner, former cabinet member Newton Baker, and New York Governor Franklin Delano Roosevelt. Roosevelt won the nomination on the fourth ballot and, breaking precedent, flew to the Democratic National Convention in Chicago to accept the nomination in person on July 2, 1932, where he promised a "**New Deal** for the American people," coining the phrase by which his administration would be known. He selected Garner to be his running mate and, promising "a New Deal for the American people" while offering very few specifics, defeated Hoover by a landslide in the November election, carrying 57 percent of the vote and 472 electoral votes.

New Deal
A term for the programs and legislation developed during Franklin Roosevelt's administration aimed at ending the Great Depression.

In the long months between the election in November and the inauguration on March 4, 1933, the U.S. economy kept getting worse. (The date of the inauguration was later changed by the 20th Amendment to the Constitution so that every president after Roosevelt was inaugurated on January 20 after a much shorter wait.) The number of unemployed workers and evicted farmers kept growing. In addition, the banking system, the heart of the nation's economic structure, faltered, and more banks closed.

Banks that had given loans to buy stocks now held worthless paper since the loans could never be repaid. Banks that had given loans to farmers now owned worthless farm land or were blocked from foreclosure by angry farmers. As more banks failed, people began to take their money out of the remaining banks. A "run on a bank," as a large number of withdrawals all at once was known, could put any bank out of business because no bank simply kept deposits in its vaults but, rather, invested the money. In 1930, 1,352 banks closed; in 1931, 2,294 more went out of business; and in 1932, another 1,453 failed. In November 1932, Nevada's governor proclaimed a "bank holiday," temporarily closing all banking before more banks got into trouble. Iowa followed in January, then Michigan, Maryland, Oklahoma, Indiana, Ohio, Arkansas, and Arizona in February. Sixteen more states closed banks at the beginning of March, and finally, on March 4, Illinois and New York—home to the nation's largest banks in Chicago and New York City—declared a bank holiday. On that day at noon, with most banks closed and most economic activity in the country at a standstill, Franklin Roosevelt was inaugurated to replace Herbert Hoover as president.

The Brain Trust and the First 100 Days

At his inauguration, the new president told the nation that it must not "shrink from honestly facing conditions in our country today." And he was blunt about what those conditions were, saying:

> Only a foolish optimist can deny the dark realities of the moment. Yet our distress comes from no failure of substance....Plenty is at our doorstep, but a generous use of it languishes in the very sight of the supply. Primarily this is because the rulers of the exchange of mankind's goods have failed, through their own stubbornness and their own incompetence, have admitted their failure, and abdicated.

But in that same address, he also insisted on his "firm belief that the only thing we have to fear is fear itself—nameless, unreasoning, unjustified terror which paralyzes needed efforts to convert retreat into advance." Given the nation's situation, many could think of quite a few things to fear, but Roosevelt made it clear that he was ready to act to address the crisis, and that alone gave people optimism—for a time.

22.1

fireside chats
Speeches broadcast nationally over the radio in which President Franklin Roosevelt explained complex issues and programs in plain language.

22.2

22.3

Roosevelt had a magnetic, optimistic personality. He used radio, still a new medium, to connect with the American people through frequent **fireside chats** and press conferences. Roosevelt had been paralyzed by polio in the early 1920s, but few Americans knew that he could not walk without help, and the media kept his secret. Radio carried the president's voice and kept his disability out of sight. Another well-kept secret was the deep strain in Roosevelt's marriage. While Franklin and Eleanor Roosevelt's personal life was often tense, as a public couple, they were extraordinary. The new first lady was often the eyes and ears of the administration, visiting desperate farmers and industrial workers, traveling down mine shafts to coal mines, speaking to audiences around the country, and bringing the nation's problems back to the White House. People responded to her on a personal level. Thousands of "Dear Mrs. Roosevelt" letters poured in to the White House. Together, Eleanor and Franklin Roosevelt projected hope to a nation that wanted desperately to believe.

The new president knew that although people were willing to give the new administration a chance, their patience was short. Banks could close for a few days, but if people could not get their money, pay their bills, keep their mortgages up to date, a worse crisis would follow. Roosevelt's economic team moved to reopen the banks. They ignored a proposal by Wisconsin Senator Robert La Follette, Jr., to nationalize the banks. Using a plan that had been drafted by officials in the outgoing Hoover administration, they convinced Congress to pass an Emergency Banking Act on March 9 that allowed those banks deemed safe to open, and permanently liquidated the weakest. After 1 week in office, President Roosevelt gave his first fireside chat, assuring people that "it is safer to keep your money in a reopened bank than it is to keep it under the mattress." The run on the banks stopped, and the newly federally approved banks remained solvent.

Three months later, Congress passed the Glass-Steagall Act that created the Federal Deposit Insurance Corporation to guarantee bank deposits. Given the role banks had played in the stock market speculation of 1928 and 1929, the Glass-Steagall Act also separated commercial banks and investment banks; the former could take deposits and make loans, with government guarantees, and the latter could invest in the stock market, at their own risk.

Early in 1932, while he was still a candidate for the presidency, Roosevelt (or FDR, as many called him) had created what he called his "Brain Trust." The original

American Voices

Letter to Eleanor Roosevelt, April 20, 1935

In her first year as the nation's First Lady, Eleanor Roosevelt received more than 300,000 letters, a large percentage of which were from young people asking for her help. Mrs. Roosevelt had become a personal symbol of caring for the Roosevelt administration, and people—particularly poor people and especially children—turned to her. From the thousands letters such as the one shown here, the needs of those who lived through the Great Depression, especially the young, also take on a human face.

Dear Mrs. Roosevelt,

    I am a thirteen year old girl and live on a farm with my mother and Step-Father we are very poor people I have lived here for five years and have wished each year for a radio but as the years go by our circumstances get worse and worse. I am wondering if I would be asking to much of you to help me obtain one. As we live in the country we wold have to have a Battery Radio. We live five miles from town, and we are poor and we have no money for boughten amusements. There is not a radio around in the country and I get terribly lonesome in summer...

    Sincerely yours, M.N.C.

Source: Robert Cohen, editor, *Dear Mrs. Roosevelt: Letters from Children of the Great Depression* (Chapel Hill, University of North Carolina Press, 2002), p. 183.

Thinking Critically

1. Contextualization

What does this letter tell you about the hopes and dreams of a 13-year-old child living in the midst of the Depression?

2. Historical Interpretation

Why would a child, or any American, turn to the First Lady for help? What does this decision tell you about Eleanor Roosevelt's public persona?

core group—Raymond Moley, a political scientist; Rexford Tugwell, an economist; and Adolf Berle, a legal financial expert, were all professors at Columbia University. Others joined or departed from the group. Although they argued with each other, the members of the Brain Trust all agreed that a lack of purchasing power was a key cause of the Depression and that a way had to be found to raise farm income and industrial wages so more Americans could buy more of what the nation could produce, thus putting more Americans back to work. They, like FDR, disliked what they called "the dole" and preferred jobs, any jobs, to welfare.

When Roosevelt came to office in 1933, the Brain Trust guided much of his policy. Some members of the official cabinet represented the older, more cautious Democratic Party establishment. However, others in the cabinet were closer to the Brain Trust, especially farm editor and inventor Henry Wallace, who became secretary of agriculture; Chicago reformer Harold Ickes, who became secretary of the interior; and Roosevelt's long-time New York State ally, Frances Perkins, who became secretary of labor and the first woman in a president's cabinet.

In what became known as the **first 100 days**, Congress passed a steady stream of new legislation. On March 13, Congress passed the Economy Act, giving the president broad powers to cut government spending. It also amended the Volstead Act to legalize beer while the country waited for the repeal of Prohibition. While the Economy Act cut federal costs—and did nothing to stimulate the economy— the amended Volstead Act not only allowed people to drink beer legally but also brought millions of dollars of new tax money into the treasury. Before the end of March, Congress established the Civilian Conservation Corps, probably the most popular New Deal agency, through which hundreds of thousands of unemployed young men worked in rural camps planting forests, pruning trees, building parks, and shoring up the nation's wild lands, thus giving many of the unemployed jobs and income to spur the economy. In April 1933, FDR, took the country off of the gold standard, replacing currency backed by gold with currency backed by the government's promise to pay. The change put badly needed money into circulation since the supply of dollars was no longer limited by the amount of gold in government or bank vaults.

In May, the president signed the Federal Emergency Relief Act that provided direct government grants to those without incomes (Hoover had provided loans). He also signed the Agricultural Adjustment Act that sought to shore up farm prices with a not-always-popular program to plow under 10.5 million acres of cotton and slaughter 6 million piglets. Many, including agriculture secretary Henry Wallace, were heartsick at the destruction of food in a nation with many hungry people, but one-third of the nation's workers were in agriculture, and the Brain Trust believed that raising farm prices by ending the surplus of agricultural products, and therefore raising the income and spending power of farmers, was the highest national priority. Before the end of May, Congress also created the Tennessee Valley Authority (TVA) to build dams on the Tennessee River that would control floods, bring electricity to rural areas that were without it, and provide jobs (see Map 22-1).

In June, in addition to the Glass-Steagall Act that regulated the banks, Congress passed the National Employment System Act, the Home Owners Refinance Act, the Farm Credit Act, the Railroad Coordination Act, and perhaps most significant, the National Industrial Recovery Act. The last act established two of the best known New Deal agencies, the Public Works Administration (PWA)—committed to large-scale construction projects across the country—and the National Recovery Administration (NRA) with a mandate to create a voluntary national network of businesses to maintain wages and prices. In 100 days, the United States had a quite different federal government than it had ever seen before. The National Recovery Administration set minimum wages and prices, outlawed child labor, and guaranteed labor the right to organize. The NRA was later declared unconstitutional, but from 1933 to 1935, the NRA, with its "We Do Our Part" signs in store windows across the nation, was a prime symbol of the New Deal.

The Civilian Conservation Corps was a very popular New Deal program that eventually put hundreds of thousands of young men to work—and gave them and their families an income—as they planted trees and built outdoor facilities around the country.

first 100 days

The first 100 days of the Roosevelt administration, beginning with his inauguration on March 4, 1933, in which the Democratic Congress passed several important pieces of legislation designed to put Americans back to work and undercut the effect of the Great Depression.

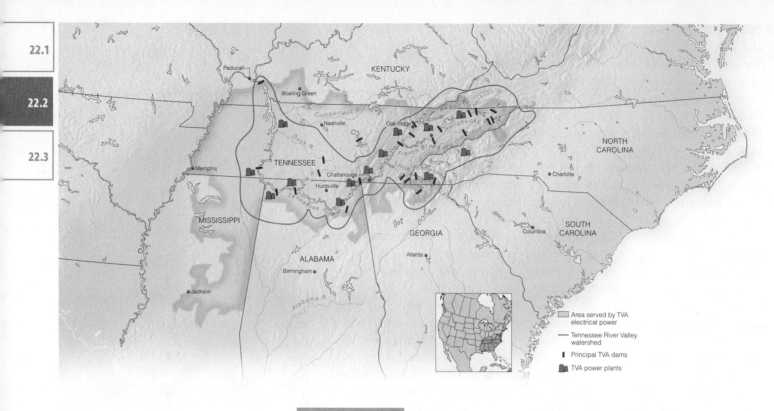

MAP 22-1 The Range of the TVA. The TVA, or Tennessee Valley Authority, built dams that controlled flooding and brought electric power to thousands of Americans living in one of the most poverty stricken parts of the nation along the length of the Tennessee River.

The Indian New Deal

The New Deal was a time of extraordinary change for many Americans, including American Indians. Like other New Deal initiatives, the changes began during the Hoover years. In 1928, Lewis Meriam led a study of federal Indian policy. Meriam's team conducted the first large-scale examination of the impact of the 1887 Dawes Act (see Chapter 16).

In his report, *The Problem of Indian Administration*, Miriam was blunt, writing, "The work of the government directed toward the education and advancement of the Indian…is largely ineffective," and, "The provisions for the care of the Indian children in boarding schools are grossly inadequate." Meriam called for moving the education of Indian children to their home and tribal context, which was done.

Roosevelt appointed social worker John Collier as commissioner of Indian Affairs. Collier came to office determined to right some of the wrongs that had been done, and by June 1934 he had convinced Congress to pass the Wheeler-Howard Act, also known as the Indian Reorganization Act. Two years later, in 1936, Congress extended the same rights to native Alaskans. This law was the beginning of what came to be known as the **Indian New Deal**. Under the Indian Reorganization Act, the government recognized the legal rights of Indian tribes (not done since 1887), including tribal right to hold reservation lands. Tribes adopted constitutions and formed governments. Tribes, not the federal government, were given the right to decide on tribal membership—not an easy issue after generations of relationships between whites and Indians. For most tribes, the Indian New Deal was a fresh start.

Indian New Deal

A series of policy changes, including the Indian Reorganization Act of 1934 that transformed government Indian policy and strengthened Indian tribal government of the reservations.

TABLE 22-1 Major New Deal Laws and Agencies

Agency/Law	Year Launched or Passed	Purpose	What Happened?
Emergency Banking Act	1933*	Initial action to save the nation's banking system	Replaced later the same year by Glass-Steagall Act
FDIC—Federal Deposit Insurance Corporation, created by Glass-Steagall Act	1933*	FDIC—to guarantee bank deposits, restore consumer confidence in banks Glass Steagall Act—to separate commercial and investment banking; banks with guaranteed deposits could not speculate in stock market	FDIC still operating, guaranteeing bank deposits Glass-Steagall separation of commercial and investment banking repealed in 1999
AAA—Agricultural Adjustment Administration	1933*	Subsidize farmers to restrict production and boost farm prices	Declared unconstitutional in 1936; replaced with farm subsidies in 1938 that still continue
Home Owners Loan Corporation and Farm Credit Administration	1933*	Provide home and farm loans to refinance mortgages	Temporary emergency measures
TVA—Tennessee Valley Authority	1933*	Build dams to stop flooding and generate electricity	Still operating
FERA—Federal Emergency Relief Administration	1933*	Provide funds for state and local relief agencies	Temporary emergency measure
NRA—National Recovery Administration	1933*	Protect prices, wages, and employment with codes for business (a major New Deal agency)	Declared unconstitutional in 1935
PWA—Public Works Administration (authorized by the NRA)	1933*	Stimulate economy by building schools, hospitals, dams, etc.	Continued until 1943 when replaced by wartime construction
CCC—Civilian Conservation Corps	1933*	Employ young men to plant forests, build roads, etc.	Continued until 1943, employing 2.5 million men, when wartime jobs eliminated unemployment
SEC—Securities and Exchange Commission	1934	Regulate the stock market	Still operating
Indian Reorganization Act	1934	Launch Indian New Deal	Much still in force
FHA—Federal Housing Administration	1934	Provide home loans	Still operating
WPA—Works Progress Administration	1935	Provide large-scale construction jobs building schools, parks, post offices	Continued until 1943 when replaced by wartime construction
Social Security Administration	1935	Support retirement pensions through payroll tax	Still operating
National Labor Relations Board created by Wagner Act	1935	Provide new rights for union organizing and free union elections	Partially repealed by Taft Hartley Act in 1947
NYA—National Youth Administration	1935	Provide jobs and support to students (officially part of the WPA)	Closed in 1943; federal work study component still operating
Fair Labor Standards Act	1938	Ensure minimum wage and maximum hours	Still operating with wage raises from time to time

* Indicates a program enacted during the first 100 days of Roosevelt's administration.

African-Americans, the Depression, and FDR's "Black Cabinet"

The Great Depression hit African-Americans especially hard. Many who had moved to northern cities were still on the bottom of the economic ladder and were often among the first to lose their jobs. As business failed and the need for goods and services declined, African-American jobs declined precipitously. In 1934, a government survey estimated that 17 percent of whites but 38 percent of blacks were out of work.

Most New Deal agencies were designed to help both blacks and whites, but in some cases, discrimination was built into the policies, and in other cases, policies that should have been fair were implemented by people who were not. The NRA, which set minimum wages for jobs, set low minimum salaries in laundry services, tobacco production,

Mary McLeod Bethune was a leader in FDR's Black Cabinet and, through her friendship with Eleanor Roosevelt, an influential voice across the administration, but she was also an influential educator and organizer in her own right.

Black Cabinet

An informal network of high-level African-American officials and advisors to the Roosevelt administration who worked together to influence government policy.

and other fields where there were large numbers of black workers. Agricultural Adjustment Administration payments often helped landlords but were not passed on, as they should have been, to help tenant farmers or sharecroppers. In the Civilian Conservation Corps, which provided jobs for unemployed young people—originally only males—some 200,000 African-American boys and young men did get jobs and work experience, but the CCC maintained rigidly segregated camps. The federal Home Owners Loan Corporation was designed to give loans to blacks and whites, but local officials of the Federal Housing Authority often decided that blacks were a poor risk and so denied loans to them.

Nevertheless, many African-Americans made significant gains during the Great Depression. Recognizing that AAA payments were being withheld, African-American sharecroppers organized the Southern Tenant Farmers Union to demand payments. African-American voters began to shift political allegiance from the "Party of Lincoln" to the Democratic Party because they were attracted to Roosevelt's New Deal Policies and especially Eleanor Roosevelt's active support as she visited black communities, advocated for black civil rights, and courted African-American voters. Blacks began to win elections to state legislatures. In 1928, Chicago's Oscar DePriest was elected to the U.S. Congress, the first black since Reconstruction. Black votes helped defeat candidates who opposed antilynching bills.

Early in his administration, Roosevelt created what came to be known as the **Black Cabinet**, a shifting and informal group. Roosevelt's (white) Secretary of the Interior Harold L. Ickes, former president of the Chicago branch of the NAACP, and Eleanor Roosevelt enlarged the size and power of the Black Cabinet. Robert L. Vann, editor of the *Pittsburgh Courier,* served as special assistant to the attorney general, and William H. Hastie, dean of the Law School at Howard University, served as a legal advisor to the Department of the Interior. Robert C. Weaver (who in the 1960s would be the first African-American in the cabinet) advised the Department of the Interior.

Perhaps the most prominent member of the Black Cabinet was Mary McLeod Bethune. Bethune was head of a school for girls in Daytona, Florida, that would become Bethune-Cookman College. During the 1920s, Bethune became president of the National Association of Colored Women, which advocated for a federal antilynching bill and for support for black women in attending training programs and college. Frustrated by what she saw as the conservatism of the NACW, she launched the more aggressive National Council of Negro Women in 1935.

At Eleanor Roosevelt's urging, Bethune was appointed as the director of the Negro Division of the National Youth Administration (NYA), where she channeled some of the NYA's considerable resources toward creating jobs for African-American youth. Bethune used her position and her friendship with Eleanor Roosevelt to organize a Federal Council of Negro Affairs to ensure that blacks in and out of the administration spoke with one voice. When Secretary of War Henry L. Stimson called a conference on women and the war effort in 1941, and failed to invite black women, she wrote to him, "We are not humiliated. We are incensed." Bethune was not going to be ignored.

The Dust Bowl and the "Okie" Experience

Unlike the many farmers who faced troubles in the 1920s, wheat farmers of Oklahoma, Kansas, and the Texas panhandle often prospered during that decade because even when the price of wheat fell they could always plow more land and plant more wheat. As the Depression worsened, however, the Plains farmers faced a unique crisis.

Eventually the ever-expanding production of wheat caught up with the farmers. The wheat harvest in the fall of 1931 was the most bountiful in history. Farmers had been planting more land, and it was exceedingly fertile. The result was that far more wheat was produced that fall than could possibly be consumed. Europe, like the United States, was in a depression. Wheat exports and wheat consumption were down. The price paid for wheat fell so low in 1931 that farmers lost money on every bushel produced. Many vowed not to plant in 1932, and probably a third of the Great Plains farmers faced foreclosures for debt or back taxes.

Then a different disaster struck. Starting late in 1932 and continuing in 1933, 1934, and 1935, farms across the Great Plains simply blew away. Year after year, the dust storms continued, but the worst storm came on Sunday April 14, 1935, known to those who lived through it as Black Sunday. The day began sunny and windless. Then in the afternoon, the wind picked up, and what looked like a purple or black wall started blowing in from the northwest. Jeanne Clark remembered that she had been outside playing when she heard a panicked call from her mother to come inside. Before she could get to the house, the storm hit. "It was like I was caught in a whirlpool," Clark said. "All of a sudden it got completely dark. I couldn't see a thing." That one storm took 300,000 tons of soil from the Great Plains and deposited it hundreds of miles away—twice as much soil as had been dug out of the Panama Canal. Clark remembered the terrible coughing that followed. A doctor said she had "dust pneumonia" and might not survive. Clark did survive, but others, mostly children and old people, died from the dust storms. Before the end of the 1930s, more than 250,000 people—two-thirds of the Plains population—simply left what had become known as the "Dust Bowl" (see Map 22-2).

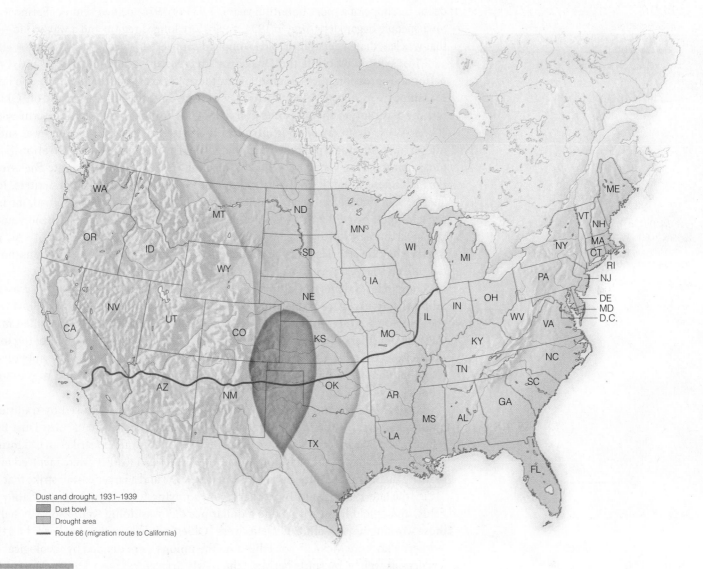

Dust and drought, 1931–1939

▨ Dust bowl

▨ Drought area

— Route 66 (migration route to California)

MAP 22-2 The Dust Bowl. Overplanting and plowing of soil with too little water led to massive dust storms that destroyed agricultural communities in states from Texas to North Dakota. Route 66, the highway from Chicago to Los Angeles, became the route by which many Dust Bowl refugees sought a new life in California agriculture.

After 1910, scores of white settlers with high hopes had come to the Great Plains and built farms in the "last frontier," encouraged by the government. Since the land was so dry, the government also doubled the homestead allotment to 320 acres. The weather could be terribly hot in the summer and cold in the winter, but the soil was rich. A few old-timers and ranchers said, "God didn't create this land around here to be plowed up." But farmers plowed and grew crops on land that had previously grown only grass.

In the 1930s, however, there was a prolonged drought, and the wells had to be dug deeper to find any water. The soil started to dry up, and then the wind, which always blows hard on the Plains, started to carry the soil away. Cattle suffocated from the dust. People rubbed Vaseline in their nostrils to protect them, and the Red Cross gave out respirator masks at school. People stuffed wet towels and sheets into cracks in doors or windows only to see their houses filled with dust anyway.

As the New Deal administration began to grapple with the Dust Bowl crisis, agricultural agents arrived in the region in 1934 offering up to $16 a head for the remaining cattle, which were either shot on the spot or shipped to a slaughterhouse in Amarillo, Texas. The government offered payments averaging $498 for a promise not to raise a wheat crop the following year. The CCC tried to build demonstration projects to reclaim the land. The reclamation projects did not work. The $498 paid off old debts, but hope of a more bountiful year in 1935 or 1936 seemed remote. Farmers and townspeople began departing in 1934, and before long, a region and a way of life—one that was less than a generation old—simply disappeared.

Most people who left the Dust Bowl moved to California. In the midst of a national Depression, they became migrant farm workers—hired hands on the farms of California's Central Valley where they were given the derogatory name of "Okies," (on the assumption that they were all from Oklahoma). For many Californians the "Okies" were desperately poor intruders in a state whose own economy was suffering terribly. Photographers working for the Farm Security Administration (FSA) took their pictures; Carey McWilliams, a young California lawyer, wrote *Factories in the Fields* describing their plight; and one of the country's best known writers, John Steinbeck, immortalized their experience in *The Grapes of Wrath*. Tom Joad, the hero of Steinbeck's novel defined what it meant to be an Okie: "Okie use' to mean you was from Oklahoma. Now it…means you're scum. Don't' mean nothing itself, it's the way they say it." Nevertheless, for the characters in Steinbeck's novel and for thousands of real-life migrants, it was also a term of pride and of grim determination.

Longtime residents of California's Central Valley feared the Okies. Mexican and Filipino agricultural workers worried, for good reason, that white Dust Bowl refugees would take their jobs. A preference for those who were native-born led many California farmers to give jobs to whites during the Great Depression, leaving longtime employees without work. Moreover, the California growers, a powerful political bloc, were happy to have more competition for jobs in the fields and to pit ethnic groups against one another other.

Mexican American and Filipino farm workers, too often ignored by traditional unions, had created their own unions. In 1933, before the arrival of most Dust Bowl refugees, 47,500 agricultural workers were involved in 37 different strikes in California's rich Central Valley. Some 5,000 mostly Mexican American workers were involved in the partially successful El Monte berry strike in June 1933 and a larger cotton strike that fall.

By the late 1930s, up to 10 workers were applying for every job in the California fields, and a field hand who made a dollar per day was doing well. Probably half of those working in the California fields were "Okies" while the other half were longtime workers who were Mexicans or Filipinos. The unions were divided by ideological differences as well as by splits between the newly arrived refugees and those who had been in the fields for a generation.

Despite the efforts of California farm workers to build unions in the field, few strikes were very successful. California agribusiness was strong and got stronger during the 1930s. The Associated Farmers of California that was founded in 1934 had resources and power far beyond anything available to the California farm workers.

Whatever one's race, working in the field was terribly hard work. Dust Bowl refugees who had owned their own farms and had viewed the future with optimism, who had bought a piano for their living room and a new Model T Ford for the family, now lived in government camps if they were lucky, and under bridges if they were not, and followed the crops from one farm to another. Most of the Dust Bowl refugees survived on the margins of society until the new industrial jobs created by World War II ended the Depression for them.

The Works Progress Administration and the Artists' New Deal

In April 1935, Congress created the Works Progress Administration (WPA) to institutionalize and expand the New Deal. Roosevelt appointed Harry Hopkins, a former settlement house worker and one of FDR's closest advisors, to lead it. The WPA's role was to move people from emergency relief ("the dole," as the president called it) to temporary, government-supported jobs and to make the government the employer of last resort. Under Hopkins's leadership, the WPA provided government-funded jobs for 8.5 million Americans at a cost of $11 billion between 1935 and 1942. WPA workers built roads, theaters, public buildings, and in some cases planned communities in every state of the Union as well as planted forests, laid out new parks, and changed the face of the countryside. Providing WPA jobs also provided opportunities for Roosevelt's political allies—usually Democrats, but in some cases, such as New York City's liberal Republican Mayor Fiorello La Guardia, also Republicans—to win political favors by handing out the coveted jobs to political supporters.

At the urging of Eleanor Roosevelt, Hopkins included jobs for artists in the WPA. In response to one critic of the artists' program, Hopkins said, "Hell, they've got to eat just like other people." In 1935 and 1936, WPA artists painted murals in post offices; provided music through symphony orchestras, jazz groups, Appalachian banjo pickers, and Texas fiddlers; staged theater productions of everything from Shakespeare to new cutting-edge works; wrote guidebooks to every part of the United States; and recorded the oral histories of former slaves, among many other projects. Besides ensuring that many artists were able to eat and practice their craft, the WPA art programs left a lasting cultural legacy, though not one without criticism.

Other federal agencies also hired artists. Rexford Tugwell, one of the most influential members of the Brain Trust, charged the Farm Security Administration with creating a "Pictorial Sourcebook of American Agricultural History." Between 1935 and 1939, a team of photographers, including several who later became famous for their work—Dorothea Lange, Walker Evans, and Ben Shahn—roamed the country creating a picture of often-hidden rural poverty.

Organized Labor, the Committee for Industrial Organization, and the Factory Floor

Many labor union leaders were not sure they trusted Roosevelt and the New Deal in the early years. However, although the primary purpose of the National Industrial Recovery Act of June 1933 was to stabilize prices, at Roosevelt's insistence, it also included a clause protecting collective bargaining through unions. The National Labor Relations Act of 1935 (the Wagner Act) sponsored by New York Senator Robert Wagner, expanded the rights of union members, outlawing "unfair labor practices" as well as giving workers the right to join a union without getting fired, rights to collective bargaining, and the right to strike. For the next decade, unions could be relatively sure that the federal government would not intervene in a strike on the side of management, as it had done repeatedly in the past. The Wagner Act did not create any unions, but it did provide a new context; labor organizers took the next steps on their own.

In 1935, when the Wagner Act was passed, only about 10 percent of American workers were union members, mostly in the skilled craft unions of the American Federation of Labor (A.F. of L.). Within the A.F. of L. some of its leaders, John L. Lewis of the United Mine Workers of America, Sidney Hillman of the Amalgamated Clothing Workers, and David Dubinsky of the International Ladies' Garment Workers Union, pushed the A.F. of L. to organize the unorganized. Lewis and his colleagues wanted industrial unions that would organize a union of all the workers in an industry such as steel or automobiles or textiles, as opposed to the craft unions that focused on a single trade—carpenters, plumbers, or electricians. But the leadership of the A.F. of L. would have none of it. They meant to protect their current members.

Lewis, Hillman, and Dubinsky created a Committee for Industrial Organization within the A.F. of L. When other union leaders within the A.F. of L. continued to resist their efforts, the Committee for Industrial Organization became the **Congress of Industrial Organizations** (CIO), a separate union and a competitor to the A.F. of L.

Congress of Industrial Organizations (CIO)
A new labor union that sought to organize industrial workers by industry, such as all automobile workers.

John L. Lewis, founding president of the CIO, could be tough, arbitrary, arrogant, and self-absorbed. He also was able to speak to workers as no one since Eugene Debs and Mother Jones. Lewis believed that by the 1930s a "mighty surge of human sentiment" was about to change industrial America.

Sometimes the "mighty surge" got ahead of those who were trying to lead it. Across the country, workers, even many who had not yet joined a union, launched a new kind of strike—the sit-down strike. Instead of walking off the job and onto the picket lines, CIO-inspired workers simply stopped work and sat down where they were. In doing so, they guaranteed that they could not be replaced by nonunion workers, and they were hard to attack without harming the machinery they were guarding. They were also much more comfortable inside the plant than outside. It turned out to be a brilliant tactic.

One of the first sit-down strikes took place in Akron, Ohio, at the Firestone Tire Plant on January 29, 1936. After the workers sat down where they were and the noise of the assembly line stopped, one worker said of the silence, "It's like the end of the world." The Firestone workers stayed where they were for 3 days and won.

The CIO reported a surge of telephone calls, "We've sat down! Send someone over to organize us!" From September 1936, through the following spring, 485,000 workers engaged in sit-down strikes. The CIO grew to 2 million members in 6 months.

For most assembly line workers fortunate enough to have jobs in the 1930s, the primary complaint was not salary. As one Chevrolet worker told a NRA investigator in 1934, "Of course, we make enough to live on while we are working, but we don't work enough time." Workers on assembly lines also complained about constant speedups on the assembly lines. In an assembly-line industry, the pace of the line ruled everything. At Flint's Fisher Body plant, a worker said, "I ain't got no kick on wages, but I just don't like to be drove."

On December 30, 1936, workers in two General Motors units in Flint, Michigan, stopped the line and sat down where they were. The Flint Sit-Down Strike had begun. By January 4, 1937, workers were sitting in at GM plants in Cleveland, Ohio; Atlanta, Georgia; Anderson, Indiana; Norwood, Ohio; and Kansas City, Missouri. It was the beginning of a long, cold winter.

On January 11, the GM management turned the heat off even though it was 16 degrees outside. Police blocked a delivery of food. A group of about 30 strikers went to the main gate and broke through a police lock to get to supporters outside. The company called the Flint police, who fired tear gas. Strikers responded by throwing door hinges, bottles, and stones at the police. The United Auto

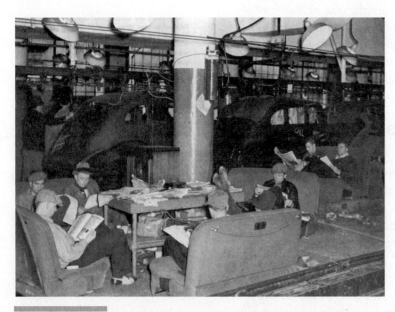

Striking workers at a General Motors factory in Flint, Michigan, sit on car seats in front of unfinished automobiles. The sit-down strike created a new form of labor union organizing.

Workers union (UAW) called it "the Battle of the Running Bulls." The wind blew the tear gas back on the police. The gas and the continuing hail of missiles from the plant infuriated them, and they began shooting at strikers and picketers. Amazingly, no one was killed. The young wife of one striker, Genora Johnson, who was herself on the picket line, remembered, "I did not know fear. I knew only surprise, anguish, and anger."

Everyone—strikers and GM management—wondered about the ability of the strikers to continue. Most of those engaged in the sit-in were not yet union members, and few of them had ever been involved in a strike before, much less a protracted sit-in. But one remembered, "It was like war. The guys with me became my buddies."

Negotiations began in mid-January and on February 11 a settlement was reached. General Motors recognized the UAW's right to represent its members, something the company had sworn never to do. It promised to negotiate in good faith on future contracts and that there would be no punishment of workers because of the sit-down. The union ended the strike. The *United Automobile Workers Journal* said of the settlement, "The greatest strike in American history has been victoriously concluded." One striker said it more modestly, "Even if we got not one damn thing out of it other than that, we at least had a right to open our mouths without fear."

Opponents of the New Deal

Not everyone celebrated the union's victory over General Motors or other results of the New Deal. In July 1934, the du Pont brothers, Pierre, Irénée, and Lammot, invited a number of business and political leaders, including the 1928 Democratic nominee Al Smith, to New York to discuss "the dangers to investors" in the New Deal. The du Ponts, who also owned a major share of General Motors, had many reasons to dislike the Roosevelt administration. They and their guests created the **American Liberty League** to oppose the New Deal.

Irénée du Pont said that the family had "followed the President in the belief that he was sincere," but thought that "the so-called New Deal" was nothing more or less than the socialistic doctrine. Al Smith, once Roosevelt's mentor, told those at a Liberty League dinner that he would probably "take a walk" (not participate) during the next presidential election and accused Roosevelt of handing the government over to dreamy professors and bleeding-heart social workers. A league publication said that the New Deal stirred up the "dragon teeth of class warfare." Other members of the American Liberty League included John J. Raskob, a former Democratic Party chair, who had been an executive at General Motors and the DuPont corporation; John W. Davis, the 1924 Democratic presidential nominee; Alfred P. Sloan of General Motors; and Sewell Avery of Montgomery Ward. (Herbert Hoover declined to join, derogatorily calling the League the "Wall Street model of human liberty.")

The National Association of Manufacturers also became a tough opponent of the New Deal. The association was created before 1900 to coordinate business opposition to labor unions. With the advent of the New Deal, leaders of the organization sought to "serve the purposes of business salvation," and by 1937, were spending $1.5 million a year on radio programs, motion pictures, bill boards, direct mail, and speakers, attacking the New Deal.

While conservative critics of the New Deal said that it was driving the country toward socialism, Roosevelt worried much more about other critics; those who thought the New Deal was not socialistic enough. The Communist Party was always unhappy with Roosevelt. Communists dismissed the New Deal as mere "bourgeois democracy." Communists created unemployment councils, led rent strikes, and defended union members and civil rights workers. Although the party was small, it was not without influence in the 1930s.

Many noncommunists also wanted to push the country further than Roosevelt wanted to go. Socialists, who were the heirs of Eugene V. Debs Socialist Party, as well as many Midwestern progressives who had supported Theodore Roosevelt in 1912

American Liberty League
Launched in 1934, the group was one of the largest and most well funded of several organizations opposed to the New Deal, which it considered socialistic.

and Wisconsin Senator Robert La Follette's bid for president in 1924, talked of a third-party challenge in 1936.

A 66-year-old Californian, Dr. Francis Townsend, proposed a federal pension of $200 per month to any person over 60 years old who would retire from work, leaving a job open for someone younger. The idea spread like wildfire. A number of candidates were elected to Congress in 1934 with Townsend's support. In addition, there were some 5,000 Townsend Clubs around the country, and 25 million people signed Townsend petitions to Congress.

While Townsend's ideas were gaining political traction, the muckraking author Upton Sinclair announced that he would seek the Democratic nomination for governor of California in 1934 based on a pledge to "End Poverty in California" (EPIC). Like the Townsend movement, the EPIC campaign took off among voters who were impatient with the New Deal. Sinclair won the nomination, received widespread support—though not from Roosevelt, who saw EPIC as an effort to confiscate private property—and helped shape the national dialogue, even though he lost the election.

More influential than Townsend or Sinclair, the "radio priest" Charles Coughlin inspired some and frightened others in the early 1930s. Coughlin had been appointed pastor of a small Catholic parish in the working class Detroit suburb of Royal Oak in 1926. Catholic auto workers formed the core of his congregation. Coughlin arranged for the local radio station to broadcast his Sunday sermons, and in 1930, their popularity led to a contract with the Columbia Broadcasting System to carry him nationally (and led the anti-Catholic Klan to burn a cross on his lawn). As the Depression worsened, Coughlin's sermons became more political. He relentlessly attacked Hoover and the nation's bankers, and he described himself as the voice of "the little people, the average man [who] was suffering." Given the size of his radio audience, Roosevelt was delighted that Coughlin supported his 1932 campaign.

After the election, the two met at the White House, but Coughlin later turned on the New Deal. He accused FDR of having "out-Hoovered Hoover" and talked of organizing his own political party. His sermons took on an increasingly anti-Semitic and isolationist tone, and some thought he was starting to sound like the new German Chancellor Adolph Hitler.

In Roosevelt's mind, however, the greatest challenge came from Louisiana's charismatic Senator Huey P. Long. Long was a product of the pine woods region of Louisiana where poverty, the Baptist church, and political independence flourished. Long's forbearers had supported the Union cause during the Civil War and Eugene V. Debs during the early 1900s. In 1928, as Al Smith was going down to defeat, Long was elected governor of Louisiana after a campaign attacking big corporations, especially Standard Oil. Long's grass-roots populism led him to attack the rich and promise opportunity for the poor. "Every man a king, but no one wears a crown," was his campaign slogan. He raised taxes on oil and gas production, built new highways, schools, and hospitals, provided free textbooks, and grew very popular and very powerful. Some said that Louisiana under Long was a virtual dictatorship. He was elected to the U.S. Senate in 1930. In Washington, he showed disdain for Democrats as well as Republicans, called the president "Frank," much to FDR's displeasure, and said that all he cared about was "what the boys at the forks of the creek think of me." There were a lot of boys and girls at the forks of a lot of creeks who thought a lot of Long. FDR considered him a dangerous demagogue.

In 1934, Long launched what he called the Share Our Wealth Society. Long promised a one-time grant of $5,000 per family and a guaranteed income of $2,500 (twice the 1934 national average) as well as educational subsidies for the young and pensions for the elderly (specifically designed to attract Townsend support) all to be paid for by seizing the wealth of the few. When people said his numbers did not add up, that there was not enough wealth to seize even if people wanted to, Long responded that his followers needed to "be prepared for the slurs and snickers of some high ups." But, he insisted, "Let no one tell you that it is difficult to redistribute the wealth of this land. It is simple."

While the Communists and Socialists did not cause Roosevelt to worry, Townsend, Coughlin, and Long did. The president worried about a dictatorship emerging in the United States, just as dictatorships had emerged as a result of the Depression in Italy and Germany. Democratic Chairman James Farley commissioned a poll that showed that a third-party ticket led by Long could lead to Roosevelt's defeat in 1936 and perhaps even a Long victory, if not in 1936 then by 1940. There was plenty to worry about. "Long plans to be a candidate of the Hitler type for the presidency in 1936," Roosevelt said. The president reshaped his political agenda to take control of the national dialogue.

The Continuing Depression and the Expanding New Deal, 1935–1939

During Roosevelt's first 100 days, indeed his first 2 years, the New Deal consisted of a series of experiments, some contradictory, some well thought out, but all designed to stem the worst of the Depression and begin a new course—to keep people from starving, to put them back to work, to get more money into circulation. In 1935 there was a shift in focus; some called it the "Second New Deal." It was not a radical change, but it did involve greater attention to long-term financial security for more Americans.

Before accepting the job as FDR's secretary of labor, Frances Perkins had insisted that the president promise to back pensions for the aging and unemployment insurance. In an early meeting, Roosevelt told Perkins, "I will authorize you to try, and if you succeed, that's fine." It was all the authorization she needed. Perkins had witnessed the tragic Triangle Shirtwaist Fire in New York in 1911 and had led the investigation that followed and helped craft some of the health and safety legislation that emerged from it. The growth and popularity of the Townsend movement gave Perkins more political clout than she might otherwise have had. If a plan could be devised that was financially viable (unlike the Townsend plan), then 1934 and 1935 was the time to get it passed.

Roosevelt worried about amassing too much power in the federal government. He insisted that the states play the lead role in unemployment insurance though he was willing to have a federal role. But he was adamant, "All the power shouldn't be in the hands of the federal government. Look—just think what would happen if all the power was concentrated here, and Huey Long became president!" Treasury Secretary Henry Morgenthau was determined that any plan be fiscally viable. But many in the administration thought Townsend had a point: the country did need to encourage older Americans to retire and leave their jobs to younger people. And Perkins was determined to get a bill through Congress.

Franklin Roosevelt signed the Social Security Act in 1935, one of the most long-lasting New Deal initiatives. Frances Perkins, the secretary of labor and its prime architect, stood behind him.

Social Security Act
Legislation that established a system of federal old-age pensions in effect to the present day.

On January 17, 1935, FDR announced plans for a Social Security program that would protect some 26 million citizens with "security against the hazards and vicissitudes of life." The proposed bill included a federal tax on employees and employers to fund the retirement system, a federal tax to help support a state-administered unemployment insurance system, and emergency grants to fund the immediate relief of the indigent elderly, Aid to Dependent Children, and modest support for public health. Since the Constitution clearly gave the government the right to tax, there was no room for a constitutional challenge to the legislation. Congress passed the Social Security Act 7 months later on August 14, 1935. The proposed **Social Security Act** included a federal tax on employees and employers to fund the retirement system. In January 1940, the fifth anniversary of Roosevelt's speech about the program, Ida M. Fuller, a 76-year-old woman living in Vermont, received the first Social Security check.

As Roosevelt prepared for the reelection battle of 1936, he also toughened his rhetoric. In his 1933 inaugural address, FDR had criticized "the rulers of the exchange of mankind's goods" for having "failed, through their own stubbornness and their own incompetence." In 1936, however, his speeches took on a harsher tone. He spoke of his "old enemies," the bankers and profiteers, and condemned their "greed" and "autocracy." He said of business leaders, "They are unanimous in their hate for me—and I welcome their hatred."

American Voices

Frances Perkins, "The Roots of Social Security," Reflecting on 1935

Secretary of Labor Frances Perkins took the lead in creating the Social Security retirement system, still in operation today. Years later, she looked back on the work she did.

[T]he real roots of the Social Security Act were in the Great Depression of 1929. Nothing else would have bumped the American people into a social security system except something so shocking, so terrifying, as that Depression....

But everything was down. Nobody could get a job. The grocer didn't employ the young boys to deliver goods any more. He couldn't afford to. The grocer himself finally went bankrupt and closed up. He had given too much credit. I mean the people who were out of work had credit at the grocery store at first and they could eat; but they couldn't pay their bills, and finally, the grocer couldn't pay his bills; and eventually somebody came and sold him out. It went on like that all the time....

In the spring of 1932, Franklin Roosevelt had gone out to Utah to the Conference of Governors....He made a speech which was full of pleasant hyperbole of one sort or another—flattery to various Governors—but at one point he began to discuss the great problems now facing this country, and he spoke about unemployment. Then he said, "I am for unemployment insurance but not for the dole."

Until we heard those words come over the wires, I wasn't sure he was going to say he was for unemployment insurance. I was afraid he was going to say he was against the dole, and nothing else....It created a great interest and a great enthusiasm among the voters, which he was not slow to catch on to. He had that kind of a mind, you know; he could feel the public pulse, and he cared about the public pulse....

At any rate, we worked all summer....It was a terribly hot summer and everybody worked hard all the time and finally we actually did bring forth a report...that recommended unemployment insurance and old-age insurance but omitted health insurance just because the experts couldn't get through with health insurance in time to make a report on it....

This, then, was the genesis of the whole bill. We did a great deal of educating by one kind of propaganda or other, chiefly hearings. Senator Wagner put it up—a bill which he called a model bill—and held public hearings in the Senate, which attracted a great deal of attention from the Senators. We had a number of senatorial committees which we asked to look into this or that. We got advice. All these actions were for the purpose, not so much of advice as of propaganda—that is, of education of the public....The result was a bill that finally was presented to Congress and, as you know, was debated very briefly....And finally, we did get the basic bill passed.

Source: Frances Perkins, "The Roots of Social Security," speech delivered at Social Security Administration Headquarters, Baltimore, Maryland, October 23, 1962, downloaded from www.ssa.gov/history/perkins5.html, January 9, 2013

Thinking Critically

1. **Documentary Analysis**

   As Perkins described it, what role did Roosevelt play in the development and passage of Social Security? What other groups and individuals were important in the process?

2. **Constructing an Argument**

   Do you agree with Perkins that without the Great Depression Social Security would never have been enacted? Why or why not?

Roosevelt attacked business leaders every chance he got during 1935 and 1936, but he did not actually *do* very much to hurt them. Nevertheless, his rhetoric stole the thunder from Coughlin's and Long's; his legislation, especially Social Security, undermined Townsend's organization; and his support for the Wagner Act created great loyalty among labor unions. As a result, Roosevelt amassed great political capital going into the 1936 presidential election.

Huey Long was assassinated in September 1935. After his death, his Share Our Wealth clubs became the Union Party, which nominated William Lemke, a congressman from North Dakota, for president. The Republicans nominated the liberal Kansas Governor Alf Landon. In spite of polls, including one by the *Literary Digest* that predicted a Landon win, Roosevelt won a stunning electoral victory in November 1936. He carried 46 of the nation's 48 states and a huge plurality of the popular vote.

As he began his second term in January 1937, the president seemed to turn the agenda back to fighting the ongoing Depression. In his inaugural address he said, "I see one-third of a nation, ill-housed, ill-clad, ill-nourished." It was a call to action but also an admission that in 4 years the New Deal had not accomplished all that it hoped for.

In spite of his extraordinary election victory and the high hopes for more permanent reform it engendered, Roosevelt accomplished far less in his second term than in the first. The sense of national crisis was not as great in 1937, and Roosevelt's own missteps got in the way.

One of FDR's greatest frustrations was the fact that a conservative U.S. Supreme Court kept undermining his efforts. Late in his first term, the court declared the NRA and then the AAA unconstitutional, as well as state minimum wage laws. Court challenges to Social Security and the Wagner Act were working their way through the lower courts. He was not sure what would come next. In early February 1937 after his reelection, Roosevelt went to Congress with a proposal that would allow him to appoint one additional Supreme Court Justice for every member who was over the age of 70—which in 1937 would mean six new justices—and similar numbers in the lower courts. The Constitution never mentions a number of justices for the court, and the number had fluctuated between five and ten. FDR's proposal was completely constitutional but politically very unwise. FDR claimed that the goal was to speed judicial review and reduce the workload of the justices. Everyone knew that, in fact, there was only one goal: to stop the court from overturning the New Deal.

To many in Congress, not only conservatives, the court-packing bill was a step toward dictatorship. For some southern senators, it would open up the way to civil rights legislation, which they always feared might someday emerge from the White House. Montana Senator Burton Wheeler, an old progressive who usually sided with the president, led the assault, claiming that the bill "cut down those guarantees of liberty written by the blood of your forefathers." The legislation was defeated by the friends of the New Deal before its enemies got a chance to join in the debate.

Ironically, while Congress defeated Roosevelt's plan to expand—or "pack"—the Supreme Court, the justices, perhaps reading the 1936 election returns, shifted ground. Chief Justice Charles Evans Hughes and Associate Justice Owen Roberts, who had both voted against the New Deal, changed their minds, first on a minimum wage law and then on the all-important Wagner Labor Relations Act, which the court found to be constitutional. The changes in the Hughes and Robert votes were dubbed "the switch in time that saved nine." After 1937, although no new justices were added, the court stopped declaring New Deal legislation unconstitutional.

Nevertheless, with the defeat of Roosevelt's court plan, the momentum behind the New Deal slowly came to a stop. Divisions in Congress engendered by the court plan never healed. Unemployment actually rose in 1937 and 1938 in the "Depression within a Depression," which most likely occurred due to Roosevelt's effort to balance the federal budget by cutting back on the federal spending that was keeping the economy moving. Congress did pass a bill to resurrect parts of the old AAA now that the court seemed more open to it. A Fair Labor Standards Act that

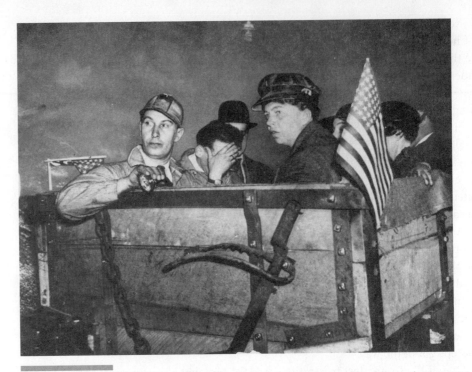

Eleanor Roosevelt could travel many places where her husband could not go. Her visits to migrant camps, African-American sharecroppers, or in this case a coal mine, highlighted the needs of many people and gave many faith in her husband's administration.

prohibited child labor and set an hourly minimum wage and a 40-hour work week also passed. However, Congress defeated a plan to expand the Tennessee Valley Authority to other regions of the country and a reorganization plan for the executive branch of the government that FDR wanted. When the president signed the Fair Labor Standards Act in June 1938, he was heard to say, "That's that." The New Deal, it seemed, had come to an end even if the Depression that launched it would run on for another year or more.

The New Deal did not end the Great Depression. The economy rebounded only as the United States prepared for World War II and government spending in preparation for war far outpaced anything that had been spent to "prime the pump" during the 1930s. Nevertheless, the New Deal changed the country. The Glass-Steagall Act and the Federal Deposit Insurance Corporation stabilized the nation's banking system, and the CCC and other agencies put people to work who desperately wanted— needed—jobs. Franklin and Eleanor Roosevelt's optimism gave people hope, and the president's commitment helped keep democratic institutions alive at a time when they were under assault not only in Europe and Asia but also in the United States. The federal government since has never shrunk to its pre-New Deal size when the Post Office was the largest government agency. Social Security and federal regulatory agencies play a continuing role in the economy and in people's lives. Including women and African-Americans in more than token positions within any administration is now the norm. The New Deal also inspired a new conservative movement and philosophy as opponents of the New Deal, especially business leaders, began to attack the new government intervention in the economy that the New Deal launched. While historians will long debate the value and the impact of the New Deal, all agree that the United States was a very different place in 1939 than it had been in 1929.

22.2 **Quick Review** Was the New Deal the best response to the Great Depression in the 1930s? What other paths might the country have followed?

THINKING HISTORICALLY

Critics of the New Deal

While Franklin Roosevelt was a very popular president, the only one in history elected to the office four times and always by large margins, at no time was his administration without opposition, especially as he faced the 1936 election. Some opponents thought Roosevelt was not moving nearly far or fast enough to use the opportunity presented by the Great Depression to restructure the American economy; others thought he was moving far too quickly and too radically.

Among those who wanted FDR to do more, Louisiana Senator Huey Long told a 1935 audience that he had "begged and pleaded and did everything else under the sun [to] try to get Mr. Roosevelt to keep his word that he gave us." But Long said he had concluded that there was no reason left to trust Roosevelt. "[H]e has promised and promised, smiled and bowed....There is no use to wait three more years. It is not Roosevelt or ruin, it is Roosevelt's ruin." In another speech, Long was especially clear on the differences, asking Iowa farmers, "Do you believe in the redistribution of wealth?" and basking in their cheers.

In contrast, the *New York Times* for August 23, 1934, carried a different story. With a headline that read, "League is Formed to Scan New Deal, 'Protect Rights,'" the newspaper reported,

"A group of prominent Democrats joined a few Republicans today to incorporate the American Liberty League, intended, according to its incorporators, to combat radicalism, preserve property rights, uphold and preserve the Constitution." For Roosevelt's old mentor Al Smith, the New Deal was becoming a danger to American liberty.

Source: *New York Times*, August 22, 1934, January 10, 1935.

Thinking Critically

1. **Constructing an Argument**

   In your opinion, which set of critics had the stronger argument, those on the left who felt the New Deal was too timid or those on the right who saw the New Deal as a threat to individual liberty and the Constitution? Why?

2. **Historical Interpretation**

   Given the vehemence with which Roosevelt was attacked from both ends of the political spectrum, what might explain Roosevelt's substantial and enduring popularity over the course of his four terms in office?

THE DEEP ROOTS OF WAR—THE UNITED STATES, EUROPE, AND ASIA

22.3 Analyze the international impact of the Depression, German and Japanese military expansion, and the initial U.S. response.

While the United States emerged from World War I relatively unscathed, much of Europe was devastated, and the Treaty of Versailles caused significant lingering pain and anger, most of all among the defeated Germans. When a worldwide Depression came, suffering, fear, and resentment all planted the seeds of another far greater conflict.

In Europe, some of the earliest signs of the postwar ill will appeared in Italy. In 1922, the leader of the ultranationalist Italian Fascist Party, Benito Mussolini, became prime minister. "Il Duce" (the leader), as he called himself, ruled Italy with an iron fist for more than 20 years. Mussolini's dream was to restore Italy's ancient glory by building prosperity and reestablishing the ancient Roman Empire, especially in North Africa, starting with Ethiopia.

For Germany, the 1920s were a terrible decade. The German Weimar Republic governed a defeated country. Hyperinflation between 1921 and 1924 made German currency virtually worthless. Shifting government coalitions were not able to create stability, especially in the face of the country's need to pay some $33 billion in reparations—payments that Britain and France used to pay their own $10 billion debt to the United States. In the late 1920s, as the worldwide depression worsened, the German economy collapsed under the load of debt payments and inflation. Banks closed in Germany and Austria. President Herbert Hoover described the German bank crisis of

1931 as "a gigantic explosion which shook the foundations of the world's economic, political, and social structure." Anger at the economic and political failure in Germany fueled old hatreds and brought a new political party to power in Germany.

Adolph Hitler's Nazi (or National Socialist) Party grew from a group of street thugs, known as Brown Shirts, in the 1920s, to a formidable group leading to Hitler's election in January 1933 as German Chancellor, with 44 percent of the vote, just before Roosevelt became president. Hitler promised that a greatly expanded German nation would provide *Lebensraum* (living space) for people of German nationality by pushing other peoples, Slavs and Jews, out of the way to make room for the "master race."

A month after coming to office, on February 27, 1933, the Nazi Party issued a decree ending free speech and assembly in Germany. They arrested Communist deputies in the German Parliament, giving themselves a solid majority there. Hitler took the title *der Fuhrer*, the leader. Later that year, just as the United States was implementing the prolabor New Deal, the Nazi government outlawed trade unions and other political parties. They authorized a new police force, the *Geheime Staatspolizei* or Gestapo, to enforce Nazi authority. In 1935, as the U.S. Congress was passing the Social Security Act and the Wagner Act, the Nazi Parliament passed the Nuremberg Decrees, which took away the citizenship of German Jews, excluded Jews from most professions and the military, and made the marriage of a Jew and non-Jew illegal. In November 1938, in a well-orchestrated attack across Germany known as *Kristallnacht* (or crystal night for all the broken glass), crowds attacked Jewish stores, homes, and synagogues while the government arrested some 20,000 Jews. The Nazi government then ordered an "atonement fine" on Jews to pay for the cost of *Kristallnacht*, closed Jewish stores, and a short time later, confiscated all Jewish property. Before long, Germany's Jews, and then those in Austria, Czechoslovakia, Poland, and other territories under German control, were being forced to wear yellow stars to identify them. They were packed into tightly controlled urban ghettos, and within 2 years, the first of them were being transported to slave labor and death camps.

Kristallnacht, November 9, 1938, was a Nazi Party-inspired attack on Jewish businesses and synagogues across Germany. It was the beginning of worse to come for Jews in Nazi-controlled countries.

While the German government was attacking its Jewish citizens, Hitler also renounced the clause in the Treaty of Versailles calling for German disarmament and began to build a new army. A year later, in March 1936, Hitler's army marched into the German Rhineland, which in the terms of the Treaty of Versailles was supposed to be kept free of troops. Two years later, in March 1938, Hitler announced that the independent country of Austria was to be known as the German province of Ostmark, and German troops marched into Austria. On March 14, 1938, Hitler rode in triumph through Vienna, welcomed as a hero by many.

Hitler did not stop there. Since the Sudeten region of Czechoslovakia had a large German population (though still a minority), Hitler claimed that they had the right under the Treaty of Versailles—which he otherwise ignored—to self-determination and should be incorporated into Germany. After a summer of negotiations and with British agreement, Hitler annexed the Sudeten region. The following spring, in March 1939, Hitler sent the German army into the rest of Czechoslovakia and made a triumphant journey to Prague.

As Nazi power grew in Germany and fascism continued its hold on Italy, the two countries formalized their alliance with the Rome-Berlin Axis treaty of November 1936. A few months earlier, in July 1936, another Fascist, Spanish General Francisco Franco, commander of the Spanish Army garrison in Morocco, led an attack on the left-leaning and democratically elected Republican government of Spain. Spain was engulfed in a bloody civil war. The governments of Germany and Italy sent planes and troops to aid Franco. The communist government of Russia and western governments sent modest aid to the Republicans. But by early 1939, the Fascists had won. Spain joined Italy and Germany, forming a powerful fascist bloc.

While Fascists were consolidating their power in central Europe, militarists in Japan were also growing in power. Japanese militarism had a strong anti-American strain as various American policies—from the exclusion of Japanese children from San Francisco schools in 1906 to the exclusion of all Japanese immigrants as a result of the 1924 immigration law—sparked continuing anger even as people in the United States forgot those incidents.

In the 1910s and 1920s, as Japanese power grew, Japan declared a goal of "Asia for Asians," which meant Japanese domination of the whole of the western rim of the Pacific Ocean to replace Britain, France, and the United States as dominant powers. Many Asians resented U.S. control of the Philippine Islands, British involvement in China and Burma, Dutch control of the oil-rich East Indies, and French control of Indochina (modern Vietnam, Laos, and Cambodia). Except in China, where Japanese advances were deeply resented, the Japanese conquests were often welcomed in the rest of Asia.

By the 1930s, Japan faced the same worldwide depression conditions as other industrialized countries. Japan saw its economic salvation in expansion. The island nation could not provide enough food for its people and lacked key natural resources such as iron and oil. If the Europeans could have Asian colonies, its leaders asked, why not Japan? In September 1932, Japan used an explosion at a Japanese-owned railway in China as an excuse to send troops into China, and they installed a puppet government in the Chinese province of Manchuria. Then in July 1937, Japanese troops captured Shanghai, the largest city in China, and the Chinese capital of Nanking. The Rape of Nanking, as the Japanese attack was called, was a brutal assault. As many as 300,000 Chinese were killed as the Japanese army raped, beheaded, machine-gunned, and bayoneted civilians. The Chinese government led by Chiang Kai-shek retreated and set up a new capital in the inland city of Chungking. Japan renamed the expanded territory in Manchuria as the Japanese province of Manchukuo. A half a million Japanese moved into the territory to farm and govern the subjected Chinese population. At the same time, Chiang's Kuomintang Party (the Nationalists) was locked in a bitter civil war with the Chinese Community Party led by Mao Zedong.

In the face of so much worldwide violence and aggression, the governments of Great Britain, France, and the United States did virtually nothing while the League of Nations proved to be a meaningless barrier to aggression. The government of France

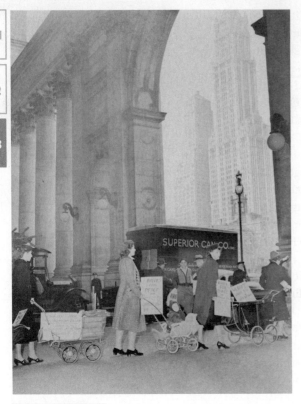

Mothers with baby carriages march for peace outside the Woolworth building in New York City, 1939.

isolationism

A belief that the United States should keep clear of nearly all involvement with the rest of the world, stay neutral and out of any foreign wars.

ordered the construction of the supposedly "impregnable" Maginot Line (named for war minister André Maginot) along the border with Germany but did little more. When Hitler's troops, in violation of the Versailles Treaty, marched into the Rhineland in 1936, Hitler wrote privately that, "If the French had then marched into the Rhineland, we would have had to withdraw with our tails between our legs." But France did not act.

The desire for peace was equally strong in Britain, driven by still-recent memories of the bloodbath of World War I. If 420,000 British soldiers could die at the single and inconclusive Battle of the Somme in 1916, the next generation was determined to avoid war. In 1933, students at Oxford University voted, "This house will in no circumstance fight for its King and its Country." In 1935, several thousand young people in Britain joined the Peace Pledge Union, opposing any British military planning. When Mussolini invaded Ethiopia in 1935, Britain, which then controlled the Suez Canal, could have cut off the Italian troops by closing the canal, but did not do so. In spite of pleas from Ethiopia, the League of Nations did nothing.

As late as September 1938, at a conference in Munich, Germany, British Prime Minister Neville Chamberlain agreed to allow Hitler's claim to the Sudetenland in exchange for a promise of peace. Chamberlain was greeted with large crowds in London when he returned promising "peace in our time." In the British Parliament, however, Chamberlain was criticized by Winston Churchill who called the Munich agreement "a total and unmitigated defeat." However, in 1938, Chamberlain, not Churchill, set British policy.

As France and Britain did nothing to stop the Fascists, most people in the United States were even more determined to keep their distance from any conflict. During the 1920s and 1930s, a significant majority of Americans wanted nothing to do with Europe's or Asia's problems. In 1935, George Earle, the governor of Pennsylvania, said, "If the world is to become a wilderness of waste, hatred, and bitterness, let us all the more earnestly protect and preserve our own oasis of liberty." Minnesota Senator Thomas Schall said more succinctly, "To hell with Europe and the rest of those nations!" While isolationism was strongest in the Midwest, many people everywhere agreed. In April 1935, 50,000 World War I veterans marched for peace and laid wreaths on the graves of three members of Congress who had voted against U.S. entry into World War I. Days later, 175,000 college students staged a strike for peace.

There were many reasons for the **isolationism** that was rampant in the United States in the 1930s. Most Americans had concluded that the many thousand American soldiers killed in the war had died for no reason. Wilson's dream of a generation of peace sustained by the League of Nations was clearly a failure, and Europeans were once again at each other's throats. Writers like John Dos Passos, Ernest Hemingway, and e.e. cummings all wrote novels about the meaninglessness of the First World War, and as Dos Passos said, "Rejection of Europe is what America is all about." In the mid-1930s, a Senate Special Committee known as the Nye Committee, chaired by North Dakota's Gerald Nye, concluded that big business had led the United States into the World War. In 1935, when President Roosevelt sought U.S. entry to the World Court, the Senate rejected the plan. Americans simply wanted nothing to do with the troubles of other nations.

In Congress, the isolationist and peace sentiment led to the passage of a number of neutrality laws designed to keep the United States out of war. A 1935 law required an embargo of arms to all belligerents in any war while (in a direct slap at Woodrow Wilson's policies) declaring that any American who traveled on a belligerent ship did so at his or her own risk. In 1936, Congress added a proviso that prohibited loans or credit to any nation at war, and in 1937, Congress explicitly extended the arms embargo to Spain.

Not every American shared the isolationist sentiments of the majority. In 1936 and 1937, several thousand young Americans, mostly from various left-leaning movements, volunteered to fight in Spain on the side of the Republican government. Volunteers named themselves the Abraham Lincoln Brigade and joined an ill-trained and ill-equipped but courageous force that fought against the Fascists. In one battle near Madrid, 120 Americans died and another 175 were wounded. By the beginning of 1939, when the last Republican units were defeated, President Roosevelt himself concluded that neutrality in Spain had been a "grave mistake…as events will very likely prove."

While the Abraham Lincoln Brigade fought and President Roosevelt began to believe that the United States would eventually have to fight Fascism in Europe, most people in the country and the Congress continued to believe that they could stay out of all entanglements. When Congress passed the 1937 Neutrality Act, they toughened the prohibition on selling arms to any side and made it illegal for Americans to travel on a belligerent ship. The law also declared that nonmilitary material—food, clothing, and so on—could be sold to a nation at war only on a "cash and carry" basis, insisting that there be no loans to belligerents and that all goods bought in the United States had to be taken out of the country in non-U.S. ships.

The neutrality legislation attempted to keep the United States out of a European war, but violence in Asia was growing. When Japan had attacked Manchuria in 1931, President Hoover's Secretary of State Henry L. Stimson proclaimed the "Stimson Doctrine": that the United States would never officially recognize the new regime in Manchukuo or any other arrangement imposed on China by force. The unstated part of the doctrine was that the United States also would not do anything much to enforce its policy. American public opinion was solidly on the side of China. The novelist Pearl Buck, author of *The Good Earth* published in 1931, and Henry Luce, the owner of the Time-Life publications, were both children of missionaries to China and between them did a lot to build public sympathy for China. In the fall of 1937, a Gallup poll showed that 59 percent of Americans favored China compared to 1 percent who favored Japan in the quest for control of Manchuria. But almost no one wanted to do more than offer sympathy to the Chinese.

In December 1937, Japanese pilots sank the U.S. gunboat *Panay* in Nanking, China. While Americans were angry, they were not angry enough to challenge Japan. After the *Panay* was sunk, Texas Congressman Maury Maverick said, "We should learn that it is about time for us to mind our own business," and a poll showed that most Americans agreed with him. While Americans wanted to stay out of war, American scrap iron and American oil continued to be shipped to Japan, strengthening that country's military. Since there was no formal war between Japan and China, the Neutrality Act did not apply, and most of the battles in Manchuria were fueled with American petroleum and bombs made of American metal. Indeed, through the late 1930s and into 1940 and 1941, Roosevelt and his cabinet feared not only American isolationists but also the wrath of Japan. If they were to cut off oil shipments—they did eventually cut metal shipments—they worried that Japan would quickly attack the Dutch colonies in Asia that were the only other potential source of oil for Japan. To keep the peace, the United States kept the oil flowing.

In the face of the Nazi attacks in Germany and then Austria and Czechoslovakia, many Jews tried to leave Europe. But leaving was not easy, and the strict quotas of the 1924 legislation made immigration to the United States very difficult. In the 1930s, the American Jewish Congress protested loudly against both the Nazi attacks and American immigration policy. The group urged boycotts of German goods and staged a mock trial of Hitler. Roosevelt felt blocked by the immigration laws though he did combine the German and Austrian quotas, allowing some additional Jewish immigration in 1936 and 1937. Britain also allowed modest immigration but resolutely opposed further expansion of the Jewish population of Palestine, then governed by Britain under a League of Nations mandate. Nazi laws limited the amount

Famed aviator Charles Lindbergh was a prominent vocal supporter of American isolationism.

of money a departing Jew could take to about $4, an amount that made a potential immigrant a pauper and therefore ineligible for admission to the United States.

After *Kristallnacht,* the November 1938 attack on Jews, New York Senator Robert Wagner and House members Edith Nourse Rogers of Massachusetts and Emmanuel Celler of New York proposed legislation that would create an expanded quota for racial and religious refugees. However, as with China, most Americans offered sympathy but little more, and Congress followed public opinion, voting the proposal down. A 1939 poll showed that 85 percent of Protestants, 84 percent of Catholics, and even 25.8 percent of Jews opposed opening the United States to Jewish refugees from Europe.

As the Nazi attacks on Jews escalated, European Jews became desperate to leave. In May 1939, the German ship *St. Louis* arrived in Havana with 930 Jewish refugees. The Cuban government refused temporary visas. The captain of the *St. Louis* then sailed up the U.S. coast, well within sight of Miami and other American cities, while negotiators tried desperately to get the U.S. State Department to allow the refugees to land. But the State Department would not agree and a Coast Guard cutter was ordered to intercept any *St. Louis* passengers who tried to go ashore. Finally in June, the *St. Louis* returned to Europe. Before the war ended, perhaps a quarter or more of the passengers had died in concentration camps. Most Americans were sympathetic to the plight of Jews, but anti-Semitism was also strong in America.

Charles Lindbergh, the aviation hero of the 1920s, became an avid opponent of any revision of the neutrality laws or any support for Jewish refugees. Lindbergh became a popular speaker at rallies of the America First Committee that had been organized in the fall of 1940 to keep the United States out of war in Europe. Father Charles Coughlin, long an opponent of the New Deal, began calling it the "Jew-Deal." For Lindbergh, Coughlin, and a significant American following, Nazism was appealing. Others, probably the majority of the supporters of the America First Committee, simply did not want any part of a war that the United States could avoid. Nevertheless, not only isolationism and ignorance but also old hatreds kept the United States from providing the support for Europe's Jews that they so badly needed.

While Americans tried to ignore developments in Europe and Asia in the late 1930s, Hitler was on the move. He understood that the faster he acted the greater his chances of success. Once Hitler invaded the rest of Czechoslovakia, Prime Minister Chamberlin, who had agreed to an earlier compromise, announced that Britain was committed to the defense of Poland and that if Hitler's forces attacked that country, his forces would be met with armed resistance.

In April 1939, Mussolini invaded Albania. Hitler made feints toward Poland. Then in August, Hitler stunned the world by signing a nonaggression pact with Joseph Stalin, the dictator of the Soviet Union (as communist Russia was known). The erstwhile enemies—Germany and the Soviet Union with radically different economic systems and ideologies—now agreed to the partition of Poland. Everyone knew what was coming next. In the State Department, one official said that the feeling in the world was like "sitting in a house where somebody is dying upstairs." Very early in the morning on September 1, 1939, President Roosevelt received a call, "Mr. President," the U.S. Ambassador in France said, "several German divisions are deep in Polish territory…. There are reports of bombers over the city of Warsaw." The President replied, "It has come at last. God help us all!"

Britain and France followed through on their promise to declare war. World War II had begun in Europe. On September 3, Roosevelt gave a radio fireside chat in which he said that the United States would remain neutral, but "[e]ven a neutral cannot be asked to close his mind or close his conscience." The country's mind was certainly not neutral. Eighty-four percent of Americans supported Britain and France, only two percent Germany. But a very large majority also wanted to stay out of the war no matter how much sympathy they might have for one side. After September 1939, more Americans, led by the president, were starting to have grave doubts that staying out of the battle was going to be possible.

22.1
22.2
22.3

22.3 **Quick Review** Considering how the United States was drawn into World War I, why might so many Americans have favored isolationism in the years leading up to World War II?

CONCLUSION

The stock market crash of 1929 was a dramatic and symbolic end to the prosperity of the 1920s, but it was not the first sign that something was very wrong with the U.S. economy. Throughout the 1920s, stock prices had risen dramatically, and by the end of 1928, the economy was showing signs of a speculative boom. Experts began to warn that a crash was inevitable, but American investors largely ignored these warnings. Finally, in October 1929, the bottom fell out of the market. Stock prices crashed and continued to crash for the next 3 years. The Great Depression was in full force.

President Herbert Hoover's response to the nation's economic woes moved in the right direction, but it was too cautious and failed to alleviate the crisis or restore confidence among Americans. In 1932, he was defeated for reelection by Franklin Roosevelt, who, once in office, took swift action to stabilize the nation's economy and its banking system, extend relief to the impoverished, and create jobs for the unemployed. Roosevelt, with the backing of the Democrats in Congress, passed nine separate pieces of legislation in his first 100 days as president. Dubbed the "New Deal," his agenda and policies provided important help for some Americans but did little for others.

The New Deal did not end the Depression, but it did provide much needed social welfare, create jobs, shore up the banking system, improve working conditions, and install protective barriers against future economic downturns. Still, the New Deal was not supported by everyone, and Roosevelt faced powerful opponents on the right (who believed that the New Deal was socialism) and on the left (who believed that the New Deal was not progressive enough). Despite such opposition, Roosevelt was popular and was reelected in a landslide in 1936.

By the end of the 1930s, the violence in Europe and Asia was demanding more and more attention. Fascists Adolf Hitler and Benito Mussolini had seized power in Germany and in Italy and had begun to threaten other states on the European continent. Similarly, Japan had begun a campaign of imperialist expansion in Asia. Most of this behavior initially went unchecked. Not until 1939, when Germany invaded Poland, did Britain and France declare war. Americans disagreed about how to respond to this aggression. At the end of the decade, U.S. involvement in another major European conflict seemed inevitable to some; however, others—probably a majority—wanted to stay out of Europe's and Asia's problems despite any sympathy they may have felt for the people in those situations.

CHAPTER REVIEW How did the Great Depression affect the United States both in the 1930s and for the future? What were the three *most* significant effects? Why?

Chapter 22   Chapter Review

THE COMING OF THE GREAT DEPRESSION

22.1 Explain the coming of the Great Depression and the initial response to it.

Review Questions

1. Comparison

Compare and contrast the stock market crash of 1929 with other factors that led to the Great Depression in the United States and worldwide. What similarities and differences do you note?

2. Contextualization

Why did Herbert Hoover find it so difficult to craft an adequate response to the Great Depression?

THE NEW DEAL

22.2 Explain the goals and results of the New Deal and the responses to change on the part of diverse Americans.

Review Questions

3. Contextualization

Why was it so important that Roosevelt stabilize the banking system as quickly as possible?

4. Historical Interpretation

What factors contributed to the growth of organized labor in the 1930s?

5. Comparison

Compare and contrast the arguments made by Roosevelt's critics on the left and the right. Why did Roosevelt worry much more about his critics on the left than his critics on the right?

6. Construct an Argument

In your opinion what were the most important accomplishments of the New Deal? What were its greatest failures?

THE DEEP ROOTS OF WAR—THE UNITED STATES, EUROPE, AND ASIA

22.3 Analyze the international impact of the Depression, German and Japanese military expansion, and the initial U.S. response.

Review Questions

7. Historical Interpretation

What connection can you make between economic events and the rise of Fascist parties to power in Germany, Italy, and Japan?

8. Contextualization

Why were so many Americans committed to isolationism?

Living in a World at War

World War II started out with disaster for the United States after Japan attacked the U.S. Navy base at Pearl Harbor, sinking much of the Pacific fleet. It would be a long time before the tide turned.

O n the morning of December 7, 1941, 350 Japanese airplanes attacked the sleeping port of Pearl Harbor, Hawaii, where much of the Pacific fleet was anchored and where planes were lined up in close formation (to protect them against sabotage on the ground). In a few short hours, 2,500 soldiers and sailors were killed, 150 U.S. airplanes destroyed, and five battleships as well as many others vessels were sunk. It was a devastating loss.

The next day, Franklin Roosevelt addressed Congress, speaking of the attack as "a date which will live in infamy." He asked for, and was given, a declaration of war against Japan. Hitler and Mussolini then declared war on the United States. The long wait was over. With the direct attack on the United States at Pearl Harbor, most isolationists and antiwar voices rallied to the president and the war effort. Every citizen would be touched by the war whether by serving in the military, working in war-related industries, or using ration stamps to buy food. It had been a long wait during the 2 years in which Roosevelt increased support for Britain, negotiated fitfully with Japan, and inched toward war. This chapter traces the story of preparation between 1939 and 1941 and the nation's full-scale involvement in World War II from December 1941 to the war's end in August 1945.

CHAPTER OBJECTIVE

Demonstrate an understanding of many aspects of World War II—military tactics, mobilization of U.S. society and the U.S. economy, and the war's impact on diverse American lives.

LEARNING OBJECTIVES

PREPAREDNESS AND ISOLATION, 1939–1941

Explain support for and opposition to the growing U.S. support for Britain and growing tensions with Japan.	23.1

MASS MOBILIZATION IN A SOCIETY AT WAR

Analyze the war's impact on widely diverse groups of Americans who fought, supported the war effort at home, or otherwise lived through the war years.	23.2

INDUSTRIAL STRENGTH, INDUSTRIAL PROSPERITY

Analyze U.S. industrial strength and productivity and its impact on the outcome of the war and on American society.	23.3

WINNING A WORLD WAR—NORTH AFRICA, EUROPE, ASIA, THE PACIFIC, 1943–1945

Explain the course of the war leading to victory in Europe and then the Pacific.	23.4

PREPAREDNESS AND ISOLATION, 1939–1941

23.1   Explain support for and opposition to the growing U.S. support for Britain and growing tensions with Japan.

When Germany attacked Poland in September 1939, Britain and then France declared war on Germany. Europe was at war. Neither Japan nor the United States intervened. After the rapid German defeat of Poland that fall, the winter of 1939–40 was known as the "Phony War" since there was so little fighting. Poland disappeared, split between Nazi Germany and the Soviet Union. Britain and France waited for an attack they knew would come—and the war did not stay phony.

The Battle of Britain

At the beginning of 1940, Hitler hinted at peace initiatives, then in April invaded Denmark and Norway and quickly defeated both. On May 10, Germany unleashed its *Blitzkrieg* (lightning war) on Holland, Belgium, and Luxembourg, bombing Rotterdam into rubble and sending in airborne and ground troops. All three countries surrendered.

On May 14, 1,800 German tanks crossed the border into France, overran the Maginot Line (see Chapter 22), which turned out to be useless, and turned toward Paris. Italy joined Germany, declaring war on France on June 10. On June 22, 1940, France surrendered. For the next several years, Germany directly governed northern France, including Paris, while a puppet government, led by the aging French World War I hero, Marshall Philippe Petain, governed the southern part of France known as Vichy France from a capital in the town of Vichy. By the summer of 1940, Hitler was the master of Europe (see Map 23-1).

Only Great Britain stood against Germany. As the German forces rushed toward Paris, they attempted to cut off a retreat by French and British armies. But 338,000 British, French, and allied troops were evacuated from the beaches of Dunkirk, leaving nearly all equipment behind. In a radio broadcast, the new British Prime Minister Winston Churchill promised, "We shall go on to the end," but he added, Britain would hold out "until in God's good time, the new world, with all its power and might, [shall] step forth to the rescue and the liberation of the old." It was a rescue that Churchill and Roosevelt tried hard to assure over the next 18 months.

After the defeat of France, Hermann Goering, Nazi air chief, announced, "The Fuhrer has ordered me to crush Britain with my Luftwaffe," and he tried hard. Bombers attacked British coastal fortifications, airfields, and then in September 1940, began the terror bombing of London. The "Blitz," as the British called it, eventually killed thousands of residents of Britain's capital—6,000 in October alone. Edward R. Murrow, the voice of the Columbia Broadcasting System (CBS) based in London, gave Americans nightly reports that "London is burning." The small British Air Force fought back. Churchill begged Roosevelt for more help. Roosevelt set about finding ways to provide it.

Moving Toward Lend-Lease Legislation

Every step that Roosevelt took brought hostility from neutrality advocates. Senior officers within the U.S. military worried that sending arms to Britain would undermine U.S. defenses. Secretary of War Henry H. Woodring was committed to a "fortress America" strategy, arming this country and ignoring the rest of the world. No one opposed Roosevelt's support for Britain more than Charles Lindbergh, a hero from his 1920s flight across the Atlantic. In October 1939, Lindbergh said, "An ocean is a formidable barrier, even for modern aircraft." The U.S. ambassador in London, Joseph P. Kennedy, predicted that Britain would quickly fall.

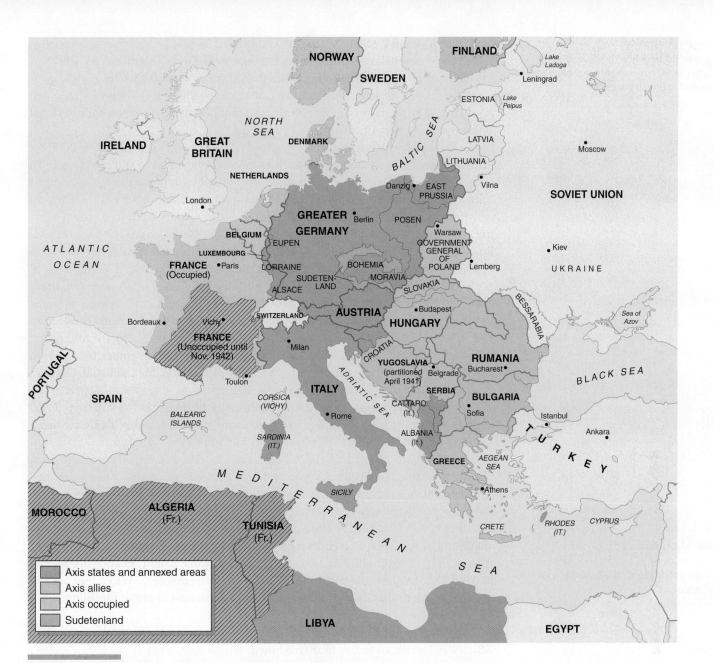

MAP 23-1 Nazi Europe, 1941. This map shows the extent of Nazi control of Europe. When one adds Vichy France and its territory in North Africa, it is clear that Hitler basically controlled the continent between Great Britain and the Soviet Union (Russia).

Republican leaders in Congress opposed any intervention, and they had a lot of public support. In July 1940, students at Yale University, supported by Midwestern business leaders, formed the **America First Committee**. Most America First supporters saw the new war as an extension of the last one, simply an intra-European battle for power and colonies. Some sympathized with the Nazis or hated Jews. Most distrusted Roosevelt.

Roosevelt argued with the isolationists in Congress, ignored his ambassador in London as someone who "has been an appeaser and always will be an appeaser," and thought Lindbergh was a Nazi. He promoted military officers who supported his efforts and sidelined others. In 1940, FDR replaced isolationist Secretary of War Woodring with longtime internationalist Republican Henry L. Stimson, who had been secretary of war in Taft's administration and secretary of state for President Hoover. Roosevelt also added Frank Knox, another Republican internationalist, as secretary of the navy.

America First Committee
Committee launched in 1940 that argued for American neutrality and for staying out of World War II.

destroyers-for-bases
An agreement between the United States and Great Britain to exchange obsolete navy destroyers for British bases.

arsenal of democracy
A phrase coined by Franklin Roosevelt for the materials needed by Britain in its fight with Nazi Germany.

four freedoms
Freedoms announced by President Roosevelt in December 1940 that became a rallying point for the causes the United States would fight for.

Lend-Lease Act
Legislation passed in 1941 for a program through which the United States "loaned" military equipment to Britain and other World War II allies for the duration of the war.

In the fall of 1940, FDR concluded a "**destroyers-for-bases**" deal, which circumvented congressional restrictions on selling ships to Britain by "trading" obsolete ships to Britain in exchange for 99-year leases on a string of British Navy bases. He pressured the navy to declare ships obsolete and defended the deal as a way to strengthen America's defenses. However, he also worried that he had exceeded his constitutional authority, and his opponents worried even more.

As war raged in Europe, the November 1940 presidential election loomed. Roosevelt broke precedent going back to George Washington and sought a third term. The Democrats, after some grumbling, mostly by supporters of Vice President John Garner, nominated Roosevelt. The Republicans, wanting to avoid having an isolationist candidate, nominated a corporate attorney and utility company executive, Wendell Willkie, an ardent opponent of the New Deal who did not disagree with Roosevelt greatly on foreign policy, though he did denounce the destroyers-for-bases deal as "the most arbitrary and dictatorial action ever taken by any president."

In the middle of the campaign, Roosevelt asked Congress to institute a military draft so the country could have a trained army ready in case of war. Many opposed the draft, but when a reporter told Willkie that, "if you want to win the election you will come out against the proposed draft," Willkie responded, "I would rather not win the election than do that." The draft became law on September 16 and, with Willkie's stance and the appointment of Stimson and Knox to the cabinet, the issue of isolationism was neutralized until late in the campaign.

Just before the election, polls showed that a majority of prospective voters preferred Willkie unless war was coming, in which case they wanted Roosevelt's steady hand. On Election Day, they chose the steady hand, and FDR won a third term.

Only a month after the election, Roosevelt received an urgent message from Churchill spelling out just how desperate things were for Britain and making clear that "the moment approaches when we shall no longer be able to pay cash for shipping and other supplies." In a fireside chat just after Christmas in 1940, Roosevelt said, "If Great Britain goes down…all the Americas, would be living at the point of a gun." The only alternative, he told his radio audience, "We must be the great **arsenal of democracy**." A week later, FDR proposed Lend-Lease legislation which would "loan" war materials to the British for the duration of the war. The president insisted, "We cannot, and we will not, tell them that they must surrender, merely because of present inability to pay for the weapons which we know they must have."

In the same speech, Roosevelt also described larger purposes for American action which was, he said, to secure **four freedoms**:

> The first is freedom of speech and expression.…
> The second is freedom of every person to worship God in his own way.…
> The third is freedom from want.…
> The fourth is freedom from fear.…

Roosevelt's "four freedoms" were very popular. Lend-Lease was much less popular. Isolationists like Montana Senator Burton Wheeler said that the plan "will plough under every fourth American boy." Newspapers like the *Chicago Tribune*, the *New York Daily News*, and the *Washington Times-Herald* all editorialized against the plan. Nevertheless, the Congress that had passed so many neutrality acts in the 1930s approved the **Lend-Lease Act** by a 60 to 31 vote in the Senate and a 317 to 71 vote in the House. Britain would get the aid that Churchill wanted.

The military preparation in 1940 and 1941 ended the Great Depression. Spending $7 billion on Lend-Lease efforts and an additional $13.7 billion on the expansion of the U.S. military (up from $2.2 billion in 1940) provided a huge stimulus to the economy, far larger than any stimulus tried during the New Deal. Nearly a million young men were drafted by early 1941, and new jobs opened everywhere, virtually ending unemployment. New or redesigned federal agencies brought business leaders into the government to manage the huge conversion to a war-oriented economy (see Figure 23-1).

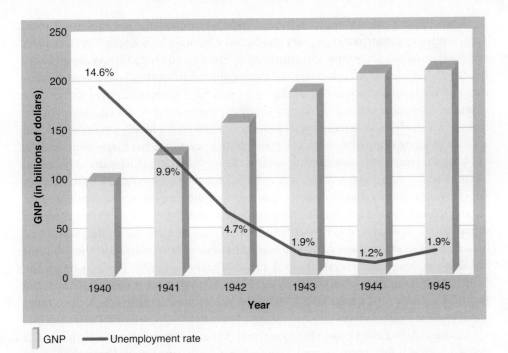

FIGURE 23-1 After 1940, the nation's unemployment rate went from almost 15 percent to fewer than 2 percent for most of the war while gross national product more than doubled from $100 billion to $200 billion.

While the United States geared up to serve as the "arsenal of democracy," Hitler suddenly attacked his erstwhile ally Russia in June 1941. While there was no love lost in the United States for Communist Russia, most Americans knew that if the Nazis defeated Russia it would mean disaster. Missouri Senator Harry S. Truman said he would not mind it if both sides lost, but he also said, "I don't want to see Hitler victorious under any circumstances." The United States extended Lend-Lease aid to the Russians.

Lend-Lease aid to Britain brought the United States close to war with Germany. German U-boats sank ships carrying goods to Britain at five times the rate that new ships could be built. The United States began patrolling the western Atlantic, guarding ships as far as Greenland before turning them over to the British Navy for escort to Britain.

In August, Roosevelt and Churchill met in Newfoundland, planned ways to work together, and issued the **Atlantic Charter** that included a somewhat vague commitment to national self-determination for other countries, nonaggression, and "the establishment of a wider and permanent system of general security"—planting the seeds of what became the United Nations. Meanwhile, patrolling U.S. Navy ships ran into conflict with German submarines. In October 1941, a U-boat attacked the U.S. destroyer *Kearny*, killing 11 sailors, the first U.S. casualties of the war. Roosevelt said, "America has been attacked." Later that month, a submarine sank the USS *Reuben James*, killing 115 sailors. War did not seem far off.

Atlantic Charter
Statement of common principles and war aims developed by President Franklin Roosevelt and British Prime Minister Winston Churchill at a meeting in August 1941.

Growing Tensions with Japan

While the United States focused on Europe, tensions were also building in the Pacific. The United States wanted to avoid a "two-ocean war," and sought peace with Japan. However, a combination of stubborn—if inadequate— support for China and a lack of careful attention did not make for an effective foreign policy. The Roosevelt administration provided modest Lend-Lease support for Chiang Kai-shek's government and allowed individual U.S. pilots to join the Flying Tigers, a volunteer air corps organized by Colonel Claire Chennault to fight for China, but continued to allow the metal and oil exports on which Japan depended.

A new generation of younger Japanese leaders, especially the war minister Hideki Tojo, wanted to ensure national glory and signed a formal alliance with Nazi Germany and Fascist Italy. Nazi puppet governments in France and Holland gave Japan badly needed access to rice, rubber, and most important, oil from Dutch and French colonies in Asia. Japan launched the Greater East Asia Co-Prosperity Sphere to free Asia from the colonial powers and to consolidate Japanese control. When Japan landed troops in French Indochina in July 1940, the United States finally cut off metal and aviation gasoline shipments, but not oil, which they saw as the last bargaining chip. As 1941 began, Japan sent a new ambassador to the United States, Kichisaburo Nomura. Nomura and U.S. Secretary of State Cordell Hull sought a way to reduce hostilities but failed. By midsummer, hard liners in Japan had won the support of Emperor Hirohito.

In October, Tojo replaced the moderate Fumimaro Konoye as Prime Minister of Japan. The new government was determined to go to war. The United States had broken the secret Japanese code and knew that war was coming. But they did not know where—perhaps an attack on American bases in the Philippines or on the British colonies in Asia, both of which were warned to prepare for attack. In fact, the Japanese military sent a huge fleet 4,000 miles across the Pacific to attack the United States itself at Pearl Harbor.

Japanese Admiral Takijiro Onishi warned that a direct attack on U.S. soil would make the Americans "insanely mad." He said that while Japan would have the advantage in a short war, in a longer war, the U.S. industrial capacity and its large supply of oil—the fuel of modern war—meant that Japan would have a very hard time of it. But Japan's leaders were confident of a quick victory.

When Japan did attack on December 7, the location was a greater surprise than the fact of the attack itself. But Japan's attack on Hawaii solidified American public opinion. Even the staunchest opponents of preparedness, including Charles Lindbergh, now supported going to war.

23.1 **Quick Review** How did the United States move from an isolationist stance to one supporting the war effort? How did the attitudes of the government and the people differ?

MASS MOBILIZATION IN A SOCIETY AT WAR

23.2 Analyze the war's impact on widely diverse groups of Americans who fought, supported the war effort at home, or otherwise lived through the war years.

For the people of the United States, the attack of December 7, 1941, changed everything. Before the war ended in 1945, 16 million Americans served in the armed forces, and 405,399 died in combat. All Americans had their lives changed by the war. At the beginning of the war, half of white Americans and 90 percent of black Americans lived in poverty. The war provided a job for everyone, and wartime jobs vastly expanded the size of the nation's middle class. Americans moved around a lot during the war. The military brought rural and urban Americans together in units that faced the same fears and hopes. Far less often, it brought people of different races together since the military of World War II remained segregated not only by race but also by gender. As the war progressed, the Great Depression became a distant memory. New prosperity and new knowledge, but also the terrible losses of a major war and new fear about distant parts of the world became central to people's lives.

Early Battles, Early Losses, 1941–1942

In the spring of 1941, a secret conversation in Washington between British and American officials (known by the code name ABC-1 or American-British Conversation Number 1) resulted in an agreement that, in the event of a two-front war, which everyone hoped to avoid, the United States would focus first on joining Britain to

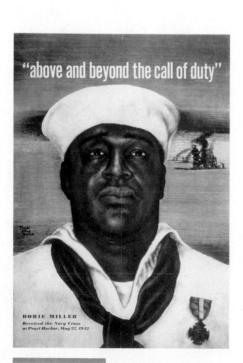

"above and beyond the call of duty"

DORIE MILLER
Received the Navy Cross at Pearl Harbor, May 27, 1942

Dorie Miller, a kitchen attendant at Pearl Harbor, was able to pull the captain of a battleship to safety and then use a machine gun to shoot at attacking Japanese planes. Although Miller was proclaimed a hero, the navy continued to limit African-Americans to non-combat roles throughout the war.

defeat Germany. As U.S. Army Chief George C. Marshall explained, "Collapse in the Atlantic would be fatal; collapse in the Far East would be serious but not fatal."

Within hours of the December 7 attack on Pearl Harbor, Japan also attacked U.S. bases in the Philippine Islands, the Aleutian Islands off Alaska, as well as Guam and Wake Islands in the mid-Pacific. Within days, Japanese pilots and troops were in the British colonies of Malaysia and Burma, French Indochina, the Dutch East Indies, and independent Thailand. To some, the Japanese were liberators, freeing them from the hated European and American colonial authorities. The Japanese had been preparing well and were a superb fighting force. British Hong Kong and American Guam and Wake Islands surrendered within a week. In February 1942, Singapore surrendered to the Japanese with 85,000 crack British troops now prisoners of war. American and British Navy forces lost the battle of Java Sea and the Dutch East Indies, and their rich oil fields fell to Japan.

In April and May of 1942, after holding out for months against impossible odds, the last U.S. troops on the islands of Bataan and Corregidor in the Philippines surrendered. Ben Steele, a young rancher from Montana who had volunteered for service, remembered that during the 99-day defense of Bataan, the Americans constantly faced starvation. After news spread that the commander in the Philippines, General Douglas MacArthur, had left for Australia, Steele and the others knew that "Only two things can happen to us now, we're going to be dead or we're going to be prisoners of war."

After surrendering, the American and Filipino troops from Bataan were forced to march 66 miles to a railroad junction where they were transported to prison camps. The march came to be known as the Bataan Death March. The Japanese captors, overwhelmed by the numbers, had been taught to hate American devils. If a prisoner fell, he was kicked, and if he did not move, killed with a bayonet. If prisoners, desperately thirsty in the hot sun, moved off the line to get water, they were shot. The surviving defenders of Bataan and Corregidor spent more than 3 years as Japanese prisoners. By the middle of 1942, Japan controlled the western Pacific from the far north to Australia, which remained in British hands.

Three days after the United States declared war on Japan, Hitler and Mussolini declared war on the United States. It was an odd move on their part. Germany, Italy, and Japan were allies—based on treaties they had signed with each other in 1936 and 1937—but if Germany and Italy had held back in declaring war on the United States, FDR would have been under great pressure to focus the war only on Japan, leaving Britain still isolated. German and Italian declarations of war allowed FDR to keep the focus on the Atlantic, which he believed was essential. The three nations at war with the United States—Germany, Italy, and Japan—were known as the Axis as opposed to the allied forces of the United States, Great Britain, and the Soviet Union, joined by exiled French troops who called themselves the Free French and forces from China and a number of other nations that allied with them.

Even though the primary American focus was on Europe, U.S. and British forces won a partial victory in the Pacific in the Battle of the Coral Sea in May 1942 when they stopped a Japanese advance to Port Moresby, Papua New Guinea. Then in June 1942, the Japanese attacked U.S. forces on Midway Island. But U.S. intelligence officers broke the Japanese code and knew that the attack was coming. In addition, U.S. pilots were learning new maneuvers that allowed direct attacks on Japanese ships. The Japanese force that was supposed to take the island lost four of its six aircraft carriers and all of its planes and pilots. U.S. forces also captured a Japanese Zero airplane, then the most modern in the war, and used it to build the U.S. Navy's new Hellcat plane, which could out-maneuver the Zero. The Hellcats began arriving in the Pacific in 1943.

Despite the successes, winning the war in 1942 was far from a sure thing. Germany and Japan both had very strong hands. German submarine commander Karl Donitz began sinking coastal shipping vessels in January 1942. New York and other coastal cities refused to turn their lights off, and the submarines used the bright city lights to target shipping. In 3 months, the Germans sunk 216 ships, half of them tankers with essential oil for Britain. Burned out ships littered the American beaches.

In the summer of 1942, German forces were besieging the Soviet Union while their planes bombed Britain. The German submarine fleet shifted from the U.S. coast to Atlantic convoys, hitting them especially hard in midocean where little help was possible. In July 1942, a convoy of 34 Allied ships headed for the Russian ports of Murmansk and Archangel was attacked in the Norwegian Sea, and 23 of the 34 ships were sunk. German Admiral Donitz was confident—and the Americans, British, and Russians fearful—that the Allied forces simply could not continue in the face of such losses.

Japan controlled the whole of the western Pacific (see Map 23-2). In August 1942, U.S. forces invaded the tactically important island of Guadalcanal in the Solomon Islands and renamed its airfield Henderson Field. A counter invasion from Japan came close to success. The reporter John Hersey, staying with the troops on the island, told readers:

> The uniforms, the bravado, the air of wearing a knife in the teeth—these were just camouflage. The truth was all over their faces. These were just American boys. They did not want that valley or any part of its jungle. They were ex-grocery clerks, ex-highway laborers, ex-bank clerks, ex-schoolboys.…[T]hey had joined the Marines to see the world, or to get away from a guilt, or most likely to escape the draft, not knowingly to kill or be killed.

But there they were. With navy support, the Marines on Guadalcanal held their position. The Japanese forces were beaten back until, in February 1943, in a move they seldom made during the war, the Japanese abandoned Guadalcanal.

Men in the Military—Volunteers and Draftees

As the war began, young men quickly found themselves in uniform. Sixteen million men had registered for the draft when the war began, more soon after, and others volunteered in anticipation of an expanding draft. The draft was administered by the **Selective Service System** through 6,443 local draft boards that decided who was eligible for various deferments—for married men, for those with children, for those in crucial war work—that were granted less and less often.

Lloyd Kilmer began life on a dairy farm but was working as a bellhop at a hotel in Rochester, Minnesota, when he heard the news of Pearl Harbor. Six months later, Kilmer enlisted in the Army Air Corps and flew combat missions over Europe until he was shot down in June 1944. U.S. troops liberated his prisoner of war camp in April 1945. Growing up in the immigrant neighborhood of East Boston, Massachusetts, during the Depression, Al Fossett ascribed his success on the high school track team to pretending that he was running after something to eat. When war came, he was stationed in British India where he served as a gunner on planes that flew supplies from India to beleaguered Chinese forces. Woodrow W. Crockett was born in Texarkana, Arkansas, and joined the army as a private in 1940. In 1942, he was assigned to the Tuskegee airmen, an African-American unit that achieved considerable distinction in World War II. He flew 149 combat missions during the U.S. invasion of Italy and received the Distinguished Flying Cross.

Most of those who served were white males like Kilmer and Fossett. The Great Depression shaped their childhood, and they liked the food and security of the army even when they were frightened. Only a minority were enthusiastic about serving while most were willing to do a job they believed needed to be done. In the process, they met a greater diversity of people than any previous generation of Americans and saw more of the world and its people.

Selective Service System
Federal agency that coordinated military conscription (the draft) beginning in World War II.

MAP 23-2 Japanese Power in the Pacific. In the early months of World War II, Japan extended its reach through much more of the Pacific region from the Aleutian Islands off Alaska to Borneo and New Guinea in the South Pacific.

Deferments, Alternative Service, and War Work

Not everyone served in the military. The Selective Service allowed local draft boards considerable discretion. Throughout most of the South, draft boards, which were nearly all white, showed a deep aversion to putting black men in uniform and giving them guns, with the result that they had to dip much deeper into the pool of white men, offering whites few deferments. Congress allowed young men to complete college so that, as one draft board member reported, "fathers in their middle thirties were being inducted from their stores, garages, and other businesses," while they saw younger single men sitting in classrooms. A November 1942 law, the Tydings Amendment, exempted agricultural workers from the draft. Men in key war industries and some who would not fight for religious reasons were also sometimes exempted.

Other Americans found themselves in new jobs they had never before imagined. Charles Briscoe's family left the Dust Bowl for California where he learned sheet metal work. In 1940, he took a job at Boeing Aircraft in Wichita, Kansas, building the super-secret B-29 long range bomber. Briscoe remembered, "We knew the B-017s and B-24s didn't have the range to get to Japan. We had to have the B-29 to win the war and get the men home from over there." At 14, Ed Powers was too young for the military, but he joined his father—who was too old to serve—in patrolling their hometown to be sure that everyone was honoring the blackout to avoid a German bombing.

Joseph Bullock was among the 43,000 conscientious objectors who in the words of Selective Service regulations "by reason of religious training and belief, is conscientiously opposed to participation in war in any form." The largest number of COs, as they were called, some 25,000 served as noncombatants in the military, providing first aid to troops under extraordinarily dangerous conditions or behind-the-lines logistical support. Those who for religious reasons could not support the war effort in any form were allowed to work in civilian public service. Bullock and the 12,000 CPS men worked on forestry projects planting trees and building roads, or staffing mental hospitals. They received no pay, had to cover their own expenses, and did not receive veteran benefits at the end of the war. A final group of some 6,000 refused out of conscience to have anything to do with the Selective Service System, and these men were sent to federal prison. Some of them, like David Dellinger, became lifelong antiwar activists. In some areas, COs were treated with respect; in others, they met deep hostility. Harry Van Dyck remembered being told, "You goddamn COs should all be shot." After the war, Bullock was told that he could not teach Sunday School because his wartime service made him an inappropriate role model for Christian children.

When 40 percent of the 21-year-olds who signed up for the first draft registration in late 1940 then got married, General Hershey announced that he would consider that recent marriages "might have been for the purpose of evading the draft." When the draft was expanded to include married men, most fathers were still exempted, leading one young couple to name their new child "Weatherstrip" because he kept his father out of the draft. However, as the need grew, fathers were also drafted, and by 1945, nearly a million fathers were in the service.

Women in Military Service

Early in the war there was some talk of conscripting women, if not for the military then for wartime industrial work. In the end, however, the United States, unlike Great Britain or the Soviet Union, left it up to individual women to decide whether they wanted to serve.

Each of the branches of the military enlisted women in special noncombat units that freed men for combat: the U.S. Army established the Women's Auxiliary Army Corps, or WAACs (later the *Auxiliary* was dropped, and they became the WACs); the

Young women begin their service as WACs during World War II.

U.S. Navy created the Women Accepted for Voluntary Emergency Service, or WAVES; the Army Air Corps set up the Women's Auxiliary Service Pilots, or WASPS; the Coast Guard launched the Women's Reserve of the Coast Guard, nicknamed the SPARS; and the Marines organized an unnamed women's branch. Some 350,000 women (compared with over 15 million men) served in uniform during World War II. Claudine "Scottie" Scott remembered her freshman year at the University of Kansas in the fall of 1940 as "a fun and exciting time," but by the following year, the world had become a much more serious place. Scott volunteered for the WAVES and was assigned to the Joint Chiefs of Staff to deliver the "log of fighting going on all over the world" to the White House every day. She was at the White House and saw President Roosevelt on the day of the allied invasion of Europe in 1944, but her focus was on the fate of her boyfriend who was part of the invading force. He was wounded but returned home, and they were married in the Veterans Hospital in Richmond, Virginia.

Martha Settle grew up in Norristown, Pennsylvania. As an African-American, she experienced racism within the War Manpower Commission. She applied, and was selected by Mary McLeod Bethune, for one of the few officer slots allowed to African-American WACs. Margaret Ray grew up in Indiana and was recruited into a small elite unit of WASPs within the Army Air Force that handled domestic military flying so men could be freed up to fly overseas. "Here I was, this farm girl," Ray remembered, "and it was so exciting." Mary Louise Roberts became a nurse with the army. She commanded a field operating room for troops during the landings in Casablanca, North Africa, in 1943 and on Anzio beach in Italy in 1944.

Rosie the Riveter and Her Friends

Just before the attack on Pearl Harbor, 12 million women in the United States held jobs—a dramatic increase from the depths of the Depression. Middle-class white women tended to be teachers, nurses, social workers, or secretaries. In the course of the war, more than 6 million more women entered the workforce. Some 2 million women went to work in previously all-male defense plants where they sometimes made up half of the workforce. Women also constituted a quarter of the workers in the converted auto industry that was producing tanks and trucks. On the West Coast, 500,000 women worked in the aircraft industry and 225,000 in shipbuilding. They made more money than most women had ever made. They took on hard jobs that before the war people thought only men could handle or from which tradition, law, and all-male unions had excluded them. But even during wartime, women were often relegated to the lower rungs of the industrial order while men took on the highest-skilled, highest-paying jobs. Drilling rivets was high-skill and high-pay work, and in spite of the "Rosie the Riveter" name and public relations posters, far more women worked in routine production jobs.

Women working in industrial plants had to develop a new fashion style that provided room for safe movement, including pants, which made movement much easier than a skirt, and short hair, which was essential around dangerous machinery. In addition, they had to develop a tough attitude in the face of catcalls and wolf whistles. Delana Jensen made 155-millimeter howitzers for the army. She was hired when the plant was still not sure whether women could handle the work, but within months, she was training men. It was exacting work and "had to be perfect…within 1/1,000th of an inch." She liked the denim coveralls and remembered, "We were living in a special time and place. There was an energy in the air and in the people. We were wanted and needed and important to the war effort."

Women working at the Douglas Aircraft Plant in Long Beach, California. Gender diversity was common as women often constituted half of the labor force in the industrial plants. Racial diversity was less common.

American Voices

Kathy O'Grady, "What Did You Do in the War, Grandma?"

In 1995 Kathy O'Grady interviewed her grandmother Katherine O'Grady who remembered the war as a time when women wanted to work in war-related industries. The pay was much better than in other jobs, and being of service to the nation mattered, as did a new found sense of freedom. Many, like O'Grady, looked back on their prewar lives as a time when they were much more naïve than they were later on.

In 1939 I lived in East Providence [Rhode Island]…I worked at Gibson's, a soda fountain at the bus stop on Westminster Street. I was very busy. Servicemen from all over used to come in. I made $15 for a 48-hour week. I bought my own clothes, paid my own expenses, car-fare, whatever I wanted, and I'd go to the movies. If you had a five dollar bill then you were very wealthy.

I met my husband while I was working at Gibson's. He had a construction job building an air base up in Newfoundland. When Pearl Harbor broke out, he came back home and we got married. All the fellows had gone into the service. His brothers were all gone. All the men were leaving. My husband had a deferment because his job was considered important to the defense, and we had a 9-month old son. But he wanted to go so badly that he quit the job.…He was shipped out to Okinawa. He was a Seabee and worked in the construction battalion which builds bases. The Seabees would go ahead of the Marines to make the landing and do all that. He went from one island to the other across the Pacific.…

After my husband went into the Seabee's I quit my job at Gibson's and went to work in a woolen mill, Lister's, which before the war was just a normal routine job. When the war started they needed wool very badly so this was considered a service job. In other words, it was important. At the mill the government used to send out all the Purple Heart soldiers to talk to us and tell us that we couldn't take time off, and pushed all this patriotism on us.…I think I got $27 a week, so it did pay more. The soldiers needed woolen blankets. At the time all servicemen were issued their clothing, their blanket, their bedroll, the whole bit. The blankets that came home after war had traveled all over the world.…We were very proud of [our work], because it meant that we were doing our part.…

After the war things changed because women found out they could go out and they could survive. They could really do it on their own. That's where I think women's lib really started.

Source: An Oral History of Rhode Island Women during World War II, downloaded from www.stg.brown.edu/projects/WWII_Women/ July 30, 2012

Thinking Critically

1. **Documentary Analysis**

   In what ways did the war change Katherine O'Grady's life?

2. **Historical Interpretation**

   What clues does the document provide about the long-term impact of the war on the place of women in American society?

Marginalization in a Democracy—The March on Washington and the War at Home

In 1940, African-Americans and Latinos continued to be excluded from the new prosperity. Three out of four African-Americans still lived in the rural South, the majority still sharecroppers. Most Latinos lived in poverty in the urban or rural Southwest. Even those who had moved from farms to small towns or cities saw themselves passed over as wartime production picked up.

In 1940, the Brotherhood of Sleeping Car Porters, perhaps the most powerful black-led organization in the United States, asked the government to avoid discrimination in the expanding armed forces. After A. Philip Randolph, long-time president of the Brotherhood of Sleeping Car Porters, and Walter White, the executive secretary of the National Association for the Advancement of Colored People (NAACP), met with President Roosevelt later that year, they believed they had a friend in the federal government, especially given Eleanor Roosevelt's commitment to civil rights.

The rapidly expanding war industries were less friendly. When the president of North American Aviation announced, "We will not employ Negroes," he spoke for many whites in management and on the shop floors of the companies. Then, in late 1940, the War Department announced its policy "not to intermingle colored and white enlisted personnel in the same regimental organization." Randolph felt betrayed, and he meant to do something about it.

Randolph proposed a massive march on Washington, initially thinking that 10,000 blacks would come to Washington, DC, to demand that the government protect their economic rights. As word spread, Randolph raised the number to 50,000 and then to 100,000. He insisted that this event would be an all-black march. "There are some things Negroes must do alone," he said. The march was called for July 1, 1941.

As it became clear that the march might be a powerful and embarrassing event, many people within the administration began to panic. They challenged Randolph's patriotism—How could he do such a thing with war imminent? What will they think in Berlin? Randolph's response was, "Oh, perhaps no more than they already think of America's racial policy." Friends within the administration tried to persuade Randolph to postpone the march, but he persisted. The only grounds on which the march could be called off, he said, would be a government order "with teeth in it" that would truly protect the economic rights of African-Americans in the new industries. Randolph won.

On June 25, 1941, Roosevelt signed Executive Order 8802 "to provide for the full and equitable participation of all workers in defense industries, without discrimination because of race, creed, color, or national origin." The order created the **Fair Employment Practices Committee** (later Commission) to enforce the policy. It was the order "with teeth in it." The march was called off. Some called Executive Order 8802 an economic Emancipation Proclamation. Executive Order 8802 was enforced unevenly but sufficiently enough to make a real difference. Sybil Lewis was a maid in Oklahoma being paid $3.50 a week before the war. She was hired at Lockheed Aircraft in Los Angeles at $48 per week. She was paired with a white woman from Arkansas, and though they certainly had their differences, Lewis remembered that they learned, "to relate to each other in ways that we never experienced before." Not all encounters were as positive.

White workers went on strike at a Western Electric factory in Baltimore, Maryland, demanding segregated restrooms. In a factory in Mobile, Alabama, shipyard workers rioted over the promotion of a black welder. Riots also took place in Detroit and New York City in 1943. Twenty-five blacks and nine whites were killed in a June riot in Detroit, and six blacks were killed in another riot in New York's Harlem. As news of these clashes spread, army bases around the world also exploded as segregated white and black units clashed in England and in the United States.

Latinos also faced exclusion and violence. The most obvious symbol of Mexican American resistance to white culture were gangs known as *pachucos*, or zoot suiters, for the exaggerated clothing— a long suit coat with baggy pants that came in at the ankles—that symbolized their defiance of social norms. During wartime frugality when most people were channeling money and resources toward the war effort, the zoot suits also seemed an unpatriotic extravagance. In June 1943, white servicemen in various boot camps in the Los Angeles area took out much of their own frustration by attacking the nearby Latino population, especially the zoot suiters. Police, for the most part, looked the other way. The **zoot suit riots** spread elsewhere until FDR intervened to stop the violence, mostly because he had been courting Mexico as a wartime ally.

In spite of riots and discrimination, and they were very real, World War II also gave African-Americans, Latinos, and American Indians new opportunities. Because of the wartime labor shortages and federal enforcement efforts, many who had previously been excluded got jobs in industries previously closed to them. Others became more politically active, and more would do so once the war ended.

Japanese Internment

In an era when many Americans sacrificed much, including their lives, other Americans, especially Japanese Americans, saw their most basic freedoms undermined by wartime hysteria. The immigration legislation of 1924 had prohibited immigration from Japan. As a result, the Japanese population in the mainland United States comprised some

Fair Employment Practices Committee
Federal agency established in 1941 to curb racial discrimination in war production jobs and government employment.

zoot suit riots
Race riots in June 1943, primarily centered in Los Angeles, in which American military personnel attacked Latinos.

While some Latinos faced hostile rioters in places like Los Angeles, others, like these Mexican-American soldiers, served in the U.S. military and believed that the war was the beginning of their successful civil rights movement.

120,000 people of Japanese descent split between some 40,000 *Issei*, or first-generation immigrants who had arrived before 1924 and were by law "aliens ineligible for citizenship," and twice as many younger *Nisei*, or American-born Japanese who were American citizens. A majority of the Issei were over the age of 50 by 1941, while many Nisei were under 18 and largely quite Americanized. The small Japanese Issei and Nisei community had remained relatively isolated. Most supported themselves by small truck farms or nurseries providing fruits, vegetables, and garden supplies all along the Pacific coast.

In the immediate aftermath of the Pearl Harbor attack, there was little overt hostility toward Japanese Americans. The usually conservative *Los Angeles Times* editorialized that the Japanese were "good Americans, born and educated as such." Speaking of the Nisei, General John L. DeWitt, head of the U.S. Army on the West Coast said, "An American citizen, after all, is an American citizen." In addition, U.S. Attorney General Francis Biddle wrote that he was determined "to avoid mass internment and the persecution of aliens that had characterized the First World War." All would quickly change their minds.

While there were 120,000 people of Japanese ancestry living on the U.S. mainland in 1941, there were 200,000 Japanese living in Hawaii, almost half of the population of the islands. After the attack on Pearl Harbor, the federal government declared a state of martial law and suspended basic rights in Hawaii. Several hundred Japanese were arrested as suspected spies and saboteurs. But the entire economy of Hawaii would have collapsed if the Japanese community had been interned, and there would have been no place to put them and no one to guard them.

The situation for the Japanese on the West Coast was very different. Their treatment dramatically contrasted not only the situation in Hawaii but also the way that German and Italian communities in the United States were treated. Unlike during World War I, the German and Italian communities were not subjected to mass discrimination during World War II. There were arrests of individuals suspected of activities supporting the country's enemies, and given the strength of the Nazi movement within the United States prior to the war, there were individuals that the government had reason to watch. All noncitizens from Germany and Italy were labeled "enemy aliens" when the war began, but FDR ordered the Attorney General to cancel the designation in the fall of 1942—just before Election Day.

When some accused Japanese Americans of spying, FBI Director J. Edgar Hoover said that such charges were utterly without foundation. Nevertheless, leaders of the California Grower-Shipper Vegetable Association, representing large-scale agriculture, did not like the competition of the small Japanese American truck farms, and one association leader declared, "We might as well be honest.…It's a question of whether the white man lives on the Pacific Coast or the brown man." Respected journalists, including Walter Lippmann and Westbrook Pegler, pushed for removal. Pegler wrote, "The Japanese in California should be under armed guard to the last man and woman right now, and to hell with habeas corpus until the danger is over." And by early 1942, General DeWitt, who had first said "An American citizen is an American citizen," was saying "The Japanese race is an enemy race and…the racial strains are undiluted." A few, very few, white voices, like the tiny Committee on American Principles and Fair Play, defended the rights of Japanese Americans. With public opinion running

Photographer Dorothea Lange, who had taken iconic images during the Great Depression, captured the pride and tragedy of this Japanese family waiting to be taken from their homes to a relocation center.

so strongly in favor of removal, President Roosevelt signed Executive Order 9066 on February 19, 1942, ordering the War Department to create "military areas…from which any and all persons may be excluded." The order did not specify which areas or which persons were to be excluded, but the result was that people of Japanese ancestry were ordered out of most of the three West Coast states.

Initially, Japanese Issei and Nisei in America were allowed to move to the Midwest or the East. The rest of the country, like Hawaii, was not covered by the internment order. Some 15,000 people voluntarily moved before General DeWitt ordered an end to such moves in late March. After that, people of Japanese ancestry were ordered to report to "assembly centers," including the Santa Anita racetrack in Southern California and the Tanforan Racetrack in San Bruno near San Francisco.

Yamato Ichihashi, a Stanford professor, described Santa Anita as "mentally and morally depressive." Families who had lived in their own homes, managed their own businesses, in some cases like Ichihashi had been involved in rich professional lives, were suddenly in armed camps, living in stables that had recently held horses, and kept behind barbed wire under the watch of armed guards. The instructions were to bring only what they could carry—no pets and no cameras.

Forced out of their homes and into the temporary relocation centers, some 100,000 Issei and Nisei were then moved a second time to 10 relocation camps scattered through sparsely inhabited regions of the West. The first to open was at Manzanar on a dried up lake bed between the coastal mountains and the higher Sierra Nevada range. In this desert location, summer temperatures were often above 100 degrees while the winter was freezing. Each family had a 20 by 20 foot uninsulated cabin.

For most of the internees, the next 3 years were a time of enforced idleness while the rest of the country worked harder than ever. Some young men volunteered to join the all-Japanese units fighting in Europe and served with distinction while their families waited for them in the camps. Other young men, offended at being asked to foreswear allegiance to an emperor they had never cared about, refused any form of service and were held as virtual prisoners at Tule Lake, California.

Some of the Japanese community challenged the process of internment. Gordon Hirabayashi remembered hearing of the order to report to the camps and thinking, "I was confronted with a dilemma: Do I stay out of trouble and succumb to the status of second-class citizen, or do I continue to live like other Americans and thus disobey the law?" He disobeyed the law and challenged it in court. In its first ruling on the legality of internment, the U.S. Supreme Court threw out Hirabayashi's challenge and he served

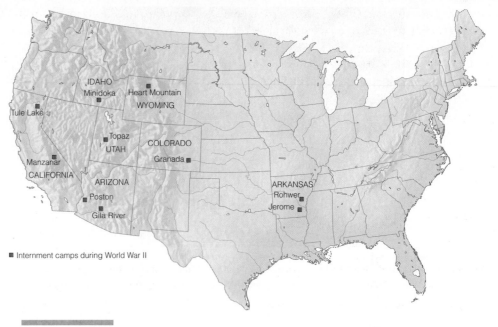

MAP 23-3 **Internment Camps.** Japanese internment camps were located in isolated areas in many parts of the United States.

Japanese internment

A federal government policy implemented by executive order through which Japanese Americans were forced to enter internment camps.

time in a prison camp. Although Justice Frank Murphy supported the court's unanimous opinion in the case, he used the occasion to write that the **Japanese internment** was the first time in history that the federal government had "sustained a substantial restriction on the personal liberty of citizens of the United States based upon the accident of race or ancestry," while noting the parallels with what Nazi Germany was doing to Jews.

A second set of cases known as *Korematsu v. United States* then began to move through the courts. In late 1944, after the presidential election and as *Korematsu v. United States* was about to be decided, the War Department declared that the original "military necessity" was now over and that those of Japanese ancestry were free to return to their homes. When the court announced its decision, it again sidestepped the specific issue, but as Hugo Black wrote in the majority decision, "All legal restrictions which curtail the civil rights of a single racial group are immediately suspect." As those who had lived in the camps returned to the West Coast, they found that their homes and businesses were long gone and that they had been excluded from the prosperity of wartime America. While the losses of those interned were estimated at $400 million, Congress provided $37 million in reparations in 1948. Only decades later, Congress voted $20,000 for each surviving internee, and in 1998, President Bill Clinton awarded the Presidential Medal of Freedom to Fred Korematsu.

> **23.2** | **Quick Review** Which groups gained the most from the United States' involvement in World War II? Which groups on the home front were hurt by the war?

INDUSTRIAL STRENGTH, INDUSTRIAL PROSPERITY

23.3 | Analyze U.S. industrial strength and productivity and its impact on the outcome of the war and on American society.

America's wartime ally, Soviet dictator Joseph Stalin, understood the key role the United States would play in World War II. Even though the Soviet Union supplied far more soldiers (and suffered almost 20 times as many battlefield deaths), Stalin said, "The most important things in this war are machines....The United States...is a country of machines." It was an accurate analysis.

A month after the United States entered the war, Roosevelt told Congress, "It will not be sufficient for us…to produce a slightly superior supply of munitions to that of Germany, Japan, and Italy." The president said the United States needed to provide "crushing superiority of equipment in any theater of the world war." Roosevelt insisted that the United States produce 60,000 airplanes in 1942 and 125,000 more in 1943, plus 120,000 tanks, 55,000 antiaircraft guns, and 16 million tons of merchant shipping. Few thought it could be done, but the goals were met.

Wartime Production

Several factors led to the extraordinary U.S. output in the machinery of war in 1942 and 1943. Compared to the rest of the world, the United States was a manufacturing giant even in the 1930s, and the United States had huge supplies of iron ore, coal, and oil. In 1937, the United States produced 4.8 million automobiles while Germany produced 331,000 and Japan only 26,000. Moreover at that point in 1937, perhaps half of all U.S. manufacturing plants were idle and a very large part of the U.S. labor force was out of work. It would not take long, once the country put itself on a war footing, for the unemployed to go to work, the plants to start up, and those already in operation to shift from peace-time to war-focused production. The War Production Board, the government agency charged with ensuring that the country produced the war materials needed, quickly prohibited the manufacture of automobiles for private use and limited other civilian manufacturing after the nation went to war. On February 10, 1942, auto workers in Detroit held a little ceremony for the last cars coming down the line then began rebuilding the machinery to make tanks and trucks. Aircraft plants, especially the giant Boeing and Lockheed plants on the West Coast, and Ford's Willow Run aircraft plant near Detroit started to turn out planes. Shipyards went to three shifts.

The United States also had an attitude toward manufacturing that greatly helped its success. German armaments minister Albert Speer told Hitler that he was worried because it was the Americans, not the Germans, who "knew how to act with organizationally simple methods and therefore achieved great results" while Germany was stuck with an "outmoded, tradition-bound, and arthritic organizational system." At the beginning of the war, Germany made 425 different kinds of aircraft, 151 kinds of trucks, and 150 different motorcycles all to exacting precision standards. The Americans made far fewer models, accepted lower standards, and got things done—a high-volume output that far surpassed allies or enemies.

Perhaps the best example of American industrial productivity was the Liberty ship, the workhorse of the merchant marine that kept Britain, Russia, and later U.S. forces in the Pacific supplied throughout the war. The Liberty ships were all built to the same standard: 440 feet long with a cargo hold that could contain 330 freight cars, 440 tanks, or 3.4 million C-rations. When the first Liberty ship, the *Patrick Henry,* was christened on December 30, 1941, just after the Pearl Harbor attack, it had taken 355 days—just shy of a year—to build. Six months later, in June 1942, it took 105 days to build a Liberty ship, and in November 1942, working around the clock, workers built the *Robert E. Peary* in less than 5 days. One engineer called the Liberty ships the "Model T of the seas," and President Roosevelt called them ugly ducklings, but they did the job.

Henry Kaiser created a huge new industrial facility in Richmond, on San Francisco Bay, where tens of thousands of workers of different races and from every part of the country, many of whom had never worked in any industry before, built these ships. The highly specific jobs of mass-produced ship building in which each worker repeated one small task over and over again took much less skill than had the jobs of elite shipbuilding workers in the past, but new workers loved the opportunities the yards provided, and the finished ships just kept coming.

The huge increase in American industrial activity was not without its problems. Early in 1942, the government took several steps to control inflation and costs. The Office of Price Administration announced a General Maximum Price Regulation in

April that made the prices of goods and services in March 1942 permanent. Known as "General Max," the regulation did help control costs and inflation. The National War Labor Board negotiated a settlement between union and management at Bethlehem, Republic, Youngstown, and Inland Steel Companies that limited wage increases to cost of living. Known as the "Little Steel agreement" (the U.S. Steel Company was "Big Steel"), the agreement became a norm throughout American industries. Although there had been several strikes in the months just before the war, most of organized labor took a "no strike pledge" for the duration of the war in return for a government policy that required industries to maintain labor contracts and union membership.

Wartime Prosperity

In spite of restrictions on wage increases, more Americans were employed and earned more money than ever before in their lives or the nation's history during World War II. Wartime rationing limited some goods. People needed ration stamps to purchase their monthly allotment of meat, coffee, tires, and gasoline, and new cars were simply not available. Housing was very hard to find, thus, many lived in cramped quarters, while extended families often moved in together. Nevertheless, Americans who could remember the Great Depression found themselves with previously undreamed-of opportunity. Laura Briggs, a young farm woman from Idaho, remembered, "We and most other farmers went from a tarpaper shack to a new frame house with indoor plumbing…[and] a hot water heater.…It was just so modern we couldn't stand it." A shipyard worker in Portsmouth, Virginia, said, "I felt like something had come down from heaven. I went from forty cents an hour to… two seventy-five an hour.…[T]he war completely turned my life around." By December 1944, Macy's department stores reported the highest volume of sales in their history.

National leaders worried about a combination of prosperity and complacency. One Pentagon officer said that Americans "have never been bombed.…They have little appreciation of the horrors of war." In December 1943, FDR told his cabinet that he sometimes thought, "One of the best things that could happen, would be to have a few German bombs fall here to wake us up." But other than isolated and utterly unsuccessful enemy efforts to fire on the Oregon coast and New York's Long Island, the continental United States was never bombed or shot at, which was a dramatically different experience from that of Britain or Russia or, of course, Italy, Germany, and Japan. Letters home from those doing the fighting were censored, and even if they had not been, many soldiers did not want to discuss the horrors of war.

Sometimes complacency had a high cost. When two inmates escaped from Auschwitz and brought stories of the Holocaust to the United States, many simply refused to believe that such things were possible. In the summer of 1943, given detailed reports of the Nazi death camps, Supreme Court Justice Felix Frankfurter simply responded, "I am unable to believe you." It was simply too horrible to contemplate. The degree to which traditional anti-Semitism played a role in some people's responses to the news about Nazi death camps, the degree to which people such as Frankfurter simply could not believe what they were hearing, and the extent to which other urgencies of the war led people to focus elsewhere has been debated ever since the war. For whatever reason—or probably many reasons—few Americans took the stories of the emerging Holocaust seriously until the end of the war demonstrated their awful truth.

Initially, the administration wanted to raise taxes to pay most of the war's cost immediately, but in the end, taxes covered about 45 percent, while loans covered the rest. Nevertheless, taxes increased significantly during the war. The Revenue Act of 1942 raised $7 billion in new taxes. In 1939, only 4 million of the richest Americans paid income tax. The 1942 law brought 13 million new tax payers into the system. The government also began payroll tax withholding in 1943, requiring employers to deduct taxes and pay them directly to the government before issuing paychecks. The rapid increases in wages and job opportunities, coupled with continued appeals to patriotism, limited objections to the new and much higher levels of taxation.

The government also borrowed money. Low-cost Series E bonds were sold, allowing many Americans to save some of what they were earning and contribute to the war effort. Larger loans were also forthcoming. Commercial banks increased their holdings in U.S. government debt from $1 billion in 1941 to $24 billion in 1945. In spite of all the borrowing and spending, the United States emerged from the war as the one remaining economic powerhouse in the world as the economies of all the other economic leaders suffered much more from the war.

23.3 | **Quick Review** How was the American experience during World War II different from that of people in Europe and Asia?

WINNING A WORLD WAR—NORTH AFRICA, EUROPE, ASIA, THE PACIFIC, 1943–1945

23.4 | Explain the course of the war leading to victory in Europe and then the Pacific.

While many Americans prospered during World War II, for those in the military, especially those in combat, World War II was a combination of long waits, boredom, and occasional moments of sheer terror, pain, and heroism.

The War in Europe, 1943–1945

In late 1942, the Russians insisted that it was time for their western allies to open a second front and attack Germany and German-occupied France directly to take the pressure off of Russia. But Churchill, remembering the terrible British losses of World War I, would not agree. Instead, Britain and America kept bombing Germany, and allied troops landed at Oran, Algeria, in November 1942 to attack German forces in North Africa, a huge diversion as far as Stalin was concerned, but it was the beginning of some victories that lifted spirits among the Allies.

In January 1943, Roosevelt went to Casablanca in North Africa to meet with Churchill, becoming the first president since Wilson to travel outside of the Western Hemisphere and the first since Lincoln to visit U.S. troops in the field. They agreed on several things: that they would continue to bomb Germany; that after North Africa, they would invade Italy, not the coast of France; and that while the United States would continue to supply Britain and Russia, a third of new forces and supplies would go to the Pacific. At a press conference at the end of the meeting, FDR also said that the Allies would accept only unconditional surrender from Germany, Italy, and Japan; there would be no intermediate peace negotiations. Then, in February 1943, the Russian Army and the Russian winter defeated the Nazi troops at Stalingrad, and the tide of war began to change. The Russian Army—known as the Red Army, which had been retreating and defending, went on the offensive. The German *Wehrmacht*—the military machine that had been undefeated in Europe since 1939—started retreating.

In the summer of 1943, American and British units began the attack on what was known as "fortress Europe"—the Nazi-controlled territory at the heart of the continent. On July 10, 1943, U.S., Canadian, and British forces, having sent coded messages that lured the Germans and Italians into defensive positions on the northern part of the Sicily, instead landed on the south coast of the island. U.S. forces under General George Patton made rapid progress across the island taking Palermo on the north coast on July 22. The effort was bolstered by welcoming crowds who helped them and shouted "Down with Mussolini." Italy's King Victor Emmanuel III dismissed Mussolini and had him arrested, but German units in Italy continued to fight. Allied forces continued a long, slow, and bitter battle up the Italian peninsula, attacking Salerno in September 1943, sustaining a long battle around Monte Cassino, making a fresh landing on the beaches at Anzio outside of Rome in January 1944, and finally taking control of Rome itself in June 1944.

World War II in Europe

- Axis powers
- Areas under Axis control, May 1941
- Allied powers
- Neutral
- Axis forces
- Allied forces: U.S.S.R.
- Allied forces: U.S. and British
- Major battles

MAP 23-4 The War in Europe. Early in the war, Nazi forces had attacked France and then the Soviet Union, but as the tide of war turned, Soviet forces moved across much of eastern Europe and into Germany itself while U.S. and British forces attacked Nazi forces in North Africa, Italy, and finally France and Germany.

While the Red Army rolled west from Russia into Poland and eventually Germany, and while American and British forces won battles in North Africa and Italy, American pilots joined their British counterparts in what became round-the-clock bombing of Germany. The British had begun bombing German military targets, first in France and then, as the planes got better, in the Ruhr Valley of Germany itself. Precision bombing in real wartime conditions was exceedingly difficult, so the British simply tried to destroy the morale of the German civilians, especially industrial workers, by bombing wherever they could—what some called terror bombing. When the Americans joined the war, they initially found the terror bombing to be abhorrent, but they worked out a compromise: the British would bomb at night, bombing wherever they could, and the Americans, with more sophisticated equipment, could bomb specified targets during the day. The first U.S. bombers began their attacks in August 1942, and by January 1943, hundreds of U.S. bombers began penetrating German airspace, hitting industrial targets like the German city of Bremen. The losses of pilots and crews were staggering. Six hundred Americans were killed in the summer of 1943, 16 percent of those who flew missions. One pilot remembered his terror when being attacked by German Messerschmitt 109s:

> The plane shook with the chatter of our guns....As other planes were hit, we had to fly through their debris....When a plane blew up, we saw their parts all over the sky. We smashed into some of the pieces. One plane hit a body which tumbled out of a plane ahead. A crewman went out the front hatch of a plane and hit the tail assembly of his own plane. No chute. His body turned over and over like a bean bag tossed into air.

And still the crews kept flying.

In November 1943, President Roosevelt left the United States for a second time, flying to Cairo, Egypt, for a third meeting with Prime Minister Churchill and then on to Tehran, Iran, for his first meeting with Stalin, which Churchill and the nominal Chinese leader Chiang Kai-shek also attended. FDR was intrigued to meet Stalin in person. At Cairo, FDR also tried to persuade Churchill that Britain must renounce its colonies in India, Burma, Malaya, and Hong Kong and promise them independence after the war as the United States was doing with the Philippine Islands. Churchill was a great wartime leader in Britain, but he was equally a lifelong British imperialist, and he was not about to be persuaded.

The Tehran Conference included discussions of the war in China. In addition, Stalin kept up the pressure for the United States and Britain to invade France as quickly as possible and promised to join the war against Japan once the war in Europe was won. The conference was also a test of the personal chemistry between Stalin and FDR. Although the U.S. president was confident of his own skill in persuading people, he confessed, "I couldn't get any personal connection with Stalin." U.S. Ambassador to Russia Averell Harriman described Stalin as someone of "high intelligence," with a "fantastic grasp of detail" and "shrewdness." Stalin, Harriman said, was "better informed than Roosevelt, more realistic than Churchill, in some ways the most effective of the war leaders. At the same time he was, of course, a murderous tyrant." Stalin wanted an absolute promise that the United States and Britain would start the invasion of Germany—code named **Operation Overlord**—in the spring of 1944. And he wanted to make sure that others knew, as he had told Josef Tito, who was leading a Communist uprising behind German lines in Yugoslavia, "whoever occupies a territory also imposes his own social system."

The Red Army, Stalin assured everyone, would not pull back from the lands it was seizing from Germany. Operation Overlord was set for May 1, 1944. In the meantime, U.S. and British planes kept bombing Germany and Germany-occupied France—6,000 bombing runs during 1 week alone in February 1944—to make it difficult for German forces to prepare for an invasion that they knew was coming. Although Roosevelt had become convinced as early as 1942 that the Nazis were killing Jews, the planes did not bomb the Nazi death camps or the rail lines to Auschwitz. U.S. planners simply could not bring themselves to believe that anything like the scale of the Holocaust was happening in spite of the fact that by 1944 they had clear evidence

Operation Overlord
U.S. and British invasion of France in June 1944 during World War II.

D-Day
June 6, 1944, the day of the first paratroop drops and amphibious landings on the coast of Normandy, France, in the first stage of Operation Overlord during World War II.

of the reality. Questions remain about why, with so many bombs being dropped, some better effort was not made to stop the trains going to those camps.

Everyone agreed that the Americans would lead the invasion of Western Europe. Roosevelt passed over several other army officers and appointed General Dwight D. Eisenhower to lead the attack. Born in Texas and raised in Abilene, Kansas, Eisenhower, better known as Ike to everyone, had spent his entire career in the peacetime army. He had been promoted to the rank of colonel months before the United States entered the war in 1941. Ike had a unique ability to get people to work together and do so with good cheer, skills that would be needed in the utmost to coordinate the American, British, and French forces involved in the invasion of Europe.

The buildup in Britain in 1943 and early 1944 was huge, with 150,000 U.S. soldiers arriving every month. The British called these American troops "overpaid, oversexed, and over here," but welcomed them not only for what they were about to do for the liberation of Europe but also for the supplies of cocoa, canned meat, candy bars, tobacco, and even toilet paper that they had. Finally, with the tides right and a break predicted in the weather, Eisenhower decided that June 6 was the time to go—and so the day became known as **D-Day**, 1944.

One young soldier, Elliott Johnson, remembered, "On the morning of June 6, we took off. I can remember the morning. Who could sleep?…I was on an LST, a landing ship tank." An armada of 6,483 vessels of all sorts of descriptions made the brief seasickness-inducing trip across the English Channel to land on several beaches in Normandy, code named Utah, Omaha, Gold, Juno, and Sword, under intense German shelling and rifle fire. Units of the U.S. 82nd and 101st Airborne divisions parachuted behind the German lines to break communications between the Germans on the beach and their commanders. In the confusion of the invasion most Allied troops were also cut off from their commanders and had to make their own decisions.

Troops landing on Omaha beach on D-Day had to use grappling irons to reach the tops of the cliffs facing them, suffering large losses. Once they got off the beaches and over the cliffs, British and U.S. troops got stuck on hedgerows, long lines of tightly planted bushes 5 to 10 feet wide that farmers in Normandy had used instead of fences and that now provided far better protection for German troops than planners had estimated. Slowly the troops broke past the initial defenses. General Omar Bradley reflected this "thin wet line of khaki that dragged itself ashore" held its ground and then started moving inland. Johnson remembered the odd scenes of battle, "Now on my way down the road I saw, on my right, these dead German boys. On my left, going across the field, is a French peasant leading a cow, cradling its head in his arms, protecting it with his body as much as possible. He had come back to get his cow, leading it away from all the noise and death." Johnson and the rest kept moving.

An iconic picture of some of the first American troops wading ashore on the beaches of Normandy, France, on D-Day, June 6, 1944, to complete the conquest of Nazi Germany.

American forces moved quickly to take control of the French towns of Brest, Lorient, and St. Nazaire and then moved on to Paris, which they liberated on August 25, 1944. A tank force under the command of General Patton headed straight for the Rhine River and Germany itself. German troops fought hard, but they were outnumbered as more troops came across the Channel. By November, the Allied forces were at the Rhine River and the border of Germany.

In December, Hitler ordered one last desperate *Blitzkrieg* and eight German divisions roared out of the Ardennes forest to surround American troops in a bulge in the Allied line near the village of Bastogne, Belgium. When the Germans called on the surrounded American forces to surrender, their commander, General Anthony C. McAuliffe, responded with one word, "Nuts!" When the German officer who received the message didn't understand it, a translator explained that it meant "Go to Hell!" With the help of tanks ordered north from Paris, the Allied forces defeated the Germans in the so-called Battle of the Bulge, and U.S. forces began moving into Germany.

As Americans moved across Germany, they discovered the full reality of the Nazi death camps. Russian units liberated the first camps early in 1945, and then in April, U.S. forces liberated Buchenwald with 20,000 prisoners. U.S. soldiers described the horror of the smell and seeing the bodies stacked up in piles. Just before the army arrived, prisoners seized control of Buchenwald, thinking, correctly, that the Nazi guards might well try to kill all of them to hide the evidence of what had been going on. U.S. forces later liberated Dora-Mittelbau, Flossenburg, Dachau, and Mauthausen camps, while British and Soviet forces liberated others. In many of the camps, the liberating armies found prisoners on the brink of starvation and weakened by disease. They also found piles of corpses, human bones, cremation ovens, and ample other evidence of the horrors that had actually taken place. The Nazis had systematically killed 6 million Jews and another 6 million people—gypsies, homosexuals, people with disabilities, and others they considered inferior humans.

Allied troops kept moving east and Red Army troops moved west. While armies marched, the bombing of Germany continued, including a controversial joint U.S.–British bombing of the city of Dresden, Germany, in February 1945 in which the resulting firestorm killed perhaps 25,000 people. The Russians were soon within miles of Berlin itself. U.S. troops finally crossed the Rhine River in March and the Elbe River in April while the Russian Army attacked Berlin. On April 30, in a Berlin bunker 55 feet underground, with Russian troops directly above, Hitler shot himself. A week later, Admiral Donitz, who had replaced him, ordered all German units to cease operation. The war in Europe was over.

As U.S. forces discovered the full extent of Nazi death camps, Americans came face to face with the terrible reality. This 23-year-old Czech victim of the Nazi camp at Flossenburg, Germany, was found by the 97th Division of the U.S. Army.

Roosevelt's Death, Truman's Leadership

Just days before the war in Europe ended, on April 12, 1945, President Franklin D. Roosevelt died. Roosevelt had led the United States longer than any president ever had or ever would. And suddenly, he was gone. In the last year of his life, Roosevelt's health was terrible. His blood pressure was dangerously high, his hands shook, and he found it hard to stand even with his leg braces. Few of those closest to him were surprised when he died on a short vacation at Warm Springs, Georgia. Nevertheless, the news was devastating. Months earlier, in November 1944, Roosevelt had been elected to a fourth term in office. Unlike the third term, he made it clear early on that he wanted to see the war through to the end. His Republican opponent was the reformist young governor of New York State, Thomas E. Dewey, but more Americans wanted continuity in a time of war. Roosevelt defeated Dewey by a comfortable margin, winning 53 percent of the popular vote and 432 electoral votes to Dewey's 99.

The November 1944 election had brought one important change, however. In 1940, Roosevelt had turned to his trusted confidant, Agriculture Secretary Henry A. Wallace, to serve as vice president. By 1944, though, many in the Democratic Party, worried that Roosevelt might not live out the next term, thought Wallace was too liberal, and convinced Roosevelt and the nominating convention to find another candidate. The compromise candidate was Missouri Senator Harry S. Truman. Truman had served in the army in World War I, tried unsuccessfully to open a clothing store in Kansas City, and then worked his way up in the Democratic political machine of his home town. He was elected to the Senate in 1934 and strongly supported the New Deal. In his second Senate term, he led a committee looking into war profiteering. He had been vice president for less than 3 months, had seldom met with FDR, and did not know many of the highest-level government secrets, including the development of the atomic bomb, when, on the afternoon of April 12, 1945, he stood in the White House cabinet room and took the oath of office as president of the United States. It would be Truman, not Roosevelt, who would lead the nation in the final months of the war and the crucial years after it.

American Voices

Alvin Kernan, *A Bluejacket's Odyssey in World War II*

Alvin Kernan went on to a successful academic career at Princeton and Yale, but in 1940, he was a 17-year-old looking for opportunity. He found it, serving in the Pacific from Pearl Harbor to the Japanese surrender. His is a story of furious battles and long waits, experiencing fear, bravery, boredom, joy, and most of all gratitude for surviving. For many who fought, World War II was not a grand campaign against fascism but a battle to keep going and survive.

In the winter of 1940–41, I stood in the deep snows of the mountains of southern Wyoming and realized that it wasn't going to work....Seventeen years old, no job, no prospects, I knew how to do only one thing, the same thing all inland mountain boys do, go to sea....Still eager to work with airplanes, I considered it a stroke of good luck that I had been assigned to Torpedo Squadron 6, part of the air group on the USS *Enterprise* (*CV-6*), one of three carriers in the Pacific Fleet....I was brought down to earth that afternoon by being put on the anchor chain work detail. Life on board ship is a constant battle with rust, in which the weapons are the chipping hammer, the wire brush, red lead, and gray paint.... Hard work, dirty, tiring, hot, and totally unrewarded....

[On the morning of December 7, 1941] The captain came on the public address system to announce that Pearl Harbor had been bombed and that we were now at war with the Japanese.

I didn't worry about being killed, but I did wonder how long I was going to have to stay in the navy now. We all disliked the Japanese and the Germans in a general kind of way, not really knowing much about them....Each sailor was given postcards to send home: two with the printed message "I am well and will write soon," and another two with "I am wounded and will write details as soon as possible." We joked that there should be a third message, "I am dead."...Death lived on an aircraft carrier operating in wartime conditions....[A] thoughtless step backward on the flight and hanger decks where the planes were turning up led to decapitation and gory dismemberment by a propeller. Planes went out on patrol and were never heard from again.

[In October 1942] A little after 0900, the public address system broke the quiet of the ship with an announcement from the bridge, "Enemy aircraft at fifty miles and closing." In the ordnance shack, just below the flight deck, we could see nothing, only listen, feel the vibrating steel deck, and slide back and forth with the steep turns that came in quick succession....As I started back across the flight deck, the guns began firing again as a single diver-bomber made a run on us. I lay flat on the deck, covering as much of my body as possible with my tin hat, trying to work my way into it, and thinking for the first time that I was likely to die, and resenting it, feeling that at nineteen I really hadn't had a chance to do most of the things people do and vowing to do them if I survived. From that moment to this, life has seemed a gift—overtime, in a way—and all the more enjoyable for it....

August 13 [1945]—they tell us that the war has ended.... There was nothing to do to celebrate, and I felt nothing, absolutely nothing—no exhilaration, no triumph, no anticipation of going home, not even the simple pleasure of having survived.

Source: Alvin Kernan, *Crossing the Line: A Bluejacket's Odyssey in World War II* (New Haven: Yale University Press, 2007)

Thinking Critically

1. Documentary Analysis

Why did Kernan join the military? How did he respond to the outbreak of war?

2. Contextualization

How would explain Kernan's lack of emotion upon hearing that the war was over? What light does his response shed on the nature of the fighting in the Pacific?

The War in the Pacific, 1943–1945

While the war in Europe was over, the war in the Pacific was far from over, and U.S. troops were preparing for what they knew would be a horrific invasion of Japan itself. After the successful seizure of control of Guadalcanal in the Solomon Islands in February 1943, commanders made the decision to skip some Japanese-held islands, leaving their troops isolated, and instead, "island hop" toward their main objective. U.S. forces moved slowly but surely toward Japan. The defeats of 1942 seemed further behind. American factories produced machine guns, ships, and airplanes at an extraordinary rate, far faster than Japan could match, and enough to supply forces in the Pacific even as the war in Europe remained the priority until it was won.

The war in the Pacific was brutal. American troops came up against Japanese soldiers who would fight to the very last. The Japanese lived by a code that prohibited

MAP 23-5 The War in the Pacific. Early in the war, Japan controlled a huge area around the western Pacific, and only a long series of sea and island battles turned the tide.

surrender. The Imperial Japanese Army's Field Service Code said, "Never give up a position but rather die," and there were no instructions for surrender. The Japanese troops knew that the Americans would always have more food, more armaments, and more back-up, but they were confident that their loyalty and fighting spirit was enough to make up for all of that.

From bombers based on Midway and on Henderson Field on Guadalcanal, from aircraft carriers, and in battles on sweltering beaches, U.S. troops kept moving. They attacked Tarawa and Makin islands in the Gilbert Islands in November 1943 and then turned them into bases for further movement. In the first 6 months of 1944, U.S. Marines took Kwajalein, Eniwetok, Truk, and Saipan. On Saipan, more than a thousand

Navajo code talkers like these fought on Pacific islands, but by communicating in the native Navajo language, were able to establish a means of communication that the Japanese, expert at breaking American coded messages, were never able to understand.

Japanese civilians and soldiers jumped to their deaths from rocky cliffs rather than surrender. In air battles during June, U.S. forces, flying new and much better planes, virtually decimated the Japanese Air Force. U.S. submarines cut off the shipment of oil from Indonesia to Japan. U.S. commanders did not stage a landing on an island until navy ships had bombarded an island for some time while planes dropped bomb after bomb. Once an island was secure, the Seabees (the navy term for uniformed construction workers) moved in and with amazing speed built airfields, shelters, and bases.

In June 1944, the United States began a campaign to retake the Philippine Islands. In October, the American and Japanese navies engaged in one of the largest sea battles in history, involving 282 ships and over 200,000 sailors off of Leyte Island. The U.S. fleet was victorious in spite of the continuing strengths of the Japanese Navy and the use of suicide *kamikaze* planes, basically planes that were used as bombs.

General MacArthur, who had left Corregidor under cover of darkness in early 1942, waded ashore facing carefully located cameras on October 20, 1944, and announced, "People of the Philippines, I have returned.…The hour of your redemption is here." In spite of MacArthur's heroics, the Japanese were able to reinforce Luzon, the main island of the Philippines, and major battles during the first 3 months of 1945 took place before the United States secured control of its former colony. Manila, the city that young service men had considered a paradise in 1941, was now a city of rubble.

In some of the fiercest fighting of the war, U.S. Marines seized Iwo Jima island in February and March 1945, moving ever closer to Japan itself. The attacks on Iwo Jima and those on some of the earlier islands were aided by Navajo code talkers who relayed messages in the Navajo language—a code the Japanese were never able to break. Iwo Jima was tiny, only 4.5 miles by 2.5 miles, but U.S. control of its airfield and radar meant that U.S. bombers going to Japan had a much shorter flight.

After a long navy bombardment, Marines landed on the beach at Iwo Jima on February 19 and sank into the volcanic sand. In spite of the bombardment, the Japanese forces on the island were still strong, and fierce hand-to-hand combat followed the landing. The Japanese refused to surrender, and many died at the hands of new U.S. flamethrowers that literally incinerated them. Associated Press photographer Joe Rosenthal took his famous photo of the Marines raising the flag on Mount Suribachi on February 23, but the fighting went on for another month. Of the 21,000 Japanese defending the island, over 20,000 died in combat.

The battle for Okinawa in April to June of 1945 was equally brutal, some 70,000 Japanese troops and 100,000 Okinawan civilians as well as almost 8,000 Americans died there. By June 1945, with the war in Europe over and after intense fighting in the Pacific, the U.S. forces in the Pacific were close to a landing on Japan itself. But it never happened.

The Atomic Era Begins

Manhattan Project
The effort, using the code name Manhattan Engineer District, to develop an atomic bomb during World War II.

While armies and navies clashed, a small team of U.S. scientists had begun work in 1942 on a top-secret venture, code-named the **Manhattan Project**. Enrico Fermi won the Nobel Prize for Physics in 1938 and used the prize money to leave fascist Italy for New York. In March 1939, Fermi warned that recent research, including his own, in atomic physics pointed to the potential development of a new form of weapon. When Fermi went to the U.S. Navy Department, a receptionist announced, "There's a wop outside." The officers who received him were not much more interested. But some of the world's best known physicists, many of whom were Jewish refugees from Nazi Germany (11 German Jewish refugees would eventually win the Nobel Prize), were determined that the U.S. government needed to act before the Nazis. A group drafted a letter to President Roosevelt, which was signed by their most well-known and respected member, Albert Einstein, and delivered in the fall of 1941. After considering the letter and the report on Nazi research, Roosevelt said simply, "This requires action." And action, top-secret action, it got.

The Manhattan Project began under a stadium at the University of Chicago, where the first chain reaction was achieved in December 1942. Then, under the scientific direction of physicist Robert J. Oppenheimer and the military oversight of General Leslie Groves, the work moved to the isolated town of Los Alamos, New Mexico, where it was easier to keep it secret. The scientists bent all of their efforts to beating Germany in the development of "the bomb," that they now knew they could build. Ironically, part way through the war, Germany suspended further research on atomic warfare because of the cost and because Hitler considered atomic physics to be "Jewish physics." However, the Americans did not know that and kept going. In Oak Ridge, Tennessee, TVA dams provided the power for the extraction of U-235 (a form of Uranium), and at Hanford, Washington, other New Deal dams, the Bonneville and Grand Coulee, drove the plants that squeezed plutonium out of uranium. With those ingredients, the engineers at Los Alamos could build their bomb.

Over 2 billion dollars was spent on the project and 150,000 people were involved, though only a tiny percentage had any idea of what they were working on. The Danish physicist Niels Bohr who had once said that the United States could not produce an atomic bomb "unless you turn the United States into one huge factory," reviewed the work in 1945 and said, "You have done just that." They had. On July 16, 1945, Oppenheimer and his team tested the first bomb in the Nevada desert. That evening, they sent a top-secret telegram to President Truman, "Operated on this morning. Diagnosis not yet complete but results seem satisfactory and already exceed expectations." Truman, who had been briefed in April, understood fully.

While people in the postwar era have debated the morality of using something of the power of the atomic bomb, few in the administration seem to have had any doubts about it. By 1945, the war had come to a point where the actors would use any weapon they could.

As scientists developed the atom bomb, regular bombs were doing their work on Japan. Boeing B-29s were dropping tons of explosives on Japanese cities. The fire-bombing of Tokyo in February and March 1945 killed almost a million people and left 8 million homeless, far more than either atomic bomb. Still, there was something unique in the use of a single bomb, harnessing the power used in the sun, for warfare.

On August 6, 1945, Air Force Colonel Paul Tibbets piloted a B-29 named the *Enola Gay* that took off from recently captured Tinian Island. The plane carried a single bomb that was dropped on Hiroshima, killing 40,000 people instantly and

This picture of Nagasaki gives some sense of the total devastation caused by a single atomic bomb on what had previously been a large urban area.

THINKING HISTORICALLY

The Decision to Drop the Atomic Bomb

President Harry Truman was clear: "The final decision of where and when to use the atomic bomb was up to me.... Let there be no doubt about it. I regarded the bomb as a military weapon and never had any doubt that it should be used." None of the president's inner circle seem to have had any doubts about dropping the atomic bomb on a major city in Japan either, and few beyond that circle knew anything about the top-secret project until news of the bombing of Hiroshima reached the world on August 6, 1945. For soldiers and sailors facing the invasion of Japan, word of the bomb's use was seen only as a blessing. The then 20-year-old sailor Alvin Kernan remembered, "Each of us felt, further, that those two bombs had saved our lives—not life in general, but our own felt, breathing life. No one who was not there will ever understand how fatalistically we viewed the invasion of Japan....[E]ach of us felt that survival was unlikely."

Some, however, did argue for a different course of action. U.S. Army Chief of Staff General George C. Marshall worried about the "opprobrium which might follow from an ill-considered employment of such force." Some senior military leaders had moral qualms about the killing of so many civilians if the bomb was dropped on a Japanese city.

Some of the physicists who helped develop the bomb also argued for a different course of action. Leo Szilard and James Franck, key researchers on the Manhattan Project, recommended that instead of dropping the bomb on a city it first be used on a "desert or a barren island" to show Japan what might be coming. They also said that once the first atomic bomb was dropped, a new arms race "will be on in earnest not later than the morning after our first demonstration of the existence of nuclear weapons," and they argued for putting international controls of nuclear weapons in place. Szilard also organized a petition signed by 68 Manhattan Project scientists, raising questions about the arms race they feared would come.

So why did Truman ignore these recommendations and order that an atomic bomb be dropped on Hiroshima and 3 days later on Nagasaki? Could he have opted for the idea of a demonstration explosion first? Was the bombing of Nagasaki necessary before the Japanese government even had time to consider the implications of the bombing of Hiroshima? At the time, and for the rest of his life, Truman insisted that he had made the decisions himself and never—then or later—had any doubts about them. Still, historians debate the reasons for his action. Because the United States had access to many Japanese secret cables, Truman knew that the country was under enormous pressure to end the war but nevertheless still had resources to keep fighting. Early in the war, President Roosevelt and the other allied leaders had agreed that only unconditional surrender by Germany and Japan would be acceptable, and in July 1945, Truman, Churchill, and Stalin reaffirmed that only the "unconditional surrender of all Japanese armed forces" would end the war and that the only "alternative is prompt and utter destruction of Japan." Truman also knew that the Soviet Union had promised to join the war against Japan once the war in Europe was over, and some have argued that Truman was determined to show Stalin the full extent of American power by defeating Japan first. U.S. military leaders estimated that the United States might lose 200,000 soldiers and sailors in the planned November invasion of Japan, and Truman certainly wanted to avoid that death toll. Some have also seen the bombing as revenge for the bombing of Pearl Harbor in 1941. Certainly, 4 years of terrible warfare had hardened everyone. Documents, most finally declassified in the 1990s, lead different historians to many different conclusions about why President Truman made the specific decisions he did. There probably will not be a final answer.

Source: See http://www.gwu.edu/~nsarchiv/NSAEBB/NSAEBB162/index.htm downloaded January 10, 2013.

Thinking Critically

1. **Contextualization**

   Given the situation Truman faced in the spring of 1945, what options, including the use of atomic weapons, did Truman have for bringing the war with Japan to a conclusion?

2. **Constructing an Argument**

   In your opinion, why did Truman decide to use atomic weapons on Japan? What evidence can you produce to support your position?

an additional 100,000 from burns and radiation. Three days, later another atomic bomb was dropped on Nagasaki. Japanese leaders debated what to do. Some diehard Japanese militarists wanted to keep fighting no matter what and saw the "peace faction" as traitors. Finally, Emperor Hirohito, who had been silent through so much of the war said, "I swallow my own tears, and give my sanctions to the proposal to accept the Allied proclamation." On August 15, Japanese radio carried a voice never heard in Japan before, that of the Emperor, who told his people that the unthinkable had come about—Japan had surrendered. World War II was over.

✳ Explore World War II in the Pacific on MyHistoryLab

WHAT WERE U.S. INTERESTS IN THE PACIFIC THEATER OF WORLD WAR II?

As the United States built its overseas colonies in the Pacific during the decades prior to World War II, Japanese leaders, who were trying to build a colonial empire for their own country, felt threatened. Industrialization and a growing population in Japan meant that the country needed more resources than the home islands could provide. Following the example of European colonial powers, Japan began its own course of expansion during the late 1800s. Soon, the empire of Japan acquired Korea, China, and islands in the Pacific as tributary colonies. Imperial competition with the United States prompted a surprise attack on the American naval base at Pearl Harbor on December 7, 1941, bringing the United States into World War II. Initially, the Japanese enjoyed military success across the Pacific, but soon the United States began to push the Japanese forces back toward the home islands. Both before and during the course of the war, the Japanese committed a number of atrocities, both

This aerial photograph shows the mushroom cloud over the Japanese city of Nagasaki on August 9, 1945. The detonation of this second atomic bomb, along with the bombing of Hiroshima, led to Japan's surrender and the end of World War II.

against military foes and civilians. In the United States, the American government removed more than 100,000 Japanese Americans and Japanese resident aliens to relocation centers in the West. Japan finally surrendered in August 1945 after the cites of Hiroshima and Nagasaki were nearly destroyed by the first atomic bombs used in combat and dropped by U.S. warplanes.

SELECTED MAJOR U.S. PACIFIC THEATER EVENTS

Year	Event	Victor
1941	Attack on Pearl Harbor	Japan
1942	Battle of Bataan	Japan
1942	Battle of Midway	U.S.
1942	Battle of Guadalcanal	U.S./Allies
1944	Battle of Leyte	U.S./Allies
1945	Battle of Iwo Jima	U.S.
1945	Battle of Okinawa	U.S./Allies
1945	Hiroshima: First Atomic Bombing	
1945	Nagasaki: Second Atomic Bombing	

KEY QUESTIONS   Use MyHistoryLab *Explorer* to answer these questions:

Analysis ▶▶▶ *How did the Japanese military initially succeed across the Pacific in the war?*

Map the progress of early Japanese victories.

Response ▶▶▶ *What atrocities did Japanese armed forces commit to various groups?*

Understand these offenses.

Consequence ▶▶▶ *How did the U.S. government violate the civil rights of its own people during the war?*

See the unfolding of the Japanese evacuation program.

As word spread of the Japanese surrender, huge crowds celebrated from San Francisco to New York City. Similar crowds celebrated in London, Paris, Moscow, and Beijing. Most people breathed a huge sigh of relief. The most terrible war in modern history was over. Few knew what the postwar world would look like.

On September 2, the U.S. battleship *Missouri* sailed into Tokyo Bay. A Japanese delegation came on board to sign the instruments of surrender while an advance unit of U.S. sailors and Marines landed to begin the occupation of Japan. It was a short, somber ceremony. A new era had begun.

> **23.4** **Quick Review** How did U.S. strategy differ in Europe and the Pacific? Why were these differences necessary? What was the key to U.S. success?

CONCLUSION

By the end of 1939, Europe was once again at war. Both Great Britain and France had declared war on Germany shortly after the German invasion of Poland. By June 1940, France had surrendered to a sustained German assault. Now Britain stood alone against fascism. At the same time, tensions mounted between the United States and Japan. Even those Americans who suspected that a war was coming hoped to avoid a war with Germany and Japan at the same time.

British Prime Minister Winston Churchill asked the United States for assistance in resisting Germany, but President Roosevelt was hampered by both the neutrality legislation of the 1930s and by public opposition to involvement in another European conflict. Through a series of complex maneuvers, Roosevelt managed to provide some military aid to Britain; however, full-scale U.S. involvement in World War II would not come until the Japanese attack on Pearl Harbor in December 1941.

During the war, 16 million Americans served in the armed forces, including 350,000 women. As the country shifted from peacetime to wartime industrial production, jobs were plentiful and Americans experienced unprecedented prosperity. Even during this time of rapid industrial expansion, racial and ethnic discrimination continued. African-Americans and Latinos, though many served in the military, were often marginalized. Ethnic hostility on the home front also resulted in the internment of 100,000 Japanese Americans living on the West Coast. By contrast, the principle of equal opportunity regardless of race, creed, color, or national origin was upheld by Executive Order 8802, which prohibited defense contractors from refusing to integrate their labor forces. Many people from previously marginalized groups were able to find new opportunities during the war, and others returned from the war determined to resist future discrimination.

During the course of the war, the Soviet Union (Russia), which had originally been allied with Germany, was then attacked by Germany. After fierce fighting in the Russian winter, Russian forces began to counterattack against Germany from the east while British and American forces attacked from the west—first in North Africa and Italy and later directly into France and Germany. After years of fighting, Nazi Germany was eventually forced to surrender, in April 1945, just after Roosevelt died in office. After the German surrender, the United States, under the leadership of Harry S. Truman, who had ascended to the presidency after Roosevelt's death, focused on the war in the Pacific, and in August 1945, Truman made the controversial decision to drop two atomic bombs on the Japanese cities of Hiroshima and Nagasaki, which became the first two cities in the world to be leveled by atomic blasts. Japan surrendered, bringing World War II to a close. In September 1945, the world entered a new era as it had only a few times in history.

> **CHAPTER REVIEW** Why was World War II a life-altering event on both personal and national levels?

Chapter 23 Chapter Review

PREPAREDNESS AND ISOLATION, 1939–1941

23.1 Explain support for and opposition to the growing U.S. support for Britain and growing tensions with Japan.

Review Questions

1. Contextualization

Why did so many Americans oppose U.S. involvement in the war in Europe? How did Roosevelt justify his efforts to aid Britain?

2. Cause and Effect

What factors contributed to the Japanese decision to go to war with the United States?

MASS MOBILIZATION IN A SOCIETY AT WAR

23.2 Analyze the war's impact on widely diverse groups of Americans who fought, supported the war effort at home, or otherwise lived through the war years.

Review Questions

3. Synthesis

What steps did the United States take to create a mass army in the early years of the war?

4. Comparison

Compare and contrast the roles of young men and young women in the war effort.

5. Construct an Argument

In your opinion, why were Japanese Americans and Japanese immigrants interned, while German and Italian-Americans were not?

INDUSTRIAL STRENGTH, INDUSTRIAL PROSPERITY

23.3 Analyze U.S. industrial strength and productivity and its impact on the outcome of the war and on American society.

Review Questions

6. Historical Interpretation

What factors contributed to the extraordinary U.S. military production during World War II?

7. Cause and Effect

How did increased industrial production affect the lives of ordinary Americans during World War II?

WINNING A WORLD WAR—NORTH AFRICA, EUROPE, ASIA, THE PACIFIC, 1943–1945

23.4 Explain the course of the war leading to victory in Europe and then the Pacific.

Review Questions

8. Historical Interpretation

What tensions between the Allies were revealed at the conferences in Casablanca, Cairo, and Tehran?

9. Comparison

How did the fighting in Europe during World War II differ from that in World War I? How would you explain the differences you note?

10. Constructing an Argument

In your opinion, was Truman's decision to use atomic bombs against Japan justified? Why or why not?

Fears, Joys, and Limits

1945–1980

The World the War Created

24

1945–1952

Members of 11th Airborne Division kneel on the ground as they watch the mushroom cloud of a 1951 atomic bomb test in Nevada. Threat of the new weapon hung over the world during the Cold War.

On August 6, 1945, the White House released a statement from President Harry Truman:

> Sixteen hours ago an American airplane dropped one bomb on Hiroshima....It is an atomic bomb. It is a harnessing of the basic power of the universe. The force from which the sun draws its power has been loosed against those who brought war to the Far East.

Thus began the atomic age, a new and previously unimagined era. The bomb brought World War II to a quick end, but it also launched the United States and the world into an uncharted arena. For people living in the United States in 1945, that announcement was but one of many extraordinary changes that year.

In early May, less than a month after Roosevelt's death on April 12, Nazi Germany surrendered. In June, the United Nations, a new international organization designed to preserve peace, held its first meeting. Then came the news of the atomic bombing of Hiroshima on August 6 and Nagasaki on August 9. Japan surrendered on August 14. World War II was over.

During the 2-day holiday that followed, Americans celebrated the coming of peace. Few had any sense of what peace would mean. People wanted to get on with their lives, even if it was hard to imagine what the new "normal"

CHAPTER OBJECTIVE

Demonstrate an understanding of the post-World War II world that emerged in the United States.

LEARNING OBJECTIVES

THE UNITED STATES IN 1945

Describe the new technology, living patterns, and political arrangements in the United States that resulted from World War II.

24.1

THE COLD WAR BEGINS

Analyze the coming of the Cold War, tensions with the Soviet Union, and McCarthyism at home.

24.2

POLITICS, 1948 AND 1952

Explain political developments that led to the elections of Truman and then Eisenhower as Cold War era presidents.

24.3

might look like. A Navy petty officer and his wife, walking hand in hand through the celebrations in Seattle on August 14, told a reporter their plans: "Raise babies and keep house!" Many returning from the war followed these plans, but they did so in a world much more complex than could be imagined on that idyllic August evening. This chapter traces the experience of those Americans who built a new world in the aftermath of World War II, describing not only their hopes and fears but also their surprises and disappointments as the postwar world took shape between 1945 and 1952.

THE UNITED STATES IN 1945

24.1   Describe the new technology, living patterns, and political arrangements in the United States that resulted from World War II.

Those who had been fighting in Europe or Asia wanted to get home as fast as they could, certainly faster than was possible given difficulties in transporting troops and managing Germany and Japan. For some women working in wartime production, it was time to welcome a long-absent husband or boyfriend, quit work, and raise a family. Other women very much wanted to continue working. For some who had moved because of the war, it was time to go home. Others who had moved wanted to stay in their new locations and have families join them. For industrial leaders, peacetime conversion meant new profits that would come from fulfilling pent-up demands for goods that had been unavailable during the war and from harnessing new discoveries related to medicines and emerging technologies. For government leaders, negotiating the international arrangements and managing the uneasy postwar alliances, especially with the United Soviet Socialist Republic (U.S.S.R.), commonly called the Soviet Union, made the postwar era one of the most difficult ever.

Science, Medicine, Technology, and the Bomb

If the nuclear physicists who designed and built the atomic bomb were in the vanguard of wartime scientific breakthroughs, biologists and medical researchers were not far behind. During World War II, the wonder drugs—penicillin and streptomycin—combated infections and resulted in a dramatic reduction in battlefield deaths. Soon after the war, medical scientists and pharmaceutical companies marketed other new antibiotics. The National Institutes of Health, which had begun as a tiny government agency in the 1930s, now led the nation's war on disease.

By 1956, 80 percent of prescribed drugs had been invented after the beginning of World War II. Vaccines ended traditional childhood diseases such as whooping cough, diphtheria, mumps, and measles. In 1955, a vaccine was found for the feared scourge of polio. For those having a hard time keeping pace with modern life, physicians offered tranquilizers, sales of which boomed. People were growing taller and living longer thanks to advances in medicine, nutrition, and hygiene. In 1940, the average American's lifespan was 62.9 years, but by 1960 it had reached 69.7. Science, it seemed, was offering the key to life itself.

For consumers, science and technology offered tangible improvements that changed daily life. In 1945, consumers were being introduced to freezers, dishwashers, automatic transmissions, and ballpoint pens. In offices, workers were beginning to use electric typewriters. Other technologies that had been developed prior to World War II —from washing machines to electric ranges to electric trains—were suddenly available after wartime production restrictions were lifted. Pent-up consumer demand and industrial availability combined quickly. What had been impossible to find during the war was now in every store.

No automobiles for private use had been produced in the United States between 1942 and 1945. But by 1947, new models were replacing the old vehicles from the 1930s. Sales of passenger cars jumped to 6.7 million per year in 1950 and to 7.9 million in 1955. General Motors, which then sold about half of all cars in America, became the first corporation to earn $1 billion in a single year. Advertising by General Motors, Ford, and Chrysler convinced people to trade in 4.5 million old cars per year in the 1950s for large, sleek new models with automatic transmissions, air conditioning, and picturesque tail fins. By 1960, 80 percent of all American families owned a car, and 15 percent owned two or more cars.

While most households had radios in 1945, only a very few had televisions (black and white, of course). Television was developed by a number of inventors, notably Philo T. Farnsworth in the early 1930s, and was introduced at the 1939 New York World's Fair. But television production stopped during World War II while factories made radar equipment. The number of television sets in American homes exploded after the war. In 1946, 8,000 homes owned a set; by 1950, 5 million; and by 1960, 45 million—or 90 percent of all American homes. In 1945, half of the nation's farm homes, where 25 million people lived, still did not have electricity to plug in a TV, but that too would change very quickly.

Hanging over all of the advances, however, was the atomic bomb. As Americans learned more about the bomb, they realized that it could end all of their improved health and new-found prosperity. Few Americans had questioned the morality of using the atomic bomb in 1945; indeed, only a tiny handful even knew that the weapon existed before its use. The few physicists who had developed the bomb understood what it meant, however. Very soon, many more came to understand the sobering reality of "the mushroom cloud" that a nuclear explosion unleashed. "The bomb" might be a new form of protection, since only the United States had it, but it was also a new threat (see Chapter 23).

Some scientists proposed the voluntary sharing of atomic technology to avoid an arms race, but President Truman decided that the safest course was for the United States to retain sole knowledge of nuclear secrets. However, in 1949, to the great surprise of many, the Soviet Union successfully tested its own atomic bomb. By that time, the wartime ally had become a potential enemy. Suddenly, with the Russian test, the idea that the United States was protected by its unique control of the bomb vanished. Before long, other nations joined the "atomic club." Great Britain, the closest U.S. ally, exploded its own bomb in 1952, France followed in 1960, and others were not far behind. Above all other concerns, however, the fear of the Russian bomb is what hung over Americans.

Officials and scientists within the Truman administration debated the development of an even more powerful weapon to counter the Russian bomb. The atomic bomb depended on nuclear fission (the splitting of an atom), but scientists knew that theoretically an even more powerful explosion could arise from nuclear fusion (the merging of atoms) to create a thermonuclear explosion—a hydrogen bomb. While virtually no one involved opposed the development of the atomic bomb during World War II, many senior scientists opposed the "super bomb." Albert Einstein, whose scientific work formed the basis for nuclear science, said that with such a super bomb, "general annihilation beckons." J. Robert Oppenheimer, who led the development of the first atomic bomb at Los Alamos, New Mexico, in 1944, opposed the larger bomb on moral and practical grounds. George Kennan, the state department official often most associated with the coming of the Cold War, argued that an arsenal of atom bombs was ample deterrent for the Soviets. Others disagreed. When President Truman asked his advisory panel, "Can the Russians do it?" even those who opposed development of the hydrogen bomb had to answer yes. The president responded, "In that case, we have no choice. We'll go ahead."

The science and the engineering involved were daunting. When many of those who had built the first atomic bombs declined to participate in the new project, a fresh team, led by Hungarian refugees Edward Teller and John von Neumann, moved ahead. The first U.S. test of a thermonuclear bomb took place on November 1, 1952, at Eniwetok Atoll in the Pacific. The predictions about the Russian capabilities also became true: the first Russian bomb was exploded in Siberia in August 1953, little more than 9 months after the first U.S. test.

The bombs that the United States and Russia exploded were powerful beyond imagination. The United States' test sent a fireball 5 miles into the sky and produced a mushroom cloud 27 miles high and 8 miles wide. Eniwetok Island disappeared, replaced by a large hole in the ocean floor. The Soviet bomb was similar. Soviet Premier Georgi Malenkov told the world that "the United States no longer has a monopoly on the hydrogen bomb." The possibility of "mutually assured destruction," influenced international diplomacy and daily life. Children practiced hiding under school desks in case of nuclear attack, (though critics wondered what good that would do in the face of a bomb that could vaporize a city.) Families built bomb shelters in their basements. The bomb was as much a part of daily life in the 1950s as televisions, new automobiles, or healthier lives.

Returning Veterans, the Baby Boom, and Suburban Homes

In August 1945, as World War II ended, 12 million American men were in the military, two-thirds of those between the ages of 18 and 34. They had been through a brutal war, and now they wanted get home and get on with their lives. Those waiting at home were equally anxious to get the troops back. It took time to organize the military governance of Germany and Japan and to arrange the transport of troops. By fall, members of Congress started to get warning letters, "No boats, no votes." Demobilization moved at a rapid pace. In less than a year, three-quarters of those in the military had been mustered out, leaving an active military of 3 million. Congress voted to cut that number to 1 million in another year.

Coming home from the war was joyous but also difficult. Soldiers and sailors, desperately tired of the killing, the dying, and the boredom of war, sometimes had a hard time adjusting to a world where life had gone on without them and in which civilians could never comprehend the horrors they had experienced. Married couples who had been apart, sometimes for 3 or 4 years, especially those who had married just before a husband shipped out, found adjustments difficult. The divorce rate skyrocketed in the late 1940s.

The government offered generous benefits to returning service men (and the few service women) to help with the adjustment. The **GI Bill of Rights** provided $20 per week for up to a year for those seeking new jobs. (The maximum payment of $1,040 for a full year was very close to the average American salary of $1,074 in 1945.) The GI Bill also offered college tuition for returning veterans, allowing a whole generation of young men to be the first in their families to attend college and prepare for middle-class occupations. In addition, the Veterans Administration made loans available for veterans to buy a house. Only later would some note that since the draft often passed over African-Americans and Latinos and excluded women, the GI Bill constituted a kind of affirmative action for white men. But in 1945, most Americans thought that these men had richly earned any favors they got.

Perhaps the greatest goal of returning veterans and the spouses and fiancées who met them was stated by the couple who wanted to "Raise babies and keep house!" They did both with amazing speed. Many veterans married very quickly, and the new couples started to have babies. In May 1946, 9 months after the end of the war, 233,452 babies were born in the United States, up from 206,387 earlier that February. In June, the number of babies was 242,302, and in October, 339,499. A total of 3.4 million babies were born in the United States in 1946, 20 percent more than were born in 1945, a birthrate unmatched in the United States in decades, though it kept climbing after that.

The speed with which returning veterans chose to marry and have children came as quite a surprise. Nothing similar had followed other wars, certainly not World War I, even though "normalcy" had been a theme of the 1920s. Nevertheless, Americans across the spectrum of class and race started having children. The population soared, and a generation known as the "**baby boomers**" became a demographic bulge whose sheer size affected many aspects of American life throughout boomer lifespans.

GI Bill of Rights
Legislation in June 1944 that eased the return of veterans into American society by providing educational and employment benefits.

baby boomers
The name given to the generation of children born to the families of returning World War II veterans between 1945 and 1960.

For white middle-class Americans, a new home located in a suburban neighborhood offered the chance to build a safe and modern life. It was to these new homes, cut off from daily interchange with their extended families but connected to others very much like themselves, that a generation of Americans moved after 1945.

Just as these new families were getting started, Abraham Levitt and his sons William and Alfred bought 4,000 acres of potato farms in the town of Hempstead, Long Island, outside of New York City. On this huge parcel of land, the Levitts built Levittown, the largest private housing project in American history. Their plan was simple: clear the land, lay out curving roads or lanes (never streets), pour concrete slabs every 60 feet along these roadways, drop off a set of construction materials at each slab—composition rock-board and plywood—then send in construction crews armed with new power tools—saws, routers, and nailers—each of whom was assigned a specific step in the construction process. At the peak of production, 30 houses were built each day. Each had a 12- by 16-foot living room, one bathroom, two bedrooms, and a fireplace. Levittown eventually included 17,400 houses that were home to 82,000 people.

Occupants moved into the first houses in Levittown in October 1947. At first, houses were sold only to veterans but soon were sold also to other families. Modest down payments and Veterans Administration and Federal Housing Authority loans brought the price of $7,990 to $9,500 within the range of many middle-class and aspiring middle-class families. Long Island's Levittown was so successful that the Levitts built two more planned communities near Philadelphia. Other developers—Del Webb in Phoenix, Joseph Kelly in Boston, Louis H. Boyar and Fritz B. Burns in Los Angeles—created similar developments that sold at an astounding pace. Between 1945 and 1960, 10 times as many houses were constructed in suburbs as in older central cities, and 95 percent of these houses were detached single family homes. Mass production that had come to automobiles in the earliest 1900s came to housing after 1945.

Architectural and social critics disliked suburban developments. The nation's best known critic, Lewis Mumford, described suburbs as,

> a multitude of uniform, unidentifiable houses, lined up inflexibly, at uniform distances, on uniform roads, in a treeless communal waste, inhabited by people of the same class, the same income, the same age group, witnessing the same television performances, eating the same tasteless pre-fabricated foods, from the same freezers, confirming in every outward and inward respect to a common mold.

For veterans and their families and those who followed after them in the 1950s, however, the new suburbs were a dream come true. Immediately after the war, a desperate housing shortage led many to double up with parents or other relatives. Half a million veterans lived in army Quonset huts or other temporary buildings. Chicago sold 250 old trolley cars as temporary homes. A home of one's own, previously often a reality only for the upper-middle class and the rich, now became a new norm. The first issue of the community newspaper in Levittown noted that "our lives are held closely together because most of us are within the same age bracket, in similar income groups, live in almost identical houses, and have common problems." The residents also made their own contribution to the baby boom to such a degree that the community became known as "Fertility Valley" and "the Rabbit Hutch."

With the end of World War II, many Americans embraced a new image of domestic bliss in a suburban home filled with children.

A house in a subdivision like Levittown, New York, was a key part of the American dream for many in the 1940s and 1950s.

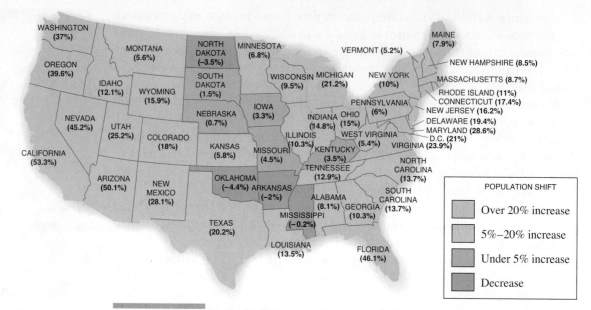

MAP 24-1 **Americans on the Move**. Many Americans moved around a lot during and after World War II, and many settled in communities distant from where they had been children. While African-Americans moved from the South to the North in large numbers, accounting for much of the population growth in states like New York and Illinois, white Americans moved from East to West, especially to California, which grew by 53 percent between 1940 and 1950.

As many in the postwar generation moved to suburbia, Americans also moved from the East to the West. Between 1940 and 1950—the years of the war and the immediate postwar era—the Sunbelt grew rapidly. Texas grew by 20 percent, Nevada by 45 percent, and Arizona and California by over 50 percent (see Map 24-1). Soldiers and sailors coming through California on the way to the Pacific liked what they saw and vowed to return. However, not all young Americans could or wanted to participate in the rush either to the suburbs or to the West. African-Americans, Latinos, and Asians were excluded from most suburban developments. Levittown specifically excluded people of color from its subdivisions for the first 20 years of the community's existence. William Levitt believed that if blacks were allowed to move in to Levittown, the whites would leave. He commented, "We can solve a housing problem, or we can try to solve a racial problem. But we cannot combine the two." As late as 1960, not a single African-American lived among the 82,000 residents of Levittown, New York.

All-white developments like Levittown were not unique. Post-World War II suburbanization was a white affair that greatly exacerbated housing segregation in the United States. Urban communities had long been segregated. Most cities had their Irish, Italian, and Jewish neighborhoods as well as neighborhoods for African-Americans, and in the Southwest, for Latinos. However, the move to the suburbs meant that many whites left the cities and many nonwhites were left behind in core urban communities with a declining tax base, declining services, and declining opportunities.

Suburbia, however, was not an attraction for all Americans. Gay men and lesbians of any race were generally excluded from suburbia unless they chose to live deeply closeted lives. One lesbian wrote, "It has never been easy to be a lesbian in this country, but the 1950s was surely the worst decade in which to love your own sex." Others simply preferred to stay in older urban neighborhoods or small towns. Women who worked, especially those who remained single or were divorced, often found the conformity of suburbia difficult. For the poets and playwrights who became the "beat generation" of the 1950s who celebrated nonconformity, suburbia was unthinkable. There was

THINKING HISTORICALLY
Observations on Levittown and Other Suburbs

In June, 1958, a sociologist, Herbert J. Gans, and his wife were among the first 25 families to move into the new Levittown development just outside Philadelphia. They lived there for the next 2 years as "participant observers" in this brand new planned suburban development. Unlike many others who wrote about suburbia, Gans noted more positive than negative observations.

About the ways that living in Levittown impacted community and social life, one resident whom Gans interviewed said:

> We didn't know before we moved here that we would entertain more, go out less. Not that we were boozehounds before, though. Not that we can't afford to go out; we just don't want to. We have a new house and want to keep it up nice; this is not work but enjoyment. I've never been more content....Working in the yard is just like fishing, so relaxing. I have more pep here.

Even if outside critics did not like what they saw in suburbia, Gans found that most of those who actually lived in Levittown did like it.

One major exception to the general sense of happiness was found among adolescents. Gans interviewed one girl who complained, "After school hours, you walk into an entirely different world. Everyone goes his own separate way, to start his homework, take a nap, or watch TV. This is the life of a vegetable, not a human being." As a result of the isolation, a car became as important to adolescents as it was to adults. One high school senior took a job to buy a car and told Gans, "I had no choice, it was either going to work or cracking up....I'll start living. I can get out of Levittown.... In plain words, a boy shouldn't live here if he is between the ages of 14–17."

While he expected to find more boredom and depression among the sometimes-isolated residents of Levittown, he did not. Gans worried about the impact of suburbanization on older cities that were losing middle-class residents and their tax base leaving behind people of color—who generally didn't or couldn't move to the suburbs—and those who were poor. But in the end, he concluded, "I should like to emphasize once more that whatever its imperfections, Levittown is a good place to live."

Source: Herbert J. Gans, *The Levittowners: Ways of Life and Politics in a New Suburban Community* (New York: Vintage Books, 1967)

Thinking Critically

1. **Documentary Analysis**
   How did Gans explain the dissatisfaction many adolescents felt with suburban living?

2. **Historical Interpretation**
   Why do you think Gans found so many suburban residents content with their new communities while most other social critics found them so negative?

---

virtually no way to get around most suburbs without a car, and for those who needed public transportation, cities remained essential. Nevertheless, starting in 1945, great numbers of American men and women moved to the suburbs and embraced life there.

The Great Migration—African-Americans Move North

While white Americans moved to the suburbs, a new generation of African-Americans moved from the South to the North. The great migration of African-Americans to the North began during World War I, continued through the 1920s, and slowed during the Depression years of the 1930s (see Chapter 21). During and after World War II, the rate of migration exploded. By 1960, half of the nation's African-Americans lived in northern cities—a huge change from the time when more than 90 percent of all blacks lived in the rural South. While the pull of northern industrial jobs and the push of southern segregation and violence remained constant from the 1920s to the 1950s, another factor accelerated the pace of movement in the late 1940s; the sharecropping system, around which the economic lives of many southern blacks had been organized from the 1880s to the 1940s, began to disappear.

On October 2, 1944, as the tide of war was turning, a crowd gathered at the Hopson cotton plantation outside of Clarksdale, Mississippi, on Highway 49 to look at a new machine that had nothing to do with the war. Howell Hopson was conducting the first public demonstration of a new International Harvester cotton picking machine. He described the scene: "An estimated 2,500 to 3,000 people swarmed over the plantation on that one day, 800 to 1,000 automobiles leaving their tracks and scars throughout the property."

The machine that the visitors had come to see changed the face of the South and changed the lives of the nation's African-Americans. The bright red picker looked like a tractor with a large metal basket on the top. As it drove down a row of cotton, the spindles mounted on the front rotated and stripped the cotton off the plants and then suctioned the cotton up to a basket. The picker could pick a thousand pounds of cotton in an hour; a good worker, only 20 pounds. Hopson said it cost $5.26 for a machine to pick a bale of cotton. A sharecropper cost $39.41 per bale. He wrote, "The introduction of the cotton harvester may have been comparable to the unveiling of Eli Whitney's first hand-operated cotton gin."

Hopson was thinking of the machine's impact on his profits. But like Whitney's invention a century and a half earlier, the machine's largest impact was on men and women of African descent. Whitney's cotton gin made slavery profitable. International Harvester's cotton picking machine made the sharecropping that had replaced slavery obsolete. A wave of 1.5 million African-Americans had moved North between 1910 and 1940, but 5 million followed between 1940 and 1960.

As people whose lives were centered in the communities, churches, and culture of the rigidly segregated South moved North, they now lived in quite different communities with changing norms. Racial discrimination, generally seen as a southern issue until World War II, became a national one. Nevertheless, opportunities in the North were better than those offered by sharecropping, and the newcomers created their own jobs and a new urban culture.

Housing in the North was even more segregated than in the South. While the Federal Housing Authority dropped explicit racial rules by the 1940s, its handbook still said, "If a neighborhood is to retain stability, it is necessary that all properties shall continue to be occupied by the same social class." In reality, that wording meant, "Don't give mortgages to black families in white neighborhoods." The white rush to segregated suburbs opened up new urban housing for blacks. Unscrupulous real estate agents made large profits while engaging in blockbusting in older neighborhoods, convincing frightened white homeowners to sell quickly and cheaply. From Boston to Los Angeles, whole city blocks went on the market at the same time, transferring the majority of homes from white to black hands in short order. Changes in the racial makeup of urban neighborhoods happened at the same time as cash-strapped cities cut back on municipal services and many banks dramatically reduced the availability of mortgages and loans for home improvements. The creation of the white suburbs and the vastly expanded urban black ghettos went hand in hand in the 1950s.

Moving from the South to an unfamiliar North could be painful for African-Americans. In *The Last Train North*, Clifton Taulbert described the longing for things left behind:

> There were no Chinaberry trees. No pecan trees....Never again would I pick dew berries or hear the familiar laughter from the field truck. This was my world now, this strange new family and their cramped quarters over the tiny grocery store they grandly called the "confectionary."

Nevertheless, they kept coming through the 1940s and 1950s. As a migrant from Tennessee to Milwaukee said, "Every train, every bus, they were coming."

Many who arrived were disillusioned. When Harvey Clark, who originally hailed from Mississippi, tried to move his family from a crowded apartment in South Chicago to a larger one just across the city line in Cicero, he was greeted by a mob and a police chief who told him to "Get out of Cicero." The chief told the agent who arranged the apartment, "Don't come back in town, or you'll get a bullet through you." The white mayor of Dearborn, Michigan, told Alabama's *Montgomery Advertiser* that "Negroes can't get in here. Every time we hear of a Negro moving in, we respond quicker than you do to a fire." As Detroit became a majority black city, its suburb of Dearborn remained 99 percent white.

Black migrants also found new freedoms and opportunities in the North. Ida Mae Brandon Gladney, who had never been able to vote in Mississippi, cast her first vote for Franklin Roosevelt in Chicago in 1940. (The black vote in Chicago carried the state of Illinois and, thus, the Electoral College for Roosevelt in that election.) Robert Joseph Pershing Foster, a physician in Louisiana, established a new practice in the rapidly expanding black community of Los Angeles in 1954 and 1955. The several million other people making the move from the states of the Old Confederacy to New York, Chicago, Los Angeles, and a hundred other cities in the North and West each had his or her own tale of the transformations taking place in every region of the country.

As they had in the 1920s, African-American artists embraced urban life and the new growing black communities of the North, few more enthusiastically than musicians like Charlie Parker and Miles Davis, shown here performing in New York City in 1947.

Latino Migrations from Puerto Rico and Mexico

While the great migration of African-Americans from the rural South to the urban North and West was occurring, migrations of Latino people were happening at the same time. The United States had won control of Puerto Rico in 1898, and Puerto Ricans had long been American citizens. After World War II, more of these Spanish-speaking citizens began moving from Puerto Rico to the U.S. mainland, especially New York City. East Harlem, long an Italian neighborhood in New York City, quickly became mostly Puerto Rican. Piri Thomas was born in New York in 1928 and described the racial discrimination faced by a young adult in Spanish Harlem in the 1950s in his 1967 memoir aptly named *Down These Mean Streets*.

In addition, the U.S. population included about 1.2 million Americans of Mexican background, and this group also grew rapidly after World War II. In the Southwest, the *bracero* (helping hands in Spanish) began during World War II to allow Mexican farm workers temporary entry into the United States to work in the agricultural fields that other Americans had left for war industries or for the military. The entry program was expanded after the war, and between 1948 and 1964, almost 5 million braceros were brought to the United States. Although they were expected to return to Mexico when the work was done, not all did, and they, along with others who walked across the hot deserts and the border, expanded the country's Mexican-American population, creating a large group, some of whom remained under constant threat of deportation.

In Southern California, growth led to new militancy in the Mexican-American community. In Santa Ana, Mexican-American parents hired an attorney and sued the Board of Education over school segregation. In 1946, the courts issued a permanent injunction against this segregation, and later, the federal appeals court directed a federal grand jury to consider an indictment against the Santa Ana board.

In Los Angeles, with the largest Mexican-American population, the Community Service Organization began to fight for political rights in 1947 and was successful in electing Edward Roybal to the Los Angeles City Council in 1949, the first time since 1881 that someone of Mexican descent had served on that body. In 1962, Roybal was elected to the U.S. Congress. Other Mexican-American organizations sprang up across the southwest, supporting a successful mine workers strike in New Mexico in 1950–1952 and building a solid base before the civil rights movements of the later 1950s while also supporting a small but growing middle-class Latino community in California and Texas.

The United Nations and the New Economic Order

While Americans were moving around the country, the rest of the planet was also in transition. Even before World War II ended, a series of international gatherings reshaped the political and economic climate of the coming postwar world.

THE INTERNATIONAL MONETARY FUND AND THE WORLD BANK In 1944, leaders in the United States and Britain were determined not to repeat the mistakes of the Treaty of Versailles. Among those mistakes, they believed, were the huge reparations imposed on the defeated Germany and the failure of the victors to ensure robust economic activity after the war.

In early 1944, Roosevelt's Secretary of the Treasury Henry M. Morgenthau invited Great Britain and the Soviet Union to join the United States in establishing a postwar economic system. Both agreed. Morgenthau then invited representatives of more than 40 wartime allies to meet at the Mount Washington Hotel in Bretton Woods, New Hampshire, in July 1944.

The resulting Bretton Woods agreement created an International Monetary Fund (IMF) for "promoting international monetary cooperation." The purpose of the IMF was to maintain exchange rates between different currencies so people could buy and sell in different countries without fear that values would fluctuate wildly (as happened in the 1930s), to provide loans to a nation that was having problems balancing payments, and to provide technical assistance to banks. The U.S. dollar was made the base on which all other currencies were calculated (and it remained so until 1971).

The Bretton Woods delegates also created the International Bank for Reconstruction Development (better known as the World Bank) to get the world on stable economic footing as quickly as possible after the devastation of the war. The World Bank was designed to support economic recovery in war-torn Europe and to reduce world poverty, especially in Latin America, Africa, and parts of Asia that did not have the economic foundation for recovery. The first loans from the World Bank were made to war-torn France in 1947, and loans were soon extended around the world.

THE UNITED NATIONS When Franklin Roosevelt and Winston Churchill agreed to an Atlantic Charter in August 1941, they called for the "establishment of a wider and permanent system of general security" (see Chapter 23). By 1944, however, Roosevelt was ready to get more specific. He proposed an international body that would include every nation but in which the most powerful ones—in his proposal, the United States, Britain, the Soviet Union, and China—would serve as the "Four Policemen." As he told reporters in the summer of 1944, if some aggressor "started to run amok," these policemen would be needed to "stop them before they got started." By 1944, the wartime alliance was calling itself the **United Nations**, and Roosevelt wanted to keep the name.

The United States invited representatives from "the four policemen" to meet at a mansion known as Dumbarton Oaks in Washington, DC. In 7 weeks, from August to October 1944, Edward R. Stettinius, U.S. undersecretary of state; Andrey Gromyko, Soviet ambassador to the United States; and Sir Alexander Cadogan, permanent undersecretary in the British Foreign Office, consulting with V.K. Wellington Koo, the Chinese ambassador to London—with whom Gromyko refused to meet directly—erected the basic structure of what would become the United Nations (UN).They agreed that the core of the new organization would be a Security Council made up of five permanent members (France was added as a fifth member) and other delegates serving on a rotating basis. The Security Council would have the real power within the UN. A majority vote of the Security Council would be sufficient to authorize military force to stop aggression. Everyone also agreed that each of the core members of the Security Council should have a veto over any such actions; the United States, Britain, and the Soviet Union were not about to allow sanctions of which they did not approve.

The planners also proposed a UN General Assembly that would permit all of the nations of the world to debate issues but that, unlike the Security Council, could not

United Nations

An international organization launched at the end of World War II with leadership from the United States, the Soviet Union, Great Britain, and China.

American Voices

United Nations Universal Declaration of Human Rights, 1948

*T*hree years after the United Nations was created, a UN Commission on Human Rights, chaired by former First Lady Eleanor Roosevelt, proposed a Universal Declaration of Human Rights. By 1948, the Cold War between the United States and the Soviet Union was fully underway, and many UN meetings were little more than shouting matches. Few expected any productive results. But Eleanor Roosevelt was able to calm the waters enough to get the document approved. The final vote was 48 in favor, zero opposed, and 8 abstentions, including the Soviet Union. Roosevelt considered the adoption of the declaration to be her most important accomplishment. While the Universal Declaration of Human Rights had no enforcement mechanism, it set a new standard of international behavior against which every nation could be measured.

PREAMBLE

Whereas recognition of the inherent dignity and of the equal and inalienable rights of all members of the human family is the foundation of freedom, justice and peace in the world,

Whereas disregard and contempt for human rights have resulted in barbarous acts which have outraged the conscience of mankind, and the advent of a world in which human beings shall enjoy freedom of speech and belief and freedom from fear and want has been proclaimed as the highest aspiration of the common people,

Whereas it is essential, if man is not to be compelled to have recourse, as a last resort, to rebellion against tyranny and oppression, that human rights should be protected by the rule of law,

Whereas it is essential to promote the development of friendly relations between nations,

Whereas the peoples of the United Nations have in the Charter reaffirmed their faith in fundamental human rights, in the dignity and worth of the human person and in the equal rights of men and women and have determined to promote social progress and better standards of life in larger freedom,

Whereas Member States have pledged themselves to achieve, in co-operation with the United Nations, the promotion of universal respect for and observance of human rights and fundamental freedoms,

Whereas a common understanding of these rights and freedoms is of the greatest importance for the full realization of this pledge,

Now, Therefore THE GENERAL ASSEMBLY proclaims THIS UNIVERSAL DECLARATION OF HUMAN RIGHTS as a common standard of achievement for all peoples and all nations…

The document then includes a total of 30 articles that elaborate the points in detail.

Source: www.un.org/en/documents/index.shtml, downloaded May 19, 2011.

Thinking Critically

1. **Documentary Analysis**

   How might the events of World War II have shaped this document?

2. **Historical Interpretation**

   What might explain the decision of the Soviet Union to abstain from voting on the Declaration?

enforce its resolutions. In addition, they agreed that there should be a secretary with a staff. Finally, they agreed that the new body should convene for the first time the following spring in San Francisco, California.

Roosevelt, mindful of Woodrow Wilson's failure to take Republicans to Versailles, appointed a bipartisan delegation to go to San Francisco, including Republican Arthur Vandenberg of Michigan, one of the most respected members of the Senate. Vandenberg's support would be crucial, and Roosevelt knew it.

Two weeks before the San Francisco meeting was to begin, Franklin D. Roosevelt died. Moments after taking the oath of office, Harry S. Truman made his first presidential decision: the conference would go ahead as scheduled on April 25. Some thought the San Francisco conference would simply be a celebration of work already done, but new tensions, especially between the United States and the Soviet Union, almost scuttled the conference. Nevertheless, most Americans wanted the United Nations to be successful, and public opinion influenced the delegates, especially Vandenberg. On June 25, 1945, the delegates unanimously approved the UN Charter. On July 28, the U.S. Senate ratified the charter by a vote of 89 to 2. The United Nations was launched.

24.1 **Quick Review** What were the most radical postwar changes domestically and internationally? Give three reasons to support each of your choices.

THE COLD WAR BEGINS

24.2 Analyze the coming of the Cold War, tensions with the Soviet Union, and McCarthyism at home.

In 1945, most people in the United States admired the Soviet Union, even if American leaders had already become wary of Stalin and his government. After meeting Stalin for the first time at Tehran in late 1943, Roosevelt said, "I 'got along fine' with Marshall Stalin." Privately, however, he confided his doubts.

The two nations were allies in World War II. American wartime propaganda talked positively about "our valiant allies." The Soviet people had withstood a murderous onslaught by Nazi forces and a terrible siege at Stalingrad. The Soviet army had done most of the fighting against Nazi Germany in World War II. Few Americans knew much about Stalin's policies within Russia, including the deadly purges of political enemies or the mass starvation that resulted from efforts toward collectivist Russian agriculture in the 1930s. Yet within a year, the Soviet Union and the United States were engaged in a **Cold War** that lasted 40 years, until the dissolution of the Soviet Union in the late 1980s. What happened to turn former allies against each other? And why did it happen so quickly?

Cold War
The political and economic confrontation between the Soviet Union and the United States that dominated world affairs from 1946 to 1989.

The Hardening of Positions: Containment, the Truman Doctrine, the Marshall Plan, and the Berlin Airlift

From the beginning of their wartime alliance, the United States and the Soviet Union had very different goals in World War II. The Soviets wanted a permanent buffer zone between themselves and Germany, and they wanted to ensure that they obtained absolute control over the countries of Eastern Europe. Having suffered so much from the war, the Soviets were also determined to take all of the machinery, munitions, and art they could from Germany. The United States wanted a rapid

This picture of American and Soviet soldiers in Germany in May 1945, just after the Nazi surrender, illustrates the friendship between the people of the two nations that developed during World War II and that ended very soon after that.

post-Nazi German recovery. In 1942, Roosevelt told Soviet Foreign Minister V. M. Molotov that, "there might be a proper time" to address the differences in war goals between the two nations, but in the midst of the war, FDR said, "the present was not the moment."

Within weeks of taking the oath of office, President Truman became convinced that the Soviets were violating promises they had made to Roosevelt and needed to be stopped. When he met with Foreign Minister Molotov for the first time, he was ready to show how tough an American president could be. When Molotov began the conversation with diplomatic chit chat, Truman immediately accused the Soviets of breaking promises they had made to FDR at the Yalta meeting. As Truman continued his tirade, Molotov responded, "I have never been talked to like that in my life," to which Truman responded, "Carry out your agreements and you won't get talked to like that." It was not an auspicious start to a new relationship. Truman later told friends, "I gave him the one-two, right to the jaw." Molotov and Stalin quickly concluded that Truman was reversing Roosevelt's policies, especially when Truman cut aid to the Soviet Union, claiming that, with the war in Europe over, they no longer needed it. But Stalin did not back down. Indeed, almost immediately after the Truman-Molotov meeting, Stalin asserted Communist control over the new governments of Poland, Romania, and Bulgaria.

In spite of Truman's tough tone with Molotov in April 1945, Truman knew that he had a weak hand in dealing with the Soviets. He sent one of Roosevelt's most trusted advisors to Moscow to try to build a better relationship, and then in July for the first—and only—time, he met face to face with Stalin in Potsdam, just outside the newly conquered Berlin. Truman and Stalin seemed to get on, and after the Potsdam meeting, Truman wrote, "I can deal with Stalin." The Americans agreed that Stalin had the right to dismantle factories in eastern Germany and move them to Russia and could arrange the government of Poland as he chose.

There were many reasons for these concessions. Most important, when the fighting in Europe ended, the Soviet army was in Eastern Europe and the American army was not. Truman knew that the American people had no stomach for maintaining an army in Europe after the war. Until the last day of the Potsdam meeting, Truman was not sure that the atomic bomb would work. Finally, with war still raging in the Pacific, Truman wanted the Soviets to keep their promise to attack Japan once the war in Europe was over.

In the year that followed the end of the war, however, both sides hardened their positions. In February and March 1946, new tensions flared. In a speech on February 9, Stalin said that the only key to future world peace was for "monopoly capitalism" to be replaced by Communism around the world. Supreme Court Justice William Douglas called Stalin's speech a "Declaration of World War III."

A week later, George Kennan, a senior diplomat in the American embassy in Moscow, sent what came to be known as the "Long Telegram" to the U.S. State Department. This widely distributed document called the Soviet government an "Oriental despotism" in which Communist ideology was merely a "fig-leaf" covering tyranny at home and rapid expansion abroad. Kennan told his State Department superiors that the Soviet Union was "a political force committed fanatically to the belief that with the United States there can be no permanent modus vivendi [accommodation between disputing parties], that it is desirable and necessary that the internal harmony of our society be destroyed, the international authority of our state be broken." He suggested that the United States should adopt a policy of **containment**, acknowledging Soviet influence where it existed but taking all necessary steps to ensure that the influence did not spread into new areas of the globe. Containment of Soviet communism would come to define U.S. foreign policy for a long time.

containment
The policy of resisting further expansion of the Soviet bloc through diplomacy and, if necessary, military action, developed in 1947–48.

iron curtain
A phrase coined by former British Prime Minister Winston Churchill in 1946 when describing the post-World War II division of Europe into two hostile segments.

Two weeks later, Winston Churchill, no longer in office but still a revered war hero, gave a speech as Truman's guest at Westminster College in Missouri in which he said:

> From Stettin in the Baltic to Trieste in the Adriatic, an iron curtain has descended across the continent. From what I have seen of our Russian friends and allies during the war, I am convinced that there is nothing they admire so much as strength, and there is nothing for which they have less respect than weakness, especially military weakness.

The image of an "**iron curtain**" dividing Europe became one of the central images of the Cold War. The call for military strength to counter Soviet strength became the foundation of a massive arms race on both sides of the iron curtain.

Not everyone in the United States agreed that a Cold War with the Soviet Union was inevitable. Three senators issued a statement saying, "Mr. Churchill's proposal would cut the throat of the Big Three, without which the war could not have been won and without which the peace cannot be saved." Former Vice President Henry Wallace, by then secretary of commerce, insisted that it was important for the United States to "allay any reasonable Russian grounds for fear, suspicion, and distrust." Privately, Truman called these critics of Churchill's speech "the American Crackpots Association."

As 1946 came to an end, more Americans were coming to the conclusion that Stalin was an evil dictator and the Soviet Union could not be trusted. Truman decided that his administration needed to speak with a single voice and dropped Wallace and Secretary of State James Byrnes from the cabinet, replacing the latter with George Marshall, who was U.S. chief of staff during the war. A year later, Truman also sponsored a reorganization of the nation's military forces in which the previously separate cabinet-level War and Navy departments were merged into a single Department of Defense that was responsible for all military matters. Truman was quickly concluding that the end of World War II did not mean the end of the need for U.S. military strength.

Meanwhile, in early 1947, Greece was in the midst of a civil war between its government and communist forces, and Turkey was resisting Soviet demands for greater control of access to the eastern Mediterranean and the Middle East. Great Britain, which had been providing support for both governments, said it could no longer afford to do so. Truman, Marshall, and Marshall's deputy, Dean Acheson, agreed that the United States needed to step in to take Britain's place in supporting resistance to communism in the region. If the containment policy meant anything, it certainly meant stopping Soviet moves into places like Greece and Turkey. The **Truman Doctrine** made it clear that containing communism would be at the bedrock of U.S. foreign policy. Needing the support of a reluctant Congress, Truman appeared in person and said, "I believe that it must be the policy of the United States to support free peoples who are resisting attempted subjugation by armed minorities or by outside pressures."

In June, the administration announced plans for massive economic aid to western Europe. The winter of 1946–47 had been the worst in years. By spring, Europe was running dangerously low on coal and food. People were cold, hungry, and desperate. Secretary of State Marshall used a Harvard commencement speech to tell the world:

> Our policy is directed not against any country or doctrine, but against hunger, poverty, desperation, and chaos....We know that in this trying period, between a war that is over and a peace that is not yet secure, the destitute and oppressed of the earth look chiefly to us for sustenance and support until they can again face life with self-confidence and self-reliance.

Truman Doctrine
President Harry Truman's statement in 1947 that the United States should assist other nations that were facing external pressure or internal revolution.

Marshall Plan
The European Recovery Program (1949), which provided U.S. economic assistance to European nations in large part to keep them out of the Soviet Union's sphere of influence.

The speech was partly true. The humanitarian goals, a campaign against hunger, poverty and desperation, were real. But the **Marshall Plan**, as it came to be called, was also directed against one country and its doctrine. People in the United States and the Soviet Union knew that the goal was to stop Soviet expansion in Western Europe.

Congress funded $13.34 billion in U.S. aid for Europe between 1948 and 1952. People were fed, economies recovered, and western capitalist democracies were established.

Stalin saw the Truman Doctrine and the Marshall Plan as a direct assault. Some Americans, notably the now-out-of-office Henry Wallace, also thought it was a needless provocation. The Soviets quickly solidified the power of a pro-Soviet regime in Hungary and arranged a pro-Soviet coup in Czechoslovakia in February 1948. Then in June 1948, the Soviet Union closed off American, British, and French access to Berlin. Before World War II ended, the Soviet Union, Britain, the United States, and France had agreed that each of them would assume military authority not only in a different quadrant of Germany but also within a different quadrant in the city of Berlin, even though Berlin itself was deep inside the Soviet quadrant. The result was a divided Germany and a divided Berlin, a precarious situation especially for the former capital city (see Map 24-2).

The Soviets saw Berlin as a useful pressure point in the Cold War. By closing off western access to the city, they could challenge the Truman Doctrine and the Marshall Plan. When they blocked all rail and highway access to Berlin in the spring of 1948, Truman decided to support the city with an airlift. In the days and weeks that followed, the **Berlin Airlift** sent hundreds of U.S. airplanes every day to Templehoff Airport in the western sector of Berlin. The city was well supplied and West Berlin withstood the siege. Eventually in May 1949, the Soviet Union relented and reestablished access to Berlin. Nevertheless, by the beginning of 1949, the iron curtain that Churchill had described was more firmly in place than ever, and the Cold War, which had been developing since 1945, was a reality.

Berlin Airlift

In 1948 and 1949, food and supplies delivered by air into Berlin to keep the city attached to western Europe.

1949—The Soviet Atom Bomb and the Fall of China

Just as the crisis in Berlin was coming to an end, the U.S. Senate ratified American membership in the North Atlantic Treaty Organization (NATO), by an 82 to 13 vote in July 1949. Fearing a Soviet invasion of western Europe, 12 nations, led by the United States and Britain, created the NATO alliance, in which each member agreed to treat an attack on any one from any source—though only one source was feared—as an attack on all. There would be no repeat by any country of Nazi Germany's attacks on the nations of Europe, one after another. The NATO treaty was the first time in history that the United States agreed to such a peacetime partnership.

Virtually nonstop flights brought vital supplies to the city of Berlin and sustained it during its isolation from June 1948 until May 1949.

Occupation of Germany and Austria, 1946–1949

☐ Land annexed by Poland
■ Land annexed by U.S.S.R.
━━ Iron Curtain

MAP 24-2 A Divided Germany. With the end of World War II, American, British, French, and Soviet forces each controlled a portion of Germany and a portion of the German capital city of Berlin as well as temporarily Austria. The arrangement would soon lead to a new crisis.

In 1955, when the Federal Republic of Germany, or West Germany, was created out of the merged British, French, and U.S. occupation zones and admitted to NATO, the Soviet Union formed the Warsaw Pact—a military alliance in eastern Europe specifically designed to counter NATO with the same guarantees of mutual assistance for its members, all of whom were under tight control by the Soviet Union. NATO and the Warsaw Pact would be more powerful entities in the coming decades than the United Nations (see Map 24-3).

MAP 24-3 A Divided Europe. As the Cold War escalated, countries within NATO and those within the Warsaw Pact, with few neutral nations, made up the new Europe.

Two further events in the fall of 1949 sped the growth of Cold War sentiment in the United States. First, in August, the Russians exploded their own atomic bomb. Then, soon after the announcement of Soviet nuclear capacity, the government of the U.S. wartime ally Chiang Kai-shek was defeated by Chinese communists. The creation of the Communist People's Republic of China under the leadership of Mao Tse-tung and the flight of Chiang's government to the island of Taiwan was a huge blow to American pride even though the United States continued to recognize the Taiwan-based government as the official voice of China until the 1970s. Chiang's government had been an important symbol to Americans since the Japanese invasion of China in the 1930s, and the United States had spent almost $3 billion to help Chiang since the end of World War II. Americans had tended to ignore the corruption and inefficiency of Chiang's Nationalist government. An internal U.S. State Department paper written in August 1949 just before the fall of Chiang's government said, "The unfortunate but inescapable fact is that the ominous result of the civil war in China was beyond the control of the government of the United States." However, many Americans—in Congress, in the media, and around the country—were convinced that the United States had somehow "lost China" and that the Truman administration was at fault. It was a sour time in a country which was not used to losses.

The Cold War at Home—Joseph McCarthy and a New Red Scare

As Americans tried to make sense of the Cold War, the Soviet manufacture of an atomic bomb, and the Communist takeover in China, some in Congress and beyond looked for internal enemies. Many politicians were worried about maintaining the security of the United States, but some in Congress sought political gain by fomenting a new Red Scare similar to the one that had followed World War I (see Chapter 21).

On January 21, 1950, Alger Hiss, a former State Department official who had been with FDR at Yalta and who helped organize the United Nations, was accused of having been a spy for the Soviets in the 1930s. One week later, Klaus Fuchs, an atomic scientist, was arrested in London and accused of turning over nuclear secrets to the Soviets. Fuchs implicated several Americans, including David Greenglass, Greenglass's sister Ethel Rosenberg, and her husband Julius Rosenberg. And little more than a week after the arrest of Fuchs, Wisconsin Senator Joseph McCarthy gave a speech in Wheeling, West Virginia, in which he claimed to have a list of active Communist Party members who worked for the federal government. People began to suspect communist infiltration everywhere. The nation was in for 5 years of fear and suspicion.

Reality was more complex than the picture of widespread subversion implied. Although the Communist Party in the United States was tiny, thousands of Americans had considered communism as an alternative to the nation's battered economic system in the 1930s. In addition, during World War II, the Soviet Union was the America's close ally in the fight against Nazi Germany. Before 1945, no one could have anticipated that helping the Soviets would be such a serious crime later in the decade.

Like many State Department officials, Alger Hiss was from the highest social strata, making him an ideal choice for those who wanted to whip up class resentment as well as anticommunism. When Hiss was accused of passing state secrets to the Soviets, he insisted on testifying under oath in front of Congress, a move that opened Hiss to a charge of libel, and even though he was never convicted of espionage, he was eventually convicted of lying under oath to Congress and served 3 years in prison. More recently available documents make it clear that Hiss had, indeed, probably been a communist in the 1930s, but when politicians like Republican Representative Karl Mundt of South Dakota said that the conviction proved that the United States "had been run by New Dealers, Fair Dealers, Misdealers and Hiss dealers" they were lumping an awful lot of other people who had never even flirted with communism in the same category. Mundt's comment did prove that, in many parts of the United States, deep resentment of the New Deal and of the eastern elite was alive and well and could easily be linked with each other and both could be linked with fears of the growing international influence of communism in the late 1940s.

Greenglass and the Rosenbergs were investigated in 1950 and charged with being Soviet spies and with passing on atomic secrets to the Soviets in 1951. Greenglass worked at the top-secret Manhattan Project, and Julius Rosenberg was a wartime engineer, and both had access to highly secret data. They were also Jewish, and even though Americans were horrified by the Holocaust, anti-Semitism was alive and well in the United States in 1950. Just as Hiss suffered for his East Coast elite status, Greenglass and the Rosenbergs suffered for their Jewish background. In the end, Greenglass served a long prison term. Ethel and Julius Rosenberg, who always maintained their innocence, were executed in 1953, the only Americans ever executed under the 1917 Espionage Act. (In the 1990s, when Soviet archives were opened and when another one of the accused coconspirators, Morton Sobell admitted that he had, indeed, been a spy, it seemed clear that at least Julius, if not Ethel, had been Soviet spies.) It was also clear that, in the atmosphere of 1950 and 1951, it was virtually impossible for them to get a fair trial.

Senator Joseph McCarthy lectured widely on the Communist menace. Although he gave few details, he successfully created great fear. In this image, he exhibits a photograph that he claims is evidence of communist infiltration during a Senate investigation in 1954.

Senator Joseph McCarthy was not the first elected official to try to make political gains by stirring up the fear of communism (in fact he came late to the process), but he stole the leadership from all the others. He had been searching for a new political issue on which to build his reelection campaign in Wisconsin, and in February 1950, he thought he had found it when he heard the national reaction to a speech in which he said, "I have here in my hand a list of 205—a list of names that were made known to the Secretary of State as being members of the Community Party who nevertheless are still working and shaping policy in the State Department."

McCarthy was far more interested in his own fame than in actually finding communists. His Senate colleagues knew him as a pathological liar who had lied about his military service (he said he had flown 30 combat missions when he had flown none; his limp was not from shrapnel, as he claimed, but from a fall), and he embarrassed them. He drank heavily, fanned the flames of homophobia, and attacked both Republicans and Democrats whom he thought were "soft on communism." Nevertheless, few were willing to challenge McCarthy while the country was caught up in the fear of communism.

McCarthy said, "The government is full of Communists." He also said that Acheson's predecessor, George Marshall, had "lost" China. For those who believed that only a conspiracy could have led to the growth of communist influence around the world, McCarthy was the perfect voice. In June 1951, he told one audience:

> How can we account for our present situation unless we believe that men high in this government are concerting to deliver us to disaster? This must be the product of a conspiracy, a conspiracy on a scale so immense as to dwarf any previous such venture in the history of man.

Only treason in high places could account for the nation's troubles as McCarthy described them.

McCarthy never did name the names on his list, and the numbers kept shifting in different speeches, but he ruined careers and frightened many into silence. His popularity seemed to protect him. In May 1950, a Gallup poll showed that 84 percent of Americans knew who McCarthy was and 39 percent believed that his attacks were good for the country. Few political leaders were willing to challenge him. However, in June 1950, Maine's Republican Senator Margaret Chase Smith and six colleagues issued a "Declaration of Conscience," saying that McCarthy was using the Senate as a "publicity platform for irresponsible sensationalism." Still, he continued for 4 more years.

When he became president in 1953, Eisenhower did not challenge McCarthy directly, but helped those who wanted to undermine him. In 1954, Edward R. Murrow, perhaps the most respected journalist in the country, did an exposé on McCarthy on his "See It Now" program on CBS television. Both the Senate declaration and the CBS program hurt McCarthy's reputation, but it was only when McCarthy decided to probe for communists in the U.S. Army that he met his match. As the army's attorney Joseph Welch grilled him, McCarthy lashed out at a young attorney who was assisting Welch, accusing him of being a Communist because he was a member of the left-leaning National Lawyers Guild. Welch exploded, "Until this moment Senator, I think I never really gauged your cruelty or your recklessness." The hearing room burst into applause. After that, on December 2, 1954, the Senate voted to condemn McCarthy by a vote of 67 to 22. He continued to serve out his term until his death in 1957, but he was a beaten man and no longer a force in national politics.

McCarthy was hardly the only leader of the Red Scare of the late 1940s and early 1950s. J. Edgar Hoover, who had been head of the Federal Bureau of Investigation (FBI) since 1924 and a participant in the government's attack on radicals after World War I, cultivated a reputation as the nation's top crime fighter, especially after FBI agents killed John Dillinger, "Public Enemy Number One," during Prohibition. But Hoover also cultivated a role as a leading anti-Communist, seeking to expose what he claimed was communist influence in the government, universities, religious groups, and later civil rights organizations. He collected files on hundreds of Americans, from members of Congress to union officials. Although President Truman complained about Hoover, insisting, "We want no Gestapo or Secret Police," he did not stop Hoover's search for subversives.

Other politicians realized that the search for Communists could lead to electoral success. The **House Committee on Un-American Activities (HUAC)** became a powerful forum for those who used the fear of communism to pursue other agendas. One of its members, John Rankin, a Democrat from Mississippi linked communism, Jews, and civil rights workers, saying of the Civil Rights Movement, "This is part of the communistic program, laid down by Stalin approximately 30 years ago. Remember communism is Yiddish. I understand that every member of the Politburo around Stalin is either Yiddish or married to one, and that includes Stalin himself." A young Republican Representative from California, Richard M. Nixon, used HUAC to build a national reputation, investigating Hiss, looking for communists in the government, and extending the search into the entertainment industry and education.

While some in the entertainment world quickly cooperated with HUAC, many fought back. Judy Garland, one of the nation's most popular stars since her childhood role in the *Wizard of Oz*, pleaded, "Before every free conscience in America is subpoenaed, please speak up!" Frank Sinatra asked, "Once they get the movies throttled ...how long will it be before we're told what we can say and cannot say into the radio microphone? If you make a pitch on a nationwide radio network for a square deal for the underdog, will they call you a Commie?...Are they going to scare us into silence?" Undeterred, HUAC continued with its hearings. Many witnesses refused to testify on the Fifth Amendment grounds that they could not be compelled to testify against themselves. Ten actors, known as the Hollywood Ten, took the more difficult route of claiming that the hearings threatened their First Amendment rights of free speech. The 10 and others were blacklisted and had their careers ruined, in spite of efforts by the Committee for the First Amendment led by Humphrey Bogart, Lauren Bacall, Katherine Hepburn, and Danny Kaye to protect them.

House Committee on Un-American Activities

Congressional committee (1938–1975) that investigated suspected Nazi and Communist sympathizers.

THINKING HISTORICALLY
Looking at the Art of the Postwar Nation

In his book, the *Unfinished City: New York and the Metropolitan Idea,* historian Thomas Bender wrote of the radical transformation of the arts after World War II, "Intellectual historians have failed to grasp the variety of artistic and critical work that characterized the 1940s, partly because concerns of the Cold War era gave precedence to certain ideological themes and political trends." Bender argues that it is also important to pay attention to the "remarkable creativity and critical discourse in the fields of painting and sculpture, photography, architecture, music, and dance."

As Bender observes, while many Americans were focused on the Cold War, others were using the arts to ask different questions about American life, especially as people came to terms with the threat of nuclear disaster after World War II. Often, artists were pointing to the confusions—some said pointlessness—of contemporary thinking as much or more than they were making overt statements about one political ideology or another.

James Agee, himself a very well-known author, was the film critic for the *Nation* magazine in the late 1940s. In a 1948 review, he wrote:

Several of the best people in Hollywood grew, noticeably, during their years away at war; the man who grew most impressively, I thought, as an artist, as a man, in intelligence, and in an ability to put through fine work against difficult odds, was [film director] John Huston.…His first movie since the war has been a long time coming, but it was certainly worth waiting for. *The Treasure of the Sierra Madre* is…about as near to folk art as a highly conscious artist can get.…I doubt we shall ever see a film more masculine in style; or a truer movie understanding of character and of men.

As a generation of young men returned from the fighting of the war and took up their day-to-day lives in the civilian work-force, some worried that perhaps they had left their masculinity behind on the battlefields. Artists, like the film director John Huston, addressed these fears. While the films of the late 1940s and early 1950s were, like all films, meant to entertain, they also helped some in the audience think through some of their greatest hopes and fears.

The abstract artist Jackson Pollock painted Convergence in 1952. Like most abstract art, the complex work leaves it to the beholder to make meaning of the lines and colors the artist offers.

Source: Thomas Bender, *Unfinished City: New York and the Metropolitan Idea* (New York: New York University Press, 2002), pp. 135–136; James Agee, "The Treasure of the Sierra Madre," *The Nation*, January 31, 1948.

Thinking Critically

1. **Historical Interpretation**

   In your opinion, what can a period's art tell us about its politics? What sort of political ideas might one see in an abstract painting or a film about masculinity?

2. **Constructing an Argument**

   How would you explain the emergence of abstract art in the era of the atomic bomb after World War II in place of the much more realistic paintings of the 1930s?

Many labor unions purged communist members. Aspiring new leaders used the accusation of communist influence to push aside older leaders. The United Electrical Workers union was replaced by a new union of electrical workers because the United Electrical was considered to be communist and was expelled by the American Federation of Labor. Civil Rights organizations, including the Urban League, the Congress of Racial Equality, and the National Association for the Advancement of Colored People (NAACP), purged communist members. Many school districts and 21 states required loyalty oaths from teachers. In 1948, the University of Washington fired three professors when they refused to answer questions about the Communist Party. Some 31 professors were ultimately fired from the University of California under similar circumstances. And the American Federation of Teachers, the leading union of elementary and secondary teachers, voted that communists should not be allowed to be members or teach in the nation's schools.

Not everyone was caught up in the Red Scare hysteria. Philip Murray, president of the Congress of Industrial Organizations, one of the nation's largest unions, wrote to President Truman in 1947 to protest that government policy did not ensure due process for accused employees. Secretary of the Treasury John Snyder protested the government's Loyalty Review Board in 1948.

George Kennan, who had played an important role in launching the Cold War, added a somber note in his *Memoirs:* "What the phenomenon of McCarthyism did… was to implant in my consciousness a lasting doubt as to the adequacy of our political system.…I could never recapture after these experiences of the 1940s and 1950s, quite the same faith in the American system of government and in traditional American outlooks that I had, despite all the discouragements of official life, before that time." Not everyone shared Kennan's pessimism, but many felt that American democracy itself had been wounded by the tactics of people like McCarthy.

War in Korea

On June 25, 1950, to the surprise of U.S. leaders, the army of North Korea attacked South Korea. Korea was a part of the world to which U.S. planners had paid very little attention. But it was the place where the Cold War turned very hot.

With the Japanese defeat in 1945, the victorious allies determined to honor Korean hopes for independence. U.S. military authorities used the same formula as they had for Germany: a divided military occupation that was meant to be temporary. Military planners agreed that the Soviet army would occupy Korea north of the 38th parallel (North Korea) and that U.S. forces would occupy the southern half of the peninsula, including the old capital of Seoul (South Korea), until a permanent plan for national unification could be achieved. It would be a long wait.

The United States backed a new government led by the 75-year-old Syngman Rhee, who was conservative, charming, fiercely independent, as well as corrupt and dictatorial. The Soviets backed an even more dictatorial 31-year-old communist, Kim Il-Sung. Both Rhee and Kim were committed to Korean unification, but on very different terms. Between the end of World War II and 1950, constant clashes between the two governments cost perhaps 100,000 Koreans their lives.

Then, in 1949 and 1950, a crisis developed. In 1949, the Soviet delegate to the United Nations, Jacob Malik, began boycotting the UN Security Council because that body continued to give the Nationalist Chinese government of Chiang Kai-shek the UN vote even though the Communist government ruled mainland China. The protest meant that the Soviet Union could not veto Security Council resolutions at a crucial moment.

At the same time, the Truman administration, worried that the United States was spread too thin, and seeing Korea as of only marginal significance, withdrew the U.S. military, leaving Rhee's government on its own. A year later in 1950, in a speech he later regretted, Secretary of State Dean Acheson described the U.S. "defensive perimeter" in Asia in a way that did not include either Korea or Taiwan. Stalin and the North Korean dictator Kim Il-Sung assumed that the United States was not prepared to defend South Korea. Kim pressed Stalin to approve an attack and Stalin agreed, though he warned Kim, "[I]f you get kicked in the teeth, I shall not lift a finger." It was all the permission Kim needed. On June 25, 100,000 North Korean troops, supported by tanks, artillery, and planes, invaded the South.

The Communist leaders had misread U.S. intentions. Truman viewed the Korean invasion through the prism of British and French inaction in the face of Nazism. He was determined to maintain the Truman Doctrine of containment of communism anywhere in the world. With the Soviets absent, Acheson appealed to the United Nations Security Council and got a unanimous vote in favor of UN action to stop the North Koreans. The Korean War was called a UN police action, although nearly all of the fighting was done by U.S. and Korean troops.

Public opinion polls showed solid support for American action, and people as diverse as Republican Governor of New York Thomas Dewey and liberal Henry Wallace (both of whom had run against Truman in the 1948 presidential election) supported Truman. Congress appropriated $10 billion.

Truman ordered General Douglas MacArthur, then commander of U.S. troops occupying Japan, to take command in Korea, and troops were rushed to Korea. Meanwhile, the North Koreans kept coming. By September, 3 months after the war began, U.S. and South Korean forces controlled only a small section of southeast Korea around the port of Pusan, known as the Pusan perimeter. Slowly, however, the U.S. forces were built up and supplies brought into Korea. American planes bombed North Korean troops heavily. The bombing wreaked havoc on Communist supply lines but also destroyed rice fields. Perhaps half the invading North Korean army were killed or wounded in the first 2 months of the war, and most of the North Korean tanks were disabled. Two to three million Korean civilians, 10 percent of the prewar population of Korea, died during the war either from bombing or from starvation because of lost rice crops.

In September 1950, under MacArthur's command, the U.S. and UN forces made a surprise amphibious landing at Inchon, on the west coast of Korea close to the 38th parallel. The Communist forces were cut off from their supplies and captured or forced to retreat. The tide of war suddenly turned, and in less than a month, the Americans advanced from the small perimeter to retake South Korea (see Map 24-4).

For MacArthur, the initial victory was only the beginning. He insisted, and Truman agreed, that the moment had come to unify the whole Korean peninsula under Syngman Rhee. The UN, with the Soviets still boycotting, agreed and MacArthur's forces began moving north, closer to the Chinese border at the Yalu River. MacArthur was confident that he could win the war and be home by December. When Truman asked about the chance of a Chinese intervention, Mac Arthur responded, "Very little." He was wrong.

By late November, as MacArthur's army continued north, a huge Chinese army attacked them. "The Chinese have come in with both feet," Truman said. This time it was the Americans that had long drawn-out supply lines. They were ill prepared for the freezing cold of a Korean winter. The Chinese wore warm, padded clothing, had fought for years in similar territory, and were adept at terrifying hand-to-hand night fighting when American planes and troops could not see them. The fighting in November and December of 1950 was brutal. Soldiers were killed as they slept or froze in the winter cold. The retreats were frightful. The U.S. Army Seventh Infantry Division lost 5,000 troops, one-third of its force, in a 3-day retreat over mountainous roads as the Chinese attacked from every angle. By January 1951, the line dividing the two armies was well south of the 38th parallel. The war settled into a bloody stalemate.

For Truman, the defeats in Korea at the end of 1950 were a diplomatic and a political disaster. Republicans now saw him as weak. Some urged the use of atomic weapons on China. General MacArthur, whom Truman despised, had strong Republican support. (MacArthur's fellow senior officers had their own opinions. When General Eisenhower was asked if he had met MacArthur he responded, "Not only have I met him....I studied dramatics under him.") In early 1951, MacArthur bypassed Truman and tried to get congressional support for a wider war. Truman had had enough. With support from the Joint Chiefs of Staff, he fired MacArthur, who had been a hero to many. Army Chief of Staff General Omar Bradley was more concerned with Europe and fearful of a land war in Asia. Bradley said Korea was the "wrong war, at the wrong place, at the wrong time, and with

U.S. troops bogged down in the snow and cold of Korea found the war far more difficult to fight than had been expected.

MAP 24-4 The Korean War. At the beginning and end of the Korean war, the peninsula was divided into two nations at the 38th parallel. However, between 1950 and 1953, the dividing line moved many times as indicated.

the wrong enemy." The new commander in Korea, General Matthew Ridgway, stabilized the defense lines and arranged better support and supplies for the troops.

The Chinese and American governments became resigned to a partial victory. Neither wanted a larger war, no matter what the two Korean governments thought. Battles for places the American troops called "Heartbreak Ridge," or "No-Name Ridge," described how those on the ground thought about what they were doing. Armistice negotiations began in the summer of 1951, but stalled over the fact that many Chinese and North Korean prisoners did not want to be returned home. It would take 2 more years, and the election of a new U.S. president, before the final armistice was signed in July 1953. More than 36,000 Americans were killed in the war, many times more Korean and Chinese troops, and probably 3 million Korean civilians. The final armistice line was not far from where the prewar line had been near Panmunjom. Sixty years later, Korea is still a tense and divided place.

24.2 **Quick Review** How did changing attitudes toward, and experiences with, the Soviet Union between 1945 and 1949 contribute to major changes in U.S. foreign policy?

24.3 Explain political developments that led to the elections of Truman and then Eisenhower as Cold War era presidents.

When Harry Truman became president in April 1945, few Americans knew much about him. Many expected Truman to merely serve out the term to which Roosevelt had been elected. Truman decided otherwise, but he had a lot of time and a lot of responsibility to manage before any thought of reelection loomed.

Riding A Tiger—Truman's First Term

As war and foreign policy dominated Truman's first months in office, Truman said he felt like he was riding a tiger. The liberal wing of the Democratic Party included New Deal activists such as Secretary of Commerce Henry Wallace and Secretary of the Interior Harold Ickes who never trusted Truman, viewing him as a product of Missouri machine politics who had been forced on FDR by the conservative wing of the party. Truman reciprocated the distrust. Looking ahead to the postwar world, Truman told Clark Clifford, one of his key advisors, "I don't want any experiments. The American people have been through a lot of experiments, and they want a rest from experiments." But Truman was not proposing any sort of Warren Harding "normalcy."

On September 6, 1945, just 4 days after the Japanese surrender, Truman proposed legislation that would implement FDR's Economic Bill of Rights, expanding the federal role in public housing, public utilities, job creation, and national health, increasing the minimum wage, offering Social Security benefits to more people, while also making the Fair Employment Practices Commission permanent. It was a sweeping agenda, delighting liberals and dismaying conservatives. Southern segregationists filibustered the fair employment bill that would have continued FDR's executive order, ensuring that employers with federal contracts could not discriminate among employees on the basis of race, and kept it from reaching a vote. Other bills were watered down by Congress. Congress turned Truman's effort to launch a national system of health insurance into the Hill-Burton Act that benefitted doctors and hospitals and private medical insurers, but did not guarantee health insurance.

While there was Democratic as well as Republican opposition to Truman's domestic agenda, the president's single most powerful opponent was Ohio Senator Robert Taft, the son of the former president, known to many as "Mr. Republican." Taft not only opposed Truman's agenda but also pushed legislation that reduced taxes, forcing cuts in government programs, and persuaded Congress in 1947, over Truman's veto, to pass the Taft-Hartley Act that lifted many of the protections organized labor had enjoyed since the passage of the Wagner Act in the 1930s.

Taft was not alone. The Republican Party was strong following World War II. As Truman understood, many people in the United States were tired of experiments, just as after World War I, many Americans simply wanted to be left alone. In the 1946 midterm elections, Republicans took control of both houses of Congress. But Harry Truman was a fighter, more of a fighter than some expected. His goal was to win a full term in his own right and elect a Democratic Congress in 1948, goals many thought unrealistic in 1946.

The 1948 Election—A Four-Way Contest

In planning his campaign for 1948, Truman sought to maintain the New Deal coalition that had elected Roosevelt four times, and even sought to expand it. He wanted to have a large plurality among white blue-collar workers, immigrant groups, farmers, and poor people. He made special efforts to court African-Americans and Jews. In 1946, he appointed a President's Committee on Civil Rights and its report, released in October 1947, led him to propose an antilynching law, a permanent fair employment commission, and laws against poll taxes and discrimination in transportation.

When the Republican Congress failed to pass these and other pieces of legislation, Truman called them "the do-nothing Congress." Under pressure from civil rights leaders, Truman overruled the objections of some of the nation's highest-ranking military officers and ordered the desegregation of the nation's armed forces in 1948. It would take several years before the last segregated regiments were phased out, but the process was underway for a dramatic change from the segregated military of World War II.

Truman also favored the establishment of an independent state of Israel. On this issue, there was deep disagreement within the administration. Secretary of State Marshall threatened to resign if the United States gave support to Israel, and most leaders of the State, Army, and Navy departments opposed recognizing the new nation. They feared that the United States would permanently alienate the Arab world, jeopardize the smooth flow of oil to the United States and Europe, and create a situation that would remain tense and untenable. Those on the White House staff tended to support creation of a Jewish state in the Middle East. Truman's own reading about the Holocaust and Middle Eastern history led him to support Israel. He got—and occasionally resented—considerable pressure from American Zionists. Thirty-three state legislatures passed resolutions favoring the establishment of a Jewish state. Truman responded to one anxious State Department official, "I have to answer to hundreds of thousands who are anxious for the success of Zionism. I do not have hundreds of thousands of Arabs among my constituents." On May 14, as the last British forces left Palestine, Zionists proclaimed the independent state of Israel. At Truman's direction, the United States immediately recognized the new government. To the surprise of many, Israel was able to defend itself successfully against an Arab attack and secure its borders and its existence.

Truman's policies from fair employment to his support for Israel also had an impact on American voters. While many African-Americans were moving into the Democratic Party and most Jewish voters were prepared to support Truman after his May 1948 decisions, the road to nomination and election that year was not easy. Many New Dealers in the Democratic Party still hoped for a more liberal or a more popular candidate.

When it became clear that Truman would win the nomination—and invite Senate leader Alben Barkley to be his running mate—Henry Wallace, former vice president and commerce secretary, bolted and set up the Progressive Party to defeat Truman, end the Cold War, and return the country to what he saw as the Roosevelt legacy.

Then, when Truman supported a convention platform plank supporting civil rights, introduced by Minnesota Senator Hubert Humphrey at the Democratic convention, 35 delegates from Alabama and Mississippi walked out of the convention waving Confederate flags and proceeded to nominate South Carolina's governor and future senator J. Strom Thurmond to run against Truman. These "Dixiecrats" were a serious threat to a party that always counted on the "solid South" to ensure national electoral victories.

The Republicans, sensing that this was their year, especially with the divisions in the Democrat ranks, nominated Governor Thomas E. Dewey of New York, the 1944 standard bearer, with California Governor Earl Warren as his running mate. The team seemed to have everything going for it and ran a cautious campaign designed to avoid mistakes. Unfortunately for the Republicans, they were too cautious and Dewey was too stiff. Alice Longworth, Theodore Roosevelt's daughter, called him, "the little man on the wedding cake." The Wallace campaign never took off and gained little support though it may have denied Truman the majority in a few crucial states, especially New York. The Thurmond campaign got virtually no support outside of the Deep South though it did carry the electoral votes of four states—Alabama, Louisiana, Mississippi, and South Carolina. Truman waged a very tough and spirited campaign against the "do-nothing Congress" and the "Wall Street reactionaries." As he campaigned, people started yelling, "Give 'em hell, Harry!" He had solid support from organized labor and farmers and held most of the New Deal coalition together. Still, the Republicans, led by Dewey, were confident of victory. But when the votes were counted, Truman won, receiving 24,179,345 votes to Dewey's 21,991,291, and 303 electoral votes to Dewey's 189. Thurmond won 39 electoral votes. Wallace none.

As he began his new term in January 1949, Truman called his agenda the **Fair Deal**. The Truman Fair Deal included repeal of the Taft-Hartley Act, support for family farmers, a more progressive income tax, federal aid to education, an increase in the minimum wage, national medical insurance as well as another try to broadening Social Security, and expanded civil rights. In his inaugural address, Truman also called for more U.S. technical assistance to developing countries. Technical assistance became known as Point Four because it was the fourth point in Truman's speech.

Even though the Democrats controlled both houses of Congress in 1949, virtually none of the Fair Deal legislation passed. Southern Democrats made sure there was no movement on civil rights, organized labor did not have enough support to overturn the Taft-Hartley Act, urban representatives saw little value in spending federal tax money on farmers, and the American Medical Association made sure that there was no national system of medical insurance such as most western European countries adopted after World War II. Point Four foreign aid passed, but the appropriations were small and the resulting technical assistance generally insignificant. Much of Truman's second term was focused on the war in Korea—which the Congress was willing to fund—and the ongoing Red Scare, which Truman did little to oppose.

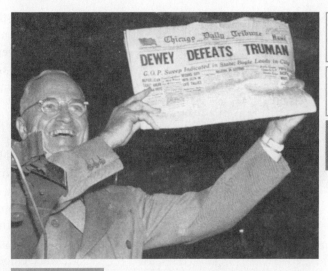

Many were confident of a Republican victory in the 1948 election, including the editors of the *Chicago Tribune,* who published this erroneous early edition over which the eventual winner, Harry S. Truman, delighted to gloat.

A War Hero Becomes President

In a belated slap at Franklin Roosevelt, the Republican Congress passed the 22nd Amendment to the Constitution prohibiting any president from serving more than two terms, and a majority of states ratified the amendment. The amendment did not apply to the sitting president, and Truman considered seeking a third term. When he was defeated in the first primaries by Estes Kefauver, a crusading senator from Tennessee, however, Truman decided that two terms was enough and dropped out of the race. In spite of his spirited come-from-behind race in 1948 and his later reputation as a tough decision maker, Truman was not a widely popular president.

The most popular person in the United States in the early 1950s was Dwight David Eisenhower, known to everyone as Ike. Born in 1890 and raised in Abilene, Kansas by pacifist parents, Eisenhower had attended West Point, seeing it as a free education for a career in engineering. Instead, he became a long-term officer in the peacetime army between the wars, moving slowly through the ranks. He was still a colonel when World War II began, but was then promoted rapidly and commanded the Allied force that defeated Nazi Germany. He probably could have had the presidential nomination of either party in 1948 but opted to become president of Columbia University and then commander of NATO forces in Europe in 1951. He managed to convey a disinterested, "above the fray" persona. Some who knew him better saw another side. General George Patton said, "Ike wants to be President so badly you can taste it."

While Eisenhower had served as a senior military commander under Democrats—Roosevelt and Truman—and tended to agree with the anti-Communist wing of the Democratic Party on foreign policy matters, he was a fiscal conservative, and the New Deal and Fair Deal programs offended his sense of the proper role of the federal government. If he was going to run, it would be as a Republican. Liberals within the Republican Party, including the 1944 and 1948 standard bearer Thomas Dewey and Massachusetts Senator Henry Cabot Lodge, were desperate to find an "internationalist" candidate who could stop the Republican front-runner, Senator Taft, an isolationist in foreign policy and a conservative on domestic issues. They courted Eisenhower who remained coy. However, primary voters made it clear that they preferred Ike to Taft: Ike defeated Taft 46,661 to 35,838 in the March New Hampshire primary even though he was still at NATO headquarters in Europe and did not campaign. After

Fair Deal
The name President Harry Truman gave to his policies to continue and extend many of the New Deal's domestic policies.

that primary, the momentum was hard to stop and Eisenhower was nominated by the Republicans in the summer of 1952—a bitter loss for Taft and his supporters.

Eisenhower asked California Senator Richard M. Nixon to be his running mate. Although the two were not close, and never were, Nixon brought balance to the ticket. Ike almost dumped Nixon at one point in the campaign because of charges that Nixon had a private, campaign fund donated by wealthy Californians. Nixon gave what became known as his "Checkers" television speech for its maudlin promise to keep the family dog, named Checkers, even though the dog had been a gift. The speech was a success, and Nixon stayed on the ticket. For the rest of his career, even after his own presidency, Nixon celebrated the day of the speech. At the age of 38, Nixon was considered young while Ike at 62 was considered old. Nixon had made his name with his search for Communists when he was a member of the House Un-American Activities Committee. In addition, he was from the West Coast while Ike's strongest support was in the East.

The Democrats nominated Illinois Governor Adlai Stevenson. Like Eisenhower, Stevenson was a strong Cold Warrior and a known internationalist who had been one of the founders of the United Nations. He had a reputation as an honest politician in a state where Democrats were often corrupt. He was more conservative than Truman on most domestic issues, especially race, and he selected Alabama Senator John Sparkman as his running mate, in part to ensure that there would be no Dixiecrat walkout in 1952. Stevenson was also very popular with many liberals, mostly because of his intelligence and wit. One said that his speeches were "simply gems of wisdom and wit and sense." Unfortunately for Stevenson's vote-getting, this skill mattered more to the party's intellectual leaders than to many in the working class-black-urban coalition that had been key to the election of Roosevelt and Truman.

The campaign was the first in which television played a major role. The Republicans made effective use of short TV spots that carried brief comments by Ike along with his famous smile. Ike also promised a nation that was desperately tired of the war, "I shall go to Korea," though it was unclear what he would do there. In November, Ike won 55 percent of the vote and carried the electoral college 442 to 89, winning even Florida, Tennessee, Texas, and Virginia, states that had voted Democrat for decades. The Republicans won small majorities in Congress.

Eisenhower fulfilled his campaign promise and went to Korea. Early in his term, he was able to conclude the peace treaty that had eluded Truman. Korea remained divided, but the conflict ended. Ike intended to create what he called "Modern Republicanism." He was a determined internationalist who kept the United States active in the UN and NATO. Under Ike, there would be no return to 1920s-style isolationism. He was determined to balance the federal budget and not likely to launch major new programs, but not roll back the major New Deal initiatives either. He once said, "Should any political party attempt to abolish social security, unemployment insurance, and eliminate labor laws and farm programs, you would not hear of that party again in our political history." He dismissed the conservative wing of the Republican Party, saying of the conservative California Senator William Knowland, "In his case, there seems to be no final answer to the question, 'How stupid can you get?'"

With Eisenhower's election, a new Republican administration was prepared to maintain many of the New Deal's domestic policies and Truman's Cold War internationalism. Individuals changed, but surprisingly little policy changed after the inauguration. Nevertheless, as the Great Depression and World War II receded and a new generation grew up with no memory of that difficult past, and as many Americans experienced unprecedented prosperity, the culture began to change. The 1950s were staid to some, surprisingly novel to others, and full of surprises for most.

24.3 **Quick Review** Aside from their political parties, how different were Truman and Eisenhower as candidates and as presidents?

CONCLUSION

The experience of World War II had a profound effect on American culture in the decade that followed the war. The federal government offered generous benefits to returning veterans, allowing a whole generation of young men to attend college, to buy homes, and to live comfortable middle class lives. Men and women, anxious to leave the war behind, married quickly and had children, a lot of children. The population soared in what was called a baby boom.

In the postwar era, the living patterns of Americans changed drastically. Many middle class white Americans left the cities for homes in newly created suburban communities. At the same time, the rate of migration of southern blacks to the urban centers of the North exploded. Many black migrants moved into city centers because they were excluded from suburban developments. Latinos from Puerto Rico and Mexico moved to American cities, notably New York and Los Angeles.

The economic gains achieved during the war continued throughout the postwar period, made possible, in part, by the position of the United States as the only remaining economic superpower in the world. Consumers, who had more money than ever, purchased goods produced by American manufacturers, achieved new levels of economic security and affluence, buying automobiles, televisions, and electric appliances in the postwar economy.

The end of the World War II also brought on new attempts at international cooperation. In an effort to create political and economic stability and a lasting peace, the United Nations, the International Monetary Fund, and the World Bank, were ushered into being.

While enjoying the remarkable prosperity of the postwar era, more and more Americans became deeply concerned about the Soviet Union and the spread of communism. The containment of communism became the bedrock of U.S. foreign policy in the Truman administration. By 1952, both the United States and the Soviet Union possessed hydrogen bombs, and the possibility of "mutually assured destruction" set off a Cold War between the two countries that would last 40 years. In Europe, the Cold War was institutionalized in the western-led North Atlantic Treaty Organization founded by the United States and Great Britain and the eastern Warsaw Pact led by the Soviet Union. America's uneasy relationship with the Soviet Union resulted in a second Red Scare within the United States itself. Fueled by the fiery rhetoric of Senator Joseph McCarthy and others, Americans began to suspect communist infiltration everywhere, and many personal and professional lives were ruined by accusations of treason, espionage, and Communist Party membership that often had little basis in reality.

In 1950, the American policy of containment was tested when North Korea attacked South Korea. The United States, with support from the United Nations, took up the defense of South Korea even after a huge army from Communist China attacked U.S. forces in the region. After fierce fighting, the outcome of the war was ambiguous. The United States and China signed an armistice that left Korea divided much as it had been since the end of World War II. With the election of a new president, Dwight Eisenhower, in November 1952, the nation that was tired of the war in Korea settled into what many hoped would be a new era of peace and prosperity even as they continued to fear the Soviet Union and the mushroom cloud of atomic destruction.

CHAPTER REVIEW | How did the actions of the United States after World War II reflect its new position as a world superpower?

Chapter 24   Chapter Review

THE UNITED STATES IN 1945

24.1 Describe the new technology, living patterns, and political arrangements in the United States that resulted from World War II.

Review Questions

1. Contextualization

How did advances in science and technology change everyday life for Americans in the 1950s?

2. Cause and Effect

What explains the rapid growth of suburbs in the 1950s?

3. Constructing an Argument

Why did the rate of African-American migration to the North explode after World War II?

4. Comparison

Compare and contrast the migration of African-Americans and Latinos in the 1950s. What similarities and differences do you note?

THE COLD WAR BEGINS

24.2 Analyze the coming of the Cold War, tensions with the Soviet Union, and McCarthyism at home.

Review Questions

5. Cause and Effect

Why did relations between the United States and the Soviet Union deteriorate so rapidly after World War II?

6. Comparison

Compare and contrast the anticommunist hysteria relating to World War I with the hysteria that followed World War II. What similarities and differences do you note?

7. Historical Interpretation

Why was the Korean War a turning point in the Cold War?

POLITICS, 1948 AND 1952

24.3 Explain political developments that led to the elections of Truman and then Eisenhower as Cold War era presidents.

Review Questions

8. Cause and Effect

How did Truman's policy initiatives during his first term impact the election of 1948?

9. Historical Interpretation

Why was Eisenhower's election a turning point in American politics?

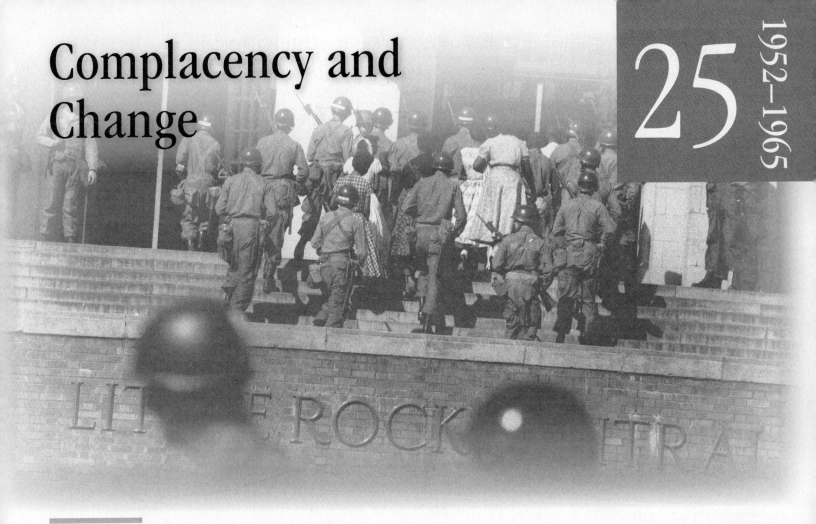

Complacency and Change

25

1952–1965

Only the arrival of federal troops assured the integration of Little Rock High School in 1957.

Dwight Eisenhower was the U.S. Supreme Commander in Europe when Harry Truman became president in the spring of 1945. In that role, he worked for Truman as he had for Roosevelt. But when Eisenhower decided to enter the Republican race for the White House and attacked Truman and the Democrats during the campaign, the relationship between the two men was deeply strained. Between Eisenhower's election victory in November 1952 and inauguration in 1953, the outgoing Truman administration had little to do with the new one. Nevertheless, once in office, Eisenhower made surprisingly few changes to Truman's policies. The Republican Eisenhower ended the war in Korea, mostly with a veiled threat to use atomic weapons, and surprisingly, solidified core New Deal policies and the Cold War.

Eisenhower's was a reassuring presence, and many considered his 8 years in office to be a time of complacency and stability in national life. However, the era was also one of extraordinary change. New technology, most of all television, changed the culture. Dissent from the dominant complacency was found in many places, most of all among the young and the more than 10 percent of Americans who were of African origin. The modern Civil Rights Movement began in the 1950s. The perceived stability and the many real changes of the 1950s are the focus of this chapter.

CHAPTER OBJECTIVE

Demonstrate an understanding of how different aspects of the 1950s, from the seeming complacency of Eisenhower's time to the growing Civil Rights Movement reshaped the United States.

LEARNING OBJECTIVES

EISENHOWER'S AMERICA, AMERICA'S WORLD

Explain the continuation of the Cold War under a new Republican administration.

25.1

A CULTURE ON THE MOVE

Explain the impact of cultural and technological changes on the country.

25.2

RACE AND CIVIL RIGHTS

Analyze the growth and impact of the Civil Rights Movement between 1954 and 1965.

25.3

massive retaliation

A policy adopted by the Eisenhower administration to limit the costs of the Cold War. Rather than keep a large military presence, the administration used the threat to use the hydrogen bomb if the Soviet Union expanded its grasp to new territory.

EISENHOWER'S AMERICA, AMERICA'S WORLD

25.1 Explain the continuation of the Cold War under a new Republican administration.

The successful test of a U.S. hydrogen bomb in November 1952, followed only months later by the successful test of a similar bomb by the Soviet Union (United Soviet Socialist Republic, or U.S.S.R.) in August 1953, meant that Eisenhower and every subsequent president would govern in a world that was quite different from any of their predecessors. While alliances like the U.S.-led NATO and the Soviet-led Warsaw Pact might position ground forces, the reality was that each of the superpowers had the capacity to destroy the other in a single stroke, and probably, for the first time in history, to destroy all life on earth. The Cold War between the United States and the Soviet Union was a daunting reality for every person on the planet in the 1950s and for a long time thereafter.

Foreign Policy in a World of Hydrogen Bombs

Early in his first term, Eisenhower lamented, "We are in an armaments race. Where will it lead us? At worst, to atomic warfare. At best to robbing every people and nation on earth of the fruits of their own toil." Eisenhower tried to diffuse the situation. In December 1953, he proposed an "Atoms for Peace" plan to the United Nations by which the United States, the Soviet Union, and the United Kingdom, would turn over some of their nuclear material to an international agency for peaceful use. However, little came of the plan. The distrust between the two superpowers was too great. Influential political leaders in the United States would not support a reduction in defense spending because they worried about the Soviets and because military spending—a total of more than $350 billion during Eisenhower's two terms—was key to defense industries and jobs in almost every congressional district in the country. So, the United States and the Soviets continued to build. The United States tested 203 nuclear weapons in the Pacific and at Nevada test sites, exposing some 200,000 civilians and soldiers to radiation and even more people to the radioactive fallout in more distant areas. The Soviets conducted at least as many tests if not more.

Along with his Secretary of State John Foster Dulles, Eisenhower tried to craft a foreign policy that kept the financial costs of the Cold War to a minimum, protected U.S. influences in key corners of the globe, and avoided war. This foreign policy comprised two key elements. The first was a policy of **massive retaliation**, announced by Dulles in January 1954. The United States was not prepared to take on the cost of keeping troops in every corner of the globe, especially after the war in Korea. Rather, the United States would try to protect the noncommunist world with programs like the Marshall Plan and the Berlin Airlift where possible, but also with the promise that if the Soviets tried to expand their sphere of influence, if they were to invade European or other countries allied with the West, then, said Dulles, the United States was prepared "to retaliate, instantly, by means and at a place of our choosing." Some called the policy "brinkmanship" since the United States was ready to go to the brink of destruction if the Soviets moved outside their sphere of influence, and the Soviets were being put on notice that the United States was prepared to use its H-bombs and use them quickly. The Soviets might have had a larger army and navy, but the United States had plenty of bombs, Polaris submarines, as well as Atlas and Minuteman rockets that could hit the Soviet Union any time and any place. From a force of 1,500 nuclear weapons, the U.S. stockpile increased to 6,000. Relying on those weapons, the country could reduce the size of the military and overall military expenditures, keep taxes relatively low, and avoid inflation yet still ensure U.S. power around the globe.

The second element in Eisenhower's foreign policy depended on secret activities organized by the **Central Intelligence Agency (CIA)**. During World War II, the United States developed the capacity to spy on and disrupt the Axis countries through the Office of Strategic Services. At the end of the war, President Truman disbanded that office. Two years later, he received congressional authorization to re-create it, now as the CIA, to spy and conduct covert operations in foreign countries that the United States feared might become communist.

In the summer of 1953, the CIA organized a coup against the elected Prime Minister of Iran, Muhammad Mussadegh, who had nationalized oil interests belonging to British companies and who some feared might have communist sympathies. With the covert help of the CIA, he was overthrown and replaced with the pro-Western Muhammad Reza Shah Pahlevi, who ruled the country for more than 20 years before being displaced by an anti-U.S. Islamic revolution in the late 1970s.

Then in June 1954, the CIA helped overthrow the democratically elected government of Jacobo Arbenz Guzman in Guatemala. Arbenz was promoting land reform by expropriating land owned by the U.S.-based United Fruit Company. Although the Arbenz administration had compensated United Fruit for the land, the company was angry, and the U.S. government feared a communist movement until CIA operatives, working with local insurgents, drove Arbenz from office. Neither action received much publicity in the United States, but the not-very-secret U.S. involvement built up significant anti-U.S. sentiment in the Middle East and Latin America. Later, in 1958, the CIA tried unsuccessfully to overthrow the government of Indonesia. In 1959, it played a role in installing a new pro-Western government in Laos. While Eisenhower knew of those actions, he may not have known about plans to assassinate the popular elected leader of the Congo, Patrice Lumumba (who was killed by dissidents before the CIA reached him), and the new leader of Cuba, Fidel Castro.

The Eisenhower administration also found itself caught up in other world crises that could not easily be handled by massive retaliation or CIA intervention. After World War II, France sought to reclaim control of its former colonies in Indochina, but many there wanted independence. In September 1945, with initial support from the United States, Ho Chi Minh proclaimed Vietnamese independence using words familiar to the Americans, "We hold these truths to be self-evident, that all men are created equal." But the French were determined to reclaim Vietnam. They installed Bao Dai, the former emperor of Annam, a part of Vietnam, as the leader in Vietnam. Ho Chi Minh's forces attacked the French. The United States, fearing a communist government under Ho and more worried about alienating France in Cold War Europe than events in Asia, sided with the French. By late 1953, the French were isolated in a fortified area, Dien Bien Phu, and facing defeat. Some, including Vice President Nixon, urged U.S. intervention, even the use of nuclear weapons. Eisenhower responded, "You boys must be crazy. We can't use those awful things against Asians for the second time in less than ten years. My God." There was no U.S. intervention at that time.

When the French were defeated in 1954, an international conference temporarily divided Vietnam into North Vietnam, to be led by Ho Chi Minh, and South Vietnam, to be led by Bao Dai and a pro-Western nationalist Ngo Dinh Diem. Elections to unify the country were scheduled for 1956. When Diem refused to participate in the 1956 elections, knowing that Ho, a national hero would win, the United States did not intervene. The United States relied on the South East Asian Treaty Organization (SEATO), a much weaker version of NATO that it had helped to create in 1955, to keep Communists out of Southeast Asia, but the organization had little effect.

The next crisis also occurred in Asia. Chiang Kai-shek's Nationalist government had been defeated on the Chinese mainland in 1949 and was ensconced on heavily fortified offshore islands, the largest of which was Taiwan, then known as Formosa. In 1954, the Communist government of China began shelling two tiny Nationalist-held

Central Intelligence Agency (CIA) Established by President Truman and expanded by President Eisenhower, the CIA was the nation's spy agency charged with keeping tabs on developments in other countries and with engaging in secret missions to advance American interests.

MAP 25-1 A World Divided. As the Cold War continued in the 1950s, the world was divided into two major spheres of influence: the West led by the United States, which included the members of NATO and other allies, and the East (see page 719) led by the Soviet Union, which included the members of the Warsaw Pact and other allied nations. Both competed for influence in the remaining neutral nations, especially in Africa.

islands, Quemoy and Matsu, just off the Chinese coast. Eisenhower wanted to protect Chiang's government, but Quemoy and Matsu were small islands that were much closer to mainland China than to Taiwan. Having seen the war in Korea, Eisenhower was determined not to fight Communist China over Quemoy and Matsu. Eventually, both sides tired of the conflict and the islands remained under Nationalist rule. Nevertheless, the incident pointed to larger possible threats.

Challenges to Maintaining Peace

In July 1955, Eisenhower met in Geneva with the new Soviet leader, Nikita Khrushchev, and leaders of Britain and France. The summit meeting, whose purpose was to reduce international tensions, produced a treaty recognizing the independence of Austria, which had been jointly occupied by the four powers after World War II, much like Germany had been. Although, the summit did not accomplish all that Eisenhower wished, many were optimistic about a new spirit of coexistence.

In February 1956, Khrushchev surprised the world with a speech—originally a "secret speech" to Soviet leaders only, but word spread quickly—in which he said that Stalin had been a tyrant who had inflicted purges, show trials, forced labor, terror, and mass executions on his people. Khrushchev declared it was time to begin the de-Stalinization of the Soviet Union. The speech was a relief to those who saw the beginning of a new era in Russia, though devastating to die-hard Communists.

Despite these advances, conflicts and differences continued to produce tensions, to which U.S. leaders were challenged to respond. In October, hostilities flared up in the Middle East. Gamal Abdel Nasser, the Arab nationalist ruler of Egypt, sought funding from both the United States and the Soviet Union to build the Aswan High Dam on the upper Nile River to irrigate new areas of Egypt, provide electricity, and promote industrialization. His flirtation with both sides angered both countries, and in 1956, Dulles cancelled the U.S. loan. Nasser responded by taking control of the Suez Canal, the essential waterway between the Mediterranean and the Red Sea that was owned by a British and French canal company and crucial to the flow of oil to Europe. Nasser said he wanted the revenue from the canal to build his dam, but his actions angered and frightened the British and French.

On October 29, with British and French backing, Israel attacked Egypt. Eisenhower was outraged. He sponsored a UN resolution demanding an Israeli withdrawal. It was an ironic moment with the United States and the Soviet Union united in opposition to Britain, France, and Israel. When the British and French ignored the UN and bombed Egypt, Nasser sank ships and blocked the canal. The United States condemned the British action and threatened to send troops to Egypt. The British never expected the United States to take a hard line. British Prime Minister Anthony Eden and Ike were wartime friends, but the president was furious. A cease fire was arranged, and the canal was reopened under Egyptian management. The Soviet Union and the United States looked good to Arab countries. Israel remained strong. Only Britain and France suffered. Eden resigned as Prime Minister, and neither Britain nor France was again a major influence in the Middle East.

In October 1956, in the midst of the Suez crisis, discontent with Soviet rule boiled over in Hungary. Khrushchev's denunciation of Stalin had raised hopes for a more liberal policy in Eastern Europe. The Soviet government granted some concessions to the Hungarians, but when they pressed for more independence, Khrushchev sent 200,000 troops and 4,000 tanks to Budapest to end the uprising. Some 40,000 Hungarians were killed and another 150,000 fled the country seeking asylum in the west. Some called for American intervention; after all, Eisenhower had talked about the liberation of "captive peoples," but the old general understood the military reality that Hungary was surrounded by other Communist nations. Most Americans seemed satisfied to label the uprising as more proof of Soviet tyranny and leave it at that.

While the Suez crisis and the Hungarian uprising were taking place, the United States was in the midst of a presidential election. The Democrats again nominated Adlai Stevenson. Although Eisenhower had a serious heart attack in 1955 and was hospitalized for 6 weeks, he had recovered fully. The Republicans again nominated their highly popular president and his not-very-popular running mate. The Democrats ran anti-Nixon television ads that they thought might be more effective than any attack on Eisenhower. Eisenhower was well liked, the country was at peace, and prosperity was evident. Eisenhower won 57 percent of the popular votes, but the outcome rested on Eisenhower's personal popularity; the Democrats carried both houses of Congress.

Neither the country nor the president expected any major change of course in the next 4 years. However, new developments on the international front presented not only new crises but also an opportunity unimagined when Ike's second term began.

A Small Satellite and a Big Impact

Sputnik
The world's first space satellite, launched by the Soviet Union in 1957.

On October 4, 1957, the Soviet Union launched *Sputnik*, a space satellite. Although *Sputnik* was small, about the size of a large beach ball, and weighed only 184 pounds, it was the first orbiting satellite ever launched into space. A month later, a much larger *Sputnik II* was launched, which carried a dog, Laika, as well as scientific and medical instruments. While the Soviet Union celebrated, Americans panicked. The Soviets were clearly winning the "space race," critics said. Democratic Senator Henry Jackson of Washington State talked of the "shame and danger" of the moment. G. Mennen

Williams, Michigan's Democratic governor, wrote of Sputnik, "It's a Commie sky. And Uncle Sam's asleep."

Because of U.S. spy flights over the Soviet Union, Eisenhower knew that although the Soviets might launch a satellite, the United States was far ahead in missile development. However, he could not say so without admitting to the spying, which he did not want to do. It was a difficult moment for an administration that worried as much about national security as they did about a race to space. Nevertheless, two important results came from *Sputnik* and the fears that the satellite induced—a new government space agency and improved education.

In 1958, the administration proposed the creation of the **National Aeronautics and Space Administration (NASA)** and before long, NASA scientists and engineers had launched the first U.S. satellite and soon closed the gap with the Soviet Union. Later NASA-led efforts resulted in human flight in space, a moon landing, a string of satellites that could be used for telecommunications (and spying), and a space shuttle that could bring cargo to replacement crews to orbiting space stations. For all of the fears of 1957 and 1958, the United States had far greater resources than the Soviets to devote to these efforts once the determination was made to do so.

The fears that resulted from the Soviet launch of *Sputnik* also had a major impact on American education. Many saw the Soviet advances in space as the result of superior Soviet education. Eisenhower proposed the **National Defense Education Act (NDEA)**, which was passed by Congress in September 1958. After many failed efforts to get federal aid for the nation's schools, funding was approved because of *Sputnik*. The NDEA provided funds to improve science education, provided scholarships, and created an education division within the National Science Foundation.

Although national worries had led to NDEA and the new curriculum materials that resulted, the 1950s had already been a time of considerable advances in education. In 1940, less than half (49%) of the nation's 17-year-olds graduated from high school. By 1950, 57.4 percent of 17-year-olds completed high school; in 1960, 63.4 percent; and in 1970, 75.6 percent graduated. Before 1950, more girls than boys had finished high school but more males than females went to college. For a time after that, graduation and college attendance ratios began to even out, though imbalance would return later. Although white graduation rates remained far ahead of those for African-American and Latino students, many more students of color attended and graduated from high school in the 1950s than ever before. Given the perceived national need, federal programs began to encourage more females to study in the sciences. At the college level, the GI Bill had generated a rapid increase in college attendance for military veterans, overwhelmingly white men, but as the decade went on, more students of all races and genders attended college. College faculty in the sciences benefitted from grants for military research, though some worried about the impact of these grants. Even before *Sputnik* was launched, a *Time* magazine article asked, "Is the military about to take over U.S. science lock, stock, and barrel, calling the tune for U.S. universities and signing up the best scientists for work fundamentally aimed at military results?"

In spite of "mutually assured destruction" and the space race with the Soviets, Eisenhower, who had seen more of war than most Americans, desperately wanted to find a path to peace, not only to avoid the economic costs of war but also to create a lasting peace. Although the July 1955 summit conference at Geneva had been disappointing, the **"Spirit of Geneva,"** and the commitment to coexistence was something on which Eisenhower wanted to build, especially in his last years in office. On October 31, 1958,

National Aeronautics and Space Administration (NASA)
A new government agency created in 1958 in response to Sputnik and specifically charged with fostering American space efforts; eventually led to the first manned moon landing and the space shuttle.

National Defense Education Act (NDEA)
Federal aid to improve education, especially science and math education, approved by Congress in 1958.

Spirit of Geneva
A perspective fostered by Eisenhower and Khrushchev that the Cold War might, at the least, be limited by their personal engagement with each other.

Sputnik I, the first space satellite.

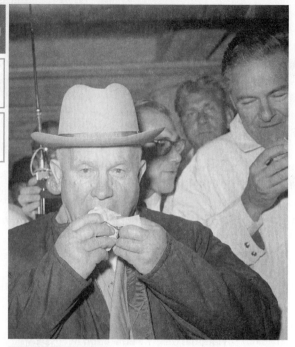

During the goodwill that emerged between the United States and the Soviet Union in 1958 and 1959, Soviet Premier Nikita Khrushchev visited the United States and was a hit on tours such as this one of an Iowa farm.

the United States announced that it was suspending nuclear testing in the atmosphere. The Soviets also suspended their testing. By 1958, atmospheric nuclear testing was found to be a health risk to millions around the world as well as an unnecessary military provocation, and the cessation was important.

When a new crisis arose over Berlin in early 1959, Eisenhower and Khrushchev managed to avoid escalation. Each of the two leaders agreed to invite the other to visit his respective country in the next year. Khrushchev's tour of the United States in September 1959 was a major success in spite of Khrushchev's ill-timed boast that "We will bury you." The two leaders agreed to another summit in Paris in May 1960. Progress seemed to be in the air.

On May 1, 1960, the progress stopped. A U-2 reconnaissance plane—the type that had been providing the kind of information about Soviet military capability that Eisenhower had kept secret—was shot down by a Soviet rocket as it flew 1,300 miles inside Russia. Khrushchev announced that the Soviets not only had the wreckage of the U-2—and it was no weather plane—but also had captured the pilot, Francis Gary Powers, alive and had found both the poison needle with which he was supposed to kill himself rather than risk capture and a pistol with a silencer that he had been supplied. "Why the silencer?" Khrushchev asked, and then answered, "To blow men's brains out! The men who supplied him with the silence gun pray in church and call us godless atheists!"

The U-2 incident dominated the Paris summit. Khrushchev insisted that Eisenhower condemn the U-2 flights and punish those responsible, which Eisenhower could not do, though he did agree to suspend the flights. Khrushchev withdrew the invitation for Eisenhower to visit the Soviet Union. There would be little talk of friendly coexistence in the next 2 years.

From Oldest to Youngest—The Transition to the Next President

While the administration dealt with the U-2 incident, the United States was in the midst of the 1960 presidential election. Eisenhower's popularity was high, and if the Constitution had allowed it and he had wanted it, he could easily have won a third term. But the Constitution had been changed and Eisenhower at 70, the oldest serving president, had no interest in a third term.

The Republican Party nominated Vice President Richard Nixon as their presidential candidate. The Democratic race was contested between several candidates, including Senators Lyndon B. Johnson of Texas, Hubert Humphrey of Minnesota, Stuart Symington of Missouri, and John F. Kennedy of Massachusetts. Many remembered the defeat of Al Smith in 1928—the last time a major party had nominated a Catholic—and wondered if Kennedy, a Catholic, could be successful. Liberals also worried about Kennedy. Eleanor Roosevelt remembered how slow he had been to attack McCarthy and how little he had done for civil rights. She preferred Adlai Stevenson. But Kennedy had several important strengths. He had extraordinary personal charisma, charming most everyone he met. He also had virtually unlimited campaign funds because of the wealth of his father, Joseph P. Kennedy, and could far outspend his opponents. Under the leadership of his brother Robert Kennedy, he had a superb campaign team. He won the Democratic nomination on the first ballot, asked Lyndon Johnson to be his running mate, and entered the general election as a strong candidate.

Nixon, having been vice president for two terms, was the better known. For the first time in American politics, the two candidates held a series of television debates.

Those who listened to the debates on radio thought Nixon had won due to the clarity of his argument. For the much larger television audience, however, Nixon seemed tired and haggard while Kennedy who arrived from California well rested and with a tan seemed at the height of new youthful vigor. In response to Kennedy's charisma, *Newsweek* reported that there were "jumpers" who leapt to see him, "runners" who chased his car, and others who simply screamed themselves hoarse. People applauded politely for Nixon.

Although Eisenhower despised the Kennedys, whom he saw as rich, ambitious, and unprincipled, his lack of enthusiasm for his vice president was hard to hide. When a reporter asked Ike to name a major Nixon contribution to the administration, he replied, "If you give me a week, I might think of one." Although he immediately recanted, the damage was done.

During the competitive campaign, Kennedy accused Eisenhower of allowing a "missile gap" to develop between the United States and the Soviet Union and promised that, if elected, the United States would expand its defenses and its missions in space. He also addressed his Catholicism in a well-received speech to Protestant clergy in Houston, Texas. Late in the campaign, when Martin Luther King, Jr., was arrested in Georgia, Nixon tried to intervene quietly, but Kennedy made a very public call to King's wife, Coretta, and Bobby Kennedy made a successful request for King's release. Many blacks, key voters in some states, decided to vote Democratic that fall. On election day, with the highest turnout since World War II, Kennedy won by one of the smallest margins in history—49.7 percent to Nixon's 49.6 percent though he won in the Electoral College 303 to 219.

On inauguration day, January 20, 1961, the youngest person ever elected president replaced the oldest serving president. The general who had commanded all allied troops in Europe in World War II was replaced by a man who had commanded a small P.T. (Patrol Torpedo) boat in the Pacific and who became a hero when his PT-109 was sunk. The new president made much of the leadership change, telling the nation, "Let the word go forth from this time and place, to friend and foe alike, that the torch has been passed to a new generation of Americans."

In the first ever televised presidential debate, John Kennedy managed to project charm and confidence to the viewers.

 Quick Review How did Eisenhower continue fighting the Cold War? How were his Cold War and domestic policies similar to or different from Truman's?

A CULTURE ON THE MOVE

25.2 Explain the impact of cultural and technological changes on the country.

During and after the 1950s, many looked on that era as one of complacency at home and trouble abroad. By 1960, however, the United States was a very different place at home from what it had been in 1950. During the 1950s, the nation became much more prosperous. In 1960, the average family income of $5,620 was 30 percent higher than it had been in 1950, and 62 percent of homes were owner occupied—up from 55 percent in 1950 and 44 percent in 1940. After the end of the Korean War in 1953, the decade was one of relative peace for the United States despite conflicts elsewhere. But the decade of the 1950s was also, as the writer Morris Dickstein noted, "a fertile period, a seedbed of ideas that would burgeon and live in the more activist, less reflective climate that followed."

The Growing Impact of Television

In 1948, Wayne Coy, a member of the Federal Communications Commission that regulated television and radio, said, "Make no mistake about it, television is here to stay. It is a new force unloosed in the land. I believe it is an irresistible force." From 104 commercial stations broadcasting to 5 million homes in 1950, television expanded to almost 600 stations received in 45,750,000 homes in 1960—almost 80 percent of all of U.S. homes.

Some of the early television programs were impressive. *Playhouse 90*, the *Goodyear Television Playhouse*, and the *Kraft Television Theater* brought serious drama to the television screen. Talented young actors, including Grace Kelly, Paul Newman, Joanne Woodward, and Eva Marie Saint, were seen by wider audiences than ever before. The *ABC Concert* carried weekly concerts by the Chicago Symphony Orchestra around the country.

Television news, though generally limited to a 15-minute program, included the *Camel News Caravan* with John Cameron Swayze and the CBS *Television News with Douglas Edwards* and brought current events into living rooms. Beginning with Truman's 1949 inauguration and Eisenhower's 1952 campaign commercials, television changed politics; people felt a new intimacy with candidates and leaders. Edward R. Murrow's *See It Now* programs brought investigative journalism to television, including coverage of Senator McCarthy's hearings.

Lighter entertainment was very successful, too. Radio had been available to many since the 1930s, and some programs, like Jack Benny's comedy routines, shifted from radio to television with little change. The long-running *I Love Lucy* show with Lucille Ball and Desi Arnaz was the most popular show on television. Other comedies, especially *The Adventures of Ozzie and Harriet*, *Father Knows Best*, and *Leave It to Beaver*, used humor to reaffirm the white, middle class, suburban lifestyle in which the wise, sometimes befuddled father supported the family while the passive (if sometimes conniving) mother stayed home to happily manage the house.

A middle-class, white family sitting at home and watching *The Lone Ranger* on television epitomized the 1950s for some.

American Voices

Newton N. Minow, Television and the Public Interest, 1961

As he began his presidency, John F. Kennedy appointed attorney and long-time Democratic Party activist Newton N. Minow to chair the Federal Communications Commission (FCC). Although Minow had little background in the media, he and Attorney General Robert F. Kennedy had strong opinions about television. In May 1961, only a few months into his tenure at the FCC, Minow gave this controversial speech to the National Association of Broadcasters, declaring that television was "a vast wasteland." While many in the television industry strongly disagreed, many critics thought Minow was on target.

Your industry possesses the most powerful voice in America. It has an inescapable duty to make that voice ring with intelligence and with leadership. In a few years, this exciting industry has grown from a novelty to an instrument of overwhelming impact on the American people. It should be making ready for the kind of leadership that newspapers and magazines assumed years ago, to make our people aware of their world....

When television is good, nothing—not the theater, not the magazines or newspapers—nothing is better.

But when television is bad, nothing is worse. I invite each of you to sit down in front of your television set when your station goes on the air and stay there, for a day, without a book, without a magazine, without a newspaper, without a profit and loss sheet or a rating book to distract you. Keep your eyes glued to that set until the station signs off. I can assure you that what you will observe is a vast wasteland.

You will see a procession of game shows, formula comedies about totally unbelievable families, blood and thunder, mayhem, violence, sadism, murder, western bad men, western good men, private eyes, gangsters, more violence, and cartoons. And endlessly, commercials—many screaming, cajoling, and offending. And most of all, boredom.

Source: Delivered May 9, 1961, National Association of Broadcasters, Washington, DC; downloaded from www.american rhetoric.com/speeches/newtonminow.htm, May 11, 2011.

Thinking Critically

1. **Documentary Analysis**
   In Minow's view, what was the most important negative impact of poor television programming?

2. **Historical Interpretation**
   What light does Minow's speech shed on the nature of the growing discontent with mainstream 1950s culture?

On *The Ed Sullivan Show*, the poker-faced Ed Sullivan introduced Elvis Presley (who Sullivan insisted be shown only from the waist up) and, later, The Beatles to American audiences. Daytime soap operas (their original sponsors were soap companies) moved from radio to television, and *Guiding Light*, *Love of Life*, and *Search for Tomorrow* provided a dash of scandal to daytime viewers. Families gathered to eat TV dinners (first marketed in 1954) on TV trays, rather than around a dining room table, to watch *Gunsmoke*, featuring a stronger and more silent Marshal Dillon than had been possible on radio, plus *Maverick*, and *Have Gun—Will Travel*, as well as detective stories, including *Dragnet*, *77 Sunset Strip*, and *Perry Mason*. Children's cartoons took over Saturday mornings. Reruns of old movies were shown in the late evening.

While some of the first programs had a single sponsor—such as the *Goodyear Television Playhouse*, the *Kraft Television Theater*, and the *Camel News Caravan*, broadcasters quickly discovered that they could make higher profits with multiple advertisers, and 30-second commercials urged Americans (always seen as white and middle class) to "see the USA in your Chevrolet," or "move up to Chrysler," and handle their indigestion with "Speedy" Alka Seltzer.

Television was rocked by not only a series of scandals in the late 1950s but also significant criticism. The most popular quiz show, *The $64,000 Question*, turned out to be rigged. Charles Van Doren, a major winner on the show, had been given answers in advance. As commercial stations focused on advertising revenue, they became increasingly cautious. One advertiser reminded the station owners, "A program that displeases any substantial segment of the population is a misuse of the advertising dollar." Since showing Americans in all of their diversity could displease some, television became bland. Even President Eisenhower said, "If a citizen has to be bored to death, it is cheaper and more comfortable to sit at home and look at television than it is to go outside and pay a dollar for a ticket." It was hardly a ringing endorsement of the new medium. The Kennedy administration would not be any more positive in its appraisal.

The Impact of the Automobile

Automobiles had been invented before 1900, mass-produced in the 1910s, and had a significant impact by the 1920s (see Chapter 21). Nevertheless, the automobile, like the TV, came to dominate American culture in the 1950s as never before.

Once wartime shortages ended, the sales of private automobiles grew rapidly. By 1960, 80 percent of American families owned an automobile (the same percentage as owned televisions). The total number of cars registered at the end of the decade was 74 million, almost double the 39 million registered in 1950. In addition, the cars were becoming larger, faster, more powerful, and much flashier. In an era of cheap gasoline, the symbolism of power, sexiness, and speed was far more important than fuel efficiency.

Automobiles needed support services and infrastructure, most of all, highways. By the early 1950s, the American Road Builders Association was able to successfully lobby for the creation of the Highway Trust Fund in which all revenue generated from automobiles, especially the tax on gasoline, could be used only to build highways with the result that, in the United States, funding for road building was ample, though funds for mass transit were more scarce. European countries used similar funds not only for roads but also for mass-transit, schools, and hospitals.

President Eisenhower, who remembered a miserable cross-country journey he had made as a young army officer on the nation's ill-maintained highways of the 1920s, adopted a plan that had been put together during the Truman administration and proposed the Interstate Highway Act, which became law in 1956. The act created the **Interstate Highway System**, a numbered network of 41,000 miles of roads from Interstate 5 in California, Oregon, and Washington to Interstate 95 that ran from Florida to Maine, connected to east-west interstates 70, 80, and 90 as well as feeder highways for which the federal government paid 90 percent of the cost (see Map 25-2). These highways made travel by car, truck, or bus much easier and cheaper than ever before. At the same time, urban, suburban, and rural sprawl was exacerbated. Suburban houses sprang up and tight-knit urban communities went into decline. Shopping malls replaced Main Street. Mass transit declined. In Los Angeles, what had once been the largest electric interurban railway in the world with 1,100 miles of track, was replaced with a system of highways using buses produced by General Motors with tires from Firestone Rubber.

New industries sprang up to service the automobile and the highway. Fast-food restaurants allowed busy drivers to pick up a meal and keep moving. Medical, legal, and insurance services for the victims of traffic accidents grew. Motels became a new place to stay, replacing grand downtown hotels that had catered to those who traveled by train or ship. Kemmons Wilson and Wallace E. Johnson opened the first "Holiday Inn" in Memphis, Tennessee, in 1952, and by 1960, there were 60,000 motels, many belonging to chains like Holiday Inn or Howard Johnson, catering to people who valued cleanliness, comfort, and the convenience of being able to drive directly to the door of a room.

Between 1920 and 1950, gasoline service stations offering fuel and automobile services, some in a grand style, became the most widely built new commercial structure in the United States. With their signs advertising Mobil, Shell, and Esso (later Exxon), they made it possible to keep cars fueled and on the move. The gasoline these stations pumped also had an impact on U.S. foreign policy as American political leaders understood the nation's love affair with the automobile and the need to maintain a steady supply of cheap gasoline, much of it from the Middle East and Latin American, if they were to stay in office.

Interstate Highway System
A national system of super highways that Congress approved at the urging of President Eisenhower in 1956 to improve car and truck travel across the United States.

MAP 25-2 The Interstate Highway System. The current Interstate Highway System is surprisingly close to the original plan approved by the federal government in 1956 for a system of super highways linking all parts of the 48 states.

Critics worried about the impact of the automobile on American culture. In *The City in History*, Lewis Mumford complained that the automobile "annihilates the city whenever it collides with it." For Mumford, it was the city, not suburban sprawl, that created community. Raymond Tucker, mayor of St. Louis also noted, "The plain fact of the matter is that we just cannot build enough lanes of highways to move all of our people by private automobile and create enough parking space to store the cars without completely paving over our cities." Nevertheless, in the 1950s, more Americans agreed with New York's master highway builder Robert Moses, who designed a series of bridges in and around New York as well as the Brooklyn Queens Expressway, the Cross Bronx Expressway, and the Long Island Expressway, and who kept advocating for more roads even as some protested.

The Boom of Religion

In the 1950s, Americans drove to church and watched religious programs on television in numbers never seen before. The religious boom of the 1950s was both a cultural and a spiritual phenomenon.

For most of the nation's history, a little over one-third of the people were involved in religious activities. However, in the 1950s, that number grew to over two-thirds, and on some Sunday mornings, more than half of all of the people in the country were in church. After World War II, Americans became active in religious organizations in numbers never seen before, and their participation kept rising for the next 15 years. Visitors from other countries were stunned by the American embrace of religion. In no other country was there a similar upsurge, certainly not in war-weary Europe. Americans identified with religious communities, built new churches at an astounding rate, especially in the new suburbs, and enjoyed songs like "I Believe," "It's No Secret What God Can Do," and "Vaya con Dios," as popular secular music. Historians continue to ask what accounted for this upsurge in religious activity. The roots of something as elusive as religious faith and as hard to discover as social conformity may be impossible to find, but the signs of the times that pointed to a more religious culture were numerous.

No one represented the religious movements of the 1950s more dramatically than Billy Graham. Graham was born on a farm near Charlotte, North Carolina, in 1918. In 1949, he led a revival in Los Angeles that brought him national attention and remained the nation's best known religious leader for the next 50 years. The Billy Graham Evangelistic Association had an annual budget of $2 million and a staff of 200 in the 1950s. It produced books, television programs, radio, and its own films. Most of all, the association organized massive religious revivals that were held in football stadiums and civic auditoriums around the country. To the frustration of some conservative supporters, Graham would not plan a religious crusade, as he called a revival, without the support of the local council of churches, which included liberal as well as conservative clergy. Graham also refused to hold racially segregated revivals, even in the Deep South.

Graham was immensely successful in bringing out thousands of people night after night. At the end of each event, individuals were invited to come forward and make a personal confession of faith to counselors who were waiting for them, as the audience sang, "Just as I Am Without One Plea." Although he was a Baptist, Graham did not worry about religious denominations and urged the converted to attend any church that appealed to them. Graham's success was such that he also became a religious advisor to several U.S. presidents.

While Graham was by far the best known and most successful revivalist of the 1950s, many others, black and white and increasingly Latino evangelists, conducted their own religious revivals in churches, tents, and fields across the United States. Oral Roberts, a Pentecostal Holiness revivalist and faith healer, built up his own media empire that rivaled Graham's. Less emotional versions of religion, including the sermons of the Presbyterian minister Peter Marshall, published in 1949 as *Mr. Jones Meet the Master* also attracted a wide audience.

A Protestant minister within the Reformed Church in America, Norman Vincent Peale, took the quest for peace of mind to a wide audience through his books, *Guide to Confident Living* published in 1948 and *The Power of Positive Thinking* published in 1952, which broke all previous records for the sales of a religious book. Peale's message was "believe in yourself" and develop "a humble but reasonable confidence." Religious groups known as the "mainstream" of American Protestantism—Methodists, Baptists, Presbyterians, Congregationalists, and Episcopalians—flourished in the 1950s with large memberships and with influence rivaling any point in their history. Reinhold Niebuhr's book, *Moral Man and Immoral Society*, challenged religious people to find ways to make ethical decisions in a complex world. Both Reinhold Niebuhr and the German-born theologian Paul Tillich appeared on the cover of *Time* magazine.

In the 1950s, American Catholics were still a minority but were more numerous than any single Protestant denomination. As white Catholics moved to new suburban communities, Catholic bishops created new parishes where none had been. Some Catholic prelates such as New York's Francis Cardinal Spellman continued to keep their distance from Protestants, but others such as Boston's Richard Cardinal Cushing found ways to reach out to non-Catholics while building Catholic churches and parochial schools at a furious rate. The walls of distrust were still high in the 1950s: parish priests warned young people not to date a Protestant, and many Protestants still saw Catholicism as inherently foreign and undemocratic. Nevertheless, many of those who sat in the pews of Catholic and Protestant churches were ready to ignore the old divides.

Monsignor Fulton J. Sheen became a popular preacher not only at Catholic religious gatherings (never called revivals) but also on television. He brought Catholic teachings into the mainstream of American culture, and his book *Peace of Soul*, published in 1949, anticipated some of the positive-thinking themes in Peale's work. Sheen restated traditional Catholic beliefs in ways that appealed to a wide audience, Catholic and non-Catholic.

While 66 percent of Americans identified themselves as Protestant and 26 percent as Catholic, only 3 percent were Jews, but Jews also participated in the religious upsurge of the 1950s. Before World War II, secularism and assimilation seemed to go hand in hand among many Jewish immigrants. Although a growing awareness of the Holocaust brought despair and cynicism to some, it brought a renewed interest in their faith to others. A new generation of leaders like Rabbi Abraham Joshua Heschel spoke of the need to link modern thinking with traditional Jewish practices and inner piety. Many American Jews wanted to rediscover their faith. The children of parents who had argued over politics now argued over theology. Attendance at synagogues reached peaks never seen before. The Orthodox, Reform, and Conservative branches of Judaism all grew.

African-American communities also had their own revivals of religion, usually quite separately from white communities. The National Baptist Convention, the African Methodist Episcopal, and the African Methodist Episcopal Zion churches, the nation's three largest African-American religious bodies, all grew during the 1950s. Black Pentecostalism flourished in northern cities as it long had in the rural South. The Church of God in Christ, founded in the 1890s, saw its largest growth in the 1950s and by 1965 had 420,000 members in 4,150 churches. The United House of Prayer for All People, led by "Sweet Daddy" Grace, promised grace in return for strict obedience to the church's teaching. In addition, Elijah Muhammad built up the **Nation of Islam** from the small Detroit Temple Number One, founded in 1931, to perhaps a community of 100,000 members.

Nation of Islam
A religious and political organization founded by Elijah Muhammad that mixed Muslim religious teachings with a campaign for African-American separatism, pride, and self-determination.

A much smaller number of Americans also looked beyond the bounds of the traditional western faiths. The inspiration of Mohandas Gandhi in India led some to look at Hinduism. From the teachings of the Vedanta Society or the California-based Self-Realization Fellowship, some people turned to yoga or transcendental meditation. Others were attracted to the Bahá'í movement, an offshoot of Shiite Islam in Iran that sought to synthesize the teachings of all world religions. Buddhism remained small in the United States in the 1950s, mostly limited to communities of Asian immigrants, though in the 1960s that status would change quickly.

As Americans became more actively engaged in their religious communities, political leaders sought to catch up. In the midst of the Cold War, they saw American religious sentiment as an important counter to atheistic communism. In 1954, Congress voted to add the phrase "one nation under God" to the Pledge of Allegiance to the Flag. A year later, Congress added the words "In God We Trust" to American paper currency. While some believers and nonbelievers found this public religiosity offensive, most Americans embraced the sort of civic religion embedded in the new pledge and coins with enthusiasm. President Eisenhower said, "Our government makes no sense unless it is founded on a deeply felt religious faith—and I don't care what it is."

Dissent

Although the 1950s have been described as a time of conformity, not everyone conformed. Born in Brooklyn, New York, in 1897, Dorothy Day joined the Socialist Party and later the IWW as a young woman, opposed U.S. entry into World War I, and was arrested for picketing the White House as she demanded the vote for women. In the 1920s, she lived a bohemian life with poets and communists in New York's Greenwich Village. Then in 1927, she experienced a dramatic conversion to Catholicism, left the man with whom she was living, and was baptized along with her new baby. In the 1930s, along with the

Catholic mystic Peter Maurin, founded the Civil Catholic Worker Movement and its related newspaper, *The Catholic Worker*, which Day edited until her death in 1980. Day embraced voluntary poverty, set up the St. Joseph's House of Hospitality in New York to provide food and clothing to those in need, and protested the buildup of nuclear arms and the wars in Korea and later Vietnam. The Catholic Worker Movement sometimes made church officials uncomfortable because it represented a voice of dissent within the Catholic Church and the larger American culture in the 1950s.

A Protestant from the rural South, Myles Horton had much in common with Dorothy Day. Horton studied with Reinhold Niebuhr and later Jane Addams, joined the Socialist Party, picketed for the International Ladies' Garment Workers' Union, and participated in endless seminars and late night discussions. In 1931, he moved back to Tennessee where he opened the Highlander Folk School "to work with people from the bottom, who could change society from the bottom." In the 1930s and 1940s, Highlander trained grass-roots leadership for the labor movement, and in the 1950s and 1960s, for the Civil Rights Movement.

These groundbreaking dissidents, however, seemed tame to many compared with the influence of rock 'n' roll, and no rock 'n' roll figure got more attention, or worried more people in the 1950s, than Elvis Presley. Presley grew up poor in Mississippi and Tennessee, learning to sing and play a guitar in his Assembly of God congregation. Music producer Sam Phillips knew that although many young white Americans loved black music, even the best of black entertainers could not break through the culture's rigid color barrier. "If I could find a white man with a Negro sound," Phillips said, "I could make a billion dollars." With Elvis, he came close.

With Phillips handling the marketing, Elvis Presley became a star. The music in "Hound Dog" and "Heartbreak Hotel" represented a new amalgam of rhythm and blues, jazz, and pop as well as the earlier rock 'n' roll of groups like Bill Haley and the Comets whose "Rock Around the Clock" sold 16 million records.

Elvis sold more than his music. His alienated look and his gyrating sexuality connected with young audiences who loved what he represented. Critics were appalled.

Elvis Presley's music and performance style captivated fans and frightened more cautious observers but transformed rock and roll music in American culture.

One said that his performances were "strip-teases with clothes on…not only suggestive but downright obscene." Exactly that sultry suggestiveness is just what made him so popular to a generation tired of conformity. When Elvis appeared on the *Ed Sullivan Show*, 54 million people watched, the largest television audience in history.

Elvis was the top musical star leading many other musicians such as black rock 'n' roll artists Chuck Berry, Chubby Checker, and Fats Domino as well as traditional pop music and jazz greats, but it was the new rock 'n' roll that defined the era. Leonard Bernstein, one of the great composers of the century, once described Elvis Presley as "the greatest cultural force in the 20th century."

Even in science, more overt attention to human sexuality challenged traditional norms in the 1950s. Alfred Kinsey, the Indiana University researcher whose book, *Sexual Behavior in the Human Male,* had produced an outcry in 1948, published *Sexual Behavior in the Human Female* in 1953, which though long and full of dry scientific data, sold 250,000 copies. While Kinsey insisted that he was simply reporting, not making value judgments, findings like the fact that 37 percent of all men and 13 percent of women had at least one homosexual experience or the fact that 50 percent of married men and 26 percent of married women had committed adultery, shocked Americans and simultaneously created an "everybody's doing it" mentality.

Hugh Hefner played into that mentality when he first published *Playboy* magazine in December 1953, which represented pure hedonistic pleasure…for men. *Playboy* linked sexuality with upward mobility and defined the good life as enjoying sex, liquor, smoking, and consumer products, without restraint. When Hefner published the first issue, with Marilyn Monroe as the centerfold, he was deeply in debt but sold enough copies that he could issue another, and by 1960, *Playboy* sold over a million copies a month.

Novelists joined in the celebration of sexuality. Grace Metalious, who had never written a book before, published *Peyton Place* in 1956, a novel that detailed scandalous affairs in a suburban context. Vladimir Nabokov, a respected writer, published *Lolita*, about the life of a young sex-addicted woman and a sex-obsessed middle-aged man. In 1958, Grove Press published an unexpurgated edition of D. H. Lawrence's *Lady Chatterley's Lover*, unavailable previously in the United States. Whatever else Americans were doing in the privacy of their homes, larger numbers of them were clearly reading much more sexually explicit material in the 1950s than in any previous generation.

Within this context of breaking from traditional cultural norms, other artists explored their own alienation in a conformist society. In J.D. Salinger's novel, *The Catcher in the Rye*, the book's teenage hero, Holden Caulfield saw adults as "phonies" who kept up pretenses that did not fit reality. Novelists like Ralph Ellison, Flannery O'Connor, Saul Bellow, Bernard Malamud, James Baldwin, John Updike, Mary McCarthy, and Philip Roth explored America's racism and the quiet desperation of many. In the late 1950s, poets and political radicals like Allen Ginsberg and Jack Kerouac took dissent to new levels. The "beat generation" challenged not only cultural pretentions of Eisenhower's America, but the artistic pretentions of its major critics. In "Howl," Ginsberg's 1956 poem, he wrote, "I saw the best minds of my generation destroyed by madness." It was Ginsberg's good luck that police in San Francisco seized *Howl and Other Poems* as obscene and forced a trial that brought Ginsberg to national attention. Kerouac's *On the Road*, published in 1957, glorified escape from expectations and conventions. Some in the 1950s found themselves embracing Kerouac's belief that, "The only people for me are the mad ones, the ones who are mad to live, mad to talk, mad to be saved, desirous of everything at the same time, the ones who never yawn or say a commonplace thing, but burn, burn, burn like fabulous yellow roman candles exploding like spiders across the stars."

25.2 | **Quick Review** How did the media play a strong role in both the conformity and rebellion of the 1950s? What other forces supported conformity or rebellion?

RACE AND CIVIL RIGHTS

25.3 Analyze the growth and impact of the Civil Rights Movement between 1954 and 1965.

Segregation, economic marginalization, and political disenfranchisement were reality for most African-Americans in the 1950s as they had been since the collapse of Reconstruction in the 1870s and 1880s (see Chapter 15 and Chapter 19). However, the African-American community never accepted segregation or second-class citizenship, and in the 1950s, it seemed as if African-American resistance to "separate but equal" burst forth in many different places at about the same time (see Map 25-3). Legal challenges to school segregation that had been building for decades achieved a major victory in 1954. Soon thereafter, long-simmering opposition to segregation in public transportation led to a year-long bus boycott in Montgomery, Alabama. Meanwhile, young African-Americans and some white supporters sat in at segregated lunch counters, organized voter registration drives, and found themselves considering significant alternatives to American culture.

The Long Road to *Brown v. Board of Education*

On May 17, 1954, the United States Supreme Court announced its unanimous decision in the legal challenge to the racial segregation of public schools, a case known as ***Brown v. Board of Education.*** Chief Justice Earl Warren wrote:

> We conclude that in the field of public education the doctrine of "separate but equal" has no place. Separate educational facilities are inherently unequal.

It had been a long road to the day of that finding.

The National Association for the Advancement of Colored People (NAACP), though founded in 1909, was often only whispered in black communities in the South throughout the 1930s, 1940s and 1950s. In the early 1950s, Anne Moody, then a high school student in Centerville, Mississippi, asked her homeroom teacher what NAACP meant. The teacher said, "You see the NAACP is trying to do a lot for the Negroes and get the right to vote for Negroes in the South." She also warned Moody, "I shouldn't be telling you all of this....It could cost me my job." The teacher was gone the following year.

In the 1930s, the NAACP began to challenge state "separate but equal" laws, bypassing state legislatures and governors with federal court cases arguing that the separate facilities were, in fact, far from equal. Two brilliant lawyers took charge of the NAACP legal effort—Charles Hamilton Houston, then dean of the Howard University Law School, and his former student, Thurgood Marshall. When Houston retired in 1938, Marshall, then just 30 years old, became the NAACP chief counsel, a position he held for 23 years. In 1961, Marshall was appointed as a federal judge serving on the U.S. Court of Appeals, and from 1967 to 1991, he served as the first appointed African-American justice of the U. S. Supreme Court.

The Houston-Marshall strategy at the NAACP was to chip away at segregation. In a 1938 case, *Missouri ex rel. Gaines v. Canada, Registrar of the University, et al.,* the U.S. Supreme Court ruled that Lloyd Gaines could not be rejected by the University of Missouri Law School on the basis of his race unless the university could offer him an equally good legal education within the state of Missouri. To offer legal education to whites but not to blacks, or to force blacks to leave the state for their education, Chief Justice Hughes said, "is a denial of the equality of legal right." In *Alston v. School Board of the City of Norfolk* in 1940, the NAACP won a ruling that said separate salary schedules for black and white teachers violated the Fourteenth Amendment. In 1950, the court issued two rulings. In *Sweatt v. Painter,* it said that separate law schools for blacks and whites were not equal, and in *McLaurin v. Oklahoma State Regents*, it ruled that segregating graduate students violated their equal protection rights. With each case, segregation was becoming more expensive for states to maintain and the arena

Brown v. Board of Education
A Supreme Court decision in 1954 declaring that "separate but equal" schools for children of different races violated the Constitution.

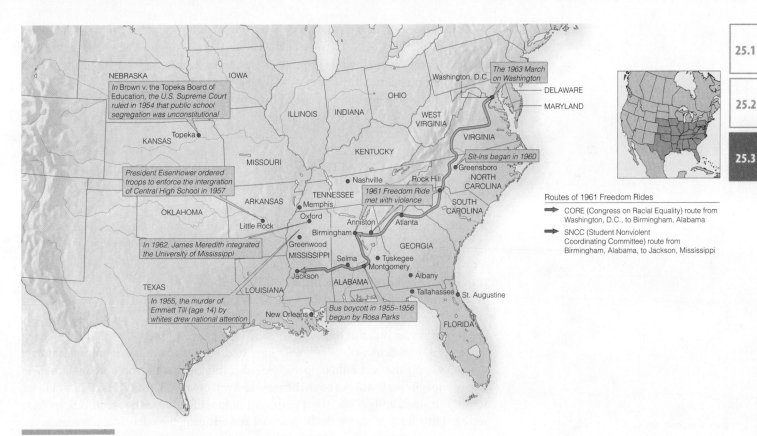

MAP 25-3 Civil Rights Events, 1953–1963. Most of the major events of the Civil Rights Movement took place in the states of the South. Some are indicated in this map.

in which it could be exercised smaller. The time was coming for a direct challenge to *Plessy v. Ferguson,* the 1896 decision by which the Supreme Court had originally approved "separate but equal" arrangements.

While the NAACP lawyers were winning cases, students at the all-black R. R. Morton High School in Farmville, Virginia, called a strike to protest conditions at their school in 1951. Although the white school in Farmville had comfortable facilities, some classes at R.R. Morton were held in tar-paper shacks, students had to wear coats to keep warm, and the teachers had to gather wood for the wood stoves. The authorities had long promised new facilities, but construction was continually postponed.

Only after going on strike did the students appeal to the NAACP. The national organization sent word that they would consider taking the case, but only if the challenge was for completely integrated schools. The students agreed and called on the adults in their community to follow them. Thus was launched one of the five cases that would be consolidated as *Brown v. Board of Education.*

The five states whose policies were challenged in the NAACP suit hired the 1924 Democratic presidential nominee John W. Davis as their attorney to defend the separate but equal policies. However, the Supreme Court agreed with the NAACP's argument that separate education always violated the 14th amendment's guarantee of "the equal protection of the laws." The unanimous 1954 decision said, "We come then to the question presented: Does segregation of children in public schools solely on the basis of race, even though the physical facilities and other 'tangible' factors may be equal, deprive the children of the minority group of the equal educational opportunities? We believe that it does."

There were those who thought that with the *Brown* decision the battle was over. Many years later, Kenneth Clark, whose testimony was central to the case, recalled ruefully, "How naïve I was!…I thought that within ten years or so, America would be free of it.…I expected southern states to resist, but I thought that their resistance would decrease and that we were on the road to some sort of functional democracy." It would take much more.

Some governors began massive resistance to school integration. The most dramatic took place in Little Rock, Arkansas, in the fall of 1957. Rather than allow the racial integration of previously all-white Central High School, the state's segregationist governor Orval Faubus ordered the Arkansas National Guard to stop nine African-American students from enrolling in the school. In a speech the night before school was scheduled to begin, Faubus said he was making the move because of a fear of violence. "Blood will run in the streets," he said, if black students tried to enter Central High.

Nine brave young students, known as the Little Rock Nine, were scheduled to test the integration of Central High School. Elizabeth Eckford remembered the terror when she found herself face to face with a white mob:

> Somebody started yelling, "Lynch her! Lynch her!"
>   I tried to see a friendly face somewhere in the mob—someone who maybe would help. I looked into the face of an old woman and it seemed a kind face, but when I looked at her again, she spat on me.

It was a harrowing experience that Eckford never forgot.

The students, the mob, and the National Guard were all recorded on national television. While President Eisenhower was no advocate of school integration, he was not about to allow an order of the U.S. Supreme Court to be flouted. He told his Attorney General Herbert Brownell, "Well, if we have to do this, and I don't see any alternative, then let's apply the best military principles to it and see that the force we send there is strong enough that it will not be challenged, and will not result in any clash." Eisenhower sent riot-trained units of the 101st Airborne. Before nightfall, a thousand U.S. soldiers were in Little Rock, securing the high school and ensuring the safety of the students.

Montgomery, Alabama

In 1955, a year and a half after the *Brown* decision, Rosa Parks finished her work day in Montgomery, Alabama, and began her bus ride home. She took a seat in the prescribed "Negro section" in the back of the bus. A few blocks later, when more whites boarded,

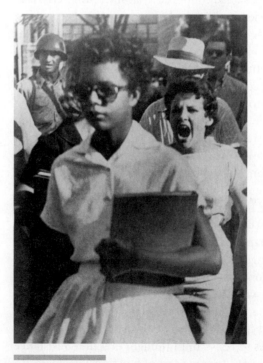

Elizabeth Eckerd, one of nine black students who sought to enroll at Little Rock Central High School in September 1957, endures the taunts of an angry white crowd as she tries to make her way to the school.

the driver, J. P. Blake, moved the line between the sections so that all of the whites could have seats. When none of the blacks moved, Blake warned them, "You better make it light on yourselves and let me have those seats." When others moved, Rosa Parks stayed where she was. "Are you going to stand up?" Blake asked. Parks said, quite simply, "No."

Blake summoned the Montgomery police who arrested Parks. When she was allowed to call home, Parks told her mother of her arrest and her mother immediately got in touch with E. D. Nixon, the acknowledged leader of Montgomery's civil rights community who was not a newcomer to making tough decisions. Nixon, then 56, was president of Montgomery's chapter of the NAACP. He worked as a porter on the railroad and was vice-president of the Alabama branch of the Brotherhood of Sleeping Car Porters, the most powerful black-led union in the United States. He had been one of the planners for the 1941 March on Washington. Nixon asked Clifford and Virginia Durr, Montgomery whites who were civil rights activists, to join him and the three went to the Montgomery jail to sign the bond for Rosa Parks' release. Within a few hours, Parks was free and at home.

The arrest of Rosa Parks in 1955 for refusing to abide by the rules of the segregated buses of Montgomery, Alabama, represented an important moment in civil rights history, one of many developments that undermined the image of the 1950s as an era of total complacency with the status quo.

Early in that evening, the matter could have ended. The court would probably have let Parks off with a small fine, and the segregated world of Montgomery could have returned to normal. But as Nixon and the Durrs talked with Rosa Parks, her husband, and her mother, the question arose: Was this incident the test case they had all been waiting for? In *Brown v. Board of Education* the year before, the Supreme Court had ruled that segregated *schools* were illegal. But what about transportation? If she were willing, if she could overcome her husband Raymond's fear that, "The white folks will kill you, Rosa," there could not be a better person than Rosa Parks for the test case they all sought.

Parks had a long history as a civil rights activist. She first tried to register to vote in 1943 when only a very tiny percentage of Alabama blacks voted. She was told she did not pass the literacy test. The same thing happened in 1944. In 1945, she hand-copied every question on the literacy test while she was taking it, in an obvious first step toward a legal challenge. Apparently, the authorities wanted to avoid a legal challenge more than they wanted to avoid her vote. She received her registration in the mail and began voting in Alabama elections in 1946. In the summer of 1955, Parks attended a desegregation workshop at Highlander. "I was forty-two years old, and it was one of the few times in my life up to that point when I did not feel any hostility from white people," Parks said.

Given her background, many have wondered whether Parks's action on the bus had been planned. She insisted it had not. But her life had prepared her for what happened. A few months later, Parks said, "There had to be a stopping place, and this seemed to have been the place for me to stop being pushed around and to find out what human rights I had, if any."

Parks, Nixon, and the Durrs retained a young African-American lawyer, Fred Gray, as her attorney. Nixon began calling the local ministers. The new minister at Dexter Avenue Baptist Church, Martin Luther King, Jr., was third on his list. Among the people Gray called that evening was Jo Ann Gibson Robinson, a professor at Montgomery's all black Alabama State College and a leader in the black Women's Political Caucus (WPC) in Montgomery, who remembered, "Telephones jangled; people congregated on street corners and in homes and talked....[but] A numbing helplessness seemed to paralyze everyone." Without consulting other leaders, Robinson and the WPC decided to call a boycott of the Montgomery buses when

Parks went on trial. She, another professor, and two students pretended that they needed to grade papers and went to their offices in the middle of the night. By 4 a.m. the next morning, using the school's mimeograph machine, they had prepared thousands of leaflets that said:

> Another Negro woman has been arrested and thrown in jail because she refused to get up out of her seat on the bus for a white person to sit down.... This has to be stopped...We are, therefore, asking every Negro to stay off the buses Monday in protest.

Between 4 a.m. and 7 a.m., Robinson and her students distributed the leaflets. They finished in time for Robinson to teach her 8 a.m. class on schedule and then distributed more leaflets.

Robinson's leaflet fell into the hands of the white *Montgomery Advertiser,* which published news of the plan on its front page on Saturday, inadvertently helping the campaign along. The story was meant to inform the white community what was afoot, but it also meant that every black knew about the boycott. Nearly all of Montgomery's blacks stayed off the buses that first day. At a planning meeting on Monday afternoon, Martin Luther King, Jr., then 26 years old, was elected president of what would be called the Montgomery Improvement Association (MIA). As president, King was the main speaker at a Monday evening service. He called on Montgomery's African-American community to protest with courage and dignity. After King's sermon, Ralph Abernathy, minister of Montgomery's First Baptist Church proposed that the boycott continue until the demands—courteous treatment by the bus operators and the seating of passengers on a first-come, first-served basis, whites from the front, blacks from the back—were met. Segregation itself was not yet challenged, only the kind of humiliating enforcement of segregation experienced by Parks. From that evening it was clear; it was not to be a one-day boycott. People would wait as long as it took.

Ultimately, it took a year-long boycott of the Montgomery buses to win the victory the black community wanted, and it took a combination of careful planning and inspirational preaching to get there. People needed courage and inspiration, but they also needed taxis and car pools to get them to work. Black-owned taxis offered reduced fares. The ministers organized car pools to help people who needed to go the longest distances.

The nation's black leadership was not enthusiastic about events in Montgomery. The Montgomery bus boycott was a spontaneous outburst that national leaders had played no role in organizing. Roy Wilkins, the long-time national leader of the NAACP invited King to address the NAACP convention in San Francisco, but also expressed deep doubts about the boycott. Thurgood Marshall openly criticized King, preferring to stick with court cases. "All that walking for nothing. They might as well have waited for the court decision," Marshall said of the boycott.

But as the year wore on, the boycott had its impact. The boycott received favorable national media attention. Fundraising became easier, and King found himself becoming a national celebrity. The aged W.E.B. Du Bois wrote that, though he still had his doubts about boycotts, if King's passive resistance could undermine American racism, it would be a huge victory. On June 4, an appeals court ruled in favor of Rosa Parks, and on November 13, 1956, the United States Supreme Court concurred. Early in the morning of December 21, 1956, 1 year and 3 weeks after Rosa Parks had refused to move, King and a few others, followed by reporters, boarded the first bus of the day. "We are glad to have you," the polite driver said.

In January 1957, King, Abernathy, and some 60 black ministers created the **Southern Christian Leadership Conference**, based in Atlanta, Georgia. The MIA had been a temporary organization focused on the bus boycott. The SCLC institutionalized the energy and the planning that had started in Montgomery and created a permanent national organization and a long-term platform for King.

Southern Christian Leadership Conference (SCLC)

The leading clergy-led voice of the southern, nonviolent Civil Rights Movement, founded in 1957 by Martin Luther King, Jr., and some 60 other black ministers, many veterans of the Montgomery Bus Boycott.

THINKING HISTORICALLY

The Many Faces of the Civil Rights Movement

Rosa Parks' refusal to give up her bus seat in Montgomery, Alabama, in December 1955 led to a year-long boycott of the buses, launched the career of a young Montgomery minister, Martin Luther King, Jr., and changed the course of American history. But the boycott worked only because of many who never became famous.

Besides Parks and King, some among the many who made the Montgomery boycott a national event:

- Claudette Colvin—A young African-American who was arrested for refusing to give up her seat on a bus 9 months before Parks but who local leaders thought was not the right candidate for a test case because she was pregnant and unmarried. Her legal appeal was later combined with that of Rosa Parks.
- E.D. Nixon—A long-time civil rights and union activist who commanded great respect in black and white communities in Montgomery.
- Clifford and Virginia Durr—White residents of Montgomery who had long supported civil rights for African-Americans at considerable personal cost and who had national connections to help the local organizers.
- Fred Gray—Then a 24-year-old lawyer in Montgomery who represented Rosa Parks. Gray had gone to law school with a private promise "to become a lawyer, return to Alabama, and destroy everything segregated I could find."
- Jo Ann Gibson Robinson and the Members of the Women's Political Caucus—Were already urging male civil rights leaders to protest Montgomery's segregated buses.
- Ralph Abernathy—A respected senior minister and an officer of the NAACP who convinced King to support the bus boycott.
- Mother Pollard—An elderly member of King's congregation who responded to her pastor's concern that she was too old to keep walking, replying, "My feets is tired but my soul is rested."
- And thousands of additional residents of Montgomery— Committed supporters who attended rallies, organized alternative forms of transportation, or simply walked to and from work for a year rather than break the boycott.

In thinking about how best to teach the history of the Civil Rights Movement, Diana Turk, a professor at New York University, said:

> Ask most middle- and secondary-level students what they have learned about the Civil Rights Movement, and most likely they will tell you a story of great leaders who, through their bravery, and inspiring words, led millions to stand with them in the struggles for freedom, equality, and Civil Rights....But...as engaging and inspiring as this tale of brave and inspiring leaders may be, much is lost when we look at history as a story of only a few individuals and their acts of heroism. As Dr. Adam Green, an historian of the black Civil Rights Movement in the United States, importantly argues, great leaders don't get very far unless they have great organizers behind them; someone needs to plan and announce boycotts and marches, set up rallies, arrange for speeches and press coverage, and spread the word about the events that together make up movements....Not only can a focus on organizers give students a sense of some of the important—and often forgotten— forces that helped shape history, but such an approach also can empower students to see how seemingly small, localized, and unheralded actions can truly change the course of human events.

Source: Diana Turk, Rachel Mattson, Terrie Epstein, and Robert Cohen, *Teaching U.S. History: Dialogues Among Social Studies Teachers and Historians* (New York: Routledge, 2010).

Thinking Critically

1. **Historical Interpretation**

   What role did each of the figures described above play in the boycott? How did their efforts reinforce each other?

2. **Construct an Argument**

   Defend or refute the following statement: "The Montgomery bus boycott proves that the most important social change is produced by action on the local level."

Students and Sit-Ins

On February 1, 1960, 3 years after the buses in Montgomery were integrated and as John F. Kennedy battled to win presidential primaries, four African-American freshmen at North Carolina Agricultural and Technical College sat down at the whites-only lunch counter of the Woolworth's store in Greensboro, North Carolina. They asked politely for service and ordered coffee. After sitting at the counter all day, they still had not received their orders. Nineteen students joined the sit-in the next day, and on the third day, they numbered 85. On the fourth day, more than 300 people joined the sit-in, expanding it to another store's lunch counter. This group action was not a well-planned event. The established civil rights leaders in neither the NAACP nor King's SCLC had been involved and, indeed, knew nothing of it until after the fact. They struggled to decide whether to support, ignore, or lead the sit-ins. But it didn't matter what they did. The student-led sit-ins that started in Greensboro spread like wildfire across the South.

Before February ended, there were sit-ins in 31 cities in eight southern states. One of the largest and longest took place in Nashville, Tennessee. After hearing of the Greensboro actions, over 500 well-dressed African-American college students walked into downtown Nashville and sat down at lunch counters in all of the major stores. The Nashville police allowed a mob to beat many of the demonstrators, and more than 60 protesters were jailed in Nashville. The mayor sought compromise and agreed to appoint a biracial committee to look at segregation in the stores. The appointment of the committee was a victory long sought by Nashville's older civil rights leaders, and it had been won by the students. By July, the lunch counters in Greensboro had also become desegregated.

While many of King's peers were not sure what to make of the sit-ins, and the NAACP Legal Defense Fund was not willing to defend those arrested, King endorsed them, seeing the sit-ins as a way to confront segregation nonviolently and directly. He continued to defend the sit-ins to an older and very wary civil rights community, and the sit-ins continued to grow in significance.

From Freedom Rides to Birmingham to Washington—"I Have a Dream," 1963

While the sit-ins continued, the U.S. Supreme Court in a 1960 ruling, *Boynton v. Virginia* declared that any segregation in interstate transportation was unconstitutional. James Farmer and others in the Congress of Racial Equality (CORE) decided to test the decision with "freedom rides" to hasten integration of interstate bus service

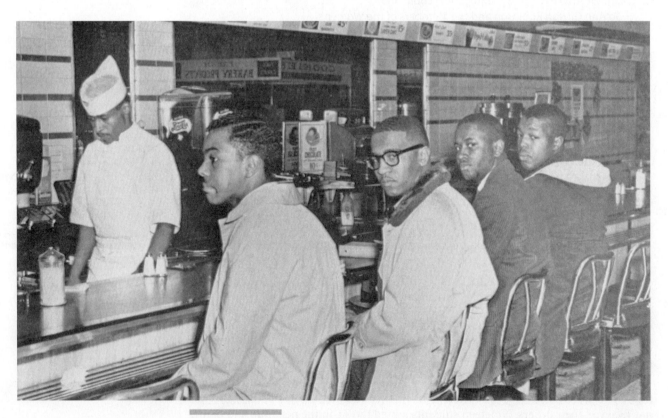

The lunch counter sit-ins, launched by these students at a segregated lunch counter in Greensboro, North Carolina, in February 1960, began a new and powerful phase of the Civil Rights Movement.

and terminals through the South. They warned the Attorney General and the FBI in advance. When the seven blacks and six whites on the two buses began their trip in May 1961, they encountered violence first in Rock Hill, South Carolina, where John Lewis was beaten when trying to enter a white rest room, then in Anniston, Alabama, where one of the buses was burned and most of the riders beaten. All of the riders were beaten again when a bus reached Birmingham, Alabama—one white rider so badly he suffered permanent brain damage. An FBI informer had reported Ku Klux Klan plans to attack the Freedom Riders, but at no point did they get any federal protection. New riders who joined the effort were also beaten and arrested. Eventually, 328 Freedom Riders were arrested in the summer of 1961.

When the new Kennedy administration called for a "cooling-off" period, Farmer responded that "blacks have been cooling off for 150 years. If we cool off any more, we'll be in a deep freeze." Finally in the fall, Attorney General Robert Kennedy convinced the Interstate Commerce Commission to order that any bus or train that crossed a state line (and thus under the Constitution became subject to federal rules) could not use any segregated facilities.

In September 1962, James Meredith became the first black to enroll at the University of Mississippi, backed by a federal court order. In response, Mississippi governor Ross Barnett promised that "No school will be integrated in Mississippi while I am your governor." Robert Kennedy thought he had a promise from Barnett to keep order on the campus, but when Barnett instead whipped up a crowd of some 3,000 whites who began throwing rocks and eventually shooting, Kennedy sent federal marshals and then federal troops, who restored order at the university.

Early in 1963, King began a campaign to desegregate Birmingham, Alabama, perhaps the most segregated city in the South. He expected resistance. King was promptly arrested during a protest—and used the time to write one of his most famous publications, "Letter from Birmingham Jail." The Birmingham police, under their chief "Bull" Connor also arrested some 3,000 protesting children and turned fire hoses and attack dogs on children and adults. Civil rights organizers also met with violent resistance elsewhere. Medgar Evers, the NAACP field secretary in Jackson, Mississippi, was murdered on his front porch that June. Riots erupted in northern cities in July. Who knew what was coming next?

The Birmingham, Alabama, police force used dogs to attack Civil Rights demonstrators, a response that brought worldwide condemnation.

Widespread television coverage brought an international outcry about the violence in Birmingham, including criticism by the Soviet Union. President Kennedy, who had been slow to act on civil rights, but feared bad publicity especially in the context of the Cold War, introduced his long-promised civil rights bill in June 1963. Kennedy told Congress that "The heart of the question is whether all Americans are to be afforded equal rights and equal opportunities." To support the proposed civil rights bill, civil rights leaders A. Philip Randolph and Bayard Rustin called for a March on Washington. On August 28, 1963, more than 20 years after Randolph first proposed a march on Washington, and 100 years after Abraham Lincoln signed the Emancipation Proclamation, over 200,000 Americans marched in the nation's capital and listened to speeches at the Lincoln Memorial.

The keynote address of the March on Washington was delivered by Martin Luther King, Jr. In words that have become immortal, King declared his hope for America in spite of all the injustice that the Civil Rights Movement was encountering. In spite of all the setbacks, King said "I still have a dream," that the situation in America could change. In the cadences of traditional black preachers, using words from Katherine Lee Bates, Thomas Jefferson, and the biblical prophet Isaiah, King preached the hope that, in America, black people and white people could, indeed, be sisters and brothers.

Martin Luther King's "I Have a Dream" speech is now iconic, but in August 1963, it took courage to make that speech not only because civil rights workers and leaders were being beaten and killed, as King would be, but also because many would think such hopes foolish and empty. Even as King spoke, it was unclear whether Kennedy or the Congress would do much to expand freedom or pass a civil rights bill.

Student Nonviolent Coordinating Committee (SNCC)
Black civil rights organization founded in 1960 that drew heavily on younger activists and college students.

The Student Nonviolent Coordinating Committee and Mississippi

On Easter weekend of 1960, some of the students who had been participating in sit-ins across the South gathered at Shaw University in Raleigh, North Carolina. Ella Baker, who helped organize the Raleigh meeting, later recalled, "Just as the sit-ins had skyrocketed or escalated without rhyme or reason, so too the response to the concept of a conference escalated beyond our expectations." James Lawson, who had played a major role in the sit-in movement in Nashville and had been expelled from the Vanderbilt University Divinity School for his efforts, also joined the Raleigh conference. He told the students that their actions were "a judgment upon middle-class conventional, halfway efforts to deal with radical social evil." The students voted to form their own organization rather than affiliate with either the SCLC or the NAACP. Thus, the **Student Nonviolent Coordinating Committee (SNCC)** was born.

No one did more to shape SNCC than Ella Baker. Baker had worked for the NAACP in the 1940s. Martin Luther King recruited her to the SCLC in the 1950s, but she found herself deeply frustrated by the male dominance of the minister-led SCLC. Her own philosophy was that "People have to be made to understand that they cannot look for salvation anywhere but to themselves." John Lewis, the youngest speaker at the March on Washington and another SNCC founder, said "We all recognize the fact that if any radical social, political, and economic changes are to take place in our society, the people, the masses must bring them about." Like many in SNCC, Lewis was distrustful of any single charismatic leader, even King. In the sit-in movement and in SNCC, Baker and Lewis found like-minded souls.

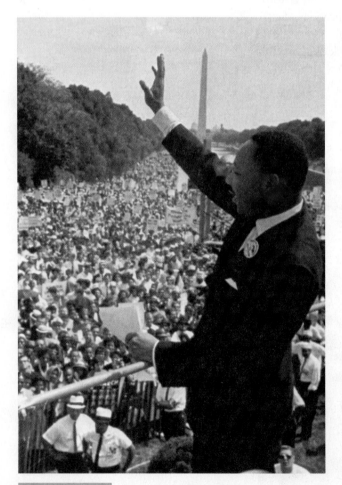

Martin Luther King, Jr., at the 1963 March on Washington.

Bob Moses arrived in Atlanta in the summer of 1960 to volunteer with SNCC during his vacation from his job as a teacher in New York City. As Moses traveled through the rural South, he met some amazing people like Amzie Moore who lived far from the centers of civil rights activity. Moses described meeting Moore:

> He was the only adult I met on this trip who had clearly fixed the students in his sights. It was as if he had been sitting there in Cleveland [Mississippi] watching the student movement unfold, waiting for it to come his way, knowing it had to eventually come, and planning ways to use it in light of his fifteen year effort, since World War II, at making changes in the cotton plantation land of the Mississippi delta.

Moses would encounter more people like Moore on his travels, and they changed him.

Moses learned that while Moore appreciated the legal work of the NAACP, integration was not his priority. His passion was the vote. Living in a congressional district that was two-thirds black, it was obvious to Moore what the vote could do. Moses wrote to the SNCC office in Atlanta, "Amzie thinks, and I concur, the adults here will back the young folks but will never initiate a program strong enough to do what needs to be done." Thus was born SNCC's focus on a massive student-led campaign for the vote. In 1961, Moses returned to Mississippi to work full time on voter registration for SNCC.

In September 1961, Herbert Lee, a supporter of the voter registration effort in Amite County, Mississippi, was shot by E. H. Hurst, a white state representative. Hurst admitted that he had shot Lee but was never prosecuted for the murder. Other murders followed.

Even when the threat of violence and murder was not imminent, people who had lived with segregation and violence all their lives were reluctant to challenge the system. In the winter of 1963–64, SNCC developed a plan to bring a thousand mostly white college students to Mississippi to help with the voter registration effort and to focus national attention on the denial of rights in Mississippi. Some SNCC field organizers worried that so many whites would undermine the strength of the black community. On the other hand, grass-roots leaders like Fannie Lou Hamer argued, "If we're trying to break down this barrier of segregation, we can't segregate ourselves." In June 1964, thousands of student volunteers, white and black, arrived for what became Mississippi Freedom Summer to register local African-Americans to vote and to demonstrate to the nation what an interracial coalition looked like. They were met with considerable hostility. Three of the volunteers, James Chaney, a black, and Andrew Goodman and Michael Schwerner, both white, were killed in late June near Philadelphia, Mississippi. There were also tensions within the movement, yet Mississippi Freedom Summer garnered national publicity for voting rights and changed the lives of many who participated.

As more blacks registered to vote, they also organized the **Mississippi Freedom Democratic Party (MFDP)** to challenge the official all-white Mississippi delegation for the August 1964 Democratic Convention at which Lyndon Johnson, then president, was to be nominated for reelection. Just weeks before the national convention, hundreds of newly registered Mississippi voters, having been turned away from the regular all-white Democratic Party meetings in Mississippi, met in Jackson and elected 68 delegates to the convention.

The MFDP succeeded in raising the denial of voting rights in Mississippi to national attention even though its delegation was not seated at the national convention. The convention made Fannie Lou Hamer, a 47-year-old Mississippi sharecropper and spokeswoman for MFDP, a national voice. Bob Moses described the MFDP delegates as "sharecroppers, domestic workers, and farmers" who were asking the national Democratic Party to truly be the party of such people" while also "taking the first step toward gaining control over their lives."

Mississippi Freedom Democratic Party (MFDP)

A separate Democratic delegation, launched as a result of the SNCC-led voter registration campaign, that challenged the right of the regular, all-white delegation to represent Mississippi at the 1964 Democratic Convention.

Fannie Lou Hamer spoke to the Mississippi Freedom Party delegation after they were barred from the Democratic Convention in 1964.

American Voices

Fannie Lou Hamer, "Testimony to the Credentials Committee," 1964

*W*hen Fannie Lou Hamer gave her testimony at the national Democratic Convention, she had come a long way from a SNCC voter registration meeting. "Until then," she said, "I'd never heard of no mass meeting and I didn't know that a Negro could register and vote....When they asked for those to raise their hands who'd go down to the courthouse the next day, I raised mine. Had it up as high as I could get it."

It was the 31st of August in 1962 that eighteen of us traveled twenty-six miles to the county courthouse in Indianola [Mississippi] to try to register to become first-class citizens.

We was met in Indianola by policemen, Highway Patrolmen, and they only allowed two of us in to take the literacy test at the time. After we had taken this test...we continued on to Ruleville...where I had worked as a timekeeper and sharecropper for eighteen years. I was met there by my children, who told me that the plantation owner was angry because I had gone down to try to register....

He said, "If you don't go down and withdraw your registration, you will have to leave." Said, "Then if you go down and withdraw," said, "you still might have to go because we are not ready for that in Mississippi."

And I addressed him and told him and said, "I didn't try to register for you. I tried to register for myself."

I had to leave that same night....

[Hamer also described her subsequent arrest:]

I was carried to the county jail and put in the booking room....

I was carried out of that cell into another cell where they had two Negro prisoners. The State Highway Patrolmen ordered the first Negro to take the blackjack [a wooden club].

The first Negro prisoner ordered me, by orders from the State Highway Patrolman, for me to lay down on a bunk bed on my face.

I laid on my face and the first Negro began to beat...I began to scream and one white man got up and began to beat me in my head and tell me to hush....

I was in jail when Medgar Evers was murdered.

All of this is on account of we want to register, to become first-class citizens. And if the Freedom Democratic Party is not seated now, I question America. Is this America, the land of the free and the home of the brave, where we have to sleep with our telephones off the hooks because our lives be threatened daily, because we want to live as decent human beings, in America? Thank you.

Source: http://americanradioworks.publicradio.org/features/sayitplain/flhamer.html, downloaded, July 8 2011

Thinking Critically

1. **Documentary Analysis**
   What light does the document shed on Hamer's motives in registering to vote?

2. **Historical Interpretation**
   What do Hamer's experiences suggest about the nature of white resistance to the Civil Rights Movement?

The North and Malcolm X

By the 1960s, half of the nation's African-Americans lived in the North, most in racially segregated urban neighborhoods. While the hopes of blacks in the South generally focused on ending the brutal segregation and on winning the right to vote, the hopes of northern blacks focused on ending segregated housing patterns, poor quality schooling, and economic marginalization. One of the most prominent voices for northern urban blacks was Malcolm X. As Marcus Garvey had done for a previous generation, Malcolm spoke of pride, self-sufficiency, and self-determination.

Malcolm was born Malcolm Little in Omaha, Nebraska, in 1925. He remembered the grinding poverty, racism, and violence of Depression Era America.

As a young adult, Malcolm pursued a life of crime and in February 1946, just before his 21 birthday, received a 10-year sentence for a string of burglaries. In his *Autobiography* he said, "I had sunk to the very bottom of the American white man's society."

While he was in prison, Malcolm experienced a religious conversion and joined the Nation of Islam, or the Black Muslims as they were commonly known. When he was released in 1952, he moved to Detroit and was soon named assistant minister at Detroit Temple Number One. The Black Muslims believed that it was important to reject traditional last names—which they saw as slave names since many came from former slave owners—and so Malcolm Little became Malcolm X. His message as a minister was, "We didn't land on Plymouth Rock, my brothers and sisters—Plymouth Rock landed on *us*!…It was a mix of pride and separation from white people— the "white devils"—along with a call for total allegiance to Allah and Allah's Messenger Elijah Muhammad.

Malcolm disdained integration and the southern Civil Rights Movement. While he was gaining fame as "the fiery Black Muslim," Malcolm was also starting to have his doubts about Elijah Muhammad. Early in 1964, he broke with the Nation of Islam and set off on a pilgrimage to Mecca as is required of every devout Muslim man. In Mecca, Malcolm found himself among Muslims from all over the world. He was transformed by the experience. When a fellow pilgrim asked him what about the Hajj had impressed him the most, Malcolm answered, "The *brotherhood*! The people of all races, colors, from all over the world coming together as *one*! It has proved to me the power of the One God." No longer would he preach separation for its own sake. He was not any less militant, but Malcolm returned from Mecca as El-Hajj Malik El-Shabazz, a devout traditional Muslim.

When he returned to New York in 1964, Malcolm explained his new beliefs. He said of his experience in Mecca, "In the past, yes, I have made sweeping indictments of *all* white people. I never will be guilty of that again—as I know now that some white people *are* truly sincere, that some truly are capable of being brotherly toward a black man." He was willing to join interracial coalitions to achieve immediate goals and would work within as well as against the political system.

Malcolm was not willing to adopt King's nonviolence and believed African-Americans needed to defend themselves. In 1964, he met Fannie Lou Hamer. When he heard her describe the beating she had received, he said, "When I listened to Mrs. Hamer, a black woman—could be my mother, my sister, my daughter—describe what they had done to her in Mississippi, I asked myself how in the world can we ever expect to be respected…and we do nothing about it?" He was not the advocate of violence that others portrayed him to be, but at one point he said, "Let sincere whites go and teach non-violence to white people!"

After his break with the Nation of Islam, he established his own independent Muslim Mosque Incorporated to preach what he believed was a truer Islam than that taught by the Black Muslims. He also established a political organization,

Explore The Civil Rights Movement on MyHistoryLab

HOW DID CONDITIONS FOR AFRICAN-AMERICANS BEGIN TO CHANGE IN THE MID-1900S?

Laws in the South known as "Jim Crow laws"—regulations that banned African-Americans and whites from, for example, marrying, dining, going to school, or socializing together—ensured racial discrimination. In the North, segregation undergirded the social structure. However, African-American leaders started to make advancements in their fight for equality in the 1950s and 1960s. Civil rights activists protested across the South, making national headlines. In the industrial cities of the North and West, large numbers of African-Americans arrived in the Second Great Migration between 1940 and 1970 as they sought better opportunities than the South afforded them. From these cities, many also began to speak out for an end to racism.

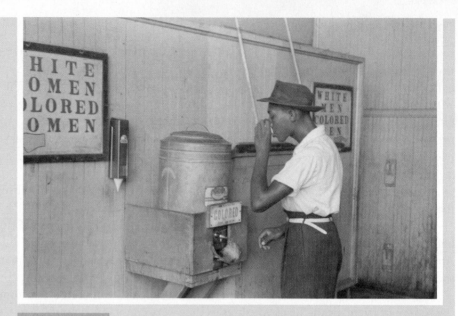

Young black man drinking from a segregated drinking fountain.

SHIFTS IN AFRICAN-AMERICAN POPULATION IN SELECTED COUNTIES, 1940–1950

County	Change, in Persons	Percent Change
Columbia County, Georgia	−1,108	−20
Cook County, Illinois	+226,822	+60
Los Angeles County, California	+142,672	+94
Quitman County, Mississippi	−2,416	−9
Wayne County, Michigan	+172,122	+70

Source: *1950 Census, Historic GIS Data: Slavery, Citizenship, & Civil Rights,* Teaching American History Project, *http://www.upa.pdx.edu/IMS/currentprojects/TAHv3/Slave_Citizen_GIS.html.*

KEY QUESTIONS   Use MyHistoryLab *Explorer* to answer these questions:

Cause ▶▶▶ *What challenges did African Americans face during the era of segregation?*

Use socioeconomic patterns to consider discrimination.

Comparison ▶▶▶ *In what parts of southern cities did African Americans live?*

Map segregation in selected urban centers.

Consequence ▶▶▶ *What was the demographic impact of the Second Great Migration?*

Consider the results of this move to the urban North and West.

the Organization of Afro-American Unity (OAAU) to advance his political agenda. His top priority, he said, was to submit "the case of the American Negro before the United Nations." Rather than focus on federal legislation, Malcolm believed that African-Americans had a case to bring their continuing marginalization before the UN, and with the support of African and Middle Eastern nations, he was confident they would win.

More important than any organization, however, Malcolm fostered a new sense of pride in a generation of northern African-Americans. He challenged the quality of education in black communities. He led demonstrations against police violence. He called on African-Americans to "control the politics in his own residential areas by voting…and investing in the businesses." He had a vision of African-Americans making international alliances with the people of the then newly independent African nations and with the Muslim world. As the scholar Manning Marable said of him, "Malcolm's great strength was his ability to speak on behalf of those to whom society and state had denied a voice due to racial prejudice."

The new Malcolm was willing to accept white coworkers, but not to be led or controlled. He dreamed that the day might come when, "In our mutual sincerity we might be able to show a road to the salvation of America's very soul." Malcolm was assassinated by Nation of Islam followers in February 1965. But he would continue to inspire great hopes long after he was gone.

25.1
25.2
25.3

Malcolm X (1925–1965) was eloquent, passionate, a courageously outspoken champion of black people, and a critic of American racism. Today he is an iconic figure memorialized in poems, song, films, books, and operas.

25.3 **Quick Review** Why were organizations like SNCC, CORE, the SCLC, and the NAACP essential to the Civil Rights Movement?

CONCLUSION

The 1950s was a decade of contrasts. For many, they were the complacent decade when Dwight Eisenhower presided over a nation that had won World War II and was happy to move to new suburban homes and domestic contentment. At the same time, threat of the hydrogen bomb greatly influenced U.S. foreign and domestic policy throughout the 1950s, and the space race with the Soviet Union prompted Americans to panic about the state of its education system. Among African-Americans, the many-faceted Civil Rights Movement transformed their lives and U.S. practices of segregation.

During the Eisenhower administration (1953–1961), the United States pursued policies that attempted to minimize the costs of the Cold War, protect the non-Communist world from Communist infiltration, and avoid armed confrontation. Key pieces of Eisenhower's foreign policy included the threat of "massive retaliation" with hydrogen bombs and the extensive use of spying and covert operations in foreign countries. When the Soviet Union launched the first space satellite, the American government responded by creating the National Aeronautics and Space Administration (NASA) to manage space exploration and by establishing new domestic programs linking education to national defense.

The 1950s were relative peaceful and prosperous for many Americans. The economy continued to grow, and many experienced a substantial increase in family income. Americans also became much more religious during the period—a phenomenon still not fully understood. At the same time, television came to dominate American popular culture. Most of the programming of the 1950s sought to reaffirm the suburban lifestyles of the white middle class, and new 30-second television commercials encouraged Americans to buy everything from Alka-Seltzer to automobiles. The automobile also rose to prominence in 1950s America, giving rise to new industries to support cars and to an interstate highway system. However, America's love affair with the automobile required a steady supply of cheap gasoline—an issue that would come to dominate American politics.

In the 1950s, although segregation, marginalization, and political disenfranchisement were commonplace for African-Americans, the modern Civil Rights Movement came into full swing. After decades of court challenges by the NAACP, the U.S. Supreme Court finally ruled in 1954 that racial segregation of public schools was unconstitutional. Civil rights protesters also successfully boycotted segregation of the public transportation system in Montgomery, Alabama, and of lunch counters across the nation.

While the Southern Christian Leadership Conference and the Student Nonviolent Coordinating Committee worked for integration and voting rights in the South, a very different civil rights leader emerged in the North. Malcolm X became a prominent northern voice for the nation's African-Americans. He rejected the integration-focused strategy of southern civil rights leaders and spoke of pride, self-sufficiency, and self-determination for blacks free from white interference. Malcolm was assassinated in February 1965, but the Civil Rights Movement, led largely by Martin Luther King, Jr., continued to press for full equality throughout the 1960s.

CHAPTER REVIEW	In what ways was the United States a different country in 1960 than in 1950? How did domestic and international events influence these changes in American society?

Chapter 25   Chapter Review

EISENHOWER'S AMERICA, AMERICA'S WORLD

25.1 Explain the continuation of the Cold War under a new Republican administration.

Review Questions

1. **Contextualization**
   What were Eisenhower's overarching foreign policy objectives? How successful was he in achieving those objectives?

2. **Cause and Effect**
   What were the most important long-term consequences of the Soviet launch of the Sputnik satellite?

3. **Historical Interpretation**
   Why did the United States and the Soviet Union find it so difficult to move past their mutual distrust and build a less confrontational relationship?

A CULTURE ON THE MOVE

25.2 Explain the impact of cultural and technological changes on the country.

Review Questions

4. **Cause and Effect**
   What were the most important consequences of the surge in automobile ownership in the 1950s?

5. **Historical Interpretation**
   How did television transform American culture in the 1950s?

6. **Create an Argument**
   How would you explain the religious boom of the 1950s?

RACE AND CIVIL RIGHTS

25.3 Analyze the growth and impact of the civil rights movement between 1954 and 1965.

Review Questions

7. **Contextualization**
   Why was Rosa Parks an ideal person to challenge Montgomery bus segregation?

8. **Historical Interpretation**
   How did students and other young people shape the Civil Rights Movement of the early 1960s?

9. **Comparison**
   Compare and contrast Malcolm X and Martin Luther King, Jr. What were the most important similarities and differences in their responses to racial discrimination and segregation?

26 Lives Changed

1961–1968

This widely publicized picture of an antiwar demonstrator putting a flower in the end of a rifle at the October 1967 March on the Pentagon reflects some of the deepest divisions of the 1960s.

CHAPTER OBJECTIVE

Demonstrate an understanding of the unique time known as "the sixties."

LEARNING OBJECTIVES

NEW VOICES, NEW AUTHORITIES

26.1 Explain the growing social protest in books, films, and student movements starting in the early 1960s.

CAMELOT, THE WHITE HOUSE, AND DALLAS—THE KENNEDY ADMINISTRATION

26.2 Analyze the successes and failures of the Kennedy administration and how they interacted with popular culture in the United States.

THE COMING OF LYNDON B. JOHNSON

26.3 Analyze the successes and failures of the Johnson administration in terms of the two issues that dominated his years in office—the launching of the Great Society programs and the war in Vietnam.

In 1960 while Kennedy and Nixon contested the presidency, a handful of white students organized **Students for a Democratic Society (SDS)**. SDS represented a new birth of activism on the part of white young people just as the Student Nonviolent Coordinating Committee (SNCC) had given voice to the activism of African-American students (see Chapter 25). The birth of groups like SDS and SNCC guaranteed that the 1960s would not be as quiet as the 1950s. As Bob Dylan, the best known folk singer of the early 1960s sang, "The times they are a changing."

Student protesters and folk singers were far from the only signs that something new was brewing in American culture after 1960. New literature signaled the change that was coming. Between 1961 and 1963, three women authors published books challenging fundamental issues: Jane Jacobs, the way cities were developing; Rachel Carson, the pollution of the environment; and Betty Friedan, the "quiet desperation" of many women's lives. They were not alone; authors increasingly challenged various aspects of American life.

The new president also represented a generational change in American politics. This chapter traces the many changes that some Americans embraced, others rejected, but few ignored as the United States experienced the decade known to many simply as "the sixties."

NEW VOICES, NEW AUTHORITIES

26.1 Explain the growing social protest in books, films, and student movements starting in the early 1960s.

Though it was formative for many, the Civil Rights Movement was only one of many challenges to American culture in the 1960s. Writers and artist had often been uncomfortable with the conformity of the 1950s, and their uneasiness took on new forms as the new decade began. Small political movements burst onto a larger stage. The result was a number of books, films, and songs that reflected and helped shape a rapidly changing culture while wide-ranging protest movements, often led by students, changed not only college campuses but also the country.

Books, Films, Music

Jane Jacobs was a writer and activist in New York's Greenwich Village when she wrote, *The Death and Life of Great American Cities* in 1961. In the opening line of that book, Jacobs said, "This book is an attack on current city planning and rebuilding." Indeed, it was an amazingly successful attack. Reflecting on the book's impact, one urban planner wrote, "When an entire field is headed in the wrong direction…then it probably took someone from outside to point out the obvious." After Jacobs, city planners in New York and most cities turned away from massive highway development, sprawling suburbs, and isolated urban high-rise buildings to focus on smaller, more neighborhood friendly options. Projects to bulldoze slums and build highways were replaced in the 1960s by the redevelopment of existing urban neighborhoods. Jacobs did not bring about this change single-handedly, but her book was a guidebook to a new generation of urban planners.

Two books published in 1962 played a similar role in other movements. Rachel Carson's *Silent Spring* is often called the bible of the conservation movement. Other people dating back to Theodore Roosevelt talked about conserving rather than taming nature, but Carson gave the preservation movement a new voice in the 1960s. While most earlier conservation efforts focused on protecting land from development, Carson described in graphic detail what pesticides were doing to birds and animals.

Michael Harrington's *The Other America*, also published in 1962, is sometimes credited with launching the Kennedy-Johnson era War on Poverty. Harrington's was far from the only voice urging a new look at the urban and rural poverty that had gone unnoticed in the affluent 1950s, but Harrington's book sold over a million copies, and the critic Dwight McDonald convinced President Kennedy to read it. In his own way, Harrington, like Carson and Jacobs, put a human face on an otherwise easily ignored domestic issue. Describing the way poverty was hidden in modern America cities, Harrington wrote, "The poor still inhabit the miserable housing in the central area….The failures, the unskilled, the disabled, the aged, and the minorities are right there, across the tracks, where they have always been. But hardly anyone else is….They have no face; they have no voice." The War on Poverty began to change that situation in 1964 and 1965.

Betty Friedan's *The Feminine Mystique*, published in 1963, played an equally central role in the development of the new women's movement of the late 1960s and early 1970s (see Chapter 27). *The Feminine Mystique* named what Friedan called the "problem that has no name": the "comfortable concentration camp" where white middle-class suburban women lived. In the late 1960s and early 1970s, a generation of women found multiple ways to break out of this and other "concentration camps."

Each of these books sold thousands, sometimes hundreds of thousands of copies. They were read by college students and people of every age bracket, and were discussed on the radio and television, in newspaper editorials, in sermons in religious communities, and around family dinner tables, bringing their ideas to many who never read them. Each book reflected changes that were already underway and, at the same time, each speeded change.

Significant Dates

1960	Kennedy defeats Nixon for U.S. president
1961	Bay of Pigs invasion of Cuba fails
	JFK meets with Khrushchev in Vienna
	Berlin Wall is built
	New Berlin crisis
1962	U.S. Supreme Court's *Engle v. Vitale* decision
	SDS Port Huron statement
	September—*Silent Spring* by Rachel Carson published
1963	Betty Friedan's *The Feminine Mystique* published
	Protests in South Vietnam; U.S. Supreme Court's *Abingdon v. Schempp* decision
	John F. Kennedy assassinated; Lyndon B. Johnson becomes president
1964	LBJ announces Great Society
	Free Speech Movement at University of California, Berkeley
	LBJ defeats Goldwater, elected to a full term as president
1965	Martin Luther King awarded Nobel Peace Prize
	Malcolm X assassinated; bombing of North Vietnam and troop increases
	LBJ signs Elementary and Secondary Education Act
	LBJ signs Medicare-Medicaid Act
	LBJ signs Voter Registration Act
	LBJ signs Immigration Reform act
1967	Martin Luther King's Riverside Speech attacking the War in Vietnam
1968	Tet Offensive in Vietnam
	Eugene McCarthy's success in New Hampshire Primary
	Robert Kennedy enters presidential race
	Johnson announces he will not seek reelection
	Martin Luther King, Jr. assassinated
	Riots in major cities
	Columbia University sit-in
	Robert Kennedy assassinated
	Democratic National Convention and riots
	Richard M. Nixon elected president

Students for a Democratic Society (SDS)
A student organization, founded in 1960, to give voice to a new wave of student protest.

Joan Baez and Bob Dylan, singing together at the 1963 Newport Folk Festival, represented a new folk music that was often linked directly to protest movements.

Films and music had possibly even more influence on Americans. In the 1960s, film and music took on a new and harder edge. Stanley Kubrick's *Dr. Strangelove* portrayed the leaders of the United States and the Soviet Union as crazed militarists willing to destroy the world. Later in the decade, *Bonnie and Clyde* (1967), *The Wild Bunch*, and *Easy Rider* (both 1969) showed a level of violence not previously seen in film, reminding audiences that this world was still a very violent one.

Many who had enjoyed the provocative rock 'n' roll sexuality of Elvis in the 1950s listened to the provocative protest folk songs of Bob Dylan and Joan Baez in the early 1960s and later to the drug-influenced acid rock of Jimi Hendrix, Pink Floyd, and the Grateful Dead in the later 1960s. Change, protest, and disengagement were increasingly reflected in film and song.

Protest songs and angry movies, however, did not completely dominate the media in the 1960s. The sentimental celebration of love and marriage, *The Sound of Music* (1965), earned $100 million, the highest gross income of any movie up to that time. *The Adventures of Ozzie and Harriet* continued to be one of the most popular TV series up to 1966. In addition, the traditional music on the *Lawrence Welk Show* and the symphonic pop music of Henry Mancini competed with folk and rock throughout the decade. The sixties were far from a unified decade, in culture or politics, but the very depth of the disunity was one of the hallmarks of the times.

The Student Movement of the 1960s

Universities had long been the location for challenges to the norms of the larger society. During the Great Depression of the 1930s, there were many student demonstrations. But the sheer numbers of students and the new attitudes of the baby boom generation who came to college in the 1960s transformed college life. In 1947, as a result of the GI Bill, college enrollments reached an historic high, and they continued to grow in each following decade.

Budgets for higher education grew even faster than enrollments. As sociologist and 1960s student activist Todd Gitlin noted, "By 1960 the United States was the first society in the history of the world with more college students than farmers." Ten years later, the nation had three times as many students as farmers. Although most of the students of the late 1940s and 1950s had been relatively quiet, the students of the 1960s were not.

Students who had founded the Students for a Democratic Society (SDS) in 1960 met at Port Huron, Michigan, in 1962 to draft a statement of their beliefs. The 1962 Port Huron statement, of which Tom Hayden, then a graduate student, was the prime author, began, "We are people of this generation, bred in at least modest comfort, housed now in universities, looking uncomfortably to the world we inherit." Recognizing their baby boom origins, the statement continued, "Many of us began maturing in complacency," but then, "[a]s we grew, however, our comfort was penetrated by events too troubling to dismiss....the Southern struggle against racial bigotry [and] the enclosing fact of the Cold War." The Port Huron statement noted, "a yearning to believe there is an alternative to the present, that something can be done to change circumstances in the school, the work places, the bureaucracies, the

THINKING HISTORICALLY

Rachel Carson's *Silent Spring*, 1962

Rachel Carson grew up in an isolated rural community 15 miles northeast of Pittsburgh on the Allegheny River. As an adult, she worked for the federal Fish and Wildlife Service while also writing independently, publishing *The Sea Around Us,* a description of life in the ocean in 1951. The book was a great success, and Carson decided to then take on a study of the impact of DDT and other chemicals on the environment. The result was Carson's most famous book, *Silent Spring,* which not only caught public imagination but also changed the way many Americans thought about the environment. *Silent Spring* was first published as a series of articles in *The New Yorker* in 1962, then published as a book that same year, and in 1963, aired as part of a CBS television series in 1963. Carson warned:

> Since the mid-1940s over 200 basic chemicals have been created for use in killing insects, weeds, rodents, and other organisms described in the modern vernacular as "pests"; and they are sold under several thousand different brand names.
>
> These sprays, dusts, and aerosols are now applied almost universally to farms, gardens, forests, and homes—nonselective chemicals that have the power to kill every insect, the "good" and the "bad," to still the song of birds and the leaping of fish in the streams, to coat the leaves with deadly film, and to linger on in the soil—all this though the intended target may be only a few weeds or insects. Can anyone believe it is possible to lay down such a barrage of poisons on the surface of the earth without making it unfit for all life? They should not be called "insecticides," but "biocides."

Along with praise for the book, Carson was criticized, most of all by the chemical industry whose products her research and writings indicted. Spokespersons for some of the major chemical companies and even some of Carson's former colleagues in the Department of Agriculture attacked the book as an effort to turn the clock back to a time when insect-born diseases, most of all malaria, killed thousands and wiped out crops causing widespread starvation.

President Kennedy, however, was impressed enough with the book to order his Science Advisory Committee to review it. When the committee confirmed her findings, Kennedy and subsequent administrations took further action, banning the domestic use of DDT. Later in 1970, President Nixon signed the legislation creating the Environmental Protection Agency to consolidate the government's efforts to protect the environment that Carson loved.

Source: Rachel Carson, *Silent Spring* (Boston: Houghton Mifflin, 1962). Two of the several studies analyzing Rachel Carson and *Silent Spring* as well as its impact on the subsequent environmental movement: Mark Hamilton Lytle, *The Gentle Subversive: Rachel Carson, Silent Spring, and the Rise of the Environmental Movement* (New York: Oxford University Press, 2007) and Priscilla Coit Murphy, *What a Book Can Do: The Publication and Reception of Silent Spring* (Amherst: University of Massachusetts Press, 2005).

Thinking Critically

1. Historical Interpretation

How might Carson have responded to critics in the chemical industry? How might the public have evaluated their criticism? How might people's jobs or political views impact their response?

2. Contextualization

Thinking about earlier conservation efforts, like those of Teddy Roosevelt, how was Carson different?

government....It is to this latter yearning, at once the spark and engine of change, that we direct our present appeal." The spark and the "yearning to believe there is an alternative to the present," would characterize the decade of the 1960s for many people, especially the young.

Not long after SDS was launched, another student movement emerged at the University of California at Berkeley. In the fall of 1964, the Berkeley administration issued a directive that student organizations that were raising funds for off-campus causes such as civil rights using tables set up on the university grounds had to move those efforts off campus. Opposition to the directive quickly united students. When petitions and meetings with the university administration did not resolve the issue, a group of students, some of whom had spent the previous summer in the South as part of Mississippi Freedom Summer, called for civil disobedience in Berkeley.

Students brought their tables back to campus and waited to see what would happen. Before long, campus police arrived and arrested Jack Weinberg who had been sitting at one of the tables, placing him in a police car. Quickly, some 3,000 students surrounded the car, and for the next 32 hours, while Weinberg sat in the car, speaker after speaker used the top of the car as a platform. The long spontaneous rally launched the free speech movement at Berkeley.

In December of that year, at a much larger student rally on the Berkeley campus, Mario Savio, a junior philosophy major who emerged as the prime voice of the student protest during the siege of the police car, told his fellow students, "There's a time when the operation of the machine becomes so odious…you've got to put your bodies upon the gears and upon the wheels, upon the levers, upon all the apparatus and you've got to make it stop." Hundreds marched into the administration building to stop the university's wheels. They sat in for two days until arrested. Berkeley remained a center of student protest.

| 26.1 | **Quick Review** How did student protest, changes in popular music, and the inauguration of John F. Kennedy symbolize the changes coming to the United States in the early 1960s? |

CAMELOT, THE WHITE HOUSE, AND DALLAS—THE KENNEDY ADMINISTRATION

| 26.2 | Analyze the successes and failures of the Kennedy administration and how they interacted with popular culture in the United States. |

The student protests were but one aspect of the changes taking place in the early 1960s. The January 1961 inauguration of John F. Kennedy (referred to often as JFK) brought the youngest president elected in the nation's history to replace the oldest. A new generation was taking charge of the country from college campuses to the White House. Kennedy partisans remembered his years in office as "one brief shining moment"—to cite the lines of the then-popular *Camelot*, a Broadway play about medieval glory to which the Kennedy's glamour was often compared. Certainly John Kennedy, his young and attractive wife Jacqueline Bouvier Kennedy, and their extended family made for a dramatic comparison with the sometimes dowdy Eisenhowers. They were able to project an image of glamour, youth, vigor (the president's favorite word, pronouncing it with his Boston accent as "vigah"), and wit. The press loved to spar with Kennedy and he with them. During the Kennedy years, the White House was the scene of gala events, concerts, and dinner parties not seen in Washington for some time. The hopes and expectations for change that arrived with Kennedy were unmistakable.

The New Frontier

Civil rights advocates also had high hopes for the Kennedy administration, believing that the new president, who had gone out of his way as a candidate to support Martin Luther King, Jr., would do more to support the cause of civil rights than Eisenhower. The Kennedy administration created a Committee on Equal Employment Opportunities headed by Vice President Johnson to look into discrimination in hiring. They hired blacks in the federal government, including some in high positions in the civil and foreign service. JFK nominated African-Americans, including Thurgood Marshall, to federal judgeships. During the presidential campaign in 1960, Kennedy promised to introduce a new federal civil rights bill if elected. But throughout 1961 and 1962, no such bill emerged from the White House. He also had promised to end racial discrimination in federal housing with the "stroke of a pen," but when no order emerged, civil rights organizers started sending thousands of pens to him.

Kennedy was slow to move on civil rights for many reasons. He could count votes in the Congress, and southern Senators with high seniority made congressional action hard to imagine. The Kennedys were also good at gauging voter interest, and in 1961

Jacqueline Kennedy and her husband made the White House a center of grace and culture as in this reception honoring Nobel Prize winners including the poet Robert Frost and the novelist Pearl Buck.

and 1962, not that many white voters seemed interested in civil rights issues. At the same time, J. Edgar Hoover hated Martin Luther King, Jr., and was convinced that he was a sexual degenerate and a Communist. He had tapes to prove extramarital activity on King's part, if nothing to show that he was a Communist. Hoover also had tapes to prove President Kennedy's considerable extramarital activities, which may well have made both Kennedy brothers reluctant to challenge Hoover, who they allowed to tap King's telephones. Whatever the reasons, the vaunted Kennedy vigor was not brought to civil rights.

In other areas, Kennedy's **New Frontier**, as he called his domestic policy, was more successful. Working closely with House Speaker Sam Rayburn, the administration was able to win an increase in the federally mandated minimum wage. At their urging, Congress also provided funds for job training and tougher regulations for testing new drugs before they went on the market. JFK was the first president since Herbert Hoover to include no women in the cabinet, but he appointed Eleanor Roosevelt to head the Presidential Commission on the Status of Women that recommended federal laws against sex discrimination. Kennedy issued executive orders ending sex discrimination in the federal civil service and signed a 1963 Equal Pay Act that mandated equal pay for equal work. In part because of his mentally ill sister, Kennedy cared deeply about mental health and, at his urging, Congress passed the Mental Retardation Facilities and Community Mental Health Act in 1963 that funded support for mental health programs.

In May 1961, Kennedy, who had been critical of the lack of interest in space exploration by the Eisenhower administration, advocated a significant increase in funding for the National Aeronautics and Space Administration (NASA) and made a promise that within 10 years the United States would safely land a man on the moon. Although Kennedy did not live to see the promise fulfilled, in 1969, the nation celebrated that accomplishment.

The chair of his Council of Economic Advisers, Walter Heller, convinced Kennedy that a tax cut would stimulate the economy leading to greater prosperity for Americans and improved standing of the Kennedy administration with voters. Kennedy fought

New Frontier
The name given to the domestic programs of the Kennedy administration (1961–1963).

hard for the tax cut and won. Nevertheless, the domestic record was disappointing to the administration, which would have liked to see faster congressional action on many of its proposals. The *New York Times* for November 12, 1963, said, "Rarely has there been such a pervasive attitude of discouragement around Capitol Hill…This has been one of the least productive sessions of Congress within the memory of most of its members."

Religion, Education, and the Courts

Just as Kennedy had his reasons for not wanting to deal with civil rights, he also had very strong reasons for not wanting to deal with the issue of religion. As the first Catholic to be elected president, he wanted to steer clear of anything that might imply his religion was influencing his work. But as with civil rights, issues of religion were bubbling.

Engel v. Vitale
U.S. Supreme Court decision that banned mandated prayers or devotional Bible reading in American public schools.

On June 25, 1962, the U.S. Supreme Court announced its decision in the case of ***Engel v. Vitale***. By a 6-1 vote, the Court declared that schools in New York State could not open the school day with prayer. The specific issue in *Engel v. Vitale* was of relatively recent origin. As the Cold War led to a fear of "godless communism," the New York State Board of Regents, which had responsibility for all public schools in the state of New York, recommended—but did not require—opening the school day with prayer. Then in 1958, the board composed a short official prayer, "Almighty God, we acknowledge our dependence upon Thee, and we beg Thy blessings upon us, our parents, our teachers and our Country." It was as inoffensive as a prayer could be, and any students who objected could be excused when it was recited. Nevertheless, the prayer caused problems. Nonbelievers did not want to say any prayer. Devout believers found such a bland prayer close to blasphemy. When Joseph and Daniel Roth asked to be excused from their Long Island classroom during the prayer because their father asked them to, they were taunted. Their father, Lawrence Roth, challenged the prayer in court. As the case was combined with others and moved through the courts, it generated public attention and anger. In the end, Justice Hugo Black spoke for the Supreme Court majority in saying, "We think that the constitutional prohibition against laws respecting an establishment of religion must at least mean that in this country it is no part of the business of government to compose official prayers."

A year later, the court went further. Edward and Sidney Schempp challenged the policy of the Abington Township School Board (Pennsylvania), which opened the school day with a Bible reading and the Lord's Prayer. In a 1963 decision, *Abington School Board v. Schempp*, the U.S. Supreme Court ruled that, no matter who composed the prayers, the school board's practices or any devotional reading of scriptures or recitation of prayers was unconstitutional. The court went out of its way to insist that the academic study of religion, including the study of the Bible "for its literary and historic qualities," was not only constitutional but also to be encouraged. However, it was not the business of government, the Court said, to lead devotional activities.

The Supreme Court's decisions provoked a fire storm. Many Americans, Protestants and Catholics, claimed that the court was "legislating God out of the public schools" and that historic practices that "had never bothered anyone" were being undermined by an unusually activist Warren court. New York Congressman Frank J. Becker proposed an amendment to the Constitution to allow voluntary prayer and Bible reading. The evangelist Billy Graham said, "The trend of taking God and moral teaching from the schools is a diabolical scheme." Alabama Governor George Wallace said, "I don't care what they say in Washington, we are going to keep right on praying and reading the Bible in the public schools of Alabama." While Catholics had once opposed devotional activities in public schools, sure that they would be Protestant, now New York Archbishop Francis Cardinal Spellman said he was "shocked and frightened" by the court's decisions. For large numbers of Americans, the decisions were the beginnings of a cultural war that would last for decades.

Kennedy's Foreign Policy—From the Bay of Pigs to the Cuban Missile Crisis

In a private conversation with his defeated rival, Richard Nixon, President Kennedy asked Nixon, "Foreign affairs is the only important issue for a president to handle, isn't it?" Kennedy said he really didn't care about the minimum wage "compared to something like Cuba." While Americans receiving minimum wage might care a great deal about it, Kennedy's focus was, indeed, Cuba, Germany, Vietnam, China, and perhaps most of all the Soviet Union. In his inaugural address, Kennedy had promised to "pay any price, bear any burden, meet any hardship, support any friend, oppose any foe to assure the survival and success of liberty." He came to office a devout Cold Warrior and remained one.

The first test of Kennedy's Cold War resolve came early. The corrupt government of Cuban dictator Fulgencio Batista had been overthrown at the beginning of 1959 in the middle of Eisenhower's second term. The new revolutionary government led by Fidel Castro was very popular in the United States during its first few months in office. Castro was welcomed in the United States and even appeared on the *Ed Sullivan Show*. Organized crime, which had enjoyed a haven for gambling and prostitution in Cuba under Batista, was driven out by Castro to the applause of most Americans. However the Cuban-American relationship quickly soured. The new revolutionary government executed a number of Batista supporters—too many, most Americans thought. As part of its land reform efforts, the Castro government seized the island's large commercial enterprises, including vast holdings of American sugar and oil companies. Unhappy business interests—legitimate and illegitimate—began a public relations campaign against the new Cuban government. Castro's communist leanings also became clearer as Cuba developed close ties with the Soviet Union. Before long, Soviet military advisers arrived in Cuba. By the time Kennedy came to office in January 1961, many considered Cuba to be a virtual satellite of the Soviet Union. The Eisenhower administration had developed plans to train a volunteer force to invade the island. Influential people, including JFK's father, former ambassador Joseph P. Kennedy, urged Kennedy to take action. While some advisers had reservations, Allen Dulles, the head of the Central Intelligence Agency (CIA), was a strong advocate, and Secretary of Defense McNamara and the Joint Chiefs of Staff approved the invasion.

On April 15, 1961, less than 3 months after JFK took office, American-based planes made an initial bombing run against the island. Two days later, a brigade of 1,400 U.S. volunteer troops landed at the **Bay of Pigs** on Cuba's south coast. The plan was for the force to connect with other Cuban anti-Castro forces that the CIA was convinced were ready to rise up against the regime. In fact, no internal revolt sprang up. Cuban defenses were strong. When the attackers called for further air support from the United States, Kennedy refused. He had become convinced that the attack was doomed. Within hours, 114 of the invaders were killed and 1,189 taken prisoner. The Bay of Pigs fiasco was a huge embarrassment for Kennedy. He took personal responsibility for the failure. He also fired Allen Dulles. For the rest of his term, Kennedy would be more cautious and less willing to trust advisers in the CIA.

Bay of Pigs
A 1961 invasion of Cuba by anti-Castro rebels backed by the Kennedy administration that was quickly defeated, much to Kennedy's embarrassment.

Kennedy's first summit with Soviet leader Nikita Khrushchev took place in June 1961 in Vienna, just 2 months after the Bay of Pigs crisis. The meeting did not go well. Khrushchev gloated over the Soviet Union's success in getting the first man into space when Yuri Gagarin orbited the earth in April. He also made threatening comments about Berlin. Khrushchev seemed to believe that the new president was weak and could be brow-beaten. In fact, his actions only strengthened Kennedy's inclination to show he could be tough. Two months later, Khrushchev ordered the construction of what came to be known as the **Berlin Wall** to separate the Soviet zone of the city from the western zone and the construction of similar barriers separating all of East Germany from West Germany. German Communists complained that their socialist system provided free education for people who then took their skills west to make more money. After August 1961, no such easy movement, nor were family visits or other travel possible.

Berlin Wall
A substantive partition built by East Germany on instructions from the Soviet Union that cut off all travel between East and West Berlin from 1961 to 1989.

MEDIUM RANGE BALLISTIC MISSILE BASE IN CUBA

SAN CRISTOBAL

LAUNCH POSITION

MISSILE-READY TENTS

MISSILE ERECTORS

LATE OCTOBER

An American surveillance plane took pictures like this one of missile facilities in Cuba that deeply worried the Kennedy administration.

By fall, Berlin had become very tense. Some Kennedy advisers suggested that the United States should use force to stop construction of the Berlin Wall. Others wondered whether access would be blocked as it was at the time of the Berlin Airlift. By the end of October, U.S. and Russian tanks faced off in Berlin. Some wondered whether World War III was about to begin. Eventually, the United States and the Soviet Union compromised. Kennedy acknowledged that he would "rather have a wall than a war," and that the Soviets had a right to build the Berlin Wall. Khrushchev did not try to close off American or western access to Berlin as Stalin had done. While the city remained a flash point in the Cold War, and the Berlin Wall stayed in place until November 1989, the Berlin crisis of 1961 passed.

The third major foreign policy crisis of the Kennedy administration—and the most dangerous—took place in October 1962. Again, the focus was Cuba. After the U.S. failure in the Bay of Pigs invasion, Cuban-Russian ties grew stronger and the Soviets sent more military personnel to Cuba. In the summer of 1962, the Soviets began building missile bases in Cuba that could house medium-range missiles pointed at the United States. As U.S. reconnaissance flights showed proof of the missiles in Cuba, it became clear that a major crisis—the **Cuban missile crisis**—was brewing.

In this crisis atmosphere, Kennedy convened an "Executive Committee" of the National Security Council. For 13 tense days in October 1962, these advisers debated the next U.S. step. Moderates led by UN Ambassador Adlai Stevenson urged restraint. Why panic about a new missile site, they asked, when the United States had missiles in Turkey and there were enough submarine-based missiles to destroy the planet?

Cuban missile crisis
A tense standoff between the United States and the Soviet Union in October 1962 at which each country stood on the brink of nuclear war over the placement of Soviet missiles in Cuba.

Hard-liners, including former Secretary of State Dean Acheson and National Security Adviser McGeorge Bundy, urged an immediate U.S. attack on the missile site. A third group, led by Robert Kennedy, opposed a surprise strike, which, RFK said, would make his brother, "the Tojo [the Japanese premiere who ordered the attack on Pearl Harbor] of the 1960s." The president agreed with his brother's position and overruled the hard-liners, but he was also determined to be tough.

On October 22, President Kennedy informed Khrushchev in both a diplomatic communication and a prime-time television speech that the United States would enforce a complete "quarantine" against future military shipments to Cuba and that the United States would meet any Soviet retaliation anywhere in the world with a "full retaliatory response." The stakes could not be higher. If a Soviet ship ran the blockade, it would be fired on by the United States. If the Soviets made a military move, the United States was prepared to fire missiles. Many worried that the world was on the brink of nuclear war. The next morning, as the first Soviet ships approached, people held their breaths. Then the Soviet freighters turned around. Secretary of State Dean Rusk said, "We're eyeball to eyeball, and the other fellow just blinked."

Behind the scenes, Kennedy and Khrushchev had come to an agreement. The Soviets agreed to remove the missiles in return for an end to the quarantine of the island and a promise that the United States would not invade. The United States also agreed to remove its missiles from Turkey but did not announce its decision. An unthinkable war had been avoided. Both leaders quickly took steps to avoid a repeat of the crisis and new communication systems—especially a "hot line" from the Pentagon and White House to the Kremlin—were set up so there would be no delay in communication in any future crisis.

Some military leaders and Cuban exiles were furious at Kennedy. U.S. Air Force General Curtis LeMay (who had commanded the bombing of Tokyo in 1945) stunned the president when he told him, "It's the greatest defeat in our history, Mr. President....We should invade today." Others wondered whether Kennedy allowed his machismo to get the best of him when the missiles in Cuba were no more of a threat than others already in place and hardly worth a world war.

While the crises in Cuba, Berlin, and then Cuba again were the most significant of Kennedy's foreign policy, the president also faced others. In spite of the 1960 campaign rhetoric in which Kennedy had accused Eisenhower of allowing a "missile gap" to develop between the United States and the Soviet Union, once in office, Kennedy acknowledged that no such gap existed. Nevertheless, the Kennedy administration increased military spending from $47.4 billion when it took office to $53.6 billion in its last budget. The United States expanded the number of Polaris submarines armed with missiles as well as the number of land-based missiles in the United States. Each side had enough missiles to destroy the world multiple times.

The administration created a new "flexible response" policy as an alternative to Eisenhower's "mutually assured destruction." They gave high priority to creating "counterinsurgency" forces, named the Green Berets, that could engage in small-scale military operations in hot spots around the world. In planning for Cuba, where the administration had a special interest, they developed Operation Mongoose, a secret CIA program to destabilize the Castro regime by contaminating Cuban sugar, causing explosions in Cuban factories, and developing at least 33 plans to assassinate Castro, all of which failed.

In addition to Kennedy's foreign policy efforts to contain communism, the administration launched a new effort at peace in Laos, support for the U.S. Agency for International Development (AID), and efforts at economic reform in Latin America and elsewhere. Kennedy also launched the **Peace Corps**, through an Executive Order, to recruit young idealistic Americans to spend 2 years abroad as volunteers working on education and development projects. In the spring of his first year in office, the president, joined by First Lady Jacqueline Kennedy, dazzled Europe.

Peace Corps
A program launched by the Kennedy administration to recruit young idealistic Americans to spend 2 years abroad as volunteers working on education and development projects.

Lyndon Johnson took the oath of office on board the presidential plane flanked by his wife, Lady Bird, and Jacqueline Kennedy, still wearing a bloodstained suit.

By the end of his first term, however, Kennedy's foreign policy legacy was mixed. Chester Bowles, who served for a time as Undersecretary of State in the Kennedy administration, said that the Kennedy inner circle were "full of belligerence" and "sort of looking for a chance to prove their muscle." A nuclear-armed world was a dangerous place to do such a thing. Nevertheless, in November 1963, in spite of ongoing tensions in Southeast Asia, Berlin, and Cuba, JFK was still immensely popular in many parts of the world, and the world was at peace. The president turned his attention to his 1964 reelection campaign.

Dallas, Conspiracies, and Legacies

The Kennedy team wanted to ensure that Texas, home of the vice president, stayed Democratic in 1964. But the Democratic Party in Texas was deeply divided. There was also deep distrust of Kennedy in Texas by 1963, indeed, even a deep visceral hatred among some Texans. In November 1963, Kennedy dreaded the trip he needed to make to build his standing in the Lone Star State.

After the president and Jackie Kennedy arrived in Dallas on November 22, 1963, they rode into the city center in a caravan, the president and First Lady along with Texas Governor John Connally and his wife in the first car, Vice President Johnson in the next one. A little after noon, as they passed the Texas School Book Depository, several shots rang out. One wounded Connally. Two hit the president. A back brace he wore for constant back pain held him erect and the second shot hit his head. By the time the president's car reached the nearest emergency room, the president was dead. A Catholic priest offered the last rites.

Vice President Lyndon Johnson had been right behind Kennedy's car and quickly understood what had happened. Neither Johnson nor anyone else knew how many people were involved in the assassination or how widespread the danger might be, so Johnson insisted that the presidential party wait until Kennedy's coffin was brought to Air Force One, still parked at the airport where it had arrived that morning. In the afternoon Johnson, flanked by his wife Lady Bird and by Jacqueline Kennedy, took the presidential oath of office. Then they flew to Washington. Kennedy's death provoked an outpouring of national grief. Suddenly, the youthful vigor that the president had projected, and the hopes that many Americans had projected onto him, seemed to dim.

Lee Harvey Oswald was arrested for the murder. His fingerprints were on the gun and he had easy access to the window where the shots were fired. Two days later, another troubled man, Jack Ruby, shot Oswald in the Dallas police station. Many suspected a widespread conspiracy. President Johnson asked Supreme Court Chief Justice Earl Warren to lead a high-level bipartisan commission to find out the truth. The commission's report—known as the Warren Report—concluded that Oswald acted alone. Not everyone was convinced; no one could confirm for sure the whole story behind Kennedy's death. Whatever the truth, a very different kind of person became president on November 22, one who would lead the administration and the country with a dramatically different style and set of priorities.

26.2 **Quick Review** What were the major accomplishments and frustrations of the Kennedy administration?

THE COMING OF LYNDON B. JOHNSON

26.3 Analyze the successes and failures of the Johnson administration in terms of the two issues that dominated his years in office—the launching of the Great Society programs and the war in Vietnam.

John F. Kennedy had been born to wealth and had attended Harvard College. As a child, he had met Franklin D. Roosevelt because his father was Roosevelt's ambassador to Great Britain. He was elected to Congress as a war hero after his small boat, PT-109 had been sunk in the Pacific during World War II, and he had served 8 years in the U.S. Senate before becoming president. Kennedy was handsome and charismatic, important factors in his election and continuing popularity.

Lyndon Johnson was born to poverty in the Texas hill country northwest of San Antonio and grew up in a small house in Johnson City when there were no sidewalks or electricity. His tough and slightly wild father served in the Texas legislature, trying hard to make ends meet, and his strong-willed mother yearned for a better life. LBJ, as he was often called, attended Southwest Texas State Teachers College. He arrived in Washington as a congressional secretary a year before Roosevelt was elected and managed to meet FDR, whom he idolized and who in 1935 appointed the then 26-year-old LBJ as the director of the National Youth Administration for the state of Texas. Johnson worked harder than any other NYA state director, got important services for Texas, and never forgot the value of government when he saw the New Deal bring jobs, electricity, and hope to people living isolated lives in rural poverty.

Johnson had a long and distinguished career in Congress before becoming vice president. He was first elected to the House of Representatives in 1937. He campaigned tirelessly and worked equally tirelessly once in office, building strong ties and coalitions. LBJ and his wife Lady Bird became a family for the sometimes lonely bachelor, Sam Rayburn, another Texan, who served as Speaker of the House for all but 4 years between 1940 and 1961. LBJ lost a primary race for a Senate seat in 1941 but won the seat in 1948. Once in the Senate, Johnson built connections to the powerful committee chairs. In 1953, at the age of 45, he was elected Democratic leader in the Senate. In 1955, he suffered a severe heart attack, recovered quickly and kept working, kept building coalitions, becoming known for the "Johnson Treatment" when he would grab a colleague by the coat lapels and hold his face an inch away while using anger, humor, and statistics to win a wavering vote. He was highly respected for his ability to get things done in the Senate, even if he was often feared and seldom liked. Few said he was handsome or charismatic. Everyone said he was effective.

Johnson hated his tenure as vice president. Many of Kennedy's inner circle, especially Attorney General Robert Kennedy made sure he was kept out of the most significant decisions. Once he became president, LBJ desperately wanted to be loved as Kennedy had been, but most of all was determined to get things done in a way that Kennedy had not been able to do. On the domestic front, he succeeded masterfully at moving his agenda along before slowly sinking into the morass of Vietnam.

The War on Poverty and the Great Society

In his first speech as president, 5 days after Kennedy was shot, LBJ mourned with the nation, but he also demonstrated a confident leadership that the country was looking for. Johnson told the Congress that he was determined to continue the "Kennedy dream" of education, jobs, care for the elderly, and "equal rights for all Americans." One could question whether, given his focus on foreign policy, those goals had actually been Kennedy's dream, but they would certainly be Johnson's. Thus, the first president from a former Confederate state insisted, "No memorial or oration or eulogy could more eloquently honor President Kennedy's memory than the earliest possible passage of the civil rights bill for which he fought so long." Congress was being put on notice that the former powerful Democratic majority leader of the Senate, now president, was determined to see his legislation passed.

The famous Johnson treatment shown here as President Johnson sought the support of Senator Theodore Green of Rhode Island.

American Voices

Lyndon B. Johnson, "Great Society Speech," 1964

Six months after he had taken the oath of office in Dallas, Lyndon Johnson gave the commencement address at the University of Michigan. He used the speech to outline a new program—a Johnson program to be known as the Great Society—to improve the quality of life for all Americans.

I have come today from the turmoil of your Capital to the tranquility of your campus to speak about the future of your country....

Your imagination, your initiative, and your indignation will determine whether we build a society where progress is the servant of our needs, or a society where old values and new visions are buried under unbridled growth. For in your time we have the opportunity to move not only toward the rich society and the powerful society, but upward to the Great Society.

The Great Society rests on abundance and liberty for all. It demands an end to poverty and racial injustice, to which we are totally committed in our time. But that is just the beginning.

The Great Society is a place where every child can find knowledge to enrich his mind and to enlarge his talents....

So I want to talk to you today about three places where we begin to build the Great Society—in our cities, in our countryside, and in our classrooms....

Our society will never be great until our cities are great. Today the frontier of imagination and innovation is inside those cities and not beyond their borders.

New experiments are already going on. It will be the task of your generation to make the American city a place where future generations will come, not only to live but to live the good life....

A second place where we begin to build the Great Society is in our countryside. We have always prided ourselves on being not only America the strong and America the free, but America the beautiful. Today that beauty is in danger. The water we drink, the food we eat, the very air that we breathe, are threatened with pollution. Our parks are overcrowded, our seashores overburdened. Green fields and dense forests are disappearing....

A third place to build the Great Society is in the classrooms of America. There your children's lives will be shaped. Our society will not be great until every young mind is set free to scan the farthest reaches of thought and imagination. We are still far from that goal....

These are three of the central issues of the Great Society....

So, will you join in the battle to give every citizen the full equality which God enjoins and the law requires, whatever his belief, or race, or the color of his skin?

Will you join in the battle to give every citizen an escape from the crushing weight of poverty?

Will you join in the battle to make it possible for all nations to live in enduring peace—as neighbors and not as mortal enemies?

Will you join in the battle to build the Great Society, to prove that our material progress is only the foundation on which we will build a richer life of mind and spirit?

Source: Lyndon B. Johnson, Speech to the Graduating Class, University of Michigan, Ann Arbor, May 22, 1964, Public Papers of the Presidents of the United States, Lyndon B. Johnson, Book I (1963-64), pp. 704–707.

Thinking Critically

1. Documentary Analysis

What are some of the specific elements that Johnson included in his definition of the Great Society?

2. Historical Interpretation

Knowing that Johnson idolized Franklin Roosevelt, what parallels do you see between the Great Society and the New Deal?

Later, after he left office, Johnson explained his approach to the presidency. "If it's really going to work, the relationship between the President and the Congress has got to be almost incestuous. He's got to know them even better than they know themselves. And then, on the basis of this knowledge, he's got to build a system that stretches..., from the moment a bill is introduced to the moment it is officially enrolled as the law of the land." And that was exactly what Johnson did. He made sure he knew who would support each bill, knew what the specific desires were of those who might be brought to support a measure, and knew how to cajole those who did not want to support it. He rewarded supporters with phone calls, personal notes, White House invitations, and special services in their states and districts, and he never hesitated to punish opponents. He came to office with a Democratic majority in both houses of Congress and a nation mourning a fallen president. He used that circumstance, plus his incredible legislative skill, to move significant legislation through an often reluctant Congress.

Johnson's first agenda was the stalled civil rights bill. Everyone expected the bill that Kennedy had submitted to be watered down. Johnson, normally the great compromiser, would not allow any tampering with the bill. He was determined to keep every section intact. He broke with his Senate mentor, Richard Russell of Georgia who led the opposition to the bill, and, instead, made an alliance with the Republican Senate Minority Leader, Everett Dirksen of Illinois. With Dirksen's help, Republicans and Democrats overcame a Russell-led filibuster. The most sweeping civil rights bill since Reconstruction was passed and signed by Johnson on July 2, 1964. It included not only provisions for equal access and equal opportunity but also specifically forbade discrimination in employment based on race, color, religion, and national origin as well as outlawed discrimination based on sex, a clause that later feminists would use most effectively. The law established a new Equal Employment Opportunity Commission to ensure enforcement.

As Johnson pushed hard for the Civil Rights Act of 1964, he also tackled a broader agenda. In his first State of the Union speech in January 1964, Johnson said, "This administration, today, here and now, declares unconditional war on poverty in America." Then in May, he used the commencement speech at the University of Michigan to describe what he called the **Great Society**, which would be how he described all of his domestic programs. Kennedy had already started efforts to attack poverty in the United States, but Johnson, the New Dealer from Texas, had seen what federally financed rural electrification did to change the lives of poor people and was passionate (see Map 26-1). He idolized Franklin Roosevelt and wanted to imitate him. He also knew that if he wanted to remain in office, he would have to face a skeptical electorate in only 11 months and he wanted to present a solid track record.

The first legislation of the war on poverty was passed by Congress in August 1964. It included provision for many of the programs later associated with the Great Society, including Volunteers in Service to America (VISTA), a domestic peace corps that recruited young people to work for a year serving in high poverty urban and rural settings; a Neighborhood Youth Corps to provide jobs for poor youth (modeled on the Civilian Conservation Corps of the New Deal era); work study loans and grants to support college students; small business loans; community action programs directed at building up grass-roots organizing ventures; Head Start to provide poor children with the same sort of readiness for kindergarten that their more well-off counterparts got at home; Neighborhood Legal Services that provided government funded lawyers for the poor; and to coordinate all of these ventures, an Office of Economic Opportunity. This impressive agenda was only a first step for Johnson, but to do more, he needed to be elected in his own right.

Johnson wanted to not only win election in 1964 but also win with such a mandate that nothing could stand in the way of his programs. Before he could do that, however, Johnson had to face a divided Democratic Party, a Republican opponent, and his own inner demons. Johnson's insecurities ran deep. He knew that the Kennedy family despised him. He knew that he did not have their urbane sophistication and that, a century after the Civil War, much of the country still distrusted southerners. He also knew—powerfully so—that he had become president—the office he had wanted all his life—only through a terrible tragedy.

Despite his concerns, however, Americans saw LBJ as the sitting president who had taken command of the situation when JFK was killed, and Johnson had no serious resistance to the 1964 nomination. Notwithstanding, Johnson was under great pressure to name Attorney General Robert Kennedy as his running mate. There was a logic to the move; Bobby (as he was always known) was keeper of the Kennedy legacy and his nomination would unite the party. Still, as Johnson later wrote, "With Bobby on the ticket, I'd never know if I could be elected on my own." In addition, Johnson deeply disliked Bobby Kennedy. He was convinced that Bobby had tried to derail his own vice presidential nomination in 1960. Eventually, LBJ informed Bobby that he

The Great Society
The name Lyndon Johnson gave to his far-reaching domestic program, which included federal aid to education, Medicare and Medicaid health insurance, immigration reform, and a Voting Rights Act.

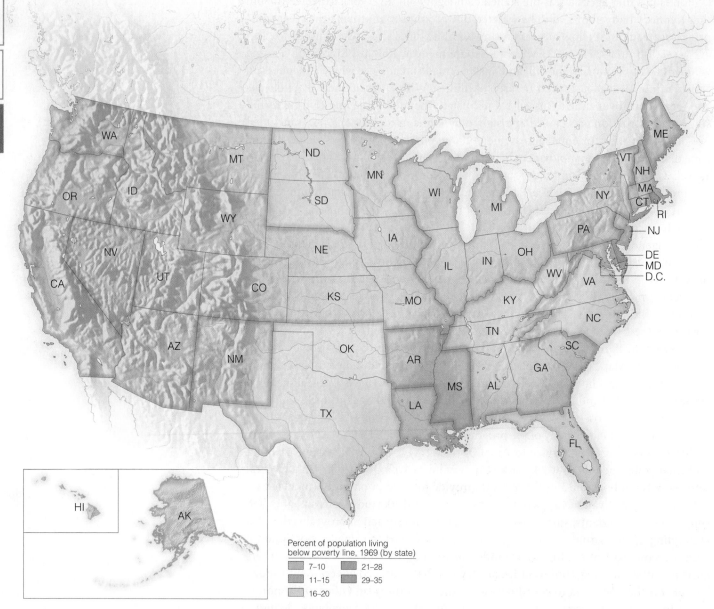

Percent of population living
below poverty line, 1969 (by state)

7–10   21–28
11–15   29–35
16–20

MAP 26-1 Americans in Poverty. This map shows the percentage and distribution of Americans living below the poverty line at the end of the 1960s.

would not be his running mate and, instead, supported him in a successful run for the U.S. Senate from New York. Johnson selected liberal Minnesota Senator Hubert Humphrey to be his vice president. Humphrey, though more liberal than Kennedy or Johnson, was also deeply loyal to Johnson, perhaps even to a fault.

The most serious challenge to Johnson's easy nomination came from the Mississippi Freedom Democratic Party (MFDP), in which grass-roots civil rights activists sought the convention seats of the regular Mississippi delegation that had been elected in white-only caucuses (see Chapter 25). Although Johnson was a supporter of civil rights, he was concerned that, if the "regular" Mississippi delegates were unseated by the Mississippi Freedom delegates and walked out, and those from

Alabama and other nearby states joined them, then it would threaten the Democrats' hold on several southern states. Johnson did not want to risk a repeat of the 1948 Dixiecrat revolt. Neither Johnson nor other party leaders understood the depth of anger that stirred the MFDP protest, nor did they see, as the MFDP leaders did, the way in which the movement represented a new form of grass-roots democracy. Neither the choice of running mate nor the MFDP challenge hurt Johnson's election chances, but both illustrated deep divides in American politics that even Johnson's masterful negotiating skills could not bridge.

The Republican Party was also deeply divided in 1964. The original front runner for the Republican nomination, New York's liberal governor Nelson Rockefeller, had left his wife of many years to marry a younger woman. At that point, the country had never elected a divorced person as president. There was also further opposition to Rockefeller's nomination. Many conservative Republicans were determined that in 1964 the party would nominate a "real conservative," and Rockefeller's main opponent for the nomination was a true conservative, Arizona Senator Barry Goldwater.

One of the most effective political advertisements of all time began with a little girl pulling petals off of a daisy and, as she finishes, the screen morphs into a nuclear explosion and ends, "Vote for President Johnson on November 3." The ad was part of an effective campaign in which Democrats painted the Republican nominee, Barry Goldwater, as ready to lead America into nuclear war.

Goldwater, an affable and tolerant individual, had friends across the political spectrum and spurned personal racial prejudice. However, he opposed civil rights legislation as an invasion of personal freedom. He felt the same way about the graduated income tax and most other government programs. Further, he called for a more aggressive opposition to communism than that taken by Eisenhower, Kennedy, or Johnson, even in places where communist regimes were well established, saying that America, "could lob one into the men's room at the Kremlin." He won most of the primary contests, and when the Republican convention met in San Francisco, the delegates were so committed to him that they shouted down Nelson Rockefeller. When Goldwater spoke, he said, "Let me remind you that extremism in defense of liberty is no vice…and that moderation in pursuit of justice is no virtue." It was just what the delegates wanted to hear. It was less popular, however, with the wider electorate.

The Democrats made good use of Goldwater's statements, developed a sophisticated television advertising campaign, and painted Goldwater as a dangerous man. Johnson won in a landslide. As he left the inaugural ball in January 1965, Johnson told his staff, "Don't stay up late. There's work to be done. We're on our way to the Great Society." The next day that work started.

In the spring of 1965, the triumphant Johnson pushed four major pieces of legislation through Congress in addition to a raft of other bills that, on their own, would have been considered significant with any other Congress. The core Great Society legislation of 1965 included federal aid to education, Medicare and Medicaid, immigration reform, and a Voting Rights Act.

Johnson knew that federal aid to education had been blocked for many years by civil rights activists out of the fear that aid might go only to segregated schools and by a deadlock between Catholic representatives, who would not support aid unless it went to parochial as well as public schools, and many Protestant representatives, who would never support aid to Catholic schools. Johnson was determined to break the deadlock. The Civil Rights Act of 1964 solved the first issue since it made it illegal for any segregated institution to receive federal aid. Johnson solved the divide on religion with a policy by which federal education funds would follow the child, whichever school the child was in. The Elementary and Secondary Education Act was submitted to Congress in January 1965 and passed in 3 months. Johnson signed it at a ceremony in front of a school that he had once attended, with one of his former teachers sitting beside him.

Every Democratic president since Franklin Roosevelt had also sought to provide federal health insurance, especially for the elderly. A coalition, led by the American Medical Association, fearing government control of medical practices, stopped every effort. However, half of all Americans over 65 had no health insurance and they, too, were a powerful constituency. Within months of being proposed, Congress created Medicare, offering basic medical insurance to everyone over 65. Arkansas Congressman Wilbur Mills, a close Johnson ally, added a provision to the Medicare bill, creating Medicaid, which provided federal funding for medical insurance to Americans living in poverty. For some old and poor people, the resulting Medicare and Medicaid legislation enabled the first visit to a medical doctor in their lives.

Even though there was not a lot of pressure to reform the nation's immigration laws in the 1960s, Johnson was determined to make immigration reform a part of the Great Society. The highly restrictive laws of 1921 and 1923 drastically limited immigration, virtually cutting off anyone from eastern Europe, Africa, or Asia (see Chapter 19). Pressure for change came from New York Representative Emanuel Celler who had tried and failed to get an exception to the old and restrictive "national origin" quotas so that Jews could flee Nazi Germany and who was now determined to change the law (see Chapter 23).

The Immigration Act of 1965 abolished the old quotas though it hardly made immigration easy. The legislation held the total number of immigrants at 290,000 (the number who were expected annually under the old law), but established priorities for education and skills rather than national origin. The law also provided an important loophole, allowing immigration above the new quota for close relatives of U.S. citizens, including foreigners who married a citizen. Although little change was expected when the legislation was signed, the new immigration law represented the beginning of a significant new era of immigration, one that matched and then exceeded the number of immigrants who came to the United States from 1890 to 1920.

The fourth major piece of legislation that Congress enacted in 1965 was the Voting Rights Act. As 1965 began, Johnson did not have additional civil rights legislation on his agenda. The Civil Rights Act of 1964 was the most significant Congressional intervention in civil rights since Reconstruction. Johnson wanted to focus in 1965 on other aspects of his Great Society and did not relish another round of conflict with Richard Russell and other southern Senators. Civil rights leaders, however, did not mean to take a back seat to anyone else's agenda.

Martin Luther King, Jr., decided to create a national confrontation around the right to vote (see Chapter 25). The 1964 Civil Rights Act banned segregation in public accommodations and the use of federal funds for any segregated institution, but it did not address the right to vote. In many parts of the Deep South, more than 90 percent of blacks were kept off the voting rolls. As they had for decades, county voting registrars used literacy tests and other techniques to make it extremely hard for a black person to register to vote, and, as Fannie Lou Hammer's eloquent testimony at the 1964 Democratic convention showed, when legal techniques failed, outright violence was used. The Mississippi Freedom Democratic Party may not have gotten seated at that 1964 convention, but they had made an impression on many Americans. King and the SCLC were determined to keep the issue of the vote for African-Americans alive. When they selected Selma, Alabama, as the site for a major confrontation, SNCC, which had focused on voting rights from its founding, agreed to join. Segregation in Selma was rigid, despite the Civil Rights Act. The city of 29,000 included 15,000 blacks of voting age. Only 355 of those black citizens were registered to vote.

The demonstrations in Selma, Alabama, and the violent response shocked the world. On Sunday, March 7, as the Selma marchers began to cross the Edmund Pettis

Bridge, sheriff's deputies charged them on horseback, clubbing people right and left. John Lewis, the head of SNCC (and a future member of Congress) was one of several people who were knocked unconscious. Pictures of "Bloody Sunday," as the day became known, were shown around the world. Two weeks later, marchers, now protected at Johnson's directive by the Alabama National Guard, finally completed a march to the state capital of Montgomery. That evening, the marchers happily sang "We have overcome." But the same evening, KKK members followed one of their supporters, Viola Liuzzo of Detroit, as she drove black marchers home from the event, and killed her. The country had had enough of this sort of violence.

Only a week after the Bloody Sunday march, Johnson went before Congress to give one of his most memorable speeches. He told Congress and the nation:

> This time, on this issue, there must be no delay, no hesitation, and no compromise with our purpose....Because it is not just Negroes, but really it is all of us who must overcome the crippling legacy of bigotry and injustice. And we shall overcome.

Hearing the first president from the South since the Civil War speak uncompromisingly of the right to vote while using the words of the civil rights movement's hymn moved many to tears.

The Voting Rights Act, which with unrelenting pressure from Johnson passed Congress by overwhelming majorities, gave the U.S. Department of Justice the right to intervene in any county where 50 percent or fewer of the eligible voters were registered—virtually all of the Deep South. Agents could monitor literacy or other tests and if necessary appoint new federal registrars. On August 6, 1965, Johnson signed the law in the same room where Lincoln had signed the Emancipation Proclamation 102 years earlier (see Map 26-2).

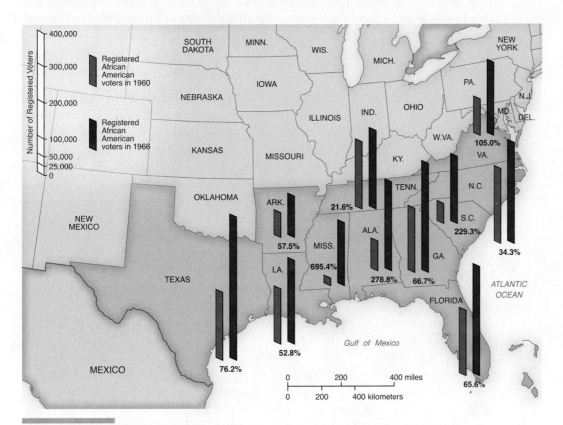

MAP 26-2 The Impact of the Voting Rights Act. This map shows the significant increase in African-American voter registration between 1960 and 1966 as a result of the Voting Rights Act.

With the Voting Rights Act, the Immigration Act, Medicare and Medicaid, and the Elementary and Secondary Education Act, and a host of other measures, Johnson was doing what he knew how to do best, getting federal legislation, federal money, and federal enforcement powers to address specific issues. He was certainly not without his critics. Many worried that the education funds were being used to expand already bloated school bureaucracies. Medicare and Medicaid seemed to be a huge new federal program that would eventually bankrupt the country. The Civil Rights and Voting Rights Acts, though popular, also created disaffection with Johnson and the Democratic Party that would, as Johnson knew, turn many southerners into Republicans.

Johnson's own personality was also a problem. Although he was a master of legislation and gave some of the most memorable speeches of any president, he was also a very difficult person. He could be crude and cruel, especially to those closest to him. George Reedy, who served as Johnson's Press Secretary and saw him close up, said, "[A]s a human being he was a miserable person—a bully, sadist, lout, and egoist....[H]is lapses from civilized conduct were deliberate and usually intended to subordinate someone else do to his will." Such behavior might be effective when arm twisting was the only way to get a bill through Congress, but they also left precious little reservoir of good will when Johnson got into trouble. After 1965, Johnson got into a lot of trouble, especially in foreign policy.

Reflecting on the Johnson administration, Averill Harriman, a senior adviser to every president from Roosevelt to Johnson, said, "LBJ was great in domestic affairs.... [I]f it hadn't been for...Vietnam he'd have been the greatest President ever." In analyses of the Johnson presidency, "If it hadn't been for Vietnam" is a steady refrain. The war in Vietnam destroyed national support for Johnson and the Great Society. The war divided Americans as no war since the Civil War. Opposition to and support for the war created a new political divide within the country and destroyed many long-standing allegiances. Cynicism about the conduct of the war became cynicism about government itself and eventually all authorities. The war cost 58,000 American lives, and many thousands more were wounded in body and mind in the turmoil of Vietnam. Whatever one's ultimate judgments about the U.S. effort in Vietnam, it is impossible to understand the history of the United States in the late 1960s and beyond without understanding the impact of that war.

Vietnam

Kennedy's foreign policy priorities were Cuba and Berlin. Until the final weeks of his life, he did not pay a lot of attention to Vietnam. When Kennedy became president, the United States had less than 1,000 troops in Vietnam, sent to train the South Vietnamese army. Slowly, JFK authorized small increases not only to train troops but also to join them on combat missions against infiltrators from the North Vietnamese Army (NVA) and their allied South Vietnamese insurgents organized as the National Liberation Front (NLF). So called counterinsurgency and strategic hamlet programs were designed to find and destroy enemy forces. Unfortunately, the violence of these missions and the corruption of the South Vietnamese regime under the leadership of the increasingly despotic Ngo Dinh Diem undermined popular support. Diem was part of a Catholic elite minority in a country where the majority was Buddhist. Although his Christianity and his anti-Communism made him an appealing figure in the United States, his despotic and corrupt administration alienated many Vietnamese.

In the summer of 1963, fierce protests were mounted within South Vietnam against the Diem regime. Quang Duc, a Buddhist monk, burned himself to death on June 11 to protest conditions, and more protests and self-immolations followed. Kennedy's new ambassador to Vietnam, Henry Cabot Lodge, Jr., lost all faith in Diem and, with Kennedy's tacit agreement, supported a military coup against Diem. The CIA-backed coup took place on November 1, and Diem and his brother were killed, something Kennedy had not necessarily expected. And then, 3 weeks later, Kennedy was dead, and some 17,000 U.S. military "advisers" were in Vietnam.

As he became president, LBJ wanted to use the office to focus on domestic policy. From the beginning, however, he felt he could not ignore Vietnam, and like Kennedy, Eisenhower, and Truman, he insisted, "I am not going to be the President who saw Southeast Asia go the way China went [to communism]." It was a fateful vow. Equally fateful was the fact that, on balance, Johnson himself was as insecure about foreign policy as he was secure about domestic policy. Winning a war was a very different thing from getting Congress to pass a bill. LBJ kept Kennedy's foreign policy advisers, and most of them were convinced that communism had to be contained around the globe. If communist North Vietnam threatened noncommunist South Vietnam, then, they believed, the United States needed to protect the noncommunist south, however unpalatable the fight might be.

Plans for expanding the war were on Johnson's desk from the day he became president and, although he eventually implemented them, he did delay expanding the U.S. involvement in Vietnam (see Map 26-3). He wanted to defeat Barry Goldwater in the 1964 elections, and part of his strategy was to paint Goldwater as a crazy warmonger. He also wanted to get the Great Society legislation through Congress. Even so, Johnson said in retrospect, "I knew from the start that I was bound to be crucified either way I moved. If I left the woman I really loved—the Great Society—in order to get involved with that bitch of a war on the other side of the world, then I would lose everything at home....But if I left that war and let the Communists take over South Vietnam, then I would be seen as a coward and my nation would be seen as an appeaser."

Johnson convinced himself that being "seen as an appeaser" in Vietnam would lead to new Soviet and Chinese aggression elsewhere, just as appeasement with Germany had led to World War II. He was intimidated by the Kennedy legacy of toughness in foreign policy and was convinced that, if he did not find a way to save South Vietnam, "There would be Robert Kennedy out in front leading the fight against me, telling everyone that I had betrayed John Kennedy's commitment to South Vietnam....that I was a coward." For a Texan who had grown up on stories of the heroes of the Alamo, being called a coward was simply beyond contemplation. Johnson's fear proved to be ironic since, 4 years later, Robert Kennedy would run as an antiwar candidate against Johnson.

Throughout 1964, LBJ increased the military advisers modestly, from 17,000 to 23,000, but he did all he could to keep Vietnam off of the front pages in the election year after the 1963 CIA-backed coup in South Vietnam. The one big exception came on August 1, when there were reports that a North Vietnamese torpedo boat fired on the U.S. destroyer *Maddox,* Johnson ordered an immediate military response. Johnson also went to Congress and asked for a resolution granting him the right to use "all necessary measures" to repel any attacks against the U.S. forces in Vietnam. The **Gulf of Tonkin Resolution** passed easily—unanimously in the House and with only two dissenting votes in the Senate—and in later years, it was this resolution, rather than any further congressional action, that presidents Johnson and Nixon used to prosecute the war. Only years later did historians discover that there was no solid evidence that anything had been fired at the *Maddox,* or a second destroyer that had come to aid it, during the August encounter, but Johnson got the power he wanted.

After Johnson's inauguration in January 1965, the military situation in South Vietnam deteriorated badly—North Vietnamese forces controlled perhaps half the land and people of the south. Johnson's key foreign policy advisers, especially Secretary of State Dean Rusk and Secretary of Defense Robert McNamara, urged a major escalation of U.S. involvement. Some, especially Undersecretary of State George Ball, opposed escalation but, in early 1965, most were calling for more troops.

In February 1965, Johnson said, "I can't ask our American soldiers out there to continue to fight with one hand tied behind their backs," and launched a major bombing campaign against North Vietnam to stop the flow of supplies to the south. As the bombing expanded—3,600 runs in April, 4,800 by June—the United States also sent more ground forces to protect the American air base at Danang. Once there, these

Gulf of Tonkin Resolution
Legislation passed by Congress in 1964 that allowed the United States to use force to protect U.S. interests in Vietnam.

MAP 26-3 The War in Vietnam. Vietnam, South and North, and sites of major battles in the U.S.-led war.

troops also engaged in battle and then needed more troops to support them. Fifty-thousand troops were in Vietnam by April of 1965, and the number rose to 75,000 by midsummer. By July, Secretary McNamara, noting that the bombing alone was not defeating the northern forces, urged that the U.S. troop strength be increased from 75,000 to more than 200,000. Johnson agreed. But he did not want to go to Congress for authorization, fearing that it would disrupt the Great Society legislation. So, he quietly asked for an additional appropriation for the war and announced a troop increase at a midday news conference devoted to other issues. The result was that although Johnson won short-term success for his domestic programs, he planted the seeds of long-term distrust.

For the next 2 years, combat in Vietnam expanded. Eventually, half a million U.S. troops were in Vietnam. Numbers at that level could be sustained only by an increased

As more and more U.S. soldiers arrived in Vietnam, they found themselves on more patrols such as the one pictured here.

military draft. Deferments became difficult to get, especially for minority and working-class men. Casualty numbers also grew, undermining morale among the troops and at home. Costs mushroomed. In 1965, the military budget was $49.6 billion; by 1968, it was $80.5 billion. Try as they might, the U.S. commanders could not get the South Vietnamese army to play a major role in the war. They avoided battle when they could and seemed to have an uncanny way of knowing where danger was and leaving those sites to the Americans.

As U.S. soldiers did more of the fighting, they also saw less purpose to what they were doing. Troops went out on search-and-destroy missions, and then came back to their bases with little to show other than a list of enemy soldiers killed. One soldier asked, "What am I doing here? We don't take any land....We just mutilate bodies." An American officer, speaking of his company's attack on the village of Ben Tre, which was suspected of harboring NLF supporters, said, "We had to destroy the village in order to save it." Destroying villages to "save" them, marching into the jungle, engaging in battles with enemy forces—battles that the U.S. troops almost always won—but then coming back to their bases while the enemy forces reorganized in the jungle were strategies that seemed pointless to most soldiers. The U.S. commander in Vietnam, General William Westmoreland, kept providing optimistic reports. Few were convinced.

Racial tensions often exploded in Vietnam. In 1965, 12.6 percent of the troops were black but 24 percent of combat deaths were of black soldiers. Black soldiers, who knew that civil rights workers were being killed in Alabama and Mississippi at home, believed that they were often being sent on the most dangerous missions. Many became increasingly angry at their fellow troops, at their officers, and at the war.

American Voices

Paul Thomas Coe, "Vietnam Letters," 1969–70

Paul Thomas Coe was a devout Mormon and a student at the University of California at Berkeley. In 1969, he lost his draft deferment. These letters reflect his experience in Vietnam.

The President of the United States March 17, 1969

To: Paul T. Coe
GREETINGS:
You are hereby ordered for induction into the Armed Forces of the United States, and to report to: Local Board No. 31 on April 16, 1969, Wednesday at 6:00 A.M. (morning) for forwarding to an Armed Forces Induction Station.

Basic Training

I'm tired of trying to rationalize things in my mind. All my beliefs seem to form a giant paradox. There is no room in my heart to justify killing, I can't ever justify the training to kill, and yet I can't justify copping out. I can't justify desertion although that seems the only logical course of action. I know inside that a time is drawing near when our families will need to draw together and the world will be in an uproar, so leaving for another country is out. The church speaks so loudly against breaking the law, and so loudly for supporting our constituted way of life that I can't justify refusing my orders. I want to do what is called of me for my country, but I can't justify the senseless loss of life.... But with every day I become more conscious of the ominous power we've given the military, and hate it so much more....

Peace on Earth
P.T.

In Vietnam

11 September, 1970

There really isn't that much I can tell you. Rain has begun and the monsoons will be here soon.... Another thing, the chow is sorry. I mean ungood food & I'm sick of dried up burnt gristly cold roast beef, nearly every day. You'd think they'd at least learn how to cook that one thing if that's all they cook, but no not them. By the way have you taught Barb [Paul's wife] to make decent gravy yet?

Miss you Mom. Give love to all.

Paul

24 Sept. 70

Rather than go out with some battalion Recon [reconnaissance] team and sit in the rain, I joined what is called the 3rd Brigade Air Cavalry. It's an instant Recon team. They insert us into trouble spots for a day or two & then extract us ... you can take anything when you know they're gonna pull you out in 2 days.

Just got back from a 3-day mission directly west of Hue about 3 ridgelines east of the A Shau Valley. We were sent in there to investigate enemy supply routes.... Then we found that the LZ [Landing Zone] we were supposed to go to was ¾ up the Ridge and washed out, so nobody could get up to it. ... We made it to the LZ & the Birds [helicopters] were beautiful. After circling for 10 minutes they figured how to get in, but they didn't like it either because there was high ground all around. But they came in anyway about 10 feet off the water ... so I threw my weapon in, grabbed that skid, pulled myself to a boulder and jumped in. Felt good. Let my legs dangle out the door all the way back....

Paul
***

DEPARTMENT OF THE ARMY
08 DEC 1970
Dear Mr. and Mrs. Coe,
By this time I am sure that you have been notified of the death of your son, Paul T. Coe. I want you to know that Paul's death came as a tragic shock to me and to all the men who knew him. On behalf of the entire company, I extend our deepest and most sincere sympathy.

On 14 November 1970, Paul was a member of a daylight patrol in the vicinity of Camp Evans, with the Headquarters Reconnaissance Platoon, when the patrol hit a booby trapped area. Your son was killed by multiple fragmentation wounds when one of the hostile booby traps exploded. I hope that it may be of some comfort to you to know that Paul died instantly and did not suffer....

Sincerely,
FRANK A. LIGHTLE
Captain, Infantry
Commanding Officer

Source: Karen Manners Smith and Tim Koster, *Time It Was: American Stories from the Sixties.* (Upper Saddle River, NJ: Pearson), pp. 27, 32, 36-39.

Thinking Critically

1. **Documentary Analysis**

   How did Coe characterize the war while in basic training? How did he view his own military service?

2. **Comparison**

   In what ways were Coe's letters similar to those written by soldiers in previous American wars? In what ways do they reflect the specific context and experiences of the war in Vietnam?

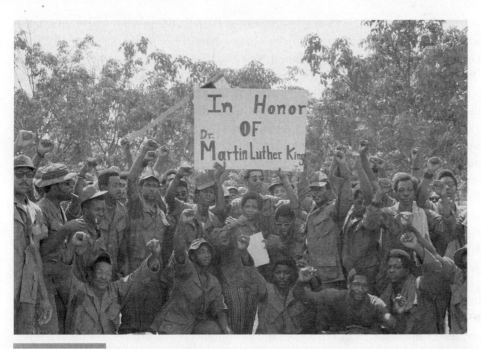

African-American troops in Vietnam who bore a disproportional share of the fighting and dying quickly lost faith in the effort.

While morale disintegrated on the ground in Vietnam, public support for the war also evaporated. By launching the war quietly, Johnson had not built public support. Many Americans had a natural tendency to support the president and the troops at first, but that support declined rapidly. Vietnam was the nation's first televised war. Television did not actually show a lot of combat; many of the battles were at night or far from cameras. Nevertheless, footage of troops going into combat as well as pictures of dead and wounded American soldiers brought the war into American living rooms. Lack of clear progress created doubt. Opposition to the war built with each news report, each draft call, and each casualty list.

While critics have rightly pointed out that no more than 20 percent of college students took part in antiwar demonstrations, and those demonstrations were mostly on elite campuses such as the University of California at Berkeley, Columbia, and Harvard, few campuses anywhere were untouched by antiwar fervor, especially as many students worried about draft calls or felt the guilt at being protected by their student status while friends went off to Vietnam. As the war escalated, those participating in campus-based teach-ins—gatherings at which experts or better informed students taught others about Vietnam—heard mostly from critics of the war. The first March on Washington to end the war took place in April 1965. At that rally, 25,000 people heard SDS president Paul Potter say, "The incredible war in Vietnam has provided the razor, the terrifyingly sharp cutting edge that has finally severed the last vestige of illusion that morality and democracy are the guiding principles of American foreign policy." In 1966, 1967, and 1968, the teach-ins became angrier and the disaffection with the government greater. As early as 1966, demonstrators were not only calling for American withdrawal from Vietnam but also waving NLF flags and chanting, "Ho, Ho Ho Chi Minh, The NLF is gonna win."

Students were far from the only opponents of the war. The Women's Strike for Peace, the Fellowship of Reconciliation, and the Catholic Worker Movement were pacifist organizations who had opposed the war from the beginning. In addition, more religious leaders began to speak out about the specific war in Vietnam. Catholic priests Daniel and Philip Berrigan and Henry Sloan Coffin, the Protestant chaplain at Yale University, became leading antiwar activists.

Established civil rights groups did not want to risk a break with the Johnson administration when LBJ was doing so much to support civil rights. Even so, SNCC was the first among them to oppose the war. A 1966 SNCC position paper attacked a war "to preserve a 'democracy' which does not exist at home." In April 1967, Martin Luther King, Jr., stood in the pulpit at New York's Riverside Church to tell the civil rights movement and the nation that he had come to see that the war was sending poor and black Americans 8,000 miles away to fight for rights that they did not have in the United States. "Somehow this madness must cease," he pleaded.

As the war continued, some opponents took their opposition to a new level. When some 35,000 demonstrators surrounded the Pentagon and tried to disrupt daily business in Washington in October 1967, the government reacted harshly with mass arrests of the protestors. Between 50,000 and 100,000 young men left the United States, most of them moving to Canada, to avoid serving in a war they thought was wrong. Many of those who moved to Canada eventually returned to the United States, especially after presidential pardons granted by presidents Ford and Carter, but some 50,000 Americans became permanent residents of Canada as a result of the Vietnam War while others stayed in neutral nations like Sweden.

In 1967, a group of young men in San Francisco announced that they were staying in the United States but refusing to cooperate with the military draft in any way. "We will renounce all deferments and refuse to cooperate with the draft in any manner, at any level," they said. Draft resistance, and a willingness to be arrested for the act, was a new stage in the protest movement. Later, Dr. Benjamin Spock (whose book on child care had been the bible for the parents of many of those now refusing the draft) and Rev. William Sloan Coffin were arrested for urging draft resistance.

Still others took their protests to other forms of direct action to try to stop the war. In May 1969, opponents of the war, including some religious leaders, walked into the offices of Dow Chemical Company, which made the napalm jelly that was used to burn, kill, and maim in Vietnam, and poured blood into filing cabinets and on office equipment to disrupt the workings of the offices.

While opposition to the war in Vietnam broadened, Johnson isolated himself with trusted advisers. He agonized about casualty reports, wept while signing letters of condolence to those who had lost a loved one in the war, and regularly got up at 4:00 and 5:00 a.m. to check on casualty figures. He never seriously considered changing course and stopped talking to those who suggested that he should. He authorized the CIA, which was only supposed to operate abroad, to spy on American antiwar leaders who he became convinced were communists, and he authorized the FBI to infiltrate and disrupt the antiwar movement. Johnson brought the army commander in Vietnam, General Westmoreland, to Washington, DC, in November 1967 to tell Americans that there was "light at the end of the tunnel" in Vietnam. By that time, fewer Americans were convinced.

1968

In 1968, the growing tensions of war, race, and change in America seemed to explode. Few were untouched by the anger and fear that the year provoked.

Two months after General Westmoreland's optimistic assessment, the light at the end of the tunnel in Vietnam dimmed considerably. On January 30, 1968, the first day of Tet, the Vietnamese lunar new year, North Vietnamese and NLF forces attacked everywhere across South Vietnam, all at once. They blew a hole in the wall surrounding the American embassy in Saigon and came close to getting into the inner compound. They attacked the distant Marine post at Khe Sanh. They took control of the old Vietnamese capital city of Hue. And they attacked American and South Vietnamese forces all over the country. Eventually, the **Tet Offensive** was beaten back, at terrible cost to the North Vietnamese. By one estimate, the North lost 40,000 troops compared to 2,300 South Vietnamese and 1,100 Americans. Even so, the North had won an important victory. Public trust in Westmoreland and Johnson was never restored. The president and the general had said that the United States was winning the war, but now it certainly looked like it was losing. Johnson's popularity dropped

Tet Offensive

A significant North Vietnamese assault on Amer ican bases across Vietnam.

from its already low 40 percent approval rating to 26 percent. Walter Cronkite, the anchor of the CBS Evening News and perhaps the most trusted journalist in the country, who had maintained careful neutrality in his reporting, traveled to Vietnam after Tet and returned to tell his viewers, "It seems more certain than ever that the bloody experience of Vietnam is to end in a stalemate." Many agreed.

When Westmoreland responded to the Tet Offensive by asking for even more troops, beyond the 525,000 Americans already in Vietnam, Johnson's new Secretary of Defense told the president, "We seem to have a sinkhole….I see more and more fighting with more and more casualties on the U.S. side and no end in sight to the action." Secretary of State Rusk, long a supporter of the war, recommended a bombing halt and an offer of negotiations with North Vietnam. Johnson hated the advice, but he could no longer ignore it.

At the same time, Johnson's lack of popularity was catching up with him. Everyone assumed that, as an incumbent president, Johnson would seek and easily win his party's nomination for another term in office. But the antiwar mood was growing, in the country and in the Democratic Party. On March 12, 1968, in the nation's first primary vote in New Hampshire, Minnesota Senator Eugene McCarthy, who had become a strong opponent of the war, won 42 percent of the votes against LBJ's 49 percent. Many who had participated in antiwar demonstrations decided to be "clean for Gene" and campaign door to door in New Hampshire. They found a ready electorate, people of many different persuasions, including those who were fed up with the seemingly endless war and those who were frustrated because LBJ seemed unwilling either to commit the force needed to win or to withdraw. The New Hampshire vote was far too close for a sitting president.

Even worse than the challenge from McCarthy, at least from Johnson's perspective, was one from New York Senator Robert Kennedy, whom Johnson loathed. Bobby Kennedy realized that McCarthy's win could mean LBJ's defeat for the nomination and that, since McCarthy had opened the way, it was a good time to challenge an incumbent of his own party. While McCarthy was little-known, Bobby was perhaps the best known politician in the country. Soon after the New Hampshire vote, Kennedy announced that he was entering the contest. For many who opposed the war, wanted further social change, and dreamed of a return to the glory days of the JFK presidency, Bobby's 1968 campaign was a dream come true. His campaign struck an emotional chord among both supporters and opponents—seldom seen in American politics.

On March 31, 1968, just weeks after the New Hampshire vote, Johnson gave a nationally televised speech. He announced plans to reduce the bombing as "the first step to deescalate the conflict." He called on Ho Chi Minh to "respond positively and favorably to this new step for peace." Then he surprised the country, perhaps himself, by adding, "I shall not seek, and will not accept, the nomination of my party for another term as your president." Johnson, the ultimate politician, knew that public trust was essential to govern. And by March 1968, he had lost that trust. North Vietnam did respond, and the road to peace had begun. It would be a long and painful road, however, one that would last far beyond the end of Johnson's term. Johnson's career and his hopes for the country had become casualties of Vietnam—though very far from the only casualties.

Four days after Johnson's surprise announcement, Martin Luther King, Jr., was shot and killed in Memphis, Tennessee, where he was supporting a strike by the city's garbage collectors. With the murder of King, the leading spokesperson for nonviolence, many felt that the cause of nonviolence itself had been damaged. Riots erupted all over America. Police arrested 20,000 people in 130 cities in the week following King's assassination. Forty-six people, 41 of them black, were killed. Urban America seemed to be coming unglued.

The riots that followed King's death reflected the deep anger in much of the African-American community. In Oakland, California, Huey Newton and Bobby Seale had founded the Black Panther Party for Self-Defense in 1966. Newton and Seale insisted that urban police forces had become occupying armies in the black community. Following a

Black Panther Party founders Huey P. Newton and Bobby Seale. The Panthers advocated a radical economic, social, and educational agenda that made it the target of a determined campaign of suppression and elimination by the police and the FBI.

California law then in place allowing unconcealed weapons, the Panthers conducted their own armed patrols of Oakland as a defense. Such an armed presence, however, almost assured violence. A 17-year-old Panther, Bobby Hutton, was killed the same month as King. Many more Panthers would be killed in subsequent years. The Panthers always remained a tiny fringe group, as popular for swagger as for their breakfast programs and their commitment to armed self-defense. Even so, while small, they were a symbol that many blacks embraced—a move away from the self-sacrificing nonviolence of King to a more angry and militant stance.

Two weeks after King's death and the urban riots, students at Columbia University, led by the SDS chapter, took over the president's office and refused to leave. Four buildings were held by white students and a fifth building, separately, by black students. The Columbia sit-in was a protest over the university's war-related research and a university plan to build a new gymnasium in the park that separated the university from Harlem. In addition, it reflected far-reaching anger toward all authorities. After 8 days, the university administration called on the police to clear the buildings and they did. The violence of the police move onto the campus—during which more than a hundred demonstrators were injured—also pointed to the deep fault lines in the nation. The mostly working-class white police were furious at the white students whom they considered privileged snobs. The student revolt at Columbia was one of many. Students protesting the war or local issues took over buildings, held mass rallies, disrupted classes, and burned war-related research materials on more than 150 campuses in the 1968–69 academic year.

In the face of this violent, some said crazy, time in American history, Bobby Kennedy continued his campaign for the presidency. On June 5, Kennedy won the California Democratic Primary. It was the capstone to his campaign. He not only championed the antiwar cause, but befriended César Chavez of the Farm Workers Union, rural whites in Appalachia, Puerto Rican immigrants living in New York City, American Indians on isolated reservations, and urban blacks in city after city, as no candidate had ever done. Then, only moments after his California victory speech, Kennedy was shot by an Arab nationalist. He died days later. As with King, many hopes died with Kennedy.

When the Democratic Party convention finally took place in Chicago in August 1968, Kennedy was dead. The McCarthy campaign had been sidelined. The party nominated Hubert Humphrey, LBJ's loyal vice president who had not entered a single primary. Humphrey had long been a darling of the liberal wing of the party, but his silence on Vietnam and his steadfast loyalty to the increasingly unpopular Johnson meant that he had lost the trust of many.

While the convention met to hear speeches and act on the nomination, protests erupted inside and outside the convention hall. Many delegates protested on the floor of the convention itself. Huge demonstrations were also planned for Chicago during convention week by demonstrators who had their own divisions. One faction, led by long-time pacifist David Dellinger, wanted a nonviolent but militant protest against the war, LBJ, and Humphrey. Another group, for whom Tom Hayden and Rennie Davis of the SDS were the most prominent, wanted a more direct confrontation that they knew might provoke police violence. Finally, a group who called themselves Yippies, led by Abbie Hoffman and Jerry Rubin, believed that the best way to protest was to make fun of the Democrats and the Chicago police in every way possible.

Chicago's mayor Richard Daley was determined to quash all demonstrations. As the convention met, the police attacked the demonstrators with tear gas and billy clubs in the glare of television cameras. They attacked delegates. They attacked the press. Nationally known reporters

Dan Rather and Mike Wallace were both roughed up. As crowds chanted, "The whole world is watching," the violence in Chicago was broadcast around the world. One McCarthy delegate described what he saw from his hotel window, "Cops chased kids off into the park and out of sight among the trees, emerged with one cop dragging a boy or girl by the leg and another cop running alongside clubbing in the groin. A man tried to carry a bleeding woman into the hotel, and they were both clubbed and thrown into the wagon."

In the aftermath of the convention, a commission appointed to investigate what had happened described it as a "police riot." The fact that this could happen, with "the whole world watching," represented how deeply divided Americans were in 1968.

The November 1968 presidential election presented three choices. First was Hubert Humphrey and his vice presidential nominee, Maine Senator Edmund Muskie, a ticket that barely seemed to limp out of the Chicago convention. Humphrey said later, "My wife and I went home heartbroken, battered, and beaten." But there were two other contenders in the 1968 race.

In what was later termed a "police riot" by an investigating commission, Chicago police officers attacked and beat demonstrators at the 1968 Democratic Party convention.

In addition, Governor George Wallace of Alabama, who had made his name blocking school integration had launched a strong third-party campaign in 1968. To the surprise of many, he qualified for the ballot in all 50 states. Wallace and his running mate, Air Force General Curtis LeMay, seemed to have broad support, ranging from the most conservative groups in the country—including the KKK and the John Birch Society—to the many white southerners opposed to racial integration to many in the North who were appalled by riots and antiwar demonstrations. With comments like, "If any demonstrator every lays down in front of my car, it'll be the last car he'll every lay down in front of," Wallace courted what he called the "law and order" vote.

Third, the Republican Party emerged from its summer convention as united as the Democrats were divided. Richard M. Nixon, who had lost to John Kennedy in 1960, spent the intervening 8 years quietly laying the ground work for a political comeback. He collected many political debts and cashed them all in to win the 1968 nomination on the first ballot. His running mate was Maryland Governor Spiro Agnew, who had once been seen as a liberal but who, especially after the Baltimore riots following King's death, had become a voice of white backlash against what he called the "circuit-riding, Hanoi-visiting, caterwauling, riot-inciting, burn-America-down" types in the black and white community. Nixon announced a "secret plan" to end the war in Vietnam and otherwise ran a carefully scripted, television-savvy, and very expensive campaign. The Republicans outspent the Democrats almost two to one.

In early fall, it seemed as if Nixon was unstoppable, in spite of Wallace's popularity. Nixon's major theme "Working Americans have become the forgotten Americans," his promise to do something different in Vietnam (no one knew what), and his success in representing anti-Johnson sentiment without getting specific all worked in his favor. An early poll gave him 43 percent of the vote to Humphrey's 28 percent and Wallace's 21 percent. Humphrey, however, ran a surprisingly strong campaign. He tried to repair the Democratic coalition, distanced himself from Johnson, and reached out to his longtime supporters. At the same time, Nixon struck some as too smooth, and a vote for Wallace seemed a wasted vote. By election day, the polls said the race between Humphrey and Nixon was too close to call.

Nixon won the November election, by a close vote of 37.7 million to 37.1 million, while Wallace took almost 10 million votes. Nixon's electoral college lead was greater: 301 to 191. The Democrats retained both houses of Congress, however. Humphrey won 97 percent of the black vote but only 35 percent of the white vote. Between them, Nixon and Wallace had won 57 percent of all of the votes, a significant backlash against Johnson's huge 1964 victory, against the war, and against the demonstrators who opposed it. In 1968, Americans were more deeply divided by race and class and region than they had been in many years, and anything approaching national consensus was a distant dream. The election results also showed that Vietnam would remain an unsolved issue for a new administration.

> **26.3** **Quick Review** How did the war in Vietnam impact Great Society programs, the Johnson presidency, and the country?

CONCLUSION

In contrast to the 1950s, which represented a time of relative stability and complacency for some Americans, the 1960s ushered in a period of intense activism and social upheaval that in one way or another touched most. Writers and artists began to criticize almost all aspects of American culture and helped set in motion the modern ecological conservation movement, the feminist movement, a new focus on poverty, and a vocal antiwar movement. Perhaps the most iconic of these movements was the student movement. In 1960, a small group of students formed Students for a Democratic Society, which sought to end war, racial injustice, and economic inequality. In its early years, members of that organization engaged in marches, protests, and other forms of direct action to counter government policies inconsistent with their stated mission.

Despite increasing social activism across the nation, President John F. Kennedy remained concerned more with foreign than domestic issues. President Kennedy and his wife Jacqueline Kennedy brought youth, charm, and energy to the White House. Although Kennedy achieved some domestic victories, he was preoccupied, to a large extent, with Cuba, Germany—especially Berlin—and the Soviet Union. After the failed Bay of Pigs invasion in 1961, Cuban ties to Russia grew. The Soviets sent military personnel to the Caribbean island, and in 1962, the Russians began building bases in Cuba for housing missiles capable of reaching the United States. A clash between the United States and the Soviet Union seemed inevitable, but the two nations reached an agreement that resolved the crisis and thereby avoided a potentially cataclysmic confrontation.

In November 1963, Kennedy was assassinated and Lyndon Johnson became president. Unlike his predecessor, Johnson attempted to focus more on domestic rather than on foreign policy issues and, in fact, was remarkably successful in advancing his domestic policy goals, which he called the Great Society. During his tenure, Congress passed the Civil Rights Act, a new immigration law, and the Voting Rights Act, as well as created Medicare and Medicaid health insurance and greatly expanded federal aid to education and the poor. Still, Vietnam was a lingering problem. As Johnson steadily increased U.S. involvement in Vietnam, opposition to the war intensified at home.

In 1968, mounting tensions in American society exploded. In the midst of the violence, at home and abroad, Johnson announced that he would not seek another term as president. Four days afterward, Martin Luther King, Jr., was assassinated and race riots broke out across the country. Two months later, Robert Kennedy was shot and killed. At the 1968 Democratic Party convention, protests erupted outside the convention hall, and the police attacked demonstrators as well as onlookers in what was later called a "police riot." While the Democratic Party was fracturing, the Republican Party seemed strong. Nevertheless, the presidential race of 1968 was a very close one. The tumultuous year ended with the election of Republican candidate Richard Nixon to the presidency.

> **CHAPTER REVIEW** The 1960s have been seen as a decade of protests. What evidence would you give for or against that assumption? How did the focus and tone of protests change from the early to the late 1960s?

NEW VOICES, NEW AUTHORITIES

26.1 Explain the growing social protest in books, films, and student movements starting in the early 1960s.

Review Questions

1. Crafting an Argument

What might explain the dramatic impact in the 1960s of books like Michael Harrington's *The Other America*? Why did similar books published in the 1950s have less influence?

2. Historical Interpretation

What changes in American society were reflected in popular film and music in the 1960s? In what ways did popular entertainment also reflect social and cultural continuity?

3. Cause and Effect

How did the growth of American colleges and universities contribute to the emergence of the student protest movements of the 1960s?

CAMELOT, THE WHITE HOUSE, AND DALLAS—THE KENNEDY ADMINISTRATION

26.2 Analyze the successes and failures of the Kennedy administration and how they interacted with popular culture in the United States.

Review Questions

4. Crafting an Argument

How would you explain the paucity of Kennedy's domestic accomplishments? In your opinion, why does he enjoy a much better reputation today than his record would seem to support?

5. Contextualization

What goals and assumptions shaped Kennedy's foreign policy?

6. Historical Interpretation

What does the public response to the Supreme Court's rulings in *Abington School Board v. Schempp* and *Engel v. Vitale* tell us about the society and culture of the United States in the 1960s?

THE COMING OF LYNDON B. JOHNSON

26.3 Analyze the successes and failures of the Johnson administration in terms of the two issues that dominated his years in office—the launching of the Great Society programs and the war in Vietnam.

Review Questions

7. Comparison

Compare and contrast Johnson and Kennedy's domestic policy agendas. How would you explain the differences you note?

8. Cause and Effect

What impact did developments in the war in Vietnam have on domestic politics in the United States during the 1960s?

9. Historical Interpretation

What divisions in American society were revealed by the events of 1968?

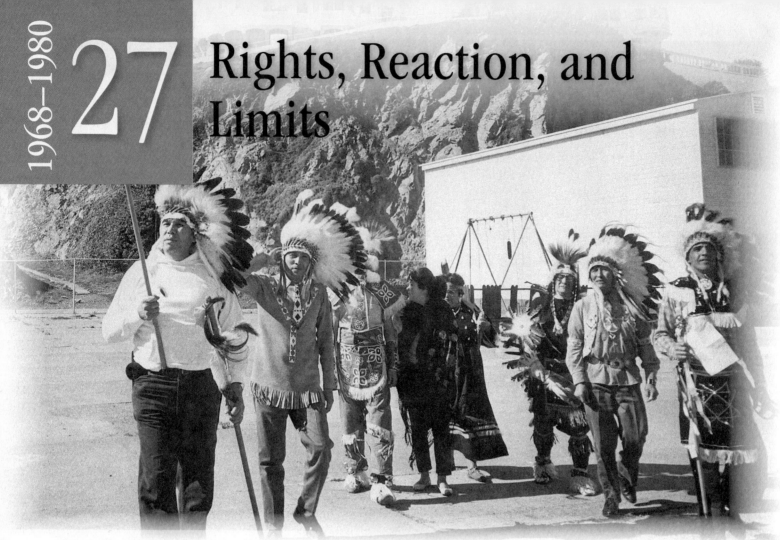

CHAPTER OBJECTIVE

Demonstrate an understanding about the mix of liberalism and conservatism that emerged after 1968.

LEARNING OBJECTIVES

THE NEW POLITICS OF THE LATE 1960s

27.1 Explain Nixon's policies and politics, domestic and international.

THE MOVEMENTS OF THE 1960s AND 1970s

27.2 Analyze the many political and cultural movements that followed in the track of the Civil Rights Movement.

THE CULTURE WARS OF THE 1970s

27.3 Analyze the reaction to the liberal and radical politics of the 1960s and 1970s and the growth of new militant conservative movements.

POLITICS, ECONOMICS, AND THE IMPACT OF WATERGATE

27.4 Explain the political impact of Watergate and subsequent developments that set the stage for the "Reagan Revolution."

Widely diverse groups of American began to protest conditions and policies that they found intolerable. Among them, members of the American Indian Movement took over the closed prison on Alcatraz Island in San Francisco Bay, claiming it as "surplus federal land" that rightly belonged to them.

Basic contradictions in American life came to the surface between 1968 and 1980. The new Republican president, elected thanks to a backlash against the unresolved war in Vietnam, initially widened the war. Nixon, elected with conservative support, also began a new era of relations with Communist China and signed some of the most far-reaching social legislation in history. While the civil rights and antiwar movements splintered, more Americans began demanding their rights in other areas. A women's movement transformed intimate relationships, the work world, and American culture. The civil rights campaigns of Latinos, Asians, American Indians, gay men, and lesbians also made their impact.

Public discourse became more divisive and angry after 1969. The new vice president, Spiro T. Agnew, called protesters "nattering nabobs of negativism." A new conservative ideology emerged, built on Barry Goldwater's campaigns but also on cultural issues, which included opposition to the Equal Rights Amendment and the growth of a new "religious right." Before the decade was over, the United States was defeated in Vietnam; Richard Nixon had resigned in disgrace; his appointed successor, Gerald Ford, was defeated in his bid for reelection; and his successor Jimmy Carter was also defeated in his reelection attempt. The decade was one that held much anger, much sordidness, and few moments of greatness.

THE NEW POLITICS OF THE LATE 1960s

27.1 Explain Nixon's policies and politics, domestic and international.

Early in 1969, Kevin Phillips, a special assistant during Richard Nixon's successful presidential campaign, published *The Emerging Republican Majority*. Phillips analyzed what he saw as the significance of the election and focused on two major changes in American politics. The new Republican Party, Phillips said, was based in "the rising insurgency of the South, the West, the New York City Irish, and middle-class suburbia." Phillips offered a detailed statistical analysis to show that the suburbs especially were overwhelmingly middle class, white, and Republican.

The elections, as Phillips described them, were a reaction against the Civil Rights Movement, which had generated considerable anger in white America and a repudiation of Johnson's Great Society. Expanded government programs and services offended people who wanted small government, who distrusted an intrusive state, and who feared racial integration.

Many found the analysis convincing even though Phillips did not assess the impact that the war in Vietnam had on the politics of 1968. Even so, many, including Lyndon Johnson, attributed the 1968 Democratic presidential losses to the war. While antiwar protesters were furious at Johnson and the Democrats for continuing the war, many other Americans were angry that the war was not being won. Anger at antiwar dissidents also ran deep. For a substantial number of Americans, celebrations of freedom from restraint—political, cultural, and sexual—were abhorrent.

The Roots of the Conservative Reaction of the 1960s

While the suburban-based conservatism was new, it was deeply rooted in the early development of suburban culture. Some Americans had long disagreed with the direction of the country. William F. Buckley's conservative journal, the *National Review* appeared in 1955. Ayn Rand's novel *Atlas Shrugged* appeared in 1957, the themes of which argued that any interference with individual rights would destroy human freedom. Ministers such as James Fifield at the First Congregational Church in Los Angeles preached that, "The blessings of capitalism come from God."

As late as 1960, there were plenty of conservatives and liberals in both parties. After the 1960 election, however, the two parties began to move in opposite directions, and over time, most liberals moved to the Democratic party while most conservatives became Republicans. The drift toward fairly rigid and uniform positions in each party was clear by the late 1960s. In the 1960s and 1970s, the conservative shift among Republicans was led by Arizona Senator Barry Goldwater, who emerged as the hero of the conservative wing of the Republicans. In his first Senate campaign in 1952, Goldwater asked audiences, "Do you believe in expanding federal government?...Do you want federal bureaus and federal agencies to take over an ever-increasing portion of your life?" If the answer was "no," then, Goldwater said, he was their man. In 1960, he criticized Eisenhower as representing a "dime store New Deal." He criticized the U.S. Supreme Court's *Brown v. Board of Education* decision as an unconstitutional federal intervention in the rights of states, and he voted against the 1964 Civil Rights Act, saying that the race relations issue "is best handled by the people directly concerned." His book, *The Conscience of a Conservative*, published in April 1960, spoke to a white middle class that was unhappy with taxes and government intrusion, no longer interested in the New Deal safety net, frightened by the Civil Rights Movement, and fiercely anticommunist. It was this conservative movement that took over the Republican Party in 1964, even though their hero went down to defeat.

Four years later in 1968, it was Goldwater's philosophy, not Eisenhower's, that Richard Nixon used to make his comeback. Nevertheless, Nixon's actual presidency

27.1
27.2
27.3
27.4

contradicted his campaign assertions. Richard Nixon himself was a jumble of insecurities and contradictions. His insecurities and his sense that there were many enemies about to attack him made it hard for Nixon to build warm personal relationships or inspire the broad popularity of presidents like Eisenhower or Kennedy. He isolated himself and often lied to hide the inner workings of his administration. Even though he had been elected as the voice of those who had supported Goldwater, his administration would be relatively liberal. Many federal programs were still popular, and Nixon was happy to support them and reap the political benefit even as he attacked liberals and liberalism as a way to win yet other voters to his side.

Nixon Domestic Policies—Liberal Legislation, Conservative Politics

Although a self-proclaimed conservative, Nixon seemed to some to be a liberal in disguise. In July 1969, Nixon led the celebrations when John F. Kennedy's goal was achieved and Neil Armstrong became the first person to walk on the moon, propelled there by American technology. In spite of the revulsion against LBJ, the 1968 election retained many Great Society Democrats in Congress. Congressional Democrats and the Republican president worked together to pass significant legislation. Johnson's 1965 Voting Rights Act was renewed in 1970. New federal funds were provided for a "war on cancer" and other medical research. Offended when she heard a group of school superintendents dismiss the educational needs of girls, Representative Edith Green of Oregon, joined by Representatives Patsy Mink of Hawaii and Shirley Chisholm of New York, proposed Title IX, which was added to the Civil Rights Act in 1972, banning sex discrimination in higher education—in sports but also in all college and university activities, and Nixon signed the law. Funds for Medicare, Medicaid, and Social Security were increased. Federal affirmative action regulations were toughened by Nixon's Department of Labor.

Nixon did much more than any of his predecessors to strengthen environmental protection. While the Kennedy and Johnson administrations had pressed passage of the Clean Air Act, Clean Water Act, and Endangered Species Act, it was under Nixon that the new cabinet-level Environmental Protection Agency (EPA) was created as well as the Occupational Safety and Health Administration (OSHA). The 1973 Endangered Species Act expanded protection for animals and plants. New Clean Air and Clean Water acts mandated the cleanup of polluted areas without regard to the cost.

Nixon also approved government support of arts and culture, particularly regional art programs and folk art. When Nixon took office, the annual budget of the National Endowment for the Arts (NEA) was $7.7 million. Many worried that Nixon, who had never shown any appreciation of art, would cut the budget, but he proposed increases each year. By the time he left office, the NEA budget was over $60 million, almost a 10-fold increase.

Nixon championed the Family Assistance Plan (FAP) that was designed by Daniel Moynihan—then a Nixon policy adviser and later a Democratic senator. It would have replaced Aid to Families with Dependent Children (known simply as "welfare" to most) with a guaranteed annual income. FAP was defeated by a combination of liberals who thought it did not provide enough money to people in poverty, and by conservatives who thought it expanded government handouts. Nixon also proposed a system of federally mandated health insurance, the only Republican to do so. Overall federal spending for people in poverty rose by some 50 percent, and total federal spending for social insurance (which always includes more middle-class than poor beneficiaries) rose from $27.3 billion in the year Nixon took office to $64.7 billion at the time of his second inauguration.

It is impossible to call anyone who presided over such spending a conservative. Nixon could be seen as the last of the New Deal presidents, and many Goldwater conservatives saw him that way and were furious with him. From Nixon's perspective, the programs were popular, he basked in the praise for what he was doing, and he remained confident that the Goldwater conservatives were certainly not going to desert the Republican Party for the Democrats.

However, Nixon was an unusually ruthless "win-at-all-costs" politician more than he was either a liberal or conservative. If a policy like increasing Social Security benefits or launching the EPA brought him votes, he was all for it. If fanning the flames of divisiveness brought more votes, Nixon fostered division. He encouraged Vice President Agnew's attacks on protestors and experts. Nixon himself condemned protestors as "the vicious and lawless elements in our society."

In planning his reelection campaign, Nixon and his campaign manager, former Attorney General John Mitchell, developed a "southern strategy" to win over Wallace voters. The administration slowed enforcement of federal guidelines for school desegregation and courted segregationist politicians. When officials in the Justice Department sought to enforce desegregation rules, Nixon wrote to John Ehrlichman, his closest aide, "Do what the law requires and not *one bit more*." He approved a plan that would involve the CIA and FBI in illegal bugging and wiretapping. He maintained a "Freeze List" of those who must never be invited to the White House and a larger "Enemies List," including reporters, politicians, and others, who should be watched regularly.

International Issues—Vietnam, China, and Beyond

Before he left office, LBJ had reduced the bombing of North Vietnam and begun the **Paris Peace Talks**. Even so, the war itself dragged on. In his presidential campaign, Nixon had promised a "secret plan" to end the war, but the end would still be a long time coming. Nixon and his National Security Adviser Henry Kissinger had a habit of bypassing the State Department and sometimes even their own staff. In Vietnam and other foreign policy arenas, the Nixon-Kissinger policies were the closely guarded work of these two men.

THE CONTINUING SAGA OF VIETNAM   In the first months of the Nixon-Kissinger tenure, the Paris Peace Talks went nowhere. Nixon expanded the bombing of North Vietnam and started bombing supply routes and North Vietnamese enclaves in neutral Cambodia. In the next 4 years, from early 1969 until the bombing ended in December 1972, more U.S. bombs were dropped on Cambodia than were dropped by the United States during World War II. The expanded bombing did nothing to break the will of the North Vietnamese leadership, though damage and civilian casualties were high. The bombing of Cambodia took a higher toll.

A year after the bombing began, Cambodia's prime minister, Lon Nol, overthrew the chief of state, Prince Sihanouk. From his exile in China, Sihanouk then urged Cambodians to join the anti-American communist resistance, the Khmer Rouge. The result was a devastating civil war in heretofore relatively peaceful Cambodia. When the Khmer Rouge—a very different communist insurgency from that in Vietnam— defeated the Lon Nol government, they launched a decade of horror in which they tried to turn the clock back to "Year Zero" and make Cambodia a preindustrial state. In the process, they killed teachers or anyone showing signs of American, Vietnamese, or western education or influence. Perhaps a quarter of all Cambodians died, and many who survived had then to live through years of 14-hour work days and constant hunger. Ironically the horror of the Khmer Rouge rule in Cambodia ended only when Vietnam invaded the country in 1978.

While Nixon and Kissinger expanded the bombing, they sought to withdraw American ground troops from Vietnam. It was, after all, sending young Americans to Vietnam that was fueling most of the resistance to the war. In May 1969, the administration announced plans to change the draft regulations so a new lottery system would give young men a better sense of the odds of their being called while reducing the overall size of the call-up "pool." Eventually, the Nixon administration moved from a draft to an all-volunteer army to reduce public resistance to Vietnam and future wars.

The administration's new policy was called **Vietnamization**. Money and arms would be sent to the South Vietnamese government so more and better trained Vietnamese troops might replace American troops. In 1969, the South Vietnamese army expanded from 850,000 to 1,000,000 troops while the first 25,000 U.S. troops

Paris Peace Talks
Talks with North Vietnam that led to an agreement by the Nixon administration to with draw all U.S. troops from Vietnam in 1972.

Vietnamization
The policy of turning the fighting of the Vietnam war over to South Vietnam in exchange for greater U.S. financial support.

were withdrawn. In the years that followed, fewer and fewer American troops were stationed in Vietnam. However, the people of South Vietnam had never embraced the war with the enthusiasm that either the South Vietnamese or American governments wanted, so it was difficult for the South Vietnamese government to rely on their loyalty.

Maintaining the morale of the U.S. troops who remained in Vietnam was very difficult. The war seemed to have no purpose. Those on leave sometimes refused to return. Desertions spiked as soldiers sought asylum in Canada or Sweden. In Vietnam, there were near-mutinies as soldiers refused to fight for strategic positions that seemed to have no value; "fragging" of officers—sometimes lethal attacks on officers by enlisted men—increased dramatically with over 1,000 reported between 1969 and 1972. Racial tensions among the troops escalated. Drug use increased. By one estimate, 40,000 of the 250,000 troops remaining in Vietnam in 1971 were using heroin. Protests against the war mounted within the army itself.

After 1968, protests against the war were larger and angrier than ever. In the fall of 1969, 600,000 to 750,000 people gathered on the Washington Mall to protest the war. When Nixon confirmed that U.S. troops had invaded Cambodia in April 1970, protests took place on 350 college campuses around the country. A quarter of all the nation's college students may have been involved. On May 4, Ohio National Guard troops opened fire at protesters at Kent State University, killing four. Two days later, local police killed two protesting students at historically black Jackson State College in Mississippi. In April 1971, 1,000 veterans of the war camped out in Washington to protest the war while they read the names of dead buddies and flung medals on the Capitol steps. One of the veterans, 27-year-old John Kerry—a future senator and presidential candidate—testified before the Senate Foreign Relations Committee. He asked, "How do you ask a man to be the last man to die for a mistake?"

President Nixon insisted that the protests made no impact on him. When students from a number of universities gathered in May 1970 to remember the four who died at Kent State, construction workers jumped into the crowd, hitting the students with

The killing of four protesting students at Ohio's Kent State University, followed by the killing of two more at Jackson State in Mississippi, change the nation's mood. The country was fighting a distant war while disagreements about that war were leading Americans to shoot and kill other Americans at home.

their hard hats. A few days later, officials of the construction unions presented Nixon with an honorary hard hat which he accepted as a "symbol, along with our great flag, for freedom and patriotism to our beloved country." A *Newsweek* poll reported that 58 percent of Americans blamed the Kent State students for the violence, only 11 percent the National Guard. The same poll showed that 50 percent of Americans approved of the invasion of Cambodia while 39 percent opposed it. The anger swirling around the war took many forms, not only protests against the war, but also anger at the protesters and anger at two presidential administrations, as much for the failure to expand the war as for making war in the first place.

Then, as the 1972 presidential election approached, the United States and North Vietnam, meeting at the so-far unproductive Paris Peace talks, agreed to a compromise. Henry Kissinger, in private meetings with the North Vietnamese negotiators, agreed that North Vietnamese troops in South Vietnam could remain there pending a final resolution. Le Duc Tho, the North Vietnamese negotiator at the talks, agreed that the South Vietnamese Thieu government could stay in place pending the resolution and that American prisoners of war—mostly bomber pilots, some of whom had been held for years—would be returned. On October 31, 1972, Kissinger announced "Peace is at hand." It turned out to be a premature announcement. South Vietnamese President Thieu, who had not been informed of the changing U.S. position, objected to the continued presence of northern troops, and after Nixon had won a second term on November 7, he backed Thieu. The war continued.

In December 1972, after his reelection, Nixon expanded the bombing of the North. More bombs were dropped in the 12-day "Christmas bombing" than in the previous 3 years. In January 1973, peace talks led back to the same agreement as had been considered in October, in spite of Thieu's continuing skepticism. On January 27, 1973, a cease-fire took effect; U.S. combat troops soon left the country. American prisoners of war were returned and went home. The direct U.S. involvement in Vietnam was over. The United States continued to provide aid for the Thieu government, kept advisers in South Vietnam, and bombed supply routes in Cambodia. But without U.S. fighting forces, the South Vietnamese government lost ground and would lose more ground in the years ahead.

CHINA While the war to stop a communist victory in Vietnam continued, Nixon, in perhaps the most surprising move of his administration, began to normalize U.S. relations with communist China. Ever since the communist victory in 1949, the People's Republic of China and the United States had remained deeply hostile to each other. The United States continued to recognize the Chinese government-in-exile on the island of Taiwan as the official government of China, in spite of the fact that the communist government based in Beijing ruled the land. Then in July 1971, National Security Adviser Kissinger made a secret trip to China and laid the groundwork for a highly publicized trip by President Nixon to China in February 1972. Nixon's every move was televised, including his handshake with Chairman Mao Zedong, his toasts with Premier Zhou En-lai, and his tour of the Great Wall.

The trip had a number of substantive benefits for all concerned. From Nixon's perspective he got a promise that China would not intervene in Vietnam. China got a promise of a smaller U.S. military presence in Taiwan. Both countries established new diplomatic channels and expanded trade and travel opportunities. For China, the trip also meant an end to decades of isolation, and for Nixon, it was a public relations boost at the beginning of an election year. Long after the trip, Nixon said, "This was the week that changed the world…a bridge across 16,000 miles and 22 years of hostilities." In a tense world, it certainly began a new era of cooperation and coexistence.

EXPANDED FOREIGN DEALINGS While Nixon's trip to China received the most publicity, U.S. dealings with the Soviet Union may have been more substantive. In September 1970, Nixon and Soviet Premier Leonid Brezhnev came to an agreement about Cuba. While the Soviet Union continued to provide Cuba with aid and the

President Richard Nixon, who had made his reputation as a staunch anticommunist, ended years of hostility between the United States and communist China with his February 1972 trip.

Strategic Arms Limitation Treaty (known as SALT I) and an Anti-Ballistic Missile Treaty (ABM)
Major treaties negotiated with the Soviet Union to reduce the world's supply of nuclear weapons.

United States continued its embargo on trade with the island, relations thawed considerably when the Soviets agreed to suspend building a submarine base there and the United States promised there would not be another invasion of the island.

A year later, the United States and Soviet leaders reduced tensions in Berlin. In May 1972, Nixon traveled to Moscow for a meeting with Brezhnev in which they agreed to a **Strategic Arms Limitation Treaty (known as SALT I) and an Anti-Ballistic Missile Treaty (ABM)** that began the process of reducing the world's supply of nuclear weapons.

Other elements in the Nixon-Kissinger foreign policy were less successful. The Six-Day War in the Middle East had taken place in June 1967, a year and a half before Nixon's election, but the new administration had to deal with the outcome. In a deceptive move, using American-supplied weapons but keeping the Americans in the dark about their intentions, Israel attacked Egypt and Syria. The Egyptian army was devastated, and Israeli troops came close to overthrowing the government of Syria until stopped by the United States at the insistence of the Soviets, who used the hotline between Washington and Moscow for the first time. Israel seized 42,000 square miles and tripled its size.

Nixon supported friendly Arab governments, especially the then "twin pillars" of Saudi Arabia and Iran. Nixon was delighted that with their oil money—much of it U.S.-supplied through massive oil purchases—Saudi Arabia and Iran could also handle their own defense and purchase American arms. When a crisis emerged in Jordan in the summer of 1970, Israel and the United States jointly defended a friendly government there. But real peace in the Middle East remained elusive.

Nixon and Kissinger sought to project American influence in other parts of the world with mixed results. They disliked India's Prime Minister Indira Gandhi and believed that India was intent on an alliance with the Soviet Union. Although Gandhi could be difficult and Indian links to the Soviet Union were real, the long-term result was a U.S. policy to strengthen ties to a military dictatorship in Pakistan. The alliance led the United States to support that government when it tried to put down a rebellion in the Bengali region that cost perhaps a million lives. It would be a long time before Indian or Bengali people warmed to the United States.

In Chile, the United States tried hard to keep a Marxist Salvadore Allende from winning the 1970 election. When he did win, the CIA kept trying to destabilize the Allende government. The efforts worked, and Allende was overthrown and killed in a military coup in 1973. The U.S.-backed military forces that overthrew the democratically elected government launched Chile on a course of years of tyranny and terror.

Finally in August 1971, almost 3 decades after the World War II leaders, meeting at Bretton Woods, New Hampshire, had made the U.S. dollar the currency against which all other would be pegged as a way to stabilize exchange rates (see Chapter 24), Nixon announced a "**New Economic Policy**" and ended that practice. In the future, the dollar would float freely in relationship to other international currencies. Nixon hoped that by cutting the dollar loose from other currencies, the new exchange rates would make it easier for people in other countries to buy U.S. goods. He wanted to bolster the economy before the 1972 election, and the economy received a valuable jolt. The long-term result of ending the stability in international exchange rates was less certain.

New Economic Policy
A policy that ended the decades long plan in which all other currencies would be based on the U.S. dollar.

27.1 **Quick Review** Nixon's policy has been described as liberalism at home and a tough Cold War stance abroad. Explain why you would agree or disagree with this position.

THE MOVEMENTS OF THE 1960s AND 1970s

27.2 Analyze the many political and cultural movements that followed in the track of the Civil Rights Movement.

The Civil Rights Movement had captivated the country's attention in the 1950s and 1960s, but it was not until the late 1960s and 1970s that many other groups of Americans formed their own movements to demand new rights and freedoms. Women, Latinos, American Indians, and members of the white counterculture all formed their own organizations, made their own demands, and pushed the society to acknowledge their concerns between 1968 and 1980.

The Women's Movement

Through the 1960s, the place of women in society remained surprisingly unchanged and unconsidered. Newspapers still ran separate listings for male and female jobs. Only a token number of women were admitted to law, medical, or other professional schools. Husbands still had to sign off on a wife's credit card application. In November 1964, Stokely Carmichael made his infamous comment, "The position of women in SNCC is prone." Women who went to Mississippi to fight for civil rights ended up doing domestic chores as well as organizing, and women in the antiwar movement found it very difficult to be seen as credible leaders. Women started to see the reality of their circumstances, and they did not like what they saw.

Women also began running for office in larger numbers than ever before. Only a tiny number of women served in state legislatures or Congress before the late 1960s. Nevertheless, during the 1960s, momentum grew as more women, and a more diverse group of women, started running for and winning elections. More women were elected to Congress, including Patsy Mink (D-Hawaii) in 1965, the first Asian woman; and Shirley Chisholm (D-New York) the first African-American woman in 1969. In 1971, Chisholm, Mink, Bella Abzug, and other women in elective and appointed offices created the National Women's Political Caucus (NWPC), a bipartisan organization to encourage women to seek office. In 1972, Chisholm also ran for president and carried 151 delegates in the Democratic National Convention. In 1975, Ella Grasso was elected governor of Connecticut, the first woman to be elected a state governor who was not following her husband.

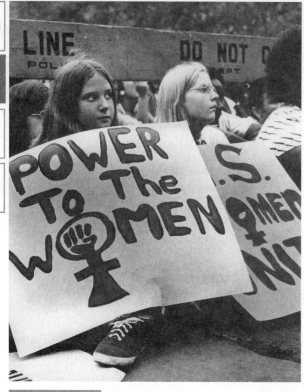

In the 1970s, many different groups of women came together to protest inequality, raise consciousness, and change the ways men and women interacted in American society.

At the end of the 1960s, some younger women began consciousness-raising groups, discussing their experiences as women as well as the emotional, political, and economic toll that sexism was taking in their lives. Like the students who founded SNCC, these younger women had far less patience with working "inside the system" than their elders. Some began to separate from larger organizations and political movements while others also separated from the men with whom they were previously aligned politically or personally.

A month after the violent demonstrations at the Democratic Convention in Chicago in 1968, Robin Morgan began organizing women to disrupt the Miss America Pageant in Atlantic City, New Jersey. The pageant was very popular in the 1950s and 1960s. Women representing each state were judged for their beauty and poise. "Miss America was perfect for us lefty Women's liberationists," Morgan insisted, "She touched capitalism, militarism, racism, and sexism, all in one fell swoop." Women who came to Atlantic City had a "Freedom Trash Can" in which they threw underwire bras, constricting girdles, copies of *Playboy* magazine, and other symbols of women's oppression. When the *New York Post* carried the story, the editors wanted to make a comparison to draft card burning, and erroneously coined the term "bra burning," though as far as anyone knows, no bras were burned in Atlantic City or at any other women's event.

A short time later, the Office of Federal Contract Compliance at the Department of Labor supported Bernice "Bunny" Sandler when she filed a complaint against the University of Maryland after she had been turned down for a faculty appointment because, she was told, "Let's face it, Bunny, you come on too strong for a woman." Sandler decided to challenge the decision. The case eventually became a nationwide class action suit against university discrimination.

In August 1970, moderate and radical feminists came together to celebrate the 50th anniversary of the women's suffrage amendment. On Women's Strike for Equality Day, fifty-thousand 50,000 women marched down New York's Fifth Avenue, including Congresswoman Bella Abzug, National Organization for Women founder Betty Friedan, and newer leaders such as Gloria Steinem and Kate Millett.

Joining Friedan and Pauli Murray, the co-founders of NOW, younger women like Kate Millett, Germaine Greer, and Gloria Steinem began their activist careers at the end of the 1960s, bringing the issues of women's struggles and women's rights to the foreground. In 1970, Florence Howe founded the Feminist Press to reissue the work of earlier feminist writers and publish the work of new women authors. In Massachusetts, 12 women founded the Boston Women's Health Book Collective and published a small booklet, *Women and Their Bodies,* in 1970. An expanded version, *Our Bodies, Ourselves,* became a best seller. A group of African-American feminists calling themselves the Combahee River Collective—in honor of a Civil War battle led by Harriet Tubman—issued a statement in 1977, saying, "Black, other Third World, and working women have been involved in the feminist movement from its start," and they wanted to be sure that "elitism within the movement" did not marginalize them. The poetry of the black lesbian feminist Audre Lorde began to gain wide circulation at the same time.

In 1972, Gloria Steinem, who had become a major voice of women's liberation, sometimes to the irritation of Betty Friedan, launched *Ms.* magazine, which turned into a mass market success when it sold 250,000 copies in its first 8 days. Too tame for some, and too much of a one-woman show for others, *Ms.* remained a voice of new ideas and important, challenging thinking. It also successfully encouraged a switch from "Mrs." and "Miss" to the marriage-neutral term "Ms." that matched the equally neutral "Mr."

Other women were lobbying state legislatures to make abortions legal. Among them was a young attorney, Sarah Weddington, who took on a Texas case that would eventually change the abortion laws of the United States. The U.S. Supreme Court heard the initial arguments of the case of *Roe* v. *Wade* in the spring of 1972. Jane Roe was a fictitious name to protect the plaintiff's identity. In January 1973, the court announced the 7-2 decision that the right to privacy prevented any state from outlawing abortion in the first two trimesters of a woman's pregnancy. *Roe v. Wade* would lead to battles about abortion and the role of the courts for decades.

Roe v. Wade
The U.S. Supreme Court's landmark 1973 decision declaring antiabortion laws unconstitutional and protecting a woman's right to choose.

Still other women endeavored to change their working conditions or to open new careers to women. In 1973, Boston office workers organized a group they called "9 to 5," which became a union. Using new federal laws against workplace discrimination, women also entered nontraditional careers in business and the construction trades that had been closed to them. Women began to appear as plumbers, bus drivers, and senior business executives.

The leaders of NOW, especially Pauli Murray, were determined to revive the struggle for an Equal Rights Amendment to the U.S. Constitution. An Equal Rights Amendment (ERA) was first proposed by the Women's Party in the early 1920s, immediately after the success of the women's suffrage amendment. By the 1970s it seemed like the next logical step. Newly elected Representative Shirley Chisholm gave a passionate speech, "Equal Rights for Women" to the House in 1969. NOW began serious lobbying of the Senate in 1970. The ERA passed by a vote of 354 to 24 in the House and 84 to 8 in the Senate. President Nixon endorsed the amendment that said simply, "Equality of rights under the law shall not be denied or abridged by the United States or by any state on account of sex." As we will see, however, as it moved through state legislatures for ratification, the ERA fell victim to a much changed political atmosphere.

The United Farm Workers, 1965–1970

César Chávez began organizing in the grape-growing town of Delano, California, in 1961. He was soon joined by Dolores Huerta. The Farm Workers Association (FWA), which later became the **United Farm Workers** union, drew on both the community organizing model developed by Saul Alinsky in Chicago and on the older tradition of a mutual benefits association within the Catholic Church. Catholic priests and nuns, Protestant ministers, and members of the United Auto Workers Union all helped the FWA grow. College students, many fresh from campus-based protest and civil rights activity, joined the effort. It was a powerful coalition, stretching far beyond the small towns of California's little noticed agricultural regions.

United Farm Workers
A union of migrant workers of California, which bargained for better salaries and working conditions.

In September 1965, Chavez, Huerta, and Larry Itliong, a leader of the Filipino farm workers, planned a coordinated effort by Filipino and Latino organizers and called a major strike for the fall harvest in Delano. A meeting of 1,200 Mexican American workers on September 16, 1965, began with a chant "Viva la Huelga! Viva la Causa!" The drawn-out Delano strike and subsequent grape boycott had begun and received widespread support across the country. It took 5 years, but on July 29, 1970, the Delano grape growers signed a contract recognizing the farm workers union as their bargaining agent. Chavez declared, "From now on, all grapes will be sweet."

The American Indian Movement—From Alcatraz to Wounded Knee

In November 1969, American Indians began a year-and-a-half siege of the abandoned federal prison on Alcatraz Island that gained national attention. Earlier, in 1964, Vine Deloria, a 30-old Standing Rock Sioux, won leadership of the National Congress of American Indians that had been founded in 1944 to support the development of Indian tribal governments. A new direction began for the nation's largest Indian organization. **The American Indian Movement (AIM)** was founded in Minneapolis among urban Indians in the late 1960s, but become a major force on the reservations in the 1970s, making some of its leaders like Russell Means and Dennis Banks national figures.

American Indian Movement (AIM)
The most widely recognized of several Native American civil rights organizations in the 1970s.

American Voices

Three Views on Women's Rights

When Betty Frieda and Pauli Murray launched NOW in 1966, they wanted the equivalent of the NAACP for women—a national organization to lobby, raise issues in the media, and reach a wide audience. In 1969, Shulamith Firestone spoke for more radical feminists through the Redstockings Manifesto. While NOW blamed a system of oppression, Redstockings blamed men. In response to both, Phyllis Schlafly challenged their basic approach and specifically the momentum building for an Equal Rights Amendment.

National Organization for Women, Statement of Purpose, 1966

We, men and women who hereby constitute ourselves as the National Organization for Women, believe that the time has come for a new movement toward true equality for all women in America, and toward a fully equal partnership of the sexes, as part of the world-wide revolution of human rights now taking place...

WE BELIEVE that the power of American law, and the protection guaranteed by the U.S. Constitution to the civil rights of all individuals, must be effectively applied and enforced to isolate and remove patterns of sex discrimination, to ensure equality of opportunity in employment and education, and equality of civil and political rights and responsibilities on behalf of women...

WE REJECT the current assumptions that a man must carry the sole burden of supporting himself, his wife, and family, and that a woman is automatically entitled to lifelong support by a man upon her marriage; or that marriage, home and family are primarily a woman's world and responsibility—hers, to dominate, his to support. We believe that a true partnership between the sexes demands a different concept of marriage, an equitable sharing of the responsibilities of home and children, and the economic burdens of their support.

Source: Ellen Skinner, *Women and the National Experience: Sources in Women's History* (Upper Saddle River, New Jersey: Prentice Hall, 2011), pp.358-360.

Redstockings Manifesto, July 7, 1969

I After centuries of individual and preliminary political struggle, women are uniting to achieve their final liberation from male supremacy. Redstocking is dedicated to building this unity and winning our freedom.

II Women are an oppressed class. Our oppression is total, affecting every facet of our lives. We are exploited as sex objects, breeders, domestic servants, and cheap labor. We are considered inferior beings, whose only purpose is to enhance men's lives. Our humanity is denied. Our prescribed behavior is enforced by the threat of physical violence.

Because we have lived so intimately with our oppressors, in isolation from each other, we have been kept from seeing our personal suffering as a political condition. This creates the illusion that a woman's relationship with her man is a matter of interplay between two unique personalities, and can be worked out individually. In reality, every such relationship is a class relationship, and the conflicts between individual men and women are political conflicts that can only be solved collectively.

III We identify the agents of our oppression as men. Male supremacy is the oldest, most basic form of domination. All other forms of exploitation and oppression (racism, capitalism, imperialism, etc.) are extensions of male supremacy: men dominate women, a few men dominate the rest. All power structures throughout history have been male-dominated and male-oriented. Men have controlled all political, economic, and cultural institutions and backed up this control with physical force. They have used their power to keep women in an inferior position. *All men* receive economic, sexual, and psychological benefits from male supremacy. *All men* have oppressed women.

IV Attempts have been made to shift the burden of responsibility from men to institutions or to women themselves. We condemn these arguments as evasions. Institutions alone do not oppress; they are merely tools of the oppressor. To blame institutions implies that men and women are equally victimized, obscures the fact that men benefit from the subordination of women, and gives men the excuse that they are forced to be oppressors. On the contrary, any man is free to renounce his superior position, provided that he is willing to be treated like a woman by other men.

We also reject the idea that women consent to or are to blame for their own oppression. Women's submission is not the result of brainwashing, stupidity or mental illness but of continual, daily pressure from men. We do not need to change ourselves, but to change men.

The most slanderous evasion of all is that women can oppress men. The basis for this illusion is the isolation of individual relationships from their political context and the tendency of men to see any legitimate challenge to their privileges as persecution.

V We regard our personal experience, and our feelings about that experience, as the basis for an analysis of our common situation. We cannot rely on existing ideologies as they are all products of male supremacist culture. We question every generalization and accept none that are not confirmed by our experience.

Our chief task at present is to develop female class consciousness through sharing experience and publicly exposing the sexist foundation of all our institutions. Consciousness-raising is not "therapy," which implies the existence of individual solutions and falsely assumes that the male-female relationship is purely personal, but the only method by which we can ensure that our program for liberation is based on the concrete realities of our lives.

The first requirement for raising class consciousness is honesty, in private and in public, with ourselves and other women.

VI We identify with all women. We define our best interest as that of the poorest, most brutally exploited woman.

We repudiate all economic, racial, educational or status privileges that divide us from other women. We are determined to recognize and eliminate any prejudices we may hold against other women.

We are committed to achieving internal democracy. We will do whatever is necessary to ensure that every woman in our movement has an equal chance to participate, assume responsibility, and develop her political potential.

VII We call on all our sisters to unite with us in struggle.

We call on all men to give up their male privilege and support women's liberation in the interest of our humanity and their own.

In fighting for our liberation we will always take the side of women against their oppressors. We will not ask what is "revolutionary" or "reformist," only what is good for women.

The time for individual skirmishes has passed. This time we are going all the way.

Source: © 2000-2013 by Redstockings, Inc.

Phyllis Schlafly, "What's Wrong with 'Equal Rights' for Women?", February 1972

Of all the classes of people who ever lived, the American woman is the most privileged.

We have the most rights and rewards, and the fewest duties....

Women's lib is a total assault on the role of the American woman as wife and mother, and on the family as the basic unit of society. Women's libbers are trying to make wives and mothers unhappy with their career, make them feel that they are "second-class citizens" and "abject slaves." Women's libbers are promoting free sex instead of the "slavery" of marriage. They are promoting federal "day-care centers" for babies instead of homes. They are promoting abortions instead of families.

Why should we trade in our special privileges and honored status for the alleged advantage of working in an office or assembly line? Most women would rather cuddle a baby than a typewriter or factory machine. Most women find that it is easier to get along with a husband than a foreman or office manager. Offices and factories require many more menial and repetitive chores than washing dishes and ironing shirts.

Women's libbers do *not* speak for the majority of American women. American women do *not* want to be liberated from husbands and children. We do *not* want to trade our birthright of the special privileges of American women—for the mess of pottage called the Equal Rights Amendment....

Source: *Phyllis Schlafly Report* 5, no. 7 (February 1972).

Thinking Critically

1. **Documentary Analysis**

   How did each author define marriage? What role did each author see marriage as playing, or potentially playing, in American society?

2. **Contextualization**

   What was the audience for each of the three documents included here? What strategies did the authors use to influence their intended audiences?

In 1973, traditionalists among the Sioux on the Pine Ridge Reservation in South Dakota staged a dramatic takeover of the village of Wounded Knee, site of the massacre of 1890. Dennis Banks and Russell Means became the spokespersons for AIM and dared the federal government to repeat the attack. The standoff lasted 71 days as AIM held the town as agents of the U.S. Marshall Service and the FBI surrounded them. In May, after an FBI agent had been seriously wounded and two AIM members killed, both sides agreed to end the siege, and the Sioux won a government agreement to reconsider the treaty rights of the Oglala Sioux.

Another demonstration soon followed when Indians staged a sit in at the Bureau of Indian Affairs offices in Washington, DC. In 1975, two FBI agents were killed in another standoff at Pine Ridge, and one of the AIM leaders, Leonard Peltier, was arrested and sentenced to prison for life, although his involvement in the violence and the verdict in his case remain hotly contested almost 40 years later.

The upsurge of Indian activity at Alcatraz, Wounded Knee, the Bureau of Indian Affairs office in Washington, and elsewhere gained more than publicity. In 1970, the Nixon administration negotiated the return of the Blue Lake in New Mexico, considered sacred by the Taos people, to the Taos Pueblo. In 1971, the Alaska Native Claims Settlement Act was passed by Congress, resolving long-standing land disputes. The 1972 Indian Education Act also provided funds for new schools that would be under tribal control. In 1973, the government began again to recognize Indian tribes as legitimate agents, starting with the Menominees in Wisconsin.

Changing Issues of Race and Diversity in the 1970s

The most dramatic scenes of the black Civil Rights Movement in the 1950s and 1960s took place in the South. In the 1970s, integration efforts moved north. Although Boston had a national reputation for liberalism, Boston's tightly knit ethnic neighborhoods could be hostile to outsiders. In 1974, federal courts found

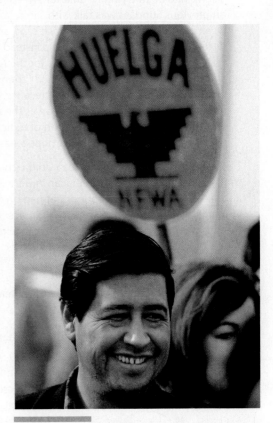

A charismatic union leader César Chávez, working closely with Dolores Huerta, became the face of the organizing effort among California migrant workers, especially the grape pickers, while the two of them built alliances to other movements.

THINKING HISTORICALLY

The Young Lords Party and the Origin of Political Movements in the 1970s

Historians have debated why so many different political movements—among women, Latinos, American Indians, gay men and lesbians, and others—emerged in the late 1960s and 1970s. In the 1950s and early 1960s, the Civil Rights Movement had been confined almost exclusively to the black freedom struggle. A new white student movement also emerged in the 1960s. In the next 10 years, it seemed, every group of Americans was starting to demand its own rights and to challenge social injustice wherever it was found.

One of the most colorful, if short-lived movement groups was the Young Lords Party, a Puerto Rican group that came into existence in New York City in 1969. Pablo Guzmán, one of the founders of the Young Lords, remembered their origins. His description of the diverse forces that led them to organize sheds light on the experience of many other groups.

In Guzmán's account, the Young Lords began with a street protest in the summer of 1969.

> "All we had been trying to do after sweeping up the streets on previous Sundays was talk with sanitation about once-a-week pickups and nonexistent trash cans, and about how to decently treat people asking for help instead of blowing them off." If protests helped win victories for the African-American community, they reasoned, why not them. But when the protest produced an angry police presence, Guzmán and his friends decided to recruit others. "It was the summer of 1969, and the first stateside organization of radical young Puerto Ricans was announcing itself—we hoped—as a political force."

They quickly learned about La Raza Unida (the people united) that was emerging among Mexican Americans in the West, about the Weather Underground that had broken off from the Students for a Democratic Society to embrace more violent tactics, and about the Black Panther Party, the militant black organization, on which the Young Lords would model themselves. They were also influenced by international connections in a world where many were challenging American dominance. Guzmán had spent a semester studying in Mexico. He said, "I left as Paul Guzman, a nervous only-child of a Puerto Rican-Cuban mother and a Puerto Rican father…I came back to the states as Pablo Guzmán."

While other groups influenced young urban Puerto Ricans like Guzmán, there were also other roots to the protest movement, as Guzmán reflected:

> But it didn't come from nowhere—my parents and my grandparents, after all, had first instilled in me a sense that there was far too long a history of injustice in this society. "Only," as my father would say later at my trial, "your mother and I never thought you would actually try to do something about it. Not on such a scale, anyhow."

But with deep roots in their own communities and with the inspiration of seeing others, the Young Lords, like the American Indian Movement or the gay men of the Stonewall Inn, were not going to remain quiet in the face of what they saw as significant injustice.

Note: Today, Pablo Guzmán is a senior journalist with CBS news.

Source: Pablo Guzmán, the *Village Voice*, March 21, 1995.

Thinking Critically

1. Compare and Contrast

How does Guzmán's description compare with the emergence of other movements described in this chapter?

2. Historical Interpretation

How much did Guzmán's family history impact what he did in comparison to other Civil Rights Movements that were developing in 1969?

that the Boston School Committee (the local name for the school board) had engaged in a deliberate policy of redrawing school district lines to maintain racial segregation, and the court ordered an immediate integration of the schools, transferring students across the city by bus, for the opening of school in the fall of 1974. Boston exploded. It was many years before peace returned to the Boston schools.

While Boston was split over school integration, New York was split over a proposal developed by community leaders, the mayor, and the Ford Foundation for local community control of public schools. In certain "experimental districts," in predominantly Puerto Rican East Harlem, and an African-American neighborhood in Brooklyn, local school boards were elected and given powers previously held by the

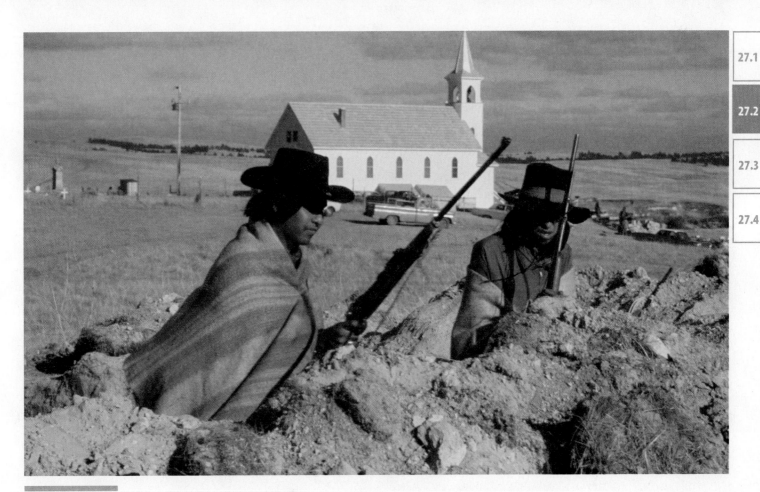

The occupation of Wounded Knee, site of the 1890 massacre, took on great symbolic significance for many American Indians.

central office. When the Brooklyn board transferred 12 white teachers out of the district in May 1968, the overwhelmingly white New York teachers union called a city-wide strike that lasted for much of the 1968–69 school year, crippled the schools, and exacerbated racial tensions in New York.

In other cities such as Detroit, Cleveland, Baltimore, St. Louis, Milwaukee, and Buffalo, whites virtually deserted the city for the suburbs. As a result, more African-Americans were elected to mayor's offices. Richard Hatcher had been elected mayor of Gary, Indiana, and Carl Stokes mayor of Cleveland, Ohio, in 1967; Tom Bradley was elected in Los Angeles, Coleman Young in Detroit, and Maynard Jackson in Atlanta, all in 1973; and Walter Washington in Washington, DC, in 1974.

Blacks and Latinos also began to seek opportunities in higher education in numbers never seen before. A growing black middle class could afford college in substantial numbers for the first time, and Johnson-era affirmative action programs opened doors. But some whites felt that affirmative action subjected them to "reverse discrimination." The arguments about affirmative action came to a head when Allan Bakke, a white applicant, was rejected for admission to the medical school at the University of California at Davis in 1973. Bakke sued, claiming that he had been denied because the university held 16 percent of the slots for minority students. In the U.S. Supreme Court's **Bakke decision** in June of 1978, four justices ruled that race-based programs were illegal and that the university had discriminated against Bakke while four justices ruled that race-based affirmative action was constitutional. The ninth justice, Lewis Powell, joined with those ordering Bakke's admission, but on much more limited grounds. Powell said that an individual could not be excluded solely on the basis of race, but that race could be a consideration. One law professor remarked, "It was a landmark occasion, but the court failed to produce a landmark decision."

Bakke decision
The U.S. Supreme Court's 1978 decision that limited, but did not end, affirmative action programs to achieve racial diversity in a university's student body.

In 1974, the U.S. Supreme Court in *Lau v. Nichols* ruled that school districts must make accommodations for students who came to school not speaking English. These accommodations could include English-immersion programs or full bilingual programs. They could not, as San Francisco had been doing, simply tell a non-English speaker like Kenny Lau to make the best of it and learn English on his own. A year later, in November 1975, Congress passed and President Ford signed the Education for all Handicapped Children Act requiring the "least restrictive" possible accommodation for students with special needs.

The 1970s were also a time in which the nature of American racial diversity began to change. In 1965, when Lyndon Johnson signed a new immigration law, only five percent of immigrants to the United States were from Asia. In the 1970s, that number climbed to 50 percent. Small Japanese and Chinese communities grew dramatically while immigrants began to arrive from India, Pakistan, and Korea. Especially in California, the growing Asian population changed state and local politics. Immigration from Latin America also increased significantly, not only from Mexico but also from many countries of Central and South American as well as the racially diverse islands of the Caribbean. With this growing racial diversity, interracial marriages became more common. A child with one Asian parent and one parent from Central America was not adequately described with traditional ethnic labels.

Out of the Closet—Stonewall and Gay/Lesbian Rights

The *New York Times* for June 29, 1969, carried an article that reported a shift in the city's gay community that would eventually spread to the nation. Of particular note, it said:

> Hundreds of young men went on a rampage in Greenwich Village shortly after 3 a.m. yesterday after a force of plainclothes men raided a bar that the police said was well known for its homosexual clientele.

Something shifted when a group of gay men, whom the police assumed would submit quietly to arrest as they had in the past, refused to do so. Many who had long kept their identities hidden stood up. Many would never return to a closeted life. In the 1970s, gay liberation became a political movement.

While the American Psychological Association (APA) had traditionally defined homosexuality as "a form of mental illness," pressure from outside and from within its own ranks led to a 1973 change when its board voted to remove homosexuality from its list of psychiatric disorders. "We will be removing one of the justifications for the denial of civil rights to individuals whose only crime is that their sexual orientation is to members of the same sex," an APA leader said.

In November 1974, Elaine Nobel was elected to the Massachusetts state legislature as the first openly lesbian or gay state representative in the United States. The following January, Minnesota state senator, Allan Spear, announced that he, too, was gay and, inspired by Nobel, would no longer keep his sexual orientation a secret. Then in 1977, Harvey Milk, a gay man, was elected to the San Francisco Board of Supervisors, symbolizing the radical change that was taking place.

A Counterculture and Its Critics—Sex, Drugs, and Rock 'n' Roll

Woodstock Music and Art Fair
A countercultural music festival that attracted an audience of over 400,000 in 1969.

The summer after Richard Nixon's inauguration, more than 400,000 young Americans gathered on August 15–17, 1969, on a farm in Bethel, New York, for the **Woodstock Music and Art Fair**. Many more would have attended if massive traffic jams and rain-induced mud had not made travel to Woodstock exceedingly difficult. Those who attended Woodstock heard Janis Joplin, Jimi Hendrix, and Jefferson Airplane as well as folk performers, including Joan Baez. Many smoked marijuana, swam in the nude, and generally enjoyed a weekend free from the constraints of traditional society. If any event stands as a symbol of the counterculture of the late 1960s, Woodstock was that event. It was also a symbol that stood closer to the end of the counterculture's life than the beginning.

Several factors helped create the counterculture's hippies of the 1960s. One was the creation of hallucinogenic drugs. The creation of a diethylamide of lysergic acid (LSD) by Albert Hoffman (no relation to Abbie Hoffman), who was seeking a way to treat schizophrenia, set a new generation on a drug-assisted search for vision quests and heightened ecstasy in body and soul. LSD was popularized by Timothy Leary and Ken Kesey as the key to the ultimate revelation or a way to "blow your mind." Music was also essential to the counterculture. Rock 'n' roll had gone through extraordinary changes in the 1960s. Two British rock groups, the Beatles and the Rolling Stones, became huge hits in the United States in the early 1960s with music that mocked mainstream music, including songs like "A Hard Day's Night." Bob Dylan moved from folk music to rock. His "Like a Rolling Stone" moved to number one on the charts. In "Sergeant Pepper's Lonely Hearts Club Band" and their first movie, *Yellow Submarine*, the Beatles embraced the psychedelic world. Finally, anger at a war that seemed always to be escalating led some, notably Abbie Hoffman and Jerry Rubin, to conclude that the best protest was street theater and humor that mocked those who they thought were leading the country to ruin.

If the counterculture had a physical home, it was in San Francisco's Haight-Ashbury district from 1966 to 1969. In Haight-Ashbury, the counterculture ruled its own small domain. Street theater could be seen on every corner. A group called the Diggers gave out free food. Relationships were casual and informal. Drugs were easily available. The summer of 1967 was declared the "summer of love," and young people from every corner of the United States streamed into "the Haight" to "make love, not war." But drugs led to too many emergency room visits and violence. Rock heroes Janice Joplin and Jimi Hendrix both died of drug overdoses in 1970 and Jim Morrison died in 1971, each 27 years old. Venereal disease spread rapidly. The free food disappeared, and the street actors went elsewhere. Utopia, it seemed, could not last long.

The Woodstock festival of 1969 was a 3-day celebration of new freedoms that were already passing for many.

27.2 **Quick Review** How might an historian account for the many political and cultural movements that emerged in the 1960s and 1970s?

THE CULTURE WARS OF THE 1970s

27.3 Analyze the reaction to the liberal and radical politics of the 1960s and 1970s and the growth of new militant conservative movements.

In the 1970s, the United States was a deeply divided nation. Among activist women there were major conflicts between feminist and with antifeminist groups. Conservative Protestants, Catholics, and Jews found new common ground, often in opposition to liberals in their own traditions. The nation's deep racial divides shifted as various groups representing specific ethnicities—whites, blacks, Latinos, Asians, and American Indians—moved in different directions.

Phyllis Schlafly and the Defeat of the Equal Rights Amendment

Perhaps no one symbolized the new political situation, what some have called the culture wars of the 1970s, as much as Phyllis Schlafly. Schlafly was born Phyllis Stewart in a middle-class family in St. Louis, Missouri, in August 1924, 3 years after Betty Friedan, another child of the Midwest. However, their paths diverged dramatically. Schlafly, deeply influenced by her Roman Catholic background and the commitment to individual responsibility she was taught as a child, became a Republican Party activist.

Throughout the 1940s and 1950s, Schlafly was a conservative activist within the Republican Party. She organized grassroots efforts for Barry Goldwater and wrote *A Choice Not an Echo*, an attack on liberals within the Republican Party.

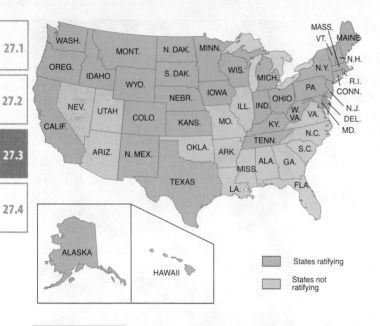

MAP 27-1 Support and Opposition to the ERA. Although the majority of state legislatures voted to approve the proposed Equal Rights Amendment to the Constitution, the amendment fell three states short of the required three-fourth's approval.

Equal Rights Amendment
A proposed amendment to the U.S. Constitution giving women equal rights with men; ratified by 35 states, three short of the needed number.

Phyllis Schlafly gave hundreds of speeches, like this one at the Illinois state capitol building, convincing enough states to defeat the proposed Equal Rights Amendment to the U.S. Constitution.

Moral Majority
One of the first large-scale organizations of the emerging "religious right," which organized support for conservative candidates and was a major force in American politics in the early 1980s.

After the Goldwater defeat, a new opportunity opened for her. In December 1971, Schlafly was invited to a debate in Connecticut. She wanted to focus on national defense, but was told that the focus would be the **Equal Rights Amendment** that was being debated at that time in the U.S. Senate. Schlafly had no opinion of the amendment, but agreed to read up on it before coming to Connecticut. She did, and the result was her decision to make opposition to the ERA her prime focus.

In 1972, as Congress was voting on the ERA, Schlafly wrote "What's Wrong with 'Equal Rights' for Women?" and then launched the STOP ERA initiative. Schlafly pulled in women whom she knew from anticommunist organizing. By early 1973, STOP ERA had chapters in 26 states. Eventually, 35 states ratified the ERA, but it fell three short of the required 38 states and was not added to the Constitution (see Map 27-1). Schlafly claimed much of the credit for its defeat. New cultural issues, including opposition to feminism, to abortion rights, to homosexual rights, and to the defense of prayer in school, as well as a particular definition of morality and law and order in the larger society, became the keys to a new conservative constituency and, for Phyllis Schlafly, a new career as an activist. For the Republican Party, they would be the keys to victory in several future election cycles.

The Rise of the Religious Right

Looking back at the 1972 election, Charles Colson, one of Nixon's prime advisers said, "It was…the first time in modern American political history that social issues became dominant." They would become even more dominant in later campaigns.

In 1978, Pat Robertson, who had founded the Christian Broadcasting Network in 1960, said that if traditionalist Catholics and evangelical Protestants, long distrustful of each other, could come together, "We have enough votes to run the country." These were fighting words and they made Robertson a central player in the religious right in the 1980s.

By far the most powerful expression of the growing religious right in the 1970s was a new organization, the **Moral Majority**, founded by Reverend Jerry Falwell, pastor of the Thomas Road Baptist Church in Lynchburg, Virginia, which claimed 17,000 members. Falwell was also president of Liberty Baptist College (later Liberty University) and host of the television *Old Time Gospel Hour,* which ran on 300 stations for an audience of some 1.5 million people.

The Moral Majority was, Falwell said, "pro-life, pro-family, pro-morality, and pro-American." It was anti-ERA, in favor of prayer in schools, the teaching of alternatives to evolution, and like some earlier secular conservative movements, intensely anticommunist. Falwell opposed U.S. foreign policy that favored the relaxation of tensions with the Soviet Union and called on the nation's leaders to fight communism. He said, "Our government has the right to use its armaments to bring wrath upon those who would do evil." Falwell, who had opposed civil rights in the 1960s said, "If you would like to know where I am politically, I am to the right of wherever you are. I thought Goldwater was too liberal." The Moral Majority helped to register perhaps 2 million new voters before the 1980 election. They were a force to be reckoned with.

27.3 **Quick Review** Were the culture wars of the 1970s—STOP ERA and the Moral Majority—reactions to earlier liberalism or something new in American culture and politics? Support your answer.

POLITICS, ECONOMICS, AND THE IMPACT OF WATERGATE

 27.4 Explain the political impact of Watergate and subsequent developments that set the stage for the "Reagan Revolution."

U.S. leadership and the U.S. economy faltered in the 1970s. The three presidents who served during that decade were ultimately viewed as flawed or weak. Nixon was driven from office in a scandal called Watergate. His successor, Gerald Ford, disappointed many, particularly for pardoning Nixon, and Ford's successor, Jimmy Carter, was unable to pull a nation out of a crisis with Iran and out of a gas crisis at home. The country, desperate for strong leadership, put its faith in a movie-star-turned-politician, Ronald Reagan, to start a new decade.

The Economic Context

The 1950s and 1960s had been decades of almost constant economic growth. During the 1960s, the nation's poverty rate dropped from 22.2 percent to 12.6 percent. The income of many Americans rose dramatically. More Americans had more to spend and more financial security than in any previous generation. While the 1970s did not see anything like a return to the financial distress of the 1930s, they were not such good times. The sense of decline was widespread.

Although the U.S. economy grew in the 1960s, the economies of other countries, especially Germany and Japan, grew more quickly. U.S corporations failed to invest in research and development as much as companies in competing countries. Americans began buying foreign-made goods that were less expensive or of better quality. U.S. manufacturers moved production to other countries where wages were lower, costing U.S. workers their jobs. In 1971, for the first time since 1900, the United States imported more than it exported.

Throughout the 1970s, unemployment continued to be much higher than in the 1960s. While high unemployment normally meant low inflation, inflation also remained high during the decade, and the combination came to be known as "stagflation." To keep taxes low and foster public support for the Great Society, while also increasing military spending for Vietnam, Lyndon Johnson had allowed government debt to grow dramatically. Nixon also did little to reduce government debt, using government programs to build popularity while keeping taxes low for the same reason. The result was continued inflation in spite of the unemployment. When federal officials tried to reduce unemployment by providing stimuli to the economy, inflation got worse. When they cut spending, unemployment soared. The country began to talk about a "misery index"—the combined harm done by unemployment and inflation. Between March and December 1974, the Dow Jones Industrial average fell from 892 to 577, a major loss for investors.

The economy was further undermined by a rapid rise in energy costs. In retaliation for U.S. support for Israel during the Yom Kippur war in October 1973, Arab members of the Organization of Petroleum Exporting Countries (OPEC) raised the price of oil on the world market. Oil, which had sold for $1.77 a barrel in October 1973, rose to $12 a barrel by the spring of 1974. Suddenly gasoline and heating oil were very expensive. Presidents Nixon, Ford, and Carter were all bedeviled by public anger over long lines at gas stations, something Americans had not experienced since World War II. Average Americans saw their disposable income decline as more money had to be spent to keep their cars running and their houses warm.

American automakers were slow to anticipate the impact of the rising prices for gasoline and kept making only large gas-guzzling cars. As a result, sales of Japanese imports, Toyotas, Hondas, and Datsuns, which had held only a small share of the U.S. auto market, soared. Steel mills, tire manufacturers, auto parts makers, and, of course, Ford, Chrysler, and General Motors, all cut back and laid off workers. Unemployment rose, especially in the Northeast and Midwest, a region that took on the new name of the Rustbelt. A 1976 *New York Times* series described the shift from the old industrial

Northwest and Midwest to the South and Southwest, "All day and through the lonely night the moving vans push southward, the 14-wheeled boxcars of the highway, changing the demographic face of America."

The rapid decline of the Rustbelt and the equally rapid growth of the South and Southwest meant many things to the United States in the 1970s. The South itself had certainly changed. It was no longer the rigidly racially segregated economic backwater it was in the 1950s. Indeed, the South was more racially integrated than the North. Tanya Tucker's 1974 song, "The South Is Gonna Rise Again," told her audience that the South would rise, "but not the way they thought it would back then. I see everybody hand-in-hand." In the new economy, Tucker sang, "I see sons and daughters of sharecroppers but they're not pickin' cotton anymore." But they were also not joining unions, and wages in the South stayed lower than in the North. Elected representatives of the new South tended to oppose what they saw as an intrusive government.

For some, the rise of the air-conditioned "Sunbelt" stretching from the Old Confederacy through the Southwest of Arizona and California, was a chance for a fresh start in fast growing cities like Houston, Texas, or Phoenix, Arizona, and the suburbs around them. For others, especially those left behind in the north, it was a disaster. In 1975–76, New York City suffered a major financial crisis. When the decline in city tax revenue and federal aid meant that the city could not pay its bills, it was forced to lay off 3,400 police officers, 1,000 firefighters, and 4,000 hospital workers. Cleveland eventually defaulted on its debts in 1978. Throughout the North, city services declined and crime spiraled.

There seemed to be relatively little that the federal government could do through the 1970s to change the economic situation or address stagflation. Tax cuts, proposed by every administration, did not have the impact that some hoped and, in the absence of corresponding cuts in federal spending, which were highly unpopular, tended to fuel further inflation. Americans found themselves in an unaccustomed era of limits, and they regularly took their anger out on political leaders of both parties.

Watergate and the End of the Nixon Presidency

When he was reelected in November 1972, Nixon seemed to be at the peak of his powers. In fact, he was beginning a long slow decline that would make his second term a torture for him, his administration, and ultimately, the country until he finally resigned in disgrace in August 1974.

Watergate

The crisis that began with a illegal break-in at the Democratic Headquarters in the Watergate complex and ended with Richard Nixon's resignation.

The constitutional crisis known as **Watergate** began with a simple burglary in June 1972. As the election campaign heated up, the special operations group known as "the plumbers," was set up within the ill-named Committee to Re-elect the President (CREEP). G. Gordon Liddy, leader of the plumbers recommended to CREEP's director, former Attorney General John Mitchell, and his deputy Jeb Stuart Magruder, that they break into the offices of Democratic Committee chair Lawrence O'Brien, which were housed in the Watergate complex in Washington, D.C., to put a tap on his telephone. Mitchell and Magruder approved the plan, but the plumbers were caught. Police found an address book on the burglars that included a number for E. Howard Hunt, a former plumber now working for CREEP, and both Hunt and Liddy were soon arrested as co-conspirators in the break-in.

The White House dismissed the whole thing as a "third-rate burglary." If Nixon had simply admitted the stupidity and fired Hunt and Liddy, perhaps even Mitchell and Magruder, the issue might have ended there. But such a move was not Nixon's style. His orders to his chief aide, Haldeman, were to "play it tough" and, most fatefully to order the CIA to stop an FBI investigation of the burglary. In those moves, the grounds for the eventual impeachment of the president were laid since the CIA order to the FBI was an obstruction of justice.

While the Democratic candidate George McGovern tried to raise the issue during the fall campaign, not much came of it. But when Hunt and Liddy went to trial in front of federal district judge John J. Sirica, the judge quickly determined that there was more to the case than a simple burglary. In addition, two *Washington Post* reporters, Carl Bernstein and Robert Woodward, also began a search for more information, including the cultivation of a secret source who they called Deep Throat. (Only decades later was it revealed that Deep Throat was Mark Felt, Deputy Director of the FBI, who was angry that the FBI had been ordered out of the case and angry at Nixon for passing him over for the director's position when the FBI's long time director J. Edgar Hoover died.)

In January 1973, just as Nixon began his second term, the Watergate burglars were found guilty in federal court. Sirica gave them all maximum sentences, but promised to reconsider if they would break their silence. One of the burglars, James McCord, started to talk to federal prosecutors. By April, not only McCord but also John Dean, Nixon's White House lawyer, and Deputy Campaign Director Magruder were talking to the Grand Jury. They also talked to staff of a Senate Select Committee, chaired by Senator Sam Ervin of North Carolina. At that point, several of Nixon's closest advisers, including Haldeman and Ehrlichman resigned. Still, proof of the president's knowledge or involvement of the affair was lacking. Then in May, the Ervin Committee started to hold televised hearings, and the nation first watched McCord accuse Dean and Mitchell, and then watched Dean accuse the White House. They also learned that Nixon had secretly taped conversations in the Oval Office to preserve a record for his memoirs.

By fall, Ervin, Sirica, and Archibald Cox, a Justice Department special prosecutor, all demanded the Oval Office tapes. Nixon refused to turn them over, claiming "executive privilege," the right of the president to keep White House deliberations confidential. On October 20, the president ordered his Attorney General, Elliot Richardson, to fire Cox as special prosecutor. Richardson refused, and Nixon fired Richardson, then fired Deputy Attorney General William Ruckelshaus. Finally, the third-ranking person at the Justice Department, Robert Bork, fired Cox. The moment was known as the "Saturday Night Massacre." Nixon surrendered only some of the tapes, including one from days after the break-in that had an "accidental" eighteen and one-half minute erasure. Public opinion started turning against the president.

The administration, so thoroughly embroiled in scandal and secrecy, was not able to pursue much else in foreign or domestic policy. It was in the middle of the Watergate crisis that Arab leaders, angry at Nixon's efforts first to reduce the dollar's value in international exchange rates (since oil was paid for in U.S. dollars) and then to support Israel, retaliated by increasing the cost of oil by some seven times. When in June 1974 Nixon tried to deflect his domestic troubles with another dramatic international trip—to Moscow to meet with Soviet leaders—the summit produced no meaningful results.

In the meantime, things seemed to go from bad to worse for the president. In October 1973, Vice President Spiro Agnew was convicted of soliciting kickbacks and forced to resign. Nixon appointed House Republican leader Gerald Ford as vice president. Ford, a popular leader with no particular ties to the White House, was quickly confirmed. As the investigation uncovered more of Nixon's dealings, the president responded, "I am not a crook." It was a low point in presidential history. But more was to come.

In March 1974, Haldeman, Ehrlichman, and former Attorney General Mitchell were indicted. Federal courts ordered that the White House tapes be turned over to the courts and to the House committee, which had begun drawing up charges that would lead to the impeachment of the president. Nixon appealed the decision about the tapes. On July 24, the Supreme Court ruled that Watergate was a criminal matter and executive privilege did not apply. The tapes had to be handed over. On July 27, Democrats and many Republicans on the House committee began voting to recommend the impeachment of the president for obstruction of justice.

Rather than face the full House vote and the trial in the Senate, both of which he now knew he would lose, Nixon went on television on the evening of August 8 and told the nation, "I have never been a quitter. To leave office before my term is completed is abhorrent to every instinct in my body. But as president, I must put the interest of America first.…Therefore, I shall resign the Presidency effective at noon tomorrow."

As the Nixon family began a sad journey to their home in San Clemente, California, Gerald Ford was sworn in as president. The nation breathed a sigh of relief that a long and distracting ordeal was over. Conservative columnist James J. Kilpatrick wrote, "The swearing-in of Gerald Ford can't come one hour too soon." At noon on April 9, Chief Justice Warren Burger, just after administering the presidential oath to Ford, turned to Pennsylvania Senator Hugh Scott and said, "Hugh, it worked. Thank God it worked." Burger was celebrating the victory of the Constitution. Ford tried hard to live up to the trust that people, liberal and conservative, now placed in him. But he did not inherit an easy situation.

Gerald Ford

Gerald Ford entered the White House with high approval ratings. He also inherited an economy that was staggering from inflation and unemployment as well as an international scene that included the last stages of the defeat of South Vietnam. Fortunately for him, there was a sense of bipartisan good will in his early days in office. George Reedy, a staunch Democrat and former press secretary for Lyndon Johnson, said, "Ford is one of the very few men in public life whose absolute honesty I do not question." Such a reputation was a precious, if limited, asset as Ford faced the nation's problems that were now his.

Ford came from Grand Rapids, Michigan. He had been an Eagle Scout, a star football player at the University of Michigan in the 1930s, and a Navy veteran of World War II. Like several other World War II veterans, including Kennedy and Nixon, Ford entered politics soon after the war, winning a seat in the House of Representatives in 1948. He gained a reputation for hard work and honesty and was elected House Minority Leader in 1965. Even so, not everyone respected him. Lyndon Johnson said that the House Minority Leader had played football once too often without a helmet. Before and during his presidency, he was often portrayed as long-winded and bumbling.

The new president believed that his top priority was to heal a wounded nation. A month after taking office, he made a controversial proposal that draft evaders be given amnesty in return for alternative service as a way to heal the divisions of the Vietnam War. Ford gave Richard Nixon a "full, free, and absolute pardon" for any crimes committed during his administration. Some hinted that Ford had made a deal with Nixon, but the new president insisted during and after his term in office that his top priority was healing the country, which included moving beyond Watergate.

Ford was convinced that the best way to counter inflation and unemployment was to get government spending under control and reduce the federal deficit. Congress, however, was very reluctant to accept any of Ford's proposals to cut federal spending. By January 1975, as the economy continued to worsen, Ford supported a tax cut. Congress approved an even larger cut than Ford had requested, and he reluctantly signed the popular bill in March 1975. He then proceeded to infuriate Democrats by vetoing a number of federal spending bills. Throughout most of the rest of his term, Ford and the Congress battled over tax and spending issues, both sides wanting tax cuts, but Ford insisting they be offset by spending cuts. Each side was determined to blame the other for ongoing economic woes and to claim the credit when the economy did improve modestly in late 1975 and early 1976. However, no one could claim that the economy was healthy during Ford's term.

In addition to economic challenges, Ford had also inherited a number of foreign policy crises. The Cold War was still very real, and when the Soviet Union expelled the author Aleksandr Solzhenitsyn in February 1974, public opinion in the United States was inflamed, undermining some of Nixon's **détente** efforts to build a new and better relationship with the Soviet Union. Ford calmed U.S.-Soviet relations when he met with Soviet premier Leonid Brezhnev and signed the Helsinki Accords, promising peaceful resolution of outstanding issues and new scientific cooperation. The Middle East, however, remained tense, and India tested its first nuclear weapon in May 1974. In addition, Kissinger, whom Ford had retained as secretary of state, supported a military coup in Argentina in 1976, as he had in Chile in 1973.

Détente
The policy of building better understanding and a more peaceful relationship between the United States and the Soviet Union.

American Voices

Gerald R. Ford, Remarks Upon Taking the Oath of Office as President, 1974

*R*ichard Nixon resigned as president on August 9, 1974, the first president in American history to do so. Nixon's elected vice president, Spiro Agnew, had already resigned and, following a new constitutional amendment, Nixon had appointed Gerald Ford to the office. Thus, when Ford became president in 1974, he was the first president in history to be unelected as either president or vice president. As he took office, he had a strong sense of the kind of national healing that the country needed from him. Moments after being sworn in, he spoke to the nation:

Mr. Chief Justice, my dear friends, my fellow Americans:

The oath that I have taken is the same oath that was taken by George Washington and by every President under the Constitution. But I assume the Presidency under extraordinary circumstances never before experienced by Americans. This is an hour of history that troubles our minds and hurts our hearts....

I am acutely aware that you have not elected me as your President by your ballots, and so I ask you to confirm me as your President with your prayers. And I hope that such prayers will also be the first of many....

I believe that truth is the glue that holds government together, not only our Government but civilization itself. That bond, though strained, is unbroken at home and abroad.

In all my public and private acts as your President, I expect to follow my instincts of openness and candor with full confidence that honesty is always the best policy in the end.

My fellow Americans, our long national nightmare is over.

Our Constitution works; our great Republic is a government of laws and not of men. Here the people rule. But there is a higher Power, by whatever name we honor Him, who ordains not only righteousness but love, not only justice but mercy.

As we bind up the internal wounds of Watergate, more painful and more poisonous than those of foreign wars, let us restore the golden rule to our political process, and let brotherly love purge our hearts of suspicion and of hate....

God helping me, I will not let you down.

Thank you.

Source: Downloaded July 1, 2011 from www.fordlibrarymuseum.gov/library/speeches/740001.asp.

Thinking Critically

1. **Historical Context**

   Beyond the Nixon resignation, what "extraordinary circumstances" might Ford be referring to?

2. **Comparison**

   Why might Americans be willing to trust Gerald Ford's words after the dishonesty of the Johnson and Nixon administrations?

Most frustrating, however, was Vietnam. The last U.S. troops had been out of Vietnam for more than a year when Ford took office, but military advisers, CIA, and State Department officers remained, and the United States continued to provide crucial aid. Congress was out of patience with the war. In March 1975, Ford briefly considered a recommendation from Kissinger to resume the bombing of North Vietnam but ultimately rejected it. Nevertheless, he was furious when in April Congress refused his request for emergency military aid to South Vietnam. In early 1975, the pro-American government of Laos fell to communists. In early April, the pro-American Lon Nol government of Cambodia fell to the Khmer Rouge. On April 29, 1975, the government of South Vietnam surrendered. As North Vietnamese tanks crashed through the gate of the presidential palace in Saigon and the last U.S. helicopters took off from the roof of the American Embassy, there was little Ford could do but attempt the rescue of some Vietnamese orphans, mostly children born as a result of relationships between Vietnamese and U.S. service personnel. The long American presence was over. South Vietnam disappeared and the communist government renamed Saigon as Ho Chi Minh City.

As the 1976 presidential election approached, Ronald Reagan, the popular two-term governor of California challenged Ford in the Republican primaries. Reagan was staunchly anticommunist, attacking Ford and Kissinger for yielding too much to the Soviet Union, and he appealed to conservative voters. But Reagan was not able to dislodge a sitting president. Ford sought to unify the party by replacing his current (appointed) vice president, former New York governor Nelson Rockefeller, on the ticket with a more conservative candidate, Kansas Senator Robert Dole, whom Reagan liked.

As the last helicopters left the roof of the U.S. embassy in Saigon in 1975, hundreds of Vietnamese who had supported the U.S. effort tried to get out. Most were left behind.

Democrats believed that after Watergate, and especially after Ford's pardon of Nixon, 1976 was to be their year, and they waged a vigorous campaign. At the beginning of the primary season, former Georgia governor Jimmy Carter was considered a long-shot in a race that involved some of the nation's best known leaders, including Washington Senator Henry Jackson and Representative Morris Udall of Arizona. To the surprise of many, Carter won primary after primary and went on to a first-ballot nomination. He selected the well-known liberal senator from Minnesota, Walter Mondale, as his vice president.

Carter started the race with a 20-point lead in the polls, but Ford was a better campaigner than many expected. In the end, Carter's focus on the continued high inflation and unemployment, the "misery index," the lingering national anger about Watergate, and Carter's success in positioning himself as the outsider won the election. The final vote was very close with Carter winning 50 percent of the popular vote to Ford's 48 percent. Ford took his loss in stride saying, "I want to be remembered as…a nice person, who worked at the job, and who left the White House in better shape than when I took over." Most agreed he deserved that tribute. Many also looked forward to a more wholesale change of national management in January 1977.

Jimmy Carter's Difficult Years—Gas Lines, Inflation, Iran

By tradition, after taking the oath of office at the Capitol, a new U.S. president leads the inaugural parade back to the White House. Normally the president rides in a limousine, but in 1977, Jimmy Carter chose to walk so he could be closer to the people, something that Carter very much wanted to have as a hallmark of his presidency. In the long campaign, Carter promised "never to tell a lie or to make a misleading statement." After the lies and cover-up of Watergate and Lyndon Johnson's "credibility gap," Carter was a refreshing change.

Jimmy Carter was born in 1924 in the still rigidly segregated South, in the small town of Plains, Georgia. His father was a successful farmer, but Plains was a small place, and Carter left it to attend the U.S. Naval academy at Annapolis, Maryland. After his navy service, Carter returned to Plains to run the family peanut farm and soon entered politics, serving in the Georgia state Senate in the 1960s. In 1970, he was elected governor of Georgia. Some civil rights leaders never trusted Carter. But in his inaugural address as governor, he said, "The time for racial discrimination is over." As governor, Carter courted the King family and created a biracial coalition that he thought should be typical of the "New South," which he sought to represent.

Jimmy Carter and his wife Rosalynn were deeply religious, active members of their Southern Baptist Church in Plains and later in Washington, DC, where Carter taught a Sunday School class. Carter's Christian faith reassured some and worried others, but his unapologetic sincerity and his equally clear commitment to the separation of church and state—uninterested in imposing his beliefs on others—tended to win him respect.

Carter's openness, his down-home style, and his fresh approach heightened his popularity. Two months into his administration, the new president had an extraordinary 75 percent public approval rating. The new administration knew from the beginning that the economy was the key to any success they would have. In spite of some modest improvements, stagflation remained a reality, and the rising costs from the energy crisis seemed to grow worse by the minute. During his first year in office, Carter proposed a large economic stimulus package that included $4 billion for public works programs. Although an economic conservative, Carter was willing to risk inflation to get a sluggish economy moving and put more Americans back to work. He also sought to end government regulations that he thought got in the way of a more robust economy. He signed the Airline Deregulation Act that ended government control of airline prices with significant benefit to consumers. Later in his term, he also supported an expansion of the food stamp program to provide food to the hungry and stimulate the economy.

Carter appointed former Republican cabinet member James Schlesinger as his special adviser on energy—later secretary of energy when Congress approved the new cabinet department—and told Schlesinger to come up with a comprehensive energy plan, and do so in 3 months. Schlesinger did, and Carter appeared on television to tell the nation of his new proposals, which included a "gas guzzler tax" on high-mileage cars, tax credits for conservation, and a total of 113 separate proposals to reduce energy consumption and increase its availability. *Newsweek* summarized the speech, "Some of the time he was Jimmy the evangelist, preaching to a nation living in energy sin. Then he was Jimmy the engineer, rattling off statistics and throwing around terms like retrofitting and cogeneration. And then he was Jimmy the leader, summoning the nation to fight the 'moral equivalent of war.'" Unfortunately for Carter, the energy plan had been developed in secret, and the Congress was far from enthusiastic about it.

Carter also tried to deal with both unemployment and inflation, but by the fall of 1978, he had become convinced that he had to make inflation his top priority. Robert Strauss, a special counselor in the White House tried with some success to "jawbone" business and labor (persuade them through public appeals) to keep wage increases and prices down. Later in 1978, Carter appointed Alfred Kahn to institute wage and price freezes. Still inflation increased. As Americans used credit cards to keep up with the increases in costs, credit card and other consumer debt grew from $167 billion when Carter took office to $315 billion in 1979, further fueling the inflationary spiral. Only late in Carter's presidency did inflation decline when Paul Volcker, chair of the Federal Reserve Board, dramatically shrank the nation's money supply, causing a major upsurge in unemployment, but that achievement, too, was at great cost to Carter's popularity.

Fueling the inflationary spiral, and causing a crisis of its own, the price of fuel just kept going up. In March 1979, the nuclear reactor at Three Mile Island in central Pennsylvania malfunctioned and the reactor core began to melt down. More than 100,000 Pennsylvania residents were required to flee. The disaster led to a national fear and disdain against nuclear energy. No new nuclear plants were built in the United States, leading to increased dependence on oil (see Map 27-2). However, oil was a volatile source of energy. The United States had long since ceased being able to produce all of the oil it needed and imported a significant amount from the Middle East (see Map 27-3). In the middle of Carter's energy crisis, OPEC increased the price of oil by 60 percent. Carter predicted that the move would cost 800,000 people their jobs in the United States. The immediate result was further inflation and very real shortages. Gas stations across the country simply ran out of gas. The public uproar was palpable, and much of the anger focused on the president.

At the end of June 1979, as Carter returned from foreign policy triumphs—the signing of the SALT II arms control agreement with the Soviet Union in Vienna and an economic summit in Tokyo, Japan—he received a call from his pollster and confidant Patrick Caddell who insisted that Carter come to Washington immediately, saying, "You have no idea how bad it is here." The president cancelled a planned vacation in Hawaii and headed to Washington. After a 10-day retreat at Camp David, Carter spoke to the nation on July 15, 1979, about what he saw as its "crisis of confidence." It was a visionary statement, but it did not shorten the gas lines or improve Carter's standing in the polls.

Some of Carter's greatest early successes came in foreign policy, but foreign policy was also the arena of his greatest failures. He announced one of his goals in his short inaugural address: "We will move this year a step toward our ultimate goal—the elimination of all nuclear weapons from this earth." To accomplish the goal, Carter sought to expand détente with the Soviet Union. He also meant to increase respect for human rights at home and abroad. Under Carter, there would be none of Henry Kissinger's *Realpolitik* stances in foreign affairs that ignored human rights or democratic institutions. Early in his term, Carter took a number of steps in all of these directions. He quickly pardoned draft evaders from the Vietnam era. He halted production of the B-1 bomber which was planned as a more advanced, and expensive, version of the B-52. He ended development of the neutron bomb. He also established full diplomatic relations with the People's Republic of China, furthering the new relationship that Nixon had begun. In 1978, Carter won Senate ratification of treaties for the eventual turnover of the Panama Canal to the Republic of Panama. All of these moves brought harsh critiques, but most Americans supported them.

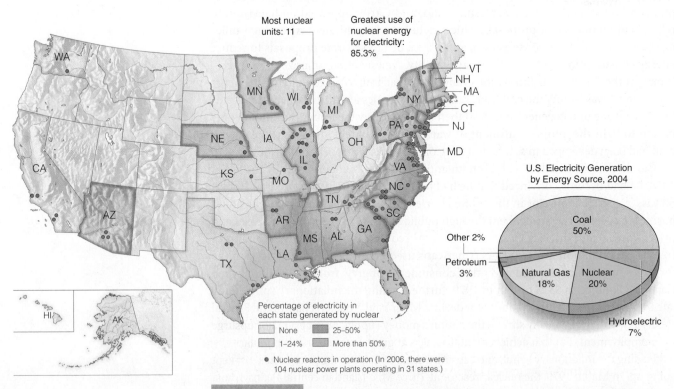

MAP 27-2 Nuclear Plants Around the United States. By 1980, the United States had 103 nuclear reactors that produced power for commercial use, supplying approximately 20 percent of the nation's electricity. After the crisis at Three Mile Island, that number would not grow.

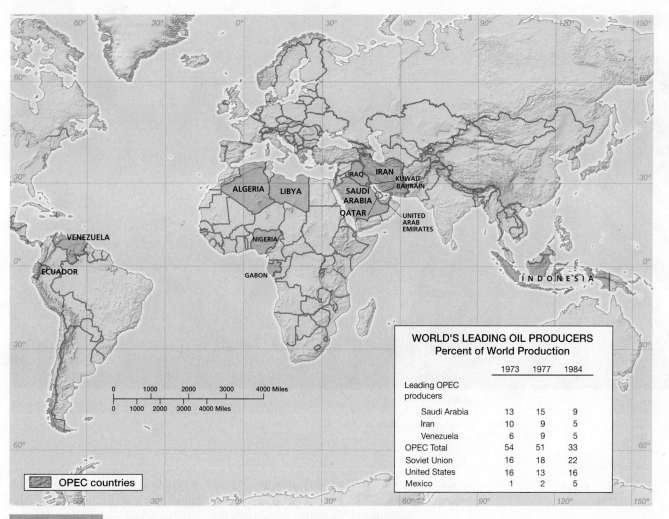

MAP 27-3 Oil-Producing Nations As the United States became more and more dependent on imported oil, it became deeply engaged with the sometimes unstable nations that produced the bulk of the world's supply.

WORLD'S LEADING OIL PRODUCERS
Percent of World Production

	1973	1977	1984
Leading OPEC producers			
Saudi Arabia	13	15	9
Iran	10	9	5
Venezuela	6	9	5
OPEC Total	54	51	33
Soviet Union	16	18	22
United States	16	13	16
Mexico	1	2	5

OPEC countries

Carter's greatest foreign policy triumph was the signing of the **Camp David Accords** between Egypt and Israel in September 1978. Carter was determined to be a Middle East peacemaker. He visited both Egypt and Israel and then invited Menachem Begin of Israel and Anwar Sadat of Egypt to come to the presidential retreat at Camp David for 13 days in September 1978. Carter remembered, "The easy, gentle atmosphere was very helpful. It kept tensions down." After some very tough negotiations, the leaders achieved a major breakthrough. The Camp David Accords included formal recognition of the state of Israel by Egypt while Israel agreed to return the Sinai Peninsula to Egypt.

Carter was dogged in his pursuit of détente with the Soviet Union. In June 1979, Carter negotiated the SALT II agreement that built on earlier agreements and placed a limit on the numbers of missiles and bombers each side would have. It was an important development; however, the effort at détente was undermined by events halfway around the world. In December 1979, the Soviet Union invaded Afghanistan to protect a beleaguered pro-Soviet government there. Carter saw the vastly expanded Soviet presence in Afghanistan as a violation of the decades-old American policy of containing Soviet communism. He ended the export of grain to the Soviet Union and ordered a U.S. boycott of the 1980 summer Olympic Games scheduled for Moscow. In spite of the fact that more than 60 other nations honored the Olympic boycott, it was a deep disappointment to athletes who had been preparing for years to compete. Carter's moves had hurt his popularity at home and had undermined his efforts toward détente.

Camp David Accords

An agreement between Israel and Egypt that brought mutual recognition between the countries and a step toward peace in the Middle East.

Carter's greatest triumph was presiding over a new peace treaty between Anwar al-Sadat of Egypt and Menachem Begin of Israel.

Iranian hostage crisis
The invasion of the American embassy in Iran by revolutionary guards who then took 66 hostages, holding them from November 1979 until January 1981.

Carter's worse foreign policy disaster, however, was with Iran. In January 1979, the government of the shah of Iran (who had been installed by a U.S.-backed coup in the 1950s) was overthrown. Ayatollah Ruhollah Khomeini, the exiled leader of the Muslim radicals, returned to Iran and created an Islamic Republic with a government that was based on religious law and that gave religious leaders like Khomeini ultimate authority. When in October the ailing shah was admitted to the United States for medical treatment, Khomeini and his followers were furious. On November 4, 1979, a mob stormed the U.S. Embassy in Tehran, taking 66 Americans hostage.

The **Iranian hostage crisis** became the dominant event of Carter's last year in office. The government froze Iranian assets in the United States, expanded the pressure on Iran, and tried every way possible to negotiate the release of the American hostages. In April 1980, feeling that negotiations were a failure, Carter approved an attack on Iran to rescue the hostages. The attack was a failure as a sandstorm and hydraulic problems disabled some of the helicopters and another crashed into a cargo plane. Eight Americans were killed but none got close to the hostages. Secretary of State Cyrus Vance resigned in protest. Later that year, after Iraq attacked Iran, the Iranian government agreed to negotiate but the process was slow. Only on the day Carter left office in January 1981, and after Reagan had taken the oath of office, were the hostages released.

The Coming of Ronald Reagan

Carter's problems with the economy, energy, and hostages formed the backdrop to the 1980 election campaign. Within the Democratic Party there was great unease with the president. His cautious economic policies and determination to balance the federal budget alienated liberals. His go-it-alone style alienated Congress. Massachusetts Senator Edward "Ted" Kennedy challenged Carter in the primaries. Public opinion polls showed a two-to-one preference for Kennedy, last of the charismatic Kennedy brothers, over Carter. But Kennedy never seemed able to articulate the reasons he was challenging

Carter. And for all of his popularity, memories persisted of the time in 1969 when Kennedy had driven a car off a bridge near Chappaquiddick on Martha's Vineyard and left a young woman, Mary Jo Kopechne, to drown. In the end, Carter defeated Kennedy for the nomination. Kennedy supported Carter in the general election, but the wounds of a tough primary fight remained. Carter stayed close to the White House and focused on the hostage crisis. The president who once prided himself on his openness and accessibility now adopted a "Rose Garden Strategy," leaving his office only rarely, even to campaign.

The Republicans entered the campaign with great confidence. The contest for the nomination quickly came down to one between former California governor and movie actor, Ronald Reagan, and former CIA director and U.S. ambassador to China, George H.W. Bush. Bush fought a tough campaign, calling Reagan's economic plan "voodoo economics." But Reagan was hugely popular with conservatives who were known as the "Republican base." He was also an effective and articulate campaigner and easily won the nomination. Reagan named Bush as his running mate. Conservatives, who had felt marginalized since Barry Goldwater's loss in 1964, believed that their day had come. Reagan was an effective campaigner, impressing many with his sunny optimism. In the one presidential debate that was held, Reagan scored points with his poise and his response "There you go again" to a Carter critique. Reagan won in a landslide. The Republicans gained 34 seats in the House, though it still had a Democratic majority, but they took over the Senate with a 53 to 47 majority that included the defeat of Democratic stalwarts Frank Church of Idaho and George McGovern of South Dakota. The Democratic Speaker of the House, Tip O'Neill said of the election, "A tidal wave hit us." Bill Moyers, who had served in the Johnson administration, said, "We didn't elect this guy [Reagan] because he knows how many barrels of oil are in Alaska. We elected him because we want to feel good." The 1980s and the time of the "Reagan Revolution" would be a very different one than the decade that had just ended.

Blindfolded American hostages are paraded outside the U.S. Embassy in Teheran by their militant captors after Iranian students stormed the embassy in November, 1979. Sixty Americans and 40 nationals from other countries were taken by the students and held captive inside the embassy.

27.4 **Quick Review** What could Ford and Carter have done to be more effective during their terms in office?

CONCLUSION

Public discourse in the United States, which had been heated in the 1960s, became even more divisive and angry after 1969. In the 1970s, new Civil Rights Movements emerged as women, gays and lesbians, Latinos, Asians, and American Indians began to demand equality and fair treatment. Against this expanding civil rights backdrop, a new conservative ideology surfaced, focusing on religion, morality, and culture. Compared with the 1950s and 1960s, the 1970s ushered in an economic downturn that undercut the security of many Americans. The 1970s also gave rise to political turmoil as one president was forced to resign in disgrace and two others lost their bids for reelection.

The new Civil Rights Movements of the 1970s resulted in advancements for many segments of the American population. Women achieved significant legislative and judicial victories, which allowed them to improve both their working conditions and their social status. Filipino and Mexican American farm workers successfully bargained for recognition of a union in California. American Indians staged protests at Alcatraz, Wounded Knee, and the offices of the Bureau of Indian Affairs, achieving modest gains with respect to civil rights and tribal autonomy. Gay and lesbian Americans began to step out of the closet, and the modern gay rights movement was born. At the same time, traditional conservatives were bewildered and angered by the rapidly shifting culture of the United States, and the so-called culture wars began. The "moral majority" organized a political response to repudiate both the civil rights agendas of the 1960s and 1970s and the Great Society legislation of Lyndon Johnson.

The Republican Party became increasingly conservative in the 1970s, but Richard Nixon was an inconsistent conservative at best. During Nixon's tenure, Title IX was added to the Civil Rights Act, the Environmental Protection Agency and the Occupational Safety and Health Administration were created, and overall government spending to aid the poor rose significantly. On the international front, Nixon authorized a relentless bombing campaign against North Vietnam and secretly expanded the fighting into Cambodia. At the same time, Nixon sought to withdraw all ground troops from Vietnam. Despite the war in Vietnam, Nixon normalized relations with Communist China and successfully negotiated two treaties with the Soviets designed to reduce the supply of nuclear weapons. Ultimately, the Watergate scandal ended Nixon's presidency. When Vice President Gerald Ford took office, he hoped to heal a wounded nation, but controversial domestic decisions and multiple foreign policy crises seriously damaged the effectiveness of his administration.

In 1976, Jimmy Carter, a little-known governor from Georgia was elected president. Carter successfully brokered a peace between Egypt and Israel. Nonetheless, ongoing economic problems at home—inflation, a high unemployment rate, and gas shortages—and his failure to secure the release of American hostages in Iran resulted in Carter's stunning reelection defeat to Ronald Reagan in 1980.

CHAPTER REVIEW How do you account for the political dissatisfaction with presidents Nixon, Ford, and Carter in the midst of so much change in the United States? What changes might have helped them? Which hurt the most?

THE NEW POLITICS OF THE LATE 1960s

27.1 Explain Nixon's policies and politics, domestic and international.

Review Questions

1. Crafting an Argument

In your opinion, how should Richard Nixon's domestic record be characterized? As conservative? As liberal? In some other way?

2. Comparison

Compare and contrast Nixon and Johnson's approaches to the war in Vietnam. How would you account for the differences you note?

3. Contextualization

What did Nixon hope to gain by visiting China in 1972?

THE MOVEMENTS OF THE 1960s AND 1970s

27.2 Analyze the many political and cultural movements that followed in the track of the Civil Rights movement.

Review Questions

4. Comparison

What similarities and differences do you see between the African-American Civil Rights Movement of the 1950s and early 1960s and the Civil Rights Movements launched by other group in the late 1960s and early 1970s? How did the fight for racial equality for African-Americans influence other movements?

5. Chronological Reasoning

How did the struggle for African-American rights change over the course of the 1960s? Why did it change?

THE CULTURE WARS OF THE 1970s

27.3 Analyze the reaction to the liberal and radical politics of the 1960s and 1970s and the growth of new militant conservative movements.

Review Questions

6. Historical Interpretation

What connections can you make between the defeat of the Equal Rights Amendment and the larger cultural and political trends of the 1970s?

7. Contextualization

What role did religious organizations play in the conservative movement of the 1970s and 1980s? How did religious organizations both facilitate the rise of conservatives to political power and help redefine the conservative movement?

POLITICS, ECONOMICS, AND THE IMPACT OF WATERGATE

27.4 Explain the political impact of Watergate and subsequent developments that set the stage for the "Reagan Revolution."

Review Questions

8. Chronological Reasoning

Why did the prosperity of the 1950s and 1960s give way to the economic downturn of the 1970s? Why did American political leaders find the economic problems of the 1970s so difficult to solve?

9. Comparison

Compare and contrast the Ford and Carter presidencies. What challenges did both presidents face?

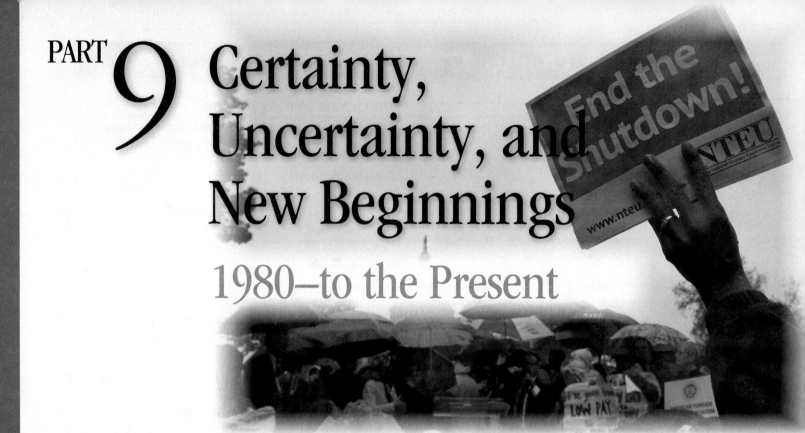

PART 9

Certainty, Uncertainty, and New Beginnings

1980–to the Present

The Reagan Revolution

No American president since Franklin Roosevelt has so dominated the nation's politics and, indeed, culture as Ronald Reagan, shown here at his inauguration in 1981.

The voters who gave Ronald Reagan his margin of victory over Jimmy Carter in 1980 were a diverse lot. Working-class whites, north and south, sometimes called "Reagan Democrats," were alienated by the civil rights and protest movements of the 1960s and 1970s. Many feared crime, which they tended to see as a "black issue," and wanted a champion of "law and order." The coalition also included middle-class and upper-middle-class suburbanites in revolt over taxes, especially rising property taxes, and government regulations that they thought were intrusive. The antitax movement led to the passage of Proposition 13 in California in 1978, a law sponsored by a private citizen, Howard Jarvis, which significantly cut California's property taxes and ultimately the state's vaunted government services. Other states copied Proposition 13, reducing taxes and public services. A third group of Reagan supporters were social conservatives—Catholics and Protestants associated with the religious right—for whom the key issues were their opposition to abortion, sexual and reproductive freedoms, gay rights, and the teaching of evolution as well as their desire for prayer in the public schools. In seeking to limit abortion or gay rights, the social conservatives wanted a more activist government, even if they otherwise favored a smaller government and lower taxes.

These diverse groups also shared a staunch hostility to communism and believed that presidents from Franklin Roosevelt to Richard Nixon had been too soft. They were united in their anger at those they considered elitist—celebrities in Hollywood, the media, universities, and the federal government. In Ronald Reagan, the former actor and two-term governor of California, they

CHAPTER OBJECTIVE

Demonstrate an understanding of the changes in government and in the larger society in the times known as the Reagan Revolution.

LEARNING OBJECTIVES

A RAPIDLY CHANGING U.S. GOVERNMENT

Explain Reagan's impact on the United States and the world. **28.1**

THE CHANGING NATURE OF THE AMERICAN ECONOMY

Explain international economic developments that shaped the United States. **28.2**

CHANGES IN THE REST OF THE COUNTRY

Explain cultural changes in the United States during the 1980s. **28.3**

Reagan Revolution

Major changes in American politics under the leadership of Ronald Reagan, including cuts in taxes and domestic spending and increased military spending.

found a hero who, they believed, would not disappoint them as had Richard Nixon. This chapter is a look at the Reagan Revolution, the wide-ranging changes in the federal government, in U.S. international relations, and in American culture that took place while Ronald Reagan was president, some with his support and some in spite of his best efforts.

A RAPIDLY CHANGING U.S. GOVERNMENT

28.1 Explain Reagan's impact on the United States and the world.

Many federal government programs that dated from the New Deal changed drastically during what came to be known as the **Reagan Revolution**. By the end of the 8 years that Ronald Reagan was president, taxes took less of people's incomes, the federal debt ballooned, and a 50-year period in which labor unions could rely on a friendly government came to an end. The Cold War, which had been the dominant element in U.S. foreign policy since the end of World War II, also ended. Both the Republican and Democratic parties emerged from the Reagan Revolution more conservative than they had been. Supporters and detractors all agreed that the presidency of Ronald Reagan was a significant turning point in the United States.

Ronald Reagan and the Reagan Coalition

When Ronald Reagan became president, he was only 1 month short of his 70th birthday, the oldest man ever elected to the office. Reagan was born in the small town of Tampico, Illinois, in 1911. His father was a shoe salesman and an alcoholic who was unsuccessful in his search for better jobs until he was hired by the New Deal's WPA. His mother, who worked as a seamstress, was a religious woman who made sure that the young Ronald and his brother were brought up in church. He said of his childhood, "We didn't live on the wrong side of the tracks, but we lived so close we could hear the whistle real loud." Handsome and popular, Reagan was elected high school class president and then student body president at Eureka College in Illinois.

Soon after college, and after a brief stint as a sports announcer in Iowa, Reagan left the Midwest for Hollywood where he appeared in 53 films between 1937 and 1953. It was steady work and it paid well. Reagan later said that he generally made two pictures per year, earning $300,000 to $400,000 per film, and would have worked harder to make more pictures if not for the high tax bite. The film work took Reagan a long way from the marginal economic status of his childhood. He married and later divorced Jane Wyman, whose Hollywood career was more successful than his; he would be the first divorced person elected president. He was popular in Hollywood and was elected president of the Screen Actors Guild from 1947 to 1952, a position he used to identify suspected Communists in the film industry. When he became U.S. president, he was the first former union president to do so. During his Hollywood years, Reagan remained a Democrat, voting for Harry Truman in 1948 and against Richard Nixon for the Senate in 1950.

In 1952 he married Nancy Davis and left a declining Hollywood career to become a spokesperson for the General Electric Company, serving as the TV host of the General Electric Theater program from 1954 to 1962. Working for GE, he also gave pep talks to workers at GE plants, touted GE products, and spoke about the corporation's views on taxes and government regulation to business groups. In his GE career, as in Hollywood, Reagan mastered the art of connecting with audiences, especially, maintaining a relaxed and genial presence in the face of lights, crowds, and distractions as well as delivering content from a script. While at GE he also changed his party registration from Democrat to Republican.

By the time Reagan left GE in 1962, he was as well-known for his political views as his acting. He supported Barry Goldwater in 1964. In a standard stump speech that came to be known simply as "the speech," Reagan said that the choice facing Americans was "whether we believe in our capacity for self-government or whether we abandon the American Revolution and confess that a little intellectual elite in a far-distant capital can plan our lives for us better than we can plan them ourselves." The speech did not elect Goldwater, but it did bring Reagan to the attention of a crucial audience—rich Republican conservatives who agreed to back him if he would run for governor of California in 1966. The incumbent governor, Democrat Edmund G. "Pat" Brown, a tough campaigner who had defeated Richard Nixon in 1962, was seeking a third term in 1966. Reagan defeated him in the fall election and won reelection as governor in 1970.

Reagan talked a more conservative line all through his presidency than he practiced while he was governor of California. While he was tough on student protests, raised tuition at California's public colleges and universities, and ousted Clark Kerr as the president of the University of California, he was willing to compromise with a Democratic legislature on other matters. He raised taxes to cover a budget shortfall as well as signed bills supporting liberalized abortion rights and bilingual education. Some of his conservative supporters were nervous about his positions but valued his skill as a campaigner. As a conservative governor of the nation's largest state, Reagan quickly became a presidential contender. He almost defeated Gerald Ford for the 1976 Republican nomination and easily defeated George H.W. Bush to win the 1980 nomination and then the presidential election against Jimmy Carter. As president, he did not disappoint most of his supporters.

Reaganomics—Supply-Side Tax Cuts, Military Growth, and Electoral Politics

Reagan came to office with three priorities: increasing military spending to ensure that the United States was significantly stronger than the Soviet Union, cutting domestic spending and government-sponsored social programs, and cutting the federal income tax. He was willing to compromise on almost everything else.

The antitax crusade had helped elect Reagan, and he surrounded himself with advisors who developed new economic theories to defend a tax cut even as he sought increased military spending. Reagan justified the tax cut with an economic theory known as **supply-side economics**. As defined by Republican congressman Jack Kemp and Democratic senator Lloyd Bentsen, supply-side referred to stimulating the economy, not by means of federal spending—the traditional approach since the New Deal—but, rather, by means of supporting the supply side—cutting taxes to foster private investment that might then lead to the creation of new jobs.

Tax cut proponents also cited what is called the "Laffer curve." Developed in the 1970s by Jude Wanniski, a correspondent for the *Wall Street Journal*, and economist Arthur Laffer, the curve meant to show that higher taxes reduced government income by reducing the incentive to work and earn taxable wages. At the extreme ends, the curve made complete sense. Zero tax would not impact work and earning in any way, and a 100 percent tax would certainly stifle most work. But the point in between, where taxes really cut into the will to work and where decreased tax rates might actually increase government income, was hard to pinpoint.

When Reagan first called for a 30 percent tax cut and used Laffer and the supply-side arguments to justify his position, his main rival for the 1980 Republican nomination, George Bush, called it "voodoo economics," and Jimmy Carter called Reagan's tax plans, "rebates for the rich, deprivation for the poor, and fierce inflation for all of us." But after he became president, Reagan dismissed criticism, saying of the economists who challenged his ideas, "They're the sort of people who see something works in practice and wonder if it works in theory." In spite of a lack of evidence in either practice or theory, the president made a tax cut his first priority, and in August, 48 congressional Democrats—their Democratic colleagues called them "boll weevils"—joined the Republican minority to pass a cut in federal income taxes that reduced the top rate on individual income from 70 to 50 percent. The president won the first of his three goals for his Reagan Revolution—the implementation of "Reaganomics," as his economic policy came to be called—in less than 100 days in office.

supply-side economics
An economic theory that to stimulate the economy the best intervention is a tax cut that would stimulate the "supply side."

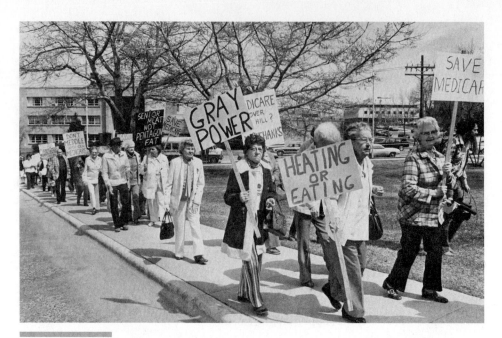

The Reagan cuts in domestic programs, including health insurance benefits for the elderly through Medicare, were not done without protest, as shown here. But few protests had a major impact on the cuts themselves.

In addition to the tax cut, Congress passed a modified version of Reagan's budget. He did not get all the cuts he wanted, but the new federal budget reduced domestic spending significantly. Reagan also used his administrative authority to cut a number of additional federal programs, including food stamps and other programs for the poor as well as Social Security benefits for people with disabilities. Some 500,000 people were removed from the Social Security disability list. Another 300,000 who had been employed through the Carter administration's Comprehensive Employment and Training Act (CETA) lost their government-sponsored jobs. The cuts were not the wholesale abolition of welfare that Reagan advocated, but they represented a substantial cut in the federal safety net that had been growing since the 1930s. At the same time, some programs such as Aid to Families with Dependent Children (AFDC) and federal tax credits for the poor actually expanded during the Reagan years.

While campaigning for the presidency, Reagan also promised to expand the military so the United States would, without question, be the most powerful nation on earth. As a candidate, he said, "You spend what you need." As president, he got congressional approval to develop a new B-2 bomber as well as cruise and MX missiles and to expand the Navy. During his first term in office, from 1981 to 1985, the total defense spending of the United States rose by 34 percent, from $171 billion to $229 billion.

Within months of the new administration coming to office, Americans understood that the change in Washington was significant, indeed, that some federal policies that had been in place since the 1930s were no longer going to continue. In addition to the tax cuts and expanded military spending, the new administration showed its attitude when the members of the Professional Air Traffic Controllers' Organization (PATCO)—the people who guide airplanes on take-off and landing—went on strike. The president told the members of the union, who were federal employees, that they had 48 hours to go back to work or they would be fired. When almost two-thirds of PATCOs members stayed out on strike, Reagan fired all 11,000 of them. They permanently lost their jobs, and the union was destroyed. People worried about the safety of air travel with so many veteran controllers gone, but the signal that this administration was going to have a different view of unions was clear. Organized labor, used to having a friend in the White House, was demoralized. Other strikes were also defeated, including an especially bitter one by the meatpackers at the Hormel plant in Minnesota in 1985–86. Union membership dropped from one-fourth of the U.S. workforce to one-sixth during Reagan's two terms. Organized labor, long a major force in American society, was on a long slow decline, something that delighted the president and his conservative backers.

In the short term, the Reagan initiatives did not improve the nation's economy. The president strongly supported Federal Reserve Chair Paul Volcker, whom Carter had appointed. Both presidents told Volcker to curb inflation no matter what the cost. Volcker did, with tough policies that sent unemployment above 10 percent in 1982, the highest since the Great Depression of the 1930s. Many people lost jobs, and new jobs were often in low-paying service sectors of the economy. Homelessness doubled while Reagan was in office from an estimated 200,000 to 400,000. The recession of the early Reagan years hurt the president's popularity, and the Republicans lost seats in Congress in the 1982 elections. Reagan, with his optimism and self-confidence, asked the nation to "Stay the Course." By 1983, the national economy started to improve and continued to do so through the last 5 years of Reagan's tenure. Economists argued whether the improvement was due to the tax cuts or expanded military spending, but in either case, a strong economy made Reagan more popular.

One result of the Reagan economic agenda was rapid growth in the federal deficit. The tax cut did not bring in as much new revenue as estimated, while the expansion of military spending more than offset cuts in domestic programs. The total federal deficit nearly tripled during the Reagan years from $914 billion to $2.7 trillion. More than one supporter saw the deficit as Reagan's greatest failure. The United States, which had been a major creditor nation since World War I, became the world's largest debtor nation. The government kept borrowing money to cover the federal deficit while individuals borrowed money—often by running up credit card debt. If some complained that Americans were maintaining a living standard beyond their means, they quickly noted that the worst offender was the U.S. government. Daniel Patrick Moynihan, once an advisor to Richard Nixon and who was a Democratic Senator from New York throughout the Reagan years, warned that the huge deficits virtually guaranteed that new federal initiatives to improve the lives of average or poor citizens were now off the table.

Reagan faced the prospect of reelection in 1984 with some significant strengths and some formidable weaknesses. To challenge him, the Democrats had, after an intense primary battle with Colorado senator Gary Hart, selected former vice president Walter Mondale as the Democratic candidate for president. In an historic move, Mondale asked New York Representative, Geraldine Ferraro, to be his running mate, the first time a woman was on the ticket of a major political party. At 73, Reagan seemed old, especially when in one debate with Mondale he seemed to lose track of a story he was telling. Reagan dismissed the issue saying, "I will not make age an issue in this campaign. I am not going to exploit, for political purposes, my opponent's youth and inexperience."

Reagan could not so easily dismiss other issues, however. Labor unions almost unanimously supported Mondale, although because of Reagan's policies they had far less clout. Most African-Americans supported Mondale, continuing a move by black voters to the Democratic Party that was speeded by Reagan's inattention to their needs. Moreover, Reagan's silence on the rising epidemic of AIDS, a new and deadly disease, created some of his toughest enemies. Even social and religious conservatives who had flocked to Reagan in 1980 were disappointed. He had done little more than talk about many of their issues such as school prayer during his first term. As president, he never gave a speech to an antiabortion audience. However, conservatives did not have another candidate.

Other developments helped Reagan in 1984. By 1983, the economy started to turn around. More Americans had jobs and people were buying more goods, often on credit, including personal computers, video cassette recorders (VCRs), and telephone answering machines that had not been available in the 1970s.

Morning Again in America
The campaign slogan of Ronald Reagan's reelection effort in 1984.

President Ronald Reagan looks to his left as a secret service agent places a hand on his shoulder and pushes the President into his limousine after he was shot leaving a Washington hotel, March 30, 1981.

Reagan also benefitted from an upsurge of popular patriotism that he had helped to foster. The space shuttle program had been years in the making since the days when Americans worried about *Sputnik* and Soviet leadership in space, but Reagan benefitted from the good will when the first space shuttle was successfully launched in April 1981. Reagan's tough line with the Soviet Union pleased anti-Communists, and the fact that at the end of his first term he was the first president since Herbert Hoover never to have met with a Soviet leader did not worry them. In June 1984, Reagan traveled to France for the 40th anniversary of the D-Day landing that ended World War II. In a series of events carefully scripted by his communications director, Michael Deaver, he led a series of jubilant and patriotism-filled celebrations honoring veterans and American power. Later that summer, the Olympics were held in Los Angeles, and Reagan led the celebrations, emphasizing how far the country had come since the boycott of the games in Moscow only 4 years before. Reagan's wealthy supporters also gave him a huge financial edge over Mondale.

Perhaps most of all, Reagan's own sunny disposition made people like him. His TV ads reinforced Reagan's message that it was "***Morning Again in America.***" His optimism was on full display when on March 30, 1981, Reagan was shot while leaving a speaking event. His press secretary James Brady was severely wounded and permanently disabled. Few knew at the time how seriously the president had been wounded when a bullet lodged in his left lung and he bled heavily. But just before entering surgery, Reagan looked at his wife, Nancy, and said, "Honey, I forgot to duck," and then asked the surgeons, "Please tell me you're all Republicans." That sort of pluck made him popular even with people who disagreed with his policies. In addition, his speaking style was extraordinary. His many years as an actor paid off. His friends called him, "The Great Communicator," and even his toughest opponents admired him. The Democratic Speaker of the House, Tip O'Neill, who tangled with Reagan on many occasions, said of him, "He may not be much of a debater, but with a prepared text he's the best public speaker I've ever seen….I'm beginning to think that in this regard he dwarfs both Roosevelt and Kennedy."

In the November 1984 vote, Reagan carried every state except Mondale's home state of Minnesota and the District of Columbia and won almost 60 percent of the popular vote. While Republicans continued to control the Senate 53 to 46, the Democrats controlled the House 252 to 182.

A year after the election, a group of Democrats, including Representative Richard Gephardt of Missouri and Governor Bill Clinton of Arkansas organized the Democratic Leadership Council. These "New Democrats" argued that there was more to the election than Reagan's personal popularity and that the Democratic Party was not going to win elections until it moved closer to the conservative mainstream. The creation of the Democratic Leadership Council was high tribute to the conservative shift in American opinion that constituted the heart of the Reagan Revolution and signaled a move away from traditional New Deal Democratic values that included significant government services, especially for those in need, and support for labor unions.

As Reagan entered his second term, people expected a repeat of the first. Reagan's top priority remained reducing taxes, and in the mid-1980s, many Democrats agreed. A bipartisan coalition passed the Tax Reform Act of 1986 that cut the number of tax brackets from 14 to two, with tax rates of 15 and 28 percent respectively, while closing many tax loopholes. Led by the president, who had begun his term cutting the tax rate for the wealthiest Americans from 70 to 50 percent, the government had now cut it to 28 percent.

After the 1986 tax bill passed, Reagan devoted more and more of his time to foreign policy. He continued to appoint conservative judges and to support deregulation and the shrinking of the federal government, but he did not present major domestic policy initiatives in his last 2 years in office. Reagan had come to office a devout Cold Warrior. But before he left office, he presided over the greatest change in U.S.–Soviet relationships since Franklin Roosevelt had granted official U.S. recognition to the Soviet Union in the 1930s.

Expanding the Cold War—From Star Wars to Iran Contra

When Ronald Reagan became president in January 1981, he had virtually no foreign policy experience. He was more sophisticated as a politician than many of his detractors (and some of his supporters) admitted. Nevertheless, he had not spent much time outside of the United States and did not know much about foreign policy. He was served by a series of weak national security advisors as well as two secretaries of state, two secretaries of defense, and a strong director of central intelligence, William Casey, all of whom disliked each other intensely, kept major developments secret from each other, and at times implemented contradictory policies. First Lady Nancy Reagan also took an active role in policy discussions, especially when she feared that conservative ideologues were taking her husband in an unnecessarily hard-line direction. It was not an administrative structure leading to crisp and clear decision making. However, in the midst of apparent chaos, Reagan himself appeared to have been a far stronger leader than perceived, one who determined the main aspects of his foreign policy even as he left the details of implementation to others.

EFFORTS TO UNDERMINE COMMUNISM   Reagan had several deeply held beliefs that would drive his foreign policy. His fierce anticommunism, which first developed when he battled with perceived Communists in the film industry in the 1940s, was reinforced by his religious faith, which was offended by Communist atheism. His ability to articulate that passionate stance against communism had been honed through his speaking career for GE and as governor. He saw communism, as he once said, as "the focus of evil in the modern world," and the United States as the exceptional carrier of goodness—the "shining city on a hill." He disliked the longstanding policy of containment that had been at the core of American foreign policy from Truman to Carter. He did not want merely to contain communism where it was. He wanted to undermine existing Communist governments.

Despite that fierce anticommunism, however, Reagan had a far greater horror of nuclear war than some of his fellow conservatives. His firm belief was that a nuclear war could "never be won and must never be fought." During his first term, he never trusted the Soviets enough to engage in serious negotiations, but he was determined to avoid nuclear war.

During his first term, Reagan was harshly critical of the Soviet Union. In a 1983 speech to Christian evangelicals, Reagan referred to the Soviet Union as "**the evil empire**." A year later, in August 1984, thinking that the microphone was turned off, Reagan said, "My fellow Americans, I am pleased to tell you today that I've signed legislation that will outlaw Russia forever. We begin bombing in five minutes." It was a joke, but the Soviets found it frightening. Reagan also ordered a massive arms buildup. Worried about U.S vulnerability and believing that any negotiations needed to be from a position of strength, Reagan supported annual increases in the military budget between 1981 and 1986. He arranged the deployment of new intermediate-range missiles in Europe in 1983 and resisted serious talks with Soviet leaders.

Reagan's goal of undermining communism where it already existed led also to other steps. In 1981, as protest movements spread in Poland and the Polish Communist government instituted martial law, Reagan imposed sanctions on Poland and on the Soviet Union: an end to landing rights in the United States for the Russian airline Aeroflot, a ban on the sale of equipment for a Soviet natural gas pipeline, and—at the petty level—termination of the special parking privileges of Soviet Ambassador Anatoly Dobrynin in the State Department garage. The administration secretly funneled some $20 million to Solidarity, the Polish protest movement, through the Vatican Bank, with the approval of Polish Pope John Paul II.

In March 1983, Reagan, against the almost unanimous advice of his foreign policy team who seldom agreed on anything, announced that the United States was going to develop a **Strategic Defense Initiative (SDI)**. As the president described it, SDI would use U.S. technological know-how to create a series of space stations armed with lasers

the evil empire
A phrase that Reagan used for the Soviet Union in particular and all Communist countries in general.

Strategic Defense Initiative
President Reagan's program to defend the United States with sophisticated technologies, also known as "Star Wars."

that would destroy any enemy missiles fired at the United States. He thought that the long-standing U.S. policy dating to the Eisenhower administration of mutually assured destruction, in which each superpower had the ability to retaliate after a nuclear attack, was essentially a commitment to mutual suicide. In 1979, Edward Teller, the lead scientist in the development of the hydrogen bomb, told Reagan that for all its ability to build and launch missiles, the United States had virtually no defense against incoming missiles. As president, Reagan was determined to create one, to make Soviet missiles "impotent and obsolete." Reagan was convinced that the United States could do it.

Senior advisors worried that SDI would be expensive, impractical, and a needless escalation of the Cold War. Critics called the whole system "Star Wars," and worried that it would militarize space, drain the treasury, and ultimately turn out to be ineffective. Military contractors, however, loved SDI. The president was committed, and throughout his two terms, research and development of the system continued.

Only long after Reagan left office did it become clear how deeply fearful Soviet leaders were of the Reagan rhetoric and arms buildup, especially SDI. The Soviets feared that SDI would make them vulnerable to a U.S attack, one they could not resist if they could not retaliate. In September 1983, a Soviet satellite mistook blips for incoming U.S. missiles and the country went on full military alert. Only the courage of a young Soviet officer, who believed that there was a computer error and who overrode the system, appears to have avoided a World War III with millions of deaths in both countries. The Cold War had never been so dangerous.

MANAGING RELATIONS IN THE MIDDLE EAST As the United States focused on the Soviet Union, the Reagan foreign policy advisors also viewed the rest of the world through the prism of the Cold War, sometimes with disastrous results. Regarding the Middle East, Reagan came to office with a generally pro-Israel point of view, a perspective that was supported by many Christian evangelicals in his political base. His team believed that Jimmy Carter's Camp David accords had tilted U.S. policy too closely toward Egypt and wanted to correct the balance. At the same time, they saw Israel, Egypt, Jordan, and Saudi Arabia as U.S. allies and were prepared to sell military aircraft to the Saudis and to supply Israel with jet bombers and military hardware. Their goal was to create a strong buffer in the Middle East against Syria and Iraq, both of which were viewed as Soviet client states (see Map 28-1).

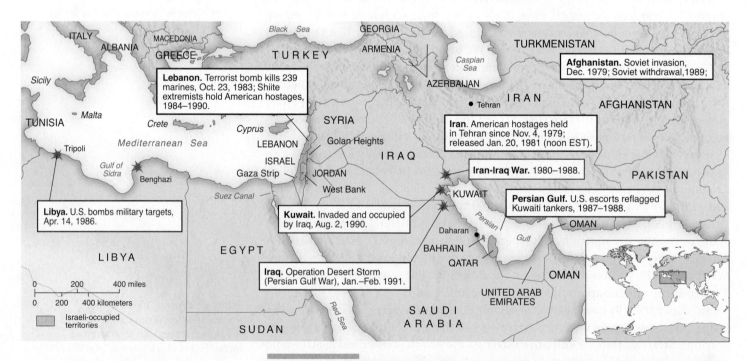

MAP 28-1 The United States and the Middle East. Events in the Middle East, Afghanistan, and northern Africa involved the United States in a series of crises during the 1980s that would only expand in the 1990s.

In Afghanistan, Reagan expanded the Carter-era efforts to resist the Soviet occupation. In 1983 and 1984, the United States provided significant aid to the Mujahedeen opposition whom Reagan called "freedom fighters." In 1985, when the Soviets escalated their involvement, Reagan ordered his military to do "what's necessary to win," and the United States began supplying the Afghan resistance with antiaircraft missiles and satellite-based intelligence on Soviet troop movements. Eventually, the Soviets withdrew from Afghanistan, leaving the CIA-backed Taliban in control of the country. It was a short-term victory but one that came with significant long-term consequences not only for the people of Afghanistan but also for the United States.

In addition, the leader of Libya was cause for concern. Libya's longtime leader Muammar Gaddafi had come to power in 1969, long before Reagan's time. Most of his North African neighbors found him to be a troublemaker, but he especially liked to create trouble for the United States. Reagan was determined to respond. In 1981, the U.S. Navy conducted exercises off the Libyan coast, and when Libyan jets attacked, the Navy shot them down. As terrorism expanded across the Middle East, Reagan was sure Gaddafi was behind much of it. When a TWA flight was hijacked in June 1985 and a West German discotheque was bombed in December of that year, killing one U.S. soldier, Reagan retaliated. In April 1986, the United States bombed Gaddafi's headquarters in Tripoli, destroying much of the Libyan air force and killing some 30 civilians including Gadaffi's 15-month-old adopted daughter. For a time, Libya was quiet, but in December 1988, a Pan Am flight was blown up over Lockerbie, Scotland, and the plot was again traced to Libya. Nevertheless, Gadaffi maintained his hold on power until 2011.

Although the hostage crisis with Iran ended the day Reagan came to office in January 1981, the United States remained hostile to Iran because of the crisis. When Iran and Iraq went to war against each other in September 1980, the United States tended to wish both sides ill. However, as the war continued, members of Reagan's National Security Council (NSC) became convinced that it might be possible to support moderates within the Iranian government and build a new U.S. relationship by supplying Iran with weapons. The United States also had good reason to believe that Iran had influence with forces in Lebanon that were holding seven U.S. citizens hostage. NSC staff, led by National Security Advisor Robert McFarlane, argued Iran might help free the hostages, which was a high priority for the president. Carrying forged Irish passports and traveling under assumed names, McFarlane and his deputy, Lieutenant Colonel Oliver North, secretly visited Tehran. In spite of U.S. policy never to negotiate for the release of hostages and despite its official arms embargo of Iran, the United States sold over 2,000 missiles to Iran in 1985 and 1986. It was the beginning of the greatest foreign policy misadventure of the Reagan administration.

Reagan and his advisers were further pulled into Middle East conflicts when Israel invaded Lebanon in June 1982. Israel's goal was to attack the Palestine Liberation Organization (PLO) presence in Lebanon and create a buffer against Syria. Reagan did not object, though he tried to get Israel to limit its engagement. Later that year, the United States sent a detachment of Marines to join an international peace effort in Lebanon. In October 1983, a truck loaded with TNT drove into the U.S. barracks killing 241 Marines. Americans, including the president, were horrified at the loss of life. The purpose the Marines were supposed to serve was always vague, and after the tragedy, the administration announced that the Marines were to be "redeployed" to ships off the coast where they moved in 1984.

In response to the experience in Lebanon, Defense Secretary Caspar Weinberger and his top military advisor and future chair of the Joint Chiefs of Staff, Colin Powell, crafted what became known as the Powell Doctrine. Henceforth, they said, U.S. soldiers would be sent overseas only as a last resort and only if the mission was clearly defined, attainable, supported by the public, and included an exit strategy, none of which had been true in the case of the deployment in Lebanon. The new restrictions would be honored more clearly in some cases than others. Toward the end of the Reagan administration, when Palestinians in the Gaza Strip and West Bank territories under the control of Israel rose up in what they called the *intifada* (or "shaking off"), the United States did little beyond urge both sides to negotiate.

DEALING WITH PERCEIVED THREATS IN LATIN AMERICA   U.S. policy in Central America, especially in El Salvador, Honduras, and Nicaragua, was also shaped by the Cold War. Since the 1920s, Democratic and Republican administrations depended on a series of Latin American dictators to create a safe climate for U.S. business and ensure that there was no Communist influence in the government of their countries. What they did to their own citizens was of less concern to American authorities. By the time Reagan had come to office, the longtime dictator in Nicaragua, Anastasio Somoza, had been overthrown by a popular uprising, and the totalitarian regime in El Salvador was seriously threatened by similar opposition. Fearing Communist influence in such popular uprisings, the Reagan administration supported the besieged government of El Salvador and sought to overthrow the new government of Nicaragua (see Map 28-2).

Jean Kirkpatrick, Reagan's United Nations ambassador, said that Central America was "the most important place in the world for us." Kirkpatrick also outlined a key Reagan policy of differentiating between authoritarian governments such as that of El Salvador, which Kirkpatrick said could in time be reformed into democracies, and totalitarian governments—particularly, the government of the Soviet Union and its client states—which she claimed would never change. Under the policy, the United States would provide support for the former and opposition to the latter.

The same month as the attack on the Marine barracks in Lebanon, October 1983, Reagan ordered U.S. troops into the small Caribbean island nation of Grenada, where a military coup had overthrown the previous government. Fearing growing Communist influence, and worried about U.S. medical students in Grenada, U.S. troops quickly defeated the coup leaders. Leaders in other countries and in the United Nations condemned the invasion as a violation of international law, but some, in and out of Grenada, were grateful for the U.S. role.

Even though a majority of the Congress wanted nothing to do with supporting Central American dictators or overthrowing governments, the administration was determined to see its will done. While rejecting a proposal to invade Cuba, made by

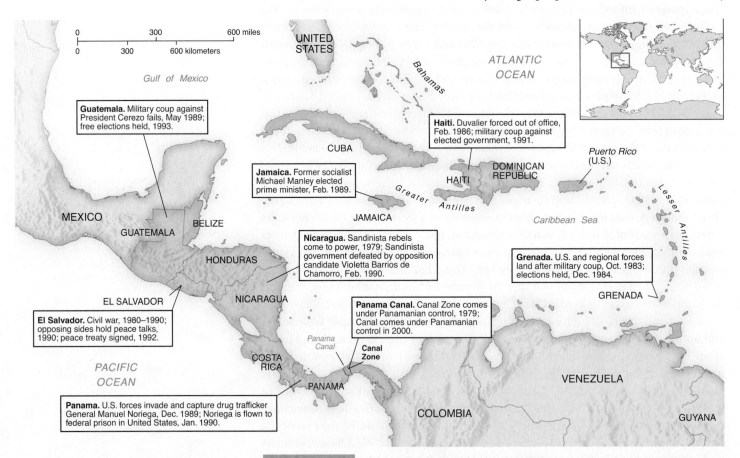

MAP 28-2 The United States and the Americas. During the Reagan and Bush administrations, the United States intervened several times in Central America, especially in Nicaragua and El Salvador, and in the Caribbean.

Alexander Haig during his short tenure as secretary of state, Reagan greatly expanded military aid and sent military advisers to El Salvador. That support was authorized even while government-sanctioned death squads assassinated critics, including the Archbishop of San Salvador, Oscar Romero, murdered while he was saying mass in 1980.

The United States also determined to intervene in Nicaragua, where the new socialist Sandinista government was committed to land reform. In December 1981, Reagan, at the urging of CIA director Casey, authorized $20 million for covert operations to support the Nicaraguan "Contras" (or counterrevolutionaries) who sought to overthrow the new government. The core of the Contra movement was a group of some 500 followers of Somoza, but it grew to an army of perhaps 10,000 who were trained in U.S.-sponsored camps in Honduras and sent back to Nicaragua with U.S.-supplied weapons to disrupt the workings of the Sandinista government. By 1984, Reagan was calling the Contras "our brothers," and he remained steadfast in their support.

By 1984, however, Congress was unhappy with the administration's Central American policy. As early as 1982, Congress passed the **Boland Amendment**, prohibiting the United States from seeking to overthrow the Sandinista government. Since Reagan insisted he was simply trying to get them to negotiate, he ignored that stipulation. But in 1984, when it came to light that the CIA had mined Nicaraguan ports, members of Congress—not only liberals but also conservatives, including Barry Goldwater—were furious. In October 1984, Congress passed stricter legislation that cut off all aid to the Contras.

With what seemed like an iron-clad prohibition of aid to the Contras, U.S. adventures in Central America seemed to be at an end. But Reagan did not give up easily. The president encouraged efforts of a young National Security staffer, Oliver North, to find new sources of aid, though it was never clear how much Reagan knew of the details of North's enterprise. Since Congress had banned government aid to the contras, North sought donations from friendly governments in Taiwan, Brunei, and Saudi Arabia and from wealthy private U.S. citizens like beer magnate Joseph Coors. At least $50 million in such aid was delivered to the Contras.

Seeking to expand the aid, North and his mentor Casey had what they termed a "neat idea." The United States was secretly selling arms to Iran. What if, they thought, the United States could make a profit on the clandestine arms shipments to Iran, and then use the funds to support the Contras? Congress would not have to appropriate any money, and no one needed to know.

The complex arrangement did not remain secret for long. In October 1986, an American cargo plane loaded with military supplies for the Contras was shot down in Nicaragua. The Sandinista government let the world know that, in spite of the two Boland Amendments, the United States was still providing significant aid to the Contras. A month later a Beirut, Lebanon, newspaper published an account, based on Iranian sources, of U.S. arms sales to Iran and the link to hoped-for hostage releases. People soon connected the two, and the scandal quickly became known as the "arms for hostages" deal or simply as "**Iran-Contra**." The matter was serious. In selling arms to Iran and in funding the Contras, U.S. laws had been broken, laws that the White House clearly knew existed. Some in Congress talked of impeachment. As with Nixon at Watergate, the question was "what did the president know and when did he know it."

As the details of U.S. activity began to emerge, the president insisted that the government, "did not, repeat, did not trade arms or anything else for hostages." He also asked Attorney General Ed Meese to investigate. Oliver North immediately began to shred documents in his office. Meese reported to the president that North had, in fact, not only sold arms to Iran—presumably to free hostages—but also used the profits to aid the Contras. National Security advisor John Poindexter met with Reagan, confirmed that Meese was right, and resigned. Reagan asked former Texas Senator John Tower to lead an investigation. A special prosecutor, Lawrence Walsh, was appointed, and Congress held hearings.

Reagan eventually had to admit, "I told the American people I did not trade arms for hostages. My heart and best intentions still tell me that it is true, but the facts and evidence tell me it is not." Many were shocked that an administration that talked so

Boland Amendment
Two Amendments passed by Congress prohibiting the U.S. government from attempting to overthrow the leftist government of Nicaragua.

Iran-Contra
A plan to secretly sell arms to Iran in exchange for the release of hostages held in Lebanon and to use the profits to provide aid to the Contra forces of Nicaragua.

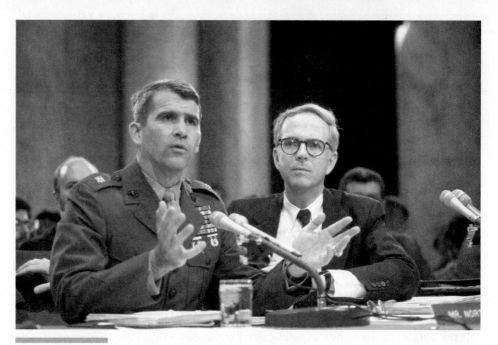

In his testimony before Congress regarding the Iran-Contra investigation, Oliver North looked and sounded like a hero in spite of the fact that he had obviously broken the law.

much about law and order was doing so many illegal things. Reagan clearly knew about the illegal sale of arms to Iran and the arms-for-hostages deals. Many also suspected that he knew about the transfer of funds to the Contras, although that was never proved. Poindexter and North insisted that the decision rested with them alone. Not everyone was convinced, but no "smoking gun" was found. North managed to testify brilliantly before Congress, portraying himself as a well-meaning patriot, and though Reagan's approval rating plummeted, talk of impeachment ended.

Walsh continued his investigation after Reagan left office and eventually secured the indictment of several officials, but Reagan's successor George H.W. Bush pardoned them. In 1994, Walsh concluded that Reagan probably should have been impeached, but by then, he was retired and ill. Iran-Contra seriously damaged Reagan's reputation. As Reagan entered his last 2 years in office, many considered his foreign policy efforts to be a failure. Between 1987 and 1989, however, the president accomplished his great foreign policy triumph.

Ending the Cold War

During his first term, as Reagan talked tough and launched the arms buildup, he also refused to meet with Soviet leaders, in part, because he saw no point in such conversations and didn't trust the Soviets and, in part, because of changes in Soviet leadership. Leonid Brezhnev, who had led the Soviet Union since Nikita Khrushchev was deposed in 1964, died in 1982. His successor Yuri Andropov died 2 years later, and the next leader, Konstantin Cherenko, died a year after that. Reagan said, "How am I supposed to get anyplace with the Russians…if they keep dying on me?" Then in 1985, a new and very different leader, Mikhail Gorbachev, came to power in the Soviet Union.

After a succession of hard-line Communists who were aging and ill, Gorbachev represented a new younger generation of reform-minded Soviet leaders who saw how desperately their country needed change. Top-down Soviet-style planning was strangling the economy. Matching the United States in military matters took a huge percentage of their nation's limited wealth. The disastrous meltdown of the nuclear reactor at Chernobyl just after Gorbachev came to office further convinced him of the need for change. Gorbachev could be as charming and optimistic as Reagan, but he was also a devoted Communist and a very tough leader. He called for major changes: *perestroika*, reform of the Soviet economic system while maintaining communism, and *glasnost*, more openness and freedom for Soviet citizens. He quickly concluded that matching the U.S. arms buildup was going to bankrupt the Soviet Union, and he sought a way to avoid the arms race.

After his reelection in 1984, Reagan was also ready to talk. By 1985, he had achieved the military buildup that he wanted and could negotiate from a position of strength. U.S. allies, especially those in Europe who lived on the front line of any conflict, were tired of Cold War tensions and increased pressure on the United States for a different policy. Nancy Reagan nudged her husband away from the hard-liners in his administration. Reagan also knew that his Cold War credentials gave him room to maneuver that another leader might not have.

By 1985, Reagan and Gorbachev were ready to work together. British Prime Minister Margaret Thatcher, known as the Iron Lady because of her ability to stand up to pressure, was a close ally and friend of Reagan. She assured him that Gorbachev was someone "with whom we can do business." Reagan and Gorbachev began a private correspondence and then met for the first time in November 1985 at Geneva where they agreed in general to a reduction in nuclear arms. The following October, they met again at Reykjavik, Iceland. There, in a small house on the ocean, they got to know each other. They talked about their lives—Gorbachev had once wanted to be an actor—their grandchildren, and their hopes for the future. At one point, they frightened their respective staff when they reached a tentative agreement to abolish *all* nuclear weapons by 2000 and then moved the date back to 1995. That agreement floundered over Gorbachev's insistence that they include SDI and Reagan's refusal. The Reykjavik summit ended in anger over Star Wars and without any agreement, but the two men had established a personal bond.

In June 1987, Reagan traveled to Berlin, the flashpoint of the Cold War. Facing the Berlin Wall at the Brandenburg Gate he demanded, "Mr. Gorbachev, tear down this wall!" The speech, which sounded much more like Reagan's old line anticommunism than the new thaw in U.S.–Soviet relations, seemed to have been as much an effort to reassure the president's conservative critics as an actual demand. But in fact, the steps that Reagan and Gorbachev were taking would lead to the end of the wall within 2 years, just after Reagan left office.

Soon after Reykjavik, the Soviet physicist Andrei Sakharov convinced Gorbachev that SDI would not work and could safely be ignored. The two leaders then authorized further negotiations on offensive weapons that led to a treaty dramatically reducing intermediate-range nuclear forces (INF) and to onsite inspections so rigorous that they frightened the American CIA.

Critics in both countries thought the leaders were moving too fast. In the Senate, North Carolina's Jesse Helms tried to stop any new treaty, and Howard Phillips of the Conservative Caucus called the president a "useful idiot for Soviet propaganda." Gorbachev, for his part, had to deal with military and civilian attacks for his "capitulationist line" toward the United States. Even so, the momentum was not going to be stopped.

At their next summit in Washington, DC, in December 1987, Reagan signed the INF treaty in a well-publicized ceremony, and Gorbachev met and mingled with American crowds like a U.S. politician. The two seemed at ease with each other. When Reagan included one of his favorite sayings, "trust, but verify," in his remarks, Gorbachev interjected, "You repeat that at every meeting." People celebrated "Gorby fever." The Senate ratified the INF Treaty by a large vote in May 1988. The two countries also made significant progress in resolving the conflicts in Nicaragua and Afghanistan, plans for joint space missions, cultural and student exchanges, and emigration and human rights. They jointly sponsored a UN resolution calling for an end to the Iran-Iraq war. The same month that the Senate ratified the INF treaty, the two leaders met for a fourth time in Moscow. They walked through Red Square, called each other "old friends," and talked with Russian citizens. When asked about his earlier Cold War speeches, Reagan said they were from "another time, another place."

perestroika
Russian for "restructuring," efforts to make the Soviet economic and political systems more modern, flexible, and innovative.

glasnost
Russian for "openness," encouragement of new ideas and easing of political repression in the Soviet Union.

This picture of President Ronald Reagan and Soviet Premier Mikhail Gorbachev having a friendly conversation in Moscow's Red Square would have dumbfounded most Americans only a few years earlier.

Before Reagan left Moscow, the United States and Soviet Union had essentially normalized their relationship. For all intents and purposes, the Cold War was over.

The Strained Election of 1988

As a candidate in the Republican primaries in 1980, George Bush had called Ronald Reagan's economic plans, "voodoo economics." While Democrats had a field day with the term once he became Reagan's vice president, Bush was a loyal member of the Reagan team, so loyal that some thought he had disappeared, but those who thought that way underestimated him considerably.

George Herbert Walker Bush was a child of privilege. His father was a successful banker and Republican senator from Connecticut. Bush attended private schools and expected to attend Yale when World War II intervened. While Ronald Reagan made war movies in Hollywood for the government, Bush flew more than 50 combat missions in the South Pacific and was shot down twice. After the war, he married Barbara Pierce, attended Yale, and then moved to Texas to make his fortune in the oil business. He served two terms in the House of Representatives from Houston. He was defeated when he ran for the Senate in 1970 but was subsequently appointed head of the Republican Party, nominal U.S. Ambassador to China after the Nixon trip, and head of the CIA for Gerald Ford.

The conservative wing of the Republican Party never trusted Bush, especially after his "voodoo economic" remarks, but also because of his lack of enthusiasm for their social issues. Disappointed that Reagan had not done more to support the social issues that were near and dear to them, some conservatives thought that the 1988 election was their chance. And Democrats, convinced that Reagan was more personally popular than his programs, believed that the end of his second term would be their chance to retake the White House. Neither challenge succeeded.

In the Republican Party, the conservative but genial Kansas senator Robert Dole challenged the vice president. And Pat Robertson, the extremely conservative religious broadcaster and head of the Christian Broadcasting Network, who had strongly supported Ronald Reagan, now resigned his ordination as a Baptist minister and campaigned for the nomination. Robertson felt that it was time to take the religious right's social and cultural issues into a presidential campaign. While Bush won the nomination on the first ballot, he embraced many of Dole's and Robertson's issues, invited a conservative, Indiana senator J. Danforth Quayle—whom many considered to be a lightweight—to be his running mate, and made a speech he would later regret, telling the Republican convention, "Read my lips. No new taxes."

Sensing possible victory, many Democrats sought the nomination. Colorado senator Gary Hart, an initial front runner, was forced out of the race after he was photographed on the yacht *Monkey Business* with the model Donna Rice—not his wife—sitting on his lap. The nomination battle came down to a contest between the Reverend Jesse Jackson, a longtime civil rights leader, and Massachusetts governor Michael Dukakis. Jackson was extremely popular in some circles and reviled in others. He was the first African-American candidate to win presidential primaries in southern states, winning five. But in the end, Dukakis won the Democratic nomination. He summed up his campaign when he told the Democratic convention, "This election is not about ideology, it's about competence."

Dukakis entered the fall campaign with a 17-point lead in the polls, a sign that people were ready for a change, but the lead quickly evaporated in what turned into a very nasty battle. Dukakis's focus on competence did not make for an inspiring campaign.

Explore the Reagan Revolution on MyHistoryLab

HOW DID THE "REAGAN REVOLUTION" OF THE 1980s SHAPE AMERICAN POLITICS?

In the presidential election of 1980, Republican Ronald Reagan won a landslide victory over Jimmy Carter. Economic stagnation and foreign policy difficulties had marked the previous years, while Reagan promised smaller government at home and stronger government abroad. In 1984, Reagan won an even more impressive victory over Democratic candidate Walter Mondale. One reason for these landslide victories was that a group of traditionally Democratic voters— white, socially conservative, blue-collar workers—changed party affiliation during the Reagan years and voted Republican. Reagan's supply-side economic policy, which included limited government deregulation and tax breaks for middle class and wealthy Americans, brought economic prosperity, but did not change the duress many suffered as other market forces saw the country move from an

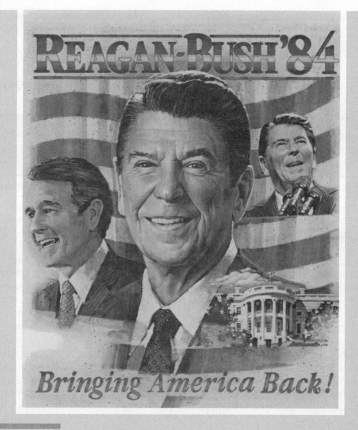

Taking advantage of a troubled economy and national mood, former California governor and actor Ronald Reagan won the elections of 1980 and 1984 for the Republican Party based on the "Bringing America Back" message.

industrial to a service economy. Abroad, the Cold War began to end during Reagan's second administration with the weakening of the Soviet Union and the erosion of communist control in its Warsaw Pact allies.

Presidential Election Electoral Results	
1980 Election	
Reagan (Republican):	489 electoral votes
Carter (Democrat):	49 electoral votes
1984 Election	
Reagan (Republican):	525 electoral votes
Mondale (Democrat):	13 electoral votes

KEY QUESTIONS Use **MyHistoryLab** *Explorer* to **answer** these **questions:**

Cause ▶▶▶ *How did support for Republican and Democratic presidential candidates change in the elections from 1976–1988?*

Chart these trends to consider their causation.

Analysis ▶▶▶ *Where did the incidence of poverty stay high?*

Map the regions where economic difficulties remained prevalent.

Response ▶▶▶ *How did the Soviet Union's collapse redraw the map of Europe and Central Asia?*

Explore the unfolding of the end of the Cold War.

American Voices

Jesse Jackson and Pat Robertson—Presidential Candidates, 1988

Pat Robertson was the most conservative candidate to seek the Republican nomination in 1988 and Jesse Jackson the most liberal to seek the Democratic. Both were Baptist ministers. Both lost to more moderate candidates and endorsed them but each also had a significant impact on their respective party platform. In speeches to their conventions they outlined their own views.

Jesse Jackson, 1988 Democratic National Convention Address	Pat Robertson, 1988 Republican National Convention Address
When I look out at this convention, I see the face of America: Red, Yellow, Brown, Black, and White. We're all precious in God's sight—the real rainbow coalition….When I was a child growing up in Greenville, South Carolina, and grandmamma could not afford a blanket, she didn't complain…she took pieces of old cloth… sewed them together into a quilt, a thing of beauty and power and culture. Now, Democrats, we must build such a quilt. Farmers, you seek fair prices, and you are right—but you cannot stand alone. Your patch is not big enough. Workers, you fight for fair wages, you are right—but your patch, labor, is not big enough. Women, you seek comparable worth and pay equity…Head Start, and day care and prenatal care on the front side of life, relevant jail care and welfare on the back side of life, you are right—but your patch is not big enough. Students, you seek scholarships, you are right—but your patch is not big enough. Blacks and Hispanics, when we fight for civil rights, we are right—but our patch is not big enough. Gays and lesbians, when you fight against discrimination and a cure for AIDS, you are right—but your patch is not big enough.… But don't despair. Be as wise as my grandmamma. Pull the patches and the pieces together, bound by a common thread. When we form a great quilt of unity and common ground, we'll have the power to bring about health care and housing and jobs and education and hope to our Nation. We, the people, can win.	Four years ago the keynote speaker at the Democratic National Convention told us that America was a tale of two cities—the "haves" and the "have-nots." The rich and the poor. The upper class and the lower class.…The Democrats have given us a clear picture of their city. They offer unlimited government, massive transfers of wealth from the productive sector of society to the nonproductive, and ever-increasing regulation of the daily lives of the people and their children. In the city of the Democratic Party, the liberal mindset reigns supreme. Criminals are turned loose and the innocent are made victims. Disease carriers are protected and the healthy are placed at great risk. In the Democrat's city, welfare dependency flourishes and no one is held accountable for his or her behavior. Society is always to blame. In the Democrat's city, the rights of the majority must always take a back seat to the clamorous demands of the special interest minorities. And yet, in their city it is always the majority that must pay the bills, through higher and higher taxes.… Ladies and Gentlemen, the Republican Party wants to write a tale of another city. We are the children of those who tamed the wilderness, spanned a continent, and brought forth the greatest nation on the face of the earth.…We see a city set on a hill. A shining light of freedom for all of the nations to see and admire. A city made great by the moral strength and self-reliance of her people.… We are Republicans, and we believe in government that is our servant, not our master.

Source: Jesse Jackson, 1988 Democratic National Convention Address, downloaded July 26, 2011 from www.americanrhetoric.com/speeches/jessejackson1988dnc.htm; Pat Robertson, 1988 Republican National Convention Address, downloaded July 26, 2011 from www.patrobertson.com/Speeches/PresidentialBidEnded.asp.

Thinking Critically

1. Documentary Analysis

What did each speaker see as the fundamental source of America's strength? What role did each assign government in making that potential strength a reality?

2. Historical Interpretation

What light do these two speeches shed on the fundamental ideological divisions in American politics in the late 1980s and early 1990s?

The comedian Mort Sahl complained that Dukakis was "the only colorless Greek in America." The Bush camp, led by Lee Atwater, ran TV ads featuring a black convicted criminal, Willie Horton, who had killed a man and raped a woman while on furlough from a Massachusetts prison. The fact that many states, including Reagan's California, had furlough policies did not make a difference. The appeal to fear was strong. In the end, Bush swamped Dukakis by a vote of almost 49 million to 42 million and 426 to 111 electoral votes and won the presidential term he had long sought.

28.1 **Quick Review** How successfully did Ronald Reagan fulfill his initial goals? How did his goals change during his term in office?

THE CHANGING NATURE OF THE AMERICAN ECONOMY

28.2 Explain international economic developments that shaped the United States.

Presidential candidates, economists, and families who gathered around the dinner table or the TV trays in the living room all debated the nature of the economic changes that were taking place in the 1980s as "Reaganomics" led to tax cuts, a reduction in government services, and fewer government regulations. Late in his term, in July 1987, President Reagan proposed what he called an Economic Bill of Rights, which he restated on several occasions:

> First is the freedom to work—to pursue one's livelihood in one's own way … free from excessive government regulation and subsidized government competition;…freedom to enjoy the fruits of one's labor…free from excessive government taxing, spending and borrowing by the government…the freedom to own and control one's property….freedom to participate in a free market… and to achieve one's full potential without government limits on opportunity.

It was a philosophy that Reagan seemed to embody in his own life story. Yet by 1987, when the president spoke, some Americans were beginning to have second thoughts.

Kevin Phillips, who helped Republican presidential campaigns from Nixon to Reagan, was among them. In his book, *The Boiling Point*, he described what he saw as Reagan's term came to an end. Reagan had been elected in 1980, Phillips said, because government was "fairly in disrepute for its swollen size and record of aggravating rather than solving problems." He continued that with the cuts in taxes and government programs, however, "[h]igh-income persons did not suffer, but middle-class voters usually worried when federal and state reductions went too far" (see Figure 28-1).

One of the striking features of the economy of the 1980s was the extraordinary fortunes made by a few individuals. In the 1980s, Ivan Boesky anticipated corporate takeovers and mergers, buying stock just before it increased in value with stunning regularity. In December 1986, Boesky was honored with a cover photo in *Time* magazine, and by 1987, he had earned a total of more than $200 million.

Michael Milken, an investor for the firm Drexel Burnham Lambert who specialized in so-called junk bonds, earned much more. Junk bonds were high-risk investments that could pay high yields. Milken arranged investments in gambling casinos and technology startups as well "leveraged buyouts" in which investors would buy a controlling share of a company—using loans arranged by Milken—and thereby take it over in spite of the will of its owners and managers. In 1987, his estimated income for that one year was $550 million.

Boesky, Milken, and other slightly lesser figures were the heroes of the 1980s. In a speech to business students at the University of California, Berkeley, Boesky said, "I think greed is healthy. You can be greedy and still feel good about yourself." But Kevin Phillips noted that, "By early 1990 The *New York Times* noted that Wall Street found an unnerving whiff of populism in the public's anger over junk-bond pioneer Michael Milken's $550-million-a-year salary."

Federal employees at the Security and Exchange Commission (SEC) became suspicious that anyone could have as much success as Boesky in guessing the direction of stock values year after year. A SEC investigation showed that Boesky was indeed getting illegal insider information about corporate takeovers and mergers. When he was charged with breaking the law, Boesky implicated Milken, whose illegal dealings were even more complex. Boesky was eventually fined $100 million, half of his fortune, Milken paid over $1.1 billion, and both served almost 2 years in federal prison. In the 1987 movie, *Wall Street*,

FIGURE 28-1 Real Family Income, 1980–1990. As this chart shows dramatically, between 1980 and 1990, the poorest fifth of Americans got much poorer, the middle groups barely held their own, and the top fifth got much more wealthy during the decade.

THINKING HISTORICALLY

A Changing World Economy

Robert Reich was a respected economist in the 1980s and would serve as secretary of labor in the 1990s. As Reagan's term came to a close, Reich looked at the Reagan tax cuts, which he argued had certainly shifted money toward the rich. However, he also said that there were larger forces at work that were reshaping the world's economy and that the real issue was that the United States could not control its economy. In 1991, Reich published *The Work of Nations* in which he said, "We are living through a transformation that will rearrange the politics and economics of the coming century....There will no longer be national economies, at least as we have come to understand that concept." Trade, finance, indeed the whole job market of the planet, Reich insisted, had become a single worldwide economy in which national policies mattered much less than in the past. "All that will remain rooted within national borders," Reich said, "are the people who comprise a nation."

In the new world, Reich believed, some were going to be much better off and others worse off. He argued that people found themselves in one of three quite different economic categories. Those who were employees in the older industries—auto or steel workers for example—found themselves with declining prospects. Well-paying jobs that had been secure were disappearing as manufacturing moved to other countries. A second group of workers, those who provided direct services—from selling hamburgers to health care workers to teachers—would keep their jobs since such services were hard to export, but would find their futures relatively flat. And finally, in the third category, those Reich called "symbolic analysts" the scientists, inventors, developers, and money managers, would do quite well, indeed better than ever before. For example, Reich noted:

> In 1960, the chief executive of one of America's 100 largest nonfinancial corporations earned, on average, $190,000 or about 40 times the wage of his average factory worker. After taxes, the chief executive earned only 12 times the factory worker's wages. By the end of the 1980s, however the chief executive earned, on average, more than $2 million—93 times the wages of his (rarely her) average factory worker. After taxes, the chief executive's compensation was about 70 times that of the average factory worker.

Clearly the Reagan tax cuts had something to do with the change but not everything.

For Reich, the larger issue was the shift from a national American economy to a unified world economy:

> All Americans used to be in roughly the same economic boat. Most rose or fell together, as the corporations in which they were employed, the industries comprising such corporations, and the national economy as whole became more productive—or languished. But national borders no longer define our economic fates. We are now in different boats, one sinking rapidly [the industrial workers], one sinking more slowly [service workers], and the third rising steadily [that of managers and inventors].

In the economy that Reich described, Americans would compete, not with each one another, but with people in the same sort of work around the world. Not everyone agreed with Reich, but it was hard to look at the nation at the end of the 1980s and not conclude that some, indeed, were sinking and others were rising quite spectacularly.

Source: Robert B. Reich, The Work of Nations: Preparing Ourselves for 21st Century Capitalism (New York: Vintage Books, 1991), p. 7 and 208.

Thinking Critically

1. **Comparison**

   How does Reich's economic analysis compare to either defenders or critics of Reagan's economic policies?

2. **Contextualization**

   How does Reich help place the changing American economy of the 1980s in an international context?

the villain Gordon Gekko gave a "greed is good" speech, based on Boesky's Berkeley talk, which became a symbol of an era.

It was not only a few high flyers who got into trouble in the late 1980s, however. Throughout much of the 1970s, the Down Jones Industrial Average had hovered just under 1,000 (that is, the average value of a share on the list was $1,000; see Chapter 22). In 1980, the average crossed the magic 1,000 line to 1,100, and from there it just kept going up along with public optimism. By 1987, the average was above 2,500. Then in October 1987, the bottom fell out as it had done before. On October 19, known as "Black Monday," the market fell by 508 points, closing below 2,000. The next day, the Federal Reserve Bank, seeking to avoid a repeat of the 1929 crash, responded, pumping millions of dollars into the market. Consumer confidence returned and the market stabilized,

The stock market crash of October 19, 1987, set off panicked selling as did every stock market crash.

but in one day, American stocks had dropped $500 billion in their value, and many investors lost their savings.

Among the victims of Black Monday was the nation's savings and loan industry. In 1982, as part of the Reagan efforts to deregulate government, most of the restrictions on savings and loan associations were removed. They were allowed to invest not only in houses and cars, which they had long done, but also in risky oil and gas ventures, real estate developments, and even junk bonds like those sold by Michael Milken. They attracted many more depositors by paying previously unheard of high levels of interest. They made huge fortunes for their executives and investors. But when the stock market, junk bonds, and then housing prices collapsed in the late 1980s, the savings and loan industry found itself in serious trouble with investments that were not worth what they owed to depositors. Some 1,200 of the nation's 4,000 savings and loans required federal help or went out of business. Since the federal government guaranteed savings and loan deposits as they did bank deposits, the government—and taxpayers—were left with the cost, which came to $500 billion or $2,000 for every American. Further investigations showed that U.S. senators had done special favors for the savings and loan industry and six senators were censured. Savings and loan owners who made fortunes were found to have stolen from their companies. William Crawford, a California official charged with investigating the scandal, said, "The best way to rob a bank is to own one."

28.2 **Quick Review** How did government policies and changes in the worldwide economic structure impact the average American in the 1980s?

CHANGES IN THE REST OF THE COUNTRY

28.3 Explain cultural changes in the United States during the 1980s.

On April 5, 1985, 3 months after Reagan's second inauguration, Michael Jackson, the most successful American rock star of the 1980s, joined in a concert, originally planned by Bob Geldof and Midge Ure, Irish and Scottish musicians, to raise funds for famine relief in Africa. The concert was broadcast around the world and raised $44 million in a production which included Jackson, Lionel Richie, Bob Dylan, Ray Charles, Billy Joel, Cyndi Lauper, Bette Midler, Willie Nelson, Paul Simon, Bruce Springsteen, Stevie Wonder, and Tina Turner.

Rock Group Duran Duran, musicians Lionel Richie, Dionne Warwick, actors Jeff Bridges and Chevy Chase, singers Bob Dylan and Harry Belafonte performing at "Live Aid '85" Concert on July 13, 1985, at J.F.K. Stadium in Philadelphia, Pennsylvania.

Three months later, on July 13, 1985, some 100,000 people attended one of two simultaneous rock concerts held in Philadelphia, Pennsylvania, and London, England. Another 1.5 to 1.9 billion people around the world watched the concerts on TV or listened on radio. At the July concert, Jackson, his guests, and an audience of many million sang *We Are the World*.

These Live Aid concerts eventually raised over $80 million for Africa. Subsequent concerts raised more money. They also symbolized new international connections. Without a time lag, people could listen to the same concert at the same time. They could also transfer money, hold meetings, and plan new enterprises, creating a worldwide culture and economy. Given the speed of travel, it did not take much longer for people to visit new places, transmit diseases, or start a new life halfway around the world.

Popular Culture—Music, Television, Theater

In addition to the fundraising—which was badly needed—the 1985 concerts also symbolized the way American rock musicians had come to dominate the world. Michael Jackson, Bruce Springsteen, and Cyndi Lauper first emerged in the 1970s and 1980s. They were joined in these concerts by others, Ray Charles, Bob Dylan, and Tina Turner, some of whom had been international figures since the 1950s. They represented diverse musical styles from Turner's start in rhythm-and-blues to Charles's jazz, to Lauper's rock, but all had become cultural icons across the United States, in major world capitals, and in isolated rural villages in Asia, Africa, and tiny Pacific islands.

The popularity of American music and American musicians was made possible, in part, by rapidly changing technologies. Michael Jackson insisted that *We Are the World* be released at exactly 3:50 p.m. Greenwich Mean Time (10:50 a.m. on the East Coast of the United States) in 8,000 radio stations around the world. The technology to transmit the music to all of these stations was new. When the Live Aid concerts were held in July 1985, one of the musicians, Phil Collins, managed to perform in person at both the London and the Philadelphia concerts thanks to the supersonic concord plane that brought him across the Atlantic faster than the speed of sound. Music Television (MTV) began broadcasting in August 1981 and built a worldwide audience for rock music. Generating these huge audiences would not have happened without the nonstop broadcasting of music videos aimed at audiences in the 12- to 34-year-old demographic who made up the bulk of those who attended the concerts or listened to the broadcasts. And after *We Are the World* had been released, it and other music from the concerts was listened to over and over by individuals using Sony Walkman personal stereos, first sold in 1979, or Sony compact disc (CD) players, which produced far better quality than older tapes and records. American music of the 1980s could be heard worldwide because American—and Japanese—technology made possible the easy and cheap distribution of quality musical sounds.

The music of the 1980s also connected with Americans, especially young Americans, and their counterparts around the globe. It was their generation's challenge to the traditional culture and its music. Where jazz, rock, and folk music all began as protests, against musical and political systems, so the music of the 1980s was its own forms of protest. African-American artists dominated the music, but they were not alone. Tina Turner, an African-American, who with her husband had headlined the Ike and Tina Turner Revue in the 1950s and 1960s, emerged after her divorce as a force in her own right in the 1980s, celebrating her energy and her sexuality with recordings like *Private Dancer* in 1984. A younger white woman, Madonna, celebrated her sometimes off-the-wall sexuality in releases like her 1984 album, *Like a Virgin*. A new generation, the children of the baby boomers, was creating a new music and a new culture of its own in the 1980s and making sure that its country, and the world, listened.

The 1980s were one of the most successful decades in the history of the film industry. The most popular film of the decade was *E.T., the Extra-Terrestrial*, a story produced by Steven Spielberg about a small creature from outer space who liked candy and wanted to "phone home." Other highly successful films of the decade included *The Empire Strikes Back* (1980), *Return of the Jedi* (1983) in George Lucas's Star Wars trilogy; *Batman*; *Ghostbusters*; and the Indiana Jones movies, *Raiders of the Lost Ark* (all in 1981) and *Indiana Jones and the Last Crusade* (1989). There were also more violent movies such as *Terminator* (1984) with Arnold Schwarzenegger and the Rambo films with Sylvester Stallone. While both Schwarzenegger and Stallone played classic "good guys," the films had plenty of blood and violence. Spike Lee directed films like *Do the Right Thing*, which explored serious issues in a thoughtful way. Martin Scorsese's *The Last Temptation of Christ*, released in 1988, generated critical acclaim but also demonstrations in front of theaters, with its portrayal of Jesus as a man with ordinary temptations. As with music, so with films, technology expanded beyond anything previously thought possible. People still watched movies in theatres, but they also watched them at home as VCRs made it possible for films to be distributed, not only to the local theatre but also to the local living room where people could watch at their leisure.

The most successful TV series of the 1980s, the *Bill Cosby Show*, reflected an updated version of the 1950s family shows. But the family in the Cosby show, the Huxtables, was led by an African-American doctor, played by Cosby. The focus on a successful African-American family in the mainstream of America, and their warm acceptance by viewers, was a clear shift. In contrast, when the lead character of *Murphy Brown*, played by Candice Bergen, had a child without being married and indicated that the father's identity was not important, the vice president of the United States, Dan Quayle, criticized the show.

African-American artists and writers also came to play a dominant role in theater and literature in the 1980s. The playwright August Wilson began producing a series of plays that explored the black experience from 1900 to 2000, including *Ma Rainey's Black Bottom* in 1985 and *Fences* in 1986. Toni Morrison's novel, *Beloved*, published in 1987, explored the evils of slavery and eventually won the Nobel Prize for Literature.

Culture Wars—The Christian Coalition and Other Critics

The cultural developments of the 1980s and 1990s in music, drama, and creative writing also produced a considerable critical response. Looking at the era, Robert Bork, a conservative legal scholar who had been denied a position on the Supreme Court by a Senate vote in 1987, published *Slouching Toward Gomorrah* in 1996 in which he blamed a decline he saw in American culture on the nation's "enfeebled hedonistic culture," its "uninhibited display of sexuality," and "popularization of violence." Many other authors, liberal and conservative, worried about what the liberal African-American journalist Carl Rowen called the "sexual rot and gratuitous violence" that led to "decadence, decay, and self-destruction" in the United States. In 1985, "Tipper" Gore, whose husband was then Democratic Senator from Tennessee, co-founded the Parents Music Resource Center after hearing her 11-year-old daughter listen to music by the recording artist Prince that she deemed profane.

The religious right was made up of people who were increasingly angry at many of the cultural trends of the 1980s and 1990s. The Moral Majority, the major political organization of the religious right, declined in the late 1980s and disbanded in 1989 (see Chapter 27). It had fallen victim to some of the more extremist statements of its founder Jerry Falwell as well as institutional mismanagement. Some commentators thought that decline would be the end of religious conservatism as a political force. They could not have been more mistaken. After Pat Robertson lost his campaign for the Republican nomination in 1988, he helped launch a new conservative religious and political organization: the Christian Coalition.

While launching the Christian Coalition, Robertson hired a young veteran of the College Republican National Committee, Ralph Reed, to run the organization on a day-to-day basis. Reed brought a steady hand as well as organizational and fund-raising skills to the Christian Coalition that the Moral Majority never had. He was a young fresh face and managed to portray himself as a moderating influence on the more extreme Robertson.

Pat Robertson was born in 1930. His father was a conservative Democratic U.S. senator from Virginia from 1946 to 1966. Robertson earned a law degree from Yale before studying for the Baptist ministry. He founded the Christian Broadcasting Network and *The 700 Club*, a religious talk show that reached millions, before he began his more overt political campaigning. In running for president and then launching the Christian Coalition, Robertson sought to resist what he saw as the increased secularization of American culture and avert what he saw as God's coming judgment on the nation's sins. Another evangelical minister, describing Robertson's supporters, said, "They have a bunker mentality. They feel modernity is against them—in matters dealing with sex, crime, pornography, education."

Ralph Reed, born in 1961, was a generation younger than Robertson. As a student, he was fascinated with the mechanics of politics and initially put off by the religious right because of their amateurishness. He was determined that the Christian Coalition would be an effective organization. The two made a strong team. By 1992, the Christian Coalition had more than 150,000 members and controlled the grass-roots Republican Party in several southern states.

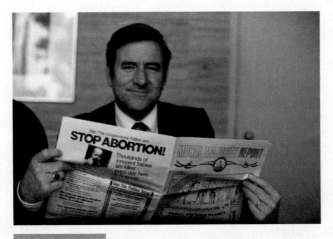

Opposition to abortion became one of the major rallying cries of the growing religious right.

By the mid-1990s, every Republican candidate for president was courting the Christian Coalition and Reed could say, "We have gained what we have always sought, a place at the table, a sense of legitimacy." His goal was more than legitimacy, however. Read and Robertson wanted to shape the nation's political agenda, from the grass roots up as much as from the top down. Pat Buchanan, who served as an advisor to Reagan in the 1980s and sought the Republican nomination in the 1990s, told Reed, "You just keep working on those school board races and leave the presidency to me." Buchanan never won a presidential nomination, but Reed told the National Press Club "There are an estimated 2,000 religious conservatives who now serve on school boards, city councils, state legislatures, and in Congress." Their impact throughout the 1990s testified to the coalition's power.

Religious conservatives were not the only critics of American culture in the 1980s and 1990s. Robert Bellah, a liberal sociologist, argued in his 1986 book *Habit of the Heart* that Americans were becoming so individualistic and consumption oriented that they were losing their ability to work together for the common good. A decade later in 1995, a Harvard scholar, Robert Putnam, published *Bowling Alone* in which he explored the impact of individualism. Americans who, in the past, joined churches, social and service organizations, and bowling leagues, now stayed home to watch television, spent less time in face-to-face gatherings of any sort, and even if they went out to a bowling alley, now did it alone. Some critics thought that Putnam and Bellah romanticized the past, but few dismissed their worries.

New Immigrants, New Diversities

In the 1980s and 1990s many who lived in the United States were very recent arrivals. In 2000, 28.4 million people, or 10.4 percent of the population of the United States, were foreign born. This increase was a significant change from the 4.7 percent who were foreign born in 1970 and marked the end of almost 50 years of very tough immigration restrictions. Immigrants they came in growing numbers in every decade. When Congress passed and Lyndon Johnson signed the Immigration and Nationality (Hart-Cellar) Act in 1965, no one expected it to have a major impact on the overall numbers of people coming to the United States (see Chapter 21). They could not have been more wrong. The 1965 law capped the number of immigrants at the same place as the older law, however, it was designed to make the process fairer. In addition to the numerical limits in the 1965 law, it provided for family reunion. If one member of a family was a legal resident or citizen of the United States, then that member could bring his or her family, regardless of the caps. By the 1990s, two-thirds of all immigrants to the United States were coming as part of family reunions.

Official government numbers showed the impact of the changes brought about by the law:

4.5 million immigrants in the 1970s
7.3 million immigrants in the 1980s
9.1 million immigrants in the 1990s

In addition, by most estimates, between 250,000 and 350,000 came to the United States every year without official documentation. In 2000, the U.S. population stood at 281 million, including some 28 million who had come between 1970 and 2000—more individuals than at any other 30-year time span in the nation's history.

The new immigrants who came between 1970 and 2000 also came from places different from immigrants of earlier eras. Before 1924, when the United States virtually closed its doors to immigrants (see Chapter 26), most immigrants had come from Europe and, unwillingly, from Africa. After 1980, most new immigrants came from Latin America and Asia. Between 1980 and 2000,

2 million people came to the United States from Europe (mostly from former Soviet states);
5.7 million people came from Asia;
4 million people came from Mexico;
2.8 million people came from other parts of Central America, and the Caribbean;
1 million came from South America;
600,000 came from Africa; and
250,000 came from Canada.

By any counting they were reshaping the country.

Immigrants moved to every part of the United States. Meatpacking plants in Kansas, potato farms in Maine, and agribusiness in southern Indiana all depended on recent immigrants who were willing to do hot, dirty, and generally low-paying work. The majority of immigrants, however, settled in relatively few areas, especially the states of California, Texas, Florida, New Jersey, Illinois, and New York. By 2000, California's population was 27 percent foreign-born as a result of a major influx of new immigrants and a modest white exodus.

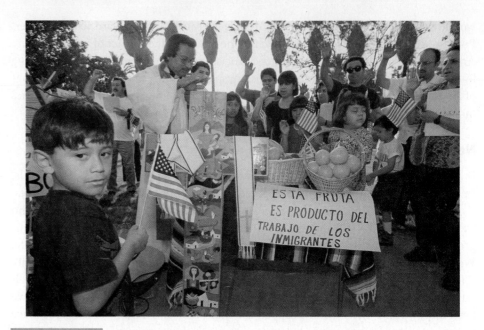

The sign at this vigil in Echo Park, Los Angeles, reads, "This fruit is the product of immigrants' labor." Members of the city's Latino community bless fruit baskets as they protest a state crack down on illegal immigration and the increase of border patrol guards.

Many immigrants also came to the United States without official approval. The borders with Mexico and Canada were hard to guard and many simply walked across. Others came on tourist visas and never left. In 1986, Congress passed legislation that President Reagan signed, giving anyone who had been in the United States since 1982 the right to seek amnesty, and 1.7 million people, most from Mexico, took advantage of the law.

Debates about immigration became intense. In campaigning for the Republican presidential nomination in 1992, Patrick Buchanan staked out the anti-immigrant views in the strongest terms. He said, "Our own country is undergoing the greatest invasion in its history, a migration of millions of illegal aliens yearly from Mexico....A nation that cannot control its own borders can scarcely call itself a state any longer." In 1986, almost three-quarters of California voters approved a law that made English the "official language" of the state. While the law had little formal meaning, it was a slap at those who spoke other languages. Some labor union leaders and workers, white and black, complained that new immigrants were taking their jobs or depressing wages in whole industries.

On the other hand, defenders of immigration argued that the American economy was dependent on immigrants who were willing to take jobs—in restaurants, agriculture, and home health care—that few native-born Americans were willing to do. Would the crops get harvested, the meat packaged, the dishes washed, and the elderly cared for if immigrants, documented and undocumented, were forced to leave? Immigrants are generally younger than the average population, pay taxes, and contribute to the Social Security system, though in the case of those who are undocumented, they may never collect benefits. Some studies, they argued, indicate that immigrants are more highly educated, more likely to be in stable families, and less likely to be engaged in crime, though other scholars disputed those numbers. While the arguments continued, people kept coming.

American Indians in the 1980s—Casinos and Rebirth

While their numbers were drastically reduced by war and disease, American Indian tribes have survived and sometimes thrived in spite of the difficulties. As restrictions on teaching American Indian languages, culture, and religion were lifted in the 1940s, 1950s, and 1960s, a surprising reservoir of an earlier cultural heritage resurfaced. For

American Voices

Caridad Rios, Adela Aguirre, and Saša Savić Talk about Their Immigrant Experiences in the United States

No single immigrant experience stands for the hundreds of thousands of people who have moved from crisis, poverty, or war to make new lives in the United States. These brief interviews with Caridad Rios, a 40-year-old native of Lake Chapala, Jalisco, Mexico; Adela Aguirre, also from Mexico; and Saša Savić from the former Yugoslavia describe some common experiences.

Caridad Rios: I don't believe I'll ever return to my country, because of them [her children]. Because how could I leave them? For better or worse they need their mother here, even if they're grown…This country is made up of immigrants. From the earliest times, immigrants came.…This country belongs to the whole world.…I have worked, now I am receiving food stamps, but who cares? I have worked, I have contributed here.

Adela Aguirre [speaking of Chinese immigrant women at the workshop she attended] The first time…that I began to notice, that I said that yes, they also feel bad, they also have problems. They also go through what I'm going through, so Adela, what are you complaining about? Yes. That was when I began to get more interested in everything. It was when I began to pay more attention to them. Because I said, I have to learn from them. I have to learn a lot from all my *companeras*, but even more from them [the Chinese women]. First of all, because they are another, they are another nationality, they have other customs, they have another language. And maybe the nicest thing they made me learn was just that, that I realized that there are people, of whatever origin or whatever nationality that will help you, will motivate you.

Saša Savić Basically I was raised in a middle-class family in the former Yugoslavia. My father was an officer in the army. So when I finished high school I served in the army, because it was mandatory for everybody to serve for 1 year. So I did that and coming out of the army there was a lot of political problems in the country. The country was in turmoil; everybody wanted to separate from each other. So since I'm from a mixed marriage—my father is Serbian and my mother Croatian—it was impossible to choose a side and say, 'okay, I want to fight in the Serbian army against Croatians or the Croatian army against Serbian. So we decided to elope; my girlfriend at the time and I decided to get married and to try to come to this country. It was very hard to get a visa at the time.…Because we said we wanted to go there on our honeymoon, we were granted a visitor visa.

Source: Kathleen M. Coll, *Remaking Citizenship: Latina Immigrants & New American Politics* (Stanford: Stanford University Press, 2010); Katherine Hanson, *Dream A New World* (Lanham, MD: Rowman & Littlefield, forthcoming).

Thinking Critically

1. **Documentary Analysis**

   What challenges and opportunities did these three immigrants associate with living in the United States?

2. **Craft an Argument**

   Defend or refute the following statement: The essential motives, experiences, and expectations of immigrants to the United States have changed very little over the centuries.

some tribes, Coyote is the perfect symbol of Indian life. Coyote is the trickster who disappears and reappears as he needs to in order to survive and thrive in new contexts. At the Spirit Mountain Casino, which is operated by the Grand Ronde Reservation in western Oregon State, a picture of Coyote dominates the gambling hall and the tribal logo. It is a fitting symbol.

Gambling transformed many American Indian communities in the 1980s. While often a subject of derision, gambling brought prosperity to many tribes that had experienced only poverty since their first engagement with Europeans. Two federal court cases, *Seminole Tribe of Florida v. Butterworth* in 1981 and *California v. Cabazon Band of Mission Indians* in 1987, made it difficult for states to limit gambling on Indian reservations. Some of those who controlled the gambling industry did not like the idea of new competitors, and Donald Trump complained about "equal treatment under the law." But the United States had always used a different set of laws for Indians, and treaty rights created a unique situation. In the court cases, tribes and their attorneys argued that the treaty rights creating the reservations gave them all the powers of any sovereign state to handle their own affairs. To regularize the new industry that was emerging, Congress passed the Indian Gaming Regulatory Act (IGRA) in 1988, and Reagan signed it. While the court cases and legislation did not give the tribes unlimited control over their own affairs, a new industry was born, one that brought prosperity to some, though not to others.

By 1994, 72 tribes were operating gambling operations in half of the states, and many more were planned. The gross income of these operations, $1.5 billion, was only a tiny fraction of the $330 billion the Americans spent on gambling, but it was a huge new source of income for tribes that had existed for generations on the economic margins.

The Pequots Foxwoods Casino produced almost $900 million in 1994, and the tribal council used the money to create other job-producing enterprises, including a silica mine and a printing plant. They bought the former Electric Boat shipyard that helped maintain the U.S. nuclear submarine fleet. Their goal was long-term economic development that was not dependent only on the gambling industry. Other tribes did the same. The Oneida Tribe of Wisconsin used the income from its slot-machine complex near Green Bay to open a chain store and a high-tech research and development firm. The Choctaws of Oklahoma used income from a bingo parlor in Durant to build a manufacturing plant, hotels, and the Choctaw Nation Travel Plaza that earned $1.4 million per month in 1992.

The new wealth allowed tribes to design their own museums, support retention of tribal languages, and maintain aspects of their culture that were otherwise being lost. They also allowed tribes to expand schools, provide new job training programs and health services, and generally support their members at a higher level. Promises of wealth also led some to "rediscover" their Indian identity. Indians who had drifted away from reservations were now returning, a change since the 1950s when a government Urban Relocation Program had led perhaps half of all American Indians to move from reservations to cities. Others who were part Indian were now claiming their Indian ties. Determining who was, and was not, a member of a specific tribe became a complex issue for some. R. David Edmunds, an ethnohistorian who himself is part Cherokee, wrote that traditionally no one questioned tribal membership, "If the Shawnees said you were Shawnee, you *were* Shawnee." By the 1990s, however, such issues had become more complex, and tribes sometimes had to make difficult decisions. Nevertheless, the new prosperity was significant.

AIDS and the Gay Community

In 1980, Acquired Immune Deficiency Syndrome (AIDS) was an unknown disease. In June 1981, the Center for Disease Control (CDC), the U.S. government's key agency for monitoring the spread of disease, reported AIDS for the first time. Later studies found that AIDS may have infected people in the United States as early as 1969, but only in the 1980s did Americans learn about what would quickly become a terrible new scourge, first identified among gay men.

By May 1982, the *New York Times* carried a story, "New homosexual disorder worries officials." At first, health officials did not know what the disease was. They were starting to discover that a cluster of symptoms were appearing in certain groups of people, especially homosexual men and intravenous drug users, but it took some time to understand what was happening. The symptoms were terrible: tumors, breathing difficulty, difficult digestion, and eventually, death. By 1984, researchers discovered the infectious agent, the human immunodeficiency virus (HIV), and understood that they were not dealing with a few isolated cases but, rather, a growing worldwide pandemic. In 1985, the CDC recorded 5,600 deaths from AIDS. Three years later, 61,816 died of AIDS. By then, researchers had also concluded that HIV was spread through contact with bodily fluids, especially but not exclusively through sex or through sharing needles or even blood transfusions that brought the blood of an infected person into contact with another. People with many sexual partners and people who routinely shared needles were especially susceptible. HIV, they also concluded, could not be spread by a hug, by touching the same material, or through the air, but many people panicked and would not come near anyone suspected of carrying the disease.

As HIV-AIDS spread—the CDC confirmed 98,835 cases by 1988—the famous and the unknown were afflicted. The actor Rock Hudson, who often played tough heterosexual male roles but was gay, announced in July 1985 that he had been suffering from AIDS since 1984. Many, including Hudson's good friend Ronald Reagan, were stunned. Hudson died in 1985. Arthur Ashe, a famous tennis star, announced in April 1992 that he had contracted AIDS through a blood transfusion in the mid-1980s and he died in February 1993. In 1987, a previously unknown teenager, Ryan White, became a national voice for AIDS victims. White, who suffered from hemophilia, had contracted AIDS from blood treatments, but was then ostracized and expelled from school in his hometown of Kokomo, Indiana. He died in April 1990. White's gentle personality made him a hero. In addition to White, Ashe, and Hudson, thousands of other Americans were suffering and dying. In some communities with large groups of gay men, especially San Francisco's Castro district and New York City's Greenwich Village, it seemed as if a whole community was dying, and those who survived spent their time caring for the sick and attending funerals.

Across the country, gay and lesbian organizations, especially ACT-UP shown here, demonstrated to demand more funding for research into the causes and cures for AIDS as well as support for immediate help to AIDS victims.

As people understood more about the disease, they also turned to the federal government for action. The government could not stop AIDS, but it could fund research that might lead to treatment and cure. The government could also spread information more effectively than any other agency, especially as it became known that using condoms during sex resulted in significantly safer, if not completely safe, sex and that using sterilized needles and not sharing them offered significant protection for drug users. But the call for government action crashed into the ideology of many of the leading players in the Reagan administration. The president's director of communications, Patrick Buchanan, had once said, "The poor homosexuals. They have declared war on nature and now nature is exacting an awful retribution." Other Reagan supporters, including Secretary of Education William Bennett, may not have agreed with Buchanan, but they strongly opposed supporting condom use. Requests by scientists at the CDC for more research funds were routinely denied.

When the U.S. Surgeon General C. Everett Koop, himself very conservative on matters of sex education, decided that it was his duty to get information out to the public on the dangers of AIDS and how to reduce those dangers, he said he realized, "I would have to skate fast on thin ice to get by political appointees who placed conservative ideology over saving lives." After Koop issued his first report, members of the Domestic Policy Council suggested "revisions" that Koop believed would undermine its effectiveness. Only in 1987 did Reagan speak publically about AIDS for the first time. Breaking a silence that had irritated many, including Nancy Reagan, the president called AIDS "public enemy Number One," but he continued to refuse to acknowledge or meet Ryan White or mention condoms until after he left office in 1989.

Gay activists became increasingly militant. In the fall of 1987, ACT-UP (AIDS Coalition to Unleash Power) staged a massive demonstration of 500,000 people in New York City. In addition, ACT-UP and other organizations, including the American Foundation for AIDS Research, continued to lobby for better public education, which in the 1990s was very effective. Eventually in 1992, Congress appropriated approximately $2 billion for AIDS research. While no cure or medical prevention has yet been discovered, important advances in the treatment of AIDS came as a result. AIDS had once been a death sentence, but by 2000, many with AIDS were living long and full lives as long as they continued to monitor their treatments carefully. In combining issues of medical science, health, sexuality, and drug use, the AIDS epidemic illustrated a tangle of cultural issues facing the nation as it entered the 1990s.

28.3 **Quick Review** How did cultural—and technological—changes in the United States in the 1980 impact each other and government policy?

CONCLUSION

The Reagan Revolution began in 1980 when Ronald Reagan defeated Jimmy Carter in his presidential bid for reelection. Reagan, supported by a broad coalition of working-class whites, suburbanites, and social conservatives, came to office with three key priorities: increase military spending, cut domestic spending and social programs, and cut the federal income tax. During the Reagan administration, all three goals were met, and both political parties, the Republicans and the Democrats, became more conservative. Many New Deal structures and programs were eliminated or drastically modified, and the combination of tax cuts and military spending increased the national debt significantly.

Reagan and his advisors rejected the idea that federal spending was the best way to stimulate a sluggish economy. Instead, they sought to foster private investment and create new jobs by cutting taxes. Relying on what they called supply-side economics, Reagan drastically reduced both taxes and domestic expenditures. Reagan's initiatives, at first, did very little to improve the nation's economy. During his first term, unemployment, inflation, and the national debt all rose steadily. But, by 1983, the economy, in the eyes of most Americans, was improving. Although the stock market was strong throughout much of Reagan's presidency, the bottom fell out in 1987. By the late 1980s, several economic events, including the savings and loan crisis, suggested that the U.S. economy was in trouble again.

Reagan came to office with very little foreign policy experience, but he quickly focused on destabilizing existing Communist governments and acted to prevent the spread of communism, especially in Latin America. As a result, the United States intervened in both overt and covert ways in many countries in the Middle East and Latin America. Later in his administration, the efforts to build new contacts within Iran and to fund the opposition to the Nicaraguan government led to what was known as the Iran-Contra scandal that seriously undermined the administration's credibility and foreign policy record. As part of his anticommunism agenda, Reagan also initiated the Strategic Defense Initiative (SDI), or Star Wars, with the intention of destroying any Soviet missiles in space before they could strike the United States. While SDI greatly troubled the Soviets, it was never a viable technology, and despite his hard-line stance against communism, Reagan forged a diplomatic relationship with Soviet leader Mikhail Gorbachev. Before he left office, Reagan and Gorbachev had essentially brought the 40-year-long Cold War to an end.

In the 1980s, the culture wars began to dominate American politics as technological changes brought the world closer together and new forms of music and entertainment dominated the culture. At the same time, the Christian Coalition gained increasing power and influence. The religious conservatives of the Christian Coalition were alarmed by liberalizing cultural trends and by the ways that immigration was transforming the country. By the end of the decade, the country had been rocked by the AIDS epidemic, which some tried to ignore but which was, indeed, one of the great public health crises in history.

CHAPTER REVIEW How did American culture and politics change during the 1980s with the advent of the Reagan Revolution and so many other changes at the same time?

Chapter 28   Chapter Review

A RAPIDLY CHANGING U.S. GOVERNMENT

28.1 Explain Reagan's impact on the United States and the world.

Review Questions

1. Contextualization

Why did working-class whites, in both the North and the South, throw their support behind Reagan in the 1980 and 1984 elections?

2. Cause and Effect

What were Reagan's domestic priorities and how did their implementation impact the economy and the federal government?

3. Construct an Argument

In your opinion, should Ronald Reagan be given credit for ending the Cold War? Why or why not?

4. Historical Interpretation

What major trends in American politics were reflected in the results of the 1988 presidential election?

THE CHANGING NATURE OF THE AMERICAN ECONOMY

28.2 Explain international economic developments that shaped the United States.

Review Questions

5. Historical Interpretation

What connections can you make between the financial scandals of the 1980s and larger trends in American economic history?

6. Construct an Argument

In your opinion, was the net impact of Reagan's economic policies positive or negative? What evidence can you present to support your position?

CHANGES IN THE REST OF THE COUNTRY

28.3 Explain cultural changes in the United States during the 1980s.

Review Questions

7. Cause and Effect

What role did technology play in the spread of American popular culture around the world in the 1980s?

8. Historical Interpretation

How and why did the Christian Coalition become a major political force in the 1990s?

9. Comparison

Compare and contrast immigration to the United States in 1900 and 2000. How would you account for the differences you note?

29 A New World Order

Bill Clinton, here surrounded by an enthusiastic crowd of supporters, was enormously effective as a political campaigner.

CHAPTER OBJECTIVE

Demonstrate an understanding of the changes in the United States as the threat of communism ended, new foreign problems arose, and new economic and technological issues shaped the country.

LEARNING OBJECTIVES

THE BUSH ADMINISTRATION, 1989–1993

29.1 Explain the New World Order that George Bush described.

THE CLINTON PRESIDENCY

29.2 Analyze the impact of the Clinton presidency and the Clinton–Gingrich conflict on the country.

TECHNOLOGY DOMINATES AN ERA

29.3 Analyze the changes in technology and their impact on U.S. culture.

On Inauguration Day, January 20, 1989, as Ronald Reagan left the White House, the nation was prosperous, his loyal vice president was replacing him, and perhaps even more significant, the long Cold War with the Soviet Union seemed to be coming to an end. George H.W. Bush would lead the nation in a very different international context than any predecessor since World War II. In April 1989, just after Bush's inauguration, the Communist government of Poland, with Gorbachev's permission, legalized the prodemocracy Solidarity and agreed to free elections. In June, for the first time in history, a Communist government was voted out of office and yielded power peacefully to its non-Communist successor. That fall, Hungary followed the same course and ousted its Communist government. Demonstrations in East Germany led to a change in leadership, and on November 9, the Berlin Wall that had divided the city, and Europe, for almost 30 years came down. With the fall of the Berlin Wall, Berliners who had never met each other embraced and celebrated. Leaders of East and West Germany talked of unification, which came 2 years later. In December, Czechoslovakia inaugurated a non-Communist government.

What had begun as a conversation between two leaders in a house in Iceland in 1986 had become, by 1989, what the new president called "a new world order." The end of the Cold War drastically changed U.S. foreign policy, and allowed

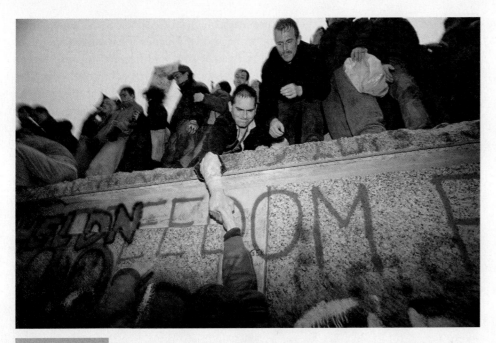

At the Berlin Wall, which had divided the city for almost 30 years, people from east and west greeted each other and celebrated a new freedom.

people to see the world differently. Tracing the changes in U.S. foreign policy and politics in the post-Cold War world as well as the domestic changes, especially those brought about by technology in the decade after the Cold War ended, is the focus of this chapter.

THE BUSH ADMINISTRATION, 1989–1993

29.1 Explain the New World Order that George Bush described.

Few people came to the White House as well-prepared to manage the rapid changes in the international situation as George H.W. Bush. As a former U.S. Ambassador to China, former head of the CIA, and former vice president, he knew the key players and understood the context of events as well as anyone. Unlike his predecessor, Bush came to office with a prime interest in foreign policy. It was an expertise that might serve him well in the rapidly changing world of the 1990s. The United States was also changing, economically and technologically, but President Bush was less prepared to deal with some of the rapid domestic changes that were taking place, which in the end cost him a second term in office.

Foreign Policy Between 1989 and 1993

Bush and his foreign policy team—Secretary of State James Baker, Secretary of Defense Richard Cheney, National Security Adviser Brent Scowcroft (a retired Air Force general), and Joint Chiefs of Staff Chair General Colin Powell—were initially skeptical of the agreements by which Reagan and Gorbachev had sought to end the Cold War, and they did not propose to reduce defense spending. However, the pace of international developments only accelerated after Bush took office. Bush maintained a hands-off policy toward the dissolution of Soviet control in Eastern Europe. He said that the United States did not want to "poke a stick in the eyes of Mr. Gorbachev." But he insisted, in spite of pleas by Gorbachev and European leaders, that Germany had the right to be united and that the new nation should be part of NATO. Bush showed less inclination to state a position when Lithuania declared independence in March 1990, leaving it to the Lithuanians and the Soviets to work out the terms of their own agreement.

While Gorbachev and Bush got to know each other, Gorbachev's own hold on power weakened. Hardliners within the Kremlin blamed Gorbachev for weak leadership as Soviet control of eastern Europe ended. In August 1991, old-line communists staged a military coup and arrested Gorbachev. Boris Yeltsin, the president of the Russian Republic, the largest and most powerful of the 15 Soviet Republics that made up the Soviet Union (or Union of Soviet Socialist Republics, the U.S.S.R.), helped defeat the coup leaders, and Gorbachev was freed and restored to power within days. However, the restoration was short-lived. In December 1991, Gorbachev announced that the Union of Soviet Socialist Republics (the Soviet Union), which had governed Russia and its neighbors since 1917, was no more. Russia, the Ukraine, and Belarus created an informal Confederation of Independent States. Other former Soviet Republics savored their independence. Gorbachev's position simply disappeared. At the Kremlin, the red hammer and sickle flag was replaced with the blue flag of the Russian Republic. The prime enemy of the United States through 45 years of Cold War was gone. While relations with Russia and the other former Soviet republics would be difficult at times, they took place in a vastly different world. (see Map 29-1).

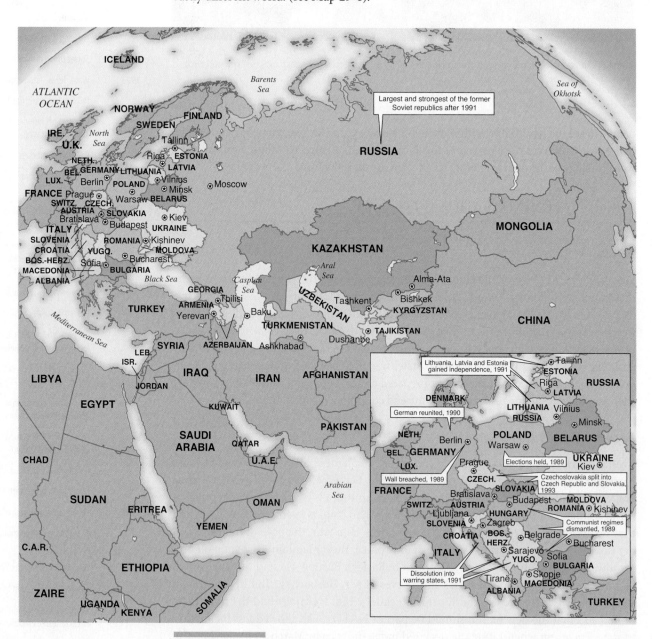

MAP 29-1 Europe After Communism. The map of Europe was radically rearranged after the Soviet Union broke apart into independent republics and the nations of eastern Europe claimed their independence from Russian domination.

While Eastern Europe went through its dramatic changes, the other Communist giant, China, was also changing. As a former ambassador to China, Bush thought he knew the country well and wanted to build closer ties. But he was taken by complete surprise in the spring of 1989, when Chinese students gathered in **Tiananmen Square** in the heart of China's capital, Beijing, to protest the communist party's tight hold and to demand more democratic governance and greater individual freedom. Such protests were unheard of in Communist China. By May, as protests had spread to 200 other Chinese cities, the government declared martial law, and then in June sent tanks and army units into Tiananmen Square, killing perhaps 3,000 students and injuring three times as many. The communist government of China was not about to follow Russia's peaceful transition to a different social system. The world, including President Bush, was horrified. For the rest of his term, Bush was torn about whether to join other nations in protest, seek to maintain and expand commercial ties with China, and respond to protests by members of Congress and the 43,000 Chinese students who were in the United States. The result was an unclear and inconsistent China policy.

In August 1990, the Bush foreign policy team was confronted by another surprising crisis in yet another part of the world. On August 1, Iraqi dictator Saddam Hussein ordered an attack on Iraq's smaller neighbor, Kuwait, and quickly took control of the country. Kuwait had been part of Iraq until 1961, and Hussein insisted he was simply reuniting what should never have been divided. U.S. ambassador to Iraq, April Glaspie, had told Hussein that the United States had "no opinion," on Iraq's border dispute with Kuwait, but she never meant that statement to mean the United States would allow Iraq to swallow its neighbor. Both Iraq and Kuwait were among the world's largest oil producers, and Iraqi control of Kuwait meant that an Iraqi dictator, whom the United States did not trust, was in control of 20 percent of the world's oil.

Tiananmen Square
Prodemocracy demonstrations involving thousands of young Chinese students.

In a very short war in early 1991, U.S. troops landed in Kuwait and quickly secured its independence from Iraq.

Operation Desert Storm
Code name for the successful offensive against Iraq by the United States and its allies in the 1991 Persian Gulf War.

Bush announced, "This will not stand." The United States negotiated with Hussein but quickly began military planning if negotiations failed. Bush gained the support of Syria, Egypt, and Saudi Arabia in insisting that Iraq must leave Kuwait. In November, the UN Security Council authorized the use of force if negotiations did not succeed. While there was significant opposition in the United States to any intervention, Congress authorized the use of force, though in the Senate the vote was a close 52-47.

On January 17, 1991, the U.S.-led **Operation Desert Storm** began. An air war showered missiles and bombs on the Iraqi forces in Kuwait and destroyed communications and electrical systems in Iraq. On February 24, U.S. Marines from bases in Saudi Arabia landed in Kuwait and in 100 hours of battle drove the Iraqi forces out of the country. Kuwait was reestablished as an independent country and a close U.S. ally. Fearing unnecessary carnage and not wanting a U.S. occupation of Iraq proper, Bush then halted all military operations. The war was over. It seemed an easy military victory, but it was not without costs.

Within Iraq, rebellions broke out against Hussein's rule. While Bush hoped they would succeed, he was not willing to intervene or to try to topple Hussein, fearing that the United States would be caught in a long-term land war in Iraq. He did, however, take action to protect the Kurdish minority in a new autonomous region within northern Iraq, announcing a "no fly zone" in which the United States would shoot down any Iraqi planes over that area, but opposition forces in the rest of the country, expecting U.S. aid that never came, were slaughtered by Hussein's troops. A U.S. boycott of Iraq led to widespread suffering within the country. Finally, the staging of U.S. troops in Saudi Arabia, site of the holiest places in the Muslim world, stirred anger among devout Muslims who hated the idea of non-Muslims in that region. Among those who were angry was Osama bin Laden, a Saudi who founded al-Qaeda, a terrorist organization, to retaliate against both Saudi Arabia and the United States.

Meanwhile, closer to home, Bush decided in December 1989 that Panama's dictator, Manuel Noriega, had to be removed. Noriega had received CIA support to oppose Communists in the region, but he had also become rich through drug trafficking and had become a brutal dictator. When his party lost a presidential election in May 1989, Noriega annulled the election. Knowing that the Carter-era treaty meant that the Panama Canal was going to be returned to Panama, Bush took no chances. On December 20, a U.S. assault team landed in Panama and took control of the country. They restored the democratically elected president of Panama, Guillermo Endara, and eventually arrested Noriega as a drug dealer and imprisoned him in Florida.

The Bush team also made other international efforts that had mixed results. The administration negotiated a **North American Free Trade Agreement (NAFTA)** that would eliminate tariffs between the United States and Canada and Mexico, but Senate confirmation of the treaty was slow in coming. Into Somalia, a nation in northeast Africa threatened by famine and chaos, the United States sent 28,000 peacekeeping troops, but could not effect large-scale changes. To the surprise of many of its own citizens, Yugoslavia, which had been relatively stable since the end of World War II, disintegrated into ethnic hostility between its Eastern Orthodox Serbian, Roman Catholic Croatian, and Bosnian Muslim communities. In response to the new crisis in Yugoslavia, the United States supported a UN peacekeeping mission, which was ineffective, and an arms embargo. Even with the Cold War over, the world remained a confusing and dangerous place.

North American Free Trade Agreement (NAFTA)
Agreement reached in 1993 by Canada, Mexico, and the United States to substantially reduce barriers to trade.

Education, Legislation, and the Supreme Court

In his inaugural address, George Bush angered the outgoing Ronald Reagan by saying that it was time "to make kinder the face of the Nation and gentler the face of the world." He also continued the Reagan assault on big government, insisting that the new "kindness" must come from a "thousand points of light," emerging from local nongovernmental groups around the country rather than from federal government programs.

Bush called himself an "education president." Where Reagan sought to abolish the Department of Education and reduce the federal government's role in education, Bush convened the nation's governors at an "Education Summit" in Charlottesville, Virginia, in the fall of 1989 to address the challenges in American public schools. The plan that emerged from Bush's partnership with the governors, who were led by Arkansas governor Bill Clinton, was called America 2000. It sought to improve the nation's schools by setting new national standards for all students.

Bush also focused efforts on two other pieces of legislation that would have far-reaching results. He supported the **Clean Air Act** that toughened air quality standards and pollution controls. It would effect huge changes in industry and begin to shift more attention to environmental issues. He also led the fight for the **Americans with Disabilities Act (ADA)** that passed Congress in 1990. The ADA outlawed discrimination in employment, public services, and public accommodations for people with disabilities. It not only transformed the face of American buildings that now had to provide wheelchair ramps, elevators, and appropriate lavatories for those with physical disabilities, but also put in motion pervasive changes in hiring practices and services that would benefit all those with disabilities, including those who were deaf and blind.

Bush's first appointment to the Supreme Court, David Souter, drew little controversy. Souter turned out to be a more liberal judge than many expected, probably including Bush, especially when he voted to affirm the court's *Roe v. Wade* decision in 1992. When Thurgood Marshall retired, Bush stirred considerable controversy by nominating Clarence Thomas. Thomas, like Marshall, was an African-American, but while Marshall had been known as "Mr. Civil Rights" and was probably the most liberal member of the court in many years, Thomas was known as an unusually conservative Republican. In his confirmation hearings, Thomas was accused of sexual harassment by Anita Hill, a black law professor and former member of Thomas's staff. Hill offered explicit testimony as to what Thomas had said and done, which was highly embarrassing to Thomas and his supporters. Hill was attacked in turn by conservatives, and Thomas called the assault a "high-tech lynching for uppity blacks," but when he was confirmed by the narrowest of Senate votes, 52 to 48, many women concluded that the male senators did not take sexual harassment seriously. While Thomas took his seat on the court, more women ran for and won elective office the following year than in any previous time, increasing their numbers in the Senate, the House, and state legislatures.

Race: From Rodney King to O.J. Simpson

In March 1991, Rodney King, an African-American, failed to stop for police on the Foothill Freeway near San Fernando, California. Los Angeles Police Department (LAPD) officers gave chase for 8 miles and finally arrested King. When King resisted arrest, four police officers beat him as he lay on the ground. A nearby resident used a home video camera to record the arrest and beating, and the video was quickly distributed around the nation. People were outraged. Although King had resisted arrest, the officers had clearly continued to beat him long after he was subdued.

The four officers on the video were arrested. Their attorneys argued that they could not get a fair trial in Los Angeles and the trial was moved to mostly rural Simi County, California. The result of the move was that the officers faced an all-white jury, unlikely in Los Angeles County. In April 1992, the jury found three of the officers

Clean Air Act
Passed by Congress in 1990 as amendments to an earlier act, required substantial restrictions on air pollution.

Americans with Disabilities Act (ADA)
Legislation that significantly improved options for people with disabilities.

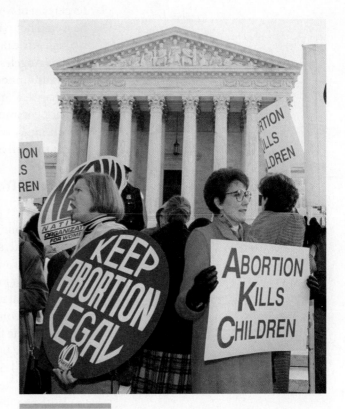

The Supreme Court's 1973 *Roe v. Wade* decision, stating that the right to privacy guaranteed in the Constitution protects a woman's right to choose an abortion, remained controversial and impacted American politics for decades to come, most of all in terms of the appointment of every new Supreme Court justice.

not guilty and deadlocked on the fourth. The acquittal released pent-up anger in the black community in Los Angeles. Riots lasting 4 days resulted in 53 deaths, 2,300 injuries, and $1 billion in property damage. Black and Latino rioters targeted whites and Asians in their neighborhoods, perhaps especially Korean storeowners. A video from the riot showed a white truck driver being pulled out of his cab and beaten. Only the intervention of other blacks who got the driver to a hospital saved his life. For many, the arrest of King, the trial, and the riot that followed illustrated just how deeply lines were still drawn between races in the United States in the 1990s.

While the events around King got the headlines, scholars and activists debated the state of race relations. Some observed that despite what happened, much had changed since the 1950s when blacks were legally barred from white schools, white bus seats, and all-white polling places in many places. Orlando Patterson, a Harvard sociologist, wrote "Relations between ordinary Afro-Americans and Euro-Americans are, in fact, the best they have ever been, although still far from ideal." Other scholars were less sure, noting that events like the beating of Rodney King and data about the educational experience of many black and Latino students confirmed that much had not changed. Andrew Hacker wrote that "A huge racial chasm remains, and there are few signs that the coming century will see it closed."

In 1994, another crisis illustrated the depth of the racial divide in the United States. O.J. Simpson, a celebrated African-American Hall of Fame former football star, was arrested in June after his divorced wife, Nicole Brown, who was white, and her white friend, Ron Goldman, were found stabbed to death just outside her condominium in an exclusive neighborhood of Los Angeles. When the police issued a warrant for Simpson's arrest, he and a friend fled in Simpson's white Bronco down the Artesia Freeway while perhaps 100,000 Americans watched on TV. Simpson eventually surrendered, and his trial continued for most of the next year. The evidence against Simpson seemed strong, but black and white Americans saw it differently. In one poll, 63 percent of whites thought he would get a fair trial while 69 percent of blacks thought he would not. The trial was a media circus. Simpson's lead attorney, Johnnie Cochran, a tough African-American trial lawyer, proved that the investigation of Simpson by the Los Angeles police was filled with racist assumptions, although he did not prove Simpson's innocence. When in October 1995 a jury acquitted Simpson of the murder charge, a majority of blacks agreed with the verdict, and celebrations broke out in black communities, while most whites were stunned. Regardless of whoever killed Brown and Goldman, the Simpson trial showed that Americans of different races were deeply divided in how they viewed the criminal justice system in the 1990s.

Economic Troubles and the Election of 1992

Bush's greatest political failure was his inability to manage the U.S. economy. After 1990, the economy went into a serious recession. During 1991 and 1992, AT&T fired 100,000 workers, GM fired 74,000, and two major airlines, Pan Am and Eastern, went bankrupt, throwing more out of work. People blamed the president. With his preoccupation with foreign policy, Bush seemed out of touch, a perception that did not help his political standing.

Bush's economic problems became an even worse political liability when he decided, in the face of the rapidly increasing government debt, that he needed to raise taxes in spite of his promise not to do so. When the top tax bracket was increased from 28 to 31.5 percent, the *New York Post* headline said, "Read my lips: I Lied." Conservative Republicans never forgave Bush.

With the Republican Party in not-quite-open revolt and the nation's economy in trouble, Democrats smelled victory in the 1992 election. Arkansas governor Bill Clinton soon emerged as a Democratic front-runner. When Clinton lost the New Hampshire primary, he called himself the "comeback kid," and campaigned harder than ever. Clinton demonstrated a combination of strengths and of weaknesses.

President Bush, future president Clinton, and independent candidate Ross Perot debated in the lively 1992 presidential campaign.

He was brilliant. Even though he grew up in poverty, he excelled in school and won scholarships to Georgetown University, was awarded a Rhodes scholarship to Oxford, and then went on to Yale Law School. At Yale, he also met and married fellow student Hillary Rodham. He was as charismatic on the campaign trail as John F. Kennedy had been. As one of the founders of the Democratic Leadership Council, he was a moderate who distanced himself from his party's more liberal members. Clinton also had his weaknesses. The explanations he gave for his rumored womanizing, draft dodging, and one-time marijuana smoking were never convincing and he earned the name "Slick Willie." But he was a tough campaigner who would not quit. He won the Democratic nomination, asked Tennessee senator Al Gore, a fellow baby boomer, to be his running mate, and in spite of a personally chaotic style, kept his campaign focused. A sign in the Clinton campaign headquarters reading "It's the economy, stupid." said it all.

An independent candidate also entered the race, eccentric billionaire H. Ross Perot. Perot described the deficit as being "like a crazy aunt we keep down in the basement. All the neighbors know she's there but nobody wants to talk about her." He said that Bush's NAFTA Treaty would produce a "giant sucking sound" of American jobs leaving the country. Although given virtually no chance of winning, Perot was the most popular third-party candidate in many years.

Bush was challenged for the Republican nomination by conservative commentator Pat Buchanan, known as the "pit bull of the Right." Bush easily defeated Buchanan for the nomination, but the attack weakened the president. The conservative dominance of the 1992 Republican convention, especially the vocal role of religious conservatives like Buchanan, alienated many more moderate voters. Throughout the fall campaign, the president seemed disengaged. It was not a close contest. Clinton won almost 45 million votes to Bush's 39 million. Surprisingly, Perot won almost 20 million votes, hurting Bush more than Clinton. Democrats retained control of the Senate 57 to 43 and the House 258 to 176.

29.1 **Quick Review** How did George H.W. Bush's foreign policy concerns evolve over the course of his presidency?

THE CLINTON PRESIDENCY

29.2 Analyze the impact of the Clinton presidency and the Clinton–Gingrich conflict on the country.

Clinton came to office with high hopes. He idolized John F. Kennedy and wanted to be remembered as another Kennedy. Clinton, the first baby boomer president, replaced Bush, the last of eight presidents who had served in World War II. He saw his coming to office as a generational change and told the country, "Today, a generation raised in the shadows of the Cold War assumes new responsibilities." He set an activist agenda, saying, "We must invest more in our own people, in their jobs, in their future, and at the same time cut our massive debt." Clinton did cut the federal deficit, dramatically. Success on other fronts, however, was more elusive.

The Early Clinton Agenda: It's Still—Mostly—the Economy

Clinton knew he owed his election to the poor state of the nation's economy. Clinton also knew that he would be reelected in 1996 only if the economic picture brightened. Having campaigned as a moderate Democrat, he surprised many when he made health care reform his first major policy initiative. Clinton, however, was convinced that reforming the nation's chaotic health insurance system would provide a significant jolt to the economy and that providing insurance for the 35 million Americans who had no insurance would help close the growing gap between rich and poor.

In spite of personal tensions in their marriage, Bill and Hillary Clinton were an especially close political team, sometimes compared to Franklin and Eleanor Roosevelt. The president appointed his wife, along with trusted associate Ira Magaziner, to lead a task force to redesign the nation's health care system. Unfortunately, the Clinton-Magaziner team made two significant errors. First, their final 1,342-page report was too long and far too complicated. Second, while they consulted hundreds of experts in developing the report, they failed to consult with Congress. In 1993, Clinton said, "If I don't get health care, I'll wish I didn't run for President." In the end, he did not get it. Conservatives in the Republican minority, led by Congressman Newt Gingrich from Georgia, attacked the plan from the day it was announced. Representatives of physicians and the insurance industry attacked the plan with TV ads and heavily financed congressional lobbying. Without strong support from a large segment of the population or the Democratic majority in Congress, the plan was doomed. In August 1994, the president announced that he was dropping the plan. It had not yet reached a single vote in Congress, but the probable outcome had become clear.

Other issues also got in the way of what Clinton wanted to accomplish. When Clinton tried to fire long-time staff members of the White House travel office for alleged improprieties, he was blocked and accused of trying to give those jobs to friends. When he tried to fulfill a campaign promise to end the ban on gay men and lesbians serving in the armed forces, he was blocked again. The resulting compromise of "Don't ask, don't tell," in which officers would not ask about sexual orientation and soldiers and sailors would keep their sexual orientation hidden or face discharge, satisfied no one.

Only weeks into the new presidency, Clinton's administration had to handle the fallout from an unexpected confrontation in Texas. In Waco, Texas, cult members led by David Koresh had blockaded themselves in their group's compound. A gun battle with agents of the FBI and Bureau of Alcohol, Tobacco, and Firearms on February 28 led to a 7-week stand-off. When the FBI became convinced that children in the compound were being abused, they attacked. Koresh ordered the compound burned, and he and more than 80 of his followers, including 21 children, were killed. It was a horrible outcome that brought significant criticism of the administration and especially of Janet Reno, the new attorney general who had approved the raid, though few knew what could have been a good outcome.

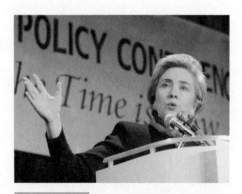

First Lady Hilary Rodham Clinton took an unusually active policy role, leading the task force to create health care legislation in 1994.

Clinton had more success on other fronts. Within 2 weeks of taking office, he signed the Family and Medical Leave Act, which Bush had vetoed twice. The law guaranteed up to 12 weeks of unpaid leave for family medical emergencies and pregnancy. In his campaign, he had promised to develop a national service plan, and Congress quickly approved Clinton's AmeriCorps, which encouraged volunteerism and promised financial support for college costs to those who gave a year of national service. In September 1994, the first 20,000 AmeriCorps volunteers were sworn in. Congress also authorized $2 billion for **Goals 2000**, the Clinton version of President Bush's America 2000 education plan to set national educational standards in core academic subjects. In addition, Congress approved a modest ban on semiautomatic assault weapons and a "Freedom of Access to Clinic Entrances Act" that required antiabortion protesters to keep some distance from medical clinics or places of worship. During his first 2 years, the Senate confirmed two of Clinton's Supreme Court nominees, Ruth Bader Ginsburg and Stephen Breyer. With their confirmation, the court's conservative drift seemed to stop.

In addition, Clinton was convinced that the huge deficit, which had grown substantially under Reagan and Bush, was creating a drag on the American economy. He was also anxious to establish his political credentials as a moderate. In August 1993, less than 7 months into office and with the health care bill still pending, Congress passed Clinton's first budget. The budget infuriated conservatives because it included a tax increase, and it infuriated liberals because it did little for federal programs. The administration's goal was simple: balance the federal budget and lower the federal debt. Clinton succeeded, and during his term in office, the total federal spending as a share of the U.S. gross domestic product dropped from 21.5 percent to 19.1 percent. Starting in 1998, real surpluses allowed a major reduction in the federal debt.

Immediately after Clinton's budget passed Congress, he turned his attention to getting congressional approval of the North American Free Trade Agreement (NAFTA), which had been negotiated by George Bush. Few gave NAFTA much chance for approval. Labor unions hated the treaty because it proposed to reduce all trade barriers between the United States, Canada, and Mexico, and the unions feared it would cost jobs. Ross Perot had based his third-party campaign on opposition to NAFTA and had succeeded in winning 19 percent of the vote. Nevertheless, Clinton believed that free trade and the development of an unfettered global economy was the key to long-term prosperity. He allied with Republicans in Congress, and against some of his closest Democratic allies, to get the treaty passed, and he signed it in December 1993.

Although Clinton saw himself as a moderate to conservative Democrat, conservative Republicans, especially those in the House of Representatives, did not think he was nearly conservative enough. Clinton also sought to undercut Republican efforts to differentiate themselves from him, which Republicans found utterly frustrating. Under the leadership of a Georgia congressman, Newt Gingrich, working with congressmen Dick Armey and Tom DeLay of Texas, House Republicans planned for the 1994 midterm elections. The House of Representatives had enjoyed a Democratic majority and a Democratic Speaker for 60 of the 64 years between 1930 and 1994. While the Senate and the White House changed hands, the House seemed permanently Democratic. But a new generation of representatives, coming mostly from suburban districts, especially in the South, where there had been few Republicans elected until the 1970s, were determined to create a Republican majority in the Congress and enact their agenda. They were very successful. In November 1994, 34 Democrats were defeated in their bids for reelection, a new Republican majority took control, and Gingrich became the Speaker of the House.

"The Era of Big Government Is Over"

With the new Republican majority and Newt Gingrich as the new speaker coming to power at the end of Clinton's second year in office, the chance for significant legislative victories for Clinton virtually disappeared. Clinton would spend much of the next 6 years either trying to hold on to past Democratic victories or doing what he and

Goals 2000
Legislation that set tough new goals over the coming decades to improve the quality of American schooling.

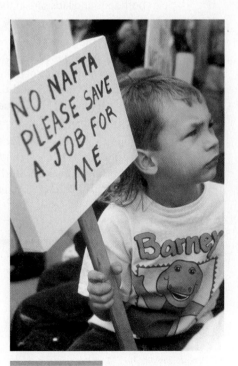

Not all Americans supported the NAFTA trade agreement. Many feared it would cost a significant number of jobs in the United States.

American Voices

Republican Contract with America, 1994

Contests for seats in the U.S. House of Representatives are traditionally local. In the 1994 campaign, however, 337 Republican candidates endorsed a common platform in a dramatic ceremony on the Capitol steps. Their "Contract with America" represented the voice of conservative Americans.

As Republican Members of the House of Representatives and as citizens seeking to join that body we propose not just to change its policies, but even more important, to restore the bonds of trust between the people and their elected representatives....

Thereafter, within the first 100 days of the 104th Congress, we shall bring to the House Floor the following bills, each to be given full and open debate, each to be given a clear and fair vote and each to be immediately available this day for public inspection and scrutiny.

1. **THE FISCAL RESPONSIBILITY ACT:** A balanced budget/ tax limitation amendment and a legislative line-item veto to restore fiscal responsibility to an out-of-control Congress, requiring them to live under the same budget constraints as families and businesses.

2. **THE TAKING BACK OUR STREETS ACT:** An anticrime package including stronger truth-in-sentencing, "good faith" exclusionary rule exemptions, effective death penalty provisions, and cuts in social spending from this summer's "crime" bill to fund prison construction and additional law enforcement to keep people secure in their neighborhoods and kids safe in their schools.

3. **THE PERSONAL RESPONSIBILITY ACT:** Discourage illegitimacy and teen pregnancy by prohibiting welfare to minor mothers and denying increased AFDC for additional children while on welfare, cut spending for welfare programs, and enact a tough 2-years-and-out provision with work requirements to promote individual responsibility.

4. **THE FAMILY REINFORCEMENT ACT:** Child support enforcement, tax incentives for adoption, strengthening rights of parents in their children's education, stronger child pornography laws, and an elderly dependent care tax credit to reinforce the central role of families in American society.

5. **THE AMERICAN DREAM RESTORATION ACT:** A $500 per child tax credit, begin repeal of the marriage tax penalty, and creation of American Dream Savings Accounts to provide middle class tax relief.

6. **THE NATIONAL SECURITY RESTORATION ACT:** No U.S. troops under U.N. command and restoration of the essential parts of our national security funding to strengthen our national defense and maintain our credibility around the world.

7. **THE SENIOR CITIZENS FAIRNESS ACT:** Raise the Social Security earnings limit which currently forces seniors out of the work force, repeal the 1993 tax hikes on Social Security benefits and provide tax incentives for private long-term care insurance to let older Americans keep more of what they have earned over the years.

8. **THE JOB CREATION AND WAGE ENHANCEMENT ACT:** Small business incentives, capital gains cut and indexation, neutral cost recovery, risk assessment/cost-benefit analysis, strengthening the Regulatory Flexibility Act and unfunded mandate reform to create jobs and raise worker wages.

9. **THE COMMON SENSE LEGAL REFORM ACT:** "Loser pays" laws, reasonable limits on punitive damages, and reform of product liability laws to stem the endless tide of litigation.

10. **THE CITIZEN LEGISLATURE ACT:** A first-ever vote on term limits to replace career politicians with citizen legislators.

Source: Downloaded from, http://www.nationalcenter.org/ContractwithAmerica.html August 2, 2011.

Thinking Critically

1. **Documentary Analysis**

   What fundamental principles and assumptions link the 10 initiatives included in the contract?

2. **Historical Interpretation**

   What does the contract tell you about the political landscape of the 1990s?

   To which groups was the contract meant to appeal? Which groups were most likely to find it objectionable?

his closest political advisor, Dick Morris, called "triangulating," finding a third point between increasingly conservative Republicans and increasingly liberal Democrats to stake out their own position, one that sometimes undercut both.

The biggest battle between the Clinton administration and the Gingrich Republicans came in late 1995, only months into the tenure of the new Congress. After several months of budget battles, Congress passed a budget that included cuts in social programs. Clinton vetoed the budget with the result that the government was briefly without a budget, forcing a partial government shut down for 6 days in

November. After temporary legislation reopened government offices later that month, the Republican House passed a budget with even further cuts, reducing funds for food stamps, Medicare, and other domestic program. Republican leaders proudly announced, "This is a fundamental change in the direction of government." Clinton again vetoed the budget, and on December 16, the government shut down for 21 days. Federal employees went without their paychecks; national parks and "nonessential" government offices closed. Only in January was a compromise reached that restored most of the cuts. Most political observers thought Clinton had won the battle, painting Gingrich as an extremist and Clinton as a cautious moderate.

In the context of this tense budget debate, Clinton went to Congress in January 1996 to give his annual State of the Union message. He announced, "The era of Big Government is over." Many Democrats wondered who had really won the budget showdown. Clinton had already promised that one of his major policy goals for 1996 was to "put an end to welfare as we know it." After vetoing more conservative legislation, in August 1996, Clinton signed the Personal Responsibility and Work Opportunity Reconciliation Act that replaced the federal government's long-standing Aid to Families with Dependent Children (AFDC) program with temporary assistance that prevented most people, except the disabled, from receiving more than 2 years of assistance, with a 5-year lifetime maximum. New York senator Daniel Moynihan called the result, which dropped 2 million black and Latino students from eligibility, the "most brutal act of social policy since Reconstruction." Fortunately, the economy was experiencing a boom time when the law was passed; the minimum wage was raised, and there were jobs to be found, at least in the short run. The long-time cost to some of the nation's poorest people was a different matter.

Clinton took other positions that disappointed liberals and heartened conservatives. He signed the **Defense of Marriage Act**, which said no state was required to recognize a same-sex marriage from another state. Since no state yet allowed same-sex marriage when the law passed, it was a symbolic move, but for gay and lesbian voters who had supported Clinton, it was a frustrating limitation that would have a greater impact in future years.

In spite of the Republican gains in the 1994 elections, the 1996 presidential election was seldom in doubt. The Republicans nominated conservative Senator Robert Dole, a decorated World War II hero and a long-time Washington insider who preferred compromise to Gingrich-style conflict. Dole had a good sense of humor but was not a strong campaigner. Clinton adopted many Republican issues and campaigned energetically. Clinton's fundraising ability meant that the two parties were closely matched in available funds, where previously, Republicans had traditionally outspent Democrats by a two-to-one margin. Perot again ran as an outsider. Clinton won 49 percent of the vote to Dole's 40 percent. Perot's vote dropped to less than 9 percent. Clinton coasted to a second term, but with Republican majorities in both houses of Congress.

In the post–Cold War era, other trends were reshaping the American political scene. By the 1990s, the majority of Americans lived in suburbs, up from only a quarter of the population in the 1950s. The combination of suburbanization and the Voting Rights Act typically led to the nation's urban centers electing liberal Democrats, often African-Americans or Latinos who reflected their districts majority, and the surrounding suburbs electing white conservatives who reflected these districts. Especially in the South and West, Republican victories often came at the cost of moderates of either party, rather than liberal Democrats, with the result that, as the Republican Party got more conservative, the Democratic Party got more liberal.

Since 1900, if not earlier, the Republican Party represented the elite, whether major corporate executives, Wall Street investors, or small town business leaders. The Democrats were the party of the working class, especially union members. The New Deal Coalition, which had kept Congress solidly Democratic for so long, included union members, urban immigrants (especially the Irish), and the white South. During the

Defense of Marriage Act
Legislation that required the federal government to ignore provisions of any state act recognizing same-sex marriages; was declared unconstitutional by the U.S. Supreme Court in 2013.

New Deal, most African-American voters, who had traditionally been Republicans after the Civil War, shifted to the Democratic Party. However, by the time Clinton came to office, much had changed. Many white southerners had turned against the civil rights movement, which they associated with the Democrats, and had become Republicans. Many white workers in the North, especially those in ethnic enclaves, were making the same transition for the same reason. In addition, union membership had fallen to below 10 percent of nongovernment workers, reducing the union vote. At the same time, more and more middle- and upper-middle-class professionals, including teachers, journalists, lawyers, and many in high-tech industries, supported the more liberal policies of the Democrats. In contrast to either 1930 or 1960, when if one knew a person's income, one could make a good guess as to their political party preference, no such guess was possible in 1990.

As the political divisions between the two parties grew sharper, the political discourse of the country grew more caustic. Angry talk radio shows drew huge audiences. Rush Limbaugh, who called women activists "feminazis" and environmentalists "environmental wackos," drew an audience of 20 million. The National Rifle Association stridently attacked any politician of either party who voted for any gun control. Common Cause sought to speak for a liberal perspective. Few spoke for moderation or even good manners. Respectful differences did not sell radio advertising. Likewise, respecting differences did not win political debates in Washington in the 1990s.

Small Wars and Dangerous Terrorists—Clinton's Foreign Policy

Clinton once said, "Foreign policy is not what I came here to do." Nevertheless, as president, he could not ignore the rest of the world. His proudest foreign policy accomplishment came early, with the passage of NAFTA, but it was far from his last foreign engagement.

Early in his first term, in September 1993, Israeli Prime Minister Yitzhak Rabin and Palestine Liberation Organization (PLO) leader Yasser Arafat shook hands in the White House after signing the **Oslo Accords**, which Norway had helped to broker. The Oslo agreement led to a suspension of the *intifada*, the Palestinian uprising that had been going on since 1987. The PLO recognized Israel's right to exist and renounced terrorism, while Israel agreed that the PLO would assume governing authority in parts of the West Bank and Gaza Strip. It was an optimistic moment for peace in the Middle East that ended all too soon when an outraged Israeli assassinated Rabin.

In 1993, events in Somalia and Haiti demanded attention. Bush had initially sent troops to Somalia to help secure peace in that war-torn region of Africa, and Clinton authorized 440 elite troops. When American troops sought to capture a warlord who had ordered the killing of Pakistani UN troops, two U.S. Black Hawk helicopters were shot down in Mogadishu and 18 Americans were killed; the body of one was dragged through the streets of the city. Clinton immediately withdrew all Americans. In Haiti, when demonstrators blocked the landing of U.S. peacekeepers in Haiti, Clinton did not try to persist, in spite of his desire to support the democratically elected president Jean-Bertrand Aristide.

In light of experiences in Somalia and Haiti, Clinton took an even more cautious stand in Rwanda when civil war broke out in April 1994. For 100 days, Hutus butchered perhaps 800,000 Tutsi and moderate Hutus who had tried to stop the genocide. The United States and the world did virtually nothing although perhaps 70 percent of the Tutsi population was killed. After he left office, Clinton said that his failure to act in Rwanda was his greatest regret, but there was little support for intervention in 1994.

At the same time, the former Yugoslavia was continuing to come apart. Slobodan Milošević, the nationalist leader of Serbia, wanted to create a new "pure" Serbian nation. He led a slaughter in which perhaps 200,000 Bosnian Muslims were killed by Bosnian and Serbian nationalists. Some 6,000 UN peacekeepers were held as virtual prisoners while the slaughter went on (see Map 29-2).

Oslo Accords
A 1993 agreement between Israel and the Palestine Liberation Organization (PLO) in which Israel agreed that the PLO could govern the West Bank and Gaza Strip in exchange for PLO recognition of Israel's right to exist.

MAP 29-2 Yugoslavia Comes Apart. In 1991–92, the nation of Yugoslavia, which had been created in the aftermath of World War I, came apart as ethnic rivalries burst into warfare.

While the United States and most of Europe did nothing, the battle continued. Finally in the summer of 1995, Clinton ordered the bombing of Serbian positions. When in July 1995 Serbia forced 40,000 Muslim refugees out of a UN safe area around Srebrenica, and then murdered some 7,000 Muslim men and boys, Clinton determined that further action was needed. In August, after further Serb attacks, the United States joined with other NATO forces in massive air strikes on Bosnian Serb positions. The bombing and NATO support for Croatian and Bosnian Muslim ground forces led Milošević to agree to join negotiations at the Wright-Patterson Air Force base in Dayton, Ohio. The **Dayton Peace Accords** led to a significant reduction of the conflict, the placement of 60,000 NATO soldiers in Bosnia, including 20,000 Americans, and the eventual war crimes trial of Milošević. In June 1999, the American commander in Europe, General Wesley Clark, convinced Clinton that the United States needed to intervene again to stop Serbian aggression in the province of Kosovo where Muslims made up 90 percent of the population. A bombing raid on the Serbian capital of Belgrade resulted in a bomb falling on the Chinese Embassy, which killed several staff members and deeply hurt U.S.–Chinese relations.

Iraq also remained an issue, even though the war with Iraq over Kuwait was over before Clinton came to office. After the CIA concluded that Saddam Hussein had tried to arrange the assassination of former president Bush, Clinton ordered a missile strike on Baghdad that destroyed the country's intelligence headquarters. The government also continued to monitor potential terrorist activity emanating from Iran or North Korea, both of which were seeking to develop nuclear weapons.

In his efforts at foreign relations, Clinton also tried to broker peace agreements. In 1995 he sought to recognize the government of Vietnam and supported a mission by three veterans of the Vietnam war then serving in the U.S. Senate, Democrats John Kerry of Massachusetts, Robert Kerrey of Nebraska, and Republican John McCain

Dayton Peace Accords
A November 1995 agreement that began the process to bring peace to the former Yugoslavia.

Good Friday Accords
A 1998 peace agreement to bring a peaceful settlement to the long-standing battles between Catholic and Protestant factions over the government of Northern Ireland.

of Arizona, all of whom testified that there were no remaining prisoners of war in Vietnam and urged reconciliation. In addition, he worked for peace in Northern Ireland and in 1994 appointed former U.S. senator George Mitchell as special envoy. Mitchell helped broker the **Good Friday Accords** of 1998, a promising breakthrough in war-torn Ireland.

Terrorism at Home and Abroad

Terrorism, both domestic and foreign, posed unique challenges because terrorists were difficult to find, to predict, and to deal with. While international terrorist acts deeply frightened the United States, a new form of domestic terrorism, though perhaps less organized, stunned the nation during Clinton's term in office. The actions of the FBI in the Waco, Texas, standoff with David Koresh had infuriated Timothy McVeigh and Terry Nichols, who believed that the FBI attack needed to be avenged. They managed to build a powerful truck bomb, and on April 19, 1995, McVeigh drove the bomb to the parking lot of the Alfred P. Murrah Federal Building in Oklahoma City and detonated it. The resulting blast killed 168 people, including a number of children in a day care center. The bombing was the largest terrorist attack in U.S. history up to that time. McVeigh and Nichols were eventually captured, and McVeigh was executed, but government officials and the public knew that they were not the only Americans so disaffected that they might turn to violence.

Four years later, two deeply disaffected teenagers, Eric Harris and Dylan Klebold, whose journals reflected their fascination with the Oklahoma City bombing, went on a rampage at their high school in Littleton, Colorado, a day after the anniversary of the earlier bombing. Their deadly rampage was the first of what would be many similar school shootings, often in suburban or rural areas and often initiated by disturbed and angry males who sought revenge against teachers and more popular students and the fleeting fame that came with such actions.

In February 1993, only a month after Clinton took office, Muslim terrorists bombed the World Trade Center in New York City, killing six. Over 1,000 people were injured in the blast and 5,000 were evacuated from the buildings. The bombing

The October 2000 bombing of the American destroyer USS *Cole* in Yemen was one of several terrorist attacks against the United States during Clinton's years in office.

THINKING HISTORICALLY

The Causes of the Columbine Shootings

On April 20, 1999, two high school students went on a shooting rampage at Columbine High School in Littleton, Colorado, killing 12 students and a teacher before committing suicide. The two had planned the day carefully and came to school well-armed with rifles and firebombs. Ever since that tragic day, and through the other school shootings that have followed in subsequent years, people have tried to make sense of what happened and why. One journalist, Neal Gabler, writing for the *Los Angeles Times* immediately after the event, asked readers to locate the tragedy in cultural and historical context:

Of all the bizarre sidelights to the horrifying massacre at Columbine High School in Littleton, Colo., Tuesday, the most bizarre may have been the story of the students trapped inside the school who called local TV stations on their cell phones and provided brief commentaries on the action. According to one report, they signed off only because they feared the intruders might be watching television themselves and thus discover the whereabouts of the cell-phone users. All of which suggests that even for the perpetrators and their victims, television was the great mediator.

By now, this is hardly surprising. Like so many real-life dramas in America, the Littleton tragedy became a media event even before the smoke had cleared and anyone knew what was really happening. Copters buzzed overhead, reporters swarmed the scene and commentators were soon delivering sententious analyses of what it all meant, giving us a sense of *déjà vu*.

But tragedies like this are media events not only because the media immediately latch onto them. Often they are media events in two far more important senses: first because the perpetrators usually seem to have modeled their behavior after certain figures in the popular culture; and, second, because the rampages seem ultimately to have been staged for the media on the assumption that if you kill it, they will come. Or, put another way, what we witnessed at Littleton was not just inchoate rage. It was a premeditated performance in which the two gunmen roamed the school dispatching victims, whooping with delight after each murder. Without pop culture, the slaughter would have been unimaginable.

Begin with the killers. In the inevitable postmortems that follow these horrors, it was reported that the outcasts Dylan Klebold and Eric Harris were part of a high school clique whose members wore long black trench coats and which dubbed itself the Trench Coat Mafia, a cinematic image if ever there was one. They were also devotees of the computer games "Doom" and "Quake," in which players prowl virtual hallways shooting virtual victims with virtual guns. They worshipped Adolf Hitler, loved Goth music, and had a special fondness for Marilyn Manson, the mordant rockstar whose satanic persona is designed to scandalize parents of his fans. In short, Harris and Klebold were creatures of pop culture.

Given how much these two seemed to have been shaped by movies, music, and computer games, it is tempting to blame the media once again for providing guidance to young would-be sociopaths....

What helped give these fantasies body is yet another new instrument of the entertainment age: the Internet. Movies provided a personal reverie for those disaffected teenagers of the past....With the Internet to connect them, teenagers are no longer silent sufferers....When you live within a virtual reality, you have to expect some addled individuals won't accept the difference between the movie or video screen and the screen of life.

Source: Neal Gabler, "Becoming Your Fantasy in Virtual Munch Beer Hall," Los Angeles Times, April 25, 1999, reprinted in Stuart A. Kallen, editor, The 1990s (San Diego, CA: Greenhaven Press, 2000), pp. 85–89.

Thinking Critically

1. **Comparison**

   What do you think about Gabler's description of teenagers in the age of cell phones, the Internet, and other new media in comparison to teenagers of other times? Does it seem accurate?

2. **Contextualization**

   In the context of the 1990s, what other factors should Gabler include in seeking to understand the Columbine shootings?

---

had been fueled by anger at the United States over its support for Israel and over the fact that U.S. troops had been stationed in Saudi Arabia near Muslim holy places. Some of the terrorists involved had gotten training from a relatively new terrorist group known as al-Qaeda.

The leader of al-Qaeda was a rich Saudi, Osama bin Laden, who had been expelled from his home country for his terrorist leanings and then expelled from Africa, where he had been living. He landed in Afghanistan and supported the country's Taliban government. In February 1998, when bin Laden called for a holy war against the west, the CIA estimated that he had some 15,000 followers, though little was known about the hard-to-find organization. In August 1998, al-Qaeda operatives managed to bomb the U.S. embassies in both Kenya and Tanzania. Most of the 223 killed and 4,500 wounded were African civilians working in or around the embassies, though 12 Americans were also killed. In October 2000, another al-Qaeda bomb ripped a hole in the hull of the Navy's USS *Cole* while it was anchored in a port in Yemen. Seventeen sailors were killed. In all, some 90 Americans were killed by foreign terrorists, mostly bin Laden's al-Qaeda, during the Clinton years. Far worse was to come in 2001, but the warning signs were there.

Scandal and Impeachment

On January 21, 1998, the *Washington Post* carried a story that surprised, but probably did not shock, the nation. The president of the United States had been involved in an affair with a young White House intern and had lied about it to his wife, to his administration, to the press, and under oath. It made for a sensational news story, and in the months that followed, the young intern, Monica Lewinsky, and the sexual escapades of Bill Clinton, remained front-page news.

Kenneth Starr, a zealous lawyer and former Republican solicitor general, was appointed as an independent prosecutor in 1994 to look into accusations that the president and Hillary Clinton's land dealings in a development at the Whitewater River in Arkansas had been improper. He spent the next 4 years, and a significant amount of taxpayer money, investigating but never discovered evidence of a crime. However, before being appointed, Starr was an advisor to the legal team assembled for a sexual harassment suit brought against Bill Clinton by Paula Corbin Jones, an Arkansas state employee who claimed that, while Clinton was governor, he had ordered a state trooper to bring her to his hotel room and sought sexual favors. Because of the trooper's role, the affair came to be known a "troopergate" in the media.

By late 1997, both the Paula Jones lawsuit and the Whitewater investigation were crawling through the legal process with no end in sight and only limited political damage to the president. Then the situation changed rapidly. A disgruntled former White House staffer, Linda Tripp, befriended Monica Lewinsky and secretly recorded their conversations as Lewinsky shared intimate details of her relationship with the president. As Lewinsky described it, she began her affair with Clinton during the government shutdown of November 1995. Tripp then shared the tapes with legal counsel for Paula Jones, who used the evidence to bolster her case that Clinton regularly engaged in extramarital affairs. She also shared the tapes with Starr. For Starr, the tapes proved that the president had lied under oath and perhaps also urged Lewinsky to lie, both federal crimes that could lead to impeachment.

Clinton denied the whole story. At a press conference a few days after the *Washington Post* story broke, he said, "I want to say one thing to the American people. I want you to listen to me. I'm going to say this again. I did not have sexual relations with that woman, Ms. Lewinsky. I never told anybody to lie, not a single time, never. These allegations are false. And I need to go back to work for the American people." Hillary Clinton denounced Starr as being part of a "vast right-wing conspiracy," and said—accurately—that he "has literally spent four years looking at every telephone call we've made, every check we've ever written, scratching for dirt."

In the summer of 1998, Lewinsky told a federal grand jury about her affair with the president and produced a semen-stained dress that she had saved. Backed into a corner, on August 17, Clinton told a federal grand jury that he had engaged in an "inappropriate" relationship with Lewinsky. That evening, he gave a TV speech in which he said, "I did have a relationship with Ms. Lewinsky that was not appropriate….It constituted a critical lapse in judgment and a personal failure." And he admitted he had "misled people, including even my wife." But he also insisted that the Starr investigation had "gone on too long, cost too much, and hurt too many innocent people."

Many, even among Clinton's closest supporters, were furious, if not at the affair, then at the lying. At a time when the country needed to deal with its economy and the terrorist attacks in Kenya and Tanzania, the president was distracted and untrustworthy. Starr and the Republican majority in Congress were eager to punish the president. Starr sent his report to the House of Representatives. In December, the House, with its Republican majority, voted to impeach President Clinton on the grounds that he had committed perjury in his original testimony to a federal grand jury and had sought to obstruct justice in the Paula Jones case. It was only the second time in U.S. history that a president had been impeached. (Nixon resigned before an impeachment vote.) According to the Constitution, removing the president is a two-part process. The House must vote on impeachment—essentially the same as a grand jury indictment—then the House acts a prosecutor while the Senate acts as the jury, with the Chief Justice of the Supreme Court presiding. In Clinton's case, the Senate was convinced that although his behavior was inappropriate, it hardly met the level of "high crimes and misdemeanors" specified in the Constitution. On February 12, 1999, the Senate rejected the charges against Clinton by a vote of 55 to 45 for the perjury charge and 50 to 50 for the obstruction of justice charge, a very safe margin since a two-thirds vote was required to convict. Five to 10 Republicans joined all of the Democrats in voting not guilty on the two charges. Clinton could focus again on being president. The Starr investigation cost $60 million.

Speaker Gingrich had been among the president's harshest critics, but the impeachment did not turn out well for Gingrich. Just before the impeachment vote, Republicans lost five seats in the November midterm congressional elections. It was the first time since 1934 that the party holding the White House showed gains in midterm elections. But the speaker, who had been an avid prosecutor of the president, was further hurt by the revelation that he, too, had been having an extramarital affair with a young staff aide. He resigned as speaker and announced that he would leave the House. The newly elected Republican Speaker, Robert Livingston of Louisiana, turned out to also be having an affair and he, too, resigned.

While many in the media were fascinated by the whole case, the American public was surprisingly indifferent. Even if many did not approve of an extramarital affair, it did not seem as big an issue as it might once have been. Clinton was hardly the first president to stray from his marriage vows. Perhaps more important, the nation was prosperous and at peace in 1999. Clinton seemed to be doing his job, whatever his personal life. As the case wound down, Starr's approval rating was 19 percent. Clinton's seldom dropped below 55 percent in his second term.

The Prosperous 1990s

Although an economic downturn brought Clinton to office, an economic upsurge kept him there. After Clinton's second year in office, the U.S. economy started to grow, and it did not stop growing for the next 6 years. Nearly all Americans were better off at the end of Clinton's term than they had been at the beginning. The signs of the new prosperity were everywhere. Of the nation's 107 million households, 106 million had a color TV by 2000, 96 million had a VCR or DVD player, 92 million a microwave, and 81 million had air-conditioning. Houses were larger than ever before. Americans were eating better as fresh, local, and seasonal foods became more widely available and more popular.

The prosperity of the 1990s was the result of many factors. Clinton's budget, which brought down the federal deficit and produced the first federal budget surpluses in decades, made more money available for investment and spending and kept interest rates low, all factors in the prosperity. Experts argued about whether Clinton' free-trade policies, like NAFTA, were helping or hurting the economy, but certainly more goods were in circulation as a result. Changes in agriculture made farms and farmers more productive so fewer people, working less land, could produce more food—and more variety of foods—than ever before—enough to feed the

United States and much of the rest of the world. The boom in technology was producing many new products and cutting the costs of items such as TVs and computers that were already on the market. In addition, easily available personal credit, at low interest rates fed the consumer spending and consumer confidence, even though it allowed people to pile up worrisome levels of debt. In his last State of the Union message in January 2000, Clinton was able to say, "Never before, has our nation enjoyed, at once, so much prosperity and social progress with so little internal crisis and so few external threats." No wonder the president remained popular and the people of the United States relatively happy.

Bush v. Gore—The Election and the Court Case of 2000

The Constitution prevented Clinton from running for a third term in 2000. Even so, he still had a remarkably high approval rating despite the affair with Monica Lewinsky that had tarnished his reputation. The logical candidate for the Democratic nomination was Vice President Al Gore. During the 8 years that Gore served as vice president, he established a solid reputation with special expertise in government operations, the use of the Internet, and the environment. Gore's 1992 book, *Earth in the Balance,* described "humankind's assault on the earth." Although Gore had worked with Clinton for 8 years, he and the president were never especially close, and Gore had been deeply offended by the Monica Lewinsky affair. He selected Connecticut senator Joseph Lieberman as his running mate, the first Jew to be on a major party's national ticket. Lieberman had also been offended by the president's behavior and said so on the Senate floor.

The two leading candidates for the Republican nomination were George W. Bush, the governor of Texas and the son of the former president, and Arizona senator John McCain. McCain was considered more liberal compared with Bush who called himself a "compassionate conservative." By March, Bush had wrapped up the nomination. Bush asked former Secretary of Defense Dick Cheney to handle the vice presidential selection and, in the end, Cheney himself became the nominee.

Gore made a fateful decision to distance himself from Clinton and did not call on the president to do much campaigning. He campaigned in favor of tough gun control legislation and for women's right to choose on abortion decisions, and he promised to keep the Social Security trust fund in a "lock box" separate from the rest of the federal budget. Many, even among his supporters, found him to be stiff and "wooden," hardly the relaxed and at-ease campaigner that Bill Clinton had been.

Bush promised a major tax cut, giving the current budget surplus back to the people. He favored allowing people to invest some of their Social Security contributions in their own stock market accounts. He promised to reform public education. He told the country that he was "a uniter, not a divider," and would work with Democrats and end the divisive partisanship in Washington. In a not-so-subtle reference to the Lewinsky affair, he promised to restore "honor and dignity" to the presidency. He talked openly about how he had overcome his own alcoholism and about his born-again Christian faith. He was a surprisingly strong campaigner in spite of his tendency to mangle the English language with statements like, "families is where our nation finds hope, where wings take dreams."

Two other candidates also entered the race: Ralph Nader, running on the Green Party ticket and critiquing the power that multinational corporations had over both Republicans and Democrats, and Patrick Buchanan, running a conservative and anti-immigrant campaign on Ross Perot's Reform Party ticket. Although Nader and Buchanan might take crucial votes away from either candidate, no one gave them a chance of winning. In addition, several other candidates representing fringe parties entered the contest; however, they posed little threat even to siphon away votes from the major contenders.

As the polls closed on November 7, 2000, results for several states were still up in the air, but later that night, the deciding vote seemed to come down to Florida. Gore had clearly won a small majority in the overall vote—a final count of 50,992,335 for

Gore versus 50,455,156 for Bush (see Map 29-3). However, American presidential contests are decided by electoral votes, and at this point in the contest, whoever won Florida's electoral vote would win the presidency. At one point, the major TV networks, using exit polls, announced that Gore had carried Florida. Later in the evening, they backed off. At around 2:00 a.m. they announced that Bush had won. Gore called Bush to congratulate him and was about to make a public concession speech. Then as new data came in, he called Bush a second time to say that any announcement was premature. By midmorning on Wednesday, November 8, everyone agreed that the election was too close to call. It would stay that way for the next 36 days.

Both campaigns assembled teams of attorneys to challenge votes and demand a Florida recount. Problems with Florida's election procedures became apparent. Some African-American voters had been intimidated or turned away from the polls. In other places where votes were counted by punch cards fed into voting machines, cards with "hanging chads," that is, cards that were not punched all the way through, were not counted, and in these places, the Gore team demanded a hand count. When Gore asked for a recount in four counties where the errors seemed especially glaring, the Bush lawyers challenged him in court. After the Florida Supreme Court sided with Gore, the Bush team took the case to the U.S. Supreme Court. On December 12, the Supreme Court ruled in a 5 to 4 decision that a recount in only four counties violated the equal protection of the law and that, given the time that had elapsed, all recounts in Florida must cease. The next day Gore conceded the election though he said he disagreed with the court's decision "with every fiber of my being." All five of the justices who voted to end the recount had been appointed by Reagan and Herbert Walker Bush (often referred to as "Bush, Sr." to distinguish him from George W. Bush). The other four justices were scathing in their dissent. The court's senior justice John Paul Stevens, who had been appointed by Gerald Ford, said, "Although we may never know with complete certainty the identity of the winner of this year's Presidential election, the identity of the loser is perfectly clear. It is the Nation's confidence in the judge as an impartial guardian of the rule of law."

	Electoral Vote (%)	Popular Vote (%)
GEORGE W. BUSH (Republican)	271 (50.5)	50,456,169 (48.0)
Al Gore (Democrat)	266 (49.5)	50,996,116 (48.0)

MAP 29-3 The Election of 2000. The presidential election of 2000 reflected how deeply divided the United States had become. The Northeast and West leaned Democratic, and the whole of the nation's midsection plus the South leaned Republican.

29.2	**Quick Review** Were Clinton's high approval ratings justified, based on his domestic and foreign policy accomplishments? Why or why not?

TECHNOLOGY DOMINATES AN ERA

29.3	Analyze the changes in technology and their impact on U.S. culture.

While Americans battled over elections and a host of social issues, a small group of Americans were transforming the world in a very different way. In the 1990s, computer use and technological innovation—from connections to the Internet to the use of cell phones—became widespread in the United States.

The Birth of New Technologies

During World War II, the military sought ways to speed the mathematical calculations to send a shell in exactly the right direction to hit an enemy target. These first computers were exactly what the name implied: machines that computed distance, velocity, and air pressure, to get a shot where it was intended to go. After the war, the U.S. Army's 1946 ENIAC computer, known as the "giant brain," performed ballistic calculations in

The ENIAC computer, created in 1946 and huge by later standards, allowed the army more computational possibilities than ever before imagined.

30 minutes that had taken 12 hours for humans to perform. With its 17,468 vacuum tubes, it was also the largest electronic apparatus on the planet. Throughout the 1950s and 1960s, similar large mainframe computers became common throughout American military bases, universities, and industry.

A whole series of postwar inventions made possible the move from large mainframe computers to personal computers. In 1947, the Bell Labs invented transistors that could replace bulky and unreliable vacuum tubes. In 1958, Jack Kilby at Texas Instruments found a way to construct a transistor and the circuitry needed to launch the pocket calculator. In 1968, Robert Noyce and Gordon Moore founded Intel to market a microprocessor that was key to personal computers. The computer giants of the day—Burroughs, Univac, NCR Corporation, Control Data Corporation, and Honeywell—dismissed Intel. Within a decade, Intel would outpace all of them.

In January 1975, the first personal computer, the MITS Altair 8800, went on the market. The MITS company promised investors it would sell at least two hundred Altair computers. It quickly sold several thousand. The Altair had its problems. MITS shipped the computer as a kit, and the buyer needed to assemble it. One early purchaser, Steve Dompier of Berkeley, California, reported enthusiastically that his Altair had arrived "in the mail at 10 a.m. and 30 hours later it was up and running with only one bug in the memory." Not everyone, however, had 30 hours to dedicate to making the new computer work. Those who did manage to successfully assemble their computers quickly realized the Altair's second problem: it didn't actually *do* much on its own. With no keyboard, no screen, and no disk drive, the Altair consisted of a case, a series of switches, and lights. It could do some things—solve mathematical problems as well as keep and sort lists. Dompier even found a way to link it to a radio and turn data into music. This early computer was a machine for dedicated enthusiasts, not the general public, but dedicated enthusiasts liked it.

One especially enthusiastic group in the San Francisco Bay area called themselves the Homebrew Club. The Homebrew Club, self-described geeks, loved the new Altair. Most were hobbyists who just wanted to have fun with the machines. But they also had a political agenda. They were rebels against the large government, universities, and corporations that dominated society and used technology, especially the giant mainframe computers, to do so. Homebrew wanted something different—a modern world in which the individual with a personal computer was more powerful than the corporation or the military or the university with its giant computers. Ted Nelson, another Bay Area geek, wrote in his 1974 self-published *Computer Lib/Dream Machines*, "I would like to alert the reader, in no uncertain terms, that the time has come to be openly attentive and critical in observing and dealing with computer systems; and to transform criticism into action....THE PUBLIC DOES NOT HAVE TO TAKE WHAT'S BEING DISHED OUT." A decade earlier, students had demonstrated in Berkeley with signs that said (mocking the instructions on cards then used in mainframe computers), "Human Being: Do not bend, spindle, or mutilate." According to Nelson, it was time to "liberate" the computer and put its power into everyone's hands.

Steve Wozniak and Steve Jobs were part of Homebrew. They decided that they should market their own kit that could outperform the Altair. They sold their first Apple I computer in 1976. However, to accomplish all they wanted—to make the computer truly a popular device that everyone could use—they needed something simpler and easier than the Altair or the Apple I. Jobs studied the styling of popular European toasters and mixers in the kitchen department at Macy's in San Francisco and designed the plastic case for what became the Apple II. The two also designed new uses for the Apple. The Apple II could be connected to a TV or a stand-alone screen and used to play computer games. It could be used for spreadsheets and word processing. Small businesses could do their own financial analysis.

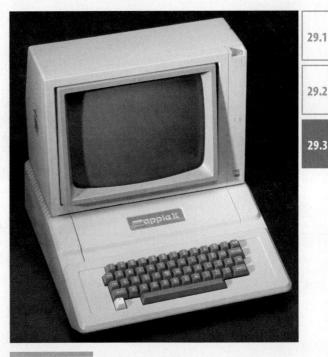

The Apple II designed by Steve Jobs and Steve Wozniak had expanded computing capabilities for both personal and business use.

Jobs and Wozniak also courted investors, including two Silicon Valley engineers, Mike Markkula and Michael Scott, who formed the core of the new Apple Company that launched the Apple II computer in 1977. Apple was a huge success. Apple Computer's revenue went from $800,000 in 1977 to $48,000,000 in 1979. That unbelievable start was only the beginning.

IBM, the largest of the computer companies, realized the money to be made in personal computers and was determined that "Big Blue," as IBM was known, not be left behind. In the 1970s, IBM's money and power came from its manufacture of office machines (the name International Business Machines actually meant something), including popular typewriters, and from leasing the large mainframe computers used by corporations and government agencies.

In the summer of 1980, IBM created a special task force independent of all the normal routines of the company to create a personal computer (PC), complete with operating system, that could compete head-to-head with Apple, and do so quickly. The task force did its work in 12 months, and the first IBM PC went on the market in August 1981. It was a huge hit. IBM made $43 million from its PC division in the first year, and the profits were soon in the billions.

The core of the IBM PC was Intel's microprocessor, a power supply from Zenith, and printers from Epson. Even though IBM was one of the largest software companies in the world, the team also decided to find a different source for the software for the PC. They turned to a Seattle-based upstart known as Micro-soft (later simply Microsoft), led by computer enthusiasts Bill Gates and Paul Allen.

Gates and Allen had written a class-scheduling program for their own high school while students there. In 1975, Gates, like the people at Homebrew, became fascinated with the Altair. He dropped out of Harvard and moved to Albuquerque, New Mexico, where the Altair was manufactured. He and Allen began writing software for the Altair and founded their company, Micro-soft, in April 1975. While Homebrew wanted to share all information freely, making personal computers part of a "people's revolution," Gates saw the potential for profit. He wrote a 1976 open letter condemning information sharing as "theft." Software, Gates insisted, should be as closely held as any computer hardware. When the IBM team approached him, Gates assured them he could produce what they needed. He bought another operating system, the "Quick and Dirty Operating System," (QDOS), adapted it to the needs of the IBM PC, and renamed it the MS-DOS (or Microsoft Disk Operating System). Rather than sell the system to IBM, Gates licensed the MS-DOS system and received royalties on every IBM PC sold. The foundation was laid by 1980 to make Bill Gates the richest person on the planet within a decade.

By 1979, even before IBM set its team to work, Steve Jobs was looking for ways to improve the Apple II. He visited the research offices of the Xerox Corporation, Xerox PARC, which was something of a mecca to computer developers. The staff was intrigued but wary of the upstart Jobs. At Xerox, Jobs saw an engineer, Larry Tesler, working with a small box that he used to move a cursor around on a computer screen. Tesler called it a "mouse," and with it, he could click on icons, open and close "windows" on the screen, and give the machine commands. The mouse was slow and bulky. The engineers at Xerox were not quite sure what to do with it. Soon, Xerox withdrew from the personal computer business—though it made a fortune selling printers that linked to PCs made by others. But Jobs felt like he had seen the future. He set a team to work designing a very different and more user-friendly mouse, and the Macintosh computer that went on sale in 1981 transformed the industry with its easy-to-operate system guided by a handheld mouse that replaced the need to key in commands.

The Y2K Scare of January 1, 2000

As the nation prepared for the calendar change from 1999 to January 1, 2000, people were strangely preoccupied with their computers. Reporting on the *ABC News*, Forrest Sawyer said:

> Surf through the Internet these days and you keep coming across a strange word, TEOTWAWKI. It stands for "the end of the world as we know it," and it refers to the effect of a tiny, seemingly innocuous computer glitch, a tiny glitch a lot of people say could literally blow the lights out on civilization.

The fear of what was sometimes called the "Y2K problem" or the "Millennium bug" was very real and illustrated how completely the United States had become dependent on computers by 2000.

The Y2K problem was relatively simple. Beginning in the 1970s, computer programmers began using a two-digit code for the date. Rather than take up additional memory for 1978, they shortened the space for the year to two digits. Everyone—and every machine—knew that "78" meant 1978. But as 2000 got closer, some computer researchers began to get very nervous. If on New Year's Day 2000 the computers suddenly thought it was 1900, who knew what might happen in term of systems malfunctioning or shutting down.

The threat was very real. The U.S. Department of Defense worried about crucial information systems shutting down. Banks worried that all information on their accounts could be lost. Electric companies worried that the electric grid, now completely computer controlled and monitored, could shut down. Hospitals worried that everything from heart monitors and breathing machines to the electricity and air conditioning in the operating rooms could stop. Internet-based businesses might not be able to operate. Ultimately, very little went wrong. Monitoring equipment in nuclear power plants in Japan failed but was repaired within a few hours. Bus ticket validation machines in Australia failed. In several countries, some cell phones stopped taking messages. In the United States, slot machines in Delaware stopped and the Naval Observatory clock briefly said that it was January 1, 19100. The problems, however, hardly resulted in the end of the world.

Some insisted that the whole Y2K crisis had been a distraction. Others knew how much work it had taken to avoid a crisis. Paul Saffo, director of the Institute for the Future in Menlo Park, California, said, "This was not hype. This was not software consultants trying to create a full employment act for themselves. This really could have screwed up our lives, and you know, a whole bunch of little geeks saved us." David Eddy, a computer programmer in Boston who first coined the term "Y2K crisis," said, "The reason nothing bad happened was that so many people put so much work into it."

American Voices

Peter de Jager and Richard Bergeon,
Countdown Y2K: Business Survival Planning for the Year 2000, 1999

As more people realized the seriousness of what could happen on January 1, 2000, if the nation's increasingly networked computers all responded as if the date were January 1, 1900, many people began to worry. Many publications raised the alarm and in the end the problem was addressed though what some in retrospect saw as a hype others believed was a true crisis averted by the hard work of many experts. In any case, books like this one were very popular in the late 1990s and spoke to the increasing public dependence on computers in many aspects of people's lives, something that had not been true even a few years earlier.

Introduction: Houston, We Have a Problem

It's New Year's Day 2000 and you're headed to your best friend's house to watch football. You're in a hurry because you don't want to miss kickoff, and you have to stop at the nearest cash machine first, because you promised to bring the beer. But instead of cash, the ATM commandeers your card, rudely informing you that it has expired.

Furious, but knowing you won't get much help on a holiday, you head to the nearest 7-11 intending to pay for your refreshments with a credit card. Pulling up to the store, you think a lot of people have the same idea, because there's a long line at the checkout counter. But the problem is not a run on beer; instead, you find out, the cash register is not working. The word, as it reaches you at the end of the line, is that the cash register is computer-based and requires a valid date to start up. And for some reason, it won't. "Some reason" is the Year 2000 problem, Y2K for short.

The preceding hypothetical—but probable—scenario is just the tip of the iceberg, and if collective public denial continues, it is an iceberg that will sink titanic computer systems worldwide. Like the unheeded warnings of disaster on the oceanliner *Titanic,* the alert to the Year 2000 problem has been sounded—on television, in newspapers, magazines, and newsletters, and via the Internet. Often, however, it has been defined simply as the inability of computers to calculate properly with 00—two zeros—signifying the new century. Further, media coverage frequently couches the issue in computer jargon, making it seem irrelevant to anyone other than programmers and information systems managers. The truth is, the Year 2000 problem will affect each of us, personally and professionally.

Source: Peter de Jager and Richard Bergeon, *Countdown Y2K: Business Survival Planning for the Year 2000*, Boston: John Wiley & Sons, 1999.

Thinking Critically

1. **Documentary Analysis**

   How do de Jager and Bergeon describe the Y2K problem?

2. **Historical Interpretation**

   In retrospect we know that the problems described in the article did not happen. Reading the chapter in 1999 how might different readers have responded? What might have led different people to respond differently?

A lot of money was spent on Y2K preparation, perhaps $100 billion in the United States and $300 billion worldwide. Old computers and operating systems were replaced. Whatever the other results, the preparation for Y2K illustrated that, beyond a doubt, by 1999 the United States and the world had become deeply dependent on computers, the Internet, the World Wide Web, and related technology, most of which had not even existed 29 or 30 years earlier.

A Connected Nation

By the 1990s, the personal computers that were being produced by Apple and IBM as well as the systems such as those made by Microsoft that made them useful, were providing people with the ability to read, write, calculate, and do much more at speeds never before thought possible. Nevertheless, for the most part, these amazing machines each still stood alone. As early as the 1940s, dreamers like Vannevar Bush, founder of the National Science Foundation, were imagining a day when, through connected systems, "The patent attorney has on call the millions of issued patents....The physician, puzzled by a patient's reactions...runs rapidly through analogous case histories...." But Bush's dream remained just a dream for almost 50 years. Only in the 1990s did it become possible for most people to make meaningful connections between individual

Internet

The system of interconnected computers and servers that allows the exchange of e-mail, posting of websites, and other means of instant communication.

World Wide Web (WWW)

Since 1991, a protocol for information use on the Internet.

computers—to share information, seek information, and combine information in heretofore unimaginable ways. Those connections were made possible by the development of the **Internet**, a massive network of smaller networks joined together. Actually, many separate developments created the Internet.

President Kennedy and his Secretary of Defense Robert McNamara were preoccupied with the question of how the president could maintain communication with the nation's far-flung military installations if a nuclear war actually happened. Without communication, the threat of massive retaliation in the case of a nuclear attack was a fiction. In the 1960s, however, government planners knew that a nuclear blast would cripple existing radio communications and knock out the nation's highly centralized telephone network. To solve the problem, the Pentagon turned to researchers at the RAND Corporation, and a RAND employee, Paul Baran, led the team that would solve the problem. A decade later, on August 27, 1976, in the parking lot of Zott's Beer Garden near Stanford University, a team of Stanford researchers sent a message from a computer in a van to another computer they had placed inside the bar. The message was received, and the first data transmission had taken place over a network. Further developments led to a much more sophisticated system.

A next crucial step in connecting computers was the development of the World Wide Web, which was achieved by Tim Berners-Lee. Berners-Lee was an English physicist working at the international physics lab in Switzerland, known as CERN, where he noted that the various scientists from different countries could not share information from computer to computer. He wanted to solve that problem. His goal was to find a way to connect computers and share information, lots of information.

In 1990, Berners-Lee found a way to create a common system so the information within files could easily be shared from computer to computer. He created a language for formatting files in hypertext so they could be read in the same way by the sending and receiving computers, and he called the language Hypertext Markup Language, or HTML. In addition, he developed a method of moving files of information, which he called the **World Wide Web (WWW)**, although in the beginning, it connected only the computers within the laboratories at CERN. By the end of 1990, the World Wide Web was up and running within the small research community at CERN. By August 1991, it was being made available at select Internet sites around the world, and by 1992, it was being used by more and more people who were creating their own websites to send and receive hypertext information through the Internet.

In the early 1990s, the WWW was still primitive, but many also saw it as revolutionary. Berners-Lee made another crucial decision. Although he could have gotten rich off of his invention, he insisted that the World Wide Web would be free. On April 30, 1993, CERN announced that anyone, anywhere in the world could use the Web without payment of royalties or legal constraints. The information superhighway, as Tennessee Senator Al Gore would call it, was launched. (Gore did not "invent" the Internet but he did coin the term "information superhighway" in 1990 and sponsored legislation to support it in Congress.)

People needed the right software on their own computers to connect to the World Wide Web. One of the earliest softwares, and the first to be available at no cost, was produced by Marc Andreesen, a 21-year-old computer science major at the University of Illinois. In January 1993, he posted an announcement that said, "By the power vested in me by nobody in particular, alpha/beta version of 0.5 of NCSA's Motif-based information system and World Wide Web browser, X Mosaic, is hereby released, Cheers, Marc." Andreesen then moved to California and was recruited by venture capitalist Jim Clark to develop a more sophisticated connection system, and in October 1994, Netscape was launched as a browser. Soon thousands of people in the United States and around the world were connecting to the Internet for the first time using Netscape Navigator to get to the Netscape home page and from there to the world. Other systems, America Online (AOL) and Yahoo!, soon followed. Before long, Bill Gates was leading

Microsoft in the development and distribution of its own Web browser. By 1998, over 45 million people—quite a jump from 15,000 in 1990—were connected to the World Wide Web. People could shop, do research, listen to music, or tour the world, without leaving the comfort of their own homes.

E-mail messages began replacing telephone calls and office memos in the late 1990s. Ray Tomlinson, a researcher working at the Defense Department inaugurated the use of @ as the core of an e-mail address. In the 1990s, people embraced the opportunity to send and receive messages at times of their own convenience rather than to have to answer the telephone. With the growth of television in the 1950s, some had worried that the printed word was in decline. After 2000, the reliance on text certainly saw a resurgence, even if in abbreviated form, as e-mail messages replaced telephone calls as the prime source of communication among Americans.

The Dot.com Bubble and Its Eventual Burst

If Y2K illustrated the degree to which almost every aspect of society had become dependent on computer technology by 2000, the bursting of the dot.com bubble illustrated how easy it was to inflate the value of every computer-related enterprise. Just as the world of electronic communications was being born in the 1990s, many people decided that the key to making a fortune was investing in the enterprise. As had happened many times before (see Chapter 22 on the stock market crash of 1929), overeager investors created a bubble that eventually burst.

In March 2000, an article in *Barrons*, the respected business magazine, asked, "When will the Internet Bubble burst?" A week later, *Business Week* ran a story on Internet stocks called "Wall Street's Hype Machine." Investors, some of whom were already beginning to have their own worries, paid attention. At the end of March and all through April 2000, stocks in high technology companies fell dramatically. Between March 10 and April 14, Yahoo! fell from 178 to 116. By the end of December 2000, nearly every technology company was down significantly. Some, like Amazon.com, recovered. Others did not. The value of specific parts of the new electronic world had shrunk, but the new electronic order was just beginning.

Google Becomes a Verb

In September 1998, two Stanford University graduate students, Larry Page and Sergey Brin, launched a new company in a garage in Menlo Park, California. They called their company Google. Page and Brin first met at Stanford in 1995, and by 1996, they had decided to search for and find information through the still-new World Wide Web. Other search engines predated Google, and others rose to challenge its dominance, but it quickly became the leader. As early as December 1998, a computer magazine was reporting Google's "uncanny knack" for producing good information very quickly, and by 2001, one could search for information on Google in 26 languages.

By December 2001, Page and Brin's company had scanned or indexed 3 billion webpages, almost 80 percent of the total then in existence. And as the number of webpages grew, Google kept scanning and indexing. When someone in any corner of the globe typed a question or a name or a topic into the google.com search page, a series of interconnected computers at Google headquarters in Mountain View, California, scanned the data and presented a list of websites to the searcher. With the advent of Google, virtually all of the knowledge available anywhere on the Internet was available at the click of a few key strokes to everyone, not just computer geeks with unlimited time and patience.

Google never charged for its services, which along with its speed, was a key to its popularity. The company's main source of revenue came from advertisements. Hotels in London may pay to get top billing when someone does a search of "London," while sporting goods companies may pay for top billing when a search is done for "sneakers." In the years after its founding, Google kept up the rapid pace of growth and change. In 2004, Google launched Google Books. The company signed agreements

Google revolutionized the ability to search for information on the internet through its powerful search engine.

with a number of prominent libraries, including Harvard, Stanford, the University of Michigan, Oxford University, the Library of Congress, and the New York Public Library to digitize *all* of their holdings. The books whose copyrights had expired would be made available online. Books still under copyright—which included most books—would have only small selections available, considered "fair use," and readers would be referred to the publisher for more. However, publishers were nervous about the fact that the whole book would be stored in Google's electronic archives, and in 2005, the Association of American Publishers sued the company for violation of copyright laws. In response, John L. Hennessy, the president of Stanford University and a member of Google's board of directors, said, "We need to rethink our copyright framework that is still a remnant of the past." The nature of copyrights and, indeed, the printed page, would be in for dramatic changes.

The Latest Technology—Winners, Losers, and Change Agents

Soon after 2000, the fast-paced technological changes were producing some clear winners: companies like Google and Microsoft and the thousands of engineers and inventors who worked in places like Silicon Valley in California or Seattle, Washington. In addition, there were also clear losers.

When the Sony Walkman cassette tape player appeared in 1979, it seemed part of a never-ending expansion of the music industry. People could buy music and listen as they walked or worked. By 2001, however, the music industry was in deep trouble. New technologies gave consumers the power to simply download the music they wanted, at no cost. In the 1990s, the bestselling album sold 15 million copies. In 1999 alone, the music industry reported profits of $14.6 billion, but in retrospect, that point was the peak year for the industry's profits. That number would fall to $6.3 billion in 2009. It was just too easy to download music, share it, and give it away. In 2001, representatives of the music industry were successful in a lawsuit closing Napster, one of the first vehicles for downloading music that had been launched in 1999, but the move was a public relations disaster because other technology for downloading made it easier and easier even without the help of Napster. If the industry was going to survive after 2001, then it would need to find a new way to create, market, and profit from music products.

Newspapers went through similar losses. After 2000, newspaper advertising, which generates most of newspaper revenue, fell dramatically, as did the actual sales of newspapers. Circulation kept dropping for most newspapers and some, like the *Los Angeles Times* and the *Boston Globe,* lost perhaps a third of all subscribers between 2000 and 2010. Many of these papers began small online versions, but readers had already become accustomed to accessing other news sites that had been designed specifically for online readers. Newspapers have yet to recover, if they ever will.

Many people also began to worry about the loss of privacy that can accompany growing information technology. Certainly, Google held a lot of information, not just on products but on people who search for information. E-mail was much easier to hack into and read than traditional letters or telephone calls, and the federal protection of privacy, especially in letters sent through the U.S. mail, did not apply to much of the new technology. Mobile phones made it easy to call from anywhere, but they also made it easy for people to track anyone's location. Privacy, as civil libertarians had traditionally defined it, was a fast-changing matter.

In the decades after 2001, technology kept changing the way people lived their lives and interacted with others. A world without e-mail or without the ability to search the World Wide Web or listen to music or follow one's friends on Facebook became virtually unimaginable. Yet before the 1990s, such a world did not exist. In that decade, the foundation for the technological future was set.

29.3 | **Quick Review** Is the expansion of technology beneficial to people, businesses, and/or governments? Why or why not?

CONCLUSION

In 1989, the Cold War came to an end and "a new world order" began to take shape. After Reagan's second term, when George H.W. Bush, a foreign policy expert, took office in 1989, he was well-positioned to see the United States through the dissolution of the Soviet Union and the end of the Cold War. But as soon as the Cold War had ended, other international crises immediately began to preoccupy the Bush administration. During his term in office, Bush sent U.S. troops to Iraq to protect the independence of Kuwait, ordered the overthrow of Panamanian dictator Manuel Noriega, and sent peacekeeping troops to both Somalia and Yugoslavia. Amid this international turmoil, the Bush administration also had to confront the increasing threat of al-Qaeda and other nonstate terrorist organizations.

While Bush focused on international issues, the U.S. economy fell into a recession, and when he raised taxes, despite an earlier promise not to do so, the conservative wing of the Republican Party abandoned him. Division within the Republican Party and the troubled economy allowed Democratic candidate Bill Clinton, whose campaign team motto was "It's the economy, stupid," to defeat Bush in his bid for reelection.

Clinton focused on two primary issues early in his administration: the economy and the nation's health care system. He managed, with the help of a Democratic-controlled Congress, to balance the federal budget, lower the national debt, and secure approval for the North American Free Trade Agreement (NAFTA), but his health care plan faltered before it reached the U.S. Congress for a vote. Two years into Clinton's first term, Republicans took control of the House of Representatives, forcing him to further moderate his positions. In his remaining 6 years in office, Clinton worked with Republicans to limit some budget cuts, end the nation's traditional welfare system, and pass the Defense of Marriage Act. Although Clinton faced impeachment stemming from charges that he had lied under oath about a sexual affair, he kept his office.

The 1990s concluded with one of the strangest presidential elections in American history. It took over one month and a decision of the U.S. Supreme Court to determine that George W. Bush, not Al Gore, would succeed Clinton as president.

With the rise of new international issues as well as economic and social issues at home, dramatic developments in technology launched a new information era. Personal computers, which first became available in the 1980s, became commonplace in the 1990s. New companies like Apple, Microsoft, and Google emerged, and existing companies like IBM and Xerox adapted to changing technologies. In the 1990s, developments such as the Internet and the World Wide Web allowed people to connect and communicate at speeds never before thought possible. These advances also ushered in an era of speculation among overeager investors. Technology stocks grew steadily throughout the 1990s, but, in March 2000, the tech bubble burst and many people lost jobs and savings. By the end of the decade, technology had become so pervasive in American life that many feared a catastrophic Y2K problem if computers malfunctioned on January 1, 2000. In addition, concern grew about the computer's impact on a range of existing institutions from the music industry to books and newspapers as well as the impact of computers on personal privacy. Nevertheless, by 2001, it was clear that the transformation of life as a result of technology was here to stay.

CHAPTER REVIEW How did changes in the 1990s connect the United States to the rest of the world to an extent unimagined at the beginning or in the middle of the 1900s?

THE BUSH ADMINISTRATION, 1989–1993

29.1 Explain the New World Order that George Bush described.

Review Questions

1. Comparison

Compare and contrast the global situation faced by the United States in 1980 and 1990. What challenges and opportunities did the changed world present to the Bush administration?

2. Contextualization

How did the power of conservatives within the Republican Party shape the Bush presidency?

3. Historical Interpretation

What do the Thomas nomination hearings, the Rodney King incident, and the O.J. Simpson trial indicate about the state of race relations in the United States at the end of the 1900s?

THE CLINTON PRESIDENCY

29.2 Analyze the impact of the Clinton presidency and the Clinton–Gingrich conflict on the country.

Review Questions

4. Contextualization

Why did Clinton feel that it was important to emphasize his departure from traditional Democratic ideas?

5. Comparison

Compare and contrast the American political landscape in 1976 and 1996. What explains the differences you note?

6. Construct an Argument

How would you explain Clinton's high public opinion ratings throughout his impeachment proceedings? What does his high ratings tell you about how the public viewed Clinton and his congressional opponents?

TECHNOLOGY DOMINATES AN ERA

29.3 Analyze the changes in technology and their impact on U.S. culture.

Review Questions

7. Synthesis

What role did new technology play in producing the prosperity of the 1990s? What other factors were important in this regard?

8. Construct an Argument

Defend or refute the following statement: "The advent of the Internet was the most important advance in communications technology since the invention of the printing press."

9. Historical Interpretation

Who were the economic winners and losers of the communications technology revolution?

Entering a New Time

The September 11, 2001, terror attack on the World Trade Center in New York and the Pentagon in Washington, DC, was a tragedy that shaped American politics for a decade.

Tuesday morning on September 11, 2001, dawned clear and beautiful on the East Coast of the United States. President Bush was in Florida, reading to a class of second graders as part of his effort to get the No Child Left Behind legislation through Congress. Most Americans were going about their business at the beginning of another workweek as memories of summer vacations faded. At 7:59 a.m. American Airlines Flight 11 took off from Boston's Logan International Airport bound for Los Angeles. In the minutes that followed, United Airlines Flight 93 left Newark for San Francisco; American Flight 77 left Washington, DC, for Los Angeles; and United Flight 175 left Boston for Los Angeles. None of those four flights made it to their intended destination.

On each of the four planes, just minutes after takeoff, hijackers took control of the flight using box cutters—then legal to carry onto a plane—as weapons. Following existing procedures, designed for hijackers of an earlier era who often sought ransom or political concessions, airline crews yielded to the hijackers, and then quickly realized the new destinations. As terrified crew and passengers used cell phones to call relatives and authorities, the planes turned back toward the East Coast. At 8:46 a.m., American Flight 11 crashed into the North Tower of the World Trade Center. Seventeen minutes later, United Flight 175 crashed into the South Tower of the Trade Center.

CHAPTER OBJECTIVE

Demonstrate an understanding of the most recent history of the United States from September 11, 2001, to the present.

LEARNING OBJECTIVES

THE IMPACT OF SEPTEMBER 11, 2001

Analyze the impact of 9/11 on the nation and on the presidency of George Bush and the impact of Bush administration policies around the world.

30.1

HURRICANE KATRINA AND ITS AFTERMATH

Explain the impact of Hurricane Katrina on the Gulf Coast.

30.2

THE FINANCIAL CRISIS OF 2008

Explain the costs and consequences of the 2008 financial crisis.

30.3

NEW LIBERALS, NEW CONSERVATIVES

Analyze the most recent political developments in the United States.

30.4

At 9:37 a.m., American Flight 77 crashed into the Pentagon. By this time, passengers on United Flight 93 had learned from cell phone calls that they were part of a massive terrorist plot. As the plane headed for Washington, DC, heroic passengers overpowered the hijackers and the plane crashed in a field in Somerset County, Pennsylvania.

Many acts of heroism occurred on that chaotic morning. Betty Ong, a flight attendant on American Airlines Flight 11 stayed on her cell phone, reporting minute by minute until the plane crashed into the World Trade Center. In New York City, Nick Gerstle, a technician for Verizon, knew CPR and thought he could be helpful at Ground Zero—the now horrific site where the twin towers of the Trade Center had stood. In the midst of the rubble, he and some firefighters found two trapped New York City police officers. He heard the officers say, "Please! Don't let us die!" And they didn't. The two officers were among the few rescued from the collapsed buildings. Julia Martinez and Margaret Espinoza were paraprofessionals—teacher aids—at the High School for Leadership and Public Service that was only a block away from the World Trade Center. They began moving two wheelchair-bound students out of the chaos, found their way blocked by debris and, with the aid of two strangers, simply picked up the girls and carried them to safety blocks away. New Yorkers, Pentagon employees, passengers on the flights, and average Americans did heroic things. That day changed history as few others had. The focus of this chapter is on the decade and more after that tragic day during which public and personal events were shadowed by what came to be called simply 9/11.

THE IMPACT OF SEPTEMBER 11, 2001

30.1 Analyze the impact of 9/11 on the nation and presidency of George Bush and the impact of Bush administration policies around the world.

In the first moments and hours after the horrific crashes, no one knew what to make of the attack on the World Trade Center and Pentagon. On first hearing the news on radio or TV, most people had the same reaction as Florence Engoran, who worked in the South Tower of the World Trade Center. When she arrived at her office on the 55th floor someone said, "A small plane hit the other building." She remembered, "I wasn't especially upset by the news," and tended to agree with her coworker who said, "Oh, just sit down, let's keep working. We have to get out some focus reports." Within minutes, however, as she saw flames and heard another crash, Engoran realized that something much more serious was happening. Although she was 5 months pregnant, Engoran headed for the stairs and walked down the 55 flights. Before she made it to the bottom, the lights were off and the stairwell was filled with dust, but she made it. Most of those working in the buildings made it out. But many did not. Handicapped people who could not walk down the stairs were stuck. People on the higher floors could not get past the fires. Some 78 police officers and 400 firefighters who had responded to the emergencies remained in the buildings trying to evacuate people when the structures collapsed. It all happened very fast. At 9:58 a.m., just 1 hour after the crash, the South Tower of the World Trade Center collapsed floor by floor, showering a wide area with rubble. Thirty minutes later, the North Tower also collapsed. What had been two of the tallest buildings in the world that morning were now simply a giant hole in the ground.

The worst violence on United States soil since the Civil War had just taken place. Nearly 3,000 people died—246 passengers on the planes; 2,600 at the World Trade Center, including workers in the two towers, police and fire rescue workers, and a few unlucky passersby; and 125 people at the Pentagon. The fear, loss, anger, and fortitude generated from that day would shape a new reality for the nation.

At 9:30 a.m., the Federal Aviation Administration grounded all flights within the United States. For the week that followed, the skies would be clear of everything but high-flying military planes. Airports would be eerily quiet. At a little after 1:00 p.m. that Tuesday, President Bush, just 9 months into his first term, addressed the nation

The twisted ruins of the World Trade Center in the aftermath of the terrorist attacks of September 11, 2001.

from an Air Force base in Louisiana, telling people that massive security measures were in effect and that the United States would "hunt down and punish those responsible for these cowardly acts," though at that point no one was quite sure who they were. At 8:30 p.m., President Bush spoke to the nation for a second time, this time from the Oval Office, asking for prayers for the families and friends of the victims and again promising retaliatory action. Ground Zero was still a mass of burning rubble and would be for weeks. The Pentagon fire was contained, but not under control. The nation tried to make sense of what had happened.

Finding the Terrorists—al-Qaeda, the Taliban, Afghanistan

In the initial confusion of the morning of September 11, no one was quite sure who was behind the attack. By early afternoon, George Tenet, the director of the CIA, informed President Bush that while the agency was still investigating, all the evidence pointed to an attack by al-Qaeda, ordered by its leader Osama bin Laden. By late that evening, when the president met with what he then called his "war council," they all agreed that plans needed to be developed to punish not only the perpetrators of the **9/11 attack** but any who harbored them.

On September 20, President Bush spoke to a joint session of Congress. He said, "Tonight, we are a country awakened to danger." He said of the government of Afghanistan that "They will hand over the terrorists, or they will share their fate." And he told the rest of the world, "Either you are with us, or you are with the terrorists." There would be no neutrals in the war on terror. The president said that the war was with terrorists, not with Islam. He insisted, "The enemy of America is not our many Muslim friends. It is not our many Arab friends. Our enemy is a radical network of terrorists, and every government that supports them." Nevertheless, the militant tone of the speech, while reassuring some, worried many. In the immediate aftermath of the attacks, international support and sympathy for the United States was high. Even nations long hostile to the United States such as Syria were expressing support. But with Bush's response, some of the support began to fade.

9/11 attack

The attack of September 11, 2001 on the World Trade Center and the Pentagon organized by al-Qaeda.

American Voices

"9/11 Memories," Michael Muskal, September 11, 2013

Everyone who lived through the day had their own experience of 9/11, one they will not forget. Twelve years later a Los Angeles Times reporter looked back on his own memories and those of others who contacted him.

Even 12 years later, the events of Sept. 11, 2001, sear Americans' memories.

In comments posted on latimes.com, people remember the tragic events of the day -- the moments, both good and bad, heroic and fearful, that are summed up by the numerals 9/11.

It was early morning when the first airplane hit one of the towers of the World Trade Center in Lower Manhattan. On the East Coast, commuters were rushing to their jobs, schools were filling with educators and students. It seemed an ordinary day until 8:46 a.m., when it wasn't.

"On 9/11/2001 I was having a national sales meeting in our offices at the World Trade Center. We had visitors from Chicago, California and New Orleans. Everyone was looking forward to getting together to recharge," writes Keith Webster of Malibu.

"At 8:45 a.m. while standing in our boardroom looking at the Statue of Liberty in the south harbor, all hell was about to break loose. We heard a pop then a swoosh. A stream of debris crossed the sky. It looked like a ticker tape parade but only a few thousand feet higher.

"In an instant, I knew what was happening, in my mind's eye an image of a terrorist walking onto my floor with a bomb vest flashed. I could see my lobby vaporized and in flames."

Webster also writes about his eventual rescue by heroic responders.

Maralynn Mash of Ft. Lauderdale, Fla., says she was at an elementary school near the World Trade Center that day.

"The children were headed toward the basement for safety when police and fire officials came into the building thinking it was empty… .But then we were directed to run … run for your lives. Teachers and students, under the guidance of an incredibly able principal, ran ahead of the second 'cloud' north on Greenwich… . What I remember is a day of bravery, a year of dedication in response to an act of cowardice. So very proud to be a New Yorker and an American."

On the West Coast, people were just waking up; many watched the tragedy in New York unfold on television. Instead of the usual fodder of second-day news, lifestyle features and celebrity pomp, viewers saw the horror of the deadliest terrorist attack on U.S. soil.

"The images of the towers crashing and exploding gave me a sense of insecurity that something like this could happen in downtown Los Angeles," writes Maricela of La Puente.

"I remember arriving at Raymond A. Villa Intermediate School in Santa Ana, Calif. It was an ordinary day. I hung out with my friends for a little bit, headed to first period, sat at my desk, the usual. I was in sixth grade at the time. Around the middle of class … my teacher put the TV on," writes Lene De Leon, now of San Antonio.

"I will never forget the images or the confusion I felt upon seeing the videos replaying over and over again. I tried so hard not to cry for fear of being made fun of, but I was hurting for all those people and my country. Everything happening was so painful to watch. The second plane hitting, people desperate for help and waving white 'flags' out of the windows, people jumping out of the windows, the towers falling. All the images were engraved in my memory and are still vivid."

They are etched onto the nation's soul nation too, and are freshly renewed every 9/11 as officials, relatives and mourners gather in New York, Pennsylvania and Washington. In all, nearly 3,000 people died.

As Kendra of Auburn, Ala., writes, "Mom said to me, 'This day will be a day to remember for the rest of your life.' "

Source: Michael Muskal, "9/11 memories: 'All hell was about to break loose'" *Los Angeles Times*, September 11, 2013.

Thinking Critically

1. Documentary Analysis

What different emotions do people remember when recalling 9/11? Have the emotions changed in the 12 years between the event and when this article was written?

2. Comparison

In what ways were the memories of those who were in or near the World Trade Center similar to and in what ways different from the memories of others who lived much farther away but shared the same moment in the nation's history?

By the time Bush spoke, CIA and U.S. Army forces had been dispatched to Pakistan and Uzbekistan to prepare for an attack on Afghanistan, whose Taliban government was protecting bin Laden and al-Qaeda. In early October, the United States attacked sites within Afghanistan while building on-the-ground alliances with Afghan warlords who were hostile to the Taliban regime. Soon, U.S. ground forces, allied with the warlords, began an assault on the Taliban government. On November 9, the northern city of Mazar-e-Sharif fell to the U.S.-led coalition forces, and a few days later, the Taliban government fled the capital of Kabul. By early December, the United States and its local allies were in control of the country, and on December 22,

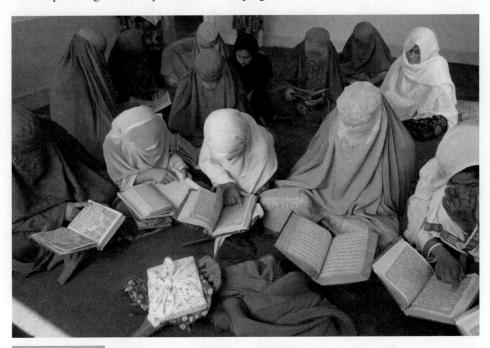 Hamid Karzai, a leader of one of the anti-Taliban factions, was installed as the new leader of Afghanistan. For the most part, however, the Taliban leaders had escaped.

Many Afghans celebrated the defeat of the austere and tyrannical Taliban even as they kept a wary eye on the Americans and on each other. Late in 2001, U.S.-backed forces attacked the remaining al-Qaeda strongholds in a region of mountainous caves known as Tora Bora. Perhaps a quarter of all al-Qaeda and Taliban operatives were killed or captured, but the rest, including bin Laden and his chief lieutenant Ayman al-Zawahiri, escaped into the lightly governed provinces on the Pakistani side of the border from which they continued to operate with considerable freedom. The United States did not track bin Laden down until May 2011, almost 10 years later.

In the aftermath of the attack, President Bush, under considerable pressure from families of victims, agreed to appoint a special commission to study the 9/11 attack and make recommendations regarding future policy. The chair of the commission, former Republican governor of New Jersey Thomas Kean, and vice chair, Lee H. Hamilton, former Democratic representative from Indiana, were careful to say, "We write with the benefit and handicap of hindsight. We are mindful of the danger of being unjust to men and women who made choices in conditions of uncertainty and in circumstances over which they often had little control." Nevertheless, they noted significant mistakes. They reported that while presidents and CIA directors are inundated with information, a lot of information had pointed to a possible large scale al-Qaeda attack. As early as December 1998, the CIA's Presidential Daily Brief for Bill Clinton said, "___ suggests bin Laden and his allies are preparing for attacks on U.S., including an aircraft hijacking." A report to George W. Bush on August 6, 2001, included a detailed note headlined, "bin Laden Determined to Strike in US." They also noted that the United States was unprepared for dealing with an attack. Although Air Force planes were launched after the first plane crashed into the World Trade Center, the pilots had no clear instructions, and the commission had great doubts that, if the passengers had not caused the fourth plane to crash in Pennsylvania, it could have been stopped before reaching Washington, DC. "The most important failure," they concluded, "was one of imagination. We do not believe leaders understood the gravity of the threat." The terrorist danger from bin Laden and al-Qaeda was not a major topic for policy debate among the public, the media, or in the Congress. It had barely come up during the 2000 presidential campaign.

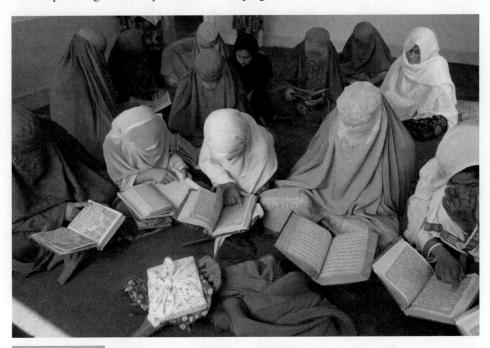

While the defeat of the Taliban brought new opportunities to many Afghans, especially women who could again study in school and take jobs, it did not bring stability to the country.

No Child Left Behind
Federal legislation requiring that all students be tested and that schools show "adequate yearly progress" in the test scores of all students.

The George W. Bush Presidential Agenda

Once in office in January 2001, George W. Bush did not waste any time implementing his own agenda. While the events of the following September would make foreign policy central to that agenda, he did not come to office with such a focus. Indeed, most early initiatives focused on domestic policy. As his administration took shape, especially his choices for members of his cabinet, many wondered about his promise to be a "uniter." He had selected a cabinet with more racial minorities and more women than any previous one, but they were a very conservative lot.

Three days after the inauguration, Bush announced that he would use the upcoming renewal of the Elementary and Secondary Education Act, first passed under Lyndon Johnson in 1965 (see Chapter 22) to change the course of federal education policy. He had campaigned on a promise to address what he called the "soft bigotry of low expectations" for poor students, and he acted quickly on that promise. He called his new proposal **No Child Left Behind** and announced he would seek a bipartisan education reform that would be "the cornerstone of my administration." In spite of the highly partisan split around his election, two of the most liberal Democratic members of Congress, Massachusetts senator Edward M. Kennedy and California House member George Miller played key roles in developing the act and shepherding it through Congress. The core of No Child Left Behind was a requirement that to receive federal funds states must develop clear standards, then test all students from the third to the eighth grade, and use the test results to measure whether individual schools and districts were making "adequate yearly progress" (AYP) in improving the education of all students and closing the "achievement gap." Although many supported the legislation, its implementation quickly generated criticism of the amount of testing involved, the constraints imposed by the regulations, and the lack of funding available for implementation.

Bush moved with equal speed on his other top priority, an across-the-board tax cut. During the campaign, he had insisted that the Clinton budget surpluses should be given directly back to taxpayers. Alan Greenspan of the Federal Reserve Board told Congress that Bush's proposed tax cut of $1.6 trillion over 10 years would not harm the economy and might do some good. There was general consensus about some sort of cut, and Bush was able to sign a phased-in tax cut of $ 1.4 trillion on June 7, 2001, less than 5 months after the inauguration. The new law cut the highest tax rate from

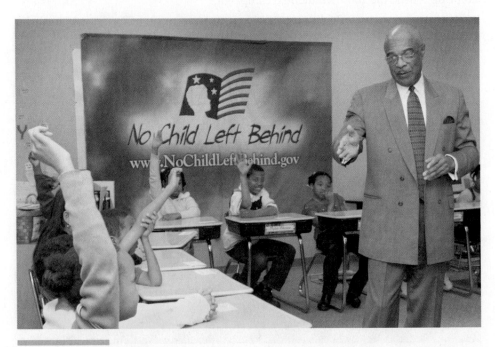

American classrooms like this one were transformed by the expectations included in the No Child Left Behind legislation. In this 2003 photo, Ron Paige, secretary of the Department of Education under George W. Bush, answers questions from students during a visit to the Skinner Magnet Center in Omaha, Nebraska.

39.6 percent to 35 percent—a significant cut, though still above the Reagan rates. It also created a new lower tax bracket of only 10 percent for the working poor, exempted many people from any federal tax, and phased out inheritance taxes. Almost immediately, many tax payers received rebate checks. Cutting taxes was a very popular policy.

The tax cut legislation, however, posed two serious problems. The first was that most of the major cuts were to be phased in, and people were impatient. Pressure mounted to speed up the implementation of the tax cuts, and in less than 2 years, Bush proposed and Congress passed the Jobs and Growth Tax Relief Reconciliation Act of 2003, which speeded tax reductions significantly. The second problem was that, with reduced taxes, the U.S. Treasury took in a lot less money. While some, especially within the administration, argued that the tax cuts were stimulating the economy and creating jobs, most economists outside of government saw little evidence for the claim. Both sides had to acknowledge that the tax cuts—along with significantly increased spending by the administration, especially after 9/11—were creating a growing federal deficit. The surpluses of the late Clinton years disappeared. For the rest of the Bush term, the federal deficit grew significantly. Some, like Vice President Dick Cheney, said "Deficits don't matter." Economists and many leaders of both parties were less sure.

Education reform and tax cuts were the most significant domestic policy agendas of George W. Bush's 8 years in office, and both were enacted during his first year. A number of other policy initiatives, however, were also important to the president. Bush came to office committed to what he called "faith-based initiatives." He believed that religious communities were often better than the federal government at delivering direct human services. Nine days after the inauguration, he proposed what he called "charitable choice" legislation that would allow religious groups to apply for federal funds as long as they were not to be used for worship or proselytizing. While legislation made it through the House, two different bills were blocked in the Senate. In frustration, Bush issued executive orders in December 2002 that prohibited federal agencies from discriminating against religious charities and established faith-based offices in several cabinet departments. For religious communities that sought federal funds, it created an especially friendly atmosphere.

Bush had also campaigned on a promise to reform Social Security, giving individuals greater choice in the investment of the funds they contributed to the Social Security system. While other priorities dominated his early years, Bush devoted a significant amount of his 2005 State of the Union speech—the first of his second term—to his proposal to allow more choice in the use of Social Security funds. By 2005, however, Bush was distracted by the war, and Democrats were far less willing to give in to the president's initiatives. Little movement happened on allowing greater choice in Social Security, and after the 2008 financial crisis, when people realized that such choices might have been financially devastating, the idea died.

Bush had little patience with conservationists. He signed legislation allowing drilling in the Arctic National Wildlife Refuge in Alaska and supported offshore oil exploration. He did not move on environmental issues or global warming. Because of his own religious convictions, he opposed stem cell research in spite of dramatic appeals from many, including Nancy Reagan. His appointments, especially to the federal courts, tended to be very conservative. While the 2000 presidential election had been fought almost exclusively over domestic issues, the events of September 11, 2001, changed everything. From then onward, foreign policy and the impact of international issues on the internal politics of the United States would be the dominant agenda of the Bush administration until his last few months in office when a new economic crisis returned attention to the domestic agenda. In the meantime, however, terrorism took center stage.

The War on Terror at Home

The *Report of the 9/11 Commission* made recommendations to tighten security within the United States and abroad. However, they noted, "Many of our recommendations call for the government to increase its presence in our lives.…Therefore, while

30.1

30.2

USA PATRIOT Act
Legislation that sought to protect Americans by authorizing significant new data gathering by the federal government.

30.3

30.4

protecting our homeland, Americans should be mindful of threats to vital personal and civil liberties." Whether the Bush administration, or the Obama administration that followed, kept the right balance has been a subject of continuing debate.

Even before the Commission finished its work, Congress, at Bush's request, passed the **USA PATRIOT Act**, which the president signed on October 26, 2001, only weeks after the attack. The act expanded not only the authority of the Department of Justice to search telephone, e-mail, medical, financial, and library records without a court order but also the authority to increase monitoring of the U.S. borders and of non-citizens within the country. It also gave the Treasury the right to monitor financial records and bank transactions. In the midst of the fears generated by 9/11, the Patriot Act passed by large majorities in both houses of Congress. Most defended the law's provisions as necessary at a time of national emergency. Nevertheless, some were deeply troubled by the bill. Richard Armey, a conservative Republican member of the House, insisted that the act have a sunset provision and expire in 5 years. Wisconsin liberal Democratic senator Russell Feingold, the only member of the Senate to vote against the law, said, "Some have said rather cavalierly that in these difficult times, we must accept some reduction in our civil liberties in order to be secure. Of course, there is no doubt that if we lived in a police state, it would be easier to catch terrorists....But that probably would not be a country in which we would want to live."

The debate about the Patriot Act continued long after it passed. In January 2003, the American Library Association, worried about increasing searches of library records, condemned the Patriot Act as "a present danger to the constitutional rights and privacy rights of library users." Others disagreed. John Yoo, who had served as one of the lead attorneys in the U.S. Department of Justice advising president Bush, and Eric Posner, a law professor, wrote a piece for the American Enterprise Institute in December 2003 in which they said, "The worst thing about the Patriot Act is its Orwellian name....If the act marginally reduces peacetime liberties, this is a reasonable price to pay for a valuable weapon against al-Qaeda." While the debate continued, President Bush signed a renewed version of the Patriot Act in March 2006, and President Barack Obama signed two further extensions of the law in 2010 and 2011.

The War in Afghanistan and Iraq

From the moment the first plane hit the World Trade Center, some people were convinced that Iraq's Saddam Hussein was somehow behind it or at least allied with al-Qaeda. Deputy Secretary of Defense Paul Wolfowitz insisted that Iraq had to be dealt with if terrorism was to be defeated. Vice President Cheney supported a U.S. attack on Iraq. Others urged caution. The CIA and others in the National Security Council initially found no "compelling case" against Iraq. Indeed, evidence showed considerable antipathy between the very religious al-Qaeda leader Osama bin Laden and a secular leader like Saddam Hussein in Iraq. So in the immediate aftermath of 9/11, the focus stayed on the al-Qaeda strongholds in Afghanistan (see Map 30-1). However, the issue of Iraq never went away.

British Prime Minister Tony Blair supported plans for an attack on Iraq, but Jack Straw, Blair's foreign minister, insisted, "Saddam was not threatening his neighbors, and his WMD [Weapons of Mass Destruction] capability was less than that of Libya, North Korea, or Iran."

As talk of a possible U.S. attack on Iraq circulated, an article appeared in the *Wall Street Journal* on August 15, 2002, by Brent Scowcroft, who had been the national security adviser in the administration of H.W. Bush. Scowcroft wrote, "Don't attack Saddam." He argued that such a war could lead to "Armageddon in the Middle East" and urged instead that the United States should "be pressing the United Nations Security Council to insist on an effective no-notice inspection regime for Iraq." Some speculated that Scowcroft's article was, in fact, a warning from Bush's father—a close friend of Scowcroft—but if it was, it came too late.

MAP 30-1 Afghanistan and Iraq. After a 2001 attack on the Taliban government of Afghanistan, the United States turned its attention to Iraq, which it attacked in 2003.

In January 2002, just 4 months after the attacks in New York and Washington, DC, Bush gave his State of the Union message in which he singled out Iraq, along with Iran and North Korea, as an "axis of evil." Bush said, "Iraq continues to flaunt its hostility toward America and to support terror.…This is a regime that has something to hide from the civilized world." A conservative columnist, Charles Krauthammer, wrote, "If there was a serious internal debate within the administration over what to do about Iraq, that debate is over."

The only remaining debate seems to have been whether the United States and Great Britain needed to seek authorization from the U.S. Congress and United Nations to attack Iraq. Although British Prime Minister Blair supported the attack on Iraq, he insisted on United Nations approval. The UN had imposed a financial and trade embargo on Iraq after it invaded Kuwait and, among other things, required it to disclose and eliminate weapons of mass destruction (WMD) and to allow UN inspections to confirm the status of any such weapons. U.S. Secretary of State Colin Powell urged seeking support from Congress and the UN. Ever since the earlier 1991 U.S. war with Iraq over Kuwait, the United States had protected Kurds in northern Iraq and maintained a boycott of Iraqi oil. Now the United States was preparing to do much more.

After considerable debate, Congress voted to authorize the use of military force if diplomacy with Iraq failed. The resolution passed the Senate by a vote of 77 to

23 and the House by 296 to 133. While almost everyone supported the invasion of Afghanistan and the attack on al-Qaeda, divisions ran deep about Iraq. The two liberal Democratic senators from Massachusetts were divided. John Kerry said, "I believe that a deadly arsenal of weapons of mass destruction in his [Saddam Hussein's] hands is a threat, and a grave threat." In contrast, the senior senator from Massachusetts, Edward M. Kennedy, voted no, as did the most senior member of the Senate, West Virginia Senator Robert Byrd. A young Barack Obama had not yet been elected to the Senate but he told a rally, "This is a dumb war."

After the congressional vote, Colin Powell took the arguments to the United Nations Security Council. Powell put his personal prestige on the line to convince the Security Council of the need to topple Saddam Hussein's government. The vote was 15 to zero in favor. France, Russia, and China, all of which had grave reservations about a war in Iraq, hoped that the authorization would force Iraq to agree to tougher inspections to avoid an invasion. With authorization from Congress and the UN, the United States, Great Britain, and a coalition of other countries, most of whom sent only token forces, went to war and toppled Saddam Hussein with lightning speed.

On March 19, 2003, U.S. forces began the war with a huge attack using bombers—over 1,500 flights a day—plus launching Navy cruise missiles. The U.S. military called it "shock and awe." After the air attack, ground forces moved across the country. By the first week in April, the airport at Baghdad fell to U.S.-led troops and U.S. tanks roared into the capital city. The Iraqi Minister of Information was captured, most of the rest of the leadership fled, and Saddam Hussein was a fugitive in the country he had long dominated. U.S. and British casualties were very low. The war, it seemed, had been won skillfully. On May 1, President Bush announced, "Major combat operations in Iraq have ended. In the battle of Iraq, the United States and our allies have prevailed." The next steps would not be so easy, however.

Securing a country as large and as tightly regulated as Iraq was no easy task. Many Iraqis who were delighted to see Hussein gone were uneasy about the role of foreign troops in their country. An Iraqi professor told American reporter Anne Garrels, "You understand, you will now have to be in complete control, and we will resent you

Under a sign proclaiming "Mission Accomplished," President Bush announced the end of combat operations in Iraq on May 1, 2004. The worst of America's difficulties in Iraq, however, were just beginning.

every step of the way." In fact, the United States never sent enough forces to manage the country once the old government had been removed. Very little planning had gone into preparation for the postinvasion world of Iraq. Most officials assumed that Iraqis would quickly return to work. As Condoleezza Rice, then the national security adviser, said, "The concept was that we would defeat the army, but the institutions would hold, everything from ministries to police forces." It did not happen.

As soon as the old authority was gone, looters began to pillage government buildings. They stole computers, televisions, and metal to be sold for scrap, which they raided from places such as towers holding communication lines and metal file cabinets filled with important documents. At the Central Bank, looters drilled into the vaults and ran out with the money, much of it in U.S. dollars or euros that could not be traced. They broke into the National Museum and carried off 15,000 ancient objects of extraordinary value.

Defense Secretary Rumsfeld responded, "Stuff happens." Most Iraqis and people around the world were less understanding. One military advisor said, "We're incompetent as far as they're concerned." In August 2003, Thomas Friedman wrote in the *New York Times*, "It would be a tragic irony if the greatest technological power in the history of the world came to the cradle of civilization with its revolutionary ideas and found itself defeated because it couldn't keep the electricity on."

In May 2003, Secretary Rumsfeld appointed a U.S. diplomat, L. Paul "Jerry" Bremer, as head of the **Coalition Provisional Authority (CPA)** to bring order to Iraq. Bremer was an experienced diplomat, but he was not familiar with the Middle East. He set up his headquarters in the fortified "Green Zone," a former Hussein palace and issued two orders that in retrospect seemed a serious mistake. Modeling the first order on the de-Nazification of Germany after World War II, Bremer ordered the de-Baathification of Iraq. The Baath Party had been Hussein's political party, the only one allowed in the country. Government officials—senior officials, police officers, and teachers—were required to be members. The order that no member of the Baath Party could work in the new administration immediately threw some 30,000 to 50,000 out of work. The idea that ministries or the police could quickly be up and running was gone.

A week later, Bremer dissolved the Iraqi army. The initial U.S. plans for a postwar government had focused on removing a few generals and then reestablishing the army since it was solid and had discipline as well as credibility inside Iraq. With his order, Bremer dissolved this source of structure and order. He also infuriated some 400,000 Iraqi soldiers who thought they had been promised that, if they would not resist the Americans, they could keep their jobs after the war. Now they were out of their jobs and had lost their pensions, but still had access to arms.

As it became clear that the United States did not have enough troops in Iraq to maintain order, Iraqis not only became angry at the Americans but also became angry at one another. Hussein's dictatorship had maintained tight control over a country whose people were deeply divided. Within weeks, members of the Sunni Muslim minority, of which Hussein was a part and which had been the nation's elite, were attacked by members of the Shiite Muslim majority. The Sunnis fought back. On August 29, two car bombs killed moderate Shiite leader Ayatollah Mohammad Baqir al-Hakim and 124 of his followers and destroyed the Mosque where they were worshipping. While Sunnis and Shiites fought in the center and south of the country, Iraqi Kurds in the north, who had been protected for 12 years by the "no fly zone" now fought to maintain their autonomy. Reprisal followed reprisal. Within months of the victory, Iraq was close to a civil war, and the Americans were caught in the middle of it. More American soldiers were killed between May and October of 2003 in "postwar" fighting than from March to May of that year in the actual invasion.

Between 2003 and 2004, U.S. forces searched the country, trying to find weapons of mass destruction and the escaped dictator Saddam Hussein. In spite of the fact that those weapons had been one of the prime reasons for going to war, none were ever found. Hussein apparently had wanted to keep up the pretense that they existed to frighten the

Coalition Provisional Authority (CPA)
The temporary governing authority for Iraq set up after the U.S. invasion in March and April of 2003.

United States and his old enemies like Iran. In fact, the weapons were not there. Bush wrote in his *Memoirs*, "In retrospect, of course, we all should have pushed harder on the intelligence and revisited our assumptions." However, Hussein himself was found not far from his hometown of Tikrit in December 2003. After an extended trial, Hussein was executed by the U.S.-backed provisional government of Iraq in December 2006.

As Iraq spiraled into civil war, U.S. soldiers complained that they had no training for serving as an occupying force. In the city of Fallujah, some 2,500 marines battled with 1,200 dissidents in street-to-street, sometimes room-to-room fighting. In the end, the U.S. forces won but then withdrew from the city, and the dissidents regrouped. Similar battles took place elsewhere. Iraqi Sunnis made an alliance with al-Qaeda. The home-grown version of al-Qaeda in Iraq, known as al-Qaeda in Mesopotamia, grew stronger as much of the country experienced anarchy. Electricity worked in Baghdad for perhaps 8 hours a day, even in the summer when air conditioning was desperately needed. Oil was being pumped only at very low levels.

Another disaster took place at a prison in Bagdad. Hussein had built **Abu Ghraib Prison** as a fortress prison for dissidents. By late summer 2003, Hussein's prisoners had been freed and the U.S. military was using the prison to hold some 4,000 prisoners of their own. They had orders from the Pentagon to "get information" from the new prisoners at Abu Ghraib. In the search for information, they humiliated prisoners by keeping some naked in front of female guards, by piling them on top of each other, and by making them crawl and bark. U.S. troops took pictures of what they were doing. In April 2004, the whole sordid mess at Abu Ghraib came to light. CBS News, the *New Yorker* magazine, and news organizations around the world, including Arab news sources like *al Jazeera,* showed the pictures and reported what was happening at Abu Ghraib. Hearing the reports, U.S. General James Mattis responded, "When you lose the moral high ground, you lose it all."

A year after the invasion, the U.S. commanding officer General Ricardo Sanchez described the situation as a "civil war" and added, "what's more, we had created these conditions ourselves." Paul Bremer said, "We've become the worst of all things—an ineffective occupier."

At home in the United States, opposition to the war and the occupation was growing. There were no weapons of mass destruction. There was no order in Iraq. There was no end in sight.

The war in Iraq dominated U.S. elections. In the 2004 presidential contest, the Democrats nominated a Vietnam-era war hero, Senator John Kerry of Massachusetts after a spirited contest in which Howard Dean, the governor of Vermont and a virtual unknown on the national stage, was the first candidate to make the Internet the core of his campaign. Although the Dean campaign's success at raising funds and recruiting volunteers did not lead to his nomination, it transformed future political campaigns. Once Kerry secured the Democratic nomination, the party united behind him and focused not only on the war in Iraq but also on Bush's handling of the economy. Kerry had voted for the war, but he had become a major critic. He called the war and the subsequent U.S. occupation of Iraq a "colossal blunder," and said that the president was "deliberately misleading the American people" about the war. Bush responded that the "world is better off without Saddam Hussein." Outside political groups supporting Bush sought to tarnish Kerry's military record. Kerry struck a chord with his criticism, but he was not a strong campaigner; indeed, one critic called him "a genius at

Abu Ghraib Prison
An Iraqi prison taken over by U.S. forces after the invasion.

Iraqi detainees wait to be released at Abu Ghraib prison, west of Baghdad in Iraq, June 2006. Pictures taken in Abu Ghraib prison of tortured prisoners circulated around the world, including in the Muslim Middle East.

self-destruction." In the end, the president won by a very small margin of 62 million to 59 million or 50.7 percent of the popular vote to Kerry's 48.3 percent. The electoral vote was also close: 286 to 251. Nonetheless, Bush had won a second term. In addition, Republicans also maintained control of Congress.

Two years later, protests against the war had grown much stronger as it continued into its fourth year. Although the president was not on the ballot, his policies were, and Democrats won a majority in both houses of Congress in the 2006 midterm elections. By 2006, the war's cost in lives and dollars was a top issue in the election. Democrat Nancy Pelosi replaced Republican Dennis Hastert as Speaker of the House of Representatives, the first woman in history to serve as speaker, and Democrat Harry Reid replaced Republican Mitch McConnell as majority leader in the Senate. Two new women were added to the Senate, bringing the total of women to 16—a then all-time high. Many thought the Republicans were going to be in trouble in the 2008 presidential election. In the meantime, President Bush knew he would face an unfriendly Congress during his last 2 years in office.

Looking at the situation in Iraq in 2006, one American official said, "We've taken Samarra four times, and we've lost it four times....We need a new strategy." In November 2006, after the midterm elections, President Bush fired Defense Secretary Rumsfeld and replaced him with Robert Gates, a less ideological administrator. A new U.S. ambassador to Iraq, Ryan Crocker, who spoke Arabic and who knew the Middle East well, was appointed. General David Petraeus was made the overall commander of military forces in the region. He developed a very different strategy in Iraq. First there was "**the surge**," an infusion of an additional 30,000 U.S. troops to provide strength in numbers. But instead of staying in fortified enclaves, Petraeus placed units in population centers. Their mission was to get to know and protect the Iraqi people to find out what their complaints were and try to respond. If troops took control of an area, they stayed and tried to build a new infrastructure. Troops felt vulnerable, and losses were high. Slowly, however, the troops and the Iraqi government began to take control of the country. By fall, one journalist reported from Baghdad, "Some shops stay open until late in the evening. Children play in parks, young women stay out after dark, restaurants are filled with families, and old men sit at sidewalk cafes playing backgammon and smoking shisha pipes." It was a peace of sorts.

the surge
A plan for the handover of authority to a new government for Iraq and an eventual orderly withdrawal of all U.S. forces.

30.1 **Quick Review** Did the War on Terror dominate George W. Bush's presidency at home and abroad?

HURRICANE KATRINA AND ITS AFTERMATH

30.2 Explain the impact of Hurricane Katrina on the Gulf Coast.

Early Monday morning August 29, 2005, **Hurricane Katrina**, one of the most powerful and deadly hurricanes in American history, hit New Orleans and the Gulf Coast of Louisiana, Mississippi, and Alabama. Hurricanes have naturally pounded Florida and the Gulf Coast since long before the first Europeans or Africans arrived, but Katrina was a natural disaster compounded by human failure. The result was hours and days of anguish for many, over 1,800 deaths, and more than $75 billion in damage.

Hurricane Katrina
A massive storm that hit New Orleans and the Gulf Coast in August 2005, leading to widespread death and destruction.

The Failure to Prepare

Only 4 years after it was founded, New Orleans was swept away by a hurricane in September 1722. In 1849, the levees protecting New Orleans failed, flooding more than 200 city blocks. Hurricanes in 1893 and 1919 flooded the city and killed many. The great Mississippi River flood of 1927 devastated the city. After the 1927 floods, the Army Corps dredged the lower Mississippi River, which made for easier transport, but changed the river's course. Development and the pumping of oil and gas from underground further degraded the Mississippi Delta, and hundreds of square miles of swampland simply disappeared under water, leaving New Orleans much more vulnerable to storms coming from the Gulf of Mexico. In 2005, a giant storm arrived.

As Hurricane Katrina began to strengthen in late August 2005, more immediate failures added dangerously to the already vulnerable area. Weather forecasters began to realize that Hurricane Katrina might be the "big one," the hurricane that people feared. Nevertheless, New Orleans Mayor Ray Nagin, Louisiana governor Kathleen Blanco, and Mississippi governor Haley Barbour all refused to issue mandatory evacuation orders. An offer by Amtrak to take people by train was ignored, and the last trains left the city with empty passenger cars. At least a quarter of New Orleans population did not own cars, and the school buses that could have been used to evacuate people sat idle and eventually flooded.

As the storm grew stronger on Sunday morning August 28, Mayor Nagin opened the Superdome, the city's massive sports complex, as a "shelter of last resort." Some 8,000 or 9,000 people moved in before the storm hit. However, most of the poorest people in New Orleans lived too far from the Superdome to get there, and no transportation was offered. Then Katrina hit.

The Storm

It started raining in Biloxi, Mississippi, around 5:00 p.m. on Sunday, August 28. By 9:00 p.m., it was raining in New Orleans and the wind was starting to pick up. By midnight, the storm surge hit Mississippi. Between 2:00 and 6:00 a.m., the wind, rain, and storm surge was pounding the Gulf Coast and New Orleans. Winds were blowing steadily at 150 miles per hour. Sometime between 3:00 and 5:00 a.m., the levees on the 17th Street Canal gave way. New Orleans lost electric power at 5:15 a.m. and telephone service at 7:11 a.m.

The hurricane's winds splintered buildings, toppled power lines, collapsed highway bridges, tore off part of the roof of the New Orleans Superdome, and stirred up waves on Lake Pontchartrain that weakened the levees. The wind also drove a huge surge of water onto the shore and up the Mississippi River. Finally, in New Orleans, the weakened levees failed and a wall of water poured into neighborhoods where it rose rapidly, destroyed buildings, and trapped people in upper floors and attics.

Examples of the power of the storm were everywhere. In St. Bernard Parish, just across the Mississippi River from New Orleans, the rising water filled St. Rita's Nursing Facility and 35 bedridden patients were drowned. In Waveland, Mississippi, where police were riding out the storm in the brick police headquarters, water filled the building and then the storm toppled it. Twenty-seven officers ended up swimming to safety, some clinging to a nearby tree for 3 hours before they were rescued. The worst destruction came in New Orleans itself, however, especially in its poorer neighborhoods. By the time Katrina hit New Orleans, almost 80 percent of its 485,000 people had evacuated. The 100,000 or so who were left were those too stubborn or too poor to go anywhere. The Lower Ninth Ward had been a working class African-American community for generations. It had strong community institutions from churches to the neighborhood bars where jazz, blues, and iconic New Orleans-style music thrived. The area was 7 feet below sea level, but the levees were designed to keep the water out. People in the Lower Ninth Ward had no transport to the Superdome, no transport out of town, and few options rather than trying to ride out the storm.

At 8:14 a.m., the Industrial Canal that brought cargo ships in but also channeled water away from the lower areas filled from the storm surge. Pumps failed, and the walls were breached. Within an hour, much of the Ninth Ward was filled with 6–8 feet of water, and the water kept rising. In a very short time, the Lower Ninth Ward was devastated.

The most famous resident of the Lower Ninth Ward was the 77-year-old Fats Domino, the famous rock 'n' roll musician. Domino, his wife, and their five children

Ninth ward residents stranded on the roof of their homes await rescue. The death and destruction that came with Hurricane Katrina was unimaginable to most Americans.

and their families were riding out the storm at their house on Marais Street. Then the water from the breech started pouring in and quickly rose to the top of first floor. The water was full of mud, sewage, oil, and stank of death. Workers would later call it a toxic stew. With 8 feet of mud-filled water destroying everything in the house and reaching the ceiling, the family ran to the attic. Some neighbors thought they had all drowned, but the water in the Domino house did not rise higher. By afternoon, a New Orleans Harbor Police rescued the family. Fats Domino, his wife, and his children joined what was by then 20,000 survivors in the Superdome. The mementos of a lifetime were gone.

The Cleanup

Few failed to notice that the worse scenes of suffering and death were in African-American communities. The New Orleans Police Department was part of the problem. Many of the officers simply deserted their posts, leaving New Orleans to its own devices. Some of those who remained offered heroic help, but others were eventually convicted of criminal activity. In addition, the Federal Emergency Management Agency (FEMA) failed to live up to its responsibilities. FEMA had been created during the Carter administration to coordinate the diverse federal agencies that might be needed in the case of a natural disaster. However, for too long during Katrina and its aftermath, FEMA did nothing. FEMA staff were asking, "Why aren't we getting the orders? Why isn't this being treated like a real emergency?" FEMA's director in 2005, Michael Brown, was a political appointee with no experience in managing any disasters. When Brown assured Mississippi Governor Haley Barbour that "FEMA had lots of hurricane practice in Florida," Barbour responded, "I don't think you've seen anything like this." It was one of the kinder statements Brown heard that week as people waited for federal help that did not come.

American Voices

Surviving Hurricane Katrina, Mary Gehman, 2005

Everyone who lived through Hurricane Katrina has their own memories. Mary Gehman shares this one.

All through the night gusts of incredibly heavy wind battered the house from the east side. It started out mild but eventually I was awakened by the noise, snug on my living room couch. I could only hope the upstairs rooms were going to hold tight.… Finally, about noon on Monday, the winds started to diminish. There were another few hours of rain and some gusts but the storm's fury had been spent.…For about an hour or two late that afternoon, after the storm had quieted and the rain stopped, I enjoyed a sense of relief and self-righteous victory. I had been right to follow my gut feeling about being able to weather the hurricane. The water outside in the street had risen higher than I had ever seen it before in my 27 years living in the alley. It flowed fast, like a roiling creek, lapping the second step of my porch.

By 5:00 p.m. that evening the creek outside my front steps had turned from a greenish grey to black, and the water was imperceptibly inching up. The flow had slowed somewhat, but there was no sign of it stopping or receding. With a sickening feeling, I watched as it came up to the threshold and began to ooze in under the front door. A few minutes later water pressed in through the baseboards: I knew we were in for a fight. The radio reported there had been a massive break in the 17th Street Canal levee and the water would rise farther before it stopped.… Hopefully, the water would stop in an hour or two.

By Tuesday 3 a.m. the water had risen to cover the second step… as I eased into it from the slick hardwood stairs, it came up above my knees to mid-thigh, well over two feet deep.…The floor boards were slippery, coated I assumed by a film of oil and filth.…

By about 3:00 that afternoon, I had pretty much made up my mind to get out. What to do about the dogs was the one remaining block. I knew the boats and helicopters that were picking people up were not taking large dogs …I glanced at the photos of my sons, their wives and my grandchildren on my night stand

and thought how useless I'd be to them were I to be found dead, my two old dogs keeping guard over me. No, I had to prioritize things in a rational manner.…

Out on the balcony I could not look at the dogs, not even as I set out a bucket of water and a dish of food for each.…It was dusk by the time a flat-bottomed boat manned by Bossier City, Louisiana, firefighters finally pulled up in the alley by the house where I was sitting on the roof peak. I scrambled down, grabbed the school bag and my purse, pulled the tall window shut behind me and handed my things down to a man in the boat. The Red Cross would be providing food and water, so no need to take more than the absolute minimum, the man in the boat assured me. The dogs pressed against me, and I petted them for the last time, my eyes welling over with tears.…All I know is that on my return to the house five weeks later, there was no trace of the dogs.…

I don't regret that I stayed through the storm—I was able to salvage a lot of important papers and items that are now of great comfort to me. The overpass will never feel the same to me as I pass over it nearly every day. My lovely dogs still haunt me. Their questioning faces swim up to the surface of my consciousness now and then—I tell them I left them for their own good. They seem to understand. They have no choice. None of us does.

Source: http://hurricanearchive.org/content/vault/survivingkatrina_2f9d906b46.pdf, downloaded August 14, 2011.

Thinking Critically

1. **Historical Interpretation**

   What does Gehman's description of the crisis tell you about her response to it?

2. **Contextualization**

   How does Gehman's descriptions of her actions fit with the actions that government leaders did or did not take regarding the storm?

By Wednesday, August 31, 2 days after the storm, two hospitals in New Orleans, Charity and University, lost their generators. It was over 100 degrees in the hospitals. With no electricity, staff and volunteers used hand pumps to keep oxygen flowing to desperately ill people. With virtually no water or supplies, only the most rudimentary medical aid was possible. Those in the Superdome were trying to survive in horrifying, primitive conditions with no sanitation and dead bodies laying exposed in hallways. Not until Thursday were thousands of people finally evacuated to Houston, Texas, where shelter was offered. New Orleans never returned to its pre-Katrina population, and a year after the storm, whole neighborhoods were virtually abandoned even as others, like the Ninth Ward, slowly rebuilt and came back to life.

30.2 **Quick Review** Based on this information, why do you think people from all over the country volunteered to help the city and people of New Orleans?

THE FINANCIAL CRISIS OF 2008

30.3 Explain the costs and consequences of the 2008 financial crisis.

The headline on the *Wall Street Journal* for Monday, September 15, 2008, was double the normal size and ran across all six columns of the paper. It said:

> CRISIS ON WALL STREET AS LEHMAN TOTTERS, MERRILL IS SOLD AND AIG SEEKS TO RAISE CASH

By the time most people read the paper, Lehman was no longer tottering; the storied bank had declared bankruptcy. Bank of America bought Merrill Lynch, and bankers and federal authorities were trying to save the American International Group (AIG). Before the day was over, the stock market fell by 504.48 points. It would fall much further. The financial exuberance of the last 2 decades had come to a sudden end.

In one extraordinary weekend, Saturday and Sunday September 13 and 14, most of the nation's leading bankers and senior government officials led by the Secretary of the Treasury Henry "Hank" Paulson tried to salvage the American economy. Although the government and the bankers failed to save Lehman Brothers, they avoided a far worse fate of massive bankruptcies and the coming of a second Great Depression. Nevertheless, they did not succeed in saving the thriving economy of the last 2 decades.

The extent of the **financial crisis of 2008** came as a surprise, even to Treasury Secretary Paulson, who had warned that a crisis was coming since becoming the top federal financial official in July 2006 and to Timothy Geithner, then the head of the New York Federal Reserve Bank. The size and complexity of the crisis that hit the country in 2008 was much more severe than they would have predicted.

The economy had been growing rapidly since the early 1990s. Interest rates had remained low in part because of policies at the Federal Reserve Bank; in part because of the Clinton-era efforts to cut the size of the federal deficit; and in part because bankers and governments in Asia, especially China, were willing to make low-interest loans to Americans and European borrowers, particularly to finance their purchases of Asian goods.

During the 1990s and later, because of policies fostered by the Clinton and Bush administrations, bankers got much more freedom from federal regulations than had been the case in any period since the Depression. In 1999, with bipartisan support, Congress passed the Gramm-Leach-Bliley Act that repealed a section of the 1933 Glass-Steagall Act. Glass-Steagall, which was passed at the height of the Great Depression, created the Federal Deposit Insurance Corporation (FDIC) to provide federal insurance for bank accounts but also required that insured banks not use their money to speculate, that is, to make risky investments. For decades, insured banks provided mortgages to families that wanted to buy a home, usually up to 80 percent of the price of a house, so people could pay off their homes over a 20- to 30-year time span. Banks were cautious in making loans, insisting on detailed documentation of a family's ability to pay back the loan. Most of the time, a bank that issued a mortgage continued to hold it until the loan was paid off.

Investment banks, like Lehman Brothers and Goldman Sachs, were free to speculate on the stock market or in other investments, but they were not federally insured; they were risking their own money, not that of the taxpayers. What had been a hard and fast divide between investment and commercial banks in 1933 had been slowly eroding and, after 1999, had became a very porous wall.

Two further developments changed the way banks operated and mortgages were issued in the United States. President George W. Bush talked of an "ownership society" in which Americans would be invested in their communities because they owned their own homes. Liberal Democrats like Massachusetts representative Barney Frank insisted that mortgages be available to allow poorer people to own their own homes.

financial crisis of 2008
A significant economic downturn that began with the housing mortgage market and ultimately led to high unemployment.

At the same time, banks found new ways to handle—and profit from—home mortgages. Rather than issue a mortgage and then hold it, banks divided mortgages into small shares—"sliced and diced" them, as some said—and then sold the mortgage shares, at a profit, to many different banks and investors. As a result, banks could invest in pieces of many different mortgages in ways that seemed to lower the risk of individual mortgage defaulting since investors held portions of many mortgages rather than the whole amount of a few. With interest rates low and mortgages easier than ever to sell to other banks, mortgage lenders also began issuing mortgages to people who never before would have been eligible. They issued mortgages with no down payment and no required documentation of income or ability to pay in what became known as the "subprime mortgage market" and then sold these mortgages at a profit. The institution that had issued the mortgage was not at risk if the person who took out the mortgage later defaulted because that institution had long since sold the mortgage, probably in pieces, to several different investors. With such easy funding available, sellers found they could ask higher prices for homes, and housing prices climbed at an extraordinary rate.

Between 2001 and 2006, housing prices kept rising, interest rates stayed low, and bankers made a lot of money. The investment bank Goldman Sachs generated an average income of $661,000 per employee in 2007. Goldman's chief, Lloyd Blankfein, earned $54 million that year. Mortgages were no longer merely for primary residences but for investment. People bought houses as investments and then sold them for higher amounts, known as "flipping," which enabled them to buy more expensive houses with the profits or simply pocket the money. Everyone seemed to be making money, and many argued that only fools were left out of the process. The situation was a classic bubble very much like every other bubble from the tulip bubble of the 1600s in Holland to the stock market bubble of 1929 to the dot.com bubble of the 1990s.

In 2006, the housing bubble reached its peak. Housing prices stopped rising. People who had bought houses they could not afford and had planned to "flip" them, could not sell them. People who had bought homes with flexible interest rates, thinking that they would refinance for a lower rate later, could not find a new mortgage. More people started defaulting on loans. As defaults grew, banks who held the mortgages started to get into trouble. Even if mortgages had been "sliced and diced," banks that owned slices of mortgages that were in default were now, themselves, in trouble. Initially, most people thought the crisis would be limited to a few mortgage lenders who had taken too many risks. They were wrong.

Before long, it became clear that large and supposedly stable investment banks like Lehman and Goldman Sachs, which held portions of many sliced loans, were in a lot of trouble. Bankers who had taken risks throughout their careers, confident that there was always a way out, could not find a way out of the crisis. Over the weekend of September 13–14, 2008, while Treasury Secretary Paulson was trying to maintain confidence, he privately called his wife to share his worries. "What if the system collapses?" he asked.

In the end, the nation's financial system did not collapse. But it did not resume the financial health that had characterized most of the 1990s and early 2000s. At the end of September, Secretary Paulson and congressional leaders put together Troubled Asset Relief Program (TARP) legislation that would stop the continuing financial collapse. When TARP was put to a vote in the House of Representatives, in spite of the support of leaders of both parties, the bailout was rejected by a 228 to 205 vote by members of both parties who did not think it was the government's business to use taxpayer money to bail out investors who had taken too many risks with their own funds. Immediately after the vote, the Dow Jones Industrial Average lost another 777 points, the biggest 1-day drop ever. Another report

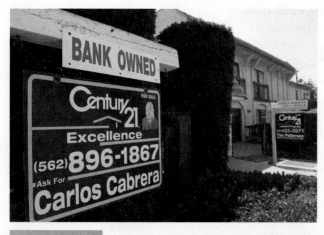

Inflated housing prices and problems with home mortgages helped cause the financial crisis of 2008. As a result, many people were evicted or forced to sell homes they could no longer afford, which produced a glut on the housing market and a significant drop in home prices and values.

indicated that 159,000 jobs had been lost in September. The crisis was spreading far beyond the banks. As credit and confidence dried up, people saw jobs, savings, and pensions disappear. The American economy seemed to be teetering badly. Finally on Friday October 3, under pressure from President Bush and from both major presidential candidates, Congress passed the TARP legislation. The law created a $700 billion fund to buy the worst of the troubled assets from the banks and stabilize the system. "We have shown the world that the United States will stabilize our financial markets and maintain a leading role in the global economy," Bush said.

In May 2009, Congress created a Financial Crisis Inquiry Commission to study the crisis. The commission held a number of hearings. At one of them, in June 2010, the financier Warren Buffett was asked who was to blame. "[I]t's a little bit like Cinderella at the ball," Buffett said. "People may have some feeling that at midnight it's going to turn to pumpkin and mice, but it's so darn much fun....There's no villain." Others thought there was some specific blame to be assigned. People blamed Lehman Brothers and other banks. They blamed the auditing companies that should have looked more closely at the account books of the banks. They blamed the repeal of Glass-Steagall. And many saw the crisis as one more in the sad long line of investment bubbles that, when they burst, hurt not only those caught up in the speculation but the economy of the whole nation and, indeed, of the world. Certainly the crisis could have been worse, and the work of the Treasury Secretary and the TARP legislation may have kept the country from another Great Depression. However, as Congressman Barney Frank said of Paulson's efforts, "You don't get any credit for disaster averted."

After 2008, unemployment rates stayed stubbornly high. In 2009 and 2010, the United States had an official unemployment rate of 10 percent, and if one counted discouraged and part-time workers, it was closer to 16 percent. Those who lost their jobs were out of work for increasingly longer periods of time. High unemployment creates its own negative cycle. For the unemployed, it is devastating. When unemployed people do not buy cars, computers, and refrigerators, the whole economy slows down. As the nation entered the 2012 election cycle, economic movement was very slow.

The crisis of 2008 also brought other economic problems to light. Firms like Lehman Brothers had been painting a rosier picture of their finances than the situation warranted, and others were engaged in much more corrupt practices. Three months after the collapse of Lehman Brothers, a New York financier, Bernard Madoff, was arrested and charged with securities fraud. Madoff's Investment Securities Company was, in reality, a giant Ponzi scheme (see Chapter 21 for information on the first such scheme by Charles Ponzi). Madoff delivered grand returns on investments made with his company, but it turned out that Madoff simply used the funds that were invested with his company to pay out high returns on older funds. He did not invest, or even save them. As long as more money kept coming in, Madoff was able to keep up the illusion of amazing success, and investors were happy. When the nation's finances seized up in the fall of 2008, Madoff was not able to keep the investments coming in, and without them, the payments could not keep going out, and the whole house of cards collapsed. Madoff was sentenced to 150 years in prison; investors lost between $10 and $17 billion.

In May 2011, another highly regarded investor, Raj Rajaratnam, head of Galleon, a multibillion dollar hedge fund, or speculative investment group, was convicted of 14 counts of securities fraud for bribing corporate employees to provide information that allowed Galleon to "guess" future stock values and make a fortune. By 2011, business leaders, and especially investors, were not highly regarded by a large segment of the American public.

Business leaders were not the only ones held in low esteem, however. Government officials, both Democrats and Republicans, were distrusted. Why, people asked, did the government bailout banks and the auto industry? Why was so much taxpayer money needed to stabilize investment banks when bankers were still getting huge bonuses but unemployment stayed stubbornly high? Were the high officials in the

Treasury Department really on the side of the average American? Some wondered when the real recovery would begin. Some wondered whether the United States was at the beginning of a permanent decline while other nations, especially perhaps China, might replace it as the world's leading financial powerhouse.

30.3 **Quick Review** How did policies, legislation, and events from the 1990s onward lead to the financial crisis of 2008?

NEW LIBERALS, NEW CONSERVATIVES

30.4 Analyze the most recent political developments in the United States.

Barack Obama was elected as a U.S. Senator from Illinois, just as George W. Bush won a second term in 2004. From the day he entered the Senate, Obama was better known than most newcomers. His upset win in a 7-way Illinois Democratic primary and his keynote speech calling for a new "politics of hope" at the 2004 convention that nominated John Kerry, followed by his continuing telegenic appearance, his life story, and his ability to rally people, all led many to notice him.

Nevertheless, he was a Senate freshman, and when the Majority Leader Harry Reid called him in for a meeting, Obama was surprised. As he headed toward the meeting, Obama told Robert Gibbs, his scheduler, "I wonder what we screwed up." But Reid stunned the young senator. As Obama recounted the meeting to Gibbs, he said, "Harry wants me to run for president....He really wants me to run for president."

Reid had certainly noticed Obama's discomfort with the Senate's slow pace, but more important, he had noticed the way Obama could connect with voters. Reid also had another reason to look carefully at Obama. The obvious front-runner for the Democratic nomination was Hillary Clinton: first lady from 1993 to 2001 and, since 2001, the U.S. Senator from New York. In the Senate, Clinton had established a solid track record. Reid liked her. Obama liked her. But a lot of Americans did not like her. Since her days as first lady and leader of President Bill Clinton's health care task force, Hillary Clinton had been a lightning rod for opposition to expanded government policies and, for some, for opposition to the role of women in politics. A lot of voters hated her. Like many Democrats, including Reid, she had voted to authorize the War in Iraq, and by 2006, it was becoming clear that, with the war going badly, such a vote was a terrible burden among liberal Democrats. Finally, for Reid and many of the Democratic Party's senior leaders, the worst nightmare was the nomination of Hilary Clinton followed by some new revelation about her husband's behavior like the Monica Lewinsky scandal that would end up bringing another Republican to the White House. They were desperate for another candidate, and in Obama they thought they had found one.

The Unprecedented Election of 2008

In modern American politics, being anointed by the party's leaders is a far cry from being nominated. Running for high office required Obama and the other candidates to slog through months of primary elections, including the Iowa caucuses and the New Hampshire primary in January, until the midsummer nominating convention. All along the way, voters are more than happy to overrule the party elite.

Obama needed to decide whether he was going to run for president or not. David Plouffe, one of Obama's inner circle of campaign leaders, warned him that he could stay in the Senate and enjoy weekends and vacations with his family or he could run for president, have every aspect of his life pried into, travel constantly, and "lead a lonely, miserable life." There was no middle ground. Obama needed time to talk it over with his wife Michelle. In the end, they were both in. Most people still considered it a long shot, but slowly, the long shot turned into reality.

In one of the first steps toward seeking the 2008 Democratic presidential nomination, then Senator Obama visited Netscape founder Marc Andreessen (see Chapter 29) and told him that he wanted to run the most sophisticated digital campaign on record. Andreessen was impressed that "the Senator was personally interested in the rise of social networking, Facebook, YouTube, and user-generated content." Several veterans of the Dean campaign also signed on to help the new campaign, and with the help of the Internet, Obama was able to raise twice the funds of his main rival, Hillary Clinton, and go on to win the nomination in spite of a long and bruising race between Obama and Clinton that remained close through the end of the primary season. Only in June was it clear that Obama had won the nomination.

It had been a historic contest. Hillary Clinton was the first woman to come so close to the presidential nomination, and Barack Obama was the first African-American to win. Perhaps, some thought, the nation was past the point where either gender or race mattered as they had in the past. Others insisted that gender and race were still very powerful forces, but in Clinton and Obama, the country had two extraordinary candidates who transcended the odds to accomplish what they did.

The battle for the Republican nomination was almost as hard fought in 2008. President Bush could not run for a third term, and his popularity had sunk as a result of the war and financial crisis. Arizona senator John McCain was the front-runner throughout the campaign. Although he had almost defeated Bush for the nomination in 2000 and was a war hero—having been a prisoner of war in Vietnam—McCain also had a hair-trigger temper and had divorced after having an affair and then remarried. The 2006 midterm Republican losses probably strengthened McCain's chances. McCain's reputation as a moderate and an independent meant that he would not be tarred with all of Bush's troubles. In spite of several primary challengers, McCain won key Republican primaries, and by March, it was clear he would be the Republican nominee for president. The only remaining question was who he would select to be his running mate.

John McCain knew that his selection of a vice presidential candidate was especially important. Obama led in fund-raising and public opinion polls. McCain needed a game-changing move. McCain wanted Connecticut's Democratic senator Joe Lieberman. Lieberman was a staunch Democrat and had served as Al Gore's running mate in 2000, but he had broken with the majority of his own party on the war in Iraq, which he supported, and he was already campaigning for McCain. His selection would reinforce McCain's credentials as an independent. But in the end, other Republicans convinced McCain that proposing a Democrat who, more important, was prochoice on the issue of abortion, would split the party. McCain rejected his friend Lieberman and selected the 44-year-old governor of Alaska, Sarah Palin. She was popular in Alaska and had all the credentials needed as a conservative Republican. Palin became a campaign sensation but her lack of familiarity with national politics, and her feuding with the McCain campaign staff probably hurt as much as it helped. When Obama asked Delaware senator Joseph Biden to be his running mate, the contrast between someone with decades of national experience and Alaska's 20-month governor could not have been greater, even if Obama also had only served in the Senate for that amount of time.

The September financial crisis played to Obama's strengths. McCain always said that economic issues were not his strong point, and when, after the Lehman bankruptcy he said, "The fundamentals of our economy are strong"—the same words Herbert Hoover had used at the height of the Great Depression—his advisors started to panic. In contrast, Obama had a comprehensive economic plan, and in the days after Lehman's collapse, he spent his time learning from people like Bush's Treasury Secretary Paulson and Federal Reserve chair Ben Bernanke, both of whom came to respect him. At the same time, the economy and the war in Iraq continued to hamper the Republicans. On Election Day, Obama defeated McCain by 53 percent to 46 percent of the vote, carrying 365 electoral votes to McCain's 173 votes. The nation, which had fought a civil war and witnessed a long civil rights movement over issues of race had just elected its first African-American president. It was an historic moment. Now people were about to see what sort of change Barack Obama had been talking about.

Obama's Agenda—Stimulus and a Health Plan

President-elect Obama asked his former opponent Hillary Clinton to serve as his secretary of state. She was reluctant to leave the independence of the Senate, but Obama pressed and Clinton took the job. Obama told Clinton, "The economy is a much bigger mess" than imagined, and he needed a very strong secretary of state to run foreign policy. He knew that while the bailout of the banks had been a first step, much more needed to be done. Nevertheless, economic experts, political leaders, and average voters all disagreed sharply about what should be done.

Obama was famous for his use of a Blackberry and an iPhone during his Senate career and his presidential campaign. Bemoaning the need to give up his iPhone for security reasons once elected president, Obama continued to use a Blackberry as well as his personal Twitter account, his MacBook Pro, and an iPad2. The world of high technology arrived in the White House in January 2009.

Immediately on taking office in January 2009, Obama proposed the American Recovery and Reinvestment Act, and it passed within weeks. The act pumped money into the economy, providing funds for road improvements, railroads, and unemployment benefits. The Recovery and Reinvestment Act was standard economics, an effort to "prime the pump" and get the economy moving by spending funds so employment would rise, private spending would pick up, and the government could step back. Unfortunately for Obama, the emergency spending piled further debts on top of those already in place, and many began to worry about the cost.

While the administration struggled with the economy, Obama also moved quickly to implement what he hoped would be his signature initiative: health care for all Americans. From Harry Truman on, every Democratic administration sought to implement **health care reform**, but every effort had failed. Obama wanted to be the Democrat who accomplished what others had failed. After a long and bitter fight, he was able to sign the Patient Protection and Affordable Care Act on March 23, 2010. Unlike the stimulus legislation, however, health care was a long fight, filled with compromises. It dominated the Congress that came to office with Obama. From the beginning the Republican minority was dedicated to defeating the measure. The Senate rule that a filibuster could stop all legislation unless 60 Senators voted to close debate provided effective leverage for Republicans and Democrats. The Senate included only 60 Democrats, so every one of them could demand special consideration and exemptions, and many did, before the final vote. The result was that the historic health care legislation passed only after a political process that discouraged almost everyone. The new law required every American to have health insurance; prohibited insurance companies from excluding anyone, including those with preexisting conditions; provided government subsidies for those who have trouble buying insurance; and penalized employers not offering health insurance. A number of state attorneys general challenged the legislation in court, but in the spring of 2012, the U.S. Supreme Court in a split decision upheld the law. Surprising its supporters, the law ended up being a political liability for a Democratic president and his party in the midterm elections of 2010 and the presidential election of 2012.

health care reform
The top priority of the Obama administration to provide universal health care for all Americans.

In November 2008, Barack Obama was elected president of the United States—a time of celebration for many.

The Rise of the Tea Party, Occupy Wall Street, and Divided Government

In part because of anger at the health care legislation, in part because of fears about the growing national debt, and in part because of a long-standing bias among Americans against big government, the huge plurality with which Obama came to office started to evaporate rapidly.

On January 19, 2010, just a year after Obama's inauguration, the growing voter anger became apparent to the nation, particularly after one of the icons of American liberalism, Massachusetts senator Edward M. Kennedy, died of a brain tumor in August 2009. Kennedy had served in the U.S. Senate since 1962, the fourth-longest Senate career in U.S. history. A special election was called to fill Kennedy's unexpired term, and almost everyone assumed that whoever received the Democratic nomination would get the job. But a little known Republican state senator, Scott Brown, campaigned hard, telling people, "It's not Kennedy's seat…it's the people's seat," and promising to be the crucial 40th vote to sustain a filibuster in the Senate against the health care legislation. Brown won easily, telling his cheering supporters on election night, "What I've heard again and again on the campaign trail is that our political leaders have grown aloof from the people, impatient with dissent, and comfortable in the back room making deals." Although Brown was not able to stop the passage of the health care law, his election was a sign that something was shifting in American politics. It was not the first such sign.

Only weeks after Obama's inauguration, protests were springing up in many different places. In Seattle, a 29-year-old woman, Keli Carender, organized a small protest rally about "the spending," whether it was Bush's TARP or Obama's stimulus. Carender told a small crowd that "I started thinking, what are we getting ourselves into? It didn't make sense to me to be spending all this money when we don't have it." Then, a little while later, on February 19, 2009, a financial news commentator, Rick Santelli, said that Obama's stimulus efforts were "promoting bad behavior" if they bailed out "the losers" who had taken out larger mortgages than they could afford. Santelli said, "We're thinking of having a Chicago **Tea Party** in July." And the name took hold.

In September 2010, between 70,000 and 90,000 demonstrators converged on the Mall in Washington, DC, to protest the health care legislation and government spending. Some wore tricolor hats to symbolize their link to the original Boston Tea Party. Some carried signs that said, "Thank you, Glenn Beck!" referring to the conservative television commentator who railed against the Obama administration. Some, alluding to fears that the health care legislation would limit treatments, carried signs that said, "Pull the plug on Obama, not Grandma." The National Tea Party Coalition tried to coordinate efforts. The Republican vice presidential nominee from 2008, Sarah Palin, adopted the Tea Party Platform and spoke at its rallies. Nevertheless, the movement was distrustful of self-proclaimed leaders. Different groups in different places did as they pleased. Tea Party candidates challenged Republicans in primary elections all through 2009 and 2010 and sometimes defeated long-standing Republican moderates. In November 2010, with solid Tea Party support, Republicans took control of the House of Representatives and made gains in the Senate. But the Tea Party candidates were of a different sort than the older Republicans, not only more conservative but also far less willing to compromise.

The Tea Party was fueled by fear about the debt, uncertainty about the economy, and anger at big institutions, most of all the federal government but also corporations and universities. Many in the Tea Party argued that the federal government should do no more than what was specifically authorized in the Constitution, and almost all of its members were generally distrustful of government programs, especially those coming from the federal government and those designed to help the poor or minority groups. It quickly became clear that the Tea Party was not going away, even though its membership might be filled with internal contradictions. Tea Party members disliked government but wanted their Social Security checks to arrive on time; they hated the new health care but loved their Medicare cards. When the outgoing Congress repealed

Tea Party
A protest group whose members sometimes modeled themselves on the Tea Party of the American Revolution and objected to the rising federal debt, Obamacare, and most government regulation.

30.1

30.2

30.3

30.4

Occupy Wall Street
A protest group that protested the rising level of student debt, the lack of job opportunities, and the fact that the economy seemed stacked in favor of the rich.

the "Don't Ask, Don't Tell" ban on gay and lesbian personnel serving in the military in late 2010, the Tea Party was divided about its response; neither the Tea Party nor the Republicans made it a major issue. Still, the Tea Party, with its focus on economic issues and anger at big government was a powerful group.

In the summer of 2011, the new Tea Party-fueled Republican majority in the House of Representatives brought the country to the brink of financial default as they refused until the last minute to raise the nation's borrowing capacity. Standard & Poor's, one of the nation's leading auditing agencies, lowered the U.S. credit rating for the first time in history because of the government's seeming inability to deal with the federal debt.

As if in response to the Tea Party, a new movement of students and other young people also emerged to protest conditions in the country. While the Tea Party took a conservative stance on economic issues, **Occupy Wall Street** was closer to the left on most issues. In September 2011, a group of young people held a rally near Wall Street in Lower Manhattan and then moved into nearby Zuccotti Park where they set up tents, a library, a communications center, and a kitchen, and planned to stay. A Canadian publication, *Adbusters,* had been calling for just such a move, and by late September it was a reality. The rallying cry of Occupy Wall Street was "We are the 99%" to differentiate themselves from the richest 1 percent, including the bankers who surrounded them in Lower Manhattan. Although those gathering in protest consistently refused to issue a manifesto or platform, Occupy was an angry response to the financial crisis and the growing gap between rich and poor in the country. They condemned the huge level of college debt that many young people were carrying and the difficulties for a new generation in getting jobs.

Before long, Occupy movements were springing up all around the country—Occupy Los Angeles, Occupy Oakland, Occupy Denver, Occupy Boston, and Occupy Rochester. In November, some 3 months after the encampment at Zuccotti Park began, New York police, on orders from the mayor, cleared the park. Mayors and police departments in other cities had generally acted sooner. Nevertheless, the Occupy movement was far from over. Through the winter and the following year, Occupy held rallies, meetings, and planning sessions. Neither Occupy nor the Tea Party was going to go away, and both would be forces to deal with. Governing a nation so deeply divided was going to be difficult. The terms of the 2012 election were set.

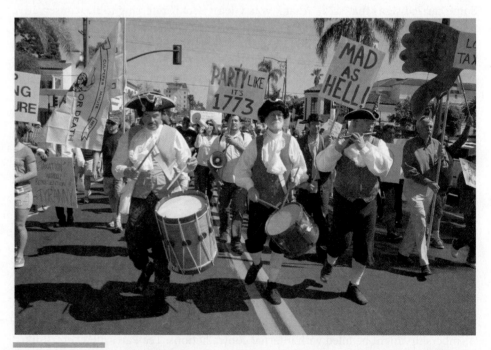

The Tea Party movement named itself after those who had dumped tea in Boston harbor in 1773 rather than pay a tax on it. Many in the modern movement shared the anti-tax, anti-government sentiments of the earlier Tea Party while some dressed the part.

THINKING HISTORICALLY

Same-Sex Marriage

On June 26, 2013, in a 5-4 opinion in the case of **United States v. Windsor**, the United States Supreme Court declared a significant part of the Defense of Marriage Act unconstitutional. Writing for the majority, Justice Anthony Kennedy said:

> DOMA's principal effect is to identify a subset of state-sanctioned marriages and make them unequal....By this dynamic DOMA undermines both the public and private significance of state-sanctioned same-sex marriages; for it tells those couples, and all the world, that their otherwise valid marriages are unworthy of federal recognition. This places same-sex couples in an unstable position of being in a second-tier marriage.

The decision was not without debate. Four justices opposed the majority. Writing for the minority, Justice Antonin Scalia said that the court should never have taken on the case and, further, that the decision would lead inevitably to the Supreme Court's declaring all state laws against gay marriage to be invalid.

Nevertheless, the majority opinion became the law of the land and, as a result, same-sex couples married in the 13 states, the District of Columbia, and under the five Native American tribal governments that approved same-sex marriage were provided all the benefits—including tax advantages, pension, and visitation rights—that all other married couples had. It was a major change and one that came very quickly.

When the Congress passed and President Bill Clinton signed the Defense of Marriage Act in September 1996, no state recognized same-sex marriage. Before the 1996 legislation, Congress had left decisions about what constituted a legitimate marriage to the states. But fearing the potential of same-sex marriage, the Republican Congress passed the Defense of Marriage Act and the Democratic President signed it. As a result, federal law said that no matter what a state did, in the eyes of the federal government (for federal income tax, for federal pensions, for benefits for spouses of government employees and armed forces personnel and many related matters) a state-sanctioned same-sex marriage was invalid.

Nevertheless, as some feared and others hoped, states started to act on their own. In 2003, the Massachusetts Supreme Judicial Court declared that state laws prohibiting same-sex marriage were invalid in that state and gay and lesbian couples began getting married there. State courts in other states, including California, Connecticut, and Iowa, issued similar rulings. Then in 2009, the Vermont legislature sanctioned same-sex marriage, New York followed in 2011, and in 2012 Washington, Maine, and Maryland passed similar laws.

Activists Phyllis Lyon and Del Martin became the first same-sex couple to be married in San Francisco on February 12, 2004. In June 2013, the United States Supreme Court said that same-sex couples could not be denied federal marriage benefits.

Same-sex marriages, illegal in every part of the United States in the 1990s, were recognized in 2013 by states comprising 30 percent of the American population and by the federal government. Opinion polls indicated that the majority of the American people agreed with the new policies. It was a rapid and dramatic change in American culture.

Thinking Critically

1. **Comparison**

   How would you compare the political mood in the United States when the Defense of Marriage Act was passed in 1996 and when it was declared unconstitutional in 2013?

2. **Contextualization**

   What other developments in American culture and political debate might help explain decisions like those of the Massachusetts Supreme Court, the Vermont legislature or in 2013 the U.S. Supreme Court? How much does context impact such decisions?

United States v. Windsor
A June 2013 Supreme Court decision that declared Americans in same-sex marriages had the same federal rights as all other married citizens.

The Election of 2012

As President Obama and the Democrats looked to the 2012 election, they did so with considerable optimism. The worst of the financial crisis was past, and the wars in Iraq and Afghanistan were at least winding down. At the same time, the president and his party were aware of some significant liabilities. The economy remained far from robust, the health care law—which some called Obamacare— remained unpopular, especially among people who resented all forms of government intrusion in their lives. Many of those who had voted for the first time in 2008 to support Obama were disillusioned with the slow pace of change and might well not bother to vote in 2012. It was going to be a close contest.

The battle for the Republican nomination was a long one. In the early stages, many wondered whether 2008 vice presidential nominee and Tea Party darling Sarah Palin would enter the race, but she never did. Once the contest for the Republican nomination got under way, former Massachusetts governor Mitt Romney, who had been a serious contender for the 2008 nomination, was always a front-runner. But many in the Republican Party thought Romney was too liberal, and a number of other candidates, including former Minnesota governor Tim Pawlenty, former speaker Newt Gingrich, businessman Herman Cann, and Representative Michele Bachmann, gave Romney a strong challenge. In the end, Romney won the nomination and asked Congressman Paul Ryan, who had earned his conservative credentials with a series of tax cutting proposals, to be his running mate.

In the fall election, Obama was generally considered to be the front-runner, but many thought the race was too close to call. In the first presidential debate, Obama performed poorly—seeming disinterested—and Romney surged. In the later debates, however, Obama came on strong. One of Romney's great strengths, his years of business experience, came to hurt him as Democrats exploited the numbers of layoffs that had taken place in Romney-owned companies. Late in the campaign, a

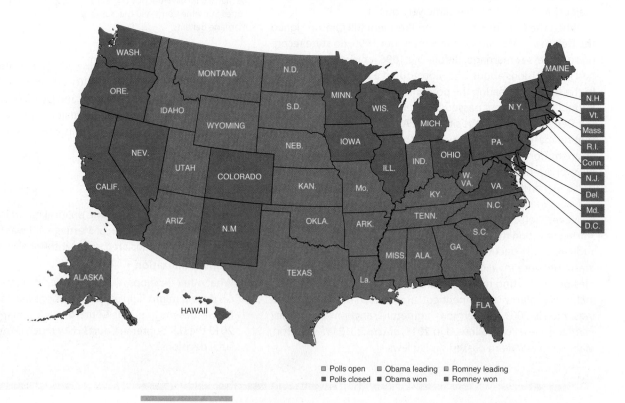

MAP 30-2 The Election of 2012. This map captures the extent of Obama's presidential election triumph and underscores the realignments of Republican red states and Democratic blue states.

private conversation in which Romney had told a group of supporters that 47 percent of the electorate would never support him because they were "dependent on the government" angered many. On election day, Obama won by a solid 51 percent to 47 percent majority and carried 332 electoral votes to Romney's 206 (see Map 30-2). The Congress, however, remained divided, with Democrats having a majority in the Senate and Republicans in the House.

At his second inauguration in January 2013, on what was Martin Luther King, Jr.'s, birthday, President Obama laid out the themes that he said would be most important in his second term. Appealing to some important moments in American history, he said, "We, the people, declare today that the most evident of truths—that all of us are created equal—is the star that guides us still; just as it guided our forebears through Seneca Falls, and Selma, and Stonewall …" and then appealing to King's memory he added, "Our individual freedom is inextricably bound to the freedom of every soul on Earth."

And he continued:

> It is now our generation's task to carry on what those pioneers began. For our journey is not complete until our wives, our mothers and daughters can earn a living equal to their efforts. Our journey is not complete until our gay brothers and sisters are treated like anyone else under the law for if we are truly created equal, then surely the love we commit to one another must be equal as well. Our journey is not complete until no citizen is forced to wait for hours to exercise the right to vote. Our journey is not complete until we find a better way to welcome the striving, hopeful immigrants who still see America as a land of opportunity—until bright young students and engineers are enlisted in our workforce rather than expelled from our country. Our journey is not complete until all our children, from the streets of Detroit to the hills of Appalachia, to the quiet lanes of Newtown, know that they are cared for and cherished and always safe from harm.

His address was not a set of policy recommendations but, rather, a way of carving out a vision.

As President Obama began his second term, the United States was more diverse than ever, with some looking optimistically toward the future and others looking nostalgically toward the past.

Former Speaker Newt Gingrich, who had contested the Republican nomination, said of Obama's speech that he "approved of 80 percent of President Barack Obama's inaugural address"; however, "the rest," Gingrich said, "was goofy left-wingism." Deciding where any consensus might be found would be more difficult than Gingrich's response might imply. Soon after the inauguration, Obama said he would use executive authority to institute action on climate change and quickly issued tough new limitations on emissions. The president had promised as much in his inaugural address, which had led Gingrich to say, "The whole section about climate change is nonsense." The divides on that issue, as on so many issues that had split the Congress and the country during Obama's first term, seem destined to continue for the foreseeable future. Many spoke of their desire for greater national unity and good will, but it remained an illusive goal.

> **30.4** **Quick Review** How have domestic issues contributed to divisions in the government and the country since 2008?

CONCLUSION

George W. Bush, in the first year of his presidency, achieved two major domestic policy goals: education reform and tax reform. But September 11, 2001, permanently shifted the focus of the Bush administration from domestic problems to international terrorism. Henceforth, the war on terror would dominate his presidency and remain a key issue for his successor in office, Barack Obama.

In the days after the September 11 attacks, it became clear that al-Qaeda and its leader, Osama bin Laden, were responsible. The Bush administration immediately developed a strategy to punish not only the direct perpetrators but also those who harbored them. When it was determined that the Taliban government of Afghanistan was protecting bin Laden and al-Qaeda, U.S. ground forces invaded the country and quickly overthrew the Taliban regime. Although the United States had forced a change in government in Afghanistan and had killed or captured many al-Qaeda operatives, both bin Laden and his chief lieutenant had escaped into Pakistan. It took another 10 years to find bin Laden, but Taliban insurgents continued to engage the U.S. military and destabilize Afghanistan and other parts of the world.

While the United States waged war in Afghanistan, the Bush administration turned its attention to Iraq. Despite the fact that neither the CIA nor the UN Nations found compelling evidence that Iraq was connected to the September 11 attacks, many in the administration favored U.S. military intervention. Ultimately, the United States and Great Britain obtained UN and congressional approval for an invasion, based on alleged Iraqi possession of weapons of mass destruction. Major combat operations in Iraq ended quickly, but the United States was ill prepared to serve as an occupying force. U.S. troops lacked clearly defined military objectives, and Iraq quickly descended into civil war. By 2004, public opinion was turning against the war. U.S. casualties were high, Iraq was in chaos, and no weapons of mass destruction had been found. Still, the U.S. mission in Iraq continued until December 2011.

From 2005 until 2008, domestic problems also plagued the Bush administration. In 2005, the federal response to Hurricane Katrina was wholly inadequate, and the U.S. economy was, in 2008, in a deep recession. The 2008 presidential election took place against this backdrop and culminated in the election of the nation's first African-American president, Barack Obama. Obama moved quickly to address the financial crisis, but while the economy was stabilized, unemployment remained high. The Obama administration's highest priority was to get Congress to approve a federal health insurance system which was signed into law in 2010. In the midst of a very slow recovery in which ordinary Americans suffered greatly, new protests including the Tea Party and the Occupy movements emerged to express voter dissatisfaction with continual war and with the economic meltdown. By the time of the 2012 presidential election, the nation was more divided than it had been in decades. Nevertheless, many liberal Americans celebrated when Obama won a second term in November 2012 and when in June 2013 the U.S. Supreme Court declared portions of the federal Defense of Marriage Act to be unconstitutional, giving people in a same-sex marriage the same federal rights as other married people. Still, the nation entered Obama's second term deeply divided on social and economic issues, and lasting resolutions seemed hard to find.

CHAPTER REVIEW How did the election of 2012 encompass issues that plagued the United States since 2000?

Chapter 30   Chapter Review

THE IMPACT OF SEPTEMBER 11, 2001

30.1 Analyze the impact of 9/11 on the nation and presidency of George Bush and the impact of Bush administration policies.

Review Questions

1. Cause and Effect

What changes in the federal government and American foreign policy of the United States followed in the wake of the attacks of September 11, 2001?

2. Comparison

Compare and contrast the war on terror with earlier, more conventional American wars. What special challenges did the war on terror present?

3. Construct an Argument

In your opinion, how will President Bush's decision to invade Iraq be viewed by future historians?

HURRICANE KATRINA AND ITS AFTERMATH

30.2 Explain the impact of Hurricane Katrina on the Gulf Coast.

Review Questions

4. Cause and Effect

How did human failure contribute to the death and destruction caused by Hurricane Katrina?

5. Construct an Argument

In your opinion, why were poor minority neighborhoods most adversely affected by the storm?

THE FINANCIAL CRISIS OF 2008

30.3 Explain the costs and consequences of the 2008 financial crisis.

Review Questions

6. Cause and Effect

What were the root causes of the 2008 financial crisis?

7. Historical Interpretation

How did the 2008 financial crisis change the way the American people saw the relationship between business and government?

NEW LIBERALS, NEW CONSERVATIVES

30.4 Analyze the most recent political developments in the United States.

Review Questions

8. Construct an Argument

In your opinion, what does Obama's election in 2008 and reelection in 2012 tell us about the state of race relations in the United States in the early 2000s?

9. Contextualization

What developments in recent American history fueled the rise of the Tea Party?

Appendix

THE CONSTITUTION OF THE UNITED STATES OF AMERICA

We the people of the United States, in order to form a more perfect union, establish justice, insure domestic tranquillity, provide for the common defense, promote the general welfare, and secure the blessings of liberty to ourselves and our posterity, do ordain and establish this Constitution for the United States of America.

ARTICLE I

Section 1. All legislative powers herein granted shall be vested in a Congress of the United States, which shall consist of a Senate and House of Representatives.

Section 2.
1. The House of Representatives shall be composed of members chosen every second year by the people of the several States, and the electors in each State shall have the qualifications requisite for electors of the most numerous branch of the State legislature.
2. No person shall be a representative who shall not have attained to the age of twenty-five years, and been seven years a citizen of the United States, and who shall not, when elected, be an inhabitant of that State in which he shall be chosen.
3. Representatives and direct taxes[1] shall be apportioned among the several States which may be included within this Union, according to their respective numbers, which shall be determined by adding to the whole number of free persons, including those bound to service for a term of years, and excluding Indians not taxed, three fifths of all other persons.[2] The actual enumeration shall be made within three years after the first meeting of the Congress of the United States, and within every subsequent term of ten years, in such manner as they shall by law direct. The number of representatives shall not exceed one for every thirty thousand, but each State shall have at least one representative; and until such enumeration shall be made, the State of New Hampshire shall be entitled to choose three, Massachusetts eight, Rhode Island and Providence Plantations one, Connecticut five, New York six, New Jersey four, Pennsylvania eight, Delaware one, Maryland six, Virginia ten, North Carolina five, South Carolina five, and Georgia three.
4. When vacancies happen in the representation from any State, the executive authority thereof shall issue writs of election to fill such vacancies.
5. The House of Representatives shall choose their speaker and other officers; and shall have the sole power of impeachment.

Section 3.
1. The Senate of the United States shall be composed of two senators from each State, chosen by the legislature thereof,[3] for six years; and each senator shall have one vote.
2. Immediately after they shall be assembled in consequence of the first election, they shall be divided as equally as may be into three classes. The seats of the senators of the first class shall be vacated at the expiration of the second year, of the second class at the expiration of the fourth year, and of the third class at the expiration of the sixth year, so that one third may be chosen every second year; and if vacancies happen by resignation, or otherwise, during the recess of the legislature of any State, the executive thereof may make temporary appointments until the next meeting of the legislature, which shall then fill such vacancies.[4]
3. No person shall be a senator who shall not have attained to the age of thirty years, and been nine years a citizen of the United States, and who shall not, when elected, be an inhabitant of that State for which he shall be chosen.
4. The Vice President of the United States shall be President of the Senate, but shall have no vote, unless they be equally divided.
5. The Senate shall choose their other officers, and also a president pro tempore, in the absence of the Vice President, or when he shall exercise the office of the President of the United States.
6. The Senate shall have the sole power to try all impeachments. When sitting for that purpose, they shall be on oath or affirmation. When the President of the United States is tried, the chief justice shall preside: and no person shall be convicted without the concurrence of two thirds of the members present.
7. Judgment in cases of impeachment shall not extend further than to removal from office, and disqualification to hold and enjoy any office of honor, trust or profit under the United States: but the party convicted shall nevertheless be liable and subject to indictment, trial, judgment and punishment, according to law.

Section 4.
1. The times, places, and manner of holding elections for senators and representatives, shall be prescribed in each State by the legislature thereof; but the Congress may at any time by law make or alter such regulations, except as to the places of choosing senators.
2. The Congress shall assemble at least once in every year, and such meeting shall be on the first Monday in December, unless they shall by law appoint a different day.

Section 5.
1. Each House shall be the judge of the elections, returns and qualifications of its own members, and a majority of each shall constitute a quorum to do business; but a smaller number may adjourn from day to day, and may be authorized to compel the attendance of absent members, in such manner, and under such penalties as each House may provide.
2. Each House may determine the rules of its proceedings, punish its members for disorderly behavior, and, with the concurrence of two thirds, expel a member.

---

3. Each House shall keep a journal of its proceedings, and from time to time publish the same, excepting such parts as may in their judgment require secrecy; and the yeas and nays of the members of either House on any question shall, at the desire of one fifth of those present, be entered on the journal.
4. Neither House, during the session of Congress, shall, without the consent of the other, adjourn for more than three days, nor to any other place than that in which the two Houses shall be sitting.

Section 6.
1. The senators and representatives shall receive a compensation for their services, to be ascertained by law, and paid out of the Treasury of the United States. They shall in all cases, except treason, felony, and breach of the peace, be privileged from arrest during their attendance at the session of their respective Houses, and in going to and returning from the same; and for any speech or debate in either House, they shall not be questioned in any other place.
2. No senator or representative shall, during the time for which he was elected, be appointed to any civil office under the authority of the United States, which shall have been created, or the emoluments whereof shall have been increased, during such time; and no person holding any office under the United States shall be a member of either House during his continuance in office.

Section 7.
1. All bills for raising revenue shall originate in the House of Representatives; but the Senate may propose or concur with amendments as on other bills.
2. Every bill which shall have passed the House of Representatives and the Senate, shall, before it become a law, be presented to the President of the United States; If he approves he shall sign it, but if not he shall return it, with his objections, to that House in which it shall have originated, who shall enter the objections at large on their journal, and proceed to reconsider it. If after such reconsideration two thirds of that House shall agree to pass the bill, it shall be sent, together with the objections, to the other House, by which it shall likewise be reconsidered, and if approved by two thirds of that House, it shall become a law. But in all such cases the votes of both Houses shall be determined by yeas and nays, and the names of the persons voting for and against the bill shall be entered on the journal of each House respectively. If any bill shall not be returned by the President within ten days (Sundays excepted) after it shall have been presented to him, the same shall be a law, in like manner as if he had signed it, unless the Congress by their adjournment prevent its return, in which case it shall not be a law.
3. Every order, resolution, or vote to which the concurrence of the Senate and the House of Representatives may be necessary (except on a question of adjournment) shall be presented to the President of the United States; and before the same shall take effect, shall be approved by him, or being disapproved by him, shall be repassed by two thirds of the Senate and House of Representatives, according to the rules and limitations prescribed in the case of a bill.

Section 8.
1. The Congress shall have the power To lay and collect taxes, duties, imposts, and excises, to pay the debts and provide for the common defense and general welfare of the United States; but all duties, imposts, and excises shall be uniform throughout the United States.
2. To borrow money on the credit of the United States;
3. To regulate commerce with foreign nations, and among the several States, and with the Indian tribes;
4. To establish a uniform rule of naturalization, and uniform laws on the subject of bankruptcies throughout the United States;
5. To coin money, regulate the value thereof, and of foreign coin, and fix the standard of weights and measures;
6. To provide for the punishment of counterfeiting the securities and current coin of the United States;
7. To establish post offices and post roads;
8. To promote the progress of science and useful arts, by securing for limited times to authors and inventors the exclusive right to their respective writings and discoveries;
9. To constitute tribunals inferior to the Supreme Court;
10. To define and punish piracies and felonies committed on the high seas, and offenses against the law of nations;
11. To declare war, grant letters of marque and reprisal, and make rules concerning captures on land and water;
12. To raise and support armies, but no appropriation of money to that use shall be for a longer term than two years;
13. To provide and maintain a navy;
14. To make rules for the government and regulation of the land and naval forces;
15. To provide for calling forth the militia to execute the laws of the Union, suppress insurrections and repel invasions;
16. To provide for organizing, arming, and disciplining the militia, and for governing such part of them as may be employed in the service of the United States, reserving to the States respectively, the appointment of the officers, and the authority of training the militia according to the discipline prescribed by Congress;
17. To exercise exclusive legislation in all cases whatsoever, over such district (not exceeding ten miles square) as may, by cession of particular States, and the acceptance of Congress, become the seat of the government of the United States, and to exercise like authority over all places purchased by the consent of the legislature of the State in which the same shall be, for the erection of forts, magazines, arsenals, dockyards, and other needful buildings; and
18. To make all laws which shall be necessary and proper for carrying into execution the foregoing powers, and all other powers vested by this Constitution in the government of the United States, or any department or officer thereof.

---

[1] See the Sixteenth Amendment.
[2] See the Fourteenth Amendment.
[3] See the Seventeenth Amendment.
[4] See the Seventeenth Amendment.

Section 9. 1. The migration or importation of such persons as any of the States now existing shall think proper to admit, shall not be prohibited by the Congress prior to the year one thousand eight hundred and eight, but a tax or duty may be imposed on such importation, not exceeding ten dollars for each person.

2. The privilege of the writ of habeas corpus shall not be suspended, unless when in cases of rebellion or invasion the public safety may require it.

3. No bill of attainder or ex post facto law shall be passed.

4. No capitation, or other direct, tax shall be laid, unless in proportion to the census or enumeration herein-before directed to be taken.[5]

5. No tax or duty shall be laid on articles exported from any State.

6. No preference shall be given by any regulation of commerce or revenue to the ports of one State over those of another: nor shall vessels bound to, or from, one State be obliged to enter, clear, or pay duties in another.

7. No money shall be drawn from the treasury, but in consequence of appropriations made by law; and a regular statement and account of the receipts and expenditures of all public money shall be published from time to time.

8. No title of nobility shall be granted by the United States: and no person holding any office of profit or trust under them, shall, without the consent of the Congress, accept of any present, emolument, office, or title, of any kind whatever, from any king, prince, or foreign State.

Section 10. 1. No State shall enter into any treaty, alliance, or confederation; grant letters of marque and reprisal; coin money; emit bills of credit; make any thing but gold and silver coin a tender in payment of debts; pass any bill of attainder, ex post facto law, or law impairing the obligation of contracts, or grant, any title of nobility.

2. No State shall, without the consent of the Congress, lay any imposts or duties on imports or exports, except what may be absolutely necessary for executing its inspection laws: and the net produce of all duties and imposts laid by any State on imports or exports, shall be for the use of the treasury of the United States; and all such laws shall be subject to the revision and control of the Congress.

3. No State shall, without the consent of the Congress, lay any duty of tonnage, keep troops, or ships of war in time of peace, enter into any agreement or compact with another State, or with a foreign power, or engage in war, unless actually invaded, or in such imminent danger as will not admit of delay.

ARTICLE II

Section 1. 1. The executive power shall be vested in a President of the United States of America. He shall hold his office during the term of four years, and, together with the Vice President, chosen for the same term, be elected, as follows:

2. Each State shall appoint, in such manner as the legislature thereof may direct, a number of electors, equal to the whole number of senators and representatives to which the State may be entitled in the Congress: but no senator or representative, or person holding any office of trust or profit under the United States, shall be appointed an elector.

The electors shall meet in their respective States, and vote by ballot for two persons, of whom one at least shall not be an inhabitant of the same State with themselves. And they shall make a list of all the persons voted for, and of the number of votes for each; which list they shall sign and certify, and transmit sealed to the seat of the government of the United States, directed to the president of the Senate. The president of the Senate shall, in the presence of the Senate and House of Representatives, open all the certificates, and the votes shall then be counted. The person having the greatest number of votes shall be the President, if such number be a majority of the whole number of electors appointed; and if there be more than one who have such majority, and have an equal number of votes, then the House of Representatives shall immediately choose by ballot one of them for President; and if no person have a majority, then from the five highest on the list the said House shall in like manner choose the President. But in choosing the President, the votes shall be taken by States, the representation from each State having one vote; a quorum for this purpose shall consist of a member or members from two thirds of the States, and a majority of all the States shall be necessary to a choice. In every case after the choice of the President, the person having the greatest number of votes of the electors shall be the Vice President. But if there should remain two or more who have equal votes, the Senate shall choose from them by ballot the Vice President.[6]

3. The Congress may determine the time of choosing the electors, and the day on which they shall give their votes; which day shall be the same throughout the United States.

4. No person except a natural born citizen, or a citizen of the United States, at the time of the adoption of this Constitution, shall be eligible to the office of President; neither shall any person be eligible to the office who shall not have attained to the age of thirty-five years, and been fourteen years a resident within the United States.

5. In case of the removal of the President from office, or of his death, resignation, or inability to discharge the powers and duties of the said office, the same shall devolve on the Vice President, and the congress may by law provide for the case of removal, death, resignation or inability, both of the President and Vice President, declaring what officer shall then act as President, and such officer shall act accordingly until the disability be removed, or a President shall be elected.

6. The President shall, at stated times, receive for his services a compensation which shall neither be increased nor diminished during the period for which he shall have been elected, and he shall not receive within that period any other emolument from the United States, or any of them.

7. Before he enter on the execution of his office, he shall take the following oath or affirmation:—"I do solemnly swear (or affirm) that I will faithfully execute the office of President of the United States, and will to the best of my ability, preserve, protect and defend the Constitution of the United States."

Section 2. 1. The President shall be commander in chief of the army and navy of the United States, and of the militia of the several States, when called into the actual service of the United States; he may require the opinion in writing, of the principal officer in each of the executive departments, upon any subject relating to the duties of their respective offices, and he shall have power to grant reprieves and pardons for offenses against the United States, except in cases of impeachment.

2. He shall have power, by and with the advice and consent of the Senate, to make treaties, provided two thirds of the senators present concur; and he shall nominate, and by and with the advice and consent of the Senate, shall appoint ambassadors, other public ministers and consuls, judges of the Supreme Court, and all other officers of the United States, whose appointments are not herein otherwise provided for, and which shall be established by law; but the Congress may by law vest the appointment of such inferior officers, as they think proper, in the President alone, in the courts of laws, or in the heads of departments.

3. The President shall have power to fill up all vacancies that may happen during the recess of the Senate, by granting commissions which shall expire at the end of their next session.

Section 3. He shall from time to time give to the Congress information of the state of the Union, and recommend to their consideration such measures as he shall judge necessary and expedient; he may, on extraordinary occasions, convene both Houses, or either of them, and in case of disagreement between them with respect to the time of adjournment, he may adjourn them to such time as he shall think proper; he shall receive ambassadors and other public ministers; he shall take care that the laws be faithfully executed, and shall commission all the officers of the United States.

Section 4. The President, Vice President, and all civil officers of the United States, shall be removed from office on impeachment for, and conviction of, treason, bribery, or other high crimes and misdemeanors.

ARTICLE III

Section 1. The judicial power of the United States shall be vested in one Supreme Court, and in such inferior courts as the Congress may from time to time ordain and establish. The judges, both of the Supreme and inferior courts, shall hold their offices during good behavior, and shall, at stated times, receive for their services, a compensation, which shall not be diminished during their continuance in office.

Section 2. 1. The judicial power shall extend to all cases, in law and equity, arising under this Constitution, the laws of the United States, and treaties made, or which shall be made, under their authority;—to all cases of admiralty and maritime jurisdiction;—to controversies to which the United States shall be a party;[7]—to controversies between two or more States;—between a State and citizens of another State;—between citizens of different States;—between citizens of the same State claiming lands under grants of different States, and between a State, or the citizens thereof, and foreign States, citizens or subjects.

2. In all cases affecting ambassadors, other public ministers and consuls, and those in which a State shall be party, the Supreme Court shall have original jurisdiction. In all the other cases before mentioned, the Supreme Court shall have appellate jurisdiction, both as to law and fact, with such exceptions, and under such regulations as the Congress shall make.

3. The trial of all crimes, except in cases of impeachment, shall be by jury; and such trial shall be held in the State where the said crimes shall have been committed; but when not committed within any State, the trial shall be such place or places as the congress may by law have directed.

Section 3. 1. Treason against the United States shall consist only in levying war against them, or in adhering to their enemies, giving them aid and comfort. No person shall be convicted of treason unless on the testimony of two witnesses to the same overt act, or on confession in open court.

2. The Congress shall have power to declare the punishment of treason, but no attainder of treason shall work corruption of blood, or forfeiture except during the life of the person attained.

ARTICLE IV

Section 1. Full faith and credit shall be given in each State to the public acts, records, and judicial proceedings of every other State. And the Congress may by general laws prescribe the manner in which such acts, records and proceedings shall be proved, and the effect thereof.

Section 2. 1. The citizens of each State shall be entitled to all privileges and immunities of citizens in the several States.[8]

2. A person charged in any State with treason, felony, or other crime, who shall flee from justice, and be found in another State, shall on demand of the executive authority of the State from which he fled, be delivered up to be removed to the State having jurisdiction of the crime.

3. No person held to service or labor in one State under the laws thereof, escaping into another, shall, in consequence of any law or regulation therein, be discharged from such service or labor, but shall be delivered up on claim of the party to whom such service or labor may be due.[9]

Section 3. 1. New States may be admitted by the Congress into this Union; but no new State shall be formed or erected within the jurisdiction of any other State, nor any State be formed by the junction of two or more States, or parts of States, without the consent of the legislatures of the States concerned as well as of the Congress.

2. The Congress shall have power to dispose of and make all needful rules and regulations respecting the territory or other property belonging to the United States; and nothing in this Constitution shall be so construed as to prejudice any claims of the United States, or of any particular State.

[5] See the Sixteenth Amendment.

[6] Superseded by the Twelfth Amendment.

[7] See the Eleventh Amendment.

[8] See the Fourteenth Amendment, Sec. 1.

[9] See the Thirteenth Amendment.

Section 4.   The United States shall guarantee to every State in this Union a republican form of government, and shall protect each of them against invasion; and on application of the legislature, or of the executive (when the legislature cannot be convened) against domestic violence.

ARTICLE V

The Congress, whenever two thirds of both Houses shall deem it necessary, shall propose amendments to this Constitution, or, on the application of the legislatures of two thirds of the several States, shall call a convention for proposing amendments, which in either case shall be valid to all intents and purposes, as part of this Constitution, when ratified by the legislatures of three fourths of the several States, or by conventions in three fourths thereof, as the one or the other mode of ratification may be proposed by the Congress; Provided that no amendment which may be made prior to the year one thousand eight hundred and eight shall in any manner affect the first and fourth clauses in the ninth section of the first article; and that no State, without its consent, shall be deprived of its equal suffrage in the Senate.

ARTICLE VI

1. All debts contracted and engagements entered into, before the adoption of this Constitution, shall be as valid against the United States under this Constitution, as under the Confederation.[10]
2. This Constitution, and the laws of the United States which shall be made in pursuance thereof; and all treaties made, or which shall be made, under the authority of the United States, shall be the supreme law of the land; and the judges in every State shall be bound thereby, any thing in the Constitution or laws of any State to the contrary notwithstanding.
3. The senators and representatives before mentioned, and the members of the several State legislatures, and all executive and judicial officers, both of the United States and of the several States, shall be bound by oath or affirmation to support this Constitution; but no religious test shall ever be required as a qualification to any office or public trust under the United States.

ARTICLE VII

The ratification of the conventions of nine States shall be sufficient for the establishment of this Constitution between the States so ratifying the same.

Done in Convention by the unanimous consent of the States present the seventeenth day of September in the year of our Lord one thousand seven hundred and eighty-seven, and of the independence of the United States of America the twelfth. In witness whereof we have hereunto subscribed our names.

[Signatories' names omitted]

Articles in addition to, and amendment of, the Constitution of the United States of America, proposed by Congress, and ratified by the legislatures of the several States, pursuant to the fifth article of the original Constitution.

AMENDMENT I

[First ten amendments ratified December 15, 1791]
Congress shall make no law respecting an establishment of religion, or prohibiting the free exercise thereof; or abridging the freedom of speech, or of the press; or the right of the people peaceably to assemble, and to petition the government for a redress of grievances.

AMENDMENT II

A well regulated militia, being necessary to the security of a free State, the right of the people to keep and bear arms, shall not be infringed.

AMENDMENT III

No soldier shall, in time of peace be quartered in any house, without the consent of the owner, nor in time of war, but in a manner to be prescribed by law.

AMENDMENT IV

The right of the people to be secure in their persons, houses, papers, and effects, against unreasonable searches and seizures, shall not be violated, and no warrants shall issue, but upon probable cause, supported by oath or affirmation, and particularly describing the place to be searched, and the persons or things to be seized.

AMENDMENT V

No person shall be held to answer for a capital or otherwise infamous crime, unless on a presentment or indictment of a grand jury, except in cases arising in the land or naval forces, or in the militia, when in actual service in time of war or public danger; nor shall any person be subject for the same offense to be twice put in jeopardy of life or limb; nor shall be compelled in any criminal case to be a witness against himself, nor be deprived of life, liberty, or property, without due process of law; nor shall private property be taken for public use, without just compensation.

AMENDMENT VI

In all criminal prosecutions, the accused shall enjoy the right to a speedy and public trial, by an impartial jury of the State and district wherein the crime shall have been committed, which district shall have been previously ascertained by law, and to be informed of the nature and cause of the accusation; to be confronted with the witnesses against him; to have compulsory process for obtaining witnesses in his favor, and to have the assistance of counsel for his defense.

AMENDMENT VII

In suits at common law, where the value in controversy shall exceed twenty dollars, the right of trial by jury shall be preserved, and no fact tried by a jury shall be otherwise reexamined in any court of the United States, than according to the rules of the common law.

AMENDMENT VIII

Excessive bail shall not be required, nor excessive fines imposed, nor cruel and unusual punishments inflicted.

AMENDMENT IX

The enumeration in the Constitution of certain rights shall not be construed to deny or disparage others retained by the people.

[10] See the Fourteenth Amendment, Sec. 4.

AMENDMENT X

The powers not delegated to the United States by the Constitution, nor prohibited by it to the States, are reserved to the States respectively, or to the people.

AMENDMENT XI [JANUARY 8, 1798]

The judicial power of the United States shall not be construed to extend to any suit in law or equity, commenced or prosecuted against one of the United States by citizens of another State, or by citizens or subjects of any foreign State.

AMENDMENT XII [SEPTEMBER 25, 1804]

The electors shall meet in their respective States, and vote by ballot for President and Vice President, one of whom, at least, shall not be an inhabitant of the same State with themselves; they shall name in their ballots the person voted for as President, and in distinct ballots, the person voted for as Vice President, and they shall make distinct lists of all persons voted for as President and of all persons voted for as Vice President, and of the number of votes for each, which lists they shall sign and certify, and transmit sealed to the seat of the government of the United States, directed to the President of the Senate;—The President of the Senate shall, in the presence of the Senate and House of Representatives, open all the certificates and the votes shall then be counted;—The person having the greatest number of votes for President, shall be the President, if such number be a majority of the whole number of electors appointed; and if no person have such majority, then from the persons having the highest numbers not exceeding three on the list of those voted for as President, the House of Representatives shall choose immediately, by ballot, the President. But in choosing the President, the votes shall be taken by States, the representation from each State having one vote; a quorum for this purpose shall consist of a member or members from two thirds of the States, and a majority of all the States shall be necessary to a choice. And if the House of Representatives shall not choose a President whenever the right of choice shall devolve upon them, before the fourth day of March next following, then the Vice President shall act as President, as in the case of the death or other constitutional disability of the President. The person having the greatest number of votes as Vice President shall be the Vice President, if such number be a majority of the whole number of electors appointed, and if no person have a majority, then from the two highest numbers on the list, the Senate shall choose the Vice President; a quorum for the purpose shall consist of two thirds of the whole number of Senators, and a majority of the whole number shall be necessary to a choice. But no person constitutionally ineligible to the office of President shall be eligible to that of Vice President of the United States.

AMENDMENT XIII [DECEMBER 18, 1865]

Section 1.   Neither slavery nor involuntary servitude, except as a punishment for crime whereof the party shall have been duly convicted, shall exist within the United States, or any place subject to their jurisdiction.

Section 2.   Congress shall have power to enforce this article by appropriate legislation.

AMENDMENT XIV [JULY 28, 1868]

Section 1.   All persons born or naturalized in the United States, and subject to the jurisdiction thereof, are citizens of the United States and of the State wherein they reside. No State shall make or enforce any law which shall abridge the privileges or immunities of citizens of the United States; nor shall any State deprive any person of life, liberty, or property, without due process of law; nor deny to any person within its jurisdiction the equal protection of the laws.

Section 2.   Representatives shall be apportioned among the several States according to their respective numbers, counting the whole number of persons in each State, excluding Indians not taxed. But when the right to vote at any election for the choice of electors for President and Vice President of the United States, representatives in Congress, the executive and judicial officers of a State, or the members of the legislature thereof, is denied to any of the male inhabitants of such State, being twenty-one years of age, and citizens of the United States, or in any way abridged, except for participating in rebellion, or other crime, the basis of representation there shall be reduced in the proportion which the number of such male citizens shall bear to the whole number of male citizens twenty-one years of age in such State.

Section 3.   No person shall be a senator or representative in Congress, or elector of President and Vice President, or hold any office, civil or military, under the United States, or under any State, who having previously taken an oath, as a member of Congress, or as an officer of the United States, or as a member of any State legislature, or as an executive or judicial officer of any State, to support the Constitution of the United States, shall have engaged in insurrection or rebellion against the same, or given aid or comfort to the enemies thereof. But Congress may by a vote of two thirds of each House, remove such disability.

Section 4.   The validity of the public debt of the United States, authorized by law, including debts incurred for payment of pensions and bounties for services in suppressing insurrection or rebellion; shall not be questioned. But neither the United States nor any State shall assume or pay any debt or obligation incurred in aid of insurrection or rebellion against the United States, or any claim for the loss or emancipation of any slave; but all such debts, obligations, and claims shall be held illegal and void.

Section 5.   The Congress shall have the power to enforce, by appropriate legislation, the provisions of this article.

AMENDMENT XV [MARCH 30, 1870]

Section 1.   The right of citizens of the United States to vote shall not be denied or abridged by the United States or by any State on account of race, color, or previous condition of servitude.

Section 2.   The Congress shall have power to enforce this article by appropriate legislation.

AMENDMENT XVI [FEBRUARY 25, 1913]

The Congress shall have power to lay and collect taxes on incomes, from whatever source derived, without apportionment among the several States, and without regard to any census or enumeration.

AMENDMENT XVII [MAY 31, 1913]

The Senate of the United States shall be composed of two senators from each State, elected by the people thereof, for six years; and each senator shall have one vote. The electors in each State shall have the qualifications requisite for electors of the most numerous branch of the State legislature.

When vacancies happen in the representation of any State in the Senate, the executive authority of such State shall issue writs of election to fill such vacancies: Provided, That the legislature of any State may empower the executive thereof to make temporary appointments until the people fill the vacancies by election as the legislature may direct.

This amendment shall not be so construed as to affect the election or term of any senator chosen before it becomes valid as part of the Constitution.

AMENDMENT XVIII[11] [JANUARY 29, 1919]

After one year from the ratification of this article, the manufacture, sale, or transportation of intoxicating liquors within, the importation thereof into, or the exportation thereof from the United States and all territory subject to the jurisdiction thereof for beverage purposes is thereby prohibited.

The Congress and the several States shall have concurrent power to enforce this article by appropriate legislation.

This article shall be inoperative unless it shall have been ratified as an amendment to the Constitution by the legislatures of the several States, as provided in the constitution, within seven years from the date of the submission hereof to the States by Congress.

AMENDMENT XIX [AUGUST 26, 1920]

The right of citizens of the United States to vote shall not be denied or abridged by the United States or by any State on account of sex.

Congress shall have the power to enforce this article by appropriate legislation.

AMENDMENT XX [JANUARY 23, 1933]

Section 1. The terms of the President and Vice President shall end at noon on the 20th day of January, and the terms of Senators and Representatives at noon on the 3d day of January, of the years in which such terms would have ended if this article had not been ratified; and the terms of their successors shall then begin.

Section 2. The Congress shall assemble at least once in every year, and such meeting shall begin at noon on the 3d day of January, unless they shall by law appoint a different day.

Section 3. If, at the time fixed for the beginning of the term of President, the President-elect shall have died, the Vice President-elect shall become President. If a President shall not have been chosen before the time fixed for the beginning of his term, or if the President-elect shall have failed to qualify, then the Vice President-elect shall act as President until a President shall have qualified; and the Congress may by law provide for the case wherein neither a President-elect nor a Vice President-elect shall have qualified, declaring who shall then act as President, or the manner in which one who is to act shall be selected, and such person shall act accordingly until a President or Vice President shall have qualified.

Section 4. The Congress may by law provide for the case of the death of any of the persons from whom the House of Representatives may choose a President whenever the right of choice shall have devolved upon them, and for the case of the death of any of the persons from whom the Senate may choose a Vice President whenever the right of choice shall have devolved upon them.

Section 5. Sections 1 and 2 shall take effect on the 15th day of October following the ratification of this article.

Section 6. This article shall be inoperative unless it shall have been ratified as an amendment to the Constitution by the legislatures of three-fourths of the several States within seven years from the date of its submission.

AMENDMENT XXI [DECEMBER 5, 1933]

Section 1. The Eighteenth Article of amendment to the Constitution of the United States is hereby repealed.

Section 2. The transportation or importation into any State, Territory, or possession of the United States for delivery or use therein of intoxicating liquors in violation of the laws thereof, is hereby prohibited.

Section 3. This article shall be inoperative unless it shall have been ratified as an amendment to the Constitution by conventions in the several States, as provided in the Constitution, within seven years from the date of the submission thereof to the States by the Congress.

AMENDMENT XXII [MARCH 1, 1951]

No person shall be elected to the office of the President more than twice, and no person who has held the office of President, or acted as President, for more than two years of a term to which some other person was elected President shall be elected to the office of the President more than once.

But this article shall not apply to any person holding the office of President when this article was proposed by the Congress, and shall not prevent any person who may be holding the office of President, or acting as President, during the term within which this article becomes operative from holding the office of President or acting as President during the remainder of such term.

This article shall be inoperative unless it shall have been ratified as an amendment to the Constitution by the legislatures of three-fourths of the several States within seven years from the date of its submission to the States by the Congress.

[11] Repealed by the Twenty-first Amendment

AMENDMENT XXIII [MARCH 29, 1961]

Section 1. The District constituting the seat of Government of the United States shall appoint in such manner as the Congress may direct.

A number of electors of President and Vice President equal to the whole number of Senators and Representatives in Congress to which the District would be entitled if it were a State, but in no event more than the least populous State; they shall be in addition to those appointed by the States, but they shall be considered, for the purposes of the election of President and Vice President, to be electors appointed by a State; and they shall meet in the District and perform such duties as provided by the twelfth article of amendment.

Section 2. The Congress shall have power to enforce this article by appropriate legislation.

AMENDMENT XXIV [JANUARY 23, 1964]

Section 1. The right of citizens of the United States to vote in any primary or other election for President or Vice President, for electors for President or Vice President, or for Senator or Representative in Congress, shall not be denied or abridged by the United States or any State by reason of failure to pay any poll tax or other tax.

Section 2. The Congress shall have power to enforce this article by appropriate legislation.

AMENDMENT XXV [FEBRUARY 10, 1967]

Section 1. In case of the removal of the President from office or of his death or resignation, the Vice President shall become President.

Section 2. Whenever there is a vacancy in the office of the Vice President, the President shall nominate a Vice President who shall take office upon confirmation by a majority of both Houses of Congress.

Section 3. Whenever the President transmits to the President pro tempore of the Senate and the Speaker of the House of Representatives his written declaration that he is unable to discharge the powers and duties of his office, and until he transmits to them a written declaration to the contrary, such powers and duties shall be discharged by the Vice President as Acting President.

Section 4. Whenever the Vice President and a majority of either the principal officers of the executive departments or of such other body as Congress may by law provide, transmit to the President pro tempore of the Senate and the Speaker of the House of Representatives their written declaration that the President is unable to discharge the powers and duties of his office, the Vice President shall immediately assume the powers and duties of the office as Acting President.

Thereafter, when the President transmits to the President pro tempore of the Senate and the Speaker of the House of Representatives his written declaration that no inability exists, he shall resume the powers and duties of his office unless the Vice President and a majority of either the principal officers of the executive departments or of such other body as Congress may by law provide, transmit within four days to the President pro tempore of the Senate and the Speaker of the House of Representatives their written declaration that the President is unable to discharge the powers and duties of his office. Thereupon Congress shall decide the issue, assembling within forty-eight hours for that purpose if not in session. If the Congress, within twenty-one days after receipt of the latter written declaration, or, if Congress is not in session, within twenty-one days after Congress is required to assemble, determines by two-thirds vote of both Houses that the President is unable to discharge the powers and duties of his office, the Vice President shall continue to discharge the same as Acting President; otherwise, the President shall resume the powers and duties of his office.

AMENDMENT XXVI [JUNE 30, 1971]

Section 1. The right of citizens of the United States who are eighteen years of age or older to vote shall not be denied or abridged by the United States or by any State on account of age.

Section 2. The Congress shall have power to enforce this article by appropriate legislation.

AMENDMENT XXVII[12] [MAY 7, 1992]

No law, varying the compensation for services of the Senators and Representatives, shall take effect until an election of Representatives shall have intervened.

[12] James Madison proposed this amendment in 1789 together with the ten amendments that were adopted as the Bill of Rights, but it failed to win ratification at the time. Congress, however, had set no deadline for its ratification, and over the years—particularly in the 1980s and 1990s—many states voted to add it to the Constitution. With the ratification of Michigan in 1992 it passed the threshold of 3/4ths of the states required for adoption, but because the process took more than 200 years, its validity remains in doubt.

SOURCES

Chapter 15 Reconstruction, 1865–1877

Federal Reconstruction Policy

By far the best source on federal Reconstruction policy is Eric Foner, *Reconstruction: America's Unfinished Revolution, 1863–1877* (New York: Harper & Row, 1988); See also Eric Foner, *The Fiery Trial*; John David Smith, *Black Voices From Reconstruction, 1865–1877* (Gainesville: University Press of Florida, 1997); Francis E. Abernethy, Patrick B. Mullen, Alan B. Govenar, editors, *Juneteenth Texas: Essays in African American Folklore* (Denton; University of North Texas Press, 1996); Henry Mayer, *All on Fire: William Lloyd Garrison and the Abolition of Slavery* (New York: St. Martin's Press, 1998); F. Douglass, "What the Black Man Wants," Sojourner Truth , 1867 speech in New York City, reprinted in Herb Boyd, editor, *Autobiography of a People* (New York: Anchor Books, 2000); and for election results www.uselectionatlas.org/RESULTS/national.php?year=1868&off=0&f=1 and www.uselectionatlas.org.

The Impact of Reconstruction

Foner, *Reconstruction*, remains a key work. See also William L. Clay, *Just Permanent Interests: Black Americans in Congress, 1870–1992* (New York: Amistad Press, 1993),; John David Smith, *Black Voices From Reconstruction, 1865–1877* (Gainesville: University Press of Florida, 1997); W. E. B. DuBois, *Black Reconstruction in America* (1903, reprinted Boston: Bedford Books, 1997); W. E. B. DuBois, *The Souls of Black Folk* (1903, reprint New York: Crest, 1961); Brenda Stevenson, editor, *The Journals of Charlotte Forten Grimke* (New York: Oxford University Press, 1988); James D. Anderson, *The Education of Blacks in the South, 1860–1935* (Chapel Hill: University of North Carolina Press, 1988); Frederick Douglass, *Narrative of the Life of Frederick Douglass: An American Slave* (1845; Cambridge: Harvard University Press, 1967); Maria S. Waterbury, *Seven Years Among the Freedmen*, cited in Nancy Hoffman, *Woman's "True" Profession: Voices from the History of Teaching* (New York: Feminist Press, 1981); Rupert Sargent Holland, editor, *Letters and Diary of Laura M. Towne* (1912; reprint New York: Negro Universities Press, 1969); and especially Ronald E. Butchart, *Schooling the Freed People: Teaching, Learning, and the Struggle for Black Freedom, 1861–1876* (Chapel Hill: University of North Carolina Press, 2010).

Terror, Apathy, and the Creation of the Segregated South

See Foner, *Reconstruction*; Nicholas Lemann, *Redemption: The Last Battle of the Civil War* (New York: Farrar, Straus and Giroux, 2006); Mary Drake McFeely and William S. McFeely, "Chronology" in Ulysses S. Grant, *Memoirs and Selected Letters* (New York: The Library of American, 1990); Charles Lane, *The Day Freedom Died: The Colfax Massacre, the Supreme Court, and the Betrayal of Reconstruction* (New York: Henry Holt, 2008); Frances Smith Foster, "Introduction" to Frances E. W. Harper, *Iola Leroy* (1892; reprinted New York: Oxford University Press, 1988); and C. Vann Woodward, *The Strange Career of Jim Crow* (New York: Oxford University Press, 1966). See also "Speech on September 3, 1868, before the Georgia State Legislature," and Frances Ellen Watkins Harper, "An Address Delivered at the Centennial Anniversary of the Pennsylvania Society for Promoting the Abolition of Slavery, 1875," reprinted in Manning Marable and Leith Mullings, editors, *Let Nobody Turn Us Around: An African American Anthology* (Lanham, MD: Rowman & Littlefield, 2000), pp. 131–134 and pp. 138–143.

Chapter 16 Conflict in the West, 1865–1912

The Tribes of the West and the U.S. Government

Two excellent studies of the Comanche Empire have recently been published, Pekka Hamalainen, *The Comanche Empire* (New Haven: Yale University Press, 2008) and S.C. Gwynne's *Empire of the Summer Moon* ();Robert M. Utley, *The Indian Frontier, 1846–1890*, Revised Edition (Albuquerque: University of New Mexico Press, 1984); Joan Waugh, *U.S. Grant: American Hero, American Myth* (Chapel Hill: University of North Carolina Press, 2009); Thomas Powers, *The Killing of Crazy Horse* (New York: Alfred A. Knopf, 2010); Nathaniel Philbrock, *The Last Stand: Custer, Sitting Bull, and the Battle of the Little Bighorn* (New York: Viking, 2010); Ellen Fitzpatrick, *History's Memory: Writing America's Past, 1880–1980* (Cambridge: Harvard University Press, 2004); David Wallace Adams, *Education for Extinction: American Indians and the Boarding School Experience, 1875–1928* (Lawrence: University Press of Kansas, 1995); Francis Paul Prucha, *The Great Father: The United States Government and the American Indians*, 2 vols. (Lincoln, 1984).

The Impact of the Transcontinental Railroad, 1869

Richard White, *Railroaded: The Transcontinentals and the Making of Modern America* (New York: W. W. Norton, 2011); Craig Miner, *The Most Magnificent Machine: America Adopts the Railroad, 1825–1862* (Lawrence, University Press of Kansas, 2010).

The Transformation of the West

Clyde A. Milner II, Carol A. O'Connor, Martha A. Sandweiss, *The Oxford History of the American West* (New York: Oxford University Press, 1994); Lewis Atherton, *The Cattle Kings* (Bloomington: Indiana University Press, 1961); E. E. Dale, *The Range Cattle Industry*, 2nd. ed. (Norman: University of Oklahoma Press, 1960); Rosenbaum, *Mexicano Resistance in the Southwest*; Andrew Bancroft Schlesinger, "Las Gorras Blancas, 1889–1891," *The Journal of Mexican American History* I:2 (Spring 1971), 94–97.

Chapter 17 The Gilded Age: Building a Technological and Industrial Giant and a New Social Order, 1876–1913

Technology Changes the Nation

The Free Library of Philadelphia, Centennial Exhibition Digital Collection http://libwww.freelibrary.org/CenCol/exh-org.htm downloaded November 29, 2010; Sean Dennis Cashman, *America in the Gilded Age: From the Death of Lincoln to the Rise of Theodore Roosevelt*, Third Edition (New York: New University Press, 1993); Pauline Maier, Merritt Roe Smith, Alexander Keyssar, Daniel J. Kevles, *Inventing America: A History of the United States* (New York: W. W.

Norton, 2006), pp. 632–634; Jackson Lears, *Rebirth of a Nation: The Making of Modern America, 1877–1920* (New York: HarperCollins, 2009).

Corporations and Monopolies

H. W. Brands, *American Colossus: The Triumph of Capitalism, 1865–1900* (New York: Doubleday, 2010); T. J. Stiles, *The First Tycoon: The Epic Life of Cornelius Vanderbilt* (New York: Alfred A. Knopf, 2009); Jackson Lears, *Rebirth of a Nation: The Making of Modern America, 1877–1920* (New York: Harper, 2009).

Lives of the Middle Class in the Gilded Age

H. W. Brands, *American Colossus: The Triumph of Capitalism, 1865–1900* is also important for understanding daily life. See also George M. Marsden, *Understanding Fundamentalism and Evangelicalism* (Grand Rapids, MI: William B. Eerdman's, 1991); George M. Marsden, *Fundamentalism and American Culture*, Second Edition (New York: Oxford University Press, 2006); Sean Dennis Cashman, *America in the Gilded Age: From the Death of Lincoln to the Rise of Theodore Roosevelt*.

Immigration

Ronald Takaki, *A Different Mirror: A History of Multicultural America* (Boston: Little, Brown, 1993); Hamilton Holt, editor *The Life Stories of Undistinguished Americans as Told by Themselves* (originally 1906, republished New York: Routledge, 2000); David Von Drehle, *Triangle: The Fire That Changed America* (New York: Atlantic Monthly Press, 2003); "Italians," in Stephan Thernstrom, editor, *Harvard Encyclopedia of American Ethnic Groups* (Cambridge: The Belknap Press of Harvard University, 1980); Iris Chang, *The Chinese in America: A Narrative History* (New York: Viking, 2003); Herbert J. Gans, *The Urban Villagers: Group and Class in the Life of Italian-Americans* (New York: The Free Press, 1962); http://www.ellisisland.org/genealogy/ellis_island_history.sap, retrieved December 12, 2010; http://www.TaylorStreetArchives.com, retrieved December 12, 2010; http://faculty.marianopolis.edu/c.belanger/quebechistory/readings/leaving.htm, retrieved December 12, 2010.

Chapter 18 Responses to Industrialism, Responses to Change, 1877–1914

Conflict in the New South

Edward L. Ayers, *The Promise of the New South*, 15th Anniversary Edition (New York: Oxford University Press, 2007).

The Politics of Conflict—From Populist Movement to Populist Party

Charles Postel, *The Populist Vision* (New York: Oxford University Press, 2007); Michael Kazin, *The Populist Persuasion* (New York: Basic Books, 1995).

Worker Protest and the Rise of Organized Labor

Nell Irvin Painter, *Standing at Armageddon: The United States, 1877–1919* (New York: W. W. Norton, 2008); Michael A. Bellesiles, *1877: America's Year of Living Violently* (New York: The New Press, 2010); James Green, *Death in the Haymarket: A Story of Chicago, the First Labor Movement and the Bombing that Divided Gilded Age America* (New York: Random House, 2006); Nick Salvatore, *Eugene V. Debs: Citizen and Socialist* (Urbana: University of Illinois Press, 1984); Elliott J. Gorn, *Mother Jones: The Most Dangerous Woman in America* (New York: Hill & Wang, 2001); J. Anthony Lukas, *Big Trouble* (New York: touchstone, 1997); Patrick Renshaw, *The Wobblies: the Story of the IWW and Syndicalism in the United States* (Chicago: Ivan R. Dee, 1967, 1999); David Von Drehle, *Triangle: The Fire that Changed America* (New York: Atlantic Monthly Press, 2003); Philip Foner, *Women and the American Labor Movement* (New York: Free Press, 1980); Thomas G. Andrews, *Killing for Coal: America's Deadliest Labor War* (Cambridge: Harvard University Press, 2008).

Chapter 19 Progressive Movements, Progressive Politics, 1879–1917

The Revolt of the Intellectuals

Nell Irvin Painter, *Standing at Armageddon: The United States, 1877–1919* (New York: W. W. Norton, 2008); Louis Menand, *The Metaphysical Club* (New York: Farrar, Straus and Giroux, 2001). A number of earlier works are also helpful in understanding the emergence of progressivism including, Samuel Hays, *The Response to Industrialism* (1957); Robert Wiebe, *The Search for Order* (1967); Gabriel Kolko, *The Triumph of Conservativism* (1963); Richard Hofstadter, *The Age of Reform* (1955); Henry George, *Progress and Poverty: An Inquiry into the Cause of Industrial Depressions and of Increase of want with Increase of Wealth* (originally 1879, reprinted New York: The Modern Library, 1929), pp. 3, 5, 405.

The Transformation of the Cities

Jay P. Dolan, *The Irish Americans: A History* (New York: Bloomsbury Press, 2008); William L. Riordon, *Plunkitt of Tammany Hall* (originally 1905, New York; E. P. Dutton, 1963); Richard Hofstadter, *The Age of Reform: From Bryan to F.D.R.* (New York, 1955); Lincoln Steffens, *The Autobiography of Lincoln Steffens* (New York: The Literary Guild, 1931); Allan Nevins, *Grover Cleveland: A Study in Courage* (1932); Don Lochbiler, "The Shoemaker Who Looked Like a King," from the Detroit News, Michigan History archive, http://apps.detnews.com/apps/history/index.php?id=175, downloaded December 28, 2010; "Samuel M. Jones," and "Brand Whitlock," Ohio Historical Society, Ohio History Central, http://www.ohiohistory-central.org, downloaded December 28, 2010; John Dewey, *The School and Society* (Chicago: University of Chicago Press, 1899); David Tyack & Elisabeth Hansot, *Managers of Virtue: Public School Leadership in America, 1820–1980* (New York: Basic Books, 1982); Mari Jo Buhle, Teresa Murphy, and Jane Gerhard, *Women and the Making of America* (Upper Saddle River, NJ: Pearson Prentice Hall, 2009); Edwin S. Gaustad, *A Documentary History of Religion in America Since 1865* (Grand Rapids: William B. Eerdmans, 1998); Jane Addams, *Twenty Years at Hull House* (originally published 1910, republished New York; Penguin Putnam, 1961); Jane Addams, *Democracy and Social Ethics* (New York: Macmillan, 1913); Jane Addams, *The Spirit* of Youth and the City Streets (New York: Macmillan Company, 1909; Champaign: University of Illinois Press, 1972); Allen F. Davis, *Spearheads for Reform: The Social Settlements and the Progressive Movement* (New York: Oxford University Press, 1967); Lawrence A. Cremin, *The Transformation of the School: Progressivism in American Education, 1876–1957* (1961).

Progressive Politics on the National Stage

Edmund Morris, *Theodore Rex* (New York: Random House, 2001); Sean Dennis Cashman, *America in the Gilded Age: From the Death of Lincoln to the Rise of Theodore Roosevelt*, third edition (New York: New York University Press, 1993); Douglas Brinkley, *The Wilderness Warrior: Theodore Roosevelt and the Crusade for America* (New York: Harper Collins, 2009); James Chace, *1912: Wilson, Roosevelt, Taft & Debs—the Election That Changed the Country* (New York: Simon & Schuster, 2004); John Milton Cooper, Jr., *Woodrow Wilson: A Biography* (New York: Alfred A. Knopf, 2009).

Chapter 20 Foreign Policy and War in the Progressive Era, 1890–1919

The most useful source for all parts of this chapter is George C. Herring, *From Colony to Superpower: U.S. Foreign Relations Since 1776* (New York: Oxford University Press, 2008). See also Jay P. Dolan, *The Irish Americans: A History* (New York: Bloomsbury Press, 2008); Adam Hochschild, *King Leopold's Ghost: A Story of Greed, Terror, and Heroism in colonial Africa* (Boston: Houghton Mifflin, 1998); Sydney E. Ahlstrom, *A Religious History of the American People* (New Haven: Yale University Press, 2004); Sean Dennis Cashman, *America in the Gilded Age: From the Death of Lincoln to the Rise of Theodore Roosevelt*, Third Edition (New York: New York University Press, 1993); Michael McGerr, *A Fierce Discontent: The Rise and Fall of the Progressive Movement in America* (New York: Oxford University Press,); John Milton Cooper, Jr., *Woodrow Wilson: A Biography* (New York: Alfred A. Knopf, 2009); and Adam Hochschild, *To End All Wars: A Story of Loyalty and Rebellion, 1914–1918* (New York: Houghton Mifflin Harcourt, 2011).

Chapter 21 A Unique, Prosperous, and Discontented Time, 1919–1929

The Prelude—The Red Summer of 1919

Frederick Lewis Allen, *Only Yesterday: An Informal History of the Nineteen-Twenties* (New York: Harper & Row, 1931); Nancy F. Cott, editor, *No Small Courage: A History of Women in the United States* (New York: Oxford University Press, 2000); Vicki L. Ruiz, From Out of the Shadows: Mexican Women in Twentieth Century America (New York: Oxford University Press, 2008).

The 1920s—The Exuberance of Prosperity

Michael A. Lerner, Dry *Manhattan: Prohibition in New York City* (Cambridge: Harvard University Press, 2007); Daniel Okrent, *Last Call: The Rise and Fall of Prohibition* (New York: Scribner, 2010); Thomas M. Coffey, *The Long Thirst: Prohibition in America: 1920–1933* (New York: W. W. Norton, 1975); Linda Gordon, *Woman's Body, Woman's Right: A Social History of Birth Control in America* (New York: Penguin Books, 1977); James Reed, *From Private Vice to Public Virtue: The Birth Control Movement and American Society Since 1930* (New York: Basic Books, 1978); Pauline Maier, Merritt Roe Smith, Alexander Keyssar, Daniel j. Kevles, *Inventing America: A History of the United States*, second edition (New York: W. W. Norton, 2006).

The 1920s—The Conflicts about American Ideals

David J. Goldberg, *Discontented America: The United States in the 1920s* (Baltimore: The Johns Hopkins University Press, 1999); John M. Barry, *Rising Tide: The Great Mississippi Flood and How It Changed America* (New York: Simon & Schuster, 1997); Daniel J. Kevles, *In the Name of Eugenics: Genetics and the Uses of Human Heredity* (New York: Knopf, 1985); *Race and Membership in American History: The Eugenics Movement* (Boston: Facing History and Ourselves); Aristide R. Zolberg, *A Nation By Design: Immigration Policy in the Fashioning of America* (Cambridge: Harvard University Press, 2006); E. David Cronon, *Black Moses: The Story of Marcus Garvey* (Madison: University of Wisconsin Press, 1955, 1969); and John Hope Franklin and Alfred A. Moss, *From Slavery to Freedom: A History of African Americans* (New York: Alfred A. Knopf, 1994).

Harding, Coolidge, and Hoover—National Politics and Policies in the 1920s

Phillip G. Payne, *Dead Last: The Public Memory of Warren G. Harding's Scandalous Legacy* (Athens: Ohio University Press, 2009).

Chapter 22 Living in Hard Times, 1929–1939

The Coming of the Great Depression

John Kenneth Galbraith, *The Great Crash, 1929* (originally 1955, republished Boston: Houghton Mifflin, 1997); Michael Bernstein, *The Great Depression: Delayed Recovery and Economic Change in America, 1929–1939* (1987); David Burner, *Herbert Hoover: A Public Life* (New York: Knopf, 1979); William J. Barber, *From New Era to New Deal: Herbert Hoover, the Economists, and American Economic Policy, 1921–1933* (Cambridge: Cambridge University Press, 1985).

The New Deal

Anthony J. Badger, *FDR: The First Hundred Days* (New York: Hill & Wang, 2008); Irving Bernstein, *A Caring Society: The New Deal, the Worker, and the Great Depression* (Boston: Houghton Mifflin, 1985); Lewis Meriam, et al., *The Problem of Indian Administration* (Baltimore: Johns Hopkins University Press, 1928); John Hope Franklin and Alfred A. Moss, Jr., *From Slavery to Freedom: A History of African Americans*, seventh edition (New York: Knopf, 1994); Sarah Jane Deutsch, "From Ballots to Breadlines: 1920–1940," in Nancy F. Cott, editor, *No Small Courage: A History of Women in the United States* (New York: Oxford University Press, 2000), p. 457–460; Timothy Egan, *The Worst Hard Time* (Boston: Houghton Mifflin, 2006), pp. 112–141; Joe Klein, *Woody Guthrie: A Life* (New York: Random House, 1980), pp. 112–141; John Steinbeck, The Grapes of Wrath (New York: the Viking Press, 1939); Manuel G. Gonzales, *Mexicanos: A History of Mexicans in the United States* (Bloomington, University of Indiana Press, 2009); David M. Kennedy, *Freedom From Fear: The American People in Depression and War, 1929–1945* (New York: Oxford University Press, 1999), pp. 254–257; Linda Gordon, *Dorothea Lange: A Life Beyond Limits*

(New York: W. W. Norton, 2009); Eric Foner, *The Story of American Freedom* (New York: W. W. Norton, 1998); Sidney Fine, *Sit-Down: The General Motors Strike of 1936–1937* (Ann Arbor: University of Michigan Press, 1969); Kim Phillips-Fein, *Invisible Hands: The Businessmen's Crusade Against the New Deal* (New York: W. W. Norton, 2009); James MacGregor Burns, *Roosevelt: The Lion and the Fox* (New York: Harcourt Brace, 1956).

The Deep Roots of War—The United States, Europe, and Asia

In my description of the roots of World War II, I have depended primarily on David M. Kennedy, *Freedom From Fear: The American People in Depression and War, 1929–1945* (New York: Oxford University Press, 1999) and George C. Herring, *From Colony to Superpower: U.S. Foreign Relations Since 1776* (New York: Oxford University Press, 2008).

Chapter 23 Living in a World at War, 1939–1945

Preparedness and Isolation 1939–1941

David M. Kennedy, *Freedom From Fear: The American People in Depression and War, 1929–1945* (New York: Oxford University Press, 1999) and George C. Herring, *From Colony to Superpower: U.S. Foreign Relations Since 1776* (New York: Oxford University Press, 2008).

Mass Mobilization in a Society at War

Kennedy and Herring remain the key sources for all sections of this chapter. See also Tom Brokaw, *The Greatest Generation* (New York: Random House, 1998); Charles E. Francis, *The Tuskegee Airmen* (Boston: Branden Publishing Company, 1993); Zachary Bullock, "Teaching Objection: How Textbooks Distort and Lie About Conscientious Objection to World War II," *Rethinking Schools*, Vol. 23, No. 3 (Spring, 2009); See individual biographies in www.navajocodetalkers.org (downloaded May 1, 2011) and www.nps.gov/pwro/collection/website (downloaded April 15, 2011); A. Philip Randolph, in Herb Boyd, *Autobiography of a People* (New York: Anchor Books, 2001), pp. 309–310; John Hope Franklin and Alfred A. Moss, Jr., *From Slavery to Freedom: A History of African Americans*, seventh edition (New York: Alfred A. Knopf, 1994), pp. 436–437; Peter Irons, *The Courage of Their Convictions: Sixteen Americans Who Fought Their Way to the Supreme Court* (New York: Penguin Books, 1990).

Industrial Strength, Industrial Prosperity

Again, Kennedy and Herring are key.

Winning a World War—North Africa, Europe, Asia, the Pacific, 1943–1945

In addition to Kennedy and herring see Michael Norman and Elizabeth M. Norman, *Tears in the Darkness: The Story of the Bataan Death March and its Aftermath* (New York: Farrar, Straus and Giroux, 2009); Elliott Johnson, "D-Day and All That," an interview in Studs Terkel, *"The Good War"* (New York: The New Press, 1984), pp. 254–264; Felix L. Sparks, "An Oral History," interview by William C. McClearn, *The Colorado Lawyer*, Vol. 27, No. 10 (October, 1998), downloaded from www.cobar.org May 8, 2011; U.S. Holocaust Museum www.ushmm.org downloaded May 7, 2011.

Chapter 24 The World the War Created, 1945–1952

The United States in 1945

James T. Patterson, *Grand Expectations: The United States, 1945–1974* (New York: Oxford University Press, 1996); David Halberstam, *The Fifties* (New York: Random House, 1993); Elaine Tyler May, *Homeward Bound: American Families in the Cold War Era*, Revised Edition (New York: Basic Books, 2008); Kenneth T. Jackson, *Crabgrass Frontier: The Suburbanization of the United States* (New York: Oxford University Press, 1985); Nicholas Lemann, *The Promised Land: The Great Black Migration and How It Changed America* (New York: Vintage, 1992); Isabel Wilkerson, *The Warmth of Other Suns: The Epic Story of America's Great Migration* (New York: Random House, 2010); Ira Berlin, *The Making of African America: The Four Great Migrations* (New York: Viking, 2010); Stanley Meisler, *United Nations: The First Fifty Years* (New York: The Atlantic Monthly Press, 1995); Alfred E. Eckes, Jr., *A Search for Solvency: Bretton Woods and the International Monetary System, 1941–1971* (Austin: University of Texas Press, 1975); Robert L. Heilbroner, *The Worldly Philosophers: The Lives, Times, and Ideas of the Great Economic Thinkers*, seventh edition (New York: Touchstone, 1995).

The Cold War Begins

James T. Patterson, *Grand Expectations: The United States, 1945–1974* (New York: Oxford University Press, 1996); George C. Herring, *From Colony to Superpower: U.S. Foreign Relations Since 1776* (New York: Oxford University Press, 2008); John Lewis Gaddis, *The United States and the Origins of the Cold War, 1941–1947* (New York: Columbia University Press, 1972); Arnold A. Offner, *Another Such Victory: President Truman and the Cold War, 1945–1953* (Stanford: Stanford University Press, 2002); Thomas G. Paterson, editor, *Cold War Critics: Alternatives to American Foreign Policy in the Truman Years* (Chicago: Quadrangle Books, 1971); Richard Hofstadter, *The Paranoid Style in American Politics and Other Essays* (Cambridge: Harvard University Press, 1996).

Politics, 1948–1952

James T. Patterson, *Grand Expectations: The United States, 1945–1974* (New York: Oxford University Press, 1996).

Chapter 25 Complacency and Change, 1952–1965

Eisenhower's America, America's World

James T. Patterson, *Grand Expectations: The United States, 1945–1974* (New York: Oxford University Press, 1996); George C. Herring, *From Colony to Superpower: U.S. Foreign Relations Since 1776* (New York: Oxford University Press, 2008); Theodore H. White, *The Making of the President, 1960* ().

A Culture on the Move

James T. Patterson, *Grand Expectations: The United States, 1945–1974* (New York: Oxford University Press, 1996); David Halberstam, *The Fifties* (New York: Random House, 1993).

Race and Civil Rights

Richard Kluger, *Simple Justice: A History of "Brown v. Board of Education" and Black America's Struggle for Equality* (New York: Alfred A. Knopf, 1975); Anne Moody, *Coming of Age in Mississippi* (New York: Laurel, 1968); Cynthia Stokes Brown, editor, *Ready from Within: Septima*

Clark and the Civil Rights Movement (Trenton, NJ: Africa World Press, 1990); John Hope Franklin and Alfred A. Moss Jr., *From Slavery to Freedom: A History of African Americans*, seventh edition (New York: Alfred A. Knopf, 1994); Henry Louis Gates Jr. and Cornel West, *The African American Century* (New York: The Free Press, 2000); Taylor Branch, *Parting the Waters: America in the King Years, 1954–1963* (New York: Simon & Schuster, 1988); Taylor Branch, *Pillar of Fire: America in the King Years, 1963–1965* (New York: Simon & Schuster, 1998); Kenneth B. Clark, interview in Studs Terkel, *Race: How Blacks and Whites Think and Feel About the American Obsession* (New York: New Press, 1992); Daisy Bates, *The Long Shadow at Little Rock* (Fayetteville: the University of Arkansas Press, 1962); James M. Washington, editor, *A Testament of Hope: The Essential Writings and Speeches of Martin Luther King, Jr.* (San Francisco: Harper San Francisco, 1986); Manning Marable, *Malcolm X: A Life of Reinvention* (New York: Viking, 2011); Malcolm X, *The Autobiography of Malcolm X* (New York: Grove Press, 1965); Kofi Natambu, *The Life and Work of Malcolm X* (Indianapolis: Alpha Books, 2002).

Chapter 26 Lives Changed, 1961–1968

New Voices, New Authorities

James T. Patterson, *Grand Expectations: The United States, 1945–1974* (New York: Oxford University Press, 1996); Todd Gitlin, *The Sixties: Years of Hope, Days of Rage* (New York: Bantam Books, 1987); Jane Jacobs Obituary, *New York Times*, April 25, 2006; Michael Harrington, *The Other America* (New York: Macmillan, 1962).

Camelot, the White House, and Dallas—The Kennedy Administration

Arthur M. Schlesinger, Jr., *A Thousand Days: John F. Kennedy in the White House* (Boston: Houghton Mifflin Company, 1965); Frederick Kempe, *Berlin 1961: Kennedy, Khrushchev, and the Most Dangerous Place on Earth* (New York: G.P. Putnam's Sons, 2011); James T. Patterson, *Grand Expectations: The United States, 1945–1974* (New York: Oxford University Press, 1996).

The Coming of Lyndon B. Johnson

For the most thorough although sometimes quite biased and still incomplete study of LBJ, see Robert Caro's multi volume political biography, *The Years of Lyndon Johnson* including *The Path to Power* (New York: Alfred A. Knopf, 1982), *Means of Ascent* (1989), *Master of the Senate* (2002), *The Passage of Power* (2012); see also Doris Kearns, *Lyndon Johnson and the American Dream* (New York: St. Martin's Press, 1976); Todd Gitlin, *The Sixties: Years of Hope, Days of Rage* (New York: Bantam Books, 1987); Alexander Bloom and Wini Breines, editors, *"Takin' it to the Streets": A Sixties Reader* second edition (New York: Oxford University Press, 2003); George C. Herring, *From Colony to Superpower: U.S. Foreign Relations Since 1776* (New York: Oxford University Press, 2008); John Hagan, *Northern Passage: American Vietnam War Resisters in Canada* (Cambridge: Harvard University Press, 2001).

Chapter 27 Rights, Reaction, and Limits, 1968–1980

The New Politics of the Late 1960s

Kevin P. Phillips, *The Emerging Republican Majority* (New Rochelle, NY: Arlington House, 1969); Lisa McGirr, *Suburban Warriors: The Origins of the New American Right* (Princeton: Princeton University Press, 2001); Kim Phillips-Fein, *Invisible Hands: The Businessmen's Crusade Against the New Deal* (New York: W. W. Norton, 2009); Bruce J. Schulman, *The Seventies: The Great Shift in American Culture, Society, and Politics* (Cambridge, MA: Da Capo Press, 2002); George C. Herring, *From Colony to Superpower: U.S. Foreign Relations Since 1776* (New York: Oxford University Press, 2008); Joel Brinkley, *Cambodia's Curse: The Modern History of a Troubled Land* (New York: Public Affair, 2011).

The Movements of the 1960s and 1970s

Susan Brownmiller, *In Our Time: Memoir of a Revolution* (New York: Delta, 1999); Sara M. Evans, *Tidal Wave: How Women Changed America at Century's End* (New York: Free Press, 2003); and Nancy F. Cott, editor, *No Small Courage: A History of Women in the United States* (New York: Oxford University Press, 2000); Barbara Smith, *All the Women Are White, All the Blacks are Men, But Some of Us Are Brave: Black Women's Studies* (New York: the Feminist Press, 1982); Florence Howe, *A Life in Motion* (New York: The Feminist Press, 2011). For the development of *Our Bodies, Ourselves*, see www.ourbodiesoutselves.org/about/history.asp, downloaded July 10, 2011; Katherine Hanson, Vivian Guilfoy, and Sarita Pillai, *More Than Title IX: How Equity in Education Has Shaped the Nation* (Lanham, MD: Rowman & Littlefield, 2009); Marshall Ganz, *Why David Sometimes Wins: Leadership, Organization, and Strategy in the California Farm Worker Movement* (New York: Oxford University Press, 2009); Ronald B. Taylor, *Chavez and the Farm Workers* (Boston: Beacon Press, 1975); Mark Day, *Forty Acres: Cesar Chavez and the Farm Workers* (New York: Praeger, 1971); Ronald Takaki, *A Different Mirror: A History of Multicultural America* (Boston: Little, Brown, 1993); J. Craig Jenkins, *The Politics of Insurgency: The Farm Worker Movement in the 1960s* (New York: Columbia University Press, 1985); Paul Chaat Smith and Robert Allen Warrior, *Like a Hurricane: The Indian Movement from Alcatraz to Wounded Knee* (New York: The New Press, 1996); William Hagan, *American Indians* (Chicago: University of Chicago Press, 1961, 1993); Joseph M. Cronin, *Reforming Boston Schools, 1930 to the Present: Overcoming Corruption and Racial Segregation* (New York: Palgrave, 2011); Jerald E. Podair, *The Strike That Changed New York: Blacks, Whites, and the Ocean –Hill Brownsville Crisis* (New Haven: Yale University Press, 2002); Shirley Brice Heath and Milbrey W. McLaughlin, editors, *Identity and Inner-City Youth: Beyond Ethnicity and Gender* (New York: Teachers College Press, 1993); Allen J. Matusow, *The Unraveling of America: A History of Liberalism* (New York: Harper & Row, 1984); Todd Gitlin, *The Sixties: Years of Hope, Days of Rage* (New York: Bantam, 1987, 1993).

The Culture Wars of the 1970s

Donald T. Critchlow, *Phyllis Schlafly and Grassroots Conservatism: A Woman's Crusade* (Princeton: Princeton University Press, 2005); Phyllis Schlafly, *Feminist Fantasies* (Dallas: Spence publishing Company, 2003); Catherine E. Rymph, *Republican Women: Feminism and Conservatism From Suffrage Through the Rise of the New Right* (Chapel Hill: The University of North Carolina Press, 2006); Leon Friedman and William F. Levantrosser, *Richard M.. Nixon: Politician, President, Administrator* (New York: Greenwood Press, 1991); Nancy F. Cott, editor, *No Small Courage: A History of Women in the United States* (New York: Oxford University Press, 2000), pp. 529–586; Edwin Gaustad and Leigh Schmidt, *The Religious History of America* (New York: Harper Collins, 2002), pp. 329–427; Bruce J. Schulman, *The Seventies: The Great Shift in American Culture, Society, And Politics* (New York: DeCapo Press, 2002).

Politics, Economics, and the Impact of Watergate

James T. Patterson, *Restless Giant: The United States from Watergate to Bush v. Gore* (New York: Oxford University Press, 2005); Timothy Moy, "Culture, Technology, and the Cult of Tech in the 1970s," in Beth Bailey & David Farber, editors, *America in the Seventies* (Lawrence: University Press of Kansas, 2004); Johnny Ryan, *A History of the Internet and the Digital Future* (London, England: Reaktion Books, 2010); Roy A. Allan, *A History of the Personal Computer: The People and the Technology* (London, Ontario, Canada: Allan Publishing, 2001); Malcolm Gladwell, "Annals of Business, Creation Myth: Xerox PARC, Apple, and the Truth about Innovation," *The New Yorker* (May 16, 2011), pp. 44–53; Jimmy Carter, *White House Diary* (New York: Farrar, Straus, and Giroux, 2010).

Chapter 28 The Reagan Revolution, 1980–1989

A Rapidly Changing U.S. Government

James T. Patterson, *Restless Giant: the United States From Watergate to Bush v. Gore* (New York: Oxford University Press, 2005); Robert Dallek, *Ronald Reagan: The Politics of Symbolism*, With a New Preface (Cambridge: Harvard University Press1984, 1999); John Ehrman and Michael W. Flamm, *Debating the Reagan Presidency* (Lanham, MD: Rowman & Littlefield, 2009); George C. Herring, *From Colony to Superpower: U.S. Foreign Relations Since 1776* (New York: Oxford University Press.

The Changing Nature of the American Economy

Kevin Phillips, *Boiling Point: Republicans, Democrats, and the Decline of Middle-Class Prosperity* (New York: Random House, 1993); Robert B. Reich, *The Work of Nations* (New York: Random House, 1991); James B. Stewart, *Den of Thieves* (New York: Simon & Schuster, 1991); Kathleen Day, *S & L Hell* (New York: W. W. Norton, 1993).

Changes in the Rest of the Country

Ed Ward, Geoffrey Stokes, and Ken Tucker, *Rock of Ages* (New York: Rolling Stone Press, 1986); Haynes Johnson, *Sleepwalking Through History* (New York: Anchor Books, 1992); Stuart A. Kallen, *A Cultural History of the United States Through the Decades: The 1980s* (San Diego, CA: Lucent Books, 1999); Justin Watson, *The Christian Coalition: Dreams of Restoration, Demands for Recognition* (New York: St. Martin's Press, 1997); Jonathan Zimmerman, *Whose America? Culture Wars in Public Schools* (Cambridge: Harvard University Press, 2002); Aristide R. Zolberg, *A Nation by Design: Immigration Policy in the Fashioning of America* (Cambridge: Harvard University Press, 2006); Daniel J. Tichenor, *Dividing Lines: the Politics of Immigration Control in America* (Princeton: Princeton University Press, 2002); Christopher L. Miller, "Coyote's Game: Indian Casinos and the Indian Presence in Contemporary America," in Sterling Evans, editor, *American Indians in American History, 1870–2001* (Westport, CT: Praeger, 2002); M.E. Melody and Linda M. Peterson, *Teaching America About Sex: Marriage Guides and Sex Manuals from the Late Victorians to Dr. Ruth* (New York: New York University Press, 1999); C. Everett Koop, *Koop: The Memoirs of America's Family Doctor* (New York: Random House, 1991); James T. Patterson, *Restless Giant: the United States From Watergate to Bush v. Gore* (New York: Oxford University Press, 2005).

Chapter 29 A New World Order, 1989–2001

The Bush Administration, 1989–1993

James T. Patterson, *Restless Giant: the United States From Watergate to Bush v. Gore* (New York: Oxford University Press, 2005); George C. Herring, *From Colony to Superpower: U.S. Foreign Relations Since 1776* (New York: Oxford University Press; Stephen Thernstrom and Abigail Therntrom, *America in Black and White: One Nation, Indivisible* (New York: Simon & Schuster, 1997); Gary Orfield and Dean Whitla, "Diversity and Legal Education: Student Experiences in Leading Law Schools," downloaded August 1, 2011 from https://gseis.ucla.edu/faculty/members/orfield;

The Clinton Presidency

Haynes Johnson, *The Best of Times: America in the Clinton Years* (New York: Harcourt, 2001); Major Garrett, *The Enduring Revolution: How the Contract with America Continues to Shape the Nation* (New York: Crown Forum, 2005); James T. Patterson, *Restless Giant: the United States From Watergate to Bush v. Gore* (New York: Oxford University Press, 2005).

Technology Dominates an Era

Y2K, though considered a significant issue at the time, has received remarkably little historical attention. American Radio Works offered a thoughtful five year retrospective, "The Surprising Legacy of Y2K" including reporting by Catherine Winter, Chris Farrell, and Ochen Kaylan from which much of this material is taken. See http://americanradioworks.publicradio.org/features/y2k/a..html, downloaded August 6, 2011. See also Robert L. Mitchell, "Y2K: the good, the bad and the crazy," *Computerworld*, December 28, 2009, http://www.computerworld.com/s/article/print/9142555/Y2K_The_good_the_bad_and_the_crazy?taxonomyName=Management+and+Careers&taxonomyId=14, downloaded August 6, 2011; John Cassidy, *dot.con: The Greatest Story Ever Sold* (New York: HarperCollins, 2002); Joe Saltzman, "Instant Communications Across Cyberspace," and David Brin, "Personal Privacy Lost to Technology," both in Stuart A. Kallen, editor, *The 1990s* (San Diego, CA: Greenhaven Press, 2000); Ken Auletta, *Googled: The End of the World As We Know It* (New York: Penguin, 2009); Johnny Ryan, *A History of the Internet and the Digital Future* (London, England: Reaktion Books, 2010); John Brownlee, "President Obama Wishes He Had Cooler Tech in the Oval Office," Geek.com, April 17, 2011.

Chapter 30 Entering a New Time, 2001– to the Present

The Impact of September 11, 2001

Damon DiMarco, *Tower Stories: An Oral History of 9/11* (Santa Monica, CA: Santa Monica Press, 2007); Thomas H. Kean and Lee H. Hamilton, *The 9/11 Report: The National Commission on Terrorist Attacks Upon the United States*, issued July 22, 2004 (New York: St. Martin's Press, 2004); Matthew Eshbaugh-Soha and Tom Miles, "George W. Bush's Domestic Policy Agenda," *The American Review of Politics*, Vol. 29, (Winter, 2008–2009), pp. 351–369 and http://miller-center.org/president/gwbush/essay/biography/print, downloaded August 6, 2011; American Library Association, "Resolution on the USA Patriot Act and Related Measures that Infringe on the Rights of Library Users," adopted January 29, 2003; John Yoo and Eric Posner, "The Patriot Act Under Fire," American Enterprise Institute, December 1, 2003; Terry H. Anderson, *Bush's Wars* (New York: Oxford University Press, 2011); George C. Herring, *From Colony to*

Superpower: U.S. Foreign Relations Since 1776 (New York: Oxford University Press, 2008); George W. Bush, *Decision Points* (New York: Crown Publishers).

Hurricane Katrina and its Aftermath

Douglas Brinkley, *The Great Deluge: Hurricane Katrina, New Orleans, and the Mississippi Gulf Coast* (New York: Harper Perennial, 2007).

The Financial Crisis of 2008

Andrew Ross Sorkin, *Too Big to Fail* (New York: Penguin Books, 2009, 2010); The National Commission on the Causes of the Financial and Economic Crisis in the United Stated, *The Financial Crisis Inquiry Report* (New York: Public Affairs, 2011); Robert B. Reich, *Aftershock:*

The Next Economy & America's Future (New York: Vintage Books, 2011); and George Packer, "A Dirty Business," *The New Yorker*, June 27, 2011, pp. 42–55.

New Liberals, New Conservatives

John Heilemann and Mark Halperin, *Game Change: Obama and the Clintons, McCain and Palin, and the Race of a Lifetime* (New York: Harper Perennial, 2010); Kate Zernike, *Boiling Mad: Inside Tea Party America* (New York: Times Books, Henry Holt, 2010); Jill Lepore, The Whites of Their Eyes: The Tea Party's Revolution and the Battle Over American History (Princeton: Princeton University Press, 2010); Todd Gitlin, *Occupy Nation: The Roots, the Spirit, and the Promise of Occupy Wall Street* (New York: HarperCollins, 2012).

Photo Credits

COVER
Library of Congress Prints and Photographs Division Washington [LC-DIG-ppmsca-15712]; Library of Congress Prints and Photographs Division Washington [LC-USZ62-19234]; Library of Congress Prints and Photographs Division Washington [LC-USZC2-1205]; Library of Congress Prints and Photographs Division Washington [LC-USZ62-35634]; Library of Congress Prints and Photographs Division Washington [LC-DIG-ppmsca-03130]

CHAPTER 15
North Wind Picture Archives/Alamy, 417; Library of Congress Prints and Photographs Division [LC-USZ62-22120], 420; Library of Congress Prints and Photographs Division [LC-DIG-pga-04115], 423; Library of Congress, Prints & Photographs Division [LC-USZ62-125422], 429; Library of Congress Prints & Photographs Division [LC-DIG-ppmsca-17564], 431; Library of Congress Prints and Photographs Division/Taylor, James E[LC-USZ62-37860], 434; Library of Congress Prints and Photographs Division [LC-DIG-ppmsca-11370], 437; Charles Phelps Cushing/ClassicStock/Corbis, 438; Library of Congress Prints and Photographs Division [LC-USZ62-119565], 441; Library of Congress Prints and Photographs Division [LC-USZ62-111152], 442.

CHAPTER 16
North Wind Picture Archives/Alamy, 449; Library of Congress Prints and Photographs Division [LC-DIG-ppmsca-13514], 450; National Archives and Records Administration [111-SC-87964], 454; Library of Congress Prints and Photographs Division [LC-USZ61-2085], 455; National Archives and Records Administration [531079], 457; Library of Congress Prints and Photographs Division Washington, D.C[LC-USZ62-3726], 458; Library of Congress Prints and Photographs Division Washington, D.C. [LC-USZ62-57524], 462; Chinese mining laborers, Idaho, 76-119.2/A, Idaho State Historical Society, 462; North Wind Picture Archives/Alamy, 467; Library of Congress Prints and Photographs Division [LC-DIG-ppmsca-03213], 468; AP Photo, 471; Art Resource, NY, 474; Library of Congress Prints and Photographs Division [LC-DIG-ppmsca-24362], 474.

CHAPTER 17
Science and Society/SuperStock, 479; Library of Congress Prints and Photographs Division [LC-USZ62-98128], 481; Library of Congress Prints and Photographs Division [LC-DIG-ggbain-02949], 485; Library of Congress Prints and Photographs Division [LC-USZ62-116999], 491; Museum of the City of New York/The Art Archive at Art Resource, NY, 493; United States Senate, 495; Library of Congress Prints and Photographs Division [LC-USZ62-67910], 500; AP Images, 502; Everett Collection Inc/Alamy, 503; Everett Collection Inc/SuperStock, 503.

CHAPTER 18
Everett Collection/SuperStock, 508; Library of Congress Prints and Photographs Division [LC-USZC4-12222], 511; Bettmann/Corbis, 512; Everett Collection Inc/Alamy, 515; Library of Congress Prints and Photographs Division [LC-DIG-pga-04170], 518; Kean Collection/Getty Images, 524; Historical/Corbis, 528; Everett Collection Inc/SuperStock, 529; Library of Congress Prints and Photographs Division [LC-DIG-ggbain-04507], 532; Everett Collection Historical/Alamy, 533.

CHAPTER 19
Library of Congress Prints and Photographs Division [LC-DIG-stereo-1s02031], 536; Lebrecht Music and Arts Photo Library/Alamy, 539; Fotosearch/Getty Images, 541; Library of Congress Prints and Photographs Division [LC-DIG-nclc-05436], 545; Library of Congress Prints and Photographs Division [LC-DIG-ggbain-12065], 546; Library of Congress Prints and Photographs Division [LC-DIG-ggbain-02864], 549; The Museum of the City of New York/Art Resource, NY, 551; Library of Congress Prints and Photographs Division [LC-DIG-ppmsca-35651], 552; Library of Congress Prints and Photographs Division [LC-DIG-ppmsca-27643], 558; Library of Congress Prints and Photographs Division [LC-DIG-hec-11546], 561.

CHAPTER 20
Library of Congress Prints and Photographs Division [LC-DIG-fsac-1a34953], 565; Library of Congress Prints and Photographs Division [LC-USZ62-55384], 566; ArtPix/Alamy, 568; Corbis, 571; Library of Congress Prints and Photographs Division [LC-DIG-ds-00353], 572; Library of Congress Prints and Photographs Division [LC-USZ62-117214], 574; Library of Congress Prints and Photographs Division [LC-DIG-ggbain-15609], 577; Library of Congress Prints and Photographs Division, 581; Library of Congress Prints and Photographs Division [LC-USZC4-1281], 584; The Art Archive/Art Resource, NY, 586; National Portrait Gallery/Smithsonian Institution/Art Resource, NY, 589.

CHAPTER 21
DIZ Muenchen GmbH, Sueddeutsche Zeitung Photo/Alamy, 596; Library of Congress Prints and Photographs Division [LC-DIG-ds-01290], 598; Library of Congress Prints and Photographs Division [LC-USZ62-123257], 601; Bettmann/Corbis, 605; Library of Congress Prints and Photographs Division [LC-DIG-ggbain-16122], 607; Library of Congress Prints and Photographs Division [LC-USZ62-54357], 607; Michael Ochs Archives/Getty Images, 611; akg-images/Newscom, 613; Everett Collection Inc/Alamy, 616; Everett Collection Inc/Alamy, 619; Fotosearch/Getty Images, 621.

CHAPTER 22
Library of Congress Prints and Photographs Division [LC-USZ62-91536], 625; Library of Congress Prints and Photographs Division [LC-USZ62-123429], 627; Gabriel Hackett/Getty Images, 628; Library of Congress Prints and Photographs Division [LC-USF33-T01-000051-M5], 631; Library of Congress Prints and Photographs Division [LC-USW3-014843-C], 634; Detroit News/PSG/Newscom, 638; Bettmann/CORBIS, 641; AP Images, 644; World History Archive/Newscom, 646; Everett Collection/Newscom, 648; Library of Congress Prints and Photographs Division [LC-USZ62-68852], 650.

CHAPTER 23
Library of Congress Prints and Photographs Division [LC-USW33-018433-C], 653; National Portrait Gallery, Smithsonian Institution/Art Resource, NY, 658; Universal Images Group/SuperStock, 662; Library of Congress Prints and Photographs Division [LC-USW33-028626-C], 666; National Archives and Records Administration, 667; National Archives and Records Administration, 674; Library of Congress Prints and Photographs Division [LC-USZ62-128309], 675; National Archives and Records Administration, 678; akg-images/Newscom, 679; Library of Congress Prints and Photographs Division [LC-USW33-059244], 681.

CHAPTER 24
Library of Congress Prints and Photographs Division [LC-DIG-ppmsca-04297], 684; Library of Congress Prints and Photographs Division [LC-USZ62-47325], 685; Harold M. Lambert/Lambert/Getty Images, 689; Hulton Archive/Archive Photos/Getty Images, 689; Frank Driggs Collection/Getty Images, 693; National Archives and Records Administration, 696; akg-images/Newscom, 699; Everett Collection/Newscom, 703; © 2013 The Pollock-Krasner Foundation/Artists Rights Society (ARS), New York; Albright-Knox Art Gallery/Art Resource, NY, 705; Bettmann/Corbis, 707; Frank Cancellare/Bettmann/Corbis, 711.

CHAPTER 25
Burt Glinn/Magnum Photos, 715; World History Archive/Newscom, 721; Bettmann/CORBIS, 722; Everett Collection/Newscom, 723; ClassicStock/Alamy, 724; Hulton Archive/Getty Images, 730; Everett Collection Historical/Alamy, 734; John G. Moebes/Corbis, 738; Bill Hudson/AP Images, 739; ASSOCIATED PRESS/AP Images, 740; William J. Smith/AP Images, 742; Library of Congress Prints and Photographs Division [LC-DIG-fsa-8a26761], 744; Library of Congress, Prints & Photographs Division, [LC-USZ62-119478], 745.

CHAPTER 26
Bernie Boston/The Washington Post /Getty Images, 748; Gai Terrell/Redferns/Getty Images, 750; ASSOCIATED PRESS/AP Images, 753; Hulton Archive/Getty Images, 756; Everett Collection/Newscom, 758; George Tames/The New York Times/Redux, 759; Democratic National Committee/AP Images, 763; Bettmann/CORBIS, 771; San Francisco Examiner/AP Images, 774; Bettmann/Corbis, 775.

CHAPTER 27
Bettmann/CORBIS, 778; John Filo/Getty Images, 782; CORBIS, 784; Jesse-Steve Rose/The Image Works, 786; Paul Fusco/Magnum Photos, 789; Bettmann/CORBIS, 791; John Dominis / The Image Works, 793; Bettmann/Corbis, 794; Bettmann/Corbis, 800; Handout/MCT/Newscom, 804; Bettmann/Corbis, 805.

CHAPTER 28
AP Photo/Luis M. Alvarez, 808; Bettmann/CORBIS, 809; AP Photo/George Lane, 812; AP Photo/Ron Edmonds, 814; Dennis Brack/Newscom, 820; AP Photo/Ira Schwartz, 822; Library of Congress Prints and Photographs Division [LC-DIG-ppmsca-19180], 823; AP Photo/Peter Morgan, 827; Ron Galella/WireImage /Getty Images, 828; Eve Arnold/Magnum Photos, 830; AP Photo/Damian Dovarganes, 832; Bettmann/CORBIS, 835.

CHAPTER 29
AP Photo/Greg Gibson, 838; Robert Maass/CORBIS, 839; AP Photo/Patrick Downs, 841; AP Photo/Joe Marquette, 843; Wally McNamee/CORBIS, 845; AP Photo/Mark Wilson, 846; Jim West/Alamy, 847; Everett Collection Historical/Alamy, 852; INTERFOTO/Alamy, 858; Science and Society/SuperStock, 859; MacX/Fotolia, 863.

CHAPTER 30
AP Photo/Chao Soi Cheong, 867; AP Photo/Beth A. Keiser, 869; AP Photo/Rahmat Gul, 871; AP Photo/Nati Harnik, 872; AP Photo/J. Scott Applewhite, 876; AP Photo/Wathiq Khuzaie, Pool, 878; Marko Georgiev/Getty Images, 881; jeff grace/LA OPINION/Newscom, 884; TANNEN MAURY/EPA/Newscom, 888; ROLLE ROD/SIPA/Newscom, 890; Liz Mangelsdorf/San Francisco Chronicle/Corbis, 891; AP Photo/Pablo Martinez Monsivais, 893.

Text Credits

CHAPTER 15

John David Smith, Black Voices From Reconstruction, 1865–1877 (Gainesville: University Press of Florida, 1997), pp. 43–44: 419; Frances Ellen Watkins Harper, "An Address Delivered at the Centennial Anniversary of the Pennsylvania Society for Promoting the Abolition of Slavery, 1875," in Manning Marable and Leith Mullings, editors, Let Nobody Turn Us Around: Voices of Resistance, Reform, and Renewal (Lanham, MD: Rowman & Littlefield, 2000), pp. 138–143: 429.

CHAPTER 16

From October 20, 1867, Record copy of the Proceedings of the Indian Peace Commission Appointed under the Act of Congress approved 7/20/1867 National Archives: 453; Charles W. Allen. Publishers' Auxiliary, 28 Nov. 1942, p. 1: 459.

CHAPTER 17

Andrew Carnegie, "Wealth," North American Review, Vol. 148, No. 391 (June, 1889): 489; Sadie Frowne, "A Polish Sweatshop Girl," in Hamilton Holt, editor The Life Stories of Undistinguished Americans as Told by Themselves (originally 1906, republished New York: Routledge, 2000), pp. 21–28: 499.

CHAPTER 18

Mary E. Lease, Speech by Mary E. Lease to the National Council of Women of the United States, Assembled in Washington, DC, Feb 24, 1891, by Mary Elizabeth Lease. In Transactions of the National Council of Women of the United States, Assembled in Washington D.C., February 22 to 25, 1891, edited by Rachel Foster Avery. (Philadelphia, PA: J.B. Lippincott & Co., 1891). pp. 157–159, found in Kathryn Kish Sklar and Thomas Dublin, editors, Women and Social Movements in the United States, 1600–2000, downloaded November 23, 2010: 520; Mary Harris Jones, The Autobiography of Mother Jones (Chicago: Charles H. Kerr, 1925: 531.

CHAPTER 19

Jane Addams, Twenty Years at Hull House (New York: The McMillan Company, 1910): 547.

CHAPTER 20

Woodrow Wilson, War Message to Congress, April 2, 1917: 583; Eugene Kennedy, A "Doughboy" Describes the Fighting Front (1918): 583.

CHAPTER 21

Source: Ellen Welles Page, "A Flapper's Appeal to Parents," Outlook, December 6, 1922; 132, 14 cited in Ellen Skinner, Women and the National Experience: Sources in Women's History (Boston: Prentice Hall, 2011), pp. 270–272: 604; Alain Locke, editor, The New Negro: Voices of the Harlem Renaissance, new Introduction by Arnold Rampersad (originally 1925, new edition New York: Simon & Schuster, 1992): 610.

CHAPTER 22

Frances Perkins, "The Roots of Social Security" October 23, 1962. United States Social Security Administration: 642.

CHAPTER 23

South Kingstown High School Oral History Project; Linda Wood and Judi Scott , Project Directors. Brown University Scholarly Technology Group, David Reville Project Manager. Interview by Heather O'Grady: 664; Alvin Kernan, Crossing the Line: A Bluejacket's Odyssey in World War II (New Haven: Yale University Press, 2007; 676.

CHAPTER 24

United Nations Universal Declaration of Human Rights, December 10, 1948: 695.

CHAPTER 25

Fannie Lou Hamer, "Testimony to the Credentials Committee" July 22, 1964. DNC Services Corporation: 742.

CHAPTER 26

Paul Thomas Coe, "Vietnam Letters," 1969–70, from Karen Manners Smith and Tim Koster, Time It Was: American Stories from the Sixties. (Upper Saddle River, NJ: Pearson), pp. 27, 32, 36–39: 770.

CHAPTER 27

Ellen Skinner, Women and the National Experience: Sources in Women's History (Upper Saddle River, New Jersey: Prentice Hall, 2011), pp.358–360: 788; The Redstocking Manifesto was issued in New York City on July 7, 1969. It first appeared as a mimeographed flyer, designed for distribution at women's liberation events. Further information about the Manifesto or other materials from th 1960's rebirth years of feminism is available from the Redstockings Women's Liberation Archives for Action at www.resdstockings.org or PO Box 744, Stuyvesant Station, New York, NY 10009: 789; Phyllis Schlafly Report 5, no. 7 (February 1972): 789.

CHAPTER 28

Jesse Jackson, 1988 Democratic National Convention Address, downloaded July 26, 2011 from www.americanrhetoric.com/speeches/jessejackson1988dnc.htm: 824; Pat Robertson, 1988 Republican National Convention Address, downloaded July 26, 2011 from www.patrobertson.com/Speeches/PresidentialBidEnded.asp: 824; Necesidades y problemas: Immigrant Latina Vernaculars of Belonging, Coalition, and Citizenship in San Francisco, California," Kathleen Coli, Latino Studies 2:1 (2004): 186– 209. Palgrave Macmillan Journals: 826; Saša Savic in Katherine Hanson, Dream A New World (Lanham, MD: Rowman & Littlefield, forthcoming: 826.

CHAPTER 29

Republican Contract With America, September 27, 1994. United States House of Representatives: 848.

CHAPTER 30

John Updike, "Nine-Eleven: New York," in Robert Fox, editor, We Were There: An Eyewitness History of the Twentieth Century (New York: The Overlook Press, 2010), pp. 343–345: 870; Mary Gehman, copyright © 2005, all rights reserved, used by permission: 882.

Index